The Reformation Theologians

The Great Theologians

A comprehensive series devoted to highlighting the major theologians of different periods. Each theologian is presented by a world-renowned scholar.

Published

The Modern Theologians
An Introduction to Christian Theology in the Twentieth Century
David Ford

The Medieval Theologians
An Introduction to Theology in the Medieval Period
G. R. Evans

The Reformation Theologians
An Introduction to Theology in the Early Modern Period
Carter Lindberg

Forthcoming

The Pietist Theologians
Carter Lindberg

The First Christian Theologians
An Introduction to Theology in the Early Church
G. R. Evans

The Reformation Theologians

An Introduction to Theology in
the Early Modern Period

Edited by

Carter Lindberg
School of Theology
Boston University

 BLACKWELL
Publishers

Copyright © Blackwell Publishers Ltd 2002
Editorial matter and arrangement copyright © Carter Lindberg 2002

The moral right of Carter Lindberg to be identified as author of the editorial material has been asserted in accordance with the Copyright, Designs and Patents Act 1988.

First published 2002

2 4 6 8 10 9 7 5 3 1

Blackwell Publishers Ltd
108 Cowley Road
Oxford OX4 1JF
UK

Blackwell Publishers Inc.
350 Main Street
Malden, Massachusetts 02148
USA

British Library Cataloguing in Publication Data

A CIP catalogue record for this book is available from the British Library.

Library of Congress Cataloging-in-Publication Data

Reformation theologians : an introduction to theology in the early modern period / edited by Carter Lindberg.
     p. cm. — (The great theologians)
    Includes bibliographical references and index.
    ISBN 0–631–21838–6 (alk. paper) — ISBN 0–631–21839–4 (pbk. : alk. paper)
    1. Theologians. 2. Reformation. 3. Theology, Doctrinal—History. I. Lindberg, Carter, 1937– II. Series.
BT27.R38 2002
230'.092'2—dc21   2001037470

Typeset in 10 on 12.5 pt Galliard
by Graphicraft Limited, Hong Kong
Printed in Great Britain by T.J. International, Padstow, Cornwall

This book is printed on acid-free paper.

Contents

Acknowledgments

I am grateful to the many people whose support and work made this volume possible. Alex Wright, previous senior commissioning editor of religion at Blackwell, initiated the project; and Joanna Pyke, Blackwell's editorial controller, has shepherded the volume to completion with her usual competence, attention to detail, and gracious flexibility concerning schedules. Finally, thanks to Clare Woodford and Laura Barry, Blackwell publishing coordinators, for their assistance with numerous details, large and small.

The contributors were a great pleasure to work with. They graciously consented to make room in their busy schedules to participate in this project. I am especially grateful to those who joined late in the game due to the withdrawals of some of the original invitees owing to serious illnesses and other problems. The volume was to include chapters on Martin Bucer and John Fisher, but unfortunately when it became apparent that these chapters would not materialize it was too late to find replacement contributors. I apologize for this impoverishment of the Reformed and Roman Catholic sections, and hope readers may begin to fill in the gaps with the entries in *The Oxford Encyclopedia of the Reformation* and the *Theologische Realenzyklopädie*.

I also wish to thank James M. Estes, professor emeritus of the University of Toronto, for both recommending Dr. Hermann Ehmer for the Brenz chapter and then translating the chapter into English. I am responsible for the translations of the chapters on d'Etaples, Luther, Melanchthon, Karlstadt, Müntzer, and Schwenkfeld. Erika Lindberg, our daughter, provided indispensable help with the translations of the French chapters on d'Etaples and Schwenkfeld. And the authors of all the translated chapters were exceedingly gracious in reading and correcting my drafts. Translation errors and infelicities – in spite of so much assistance – remain my own.

Carter Lindberg
Boston, 2001

Contributors

Gillian T. W. Ahlgren is associate professor of theology at Xavier University in Cincinnati, Ohio. She is the author of *Teresa of Avila and the Politics of Sanctity* (1996), and the forthcoming *Digo Yo, Francisca: Proclaiming Reform in Sixteenth-Century Toledo*, as well as numerous articles on women in sixteenth-century Spain.

Oswald Bayer is professor of systematic theology at the University of Tübingen and editor of the *Neue Zeitschrift für systematische Theologie und Religionsphilosophie*. His numerous articles have appeared in a variety of European and American journals. The more recent of his many monographs include *Theologie (Handbuch system-atischer Theologie 1)* (1995), *Freiheit als Antwort: Zur theologischen Ethik* (1995), and *Gott als Autor: Zu einer poietologischen Theologie* (1999).

Guy Bedouelle, OP is professor of church history at the University of Fribourg, Switzerland, and President of the Dominican Center of Studies, Le Saulchoir, Paris. Besides his publications on Lefèvre d'Etaples, he is the author (in collaboration with Patrick Le Gal) of *Le "divorce" du roi Henry VIII, Textes et documents* (1987) and (in collaboration with Bernard Roussel) *Le temps des Réformes et la Bible* (1989). He is also the editor of volume 83 of the *Collected Works of Erasmus in English* (1998) for which he provided the Introduction and the annotations on the *Apologia ad Fabrum*.

Peter Newman Brooks, fellow emeritus of Robinson College, Cambridge, was lecturer in Church History in the Cambridge Faculty of Divinity from 1970 to 1998. He is currently professor of Reformation studies and director of graduate studies at Cranmer Theological House, Shreveport, USA. His many publications on the continental and English Reformations include editing *Seven-Headed Luther* (1983), *Cranmer in Con-text: Documents from the English Reformation* (1989), and his monograph *Thomas Cranmer's Doctrine of the Eucharist* (2nd ed., 1992).

J. Laurel Carrington is professor of Renaissance and Reformation history at St. Olaf College, Minnesota. She is currently working on the annotations for Erasmus's *Epistola contra Pseudoevangelicos* and *Epistola ad Fratres Germaniae Inferioris* for volume 78 of the *Collected Works of Erasmus.*

Hermann Ehmer is Director of the Landeskirchliche Archiv of the Evangelische Landeskirche in Württemberg and lecturer on Württemberg church history at the University of Tübingen. From 1977 to 1988 he was the manager of the Wertheim Staatsarchiv. He is also the coeditor of the *Blätter für württembergischen Kirchengeschichte* and of the *Quellen und Forschungen zur württembergischen Kirchengeschichte.* He has contributed numerous publications in the areas of the history and church history of Baden-Württemberg.

Daniel F. Eppley is assistant professor of the history of Christianity at McMurry University in Texas. His doctoral dissertation (University of Iowa, 2000) is titled "A Convenient Faith: Royal Supremacy and the Definition of Christian Doctrine in Tudor England." His recent research focusses on the defense of the royal supremacy in Tudor England.

Bruce Gordon is lecturer in modern history at the University of St. Andrews and associate director of the St. Andrews Reformation Studies Institute. He is the author of *Clerical Discipline and the Rural Reformation* (1992), editor of *Protestant History and Identity in Sixteenth-Century Europe* (2 vols., 1996) and, with Peter Marshall, editor of *The Place of the Dead: Death and Remembrance in Late Medieval and Early Modern Europe* (2000). He is currently writing a book on Zwingli.

Scott Hendrix is James Hastings Nichols professor of Reformation history and doctrine at Princeton Theological Seminary. He is the author of numerous articles on Luther and Rhegius as well as *Luther and the Papacy: Stages in a Reformation Conflict* (1981), *Tradition and Authority in the Reformation* (1996), and, with Günther Gassmann, *The Fortress Introduction to the Lutheran Confessions* (1999).

Frank A. James, III is professor of historical theology at the Reformed Theological Seminary, Orlando Florida, and regular visiting professor of Reformation history at the Centre for Reformation Research, Oxford. His publications include *The Peter Martyr Reader*, coedited with J. P. Donnelly and J. C. McLelland (1999), *Peter Martyr Vermigli and Predestination: The Augustinian Inheritance of an Italian Reformer* (1998), and *Via Augustini: The Recovery of Augustine in the Later Middle Ages, Renaissance and Reformation*, coedited with Heiko A. Oberman (1991). Since 1996, Professor Frank has been general editor of the Peter Martyr Library (with J. C. McLelland and J. P. Donnelly).

Ralph Keen is associate professor of religion at the University of Iowa School of Religion. He is the editor and translator of *Responsio ad Johannem Bugenhagium Pomeranum* (1988) and the author of *Divine and Human Authority in Reformation Thought: German Theologians on Political Order, 1520–1555* (1997). He is presently working on a comparative study of varieties of sixteenth-century Catholicism.

Robert Kolb is professor in the Institute for Mission Studies at Concordia Seminary in St. Louis. He is the author of numerous books in the field of Reformation studies, including *Luther's Heirs Define His Legacy* (1996) and *Martin Luther as Prophet, Teacher, and Hero: Images of the Reformer, 1520–1620* (1999). His most recent work, with Timothy Wengert, is a new translation of *The Book of Concord, The Confessions of the Evangelical Lutheran Church* (2000).

Carter Lindberg is professor of church history at the Boston University School of Theology. He is the author of the textbook, *The European Reformations* (1996), and *Beyond Charity: Reformation Initiatives for the Poor* (1993), and editor of *The European Reformations Sourcebook* (2000).

Peter Matheson is fellow of the Department of History and principal of the Theological Hall at the University of Melbourne. In addition to his studies and translations of Argula von Grumbach, he is the translator and editor of *The Collected Works of Thomas Müntzer* (1988). His most recent books are *The Rhetoric of the Reformation* (1998), and *The Imaginative World of the Reformation* (2000).

Elsie Anne McKee is Archibald Alexander professor of Reformation studies and the history of worship at Princeton Theological Seminary. In addition to her publications on Katharina Schütz Zell, her books include *John Calvin on the Diaconate and Liturgical Almsgiving* (1984), *Elders and the Plural Ministry: The Role of Exegetical History in Illuminating John Calvin's Theology* (1988), and *Diakonia: In the Classical Reformed Tradition and Today* (1989). With B. Armstrong, she is editor of *Probing the Reformed Tradition: Historical Studies in Honor of Edward A. Dowey, Jr.* (1989).

Gregory J. Miller is associate professor of history at Malone College, Ohio. Since his dissertation, *Holy War and Holy Terror: Views of Islam in German Pamphlet Literature 1520–1545* (Boston University, 1994), much of his work has focussed on early modern European responses to Islam. He is currently writing a book on Zwingli's successor, Theodor Bibliander.

Richard A. Muller is professor of historical theology at Calvin Theological Seminary, Grand Rapids, Michigan. His extensive studies of Reformed Orthodoxy include *Christ and the Decree: Christology and Predestination in Reformed Theology from Calvin to Perkins* (1988), *God, Creation, and Providence in the Thought of Jacob Arminius* (1991), and *Post-Reformation Reformed Dogmatics* (2 vols., 1987, 1993). His most recent study is *The Unaccommodated Calvin: Studies in the Foundation of a Theological Tradition* (2000).

Oliver K. Olson, emeritus professor of theology, Marquette University, was a career chaplain in the US navy. His *Matthias Flacius and the Survival of Luther's Reform* is forthcoming.

John W. O'Malley, SJ is professor of church history at Weston Jesuit School of Theology. Author of numerous studies on Reformation subjects and early modern

Catholicism, his most recent books include *The First Jesuits* (1993) and *Trent and All That: Renaming Catholicism in the Early Modern Era* (2000).

Heinz Scheible is director of the Melanchthon-Forschungsstelle, Heidelberger Akademie der Wissenschaften, where he is engaged in the preparation of the critical edition of Melanchthon's correspondence. Among his many studies are the articles on Melanchthon in *The Oxford Encyclopedia of the Reformation* and the *Theologische Realenzyklopädie*, and the major biography, *Melanchthon: Eine Biographie* (1997).

Gottfried Seebass is professor of church history at the University of Heidelberg and serves as an editor of numerous scholarly works including the *Theologische Realenzyklopädie*. The wide range of his contributions to Reformation studies may be sampled in the recent collection of his essays edited by Irene Dingel, *Die Reformation der Aussenseiter. Gesammelte Aufsätze und Vorträge* (1997).

André Séguenny is research fellow at the Centre National de la Recherche Scientifique, University of Strasbourg. He is editor of the *Bibliotheca Dissidentium* series (20 vols. to date), and author of *The Christology of Caspar Schwenckfeld* (1987) and *Les Spirituels: Philosophie et religion chez les jeunes humanistes allemands au seizième siècle* (2000).

Sjouka Voolstra is professor of Mennonite history and theology at the Mennonite Seminary (Amsterdam) and at the University of Amsterdam. His publications on Menno Simons include *Het Woord is vlees geworden. De melchioritisch-menniste incarnatieleer* (1982) and *Menno Simons: His Image and Message* (1997).

Jared Wicks, SJ has been active in the study of Reformation theology since his dissertation on Luther under Erwin Iserloh at Münster (1967). A number of his essays appeared in his *Luther's Reform: Studies in Conversion and the Church* (1992). Besides his studies on Cajetan, he has contributed entries on sixteenth-century Catholic theologians for the *Encyclopedia of the Reformation* (1995). He currently teaches in the Faculty of Theology at the Gregorian University, Rome.

Randall C. Zachman is associate professor of Reformation studies in the Department of Theology at the University of Notre Dame, where he is also Director of the MA and MTS programs in theology. He is the author of *The Assurance of Faith: Conscience in the Theology of Martin Luther and John Calvin* (1993) and numerous articles in various theological journals.

Alejandro Zorzin, a pastor in the Iglesia Evangélica del Rio de la Plata, Argentina, has recently accepted a pastoral position in Germany. His dissertation on Karlstadt appeared under the title *Karlstadt als Flugschriftenautor* (1990). His "Escatología apocalíptica en la Reforma protestante del siglo XVI" is in the volume he coedited, *Escatología y espiritualidad: expectativas ante el nuevo milenio* (1999).

Abbreviations

ARG	*Archiv für Reformationsgeschichte / Archive for Reformation History*
BSLK	*Bekenntnisschriften der Evangelisch-Lutherischen Kirche*, Göttingen: Vandenhoeck & Ruprecht, 1963
BSRK	*Bekenntnisschriften der Reformierten Kirche*, Leipzig, 1903
CH	*Church History*
CHR	*Catholic Historical Review*
CO	*Ioannes Calvini opera quae supersunt omnia*, ed. Wilhelm Baum, Edward Cunitz, and Eduard Reuss, 59 vols. (vols. 29–87 of *CR*), Brunswick: A. Schwetschke & Son (M. Bruhn), 1863–1900
CR	*Corpus Reformatorum: Philippi Melanchthonis opera quae supersunt omnia*, ed. K. Bretschneider & H. Bindseil, 28 vols., Halle: Schwetschke, 1834–60
CS	*Corpus Schwenckfeldianorum*, 19 vols., Leipzig and Pennsburg, PA, 1907–61
CTJ	*Calvin Theological Journal*
CTM	*The Collected Works of Thomas Müntzer*, trans. and ed. Peter Matheson, Edinburgh: T. & T. Clark, 1988
CW	*The Complete Works of St. Thomas More*, New Haven & London: Yale University Press, 1963–97
FC	Formula of Concord
JEH	*Journal of Ecclesiastical History*
LQ	*Lutheran Quarterly*
LuJ	*Lutherjahrbuch*
LW	*Luther's Works*, American edition, ed. Jaroslav Pelikan and Helmut Lehmann, 55 vols., St. Louis and Minneapolis: Concordia Publishing House and Fortress Press, 1955–86
MBW	*Melanchthons Briefwechsel: Kritische und Kommentierte Gesamtausgabe. Regesten*, ed. Heinz Scheible, 8 vols. to date, Stuttgart–Bad Cannstatt: Frommann-Holzboog, 1977–

MBW.T1	*Melanchthons Briefwechsel: Kritische und Kommentierte Gesamtausgabe. Texte*, ed. R. Wetzel, 2 vols. to date, Stuttgart–Bad Cannstatt: Frommann-Holzboog, 1991–
MSA	*Melanchthons Werke in Auswahl (Studienausgabe)*, ed. R. Stupperich, 7 vols., Gütersloh: Gerd Mohn, 1951–75
MSB	*Thomas Müntzer, Schriften und Briefe*, ed. Günther Franz, assisted by Paul Kirn, Gütersloh: Gerd Mohn, 1968
NZSTh	*Neue Zeitschrift für systematische Theologie*
OER	*The Oxford Encyclopedia of the Reformation*, ed. Hans J. Hillerbrand, 4 vols., New York: Oxford University Press, 1996
OS	*Ioannis Calvini opera selecta*, ed. Peter Barth, Wilhelm Niesel, and Dora Scheuner, 5 vols., Munich: Chr. Kaiser, 1926–52
SCJ	*Sixteenth Century Journal*
Tappert	*The Book of Concord*, ed. Theodore Tappert, Philadelphia: Muhlenberg Press, 1959
TRE	*Theologische Realenzyklopädie*
WA	*D. Martin Luthers Werke. Kritische Gesamtausgabe*, 60 vols. to date, Weimar: Böhlaus Nachfolger, 1883–
WA Br	*D. Martin Luthers Werke. Kritische Gesamtausgabe. Briefwechsel*, 15 vols., Weimar: Böhlaus Nachfolger, 1930–78
WA TR	*D. Martin Luthers Werke. Kritische Gesamtausgabe. Tischreden*, 6 vols., Weimar: Böhlaus Nachfolger, 1912–21
Z	*Huldreich Zwinglis sämtliche Werke*, ed. E. Egli et al. (vols. 88– of *CR*), Berlin, Leipzig, and Zurich, 1905–
ZKG	*Zeitschrift für Kirchengeschichte*
ZThK	*Zeitschrift für Theologie und Kirche*

Introduction

Carter Lindberg

It is through living, indeed through dying and being damned that one becomes a theologian, not through understanding, reading, or speculation. Martin Luther (*WA* 5:163, 28f.)

The purpose of *The Reformation Theologians* is to introduce the theologies of selected theologians of the sixteenth-century Reformations to students of historical theology, church history, and the history of Christianity as well as to all persons interested in "how we got this way." In addition to this historical goal, there is also a contemporary interest. In the words of Bernd Moeller: "We need the spiritual and intellectual energies that the Reformation has to offer. Moreover, the Christian life, the church, and contemporary theology have so many ties to the Reformation that for our own self-knowledge we should always be aware of this relationship, and should continually examine it and test its relevancy for today."[1]

The selection provides as inclusive a range of theologians as possible within the limitations of a single book of reasonable length. The cast of characters includes professors of theology and persons without formal theological education, clergy and laity, men and women, and advocates of nearly all the reforming options of the "long" sixteenth century (1400–1600). The "usual suspects," of course, are here. In the words of Heinz Schilling, "In the beginning were Luther, Loyola, and Calvin."[2] But, of course, these Reformers were not "the beginning" in the sense of being sui generis. They and their contemporaries did not drop full-blown from heaven but rather were nurtured in the context of late medieval theology and piety, and stimulated by the contributions of humanism. Space, however, precludes more than a bow in the direction of these influences by the inclusion of Lefèvre and Erasmus.[3]

Many others besides medieval theologians and humanists were regretfully excluded. Some of the "excluded" have at least cameo roles in the following essays; others remain in the wings. There will always be "Reformers in the wings," as David Steinmetz so aptly titled his effort to expand our horizon of reformers. Indeed, there were so many Reformation theologians that a series of studies devoted only to Reformation dissidents recently published its twentieth volume.[4] Much has been accomplished in recent years to provide a long overdue public stage for, or at least to shine more light upon, those "in the wings" who preached and wrote and legislated for reform, including women.[5]

Yet even a cursory scan of the recently published *Oxford Encyclopedia of the Reformation*, let alone the magisterial German *Theologische Realenzyklopädie*, still in process, reveals the limitations of the present selection. Other Reformers – lumped under the rubric of the "common man" – who were clearly more than just a Greek chorus on the Reformation stage also remain beyond the scope of this text.[6]

The stage itself was also of great significance for both the roles of the Reformers and how they played them. Our focus is on the theologies of the Reformers, but we dare not forget, as Luther himself so vividly stated, that these theologies developed in the midst of life.

> Very little in the Reformation was stable. Not only did the formulation of religious ideas take place amidst wars, persecution and plague, but the very language which the evangelical groups conscripted to their cause formed a brilliant prism, whose diverse colours transformed as it was manipulated. Terms such as church, authority, nation and even reformation itself were variously and often in contradictory ways used in the sixteenth century.[7]

The keen awareness that theologies cannot be abstracted from their historical contexts was already expressed by Bernd Moeller's 1965 warning that the Reformation is too important to be left to the systematic theologians. Without sensitivity to "the Reformation as history," Reformation theology itself may be oversimplified. "After all, this theology had such a great impact in history precisely because it was intricately interwoven into history."[8] Richard A. Muller has more recently made the same point with regard to Calvin. "A clever theologian can accommodate Calvin to nearly any agenda; a faithful theologian – and a good historian – will seek to listen to Calvin, not to use him."[9] The following chapters therefore should be read in conjunction with historical surveys and studies.[10]

Moeller's call for a historical view of the Reformation continues to find a receptive audience, especially among English-speaking scholarship where social history has been ascendant for nearly a generation now. The social historical approach to the Reformation emphasizes the centrality of communal, political, economic, and social goals that stimulated collective behavior. Thus a leading social historian of the Reformation, Thomas A. Brady, Jr., suggests that "perhaps the time has come for a new approach ... the Reformation as an adaptation of Christianity to the social evolution of Europe."[11] The proposals for this are legion: the Reformation as "urban event," "anticlerical event," "ritual event," "communal event," "confessional and social disciplining event," and even "pyschological event."[12] Without gainsaying these and similar approaches, our motif is the Reformation as theological event. John O'Malley's comments about François de Sales, Filippo Neri, and Teresa of Avila may be applied to the Reformation theologians as a whole: "These individuals and phenomena can be studied from many perspectives, but is it not incumbent upon us to study them for what they head-on purported to be about, the sacred?"[13]

Thus it is time to affirm once again, with due appreciation for historical contexts, that theological ideas matter, and that theology may be a motor for historical events and not just driven by them. To think otherwise is an anachronistic "Alice in Wonderland" view of the Reformation in which theology is only the linguistic cloak for the Reformers' "real" motivations. Indeed, it was precisely theology that enabled the reform impulse effectively to cross social and political polarizations.[14] As recently as 1989, Steven Ozment wrote: "The study of the Reformation still awaits a Moses who can lead it through the sea of contemporary polemics between social and intellectual historians and into a historiography both mindful and tolerant of all the forces that shape historical experience."[15]

More words of caution are in order. Our title is not as straightforward as it seems. It should be clear by now that the definite article, "The," does not mean that only those in our volume are Reformation theologians. Also, recent scholarship raises questions about both "Reformation" and "theologians." "Reformation" – how is this word defined and used? "Theologians" – what criteria delineate a theologian? Let us begin with the last and work back to the first, at the same time being aware that these terms are also intimately related.

Theologians

What makes a theologian? More to the point for the figures in this text: "What makes a person a Christian?"[16] Their answers varied and sometimes conflicted, but they agreed that theology is not an abstract intellectual exercise but rather the application of the living voice of the gospel to the lives around them. Theology is for proclamation.[17] It is noteworthy that – sharply put – the Reformation began as a pastoral event rather than as an academic discussion among professors of theology. In this sense, the Reformers stand in continuity with the early church's understanding that "believing" is rooted in "worship" – *lex orandi, lex credendi*.[18] For the Reformation theologians there is an "indissoluble intertwining of affect and intellect, piety and erudition, prayer and thought. . . . *Theology proceeds from worship and returns to it.*"[19]

Note, therefore, in the following chapters the consistent concern to provide works of instruction and edification in the vernacular, as well as the drive from Lefèvre on to make the Scriptures and liturgical materials available in the languages of the laity. The great majority of Luther's first publications were in German rather than the Latin of academe, and were sermons and devotional writings addressed to the fundamental issues of the religious life: the need for God's love and acceptance, and the anxiety before death.[20] Luther first became known not so much as a church rebel, nor even so much as a learned theologian, but rather as a pastor and reformer of the spiritual life.[21]

> Theology was no longer kept under lock and key in academic institutions, but had become the *cause célèbre* of a new public awareness. . . . [T]heology, seen as both the knowledge of faith and practical wisdom applicable to the problems of life, was to be brought out of the monasteries and universities into the streets and city halls. . . . [Luther] succeeded in freeing scholarly theology from the Babylonian captivity of secret and secretive academic debate.[22]

The same point may be made of other Reformers. They gained their audience through devotional and pastoral works, a point often overlooked in the modern interest in their theological systems. In fact, even a doctrinal emphasis such as pre-destination was in its Reformation context not a theological abstraction but an expression of pastoral care that lifted the burden of proof for salvation from human shoulders and placed it squarely on God, where it belongs. The conviction that God is in charge of the universe afforded those in spiritual turmoil and those being persecuted for their faith "unspeakable consolation."[23]

Our representative theologians agreed that the Word of God, God's address to humankind, takes precedence over words about God. Yet, as the following chapters make clear, they did not always agree on the interpretation and application of that Word. Indeed the content of the proclamation was so crucial, that it became church-dividing. With salvation at stake, Reformation theologians were rarely timid in their assertions.[24]

Thus we are reminded that as highly trained in theology as some of our examples were, they remained "innocent" of our contemporary methodological interest in "objectivity." The modern academic ideal of bracketing personal commitment in order to provide comparative and alternative views for discussion or on the supposition that all is relative or that content is discovered through dialogue was alien to the minds of most of our examples. Equally alien was the modern apologetic effort to make the Christian faith "plausible." Indeed, for Reformation theologians, the electrifying power of the gospel – God's justification of the godless – was totally implausible.[25] Hence Luther's sharp response to Erasmus's philosophical reflections on the freedom of the will: "The Holy Spirit is no Skeptic, and it is not doubts or mere opinions that he has written on our hearts, but assertions more sure and certain than life itself and all experience."[26] Such a stance may be offensive to modern ears, but it reminds us that for the Reformation theologians the truth of God's promise was at stake – at times even literally, for the person who proclaimed it![27]

Reformation

Given the Reformers' conviction that the Word of God "is most certainly true," but that its proclamation became church-dividing, is the title of our text misleading? Was there one Reformation or many? The image of the unity of the Reformation is nicely illustrated by a 1521 Zurich woodcut, "The Godly Mill," and a 1617 Dutch broadside, "The Light of the Gospel Rekindled by the Reformers."[28] The two illustrations roughly suggest both the time-span and continental breadth of the Reformation. The former depicts a grain mill that, as the full title states, "operates by the grace of God." In the upper left corner the flame of the Holy Spirit descends from God the Father and propels the mill wheel. Christ stands by the grain hopper and pours into it the four Evangelists and Paul. Erasmus, whose edition of the New Testament was so helpful to Luther and whose humanism was influential upon Zwingli, is the miller shoveling the meal of the gospel into a sack. Behind Erasmus stands Luther, kneading the meal into the bread of evangelical teaching that is then distributed by another figure (Zwingli?) to representatives of the ecclesiastical establishment, who reject it. Above the heads of the recalcitrant clergy and pope is a bird croaking "ban, ban" (Luther was banned on January 3, 1521). A large figure of "Hans the Hoeman," the symbol of the peasantry, looms behind the Catholic clergy, wielding a flail to protect the proclamation of the gospel and to threaten the representatives of the ecclesiastical establishment.

The Dutch broadside depicts 16 Reformers (Luther, Calvin, Melanchthon, Beza, Bucer, Bullinger, Vermigli, Knox, Jerome of Prague, Zwingli, Hus, Wyclif, Zanchi, Perkins, Flacius, and Oecolampadius) crowded around a table with a group portrait of six others (George of Anhalt, John à Laski, Farel, Sleidan, Marnix, and Junius) on the wall behind them. This harmonious union of Reformers, including their "forerunners," Wyclif and Hus, are presented in a kind of Last Supper scene. In the place of Christ is Luther, with a bible open upon the table, flanked by Calvin, also pointing to a book (bible?). Opposite them, in the place of Judas, are a cardinal, a devil, the pope, and a monk, who represent the fourfold form of Catholic false faith. There is a blazing candle in the center of the table, also set upon a bible, that signifies the truth of divine light brought into the open by the Reformers. The Catholic opponents are depicted as the servants of darkness who are attempting in vain to blow out the candle.

These pictures raise all the issues about the Reformation now debated by modern historians and theologians: unity or plurality? If unity, in what did it consist? How long did the Reformation last – a *longue durée* including the late Middle Ages or an episode between 1517 and 1525? Furthermore, these triumphalist representations of the Reformation, and their continuation in more recent "Whiggish" interpretations,[29] do not merely omit Catholic reform but portray the Catholic establishment arrayed with all the forces of evil and obscurantism against reform. The Dutch broadside also illustrates roots of reform – a so-called "First Reformation" – in Wyclif and Hus, a claim once again coming to the fore among their descendants.[30] The pictures are also significant for what they do not portray. "The Godly Mill" does depict the "common man" in the form of the peasant defender of the first Reformers, but the Dutch engraving omits the "common man," and gives no hint of either the so-called Radical Reformers such as Karlstadt and Müntzer or lay theologians such as Schwenckfeld and Argula von Grumbach.

Was there one Reformation or many Reformations? Was there a unified Reformation theology to the extent that we can speak of "Reformation theology" and "Reformation theologians"? Scholarly debate has swirled around these questions for some time, and has not yet concluded. In an extended review of *The Oxford Encyclopedia of the Reformation*, Merry Wiesner-Hanks, one of its editors, states that the *Encyclopedia* reflects the demise of older "orthodoxies" of Reformation scholarship and the rise of new approaches.[31] The "old orthodoxies," both topical and methodological, include the older textbook assumption that the Reformation was bracketed by the *Ninety-five Theses* (1517) and the *Peace of Augsburg* (1555).[32] This time frame focussed the Reformation in the works of a few theologians, hence isolating the Reformation from both early modern social and economic history and continuity with the medieval age. The new approaches that Wiesner-Hanks highlights include awareness of the importance of the institutions created in the latter half of the sixteenth century as well as such topics as "confessionalization," "social disciplining," and "popular religion."[33] Regarding the question of the one and the many Reformation(s), she points to the present

> stress on diversity within Protestantism and Catholicism, on a Reformation that was . . . "pluriform and polycentric"[34] . . . This is not only a Reformation made up of a number of subsidiary Reformations – peoples', urban, communal, princes' – but a Reformation in which these subsidiary movements did not occur in a neat chrono-logical progression, but were interwoven and synchronic. There is no reassuring chain of begats here, nor strong Hegelian dialectic, but a variety of ideas, plans for action, and significant players.[35]

Theologically this is evident in the different understandings of that Reformation watchword *sola scriptura*. Whereas Luther understood Scripture as God's promise, Karlstadt and then the South German and Swiss Reformations viewed Scripture as God's law or blueprint for society.

> To search for unity in the Reformation leads in a false direction, certainly for the years from 1519–1530. The pursuit obscures at least three revolutionary changes: 1. the development of multiple reformation theologies; 2. the rise of autonomous political movements like the Knights' Revolt, the Peasants' Revolt and urban uprisings; 3. divergent interpretations of the goals of the Reformation by various social groups.[36]

However, it is premature to assume that the debate over the plurality of the Reformation is settled. Recently in Germany, three church historians locked horns over whether it is legitimate to speak of *the* Reformation rather than a plurality of impulses, movements, confessions, and interests. Bernd Moeller argued for the unity of the Reformation on the basis of the reception of Luther's theology of justification by grace alone, facilitated by the massive publication of his pastoral and sermonic writings. "Grosso modo the Reformation is tantamount to the reception of Luther."[37] In response, Dorothea Wendebourg argued that the "unity" of the Reformation is a construct imposed upon a plurality of reforming movements by the Counter-Reformation. With reference to the Dutch engraving depicting Protestant harmony mentioned above, she stated: "[It is] a beautiful image of Reformation unity, but we know that it wasn't so. Not harmony, but conflict, not community but refusal of communion fellowship in the Lord's Supper – that was the reality." Further-more, the "left wing" of the Reformation, including such figures as Karlstadt and Müntzer, the Swiss Anabaptists, and German Spiritualists, was not only criticized but also persecuted by the Magisterial Reformers.[38] Thus it was the Counter-Reformation's "pox" on all the reforming houses that projected "unity" upon the disparate movements.

On the other hand, Wendebourg's claim appears dubious in light of the fact that the term "Counter-Reformation" itself stemmed from Protestant anti-Catholic bias. "The first names for the epoch were devised by Protestants. The model and standard for understanding Catholicism was what happened in Protestantism. Thus 'Counter-Reformation' and 'Catholic Reformation.'"[39] Ironically, these Protestant labels for early modern Catholicism projected a unity upon it that obscured its own diversity and complexity.[40] The continuation of the Protestant model for defining the Reformation may be seen in repeated efforts to locate the unity of the Reformation in the doctrine of justification.

Martin Brecht and Berndt Hamm, challenged by Ulrich Gäbler's claim that the concept "Reformation" eludes definition because of theological diversity,[41] argue that there is a consistency in Reformation theology that is historically rooted in the emphasis upon justification as the center and limit of theology. After a discussion of variations on this theme, Brecht states that for Luther, Zwingli, and Calvin: "The essential solidarity exists in the doctrine of justification through faith alone and in the related anthropology of the justified sinner. Where this central teaching is not shared, for example by many representatives of Spiritualism, one is not able to speak of reformatory theology."[42]

Hamm, who adds Melanchthon to Brecht's "big three," posits that recent studies have so emphasized the diversity within the Reformation that it is increasingly difficult to maintain and delineate a core Reformation theology, especially in relation to the doctrine of justification. Consequently, either a common Reformation theology fades from view or the theology of grace is so weakly formulated that a clear demarcation from the Catholic understanding of grace no longer appears possible. "At this point resigned historians meet euphoric ecumenists, who in any case are of the opinion that the doctrine of justification is not church dividing."[43] The latter part of Hamm's point is of interest in light of the theological controversy in Germany over the recent Lutheran–Roman Catholic "Joint Declaration on the Doctrine of Justification."[44] There is a sense in which the controversies of the present are fought through the controversies of the past.[45] Historical study might well carry the same inscription found on a car's passenger-side mirror: "Caution, objects in mirror are closer than they appear." Theologians read the Reformation sources with an eye on contemporary faith and life.[46] In short, theologians are not antiquarians.

More recently, Scott Hendrix set forth his agreement with Moeller, and upped the ante. "A broader definition of the Reformation's agenda is needed in order to ground both its coherence and its significance, for not only has the unity of the Reformation been challenged, but also its significance." Common to all the Reformers was the desire "to uproot the old religion and plant the new."

> [I]s it possible to speak meaningfully of one Reformation with a common agenda? I believe one can do this if the agenda – rerooting the faith in Europe – is seen as the common goal of the Reformation and the disagreements are understood to be different conceptions of how this rerooting could best be accomplished. Protestants and Catholics agreed that the abuses of medieval piety should be abolished, but they disagreed, as did Protestants among themselves, about the extent of that abolition.

In short, differences among the theologians "have to be understood as differences in strategy and not as competing interpretations of Christianity."[47] Hendrix's displacement of theological differences by differences of tactics or strategies echoes earlier claims that it was strategy, not theology, that separated Luther and Karlstadt in the early phase of the Reformation in Wittenberg.[48]

Hendrix illustrates his bold move to create a procrustean bed for Reformation theologians by reference to Cranach the Younger's famous painting of the vineyard of the Lord in the Wittenberg town church. Yet what is immediately striking about

Cranach's late Reformation painting is that the vineyard is divided into two parts. On the left side, the pope and his followers are destroying the vineyard, whereas on the right side, Luther and his followers are restoring and tending it. The didactic and polemical use of artwork in the Reformation period may indeed express Reformation "oneness," but far more often than not that unity is confessionally specific and exclusive.[49]

Furthermore, one need not look hard or far for sharp and mutual condemnations between Reformation theologians. Not without reason, Melanchthon is said to have sighed on his deathbed that finally he would be delivered from the *rabies theologorum*, "the madness of the theologians." Luther referred to Karlstadt as a theologian who had "swallowed the Holy Spirit, feathers and all," and to Müntzer as the devil incarnate. These feelings were mutual.[50] In an apparently mellower mood, Luther summarized his evaluation of others in the slogan: "Substance and eloquence = Philip [Melanchthon]; eloquence without substance = Erasmus; substance without eloquence = Luther; neither substance nor eloquence = Carlstadt."[51] Erasmus wrote to Bucer that one of the reasons he had not joined the evangelical movement was

> the constant in-fighting between the leaders. Leaving aside the Prophets and Anabaptists, just look at the spiteful pamphlets written by Zwingli, Luther and Osiander against each other. . . . The Gospel would have looked good to everyone if the husband had found it made his wife nicer, if the teacher saw his student more obedient, if the magistrate had seen better-behaved citizens, if the employer found his employees more honest, if the buyer saw the merchant less deceitful.

Similarly the humanist Willibald Pirckheimer wrote: "I confess that I initially also was a good Lutheran, as was also our blessed Albrecht [Dürer], for we hoped the Roman knavery as well as the roguishness of the monks and parsons would be improved. But as one watched and waited, matters got worse. . . ." And Calvin wrote to Bullinger concerning Luther's "inordinately passionate and brash character," and warned "that if you engage in battle with him nothing is achieved except provision of entertainment for the unbelievers." But Calvin also appealed to Bullinger to remember "what a great man Luther is, and by what extraordinary spiritual gifts he is distinguished."[52]

In general, the humanists were disappointed that the Reformation did not markedly improve morality. But as Luther himself made clear, *the* issue of reform was not the ethical regeneration of society but the proclamation that salvation is received, not achieved. The very point of justification by grace alone is that discipleship is not dependent upon its results.

> Doctrine and life are to be distinguished. Life is as bad among us as among the papists. Hence we do not fight and damn them because of their bad lives. Wyclif and Hus, who fought over the moral quality of life, failed to understand this. . . . When the Word of God remains pure, even if the quality of life fails us, life is placed in a position to become what it ought to be. That is why everything hinges on the purity of the Word. I have succeeded only if I have taught correctly.[53]

Luther stated the importance of theology even more sharply: "Doctrine directs us and shows the way to heaven. . . . We can be saved without love . . . but not without pure doctrine and faith." Doctrine and life are incomparable; and therefore the devil's argument about "not offending against love and the harmony among the churches" is specious.[54]

It is clear from the above sketch that while there are broad areas of consensus there is not harmony or unity among the proliferating studies of Reformation history and theology. We should not therefore expect the following essays to exhibit what the field as a whole has not achieved. Contributors agreed to address specific theological subjects such as justification and sanctification, hermeneutics, ecclesiology, sacraments, and ethics, but had a free hand to develop the significance and reception of their assigned theologian. Thus each chapter stands on its own, but at the same time sheds light – and perhaps some heat – upon the other chapters. The advantage of a collection such as this is that readers are *not* subjected to a one-dimensional perspective normed by a particular Reformer, but rather are provided with multiple views of Reformation theologians. Read as a whole, this volume provides a window on the theologies of the Reformation period as well as the passionate commitment of our subjects to "reroot" the Christian faith. In a broad sense they all shared a commitment expressed by the motto *ecclesia semper reformanda* – the church always reforming. What they contribute to our own participation in the ongoing reform of the church is the crucial importance of theology to this task.

Notes

1   Bernd Moeller, "Problems of Reformation Research" in his *Imperial Cities and the Reformation: Three Essays*, trans. H. C. Erik Midelfort and Mark U. Edwards, Jr. (Durham, NC: Labyrinth Press, 1982), 16. Francis Higman makes the point that a contribution of church history is enabling a better understanding of contemporary society. Francis Higman, *Lire et Découvrir. La circulation des idées au temps de la Réforme* (Geneva: Droz, 1998), 14.

2   Heinz Schilling, "Luther, Loyola, Calvin und die europäische Neuzeit," ARG 85 (1994), 5–31, here 9. Schilling continues: ". . . with such a sentence a book on the early modern period may begin. . . ."

3   Heiko A. Oberman has stimulated much of the research on the late medieval context of the Reformation. See his *The Harvest of Medieval Theology: Gabriel Biel and Late Medieval Nominalism* (Cambridge, MA: Harvard University Press, 1963) and *Werden und Wertung der Reformation: Vom Wegestreit zum Glaubenskampf* (Tübingen: Mohr, 1977). See also Charles G. Nauert, Jr., *Humanism and the*

Culture of Renaissance Europe (Cambridge: Cambridge University Press, 1998), 144:

> The true programme of Christian humanism, which concerned humanistic studies as an essential part of religious renewal and concentrated on both pagan and Christian Antiquity as a source of inspiration, was essentially the creation of two men, the French humanist Jacques LeFèvre d'Etaples (c.1460–1536) and the Dutch humanist Desiderius Erasmus of Rotterdam (1467?–1536), with Erasmus being by far the more important.

4   *Bibliotheca Dissidentium: Répertoire des non-conformistes religieux des seizième et dix-septième siècles*, under the general editorship of André Séguenny (Baden-Baden and Bouxwiller: Valentin Koerner). Besides David C. Steinmetz, *Reformers in the Wings* (Philadelphia: Fortress Press, 1971), see the similar efforts by B. A. Gerrish, ed., *Reformers in Profile: Advocates of Reform 1300–1600* (Philadelphia:

Fortress Press, 1967); Martin Greschat, ed., *Gestalten der Kirchengeschichte: Die Reformationszeit*, 2 vols. (Stuttgart: Kohlhammer, 1981); and Hans-Jürgen Goertz, ed., *Profiles of Radical Reformers: Biographical Sketches from Thomas Müntzer to Paracelsus* (Kitchener: Herold Press, 1982).

5   See Merry Wiesner, *Women and Gender in Early Modern Europe* (Cambridge: Cambridge University Press, 1993). See also her chapter "Family, Household, and Community" with bibliography in Thomas A. Brady, Jr., Heiko A. Oberman, and James D. Tracy, eds., *Handbook of European History 1400–1600* (Leiden: E. J. Brill, 1994), vol. 1: 51–78. A special edition of *The Sixteenth Century Journal* (31/ 1 [Spring 2000]) is devoted to "Gender in Early Modern Europe."

6   See Heiko A. Oberman, "*Die Gelehrten die Verkehrten:* Popular Response to Learned Culture in the Renaissance and the Reformation" in his *The Impact of the Reformation* (Grand Rapids: Eerdmans, 1994), 201–24, here 224: "Reformation propaganda found a ready and alert audience, as is succinctly formulated in one of the most impressive Reformation pamphlets: 'Don't believe them when they say, "ja, die bawrenn verstehen die sach nicht."'" Luther's self-consciously broad appeal is reflected in his statement that "in my office of teacher, a prince is the same to me as a peasant." LW 46:75; WA 18:393, 22f., cited by Hans-Christoph Rublack, "Reformation und Moderne. Soziologische, theologische und historische Ansichten" in Hans Guggisberg and Gottfried Krodel, eds., *The Reformation in Germany and Europe: Interpretations and Issues* (Gütersloh: Gütersloher Verlagshaus, 1993), 17–38, here 29. More than any other contemporary scholar, Peter Blickle has striven to bring "the common man" center stage. See his *The Revolution of 1525. The German Peasants' War from a New Perspective*, trans. Thomas A. Brady, Jr. and H. C. Erik Midelfort (Baltimore: Johns Hopkins University Press, 1981); *Communal Reformation. The Quest for Salvation in Sixteenth-Century Germany*, trans. Thomas Dunlap (Atlantic Highlands: Humanities Press, 1992); and *From the Communal Reformation to the Revolution of the Common Man* (Leiden: E. J. Brill, 1998). For critical responses to Blickle's work see the reviews by Mark U. Edwards, Jr. in *Historische Zeitschrift* 249 (1989), 95–103, and *CHR* 79/2 (1993), 332–3.

7   Bruce Gordon, "The Changing Face of Protestant History and Identity in the Sixteenth Century" in Bruce Gordon, ed., *Protestant History and Identity in Sixteenth-Century Europe*, 2 vols. (Aldershot: Scolar Press, 1996), 2:7. For lively description and analysis of Reformation rhetoric see Peter Matheson's *The Rhetoric of the Reformation* (Edinburgh: T. & T. Clark, 1998) and *The Imaginative World of the Reformation* (Edinburgh: T. & T. Clark, 2000).

8   Moeller, "Problems of Reformation Research," 7. This essay originally appeared as "Probleme der Reformationsgeschichtsforschung," *ZKG* 14 (1965), 246–57.

9   Richard A. Muller, *The Unaccommodated Calvin: Studies in the Foundation of a Theological Tradition* (New York: Oxford University Press, 2000), 188.

10 See for example: Thomas Brady, Jr., Heiko A. Oberman, and James D. Tracy, eds., *Handbook of European History 1400–1600: Late Middle Ages, Renaissance and Reformation*, 2 vols. (Leiden: E. J. Brill, 1994/5); Euan Cameron, *The European Reformation* (Oxford: Clarendon Press, 1991); Carter Lindberg, *The European Reformations* (Oxford: Blackwell, 1996) and companion volume, *The European Reformations Sourcebook* (Oxford: Blackwell, 2000); Steven Ozment, *The Age of Reform 1250–1550: An Intellectual and Religious History of Late Medieval and Reformation Europe* (New Haven: Yale University Press, 1980); and Andrew Pettegree, ed., *The Reformation World* (London and New York: Routledge, 2000).

11 Thomas A. Brady, Jr., "Social History" in Steven Ozment, ed., *Reformation Europe: A Guide to Research* (St. Louis: Center for Reformation Research, 1982), 161–81, here 176. See also Heiko A. Oberman's comments on "the loaded language of social analysis" in his *The Impact of the Reformation*, 179–83.

12 The literature is too extensive to list in detail, but representative scholars associated with these designators include: A. G. Dickens, Hans-Jürgen Goertz, Robert Scribner and Susan Karant-Nunn, Peter Blickle, Heinz Schilling, and Erik Erikson. For overviews see Walter Ziegler, "Sozial- und Religionsgeschichte in Deutschland in der frühen Neuzeit. Eine historiographische Bilanz," *ZKG* 110/3 (1999), 372–85; and Craig Harline, "Official Religion – Popular Religion in Recent Historiography of the Catholic Reformation," *ARG* 81 (1990), 239–57.

13 John W. O'Malley, *Trent and All That: Re-naming Catholicism in the Early Modern Era* (Cambridge, MA: Harvard University Press, 2000), 139.

14 Berndt Hamm, "Reformation 'von unten' und Reformation 'von oben': Zur Problematik reformationshistorischer Klassifizierungen" in Guggisberg and Krodel, *The Reformation*, 256–93, here 289. See Heiko A. Oberman, *The Reformation: Roots & Ramifications*, trans. Andrew Colin Gow (Grand Rapids: Eerdmans, 1994), 203:

> The de-confessionalization of Reformation history has brought forth more balanced judgements, but there is also a price to pay. The events of the first half of the sixteenth century are no longer subjected to narrowly dogmatic interpretation, but theological interpretation has also been banished. . . . [T]hose frequently proclaimed as the "true reformers", [are] those not motivated by theological considerations. They are often presented as the "real" agents, seen from the social perspective, behind the progressive, forward-looking decisions and events of the Reformation.

Older Marxist historiography understood theology as the language of the time for social and economic issues. But see also Tom Scott's critique of Blickle's affirmation of the role of theology in the Communal Reformation: "In a sentence, I believe that it was possible to achieve a Communal Reformation without the introduction of evangelical religion." Tom Scott, "The Communal Reformation between Town and Country" in Guggisberg and Krodel, *The Reformation*, 175–92, here 192.

15 Steven Ozment, ed., *Religion and Culture in the Renaissance and Reformation* (Kirksville: Sixteenth Century Journal Publishers, 1989), "Introduction," 4. However, Ozment also noted (3): "To a remarkable degree, religion emerged as the unifying theme of the conference, far more than either 'cities' or 'culture.' "

16 In Luther's "Letter to the Christians at Strassburg in Opposition to the Fanatic Spirit" (1524) he wrote:

> My sincere counsel and warning is that you be circumspect and hold to the single question, what makes a person a Christian? Do not on any account allow any other question or other art to enjoy equal importance. When anyone proposes anything ask him at once, "Friend, will this make one a Christian or not?" If not, it cannot be a matter of major importance which requires earnest consideration. *LW* 40:67–8

17 See Gerhard O. Forde, *Theology is for Proclamation* (Minneapolis: Fortress Press, 1990). See also Oswald Bayer, "Geistgabe und Bildungsarbeit," chapter 21 in his collection *Gott als Autor: Zu einer poietologischen Theologie* (Tübingen: Mohr Siebeck, 1999).

18 The abbreviated version of Prosper of Aquitaine's (c.390–c.463) *ut legem credendi lex statuat supplicandi* – "the rule of prayer should lay down the rule of faith." See Jaroslav Pelikan, *The Christian Tradition: A History of the Development of Doctrine*, vol. 1: *The Emergence of the Catholic Tradition (100–600)* (Chicago: University of Chicago Press, 1975), 339.

19 Oswald Bayer, *Theologie*, vol. 1 of *Handbuch Systematischer Theologie*, ed. Carl Heinz Ratschow (Gütersloh: Gütersloher Verlagshaus, 1994), 18.

20 See, for example, Jared Wicks, SJ, "Applied Theology at the Deathbed: Luther and the Late-Medieval Tradition of the *Ars moriendi*," *Gregorianum* 79/2 (1998), 345–68.

21 Bernd Moeller, "Die Rezeption Luthers in der frühen Reformation" in Berndt Hamm, Bernd Moeller, and Dorothea Wendebourg, *Reformationstheorien: Ein kirchenhistorischer Disput über Einheit und Vielfalt der Reformation* (Göttingen: Vandenhoeck & Ruprecht, 1995), 16–17. See also Oswald Bayer, "Luther's Ethics as Pastoral Care," *LQ* 4/2 (Summer 1990), 125–42. See Mark U. Edwards, Jr., *Printing, Propaganda, and Martin Luther* (Berkeley: University of California Press, 1994), 164: "Thanks to these largely pastoral and devotional works, Luther became Germany's first best-selling vernacular author, speaking to a far wider audience than, say, the humanists who had used the press before him."

22 Oberman, *The Reformation*, 207. See also Higman, *Lire et Découvrir*, 87–106, 179–200, 531–44.

23 Article 13 of the *Belgic Confession of Faith* (1561). See Lindberg, *The European Reformations Sourcebook*, 208.

24 See Harding Meyer, " 'Delectari assertionibus' On the Issue of the Authority of Christian

Testimony" in Carter Lindberg, ed., *Piety, Politics, and Ethics: Reformation Studies in Honor of George Wolfgang Forell* (Kirksville: Sixteenth Century Journal Publishers, 1984), 1–14.

25 See Gerhard Sauter, "Rechtfertigung VI" in *TRE* 28 (1997), here 342–44, with English translation in *LQ* 11/1 (Spring 1997), here 83.

26 *LW* 33:24. Also, *LW* 33:21, "Nothing is better known among Christians than assertion. Take away assertions and you take away Christianity." See Leif Grane, *Martinus Noster: Luther in the German Reform Movement 1518–1521* (Mainz: Zabern Verlag, 1994), 294: "With very few exceptions his [Luther's] theology was no obstacle because they [humanists] at first had no base on which they could make up their minds about it – unless they began to realize that without theology in the sense of *assertiones* it would never be possible to pass from talking to acting."

27 Martyrologies representing all parties in the Reformation conflicts became in themselves theologies of history showing the continuity, and thereby authenticity, of the present-day church under the cross with the suffering of the early church. See for example, David Watson, "Jean Crespin and the Writing of History in the French Reformation" and Andrew Pettegree, "Adriaan van Haemstede: the Heretic as Historian," both in Bruce Gordon, ed., *Protestant History and Identity in Sixteenth-Century Europe*, 2 vols. (Aldershot: Scolar Press, 1996), 39–58, 59–76; Robert Kolb, *For All the Saints. Changing Perceptions of Martyrdom and Sainthood in the Lutheran Reformation* (Macon, GA: Mercer University Press, 1987); and Brad S. Gregory, *Salvation at Stake: Christian Martyrdom in Early Modern Europe* (Cambridge: Harvard University Press, 1999).

28 Both illustrations are in Lindberg, *The European Reformations*, 176, 378. The Dutch broadsheet is also described and discussed in Dorothea Wendebourg, "Die Einheit der Reformation als historisches Problem" in Hamm, Moeller, and Wendebourg, *Reformationstheorien*, 30–51, 31–2.

29 See Philip Benedict, "Between Whig Traditions and New Histories: American Historical Writing about Reformation and Early Modern Europe" in Anthony Molho and Gordon S. Wood, eds., *Imagined Histories: American Historians Interpret the Past* (Princeton: Princeton University Press, 1998), 295–323.

30 See the arguments advanced by Czech theologians that the "first" Reformation was initiated by Hus, and that therefore the sixteenth-century Reformation was the "second" Reformation. Much of this material is available in the publications of the "Prague Consultations," a multilateral ecumenical dialogue sponsored by the World Alliance of Reformed Churches and the Lutheran World Federation. My critical responses are "A Specific Contribution of the Second Reformation" in Milan Opocenský, ed., *Towards A Renewed Dialogue: Consultation on the First and Second Reformations* (Geneva: World Alliance of Reformed Churches, 1996), 39–62 and "Towards a More Comprehensive and Inclusive View of the Reformation and Its Significance for Today" in the "Prague VI" Consultation (forthcoming). Zdenek David suggests that the preoccupation of Czech historians and theologians with expanding the concept of the Reformation to include the Utraquist movement is a misguided tendency that may be a central European variant of the Whig interpretation of history. Zdenek David, "The Strange Fate of Czech Utraquism: The Second Century, 1517–1621," *JEH* 46/4 (October 1995), 647–8.

31 Merry Wiesner-Hanks, "Traditional Orthodoxies and New Approaches: An Editor's Perspective on the Oxford Encyclopedia of the Reformation," *CH* 67/1 (March 1998), 107–13. See also the review by Mickey Mattox in *LQ* 14/2 (Summer 2000), 225–30.

32 See, for example, the classic textbooks of the prior generation: Harold J. Grimm, *The Reformation Era 1500–1650* (New York: Macmillan, 1954; revised 1965), and G. R. Elton, *Reformation Europe 1517–1559*, 2nd edn, with an Afterword by Andrew Pettegree (Oxford: Blackwell, 1999). The first edition was in 1963. Pettegree remarks that Elton's narrative presentation of the Reformation "as a drama formed principally through the conflicts of its leading actors" went out of fashion with the rise of social history in the sixties. "No history of the sixteenth century would now begin as Elton does, with Martin Luther, nor even with the Reformation; though thankfully, the contrary fashion for writing the history of the age almost without mentioning Luther seems also to have passed." Pettegree, "Afterword," 236.

33 For introductions to these approaches see Heinz Schilling, "The Reformation and the Rise of the Early Modern State" in James

D. Tracy, ed., *Luther and the Modern State in Germany* (Kirksville: Sixteenth Century Journal Publishers, 1986), 21–30; Heinz Schilling, "Confessional Europe" in Brady, Oberman, and Tracy, *Handbook*, 2:641–81; R. Po-Chia Hsia, *Social Discipline in the Reformation: Central Europe 1550–1750* (London/New York: Routledge, 1989). Reviews of the debate over confessionalization include Joel Harrington and Helmut Walser Smith, "Confessionalization, Community, and State Building in Germany, 1555–1870," *Journal of Modern History* 69/1 (1997), 77–101), and Thomas Kaufmann, "Die Konfessionalizierung von Kirche und Gesellschaft," *Theologische Literaturzeitung* 121/11 (1996), 1008–25; 121/12 (1996), 1112–21. See also Susan Karant-Nunn, *The Reformation of Ritual: An Interpretation of Early Modern Germany* (London and New York: Routledge, 1997) and Robert W. Scribner, "Elements of Popular Belief" in Brady, Oberman, and Tracy, *Handbook* 1:231–62.

34   David Lotz, "Protestantism: An Overview" in *OER* 3:352.

35   Wiesner-Hanks, "Traditional Orthodoxies," 111.

36   Miriam U. Chrisman, "The Reformation of the Laity" in Guggisberg and Krodel, *The Reformation*, 627–46, here 627.

37   Bernd Moeller, "Die Rezeption Luthers in der frühen Reformation," in Moeller, Hamm, and Wendebourg, *Reformationstheorien*, 10. See also Thomas A. Brady, Jr.'s review in *SCJ* 27/1 (Spring 1996), 286–9; I have used Brady's translation.

38   Wendebourg, "Die Einheit," 32.

39   O'Malley, *Trent and All That*, 120.

40   Ibid., 121–2.

41   Ulrich Gäbler, *Huldrych Zwingli: His Life and Work*, trans. Ruth Gritsch (Minneapolis: Fortress Press, 1986), 47:

In view of the diversity of theological positions among sixteenth-century Protestants, the concept "Reformation" cannot be precisely defined historically. Although earlier – and still today, in confessional Lutheran research – it was commonly equated with the theology of the Wittenberg reformer, the precise meaning of the term is increasingly obscured in the literature. If the term is used anyway, it is to point out that what happened was

disengagement from the traditional church and its doctrine. With regard to content, various ways of dealing with this newly won viewpoint can be imagined. Luther's theology was probably the most significant force, but it was in no way the only effective one.

Martin Brecht, "Theologie oder Theologien der Reformation?" in Guggisberg and Krodel, *The Reformation*, 99–117, here 99; Berndt Hamm, "Was ist reformatorische Rechtfertigungslehre?," *ZThK* 83/1 (1986), 1–38, here 2, n. 3.

42   Brecht, "Theologie," 116.

43   Hamm, "Was ist reformatorische Rechtfertigungslehre?" 2.

44   For the statement and commentary see *Joint Declaration on the Doctrine of Justification: A Commentary by the Institute for Ecumenical Research, Strasbourg* (Geneva: Lutheran World Federation, 1997). The controversy was widely covered in public media such as the *Frankfurter Allgemeine Zeitung*, as well as theological journals. See my "Do Lutherans Shout Justification But Whisper Sanctification?," *LQ* 13/1 (1999), 1–20, here 13–14, 19. See also Johannes Brosseder, Ulrich Kühn, and Hans-Georg Link, *Überwindung der Kirchenspaltung: Konsequenzen aus der Gemeinsamen Erklärung zur Rechtfertigungslehre* (Neukirchen-Vluyn: Neukirchener Verlag, 2000) and Eberhard Jüngel, ed., *Zur Rechtfertigungslehre*, Beiheft 10, *ZThK* (1998).

45   O'Malley, *Trent and All That*, 80, 82. Hamm, "Was ist reformatorische Rechtfertigungslehre," 2, makes the point that our questions about the Reformation get caught up in the contemporary evangelical churches' search for identity.

46   Histories of interpretations of the Reformation document that personal and ideological involvement in historical studies is by no means limited to theologians. See for example, A. G. Dickens and John M. Tonkin, *The Reformation in Historical Thought* (Cambridge, MA: Harvard University Press, 1985). That personal involvement with the past extends to other eras as well is illustrated by Norman F. Cantor, *Inventing the Middle Ages: The Lives, Works, and Ideas of the Great Medievalists of the Twentieth Century* (New York: William Morrow, 1991).

47   Scott Hendrix, "Rerooting the Faith: The Coherence and Significance of the Reformation,"

Princeton Seminary Bulletin 21/1 (n.s., 2000), 63–80, here 64–5, 67, 72, 73. O'Malley, *Trent and All That*, 76, points out that the Catholic scholar, H. Outram Evennett, made a comparable point well over a generation ago when he claimed "that both the Reformation and the 'Counter-Reformation' were two different outcomes of the same general aspiration toward 'religious regeneration' that pervaded the late fifteenth and early sixteenth centuries." Hendrix, 71, credits Jean Delumeau's thesis on the Catholic Reformation as Christianization (*Catholicism between Luther and Voltaire* [Philadelphia: Westminster Press, 1977]) for stimulating his own argument. On Delumeau see John W. O'Malley, *Trent and All That*, 100–3, and his references to Michel Despland, "How Close Are We To Having A Full History of Christianity? The Work of Jean Delumeau," *Religious Studies Review* 9/1 (January 1983), 24–33; Robert Birely, SJ, "Two Works by Jean Delumeau," *CHR* 77 (1991), 78–88; and Heiko A. Oberman's review in *SCJ* 23/1 (1993), 149–50.

48 See Ulrich Bubenheimer, "Scandalum et ius divinum. Theologische und rechtstheologische Probleme der erste reformatorische Innovationen in Wittenberg 1521/22," *Zeitschrift*

der Savigny-Stiftung für Rechtsgeschichte 90 (1973), 263–342, here 287: "The legal theological problem of the Wittenberg reform movement was a problem less of the contents of the reforms than strategies of reform." James S. Preuss, *Carlstadt's 'Ordinaciones' and Luther's Liberty: A Study of the Wittenberg Movement 1521–22* (Cambridge, MA: Harvard University Press, 1974), 2: "It is the contention of this study that the fundamental issues in 1521–22 were issues of religious *policy*. . . . To be sure, the theologies of Carlstadt and Luther were by no means identical in 1521–22, but neither were theological differences the decisive reason for their separation."

49 See Andrew Pettegree, "Art" in Pettegree, *The Reformation World*, 461–90, with reference to the vineyard painting on 477.

50 For a review of their mutual condemnations see my "Theology and Politics: Luther the Radical and Müntzer the Reactionary," *Encounter* 37/4 (Autumn 1976), 356–71.

51 *WA TR* 3:619; *LW* 54:245. Cited by Moeller, "Problems of Reformation Research," 11.

52 Lindberg, *The European Reformations Sourcebook*, 262–5.

53 *LW* 54:110.

54 *LW* 27:41f.

Bibliography

Brady, Thomas A., Jr., *Communities, Politics and Reformation in Early Modern Europe*, Leiden: E. J. Brill, 1998. Collection of previously published essays. See especially Chapter 1: "Prolegomena: Social History of Early Modern Europe."

Dickens, A. G. and John Tonkin, with Kenneth Powell, *The Reformation in Historical Thought*, Cambridge, MA: Harvard University Press, 1985. Comprehensive historiography of interpretations of the Reformation from the sixteenth century to the present.

Dixon, C. Scott, ed., *The German Reformation: The Essential Readings*, Oxford: Blackwell, 1999. Collection of key interpretive essays by major scholars.

Engen, John Van, "The Christian Middle Ages as an Historiographical Problem," *American Historical Review* 91/3 (1986), 519–52.

Greengrass, Mark, *The European Reformation c.1500–1618*, London and New York: Longman, 1998. An excellent resource on every aspect of the Reformation.

Guggisberg, Hans R. and Gottfried Krodel, with Hans Füglister, eds., *The Reformation in Germany and Europe: Interpretations and Issues* (special volume of the *Archiv für Reformationsgeschichte*), Gütersloh: Gütersloher Verl.-Haus, 1993. Papers from an international forum on all aspects of contemporary Reformation research, including theology.

Luebke, David M., ed., *The Counter-Reformation: The Essential Readings*, Oxford: Blackwell, 1999. Collection of key interpretive texts by major scholars.

Maltby, William S., ed., *Reformation Europe: A Guide to Research II*, St. Louis: Center for Reformation Research, 1992.

McGrath, Alister, *Reformation Thought: An Introduction*, 3rd edn, Oxford: Blackwell, 1999. Useful appendices list English translations of Reformers' writings, bibliographical resources, chronology, etc.

O'Malley, John W., *Trent and All That: Renaming Catholicism in the Early Modern Era*, Cambridge,

MA: Harvard University Press, 2000. Comprehensive review of the historiography of "early modern Catholicism."

——, ed., *Catholicism in Early Modern History: A Guide to Research*, St. Louis: Center for Reformation Research, 1988.

Ozment, Steven, ed., *Reformation Europe: A Guide to Research*, St. Louis: Center for Reformation Research, 1982.

German handbooks provide comprehensive introductions to the literature and issues of Reformation studies. See, for example:

Blickle, Peter, *Unruhen in der Ständischen Gesellschaft 1300–1800* (Enzyklopädie Deutscher Geschichte, Bd. 1), Munich: Oldenbourg, 1988.

Goertz, Hans-Jürgen, *Religiöse Bewegungen in der Frühen Neuzeit* (Enzyklopädie Deutscher Geschichte, Bd. 20), Munich: Oldenbourg, 1993.

Lutz, Heinrich, *Reformation und Gegen-Reformation* (Oldenbourg Grundriss der Geschichte), 3rd edn, Munich: Oldenbourg, 1991.

Schilling, Heinz, *Die Stadt in der Frühen Neuzeit* (Enzyklopädie Deutscher Geschichte, Bd. 24), Munich: Oldenbourg, 1993.

Schmidt, Heinrich Richard, *Konfessionalisierung im 16. Jahrhundert* (Enzyklopädie Deutscher Geschichte, Bd. 12), Munich: Oldenbourg, 1992.

See also volumes 7–8 of the French handbook, *Histoire du Christianisme*, under the general editorship of J.-M. Mayeur, Paris: Desclée, 1992.

Humanist Theologians

Jacques Lefèvre d'Etaples (c.1460–1536)

Guy Bedouelle, OP

Faber Stapulensis, Jacques Lefèvre, was born about 1460 in Etaples in Picardy, the northern French province from which came Farel and Calvin. Though a priest, he was never a doctor of theology, a point that his theologian adversaries such as Noël Beda would not hesitate to emphasize. Nevertheless, he rightly deserves to be ranked among the theologians of his time, especially because of the influence he exercised upon his contemporaries, due perhaps as much to his person or center of interest than to his specific ideas.

We know him by his writings, which were widespread during his time, but which after his death were for all practical purposes not well known and of little influence. In distinction from Erasmus, we have very little of his correspondence, although the numerous dedications addressed and received permit the drawing of a sufficiently complete portrait of him.[1]

This serene and peaceful man, friend of cloisters and books, had an eventful enough life, and its evolution knew numerous stages, reflected by the different circles of his entourage. This is why it is essential to begin by tracing the influences upon his theological thinking and the different periods of his life. After this, we shall examine his hermeneutics and some themes of his theology.

The Four Circles of Lefèvre d'Etaples

Lefèvre is one of the most precocious and most famous figures of French humanism, studiously applying himself to return *ad fontes*! The return to the sources, in his case, may appear eclectic but it is unified by a vision of spiritual theology. In fact, Lefèvre found himself at the confluence of divers interests that were like successive stages in his intellectual itinerary: first philosophy, then medieval spirituality and patristics, and finally Holy Scripture. At each stage he was at first surrounded by teachers but soon by friends and disciples. It has been noted that the devotion Lefèvre aroused throughout the course of his career was so extensive that Erasmus appeared jealous at times of those "Fabristae." His disciples came from far – Hungary and Poland – and near, and were true friends in spite of age differences.

Paris

Lefèvre was a student and then a professor at the Collège du Cardinal-Lemoine in Paris. During his visit to Italy in 1492, he encountered the Aristotelian Barbaro, the Platonist Ficino, and Pico della Mirandola, who was attempting a synthesis of the two traditions. On his return, Lefèvre became the "restorer" of Aristotle, annotating the whole of the latter's work, but he also was interested in the hermetic writings and in Pseudo-Dionysius. He retained the most mystical writings of the Middle Ages, for example those of Richard of Saint Victor, Ramon Lull, Ruysbroeck, and Hildegard of Bingen. As for patristics, although he himself edited *The Pastor* of Hermas, he had a circle of disciples working for him. These books, published by the first Parisian printers (W. Hopyl, J. Higman, H. Estienne, and Josse Bade), are characterized by a labor of editing, translation when needed, and annotations according to a pedagogical method he maintained to the end of his life. His works are further unified by his concern for the communication of his Christian convictions. According to a comment in his 1505 Preface to Ramon Lull's *Contemplations,* this editorial activity was a vocation that substituted for the call to the monastic life for which his health made him unfit. His work as editor culminated with three volumes of the works of Nicholas of Cusa in 1514, of which he was the chief architect, supported by a veritable team of scholars including Reuchlin and Beatus Rhenanus.

Lefèvre gradually abandoned this sphere of interests in order to devote himself exclusively to the Bible. He did so in three stages, comparable to three "conversions," becoming commentator, translator, and, with his disciples, preacher. From 1509, when he was in contact with Josse Clichtove – his earliest disciple – Charles de Bovelles, Alain de Varènes – who later kept their distance – and François Vatable, Lefèvre resided at the abby of Saint-Germain-des-Prés in Paris, where he had been called by Guillaume Briçonnet. There he presented in synoptic form five Latin versions of the Psalter, the *Quincuplex Psalterium,* a work whose annotations by both Luther and Zwingli we know.[2] This work, wonderfully printed by Henri Estienne, was re-edited by Lefèvre in 1513. The year before, he had published a commentary on the Pauline epistles that certainly constituted a turn in his theological thinking and which was read as a work announcing the intuitions of the Protestant Reformation. This work is of major importance for dealing with his theology.

In the second edition, curiously antedated to 1515, he responded to Erasmus's comments in the *Annotationes* of the *Novum Instrumentum* of 1516, that gave rise to a dispute over interpretation.[3] The error of the publication date was probably only the printer's mistake, but the importance of this controversy may not be underestimated to the extent that, as we shall see, Erasmus, outraged by this public contradiction, was able to detect and reveal certain weaknesses of the Parisian humanist's exegesis. Another controversy centered on who was right concerning the liturgy that made Mary Magdalene into one person whereas the Gospels, Lefèvre maintained in terms of the tradition, apparently distinguished three Marys.[4]

In any case, these disputes between humanists – and it was also one of the arguments of Erasmus – became a card in the hand of the professional theologians who were on the alert for divisions among the partisans of belles-lettres, and attentive to their mistakes. To protect himself from these attacks, Lefèvre left Saint-Germain-des-Prés, but remained fully at the service and under the protection of his former student, Guillaume Briçonnet, who invited him to follow him to Meaux where he became the bishop.

Meaux

In 1521, after arriving in Meaux, Lefèvre, who became a sort of episcopal vicar to Briçonnet, began his commentary on the four Gospels. A circle of disciples formed around him composed of François Vatable, one of the best Hebraists of his day; Gérard Roussel; Michel d'Arande, an itinerant preacher supported at the Court by the sister of the king, Marguerite d'Alençon; Martial Masurier, a doctor of the Sorbonne; and at certain times, Guillaume Farel. It can be said that this circle constituted a laboratory of preaching. Lefèvre and his disciples composed a collection of homilies on the pericopes for Sundays and the major festivals that by its simple, pastoral style and unique recourse to Scripture broke with the contemporary sermonic style of inexhaustible divisions, taken from scholastic usage, or occasional ludicrous anecdotes and exempla. In place of such homiletic pedantry, Lefèvre and his colleagues concentrated on the proclamation of the Christian faith and its mysteries. Lefèvre also translated the New Testament into French in order to facilitate its reading by the people.

In a second stage that began in April 1523, the circle of disciples was modified. Though Roussel, d'Arande, and Masurier remained, there were now present more radical figures such as Matthieu Saunier or Jacques Pauvan, who was burned at the stake in Paris in 1525. There was also Pierre Caroli, a doctor of the Sorbonne, who oscillated between Rome and Geneva. This is why, in the context of the penetration of Lutheran ideas into France, the attacks of the Paris Theology Faculty became incessant, and Lefèvre's commentary on the Gospels was subjected to examination. Briçonnet, as early as October 1523, forbade his diocesan priests to possess Luther's works. This is the time frame for dating two letters by Lefèvre to Guillaume Farel, then in Basel, which affirm his sympathy "for that which comes from Germany," and his admiration for the Reformation theses of Breslau composed in April 1524 by Johannes Hess, which he found "consonant with the Spirit."[5]

Meanwhile, King Francis I, taken prisoner at Pavia and imprisoned in Madrid, who through his sister, Marguerite, was the protector of Lefèvre, was no longer able to act. Thus Lefèvre and some members of his circle at Meaux considered they had to leave the diocese and find a refuge in Strasbourg.

Strasbourg

In Strasbourg, which he reached at the end of October 1525, Lefèvre composed his commentary on the "Catholic Epistles," published in 1527, the last work signed by his name. But above all, he pursued the French translation of the Vulgate Bible that would lead to a complete version of the Bible in French. It was printed in Antwerp in 1530. This translation, at least the New Testament part, largely inspired the celebrated translation by Pierre Olivétan, Calvin's cousin, requested by the Waldensians at their Synod of Chanforan in 1532. Lefèvre's translation would also influence future generations of Catholic translations at Louvain. Francis I, now released from captivity, recalled Lefèvre to France, to where he returned in April 1526. He had spent about six months in Strasbourg, a city engaged in a relatively peaceful transition to the Reformation, even though the reforming preachers had to overcome tensions due to both the prudence of the civil authorities and the more radical ideas of the numerous German refugees from the Peasants' War. It is known that during this time profound liturgical innovations had been introduced under the pressure of this reforming group.

Strasbourg bordered on another milieu to Lefèvre, even though he was accompanied by Gérard Roussel and Michel d'Arande of the Meaux group and Guillaume Farel was already present there. The city was at least marked, if not dominated, by Martin Bucer, who had arrived in May 1523, left his Dominican order, married, and already manifested the power and ingenuity of his theology. The circle Lefèvre found there included Matthias Zell, the Cathedral preacher; Wolfgang Capito, who had arrived from Basel and in whose home Lefèvre found lodging; and also François Lambert of Avignon and Caspar Hedio. At this time, when Bucer was preparing his commentaries on the Synoptic Gospels, there was a veritable exegetical school in Strasbourg whose members devoted themselves to editing, translating, writing commentaries, and also teaching. Discussions on the Bible and theology were not lacking, as witnessed by Bucer's remembrance in a letter to Boniface Wolfhart, future Reformer of Augsburg: "You remember, Boniface, that discussion I had with you in Capito's large house, opposite the Saint-Pierre-le-Jeune graveyard, in front of the windows of the heated room where Lefèvre was."[6]

If we believe a letter written in December 1525 by Gérard Roussel to a correspondent in Meaux, the French were enthusiastic about what they saw in Strasbourg "where Christ alone is worshipped."[7] However, judging by the disappointed remarks of Pierre Toussain, former canon of Metz, written to Oecolampadius in July 1526, neither Lefèvre nor Roussel was apparently ready to take steps to transport this development back to France. According to Toussain, the two men, once they had returned to France, considered that "the hour [had] not yet arrived."[8] Lefèvre, being able once again to benefit from royal protection, had indeed returned to France.

Nérac

In May 1530, after having been for a while the tutor to the children of Francis I in Blois and royal librarian, Lefèvre requested permission to retire. The hardening of religious policy, symbolized by the execution of Louis de Berquin in April 1529, but also the age of the old humanist, were probably the reasons for this request. Lefèvre finished his life in Nérac, at the court of Marguerite, who in 1547 became Queen of Navarre. He was there in the company of his faithful friends Michel d'Arande and Gérard Roussel, no doubt because a common affection and admiration linked them to the poetically talented sister of Francis I, "Marguerite of the princesses," as she was called in his 1547 collection of works. It was the Queen of Navarre who there played the principal role at that time when she published *The Mirror of the Sinful Soul*. Clément Marot arrived in December 1534 after the affair of the placards, and remained there until March 1535. It seems that when Bonaventure des Périers entered the service of Marguerite and arrived in Navarre at the end of 1536, Lefèvre had already been dead for some months; perhaps he died in March.[9]

Lefèvre made no declaration of a break with the Roman Church, but neither did he make any statements of retraction or conformity to the doctrines of the Church as apparently Rome requested of him. It appears, moreover, that in 1525 Erasmus had intervened in his favor with the Roman proceedings, if one may judge by a sufficiently cryptic phrase by Gian-Matteo Giberti, datary of Pope Clement VII, in a letter of November 27, 1525.[10]

Only a close reading of Lefèvre's works may provide the keys of a very nuanced thinking that strove for balance in pursuit of concord and harmony. One must take into account, of course, the last ten years of his life, during which he did not publish much beyond his complete translation of the Bible into French. One can understand, then, how his case – and particularly his silence – has been made the object of divergent interpretations encountered in his historiography.[11] In considering Lefèvre as a theologian, it is advisable to take into account not only the evolution of his thought but also its constant elements, such as the Apostolic Fathers, Pseudo-Dionysius, Christian Cabbala, the mystics, and also Nicholas of Cusa, in his endeavor to reconcile thought for a "Catholic Concordance."

The Biblical Hermeneutic

Lefèvre's *Prefaces* to his biblical works trace a path toward an increasingly Christocentric interpretation of Scripture. As early as his *Quincuplex Psalterium* (1509), Lefèvre proposed a hermeneutic based on the coincidence of the literal meaning and the spiritual sense becoming the "true" literal sense of Scripture. "We call literal the sense that agrees with Spirit and that the Holy Spirit reveals to us."[12] Similarly, in his teaching of Aristotle, Lefèvre distanced himself from the medieval commentaries and glosses; he rejected the traditional fourfold sense of Scripture: "Thus the literal sense and the spiritual sense coincide, [so that the true sense is] not that which is called allegorical or tropological, but that which the Holy Spirit certifies speaking through the prophet."[13] He maintained this even if in the second edition of 1513, an incidental clause, sounding like a weak contradiction, opportunely specifies that he does not want to deny "the other allegorical, tropological, or anagogical senses, especially there where the subject requires it." In the previous year, in the commentary on the Pauline epistles, he declared that the four senses dear to the Middle Ages should not be looked for anywhere in the Scriptures, but may be useful for the comprehension of certain passages (on Gal. 4:24). It may be seen that he opposes, not without reason, the systematic and, hence, artificial usage of the plurality of senses that gives a mechanical aspect to the late medieval biblical commentaries. In fact, if the traditional terminology is retained, Lefèvre, especially in his commentaries on the Gospels, often slides toward allegory.

However, Lefèvre's biblical hermeneutic clearly achieves a sort of theological recentering that may claim originality, even with regard to his reading of the Church Fathers. He proposed a search for a unified sense of Scripture, at once literal and spiritual, that would lead to a strictly Christological reading of the Bible. In his 1524 Preface to a Latin Psalter that he enriched by Hebrew readings, Lefèvre wrote with pious enthusiasm: "Christ is the Spirit of the entire Scripture. And Scripture without Christ is only writing and the letter that kills." He deduced a kind of history of salvation by a deep comprehension of the secrets of Holy Scripture. "The Holy Spirit leaves absolutely nothing in the shadows for the world, and preaches all the mysteries of Christ."[14] An interpretation that will not be Christological is not possible since Christ the Savior is "the only truth."[15]

Nevertheless, in its turn, by its systematization, this biblical hermeneutic, by always searching for "the most divine" sense, does not avoid narrowing meaning, though it desires to return to the center of theology. Indeed, even if the perspective that looks to Christ is in fact the key to Scripture, it appears in Lefèvre's usage to be too narrow to take account of the rich abundance of Scripture; it is as if he desired to twist the interpretation, and if he confused movement toward unity and uniformity. An example may make this understandable. When, in the 1515 edition of the *Quincuplex Psalterium*, Lefèvre wants to interpret the Psalm *Miserere* (Psalm 50 in the Vulgate), he renounces the expression of David's repentance, one of the most celebrated phrases in the liturgical and spiritual tradition, declaring that he "has not found prophecy there, and that there is no worthwhile explanation to seek there." The reason is that this Psalm makes allusion to the sin of him [Christ] whom it declares, and Lefèvre's interpretive key prevents him from being able fully and entirely to hear of Christ who was made man "in all things except sin."

He has the opposite issue in the interpretation of the Cabbala, where philology and theology meet and mingle; where the words, by the slant of the Hebrew letters, express by themselves the divine. Lefèvre devoted himself to long passages on the names of God, as did Reuchlin and other Christian Cabbalists.[16]

Lefèvre desired to deploy in all its breadth the interpretive sense that would reconcile the letter and the spirit, and provide a unifying role. He used it therefore for "the concord of the Scriptures." "It is the accord, the concord of the Scriptures, with which we are concerned, which guides us."[17] The play of cross-references, of echoes throughout the Bible, of concordances, became a hermeneutical principle. One can understand that the Reformers would have seen this as implementing *sola Scriptura*, the reading of Scripture by Scripture; but Lefèvre's approach is much more Neoplatonist, by an affinity to Pseudo-Dionysius, Nicholas of Cusa, and Pico della Mirandola. This concord makes comprehensible the articulation of the two divine covenants, the old and the new, by passing from the veiled to the unveiled, from the closed to the open, by means of the "key of David," the Christ.

Christ the Mediator, our reconciliation, is He who opens the Scriptures to us as the principle of concord. The unity of the Bible is formed around the Word, and the harmony of interpretation becomes the image of celestial harmony. If this vision is grandiose and proves to be necessary in the midst of the controversies at the beginning of the sixteenth century, the implementation of the Parisian humanist's exegesis could have appeared too audacious for the scholastic theologians but also too one-sided for his humanist friends. The latter is evident in his dispute with Erasmus.

When, in his Latin translation of Hebrews 2:7, Lefèvre cited Psalm 8:6, following a rare reading in the manuscripts that he considered more faithful to the Hebrew, he did so not primarily as an exegete but according to his Christological vision. He preferred *minuisti eum paulominus a Deo* (you have made him a little less than a God) to the received text *minuisti . . . ab angelis* (you have placed him below the level of the angels). Lefèvre's textual choice had a decisive importance for him that Erasmus, who criticized him in 1516, apparently did not comprehend. Erasmus realized that in Lefèvre's reading Lefèvre did not hesitate to accuse him of impiety because he wrote things "unworthy" of Christ. Lefèvre had the impression that the traditional reading of the text posited that God had made Christ lower than the angels, but that did violence to Christ's transcendence or to the divine nature of Christ – since the Psalm was used Christologically. In his *Apologia ad Fabrum Stapulensem* (1517),[18] Erasmus indicated he was deeply wounded by this accusation that clearly was close to the charge of heresy. He then cruelly enumerated the weaknesses of Lefèvre's knowledge of Greek, highlighting certain contrary meanings and many naivetés, which he had already pointed out in the translation of Paul. What is more, he emphasized equally the gaps in the substance of Lefèvre's patristic interpretation, and especially the error of perspective in subordinating the under- standing of Scripture to a vision, that if not docetic, at least tends toward a certain monophysitism. Erasmus affirmed that in fact Christ had been put below the angels, but that this does not contravene Lefèvre's "principle of dignity" since the Passion, sufferings, and death of Christ are in fact humiliation and abasement; but it is precisely by the humiliation of the Cross that our salvation arises.

Thus, Lefèvre's hermeneutic of the "principle of dignity" was the source of his piety and spirituality, but also his limitation. It is encountered again in the dispute over the "Three Marys" in which, against John Fisher and others, Lefèvre refused the oneness of the personage of Mary Magdalene, popularized by the liturgy and popular devotion. If Lefèvre in this case had good exegetical reasons for his argu- ment, his motivations were primarily spiritual: a sinner could not be given the honor of being the first witness to the Resurrection. Lefèvre therefore insisted on a unitive vision, sensitive to the harmony of contemplation, against a more Augustinian view, sensitive to the paradoxes of grace; even though at the same time he had formulas close to the Reformers on *sola gratia*.

Justification, Faith, and Works

The doctrines of justification, faith, and works were profoundly divisive issues of the Reformation period among Protestants as well as Catholics. Lefèvre's understanding of these doctrines appears on the one hand in his commentaries on the Epistles of Paul of 1512 – thus well before the eruption caused by Luther's *Ninety-five Theses*, and, on the other hand, in his commentaries on the so-called Catholic Epistles com- posed in 1525 and published in 1527, by which time theologians were in complete turmoil over these subjects. When those texts are chosen, one finds some of the matters in the commentaries on the four Gospels (1522). The literary genre of the biblical commentary, the genre of annotations and paraphrase, like that of Erasmus, does not lend itself to an organized and synthetic presentation of the theological thought of Lefèvre, which ought not be excessively systematized.

That is why, for example, one finds different approaches when he speaks of justification. Lefèvre stated that there are two justifications.[19] In the 1512 commentary on Romans 3:19–20, he distinguished in dialectical terms between the justification of the law and that of faith. The former operated by works; the latter by grace. But he added that it is necessary to seek both, but above all the second, which is favored by the gospel, whereas the former is advocated by the philosophers. But in 1522, on John 1:29, Lefèvre distinguished a universal justification and another particular and personal one which are as inseparable as heat is from light.

Already in the *Quincuplex Psalterium*, the expression *sola gratia* frequently arises, notably in relation to Psalms 6, 12, and 24; but at that time the accent is put more on the believer's acceptance of God's mercy than on faith properly so-called, without anything evidently opposing them. In any case, blessedness does not come from works but from God himself (on Ps. 127:2). Thus the Reformers' intuition was indeed present by the way Lefèvre read Holy Scripture and it is understandable how, in annotating the *Quincuplex*, the Doctor of Wittenberg was already able to formulate his own theology.[20]

Nevertheless, Lefèvre insisted on the salvific importance of works in the Christian life in a way that Luther could not accept.[21] In fact, the Parisian humanist regarded works to be necessary for the preparation, retention, and augmentation of justification.[22] Without works we can lose the grace of justification (on Rom. 3:28). At the same time, Lefèvre affirmed in a very Lutheran manner that works done outside of faith, even inspired by human love, in spite of appearances are not good works (on Jas. 2:18). Therefore, everything gravitates around faith, but it can be seen that Lefèvre chose a difficult balance of faith and works.

It appears to me that the explanation is again to be found in Lefèvre's hermeneutic. Lefèvre found both perspectives in the New Testament, that of Paul in Romans and Galatians, and that of James. Nothing is more strange to his thought than to introduce "a canon within the canon of the Scriptures." He took Scripture as a whole that cannot be inconsistent. In this sense his attitude is profoundly Catholic. If there seems to be opposition, it can only be apparent. It is necessary to affirm *sola gratia* like Paul, and the necessity of works like James. His ideal of a vocation of reconciliation and unity required of him that he hold both positions, explicating that Paul opposed those who considered themselves justified by works, and that James opposed those who believed they were saved without works. In fact, one must not put his confidence either in faith or in works, but solely in God (on Rom. 4:2).

This is why, in his commentary on James in 1525, Lefèvre multiplied the expressions indicating the concordance, speaking of "the work of faith," "the works of faith," "faith living and working." In other words, he insisted on the reciprocal inclusion of faith and works, indicating in some way that faith without works is not faith, and that works without faith are not works. A similar paradoxical tension can also be found in Lefèvre's affirmed refusal of a theology of merit and the affirmation of free will (on Rom. 11:11).

The Sacraments

In the area of the sacraments it would also be rash to want to find in Lefèvre a discursive treatise on the medieval seven sacraments which would be confirmed by the Council of Trent 30 years after his commentaries. In the meanwhile, Lefèvre formulated some notations in dependence upon the biblical texts.

Lefèvre nearly always named baptism the *lavacrum regeneratis*, the bath of regeneration, according to the passage of Titus 3:5 that insists on the gratuitousness of salvation. Lefèvre never ceased to emphasize that baptism is there not only for the pardon of sins, but for the sanctification that is none other than filial adoption in Christ, our reconciliation with God in Him (on 2 Cor. 5:18). The Church is the "communion of the regenerate," in the proper sense of the second birth (on Ps. 132). If the ceremony of baptism requires a triple immersion, this symbolizes the role of the Trinity, but also the three days of Christ in the tomb before the Resurrection (on Rom. 6:4). This trinitarian reality is recalled by Lefèvre when he commented that the baptism of Christ is itself "our purification, our justification, and our sanctification" (on Mt. 3:16–17).

In the *Quincuplex Psalterium*, the Eucharist is qualified as the provisions for life eternal (*viaticum vitae aeternae*) (on Ps. 4:8), it gives nourishment for the voyage, for the crossing toward eternal life. The Psalms which make allusion to the manna given by God in the desert are therefore accounts of the Eucharist (on Ps. 22:5). In his exposition of Psalm 110, Lefèvre qualified the Eucharist as the very holy, very august sacrament and memorial of redemption. A more extensive reflection can be found in his commentary on Hebrews 5. The Eucharist is a memorial and remembrance (*memoria et recordatio*) of the unique sacrifice of Christ on the Cross, but it would be difficult to deduce from this that Lefèvre denies the sacrificial aspect of the Mass. In 1509, he spoke likewise of the "new sacrifice" (Ps. 49:15), the sacrament of the Eucharist was defined as "memorial and confession (in the sense of recognition) of the benefit received" (Ps. 49:16). In 1512, he specified that the new rite was performed by virtue of a unique oblation that was symbolically imitated until the end of the world (Heb. 10:11). It does not seem that by the phrase "symbolic rite," Lefèvre would have had to be thinking along the lines of Zwingli's commemorative sacramental theology.[23] It is true that Lefèvre did not at all go into the question of transubstantiation, which is what a controversialist theologian of his time would have done. It can be imagined that having read Scripture by itself, Lefèvre did not encounter the idea in the Scripture passages on which he commented. He did not refuse to understand the Discourse on the Bread of Life in a sacramental sense, but recalled that it is not the receiving of the sacrament that counts, but the reality of the sacrament that alone enhances the grace that leads to faith (on Jn. 6:53).

One finds here and there an allusion to Confirmation (for example on Ps. 22:7) as that holy oil that introduces one into the realm of the priests, that is, as an allusion to the priesthood of the faithful. Whatever may be Lefèvre's interpretations of Matthew 16:18–19, following that of Augustine, and of John 20:22–3, which he did not apply to the sacrament, he understood Hebrews 10:16 in relation to Matthew 18:18 as an allusion to penitence, to confession (in the sense of a sacramental) and to the absolution by the priest. But he did not do so without recalling in solemn terms that the pardon received comes from the unique oblation of Christ who, in a superabundant manner, has made satisfaction for the sins of the entire world. This confession must be made to God in faith (on Jas. 5:16). But the astonishing importance Lefèvre gave to Purgatory must be noted, finding it in texts where the tradition had not seen it (such as Mt. 5:22–3, Mt. 18:23, Lk. 16:19–31), but not mentioning it in his comments on 1 Corinthians 3:13–15, one of the classical sources for the traditional doctrine.

Extreme Unction, the sacrament that was given to the dying on the basis of James 5:15, was criticized by Luther but apparently accepted by Lefèvre, whose goal was to correct the tradition. He considered that the presbyteroi must comprise, like the "elders," the seniors of the church. In 1525, Lefèvre deplored that instead of holy persons one called on priests, no matter who they were, to anoint with oil those near death, whereas the text of the epistle makes clear allusion to the ill. But the times were so bad that one hesitated to appeal for help on this occasion of invoking the name of Jesus Christ. For him, the oil that is mentioned in the text of James is spiritual, not physical, even if this usage cannot be formally excluded. What counted for him, and what was lacking, is the faith of him who prays over the ill person, and the faith of the latter. Lefèvre then invited a reform of the practice of unction for the dying, which would also be denounced at the Council of Trent in 1547.

Lefèvre's theology comes to light through discrete touches, little by little, as the occasion presents itself in the texts on which he comments. It is true that in Meaux he certainly had to deal with a pastoral practice that his activity as professor and as editor of texts did not permit him to be engaged in. The homilies composed in the group that he animated may provide another light, but one cannot approach these texts without some caution.

The Doctrine of the Epistles and Gospels

Most writers who treat the thought of Lefèvre d'Etaples put the works signed by his name on the same level with those which, from 1523 on, essentially his translations of the Bible into French, have been attributed to him. They draw arguments from the anonymous collection of homilies in French published first under the title *Epîtres et Evangiles pour les cinquante et deux semaines de l'an*, printed by Simon du Bois without place and date (but without doubt printed first in Paris in 1525/6 and then in Alençon between 1530 and 1533), then, under a title very slightly different and in a very interestingly enlarged form, printed by Pierre de Vingle, also without place and date, but very likely in Lyon in 1531 or 1532. This text was attributed by the Censor of the Paris Theology Faculty in 1525 to Meaux, and by inference to Jacques Lefèvre d'Etaples. External criticism, but above all internal criticism, that is to say, the doctrine found there, indicates without doubt that these homilies come from the disciples of Lefèvre, probably above all from Gérard Roussel, who had a major role in the composition of the short sermons that were perhaps conceived as models for the renewal of preaching that Bishop Briçonnet had desired to promote in his diocese. It is no less certain that even if the resemblance between these homilies and Lefèvre's biblical commentaries is not striking, the inspiration of the

Parisian humanist remains undeniable. In order to be at the same time complete but also precise, it is advisable now to indicate the orientation of the composition independent of Lefèvre himself.

This collection that proposed a homily called "exhortation" for each of the liturgy's Scripture passages, i.e., the Epistle, that is, the first reading, and the Gospel of the Mass, is one of the finest theological texts in the French language of that time. Without polemic, apart from some traits found more in the additions in the second edition, clear and centered on the edification of the faithful, these texts are a jewel of "evangelical" literature in French.

Though most of the biblical books are cited, often for the very reason of commenting on the text, a large part consists of the Psalms, and for the New Testament, the Epistle to the Romans, 1 Corinthians, and the Epistles of the Captivity (Ephesians, Philippians, Colossians, Philemon); the recourse to patristic or medieval sources is practically non-existent apart from some allusions to the Roman liturgy. Some rare references to the Church Fathers, essentially Augustine, are made in the additions to the second edition.

Since it concerns presenting to the Christian listeners the meaning of the Scripture passages that they just heard, the homilies consider that what matters above all is the search for the "secrets of God."[24] It is the Holy Spirit who will illumine, not so much the preacher, but "all the hearers." Yet curiosity must not be pushed too far. Certain secrets remain reserved to the wisdom of God,[25] such as the restoration of the kingdom of Israel or the Day of Judgment, when the dark secrets of consciences shall be revealed.

It is necessary then to strive for understanding Scripture by a spiritual intelligence that requires the rejection of that which is often too human in the interpretation given in commentaries or sermons. It is necessary to search for the pure wine and not that diluted by water, for the good grain without the tares, the expression that in the gospel refers to the "traditions, doctrines, and inventions of the scribes and the pharisees."[26]

The genuine door to Scripture is the Word of God itself. It is the proper key to itself, proposed to all, for "to each Christian full authority and irrevocable power is given to judge all human doctrine, all the commandments, all human decrees and statutes, to determine if they conform to the Word of God or not."[27] There is the foundation of "the Church of the faithful." The Christian is the one who is justified by faith, splendidly defined albeit censured by the Paris Theology Faculty in 1525: "If you believe that Jesus Christ is raised from the dead for your justification, his resurrection is yours and your justification, and you are truly justified."[28]

But then the homilies develop a theology of living faith, of faith that works by love. This is what must be understood by the wedding garment demanded of those invited to the marriage festivities (Mt. 22:2–14). That garment is faith active in love [*charité*].[29] We then find noticeably the same doctrine that Lefèvre developed in his contemporaneous commentary on the Epistle of James, and that he situated midway between the Reformation theology of justification by faith alone and the importance accorded to works.

The homilies of Lefèvre and his disciples insisted on a traditional theme in medieval theology but which did not appear to have been well understood by the Parisian theologians at the beginning of the sixteenth century: the unity of all three theological virtues of faith, hope, and love [*charité*]. "Since seeing that God is Wisdom, our works are done in faith; seeing that He is Power, they are accomplished in hope; seeing that He is Goodness, they are done by ardent love."[30]

These texts rarely speak of the sacraments, of the worship service, or of the invocation of the saints, nor do they speak much of the Church visible in its hierarchy and its rites. For the homilies of the diocese of Meaux, "the true house of God is the heart, the soul, and the mind of the Christian where God wills to be served by prayer and worship in spirit and truth."[31] The Christian Church is therefore composed of saints, of the elect who proclaim the secrets of the Word, that is to say, the coming of Christ in our flesh and of its redemption.

Thus to be sanctified consists of being and becoming an imitator of Christ. If we live according to the works of the Spirit, "we shall be true imitators of God and of Jesus Christ."[32] This signifies what is necessary to participate in the sufferings of Christ: "to be companions of his sorrows." Finally, we are to conform to his death in dying to our sins and to our concupiscence, ready to give our life for our brothers through love because the entire life of the Christian is to endure suffering."[33] Here one recognizes the theme of the *imitatio Christi*, so cherished at the end of the Middle Ages, and more precisely the conformity to Christ by which Lefèvre expressed his Christian anthropology.

Conformity to Christ

Beyond the imitation of Christ, beyond even the conformity to Christ in his activity, the Christian for Lefèvre is called to take the form of Christ, "Christiformity." Inspired by Galatians 4:19, this term is found in the authors to whom Lefèvre was attached and whom he had edited, Dionysius and Nicholas of Cusa. Lefèvre used the term in all of his Scriptural commentaries, above all in that on Paul.[34] It could be said that he rediscovers the Christological aspect of divinization so dear to the Greek Fathers.

As like is known by like, so the re-creation by Christ cannot be conceived except by comparison to him (on Jn. 13:35). In glory we shall be entirely conformed to Christ, but our glory in this world is to conform to Him in our whole person (on Rom. 8:26). The works of mortification that the Christ imposes aid in reproducing the interior Christiformity (on Col. 3:12). Likewise, prayer is the act of one who is trying to conform to Christ by the Spirit (on Rom. 8:23).

As in all bodies, there must be a certain proportion between the body and its members under penalty of having to deal with a monster. In the body of Christ this proportion, this harmony, is called Christiformity (on Col. 3:1). Lefèvre's Christian anthropology thus takes the Pauline expression (Gal. 2:20): It is no longer I who live, it is Christ who lives in me. This is well expressed in the Preface written by Lefèvre to the second part of the French translation of the New Testament, dated from Meaux, November 6, 1523: "Let us go then to Jesus Christ in complete confidence. He must be our thought, our speech, our life and salvation, and our all."[35]

Lefèvre was indisputably a theologian, not because he was according to our modern categories an exegete, a dogmatician, or a moralist, but because he unified his reading of Scripture by a spiritual, Christological vision. At times disconcerted in his choices and arguments, he appears nevertheless until 1527, the date of his last publication, and even up to 1532, if he is recognized in the second edition of the homilies for the diocese of Meaux, to adopt a middle position that appears to correspond to his temperament and to his ideal of concord, and in a time when the confessional frontiers in France were not yet well defined. He was the leader, discrete yet resolute, of the "evangelical" movement for whom a renewed and unified reading of the Bible ought to be enough for the needed reformation of the Church.

Notes

1 Eugene F. Rice, *The Prefatory Epistles of Jacques Lefèvre d'Etaples and Related Texts* (New York and London: Columbia University Press, 1972).

2 For Luther, see *Annotationes Quincuplici Fabri Stapulensis Psalterio manu adscriptae* (1513), *WA* 4:466–526; for Zwingli, see *Corpus Reformatorum* 99, *Sämtliche Werke* 12:280–91. Editor's note: Zwingli's "allusion to Lefèvre, whose *Psalterium quincuplex* Ulrich possessed and used. His copy, beautifully printed in 1513, with its wide margins in which is inserted here and there the fine hand of the reformer, is to be found at Zurich. . . ." Jean Rilliet, *Zwingli: Third Man of the Reformation*, trans. Harold Knight (Philadelphia: Westminster Press, 1964), 99.

3 See Anne Reeve, ed., *Erasmus' Annotations on the New Testament. Galatians to the Apocalypse* (Leiden: E. J. Brill, 1993), 706–13 for the developments concerning the note on Heb. 2:7.

4 Editor's note: Lefèvre "contended, on the basis of the evidence of the New Testament and the patristic writings, that the Mary Magdalene celebrated in the church calendar was a figure compounded of three different women, namely, Mary of Bethany, the sister of Martha . . . , Mary Magdalene . . . , and the unnamed woman who had been forgiven much and had annointed Christ's feet. . . ." Philip Edgcumbe Hughes, *Lefèvre: Pioneer of Ecclesiastical Renewal in France* (Grand Rapids: Eerdmans, 1984), 118.

5 A. J. Herminjard, *Correspondance des Réformateurs de langue française*, I (Geneva and Paris: H. Georg and M. Lévy, 1866), letter 98, 206–9; letter 103, 219–31.

6 It was concerning a discussion of the Lord's Supper that Bucer evoked in this letter of 1532. See J. V. Pollet, *Martin Bucer. Etudes sur sa correspondance* (Paris: Presses Universitaires de France), I:114.

7 Herminjard, *Correspondance*, I, letter 168, 411.

8 Herminjard, *Correspondance*, I, letter 181, 447.

9 Herminjard, *Correspondance*, III, letter 544, 300–400.

10 P. S. Allen, *Opus epistolarum Erasmi*, VI (Oxford: Oxford University Press, 1926), Ep. 1650a; 234–5, lines 14–18.

11 While Renaudet has rightly seen Lefèvre d'Etaples as one of the principle actors of Parisian humanism, Protestant historiography has made him a proto-Reformer, even one of the first French-speaking Reformers. Bèze inscribed his portrait in his *Icones* in 1580. Such was the position of C. H. Graf (1842 and 1852) who based his position on the Pauline commentaries; by A.-L. Herminjard (1868); E. Doumergue (1899); J. Barnaud (1900 and 1936); N. Weiss (1919); H. Doerries (1925); K. Spiess (1930); J. Panier (1935); and F. Hahn (1938). It was contradicted by the Catholic historians E. Amann (1926) and P. Imbart de La Tour (1944). The question was, so to speak, "de-confessionalized" by Richard Stauffer in a 1967 article, "Lefèvre d'Etaples, artisan ou spectateur de la Réforme?," reprinted in *Interprètes de la Bible* (Paris: Beauchesne, 1980), 11–29. In 1970, Carlo Ginzburg tried to make him a "Nicodemite" (*Il Nicodemismo* [Torino: Einaudi, 1970]).

It is necessary to distinguish numerous issues: Lefèvre's relations with the Reformers; the facts or legends which surrounding his final years; and the exact content of his thought. Lefèvre's letters of 1524 and 1525 to Farel, mentioned above, show an admiration for Oecolampadius and Zwingli, and mention the works of Melanchthon, Myconius, and Brunfels. After the visit to Strasbourg, there is hardly any trace of his opinions, though they were probably close to those of Marguerite of Navarre who welcomed him. The visit of Calvin to Nérac in order to meet Lefèvre is mentioned only in the life of Nicolas Colladon (*Corpus Reformatorum* 49, *Opera Calvini* 21, col. 57). The opinion, spread about at the beginning of the seventeenth century, that late in life Lefèvre expressed regret at not having the courage to break with Rome seems scarcely probable. Bayle himself (*Dictionnaire* [Amsterdam, 1730, II, 469–70]) tends to doubt it.

12 Rice, *The Prefatory Epistles*, 194.

13 Ibid., 194.

14 Ibid., 473.

15 Ibid., 437.

16 François Secret, *Les kabbalistes chrétiens de la Renaissance* (Paris: Dunod, 1964), 150–64.

17 Rice, *The Prefatory Epistles*, 196.

18 The critical edition by Andrea W. Steenbeek (Amsterdam: Elsevier, 1994).

19 In no case did it concern double justification, so to speak of one justification in two times, elaborated in the circles of Contarini, discussed at the interconfessional Colloquy of Ratisbon in 1541, and rejected by Luther as well as by the Council of Trent.

20 Guy Bedouelle, *Le "Quincuplex Psalterium" de Lefèvre d'Etaples. Un guide de lecture* (Geneva: Droz, 1979), 233–40.

21 "Even Stapulensis, a man otherwise spiritual and most sound – God knows – lacks spiritual understanding in interpreting divine Scripture; yet he definitely shows so much of it in the conduct of his own life and the encouragement of others." Letter to Spalatin, October 19, 1516. *LW* 48:26; *WA* Br 1:90.

22 Charles-Henri Graf, *Essai sur la vie et les écrits de Jacques Lefèvre d'Etaples* (Strasbourg, 1842; repr. Geneva: Slatkine, 1970), 67; Hughes, *Lefèvre*, 87.

23 As suggested by Hughes, *Lefèvre*, 87.

24 "Evangile de la Pentecôte" in G. Bedouelle and F. Giacone, eds., *Epistres et Evangiles pour les cinquante-deux dimanches de l'an* (Leiden: E. J. Brill, 1976), 210.

25 "Epistle for Ascension" in ibid., 199.

26 "Evangile du mardi de Pentecôte" in ibid., 223.

27 "Evangile du 8eme dimanche après la Pentecôte, ajout de 1531/1532" in ibid., 269.

28 "Evangile du 24eme dimanche après la Pentecôte" in ibid., 269.

29 "Evangile du 20eme dimanche après la Pentecôte" in ibid., 337.

30 "Epître du 11eme dimanche après Pâques" in ibid., 193.

31 "Evangile de Fête de la Dédicace, ajout de 1531/1532" in ibid., 391.

32 "Epître du 5eme dimanche après la Pentecôte" in ibid., 251.

33 "Epître du 16eme dimanche après la Pentecôte" in ibid., 315.

34 Hughes, *Lefèvre*, 192–7, has translated into English the most important texts where Lefèvre expresses this notion.

35 Rice, *The Prefatory Epistles*, 461.

Bibliography

Reprint Editions of Lefèvre's Works

Quincuplex Psalterium (1513), Geneva: Droz, 1979. Supplemented by the "Companion Volume" by Guy Bedouelle, *Le "Quincuplex Psalterium" de Lefèvre d'Etaples. Un guide de lecture*, Geneva: Droz, 1979.

S. Pauli Epistolae XIV cum commentarius (1512), Stuttgart: Frommann-Holzboog, 1978.

Epistles et Evangiles pour les cinquante-deux semaines de l'an. Text of 1525 edited by M. A. Screech, Geneva: Droz, 1964. Augmented by the 1532 text edited by Guy Bedouelle and F. Giacone, Leiden: E. J. Brill, 1976.

The other works of Lefèvre may be found in the early history holdings of the major libraries. This is because there are numerous editions in the first half of the sixteenth century, but their publication ended, with rare exceptions, around 1560. A nearly complete bibliographical listing is in the important study by Eugene F. Rice, Jr., *The Prefatory Epistles of Jacques Lefèvre d'Etaples and Related Texts*, New York: Columbia University Press, 1972.

General Studies

Bedouelle, Guy, *Lefèvre d'Etaples et l'intelligence des Ecritures*, Geneva: Droz, 1976.

Hughes, Philip Edgcumbe, *Lefèvre: Pioneer of Ecclesiastical Renewal in France*, Grand Rapids: Eerdmans, 1984.

Renaudet, Augustin, *Préréforme et humanisme à Paris pendant les premières guerres d'Italie*, Paris, 1916, re-edited 1953, repr. Geneva: Slatkine, 1981.

Discussion of Lefèvre's works by Bernard Roussel in *Revue d'histoire et de philosophie religieuses* 60 (1980), 465–85; and Jean-Pierre Massaut in *Revue d'histoire ecclésiastique* 78 (1983), 73–8. See also Guy Bedouelle, *Dictionnaire de spiritualité*, IX, 1976, cols. 520–5, and *TRE*, X, 1982, 781–4.

Particular Studies

Bedouelle, Guy, "Lefèvre d'Etaples et Luther. Une recherche de frontières. 1517–1527," *Revue d'histoire et philosophie religieuses* 63 (1983), 17–31.
——, "Une adaptation anglaise des Epistres et Evangiles de Lefèvre d'Etaples et ses disciples," *Bibliothèque d'Humanisme et Renaissance* 48 (1986), 723–34.

Hufstader, Anselm, "Lefèvre d'Etaples and the Magdalen," *Studies in the Renaissance* 16 (1969), 31–60.

Massaut, Jean-Pierre, *Critique et Tradition à la vielle de la Réforme en France*, Paris: Vrin, 1968.

Rice, Eugene F., "The Humanist Idea of Christian Antiquity," *Studies in the Renaissance* 9 (1962), 126–60.

Veissière, Michel. *L'évêque Guillaume Briçonnet (1470–1534)*, Provins: Société d'histoire et d'archéologie, 1986.

Desiderius Erasmus (1469–1536)

J. Laurel Carrington

The life of Erasmus of Rotterdam spanned a period of transition and turmoil, in which he himself played no small part. Recognized as the prince of humanists, the leading biblical scholar of his age, and a powerful advocate of church reform, he nevertheless came under devastating attack from both the Catholic theologians of Louvain and Paris and the adherents to Luther's evangelical reform. While he is best known to readers today for his satirical *Praise of Folly*, during his own time he made his mark with pedagogical works and the critical edition of the Greek New Testament, the *Novum Testamentum*, complete with a new Latin translation and a full set of annotations.

As a humanist, biblical scholar, and reformer, Erasmus emphasized the primacy of language both in understanding God's communication of himself to humankind and in cultivating the appropriate response to that message. The approach to religion that he advocated in works such as the *Colloquies* and the *Enchiridion militis Christi* emphasized inner conviction over outward ceremonies, thus attracting the interest of reform-minded people all over Europe, as well as the suspicion and even fury of Catholics of a more conservative cast. Many of those whom Erasmus influenced during the first two decades of the sixteenth century, in some cases younger scholars who worked closely with him on his *Novum Testamentum*, would be attracted to Luther's reform, perceiving him as a kindred spirit to Erasmus. At the same time that Erasmus's younger colleagues were hoping that he himself would join with them and Luther, Catholics, including Popes Leo X, Adrian VI, and Clement VII, would alternately request and demand that he write forcefully against Luther. Thus, from the time of Luther's attack on the church to the end of his life, Erasmus, who at all points professed his loyalty to the Roman Church, struggled to establish his identity against the pressures that mounted against him on all sides.

Early Years

Born in Gouda as the illegitimate son of a priest and a physician's daughter, Erasmus received an education typical of his time at Gouda, Deventer, and 'sHertogenbosch.

His teachers at Deventer were members of the Brethren of the Common Life, and under their influence Erasmus grew up in an environment shaped by a belief in simplicity, practical piety, work, and service, eschewing the more complex speculations that characterized the university theologians. Some of these convictions appeared in his adult writings, although he spoke disparagingly of the education he received at Deventer, claiming that he was taught Latin by the method typical of schools not enlightened by humanist pedagogy, including much rote memorization punctuated by severe punishment for mistakes. Still, it was there that he first encountered humanist thought, classical literature, and a famous representative of humanism in the person of Rudolf Agricola, a poet and friend of the school's rector, Hegius.

In 1487 Erasmus joined the Augustinian order of canons regular at Steyn. Over the next seven years he continued his education on his own by reading widely in classical authors from the monastery's library, and working assiduously to improve his own writing. Regular exchanges of Latin epistles with fellow canons testify that companions shared his interests. The library was extensive enough to have on hand the *Elegantiae* of the Italian humanist Lorenzo Valla, whom Erasmus may also have encountered at Deventer. He early on became enthralled with that scholar's critical intellect, his expertise in the history of the Latin language, and his ability to use his expertise in a philological examination of texts. Nevertheless, Erasmus grew restless at the monastery, and in 1495, with the permission of his order, he left, eventually to study theology at the University of Paris under the patronage of the bishop of Cambrai.

His time in Paris exposed him to the rigors of scholasticism, which he thoroughly disliked. It also proved to be an opportunity for him to expand his contacts within the world of letters he so eagerly desired to join, and to get his own writing into circulation. He never completed his doctoral work at Paris, but was later awarded a doctorate in theology from the University at Turin. In 1499 he traveled to England with the help of a new patron, the lord of Mountjoy. This visit turned out to be a turning point for him, for here he encountered Thomas More and John Colet, and heard the latter's lectures at Cambridge on St. Paul's epistles.[1] From that point on, Erasmus turned his interest in literature to biblical scholarship, which became his lifelong pursuit.

Christian Humanism

A rubric that is commonly associated with Erasmus's approach to spiritual renewal is "Christian humanism." As a humanist, Erasmus was drawn to the pagan literature of ancient Greece and Rome, which he believed was an essential component of the development of a well-formed mind. As a Christian humanist, Erasmus worked to draw together both pagan and Christian sources to effect a transformation of the spirit through language. He regarded the language of Scripture as paramount, yet the pagan classics served a purpose as well. Through mastery of the good literature of the past Christians could learn how to love both what is morally good and the truth that Christ had prepared for them, something they would never be inspired to do through reading the crabbed and distorted Latin of the Scholastic theologians.

An early work, the *Antibarbari*, is a defense of *bonae litterae* against those forces in Christendom that would suppress the classics. Originally drafted around 1488, the *Antibarbari* was revised and eventually published in 1520. While the circumstances of Erasmus's life had changed greatly in the intervening years, his basic convictions had not. He believed that there was an integral connection between the quality of language in which a message was expressed and the reader's or hearer's ability to grasp that message, not only in the mind but in the heart as well. This connection was particularly important in communicating the sublime truth of the gospel message. In this conviction Erasmus traced his legacy to Jerome, whom he professed to prefer to Augustine, and whom he regarded as a model for his own vocation. Through his work on the Vulgate and his many commentaries, letters, and other writings, Jerome applied his substantial learning to the cause of promoting the gospel. One of Erasmus's most important scholarly endeavors, the first upon which he embarked in the aftermath of his visit to England, would be a critical edition of the works of Jerome, begun in 1500 and eventually published in 1516.

In response to those who asserted there was nothing good for Christians in pagan literature, Erasmus claimed that Christians acquired the tools for understanding the gospel from the ancient world of pagan Latinity. "To such an extent is it true that we Christians have nothing we have not inherited from the pagans. The fact that we write in Latin, speak it in one way or another, comes to us from the pagans; they discovered writing, they invented the use of speech."[2] More than that, God intentionally planned that those people who lived before Christ would develop these skills to pave the way for Christians to fulfill God's will.[3]

In the *Enchiridion Militis Christiani* (1503), Erasmus further developed the principle that a combination of pagan and divine reading can educate the Christian in the ways of Christ. He warned that to rush into scriptural study without adequate preparation is a form of arrogance. "[Pagan] writings shape and invigorate the child's mind and provide an admirable preparation for the understanding of the divine Scriptures, for it is almost an act of sacrilege to rush into these studies without due preparation." Yet he also advised the reader not to linger too long with such literature, but to do so "more in the manner of a foreign visitor than a resident,"[4] always keeping one's eye on the true calling of oneself to Christ. The 1522 Colloquy *The Godly Feast*, in which one of the characters confesses that "when I read such things of such men, I can hardly help exclaiming, 'Saint Socrates, pray for us!',"[5] makes an even stronger case for the value of pagan learning.

Erasmus's Christian humanism is the logical extension of his anthropology, which emphasizes that aspect of human nature which is amenable to instruction by the divine preceptor, Christ, through whatever means Christ chooses. In the *Enchiridion* Erasmus attributes a dual nature to man, body and soul, the beast and the divine, which in their original state were combined in perfect harmony. This harmony was destroyed by sin, and thus body and soul are in a state of discord in human life. However, in the same text he proposes as an alternative vision a tripartite division of man into body, soul and spirit, following Origen who, along with Jerome, was a favorite source for Erasmus. According to this division, the soul is intermediate between the body and the spirit. Neither body nor spirit can be other than what it is, but the soul, which can ally with either the upper or the lower nature, is open to persuasion. It is to the soul, that which makes us truly human, that our education most properly applies, for the body cannot use it and the divine spirit does not need it. Language, the medium for teaching and persuasion, must bring the mysteries of heaven to life for human understanding at this level.

Reading Scripture is the key to understanding the divinity to which God wants human beings to aspire, but the reader must know how to approach Scripture in order to understand it. Erasmus's advice is to look to the allegorical rather than the literal meaning of Scripture, following in the footsteps of the ancient interpreters Paul, Origen, Ambrose, Jerome, and Augustine. Of the Scholastics, Erasmus says, "I notice that modern theologians are too willing to stick to the letter and give their attention to sophistic subtleties rather than to the elucidation of the mysteries, as if Paul were not right in saying that our law is spiritual."[6] Scripture, like human nature, has its body and its spirit, and Erasmus in the *Enchiridion* shows how an education rich in the literature of the classics can help a reader of Scripture approach it in the proper way.

Much of Erasmus's effort as a scholar thus went toward helping students achieve a wide knowledge of the classics. His most important work in this endeavor was the *Adagia*, a compilation of commonplaces from the ancient world, with explanations of their origins and meanings. The *Adagia*, which like so many of Erasmus's major works was revised and expanded repeatedly throughout his life, was first published in Paris in 1500, containing 818 entries. The work underwent a major expansion in Venice in 1508, when 3,260 adages came out of the Aldine Press. Erasmus published a further revision with the Froben Press in Basel in 1515, including several comment-aries that took the form of significant essays in their own right.

Philosophia Christi

Erasmus returned to Paris from England filled with enthusiasm not only for biblical scholarship, but for Neoplatonism as well. Over the next several years he moved frequently, from various locations in the Netherlands (where he wrote the *Enchiridion*), then back to England, and finally in 1506 to Italy once more, stopping first in France. He received his theological degree on this trip, in addition to meeting the publisher Aldus Manutius in Venice, where he turned out the enlarged edition of the *Adagia*. Once that task was completed, he left Italy abruptly when he received an invitation to return to England in 1509 with the accession of Henry VIII to the throne, an event that Erasmus and his English friends welcomed as the dawning of a golden age for scholars. It was during his stay there that he hastily wrote his most famous work, the *Praise of Folly*.

At this point in his life, in his early forties, Erasmus had developed his distinctive program for religious renewal, which is most succinctly defined as his *philosophia Christi*. The term itself is a repudiation of the scholastic culture that dominated the approach to philosophy in the universities; for his part, Erasmus would insist, the only philosophy that matters is the philosophy of Christ. It is in the *Paraclesis*, the introduction to Erasmus's 1516 edition of the New Testament, that we find perhaps the most consummate expression of the *philosophia Christi*. Several themes emerge as characteristic of Erasmus's approach. First, it is strongly Christocentric; all things point to and refer back to Christ. Erasmus wrote: "Certainly He alone was a teacher who came forth from heaven, He alone could teach certain doctrine, since it is eternal wisdom, He alone, the sole author of human salvation, taught what pertains to salvation, He alone fully vouches for whatsoever He taught, He alone is able to grant whatsoever He has promised."[7] While the historical person of Christ certainly effected all of these things, the Christ to whom Erasmus wishes to introduce his readers is the Christ who is revealed in the written word of Scripture. Indeed, in the *Enchiridion*, Erasmus claims that the people who encountered Christ in the world did not understand him so well as those who are able to encounter him in the writings of Scripture, which present him to readers in all of the essentials of his being.

The second theme of overriding importance for Erasmus is the primacy of the inner life over the details of doctrine or ceremony. Again, from the *Paraclesis*: "In this kind of philosophy, located as it is more truly in the disposition of the mind than in syllogisms, life means more than debate, inspiration is preferable to erudition, transformation is a more important matter than intellectual comprehension."[8] This tendency to stress inward devotion and personal transformation inspired the later Reformers. Yet at the same time Erasmus's lack of regard for the intellectual comprehension of doctrine would ultimately get him into trouble with Luther when the two of them battled over the question of the freedom of the will.

In the *Sileni Alcibiadis* adage, Erasmus upholds the value of what is hidden over what is obvious, deploring the preference on the part of theologians and churchmen for the flashy and worldly kind of success. Riches, honor, military might – all must give way to the inner word, the grasping of Christ's true message. In the *Ratio verae Theologiae*, the introduction to the 1519 edition of the *Novum Testamentum*, Erasmus will claim that "This is your first and only goal; perform this vow, this one thing: that you be changed, that you be seized, that you weep at and be transformed into those teachings which you learn."[9] That biblical study should be transformative is key to his approach, which privileged the language of Scripture at the same time it demanded the reader look beyond the surface to the message within. Scripture itself must never be approached as a set of discrete passages torn out of context, but rather each passage must be read and understood in an awareness of the essential unity of the whole.

A third tendency is Erasmus's essentially optimistic view of human nature, which is the basis for his praise of the pagan classics as having value for Christians, even as he upholds Christian philosophy above all other. Again, in the *Paraclesis* he writes, "Moreover, what else is the philosophy of Christ, which He himself calls a rebirth, than the restoration of human nature originally well formed?"[10] For many readers, this emphasis suggests that Erasmus was primarily concerned with ethical philosophy rather than with the kingdom of Heaven. However, the philosophy of Christ is not reducible for Erasmus simply to the classical concept of the "good life," for the inner transformation is a spiritual one, not simply a moral one. While Erasmus, unlike Luther, wished to reserve to human agency a role in preparing the individual to receive God's grace, his most profound commitment was to the individual's transformation through love of Christ into someone capable of rising beyond the flesh to the things of heaven. It is the role of language to communicate God's love, and to transform the hearers of the message into joyous recipients of God's Word. Erasmus would see the Christian "praying more than arguing and seeking to be transformed rather than armed for battle, [whereby] he would without a doubt find that there is nothing pertaining to the happiness of man and the living of his life which is not taught, examined, and unraveled in these works."[11]

Erasmus's Christology

While Erasmus believed that Christ is most vividly present to Christians through Scripture, he also believed that the Christ that is embodied in Scripture was also embodied in his life on earth. Thus, his understanding of Christ is strongly incarnational. In a 1499 exchange with John Colet, Erasmus disputed Colet's interpretation of Christ's request in the Garden of Gethsemane that God remove the cup of suffering from him (Mt. 14:36). Colet suggested that this passage indicated Christ's reluctance to see the Jews commit the sin of murdering him rather than reflecting Christ's experience of the fear of death. Erasmus had no difficulty in seeing Christ in his human nature as subject to all of the infirmities of the flesh, including hunger, thirst, fatigue, and fear, whereas Colet objected to the suggestion that Christ experienced even a moment's unease about his impending sacrifice.

Erasmus's treatment of Christ's human nature in this exchange is consistent with his Christology throughout subsequent writings. The *Sileni Alchibiadis* adage, for example, draws a parallel between the statuettes from the ancient world that would be crude and ridiculous on the outside but reveal inside the figure of a god. Christ is like that, Erasmus claimed: in the world he appeared to us as a carpenter and itinerant preacher, a person of no importance or education, poor and unimpressive. Underneath the surface, however, we find the god within. A similar theme would inform Erasmus's representation of Christ in the *Praise of Folly*, which also makes use of the Silenus analogy. In both pieces, Erasmus represented Christ's humble status in life as a repudiation of the values of the world. To people who value wealth, honors, and glory, Christ's sacrifice on the cross is nothing short of folly. Stressing the ignominy of Christ's crucifixion increases the ultimate glory that results in a realization of the reversal of value between the world's wisdom and the divine folly of Christ.

The Sacraments

The relationship between outer sign and inner truth appears in Erasmus's work to be alternately one of opposition and of harmony. In the *Explanation of the Creed*, Erasmus writes that "the sacraments, through certain sensible signs, infuse invisible grace in harmony with those outward signs."[12] While the sacraments are signs of grace, however, they are not its cause. They possess a twofold nature in their physical and spiritual aspects, of which Erasmus consistently emphasized the latter over the former. At the same time he did not repudiate the outer sign, but rather claimed that both the sign and the grace it signified must be in harmony. Nonetheless, Erasmus's approach to the sacraments was the source of criticism and misunderstanding by Protestants and Catholics alike. The former mistakenly believed him to be of their persuasion, while the latter challenged his interpretations as contrary to church teachings.

A case in point is Erasmus's view of matrimony. In 1518 he published the *Encomium matrimonii,* a work that was actually written much earlier, in 1497 or 1498. The work was attacked by Jan Briart, vice-chancellor of the University of Louvain. Erasmus was at that time living in Louvain, where he experienced increasing tension in his relationship with the university's theologians; he would eventually move to Basel in November 1521. At issue for Briart was the fact that Erasmus placed such a high value on marriage that he did not consider it to be second to celibacy in its dignity. While Erasmus did hold that virginity, preserved in a spotless condition as a vocation rooted in love, was the best way of life, he believed that most of those living under vows of celibacy did not maintain sexual purity, but rather simply avoided the state of matrimony.

Erasmus's views are explicit in the *Colloquies,* which include a series of dialogues concerning the married state. Here he suggests that for most people, entering into matrimony is the natural thing to do. The Colloquy entitled "The Girl with no Interest in Marriage" is a dialogue between a suitor, Eubulus, and a young woman, Catherine, whom he seeks to persuade to marry him. Catherine, however, has her heart set on the cloister. The arguments Eubulus makes in favor of marriage are that the cloister does not necessarily entail the ideals she has in mind – "All the veiled aren't virgins, believe me."[13] Second, he disapproves of her taking monastic vows in opposition to her parents' wishes that she marry. Third, there is a danger in taking a vow that cannot be rescinded, at a time in youth when inexperience can compel bad choices. Finally, in her present state she can still worship God in every way that she could in the cloister, but with freedom rather than under the compulsion of vows. "The Repentant Girl," a companion piece to "The Girl with No Interest in Marriage," features the same young woman as sadder but wiser, having entered the cloister only to leave in a state of disillusionment, fortunately without yet having made her profession.

For Erasmus, the sacramental quality of marriage lay in the bond between husband and wife. His position here is consistent with his understanding of the sacraments in general, emphasizing the need to approach them with spirit and mind engaged, rather than simply relying on a ritual. A sacrament such as penance, for example, was not effective without genuine contrition, and while Erasmus did not discourage auricular confession to a priest, he was critical of the manner in which confession was frequently handled, pointing out that the true confession took place between the repentant sinner and Christ. In the Colloquy "The Shipwreck," Adolphus, a survivor of a shipwreck, recounts his preparations in the hour of peril: "Seeing everything in an uproar, I confessed silently to God, condemning my unrighteousness before him and imploring his mercy."[14] Adolphus refused to invoke the protection of the saints, preferring to put himself in the hands of God the Father.

Erasmus upheld the practice of infant baptism, but while he believed that baptism was important as an entry into the faith community, it was in itself not sufficient without effort on the part of the individual to live a godly life in fulfillment of the baptismal covenant. The sacrament of penance was the means by which sins that threatened one's standing with God could be overcome. In regard to the Eucharist, which will be discussed more completely below, he believed in the Real Presence, although in his 1516 annotations on Mark 14 and 1 Corinthians 11 he seemed to claim that there was no biblical support for this in the words of institution.

New Testament Scholarship

Just as the sacraments have their outer ritual and their inner meaning, Scripture has its letter and its spirit. Erasmus believed that all education must have as its goal the training of readers to understand Scripture, and thus the consummate achievement of his life was his New Testament scholarship, of which his own edition of the New Testament was the most significant.

This endeavor consisted of an edited version of the Greek New Testament, a Latin translation, and a set of annotations. Of these three components, it was the annotations that were the core of the enterprise. They do not comprise a running commentary, but rather a set of notes on the text to help readers understand it. In later editions, however, Erasmus found himself elaborating on certain points of contention, to the degree of turning some of them into lengthy excursions into theology. The Greek edition, pulled together from a compilation and comparison of as many of the oldest manuscripts Erasmus could find, allowed scholars to consult the original in reading through Erasmus's textual notes to evaluate his conclusions for themselves. Finally, the purpose of the Latin translation was to give readers an opportunity to see how careful scholarly consideration might lead to language other than the familiar Vulgate version. In presenting his translation, Erasmus never saw himself in the role of altering the work of Jerome, but rather of seeking to restore it.

Erasmus's New Testament went through five editions in his lifetime, in 1516, 1519, 1522, 1527, and 1535. In each case he added to the annotations in response to critics and as his sense of the work developed. The 1516 edition, called the *Novum Instrumentum*, appeared with the *Paraclesis* and an *Apologia*, as well as another introductory writing, entitled the *Methodus*, which was expanded and renamed the *Ratio verae Theologiae* for the 1519 edition. Erasmus based his work on several contentions. The first was that the text of the Vulgate was seriously corrupted by an accumulation of scribal errors, thereby leading to false interpretations of key passages. The second was that linguistic usage had changed significantly from the time of Christ, and that modern readers needed help understanding the original sense of the language. In particular, knowledge of the Greek of the first century was necessary not for all readers, but for scholars seeking to clarify the Bible's meaning for ordinary readers. In addition, ignorance about the historical context in which the Scriptures were written created misunderstandings.

In taking this approach, Erasmus applied textual and historical criticism to Scripture that purported to treat this work as any other ancient text, vulnerable to historical change and textual corruption. Critics feared that in so doing, he undercut the universality and timelessness of Scripture. Yet Erasmus was not the only scholar of his time pursuing textual scholarship; the French humanist scholar Jacques Lefèvre was working on a set of commentaries, while in Spain a group of scholars was assembling the Complutensian Polyglot, which would be published in 1520. Erasmus felt a close association between his own work and that of Lorenzo Valla, whose *Adnotationes* on the New Testament Erasmus had published in 1505. But the predecessor with whom he drew the strongest connection was Jerome.

Critics of Erasmus's New Testament included the Englishman Edward Lee, who supplied a detailed list of complaints with Erasmus's editorial decisions; the Louvain theologian Maarten van Dorp and his colleagues; and the Spaniard Diego Lopez Zuñiga. Even Lefèvre, with whom Erasmus had so much in common, fell out with him in the course of a controversy that would cause Erasmus serious personal hurt. Noël Beda, syndic of the University of Paris, and Girolamo Aleandro, with whom Erasmus had shared a room in Venice, became his lifelong adversaries. Underlying their responses to specific passages was the feeling that challenging the Vulgate was tantamount to heresy, given the canonical status of that text. Another focus of opposition was Erasmus's emphasis on original languages, in this case Greek. Critics charged that it was not only unnecessary (claiming that Greek manuscripts were even more likely to be corrupt than Latin ones since the split between the Roman and Greek Orthodox Churches), but dangerous, because it encouraged impious questioning of the traditional understanding of the text. In his commentaries on the Greek text, Erasmus had raised direct challenges to medieval interpreters such as Peter Lombard, who was the backbone of scholastic exegesis. He often was caustic in his denunciation of their methods as well as their conclusions, never failing to counter these with his own conclusions based on the original Greek.

Two of his interpretations especially came under fire. The first was his translation of John 1:1: "In initio erat *sermo*," translating the Greek *logos* as *sermo*, implying discourse, conversation, in place of the Vulgate *verbum*. Erasmus wrote a lengthy apologia explaining his reasoning. The second is the famous *Comma Johanneum*: 1 John 5:7: "For there are three who bear witness in heaven, Father, Word, and Holy Spirit: and these three are one." Erasmus claimed that this passage did not occur in any of the Greek manuscripts he consulted, thus prompting accusations that he was an Arian. His 1519 edition did not include this verse, but following the subsequent outcry he reinserted it in the 1522 edition.

In addition to the *Novum Testamentum*, Erasmus provided a set of *Paraphrases* of most of the books of the New Testament. As in the case of the *Novum Testamentum*, Erasmus claimed that modern readers ignorant of the historical and linguistic context of the New Testament might be either misled or put off by reading the Holy Scriptures without the aid of an interpreter. His *Paraphrases* thus were to be taken in two senses, as an alternative rendering of Scripture and as a commentary on it. The *Paraphrases* were widely read and did not occasion the same degree of controversy that bedeviled reception of the *Novum Testamentum*. However, they did not escape censure from several of his enemies, including Noël Beda, who pursued a long correspondence with Erasmus and publicly denounced him as a "clandestine Lutheran" in 1529.

The Debate With Luther

Whatever difficulties Erasmus had with critics during the second decade of the fifteenth century only intensified with Luther's eruption onto the world stage. As the crisis precipitated by Luther became increasingly serious, Erasmus found himself under severer pressure to take a stand. His letters throughout the early 1520s are filled with the struggle to identify himself in reference to Luther. In a December 1520 letter to

Frans van Cranevelt, for example, he complains of those enemies who seek to blame Erasmus for the debacle: "They thought this a pretty trick . . . to put Luther and Erasmus in double harness – like yoking an ox with a fallow deer."[15] In January 1521, Pope Leo X himself admonished Erasmus to take up his pen against Luther. Erasmus vainly professed that he was neither Luther's enemy nor his secret supporter. As a loyal Catholic, he believed that the proper way to deal with Luther was through reason and persuasion, not by force, and for that reason he disapproved of the issuing of the bull *Exsurge domine*. However, Erasmus was also dismayed at Luther's violent invectives, and at the prospect that the literary studies he valued so highly were being undermined by the threat that Luther posed to established authority.

It was Luther who first perceived the true distance between them, commenting in 1523 to Oecolampadius that Erasmus gave little weight to things of the spirit.[16] Erasmus, hearing of this judgment, wrote in a letter to Zwingli that he was at a loss to understand it, "for I am under the impression that I have maintained almost all that Luther maintains, only without his violence and abstaining from some riddles and paradoxes."[17] The "riddles and paradoxes" doubtless referred to Luther's denial of free will. Yet even as Erasmus wished to remain neutral, both Reformers and Catholics were making it impossible for him to keep peace with either faction, the one trying to manipulate him into making common cause with them, the other attempting to bully him into helping their agenda of destroying Luther.

By February 1524, Erasmus was privately circulating the *De libero arbitrio*, and in April that year Luther, having gotten wind of it, wrote to Erasmus, warning him to limit his activities to those areas in accordance with his gifts, and not get involved in controversy with him.[18] At the same time Pope Clement VII wrote to Erasmus expressing his pleasure at the news that Erasmus had written against Luther.[19] Erasmus responded to Luther in early May saying that he had not attacked him in print; however, the work was published in September. The controversy that ensued would be bitter and painful for Erasmus, leaving him with a strong antagonism toward Luther.

The *De libero arbitrio* is not just an exposition of Erasmus's position on the question of freedom of the will, but a manifesto demonstrating his most strongly held convictions. These convictions have as much to do with the manner in which consensus in the institutional church is achieved and with Erasmus's approach to biblical interpretation as with the theological issue under discussion. In his introductory comments, Erasmus writes that he is not interested in having a wrestling match, in insulting Luther, or (as his Catholic friends might prefer) attempting to destroy him. Indeed, as he points out, "I take so little pleasure in assertions that I will gladly seek refuge in skepticism whenever this is allowed by the inviolable authority of Holy Scripture and the church's decrees; to these decrees I willingly submit my judgment in all things, whether I fully understand what the church commands or not."[20]

This is a much-misunderstood passage, and one that would attract that angry scorn of Luther. Erasmus was not describing himself as a skeptic but rather declaring his willingness to allow the church to rule in matters of doctrine. Throughout the *De libero arbitrio*, Erasmus affirmed the consensus of the church, past and present, over the assertions of an individual. Erasmus, out of respect for Luther's unwillingness to consider any authority other than Scripture, was willing to base his defense of free will entirely on scriptural authority. But he commented that

> if Luther and I seem to be evenly matched on the basis of scriptural testimonies and sound arguments, [readers] should take into consideration the long list of highly learned men approved by the consensus of very many centuries, all the way up to our own day, most of them commended by their exemplary life as well as by their admirable learning in the Scriptures.[21]

In advancing the authority of so many learned men, as Erasmus did, he likewise claimed that his belief in the goodness of God would not permit him to imagine that they had been deceived in such a matter as this for the history of the church. One other significant argument that he made in the introduction was a pragmatic one: even if Luther's version of reality were true, what would be the effect of publishing it to all and sundry?[22]

Erasmus's position on freedom of the will itself is based on his anthropology, which as we have noted is essentially an optimistic vision of human nature. The fall has obscured the excellence of God's creation in human nature, but not destroyed it. Thus Erasmus was able to define free will as "a power of the human will by which man may be able to direct himself towards, or turn away from, what leads to eternal salvation."[23] In other words, humans have something to contribute to their salvation, even if in their contribution they must be accompanied at each stage by God's grace. Erasmus distinguished four types of grace. First, there is natural grace, describing our created nature that maintains itself in spite of the corruption of sin. Next is special or operating grace, that allows us to feel repentance and moves us to attempt to improve ourselves. Justifying or cooperating grace follows upon the believer's efforts, thus making him or her acceptable to God. Finally, the Christian needs the "gift of perseverance," or completing grace, to keep him or her in that state. In this fourfold approach, Erasmus revealed his debt to his scholastic education.

To support his position, Erasmus developed arguments based on Scripture that reflect his hermeneutical convictions. Above all, Scripture is not to be interpreted in a manner that intentionally distorts it from its most obvious meaning. Thus, in any part of Scripture in which God commands something, he must be operating under the expectation that people can act on his command.

> What is the meaning of the many parables about keeping the word of God, running out to meet the bridegroom, about the thief breaking in by night, the house that must be built on rock? Surely they spur us on to strive, to be eager and diligent, so that we do not neglect God's grace and perish. They will seem meaningless or superfluous if everything is referred to necessity.[24]

Even in cases that appear to argue against free will, Erasmus believed that God uses an individual's tendency to evil in accordance with that individual's deserts. "But when God gives people over to their own depravity, he does so because of their previous deserts. . . . But where absolute, perpetual necessity obtains, there can be no question of deserving reward or punishment."[25]

Luther made short work of these arguments in his *De servo arbitrio*, which was scathing in its rejection of Erasmus's effort. He brushed aside Erasmus's pragmatic concerns as irrelevant to the absolute need for Christians to know and to preach the truth to the ends of the earth. That truth, which the Bible unambiguously proclaims, is that not only do humans have no free will, but they have no righteousness, for even their very efforts at good deeds are grounded in sin. Luther dismantled Erasmus's case as leaving free will with so negligible a role to play as to be virtually nonexistent. Erasmus responded with two lengthy treatises, the *Hyperaspistes* I and II, in which he lashed out at Philip Melanchthon as well as Luther, although he otherwise managed to maintain a cordial relationship with Melanchthon throughout his life.[26] But the quarrel with Luther left a lasting mark on Erasmus, and in the last decade of his life he grew increasingly pessimistic in his evaluation of the state of the world.

The Later Erasmus

In addition to the controversy with Luther, Erasmus experienced a breakdown in his relationships with former friends and colleagues, mostly men of the generation younger than himself, some of whom had participated with him in work on the New Testament. Throughout the 1520s, Erasmus came into either direct or indirect conflict with Ulrich von Hutten, Johann Oecolampadius, Wolfgang Capito, Konrad Pellicanus, Caspar Hedio, and Martin Bucer, among others.

During the same period Luther himself was embroiled in the eucharistic controversy. Erasmus would be drawn into this quarrel because of several passages from his annotations, *Paraphrases*, and the *Enchiridion* that appeared to the sacramentarians to support their position.[27] An associate of Zwingli's in Zurich, Leo Jud, went so far as to claim publicly that Erasmus was in covert agreement with them but was too cowardly to admit it openly.[28] Erasmus was prompted to write a pamphlet of his own in an effort to rebut these charges,[29] and to pour out his sense of outrage and frustration in his correspondence. Yet the sacramentarians were not entirely unreasonable in their assumptions; in a guarded response to Oecolampadius's treatise on the Lord's Supper, Erasmus wrote to the town council of Basel in October 1525 that "the work is learned, well-written, and thorough. I would also judge it pious, if anything could be so described which is at variance with the general opinion of the church, from which I consider it perilous to dissent."[30] This letter would cause serious misunderstandings, as people would conclude that Erasmus in his heart agreed with Oecolampadius's position, but was afraid to defy the authority of Rome. Not so, Erasmus would reply: his loyalty to Rome was based not on fear but on his heartfelt belief that, for all its faults, the Roman Church remained the one, true church.

The most comprehensive expression of Erasmus's alienation occurred in his quarrel with the Strasbourg reformer Martin Bucer, who was, ironically, an early admirer of Erasmus. The main documents include Erasmus's *Epistola contra Pseudevangelicos*, written at the end of 1529, an anonymous reply by Bucer entitled *Epistola Apologetica* published in March 1530, and a rebuttal by Erasmus under the title of *Epistola ad Fratres Germaniae Inferioris*, which appeared in August 1530. The first of these was occasioned by Erasmus's frustration with a younger scholar and friend, Gerald Geldenhouwer, who had cited passages from earlier texts by Erasmus out of context to support an argument of his own. The *Epistola contra Pseudevangelicos*, beginning as a rebuke to this young man, quickly expanded to include a generalized rebuke against similar tactics employed by others of the reforming party. Ultimately the letter launched a broadly-based attack on all aspects of the doctrines and lives of the Reformers in order to prove that these people do not represent the true meaning of the gospel message.

Erasmus's initial attack mingled personal concerns with the larger question of what may be the appropriate way to bring about much-needed change in an institution. He expressed his most serious charge with a metaphor from the gospel: "You pluck out the tare along with the wheat, or, to put it more rightly, you pluck off the wheat instead of the tare."[31] Beyond attacking what is bad in a way that endangers the good, the Reformers have actually thrown out the good and retained or increased the bad. "They have rejected the distinction of foods, along with fasting, but all the same they eagerly indulge in drunkenness; and so some have escaped Judaism only to start becoming Epicureans. They trample on ceremony, but add nothing to spirituality; in fact, it has greatly decreased, in my judgment."[32]

Erasmus was particularly dismayed by the manner in which the evangelical attack has polarized Christendom, thus restricting the freedom of everyone to contest the very abuses the Reformers claim to find most abhorrent. The thrust of Erasmus's argument is pragmatic in nature: the Reformers, by relentlessly attacking the established church, have only made things worse, and in addition, they show no understanding of how to teach Christian behavior to others, particularly in their failure to provide a good example. But Erasmus's complaints about personal morals serve not only to expose the Reformers as hypocrites, but also to provide the basis for his critique of the efficacy of their doctrine: if they were real Christians preaching the true gospel they would be humble, continent, sober, and mild in demeanor. In addition, toward the end of the *Epistola* Erasmus employs an argument based on history: the early church, he claims, is not an appropriate model for people to follow today. Thus Erasmus contrives to attack the foundations of the Reformers' cause as well as the manner in which it has been carried out.

In his answer, Bucer makes every effort to portray the beliefs and practices of the evangelicals in as inoffensive a light as possible, the upshot of his strategy being to show that the evangelicals are not the wild extremists that Erasmus has claimed. This strategy demands Bucer focus at least in part on what the evangelicals have in common with the traditional Church, enabling readers to imagine that the Reformers are not so much cutting themselves off from past practices as calmly and reasonably shifting their emphases to something more suitable. In the *Epistola ad Fratres Germaniae Inferioris*, Erasmus loses no time in dismissing Bucer's claims. To the contention that the evangelicals recognize much that was good and holy in the church's history, Erasmus only responds:

> They who teach that baptism is not necessary for anyone's salvation, who teach that in the Eucharist there is nothing but bread and wine and many other similar things, who say that the old doctors of the church taught pure nonsense, and that there is a danger that they are all in Hell, how do they represent the church if not as blind?[33]

He repeats such blunt summaries of the Reformers' views often, thus bypassing entirely the mediating language in which Bucer has attempted to recast the essence of his party's goals.

The exchange represents the ultimate failure of hope for a bridge between Erasmus's moderate, humanistic approach to reform and the challenge of the evangelicals. Erasmus's approach, which combined a sharp critique of abuses and superstitious practices with a piety that was deeply personal, seemed for many of his contemporaries to hold out the promise of change within the church that would improve it while cherishing its traditions and protecting its authority. As a champion of the humanist cause of "good letters," Erasmus was at the same time a powerful advocate of a spiritual renewal based on an immersion in Scripture, seasoned by a liberal education in the classics. Martin Luther's challenge, however, struck at the heart of the Roman Church in his attack on the freedom of the will. Erasmus's 1524 debate with Luther exposes the abyss between Erasmus's Christian humanism and Luther's evangelical theology. The exchange with Martin Bucer reveals Erasmus's rejection of the Reformers' positions concerning the sacraments, ecclesiology, and political authority, as well as their moral stature. In drawing up evidence to support his complaints, Erasmus presents a detailed interpretation of the sweep of Christian history as well as the events of the previous decade, which demonstrates that whatever sympathy he may have had with the Reformers in earlier years was by now utterly exhausted.

In the spring of 1529, Erasmus left Basel, which had gone over to the reform, to settle in Freiburg. There he spent most of the remainder of his life, returning to Basel just before his death. By the time he died in July 1536, he had long since come to believe that events had passed beyond his ability to influence them, for better or worse. Yet his influence far surpassed what he could have imagined even in the glory days of his prime. The legacy of his pedagogical work, his biblical scholarship, and his humanist-inspired reform has inspired and informed readers from the sixteenth century to the twenty-first.

Notes

1 The question of Colet's influence on Erasmus has recently been subject to considerable revision. Frederic Seebohm, in *The Oxford Reformers* (London: J. M. Dent & Sons, 1914), claims that Colet substantially inspired Erasmus's approach of applying classical philological methods to Scripture. However, a more recent biography by John Gleason, *John Colet* (Berkeley: University of California Press, 1989), argues that Colet's influence on Erasmus was minimal. Richard Marius, *Thomas More: A Biography* (New York: Knopf, 1985) also raises questions about the reputed intimacy between More and Erasmus.
2 *CWE* 23, 57:23–6.
3 *CWE* 23, 61:8–12.
4 *CWE* 66, 33.
5 *CWE* 39, 194:33–4.
6 *CWE* 66, 33–4.
7 John C. Olin, *Christian Humanism and the Reformation* (New York: Fordham University Press, 1987), 95.
8 Olin, *Christian Humanism*, 100.
9 Hajo Holborn, *Ausgewählte Werke*, 180:22–4, cited in Marjorie O'Rourke Boyle, *Erasmus on Language and Method in Theology* (Toronto: University of Toronto Press, 1978), 73.
10 Olin, *Christian Humanism*, 100.
11 Olin, *Christian Humanism*, 102.
12 *CWE* 70, 340.
13 *CWE* 39, 289:36.
14 *CWE* 39, 357:15–16.
15 Ep. 1173, *CWE* 8, 133:136–8.
16 *WA Br* 3: 96:12–25.
17 Ep. 1384, *CWE* 10, 84:92–8.
18 Ep. 1443, *CWE* 10, 246:74–8.
19 Ep. 1443B, *CWE* 10, 250:8–12.
20 *CWE* 76, 7.
21 *CWE* 76, 15.
22 *CWE* 76, 13.
23 *CWE* 76, 21.
24 *CWE* 76, 42.
25 *CWE* 76, 52.

26 A recent study by Timothy J. Wengert, *Human Freedom, Christian Righteousness* (New York: Oxford University Press, 1998), argues that the relationship was far less cordial than assumed; see, however, reviews of the book by Laurel Carrington and by John Payne in *Erasmus of Rotterdam Society Yearbook Twenty* (2000).

27 Some of the passages in question are from the Fifth Canon of the *Enchiridion*, the annotations on Mk. 14, parts of the *Paraphrase* of 1 Cor. 10 and 11, and the *Paraphrase* of Acts 2:42.

28 The pamphlet was entitled *Des hochgelerten Erasmi von Roterdam unnd Doctor martin Luthers maynung vom Nachtmal unnsers herren Ihesu Christi neuwlich aussgangen auff den XVIII tag Aprellens.*

29 This is the *Detectio Praestigiarum. ASD* IX-1 233–62.

30 Ep. 1636, *CWE* 11, 343:3–344:6.

31 *ASD* IX-1 292:239–40.

32 *ASD* IX-1 292:266–70.

33 *ASD* IX-1 402:609–12.

Bibliography

Primary Sources

Allen, P.S., ed., *Opus epistolarum Des. Erasmi Roterodami*, 12 vols., Oxford: Clarendon Press, 1906–58.

The Collected Works of Erasmus, Toronto: University of Toronto Press, 1974– (cited as *CWE*).

Holborn, Annemarie and Hajo, *Desiderius Erasmus. Ausgewählte Werke*, Munich: C. H. Beck'sche, 1974.

Leclerc, Jean, ed., *Des. Erasmi Roterodami opera omnia*, 10 vols., Leiden: 1703–6.

Olin, John C., ed., *Christian Humanism and the Reformation: Selected Writings of Erasmus*, 3rd ed., New York: Fordham University Press, 1987.

Phillips, Margaret Mann, *Erasmus on his Times: A Shortened Version of* The Adages of Erasmus, Cambridge: Cambridge University Press, 1967.

Reedijk, C., et al., *Opera omnia Des. Erasmi Roterodami* (Amsterdam: North Holland Publishing Co., 1969– (cited as *ASD*).

Thompson, Craig R., *The Colloquies of Erasmus*, Chicago: University of Chicago Press, 1965.

Secondary Sources

Augustijn, Cornelius, *Erasmus: His Life, Works, and Influence*, Toronto: University of Toronto Press, 1991.

Bataillon, Marcel, *Erasme et l'Espagne: Recherches sur l'histoire spirituelle du XVI‘ Siècle*, 3 vols., Geneva: Droz, 1991.

Bentley, Jerry H., *Humanists and Holy Writ: New Testament Scholarship in the Renaissance.* Princeton: Princeton University Press, 1983.

Boyle, Marjorie O'Rourke, *Erasmus on Language and Method in Theology*, Toronto: University of Toronto Press, 1978.

——, *Rhetoric and Reform: Erasmus' Civil Dispute with Luther*, Cambridge, MA: Harvard University Press, 1983.

Chantraine, Georges, SJ, *"Mystère" et "Philosophie du Christ" selon Érasme*, Gembloux: Editions J. Duculot, 1971.

Chomarat, Jacques, *Grammaire et Rhétorique chez Erasme*, 2 vols., Paris: Société d'Edition "Les belles lettres," 1981.

Hoffmann, Manfred, *Rhetoric and Theology: The Hermeneutic of Erasmus*, Toronto: University of Toronto Press, 1994.

Kohls, Ernst-Wilhelm, *Die Theologie des Erasmus*, 2 vols., Basel: Helbing & Lichtenhahn/Friedrich Reinhart Verlag, 1966.

Margolin, Jean-Claude, *Érasme: Précepteur de l'Europe*, Paris: Julliard, 1995.

McConica, James K., *Erasmus*, Oxford: Oxford University Press, 1991.

Pabel, Hilmar M., ed., *Erasmus' Vision of the Church*, Kirksville: Sixteenth Century Journal Publishers, 1995.

Payne, John, *Erasmus: His Theology of the Sacraments*, Richmond: John Knox Press, 1970.

Rummel, Erika, *Erasmus's Annotations on the New Testament: From Philologist to Theologian*, Toronto: University of Toronto Press, 1986.

——, *Erasmus and his Catholic Critics*, 2 vols., Nieuwkoop: De Graaf, 1989.

Tracy, James D., *Erasmus: The Growth of a Mind*, Geneva: Droz, 1972.

——, *Erasmus of the Low Countries*, Berkeley and Los Angeles: University of California Press, 1996.

Wengert, Timothy J., *Human Freedom, Christian Righteousness: Philip Melanchthon's Exegetical Dispute with Erasmus of Rotterdam*, New York: Oxford University Press, 1998.

Lutheran Theologians

Martin Luther (1483–1546)

Oswald Bayer

Luther saw himself and his work in the perspective of the rupture of the times, the rupture between the old and new aeon – between the end of the old world, the fallen creation, and the new world, the renewed creation.

The old world was convulsed by a last desperate effort directed against the gospel that had overpowered evil and vanquished it. In defiance of these evils of the last days, Luther fought tirelessly against the Roman papacy[1] as well as the Enthusiasts. He also encountered God himself as his enemy whose omnipotence working all in all, good as well as evil, is inextricable to us. Yet, in spite of Luther's conviction of the imminent end of the world, he intentionally presented his marriage and the establishing of a family – in the midst of the Peasants' War – as a sign of his faith in God the Creator. "If I can manage it, before I die I will still marry my Katie to spite the devil. . . . I trust they [the peasants] will not steal my courage and [my] joy. . . . In a short while the true judge will come."[2]

The source of Luther's trust and strength in the midst of these theological and social conflicts was the Crucified himself: the certainty that God is Man. The crucified God – "Immanuel," "God is with us" – bears and overcomes the night of sin, death, and hell by the power of his love. He is "with us in the muck and work of our lives so much that his skin smokes."[3] At the same time the God, who FORGIVES SIN,[4] tears us away from ourselves and places us outside ourselves that we may be supported by that which is outside us (*extra nos*) – the Word of the Cross.

That is why Luther had no biographical interest in his own person. The course of his own life and the general course of the world were for him submerged entirely in the course of the Word of God. The authoritative frame of reference within which Luther's life and work are properly perceived is his focus on the "course of the gospel," the history shaped and effected by the Holy Scriptures; what he called the dramatic epic poem of the "divine Aeneade," the book of experiences.[5]

Luther's apocalyptic understanding of creation and history opposes modern concepts of progress. For Luther the only progress is return to one's baptism, the biographical point of rupture between the old and new worlds. Creation, Fall, redemption and completion of the world are not a sequential advance, one after the other, but perceived in an intertwining of the times.

For Luther the rupture of the times cast in sharp relief the tensions between faith and sight, between the God revealed in Christ and the God hidden in absolute majesty. These tensions created anxiety and attacks of desperation that Luther knew as *Anfechtungen*. By these temptations and trials he was driven to the Word, which, as the power of God's prevenient answer, addresses the cry of *Anfechtung* to the incomprehensible God where he may be grasped – in the Word of his promise that may be tasted in the Lord's Supper.

Luther's Concept of Theology

Luther used the word "theology"[6] with striking emphasis and on occasion with programmatic emphasis – as in the phrase *theologia cruces* (theology of the cross)[7] – in correspondence to the three main epistemological questions that came to him from Gabriel Biel.[8] In response to this scholastic tradition, Luther understood theology first as wisdom gained from experience, *sapientia experimentalis*,[9] fostered by "prayer, meditation, and trial."[10] Second, he sees the unity of theology, its "subject," in the dramatic event of justification. Third, he explodes the scholastic alternatives of whether theology is speculative or practical, and sets forth a fundamental third option: faith as passive life (*vita passiva*).[11] This is "so that we are not seduced either by the active life (*vita activa*) with its works or by the contemplative life (*vita contemplativa*) with its speculations."[12] Thus the dominant binary schema of theory and praxis is broken and replaced by a threefold schema according to which both, metaphysics and ethics, are grounded in a third, a pathos, and thus are critically limited.

Luther's concept of theology is primarily not a *scholastic* but rather a *monastic* theology. What is primary for Luther is not that theology of university disputations (of which he himself was certainly a master), but rather a pastoral theology marked entirely by the Word of address that creates faith through the use of Scripture and thereby occasions the formation of passions. This theology as meditation on the text also shapes Luther's catechetical systematics.[13] The centrality of the *monastic* element in no way implies the exclusion of the *scholastic* element. Theology as meditation on the text and exegesis of Scripture exists for Luther within the educational coherence of the medieval trivium of grammar, dialectic, and rhetoric, with an emphasis upon grammar. Conflicting interpretations are decided by adhering to the biblical letters in which the Holy Spirit is incarnated, who has "his own grammar."[14] With Johann Georg Hamann one can succinctly formulate: For Luther theology is "the grammar of the language of the Holy Scripture."[15] Luther perceived the relationship of theology and philosophy in a differentiated way, not only in the rejection of Aristotle and his commentaries, but also in a positive reception, the intensity of which has only recently been discovered.[16]

Luther's concept of theology comprises a theoretical revolution that explodes the scholastic concept of theology. This revolution is grounded in how Luther, in conversation with the biblical texts, perceives the vital importance of temporality and language to the knowledge of God, indeed of God himself. He understands theology therefore not as a science of principles or essence, but rather as a science of history and of experience. To Aristotelian ears, *sapientia experimentalis*[17] is a *contradictio in adiecto*, a "square circle." According to Luther, however, "theology is an infinite wisdom because it can never be completely learned."[18]

The Subject of Theology: Man the Sinner and God the Justifier

From Thomas Aquinas to Wolfhart Pannenberg many regard the subject of theology simply and without conditions as "God." "God" is "the essential subject of theology."[19] According to Pannenberg, everything that theology thematizes, it thematizes "under the perspective of its relatedness to God (*sub ratione Dei*)."[20] In this sense theology is the "science of God."[21]

In opposition to that definition, Luther's concept of theology appears intolerably narrow: "The proper subject of theology is man guilty of sin and condemned, and God the Justifier and Savior of man the sinner."[22]

This communicative relationship of God and man is in no way self-evident, but astonishing. This becomes clear by Luther's sharp contrast of God and man. He speaks not of an association, but of a dissociation, a separation – the divorce, the deadly divorce – of God and man. In this dissociation the naked God clashes with the naked man. The "naked God" (*nudus deus*) is God "in his absolute majesty," "the absolute God" (*Deus absolutus*)."[23] One can have nothing "to do" with this "naked God"; one cannot "associate," "deal," or "speak" with him; one cannot have faith in him. However, this dissociation does not allow the "naked man" (*nudus homo*) any rest. He experiences the *deus nudus* as his enemy. Thus the dispute between the sinful man and the justifying God is above all the "struggle"[24] over who is in the right. Such a dispute is no harmless correlation of the knowledge of God and the knowledge of the self. For it is not certain from the outset who this is who is over against man. Is it God or the Devil? Did Jacob at Jabbok wrestle with a demon or with Jahweh?[25] Whether the person's opponent is God or the Devil is decided by the certainty of the Word and thereby in an implied Christology. A beneficial and truly communicative relationship rather than a destructive encounter between God and the person is a relationship in the Word; it occurs in verbal exchange and communication (*in sermonibus tuis*). The kind of mediation is more narrowly determined when Luther emphasizes that here God is not naked, but "dressed and clothed in his Word and promises, so that from the name 'God' we cannot exclude Christ."[26] In Christology it becomes explicit who is related to whom in which medium. It is "the proclamation of the gospel through which he [Christ] comes to you or through which you are brought to him."[27]

The story of Jacob's struggle at Jabbok shows in the most graphic way what is involved in the coming together of the justifying God and the sinner. In this struggle for life or death concerning mutual recognition, faith "makes" God (*facit deum*): "Faith is the creator of the Deity." Unbelief, however, makes an idol. To be sure, this all takes place "in us,"[28] not in the nature of God. In this dispute between the sinner and the justifying God – thus between God and faith, not in the projection of unbelief and its dependence upon self-created idols – Jesus Christ is present as true God and true man. The office and the work of Christ is to abolish the clash of the *deus nudus* and the *homo nudus*; to vanquish such deadly confrontation so that God speaks to the sinner, mercifully saving him from death, not the least of which is the self-distortion that is the origin of the worship of idols. In just this way Word and faith – in which man the sinner and God the justifier come together – are proved as the matter and subject of theology: "For God does not deal, nor has he ever dealt, with man otherwise than through the Word of promise. We in turn cannot deal with God otherwise than through faith in the Word of his promise."[29]

Promissio: The Reformatory Turn in Luther's Theology and Its Permanent Center; Law and Gospel

The reformatory turn in Luther's theology is not sufficiently explained by the causative understanding of the righteousness of God (*iustitia dei*) as such (that is, that God is righteous in that he makes us righteous), because that is an element of the Augustinian tradition and therefore does not properly designate the distinctively reformatory. It resides rather in the understanding of God's promise[30] as Luther painstakingly found it, above all in the Pauline texts. The context was Luther's profound investigation of the sacrament of penance, impelled by the urgent problem of indulgences. Luther initially understood the priestly words of absolution *Ego te absolvo* ("I absolve you of your sins") as an act of speech, which confirms something existing, a declaratory act. The priest sees the sinner's repentance, takes it as a sign that absolution has already occurred to the penitent inwardly, who is nevertheless still unaware of this divine justification, divine absolution. The priest thus lets God's absolution appear as such; he confirms it – to the ascertainment of the person absolved. Thereby the word of absolution is understood as a judgment in the sense of a statement.

With that understanding, Luther remains wholly in the framework of the classical understanding of language, above all that of the Stoics, which Augustine inherited and which still widely prevails. Subsequently language is a system of signs, referring to things or signs that express an emotion. In both cases, the sign – as statement or expression – is not the matter itself.

That the verbal sign itself is already the matter itself, that it presents not an absent but rather a present matter, that was Luther's great hermeneutical discovery, his reformatory discovery in the strict sense of the word. He made this discovery first of all in his investigation of the sacrament of penance (1518). That the sign itself is already the matter and event itself means in view of absolution that the sentence "I absolve you of your sins" is not merely a declaratory judgment of what already is, thus presupposing an inner, proper absolution. The word of absolution is rather a verbal act, which first creates a relationship – between God in whose name it is spoken, and the person to whom it is spoken and who believes the promise.

This verbal act is an active, efficacious Word that creates community and thereby liberates and makes certain. *It does what it says; it says what it does.* Luther also discovered the same effective Word in the institutions of baptism and the Lord's Supper – similarly in the stories of Christmas and Easter ("Fear not!"). Indeed,

Luther, as his rendition of Psalm 33:4b shows ("What he promises, he certainly keeps"), understood the entire Bible, including the creation story, as promise. God's promise is the concrete manner in which he presents himself: "I am the Lord your God!" and in which Jesus Christ is present as God's Word: reliable and definite – definitively liberating and making certain.

This unequivocal meaning can only be reached when the gospel as giving promise – "Take and eat!" (Gn. 2:16; 1 Cor. 11:24) – is distinguished from the demanding and the sin-convicting law. For Luther the gospel is the "other" word,[31] the second and final, ultimately valid Word. In retrospect Luther reported: "When I found this distinction between law and gospel, I broke through."[32] Here the breakthrough to the reformatory turn and discovery occurred.

That, in brief, characterizes the jumping-off point of the reformatory turn in Luther's theology. Everything else is oriented to it: the Word of gift and promise with which God creates the world; the Word which calls me and all creatures into life; the Word which gives in baptism and in the Lord's Supper the promise of new and final community; the Word which rights the upside-down world and brings it back to himself. In this focus and breadth, the justification of the godless (Rom. 4:5) is to be perceived through the Word alone, by grace alone, by Christ alone, through faith alone.

Creation as the Foundation and Preservation of Community

For Luther the creation is the promised world.[33] The entire world is the medium of a promise to me, in and through which I am addressed by God himself. I am placed in it, enjoy my life in the space and time granted me, in the rhythm of night and day, summer and winter, youth and age. Whoever closes himself to the promised world and community, will find that his own heart, mouth, and hand are now closed: the entire world becomes too narrow for him. He becomes anxious and thereby suffers God's wrath. Whoever closes himself or herself to the creation does not hear and perceive the world as promised, but loses it as a home and gains it as a desert. If the world is not believed as promised, it is experienced as merciless law; it becomes "a thousand deserts mute and cold."[34] In such silence and such coldness I experience God's wrath. All creatures about me – even a rustling leaf that terrifies me (Lv. 26:36) – bear witness to and speak this wrath, but most of all my own heart in its presumption and desperation (Jer. 17:9), alone and lonely, distorted in itself. Man possessed by himself cuts off his own life. This is the original sin, the sickness unto death.

We receive the gift of life including the space and time presented to us with the address: "You may eat from all of this" (Gn. 2:16). The freeing of space for life occurs for Luther in the permitting and inviting Word of God. Addressed by such a promising Word one can answer. One answers in accepting God's gift, which grants community and praises God as the giver of all good. The praise of God does not occur in an abstract and direct encounter with God, but rather is mediated through the disclosed and preserved world, especially in the astonishing encounters with one's fellow creatures.

When Luther understands the entire creation as God's promise and gift, this understanding is gained from his understanding of the gospel and sacraments. Above all, it is the gift-Word of the Lord's Supper that Luther has in his ears, before his eyes and in his heart when he perceives every act of the Trinitarian God is a giving promise and a promising giving.

In overflowing goodness, the Creator creates the necessary space for life – not by contracting and withdrawing himself to avoid impinging on the independence of his creatures, but by expanding himself to enable relationships, communications, exchanges, and community. He fulfills everything and pours himself out in giving virtue free from envy.

With these presented spaces for living, man and woman use the freedom promised them in order to sustain their environment. They are enabled to "give names" (Gn. 2:19f.), namely, to order and to structure their world. This occurs in three estates.

World Order: The Three Estates; "Natural Theology"

With his doctrine of the three estates, Luther interprets the biblical creation story in terms of a theology of creation, a theology of sin, and social ethics. The three estates – church, household, and government (*status ecclesiasticus, status oeconomicus, status politicus*) – are not sociological concepts of classification, but rather characterize the fundamental life forms by which God's promise of creation constitutes human being.

The fundamental estate is the *status ecclesiasticus* – the estate through which God addresses man who is called to a grateful free answer. Being human exists in that the person is addressed and therefore can hear and in responding can speak, but also must be responsible. In the divine address and the expectation of the human answer resides the basic event of worship, of honoring God, the foundation of religion, of the church understood as an order of creation. All persons and all religions belong to it. Every person belongs as such – this defines him or her as human – to the church as an order of creation, which, to be sure, is totally corrupted by human ingratitude, by sin.

The second estate is the household or the economy. It is embedded in the basic estate – the church as an order of creation, consisting of Word and faith or Word and unbelief – permeated by it and embraced in it. Luther speaks of the economy in terms of the relationship of parents and children, of husband and wife, of man and the soil, thus of work procuring daily bread.

Luther did not wish to recognize the third estate, the political realm, as an order of creation but only as an estate first made necessary by the fall into sin, thus an "emergency order." He did this, although he knew that politics is grounded in the economy, in the consequence of the household estate.

The fall into sin not only brought about the state with its coercive means for maintaining right order, but also corrupted the two unequivocal orders of creation: the church, and the household or economy. But while all three are depraved, they are not destroyed; even as corrupted they remain embraced in God's promise and therefore holy. What matters is that the power of the creating and forgiving Word of God may be recognized and believed even in and through their distortion.

Luther's conception of the church as an order of creation provides at the same time his understanding of the "universal" experience of God, i.e., "Natural Theology." The permitting promise of life in the biblical story of creation, "You may eat of everything" (Gn. 2:16), and the self-presentation of God, "I am the Lord your God" (Ex. 20:2), coincide and are valid for everyone. This one fundamental promise and the commandment to have no other gods (Ex. 20:3), as well as the threat of death to protect the promise of life (Gn. 2:17), show a peculiar "Natural Theology" and at the same time a phenomenology of religion. Luther takes into account, in the sense of Rom. 1:18–3:20, a relationship with God experienced and lived by every person; a relationship which is actually and practically always corrupted, misguided, and distorted; it is a mis-relation. Reason – not primarily theoretical reason but the practical reason directed by the power of imagination – always grasps after God but always misses. Thus Luther comments on Jonah 1:5 ("And the sailors were afraid and cried out, each to his god") "that these people in the boat all know of God," "but no one knows God."[35] It is the office of Christ to make God known with certainty.

The Image of God in Man; Reason and Free Will

The three estates mark the realm of responsibility of man addressed by God, placed in the world as the image of God, empowered by the Creator through language and reason to share "rule" over fellow creatures (Gn. 1:28). Human beings are thus "put" in the world in order to "cultivate and preserve" it (Gn. 2:15). Reason, understood as language, is – as far as civil righteousness (*iustitia civilis*) is concerned – not extinguished by the fall into sin, but "rather confirmed."[36] In spite of sin, reason is the "inventor and mentor of all the arts, medicine, laws, and of whatever wisdom, power, virtue, and glory human beings possess in this life."[37] In this connection, Luther cannot praise highly enough reason and free will. Within the realm of civil righteousness, reason is to a certain degree "something divine."[38] On the other hand, reason is a "whore" – perverted – when it arrogates to itself alone judgment in questions of faith and salvation; then reason is to be "slaughtered" by faith.[39]

Sin and the Bondage of the Will

Just as the essence of being human consists in living in faith, so in unbelief the person is not what he or she was created to be. In unbelief, in sin, there is an indissoluble link of destiny and guilt, fate and freedom. For Luther, in the wake of the anti-Pelagian Augustine, the connection of original sin and bondage of the will is constitutive. Already in thesis 13 of the *Heidelberg Disputation* (1518), the radical doctrine of sin is constitutively linked to an emphasis upon the unfree will: "Free will, after the fall, exists in name only. . . ."[40]

The stone of offense for Luther is Erasmus's thesis: "that we may apply our wills to grace, or turn away from it."[41] "[B]y free choice in this place we mean a power of the human will by which a man can apply himself to the things which lead to eternal salvation, or turn away from them."[42] Luther opposed this thesis as sharply as possible.[43] The turn to salvation, faith, is in no way a human work but rather is God's work alone, the completion of which – precisely because God is omnipotent – no one can hinder. God is not only willing to keep what he promises, but he is also able to do it. If salvation were not entirely and solely in God's hands, I would – even if only in the slightest bit – have to have a say in and to cooperate in my salvation. Thus I would, on this single point alone, certainly the Archimedean point, have to fend for myself. Then uncertainty would enter which would destroy the certainty of salvation,[44] and thereby also deny the radical nature of sin.

The sinner first of all despises his food, does not see the gifts given him. He who believes, "tastes and sees that the Lord is friendly" (Ps. 34:8); he has an eye for God's kindness. He who has not, does not believe; he sins. Sin is not primarily transgression of a prohibition (*peccatum commissionis*), but rather disregarding an exhibition and overlooking an offered gift (*peccatum omissionis*). The characteristic of the old man, the sinner, is that he is not able to see what is given to him.[45] The mark of radical anxiety about existence is that it fails to see, it misses and omits the present. Ingratitude is the main sin.

Sin is the perversion of creatureliness. Luther speaks of a "perversion" (*invertere*).[46] The essence and work of the Devil, the Confusor, is that he perverts the creaturely. The "world turned upside down" "drowns in its blindness;"[47] it is creatureliness curved in upon itself. The person seeks in the last resort to pass judgment upon himself, thereby making God a liar and erecting his own judgment upon himself and his fellows as an idol in his heart.[48] He himself imagines that upon which his heart depends. Thus Luther defines man as "a rational animal which has a heart that imagines."[49]

The Evil One; God as the Devil; God's Wrath

Sin as evil comes through the sinner into the world. God is not the cause of sin. The cause is man alone in his freedom. Therefore he is guilty and must himself bear responsibility. He has, however, already forfeited his fundamental freedom. Luther confesses with Psalm 51:7: "I – I myself – I was conceived in sin!"[50]

In this evil which is by no means anonymous, but on the contrary is confessed in the most individual manner, however, works the omnipotence of the Creator. For even in sin the sinner has his life from his Creator. For God is not idle, but rather "active to the utmost"[51] – like water flowing unstoppable but to a false mill. "Since, then, God moves and actuates all in all, he necessarily moves and acts also in Satan and the ungodly. But he acts in them as they are and as he finds them; that is to say, since they are averse to God and evil, and caught up in the movement of this divine omnipotence, they do nothing but averse and evil things."[52]

For Luther the inevitable concept is that if – against gnosticism and Marcionitism – God is to be confessed and conceived as the one and only God, and if his creative power is omnipotent, this working power also must be effective in the uncomprehending and anti-godly. Thus God works all in all:[53] evil as well as good (Lam. 3:38), life as well as death, light as well as darkness (Is. 45:7), love as well as hate (Eccl. 9:1), fortune as well as misfortune (Am. 3:6).[54]

Here Luther's speech concerning the Devil may be understood in its radicality. The Devil, humankind's bitterest enemy, who constantly and everywhere assails and afflicts people, is nothing other than the mask of the Almighty God in his dreadful hiddenness. In my profoundest *Anfechtung*, God himself becomes my enemy (Jb. 13:24; 16:7–14) and I can no longer distinguish at all between God and the Devil, and I "do not know whether God is the Devil or the Devil is God."[55]

God in his terrifying hiddenness cannot be defined, "understood," or even defended. Thus for Luther in contrast to Leibniz, theodicy is not a dispute in the forum of understanding and critical reason *about* God, but rather as with Job it is a litigation *with* God. It concerns reliance upon God against God; a complaint in which it is necessary to appeal to God against God,[56] relying upon the God revealed in the gospel, for "to search for God outside Jesus is [to find] the Devil."[57] Only through Christ received in the Holy Spirit may God the Father be seen in the heart; only here the uncertainty and ambiguity of the experience of God is overcome. Here as well is overcome God's incomprehensible wrath, effective with his terrifying hidden-ness, as his comprehensible[58] wrath over against man as sinner. Christ is the "mirror of the Father's heart. Apart from him we see nothing but an angry and terrible Judge. But neither could we know anything of Christ, had it not been revealed by the Holy Spirit."[59]

Through the Son, our Lord: God as Mercy and Love

Luther's Christology is manifest in an exemplary way in his hymn "Dear Christians, Let Us Now Rejoice."[60] The hymn tells of God's unexpected act of liberation, his katabatic movement in which he promises and gives himself; it tells of the upheaval into life that occurred with Easter eve; in brief, it tells the event of salvation. Both parts of the story of liberation are linked together according to the paradigm of complaint-response as presented in Psalm 22.

In stanzas 2 and 3, the complaint – that of the old sinful and lost man – reaches a crescendo in the cry of Romans 7:24 ("Wretched man that I am! Who will rescue me from this body of death?"). This complaint of the old man, who has also dragged the rest of creation into ruin (Rom. 8:18–25), is so radical that it not only encompasses the experience of modern man, who in seeking self-realization is anxious about his identity. Rather these experiences are in the first place given an appropriate language by that Pauline lament and its Lutheran formulation.

The complaint is read as the story of the descent into a hell of self-knowledge. This story tells of grounding existence in one's self, the self-absorption in which the self is closed in upon itself – indeed, so closely that it loses its breath, and yet its sickness does not lead to death, but eternally torments itself in its self-entanglement. In this ontology of self-existence is working the condemning and eternally killing law, with which I am inevitably afflicted for – in the midst of the whole of humanity lost and a creation cast into ruin – I have defined myself through my acts. This *ontology* is an *ontology of self-justification*. The narcissism of the modern era[61] has a still more terrifying visage than it had in Luther's time, which had incorporated the Aristotelian understanding of justice positively in its doctrines of sin and grace and thereby confirmed self-justification. Indeed, at the time of Aristotle himself, whose metaphysics of the world of works expressed a cosmic and social piety, man, while absorbed in works, was still not nakedly entangled in himself.

The second part of the hymn (stanzas 4–10) tells of deliverance. Soteriology appears as Christology and the doctrine of the Trinity. God's self-sacrifice, expressed theologically as trinitarian self-commitment, anticipates an answer to the complaint of the old and lost man. From the depths of hell the person who is crying out is heard and from the outset integrated in the inner conversation of God. The conversation between Father and Son, Son and Father is no speculative trinitarian theological concept, but rather is from the beginning an effective event to the sinner, related as "mercy." The entire being of God is understood as self-giving promise, which the Son promises to the man lost in death: "Hold thou to me . . . I give myself entirely for thee. . . ."

"Then God was sorry on his throne. . . ." God's turn to the sinner occurs by God's mercy alone – from his creative power that saves from all evil, sin, death, and hell. Humankind's complaints and questions are heard and answered from eternity. But the answer and salvation, to be sure, happen historically through the resurrection of the crucified Jesus, which, also historically, is (concentrated in the bodily Word of baptism and the Lord's Supper) communicated to us in the present.[62] Jesus Christ as *Christus praesens*, heard and grasped in this bodily Word of promise, comes to man and incorporates him into Christ, into his body, and into his history. This communicative being of Jesus Christ in faith is nothing other than the communicative being of God himself. Out of his groundless love and mercy, God as the Father through the Son in the Holy Spirit promises himself to man, committing himself totally, sharing his being, keeping nothing for himself, giving everything.[63]

The Holy Spirit; the Church

The appropriation of the saving work of Jesus Christ as faith in him is no achievement "by our own reason and strength,"[64] but rather the work of God himself alone, the work of God the Holy Spirit. "No one can say 'Jesus is Lord' except by the Holy Spirit" (1 Cor. 12:3). The Holy Spirit has called me by the gospel[65] as an individual – not in isolation, rather in the midst of "the whole Christian church on earth." Through "this gospel and the sacraments," "God gives the Holy Spirit who in those who hear the gospel, creates faith." He does this indeed "where and when he wills," but when he does it, he never does it without the external "bodily Word."[66]

"Where the Word is, there is the church."[67] This is the principle of Luther's understanding of the church. The Word is Jesus Christ himself[68] in his presence, as he, mediated by wordly means, promises himself in baptism and as gift in the Lord's Supper ("This is my body given for you!") and in the absolution.

Luther sees the signs of this church of the Word in seven "holy and salvific things," seven "means of salvation." The church as the *sanctorum communio* is "externally known" by the "Word," especially in its forms of "baptism," the "Lord's Supper," and the "keys" as well as in its "ministries," its "service of the Word," further public "prayer," confession (including "the public expression of the catechism"), and the "cross" suffered for the sake of the gospel.[69] These "external signs"[70] do not refer to something interior, but rather in, with, and among them the church is not only recognized but also constituted. The marks of recognition are essential marks. "But you must adhere to and follow this sure and infallible rule: God in His divine wisdom arranges to manifest Himself to human beings by some definite and visible form which can be seen with the eyes and touched with the hands, in short, is within the scope of the five senses. So near to us does the Divine Majesty place Itself."[71]

The signs of the church are all together "holy and salvific things," seven "means of salvation" whereby the Holy Spirit sanctifies his people according to the first table of the law. Luther further asks whether those who in their estates exercise obedience as love corresponding to the second table of the law are not then also to be considered as an "external sign" "by which one recognizes the holy Christian church, namely there where the Holy Spirit sanctifies us also according to the other table of Moses."[72] Thus the estates, inasmuch as elementary life is grasped and determined by the seven last commandments, could be named "seven holy and salvific things" – seven means of salvation![73] However, then Luther raises the objection: They can "not be regarded being as reliable" as the seven "holy means of salvation" in which Jesus Christ himself is present as the church, "because even some heathen too practice these works and indeed at times appear holier than Christians."[74] In this way Luther seeks to distinguish between, on the one hand, creation and preservation, which God carries out also through the work of the heathen; and, on the other hand, salvation as it mediates itself with certainty in Christ's Word, and thus to clarify the question of orthopraxy.

Faith and Good Works

"First of all there is God's Word. After it follows faith; after faith, love; then love does every good work, for it does no wrong, indeed it is the fulfilling of the law."[75]

Luther fully understands himself as an interpreter of Paul when he says "that a man is justified without works – although he does not remain without works when he has been justified."[76] If "faith justifies without any works," it does not follow "that men are therefore to do no good works, but rather that the genuine works will not be lacking."[77] The law is not abolished but rather it is fulfilled. It concerns doing everything "from the bottom of your heart. But such a heart is given only by God's Spirit who fashions a person after the law, so that he acquires a desire for the law in his heart, doing nothing henceforth out of fear and compulsion but out of a willing heart."[78]

Luther never tires of emphasizing the freedom and spontaneity of the new obedience, of the hearing and acting of the reborn. What counts is "faith active in love" (Gal. 5:6). The relationship of faith and love is expressed in the double thesis of *The Freedom of a Christian*: "A Christian is a perfectly free lord of all, subject to none. A Christian is a perfectly dutiful servant of all, subject to all."[79] The Christian is not a species of humankind or a religious person, but rather just a person, the liberated person. In faith the Christian lives outside him or herself, in God – thereby freed from having to seek identity and self-realization. Therefore he can now afford to be the servant of all, not only of all persons but of all things.

The thrust of Luther's entire tract on Christian freedom is nothing other than his exegesis of the one Pauline verse: "For though I am free with respect to all, I have made myself a slave to all" (1 Cor. 9:19). Not: although I am free, but rather because I am free. Luther at the same time claims to interpret Paul's text in Romans 13:8–10 concerning the fulfillment of the law through love. Through faith, the freedom to serve in love is received

> so that we henceforth have no law nor owe anyone anything other than love (Rom. 13:8); and that we do good to our neighbor just as Christ through his blood has done to us. Therefore all laws, works, and commandments are required of us in order thereby to serve God, . . . Thus we shall do the laws, works, and commandments which are good and required of us in service of the neighbor just as the temporal authorities in their governance obey, follow, and serve, feeding the hungry, helping the needy. . . .[80]

Luther did not limit himself to an isolated interpretation of Paul as claimed by the frequently encountered misunderstanding of his theology and of Article 4 of the *Augsburg Confession*. That the law is fulfilled in love and mercy leads to the broadest social connections.

The Two Ways of Government (*Regimente*)

The doctrine of the three estates described above receives a far greater emphasis in Luther's self-testimony than the doctrine of the two ways of government. The latter is not found in his testamentary texts.[81] If attention were paid to this in the interpretation of Luther, many futile discussions would be avoided. There exists the danger in relation to Luther's doctrine of the two ways of God's government of abstracting sexuality, marriage, family, education, schools, and economics into the political arena as a "temporal" realm opposed to the "spiritual" realm, or of reducing the teaching to an opposition of state and church.

Nevertheless, Luther's clear distinction between the two ways of God's government deserves particular attention, for it stamps his entire theology of reformation. In light of its reception in the twentieth century, it should be noted that it is not a static and constant distinction. Rather, it is to be regarded solely as an interim measure in the rupture of the times, and will be abrogated with the end of the world. The doctrine takes into account that not all persons are Christians, and that even the Christian himself as the new man has up to the time of his death to relate to the old, sinful man who has need of the law.

Luther's distinction of the two ways of God's government is classically set forth in his *Temporal Authority: To What Extent it Should be Obeyed* (1523). In the first part of this writing, Luther compares the divinely instituted system of law that is not without compulsion (Rom. 13:1–7) to the non-aggressive stance expected of Christians by the Sermon on the Mount (Mt. 5:39). As Christians, i.e., insofar as they belong to God's spiritual governance in which God rules by Word and faith, they do not need the law and its compulsion. Nevertheless, they are subject to temporal authority – not out of fear but rather from understanding and for the sake of responsibility for the neighbor. God has "ordained two governments: the spiritual, by which the Holy Spirit produces Christians and righteous people under Christ; and the temporal, which restrains the un-Christian and wicked so that – no thanks to them – they are obliged to keep still and to maintain an outward peace."[82] In the second part of the treatise, the limits of the commanded obedience are outlined. Only "bodily" obedience in external things is commanded, the temporal authority may give no law to the soul. For "no one can or shall compel faith."[83] The third part of the treatise, an instruction for princes, shows that the distinction and classification of the two governments has its original place in the instruction of the conscience of those politically responsible.

The distinction of God's two ways of government can hardly be overvalued in its total theological, in particular social-ethical significance. It serves the orientation of the Christian who believes in the completion of the world (John 19:30), but who still does not yet see it and thus must behave accordingly.

The Completion of the World and the Trinity

In the eschaton the three-in-one God shall be all in all (1 Cor. 15:28). Then the distinction between the two governances together with the distinction of law and gospel shall be transcended; then we shall also no longer be afflicted by the over-whelming, incomprehensible hiddenness of God which presses upon us to our death. But for now the difference between faith and sight (2 Cor. 5:7) remains; it may be neither conceptually nor, even less so, existentially mediated and in any manner "overcome." It may only be meaningfully marked: linguistically endured and held open – in complaint and petition. In the liturgy of worship the rupture between the old and new worlds is acted out. A theology oriented to the liturgy of worship is not captive to a speculation unmindful of time and situation, and will not express in thought what in lived faith remains for so long an open wound until we view the countenance of the three-in-one God without *Anfechtung*.[84]

This vision of God is the perception of his righteousness. The "light of glory," so Luther concludes his *The Bondage of the Will*, "will show us hereafter that the God whose judgment here is one of incomprehensible righteousness is a God of most perfect and manifest righteousness."[85] This light of glory will enlighten and clarify that what remains inconceivable not only in the light of nature, but all the more in the light of grace: the terrible hiddenness of God. Thus, the light of glory resolves the question of theodicy. "On that day," promises the Johannine Christ in his farewell address, "you will ask nothing of me" (Jn. 16:23).

With this eschatological perspective Luther, along with his christological– soteriological perspective (presented earlier), prevents speech of the three-in-one God from becoming speculative. Luther preserves this mystery by grasping it as a "trialogical" language-event. In its clearest form this occurs in Luther's reformatory exegesis of the Johannine prologue: God is the Word that he speaks in, with, and to himself, that remains in him and in no way may be separated from him.[86] "That is exactly as it is with God. His word is so much like himself, that the godhead is wholly in it, and he who has the word has the whole godhead."[87] The Word "brings with itself the entire godly nature."[88] Thus God's "being" is Word, namely already in itself the power of communication – a power that empowers us to communication. In himself, God is communication in the internal relationship of Father, Son, and Spirit – in himself eternally rich in his relationships, God is no opaque substance or monad, no monarchical being. In his internal moving, speaking, hearing, and answering as Father and Son, to whom the Spirit listens, in order to convey to us what is heard – the whole being of the three-in-one God is the one and only communication to me together with all creatures. This communication of God himself is an event of complete devotion and a trustworthy, binding promise, concerning which Luther spoke in the most impressive way in his "Confession" (1528).[89] *The trinitarian being of God is the inner structure of promise.*

Notes

1 "On the three hierarchies: church, worldly regiment and household and that the pope is under none of these but is the enemy and persecutor of all of them," *WA* 39 II: 39–91. Luther's polemic against the papacy must be critically viewed today because Luther's judgment of the papacy as the Antichrist no longer applies to the contemporary Roman Catholic Church.

2 *WA Br* 3:482, 81–3; *LW* 49:111–12.

3 *WA* 4:608, 32–609, 1.

4 Of all the verses in his bible, Luther distinguishes only this one phrase with capital letters. In a marginal gloss, he calls this clause "the main part" and the "central place of this epistle and of the entire Bible." See Martin Schloemann, "Die zwei Wörter. Luthers Notabene zur Mitte der Schrift," *Luther* 65 (1994), 110–23.

5 See *WA TR* 5:168, n. 7; *LW* 54:476.

6 Conceptually Luther stood within the Areopagite tradition, whose *theologia negativa* he sharply criticized (e.g., *WA* 5:163, 25f.), insofar as it seduces one to speculation, but which he emphatically affirmed where it, as with Tauler, is lived as *vita passiva*.

7 *WA* 1:613, 22; *LW* 31:225; *WA* 1:290, 39f.; 57 III:79, 20; 1:354, 28; cf. 1:354, 21f.; *LW* 31:40; *WA* 1:614:17–27; *LW* 31:227.

8 Gabrielis Biel, *Collectorium circa quattor libros Sententiarum* I: *Prologus et Liber primus*, coll. Martino Elze and Renata Steiger, eds. Wilfredus Werbeck and Udo Hofmann (Tübingen: Mohr, 1973), 8: "We summarize the Prologue . . . [where] he discusses the question chiefly in three points: namely, theology in itself, in

relation to its unity, and in relation to its object."

9 *WA* 9:98, 21.

10 *WA* 50:658, 29–660, 30.

11 *WA* 5:166, 11 (*passiva vita*).

12 *WA* 5:85, 2f.; Archiv zur Weimarer Ausgabe 2:137, 1f.

13 See Oswald Bayer, *Theologie* (*Handbuch Systematischer Theologie* 1) (Gütersloh: Gütersloher Verlagshaus, 1994), 106–14.

14 *WA* 39 II:104, 24.

15 Bayer, *Theologie*, 13, 124. See J. v. Lüpke, "Theologie als Grammatik zur Sprache der heilige Schrift," *NZSTh* 34 (1992), 227–50.

16 Theo Dieter, *Der junge Luther und Aristoteles* (Berlin and New York: De Gruyter, 2001).

17 *WA* 9:98, 21. See the exegesis of Psalm 51:2 (1532): "Cognitio dei et hominis est sapientia divina et proprie theologicae," *WA* 40 II:327, 11; *LW* 12:311, and *WA* 39 I:176, 5; *LW* 34:138.

18 *WA* 40 III:63, 17f.

19 Wolfhart Pannenberg, *Wissenschaftstheorie und Theologie* (Frankfurt/Main: Suhrkamp, 1973), 300.

20 Ibid., with specific reference to Thomas (*STh* I, q. 1, a 7c). See Wolfhart Pannenberg, *Systematische Theologie*, vol. 1 (Göttingen: Vandenhoeck & Ruprecht, 1988), 15.

21 Pannenberg, *Wissenschaftstheorie*, 299–348: Chapter 5 (the substantive center of the entire book): "Theologie als Wissenschaft von Gott."

22 *WA* 40 II:328, 1f. This definition of the subject coincides exactly with Luther's emphasis

that the central biblical message is the forgiveness of sins. See *WA* 40 II:385, 9.

23 *WA* 40 II:330, 1, 12, 17; *LW* 12, 312.

24 *WA* 40 II:326, 36.

25 See *WA* 14:433–57; *WA* 24:566–81; *WA* 44:93–116.

26 *WA* 40 II:329, 7; *LW* 12:312f.

27 *WA* 10 I/1:13, 21.

28 *WA* 40 I:360, 5f. (on Gal. 3:6; 1531); *LW* 26:227: Faith "is the creator of the Deity, not in the substance of God but in us."

29 *WA* 6:516, 30–2; *LW* 36:42.

30 See Oswald Bayer, *Promissio. Geschichte der reformatorischen Wende in Luthers Theologie* (1971; 2nd ed. Darmstadt: Wissenschaftliche Buchgesellschaft, 1989).

31 *WA* 7:24, 9f (Thesis 9).

32 *WA TR* 5:210, 15f (Nr. 5518); *LW* 54:442–3.

33 Oswald Bayer, *Schöpfung als Anrede. Zu einer Hermeneutische Schöpfung* (2nd ed. Tübingen: Mohr, 1990).

34 Friedrich Nietzsche, *Der Freigeist*, 1st part: Abschied, 3rd strophe in idem, *Werke*, Kritische Gesamtausgabe, eds. G. Colli and M. Montinari, VII, 3 (Berlin and New York: De Gruyter, 1974), 37. (Aus den Nachgelassenen Fragmenten, Fall 1884: *KGW* VII, 3, 28 [64].)

35 *WA* 19:208, 21f.

36 *WA* 39 I:175, 20f.; *LW* 34:137.

37 *WA* 39 I:175, 11–13; *LW* 34:137.

38 Ibid.

39 *WA* 40 I:362, 15 on Gal. 3:6.

40 *WA* 7:445; *LW* 31:40.

41 Erasmus, *On the Freedom of the Will*, in E. Gordon Rupp, Philip S. Watson, et al., trans. and eds., *Luther and Erasmus: Free Will and Salvation*, Library of Christian Classics, vol. 17 (Philadelphia: Westminster Press, 1969), 53; Erasmus von Rotterdam, *De libero arbitrio Diatribe*, 2 a 11.

42 Ibid., 47; 1 b 10.

43 *WA* 18:667, 29–668, 3; *LW* 33:112f.

44 *WA* 18:783, 17–39; *LW* 33:288–9.

45 *WA* 40 III:240, 5f. on Ps. 127:2.

46 *WA* 46:494, 14.

47 Tappert, 413, 21; *BSLK* 649, 26–8.

48 *WA* 7:25, 14–18; 7:54, 13–15; *LW* 31:350.

49 *WA* 42:348, 37–42; *LW* 2:123.

50 *WA* 26:503, 32; *LW* 37:363.

51 *WA* 18:747, 25 (see 711, 1); *LW* 33:178.

52 *WA* 18:709, 21–4; *LW* 33:176.

53 *WA* 18:685; *LW* 33:140.

54 See especially Hans-Martin Barth, *Der Teufel und Jesus Christus in der Theologie Martin Luthers*, *FKDG* 19 (Göttingen: Vandenhoeck & Ruprecht, 1967).

55 *WA TR* 5:600, 11f. See Thomas Reinhuber, *Kämpfender Glaube: Studien zu Luthers Bekenntnis am Ende von De servo arbitrio* (Berlin and New York: De Gruyter, 2000), 56–62.

56 *WA* 19:223, 15f. See *WA* 5:204, 26f.

57 *WA* 40 III:337, 11 (on Ps. 130:1; 1532/3).

58 On this important distinction between the understandable and incomprehensible wrath of God, see Reinhuber, *Kämpfender Glaube*, 91–102.

59 Tappert, 419:65.

60 *WA* 35:133–5; *LW* 53:217–20.

61 See Oswald Bayer, "The Modern Narcissus," *LQ* 9 (1995), 301–13.

62 In this communication, the liberation occurs, as expressed in the tract *The Freedom of a Christian*: "The joyous exchange and struggle. . . . Here this rich and divine bridegroom Christ marries this poor, wicked harlot, redeems her from all evil, and adorns her with all his goodness. Her sins cannot now destroy her, since they are laid upon Christ and swallowed up by him," *WA* 7:25, 34–6, 12; *LW* 31:352.

63 *WA* 26:505, 38–506, 12; *LW* 37:366.

64 Tappert, 345.

65 Tappert, 345; *WA* 30/1:250, 2–18.

66 Tappert, 31.

67 *WA* 39 II:176, 8f. "God's Word cannot be without God's people." *WA* 50:629, 34f.; *LW* 41:150.

68 "We will not grant nor yield to them this metaphysical distinction and difference spun out of reason. Man preaches, threatens, reproves, frightens, and consoles, but the Holy Spirit works. The servant baptizes, absolves, and administer the Supper of our Lord Christ, but God cleanses the heart and forgives sins. Oh no, not with nothing; but we also conclude: God himself preaches, threatens, reproves, frightens, consoles, baptizes, administers the Sacrament of the Altar and absolves. . . ." *WA TR* 3:673, 31–6.

69 *WA* 50:628, 32–642, 32; *LW* 41:149–65.

70 *WA* 50:643:6.

71 *WA* 42:626, 15–19; *LW* 3:109.

72 *WA* 50:643, 6–19; *LW* 41:166.

73 *WA* 50:643, 36f.; *LW* 41:167.

74 *WA* 50:643, 26–9; *LW* 41:167.

75 *WA* 6:514, 19f.; *LW* 36:39. "We do not become righteous by doing righteous deeds, but having been made righteous, we do righteous deeds," *WA* 1:226; *LW* 31:12.

76 *WA DB* 7:16, 17–19; *LW* 35:374.
77 *WA DB* 7:16, 35–8; *LW* 35:374.
78 *WA DB* 7:4, 31–4; *LW* 35:367.
79 *WA* 7:21, 1–4; *LW* 31:344.
80 *WA* 12:157, 6–14. Cf. *WA* 26:505, 11–15.
81 See the "Schmalkald Articles" (*WA* 50:195, 18–23) and the Catechism (especially *WA* 301:397, 1–3 and 147, 22ff.), where the doctrine of the three estates is terminologically and substantively preferred.
82 *WA* 11:251, 15–18; *LW* 45:91.
83 *WA* 11:264, 23; *LW* 45:106.
84 With Luther may be learned that and how this circumstance constrains and determines the place of the doctrine of the Trinity in dogmatics so that it becomes clear that the doctrine of the Trinity must be distinguished from a "general" doctrine of God and anthropology. See Oswald Bayer, "Poietological Doctrine of the Trinity," *LQ* (forthcoming).
85 *WA* 18:785, 35–7; *LW* 33:292. This conclusion, in the context of the preceding few pages and his preface to the book of Job (*WA DB* 10/1:4; *LW* 35:251–3), is in my opinion the most apt articulation of the whole point of eschatology.
86 Cf. *WA* 10/1/1:186, 12f.
87 *WA* 10/1/1:188, 6–8; *LW* 52:46.
88 *WA* 10/1/1:188, 12–14.
89 See above, n. 63.

Bibliography

Primary Sources

See *LW* and *WA*.

Secondary Sources

Brecht, Martin, *Martin Luther*, 3 vols., Minneapolis: Fortress Press, 1985–93.
Forde, Gerhard, *On Being a Theologian of the Cross: Reflections on Luther's Heidelberg Disputation, 1518*, Grand Rapids: Eerdmans, 1997.
Forell, George W., *Martin Luther: Theologian of the Church*, St. Paul: Luther Seminary, 1994.

Junghans, Helmar, ed., *Leben und Werk Martin Luthers von 1526 bis 1546*, Berlin: Evangelische Verlagsanstalt, 1983.
Kolb, Robert, *Martin Luther as Prophet, Teacher, and Hero: Images of the Reformer, 1520–1620*, Grand Rapids: Baker Books, 1999.
Lohse, Bernhard, *Martin Luther: An Introduction to His Life and Work*, Philadelphia: Fortress Press, 1986.
——, *Luther's Theology*, Minneapolis: Fortress Press, 1999.

Philip Melanchthon (1497–1560)

Heinz Scheible

Melanchthon, longer than any other Reformer, experienced and actively shaped the events of his time. His books have been read by more people throughout Europe perhaps than those of Luther or Calvin. Thus it is of the greatest importance to become acquainted with his own thought and endeavors before asking about his agreements or differences with other Reformers, in particular, Luther.[1]

Melanchthon is usually referred to as "humanist and Reformer." Now there was no Reformer who was not likewise a humanist; every educated person at that time was to some extent a humanist. Nevertheless, Melanchthon, more than any others, taught theological and humanist-philosophical subjects throughout his entire career, and through innovative textbooks enriched and influenced students who later worked as pastors, teachers, and politicians. In this respect, the designation "humanist and Reformer" is not inappropriate.

When Melanchthon arrived in Wittenberg he had already successfully completed studies in scholastic philosophy and humanism. Nevertheless, he immediately began a student relationship with Luther, his senior colleague, who was at the point, in the sense of the humanist motto "*ad fontes*," of raising to public awareness the biblical sources against the abuses of church practices. Melanchthon helped him in this connection.

The Young Humanist

Melanchthon was born on February 16, 1497 in Bretten in the Electoral Palatinate. His mother, Barbara Reuter, belonged to the Bretten upper class. His father, Georg Schwarzerdt, came from Heidelberg, where he was a highly qualified armorer in the service of Philip, the electoral prince of the Palatine, whose name was given to his firstborn son. Philip's intellectual aptitude was early recognized and promoted. A private tutor gave him a competent command of Latin. After the deaths of his father and grandfather, the 11-year-old Philip and his younger brother were brought to Pforzheim, where they lived with Reuchlin's sister, a family relative. There Philip attended the famous Latin school of Georg Simler, one of the first Greek scholars in

Germany. It was Reuchlin who not only strongly encouraged the young Philip but conferred on him the humanist name "Melan-chthon," a Greek translation of the German "Schwarz-erde."

Melanchthon entered the University of Heidelberg on October 14, 1509, and on June 10, 1511 he received a "Bachelor of Arts" after completing the traditional course of studies in the shortest possible time. He began his studies in Tübingen on September 17, 1512, and was promoted to "Master of Arts" on January 25, 1514. In Heidelberg he had learned the *via antiqua*; at Tübingen he studied the *via moderna*. He also attended lectures in theology, but his major focus was the Greek language. In 1516 Melanchthon published his first academic writing, a lengthy introduction to an edition of Terence that gained the notice and commendation of Erasmus. In return, Melanchthon sent Erasmus an elaborate Greek poem. Erasmus and Melanchthon never met, but they corresponded in spite of the estrangement that developed through Melanchthon's connection with Luther; at the end there was mutual respect.

In 1518, on the recommendation of Reuchlin, Melanchthon received a call to the chair of Greek in Wittenberg. His inaugural lecture won the admiration of the entire audience, especially Luther.

Luther's Zealous Student

Melanchthon understood his professorship in Greek language and literature to include responsibility for the New Testament. Occasionally he also substituted in the chair of Hebrew. When, soon after his arrival in Wittenberg, he took up a regular course in the Faculty of Theology, this was not so unusual for a Master of Arts. However, the dynamics of his theological studies was excited by his encounter with Luther. Each inspired the other. It is indeed rare that two such great intellectuals should come together in this way and should be so ready to collaborate.

In June and July 1519, Melanchthon accompanied Karlstadt and Luther to the Leipzig disputation with Johann Eck. There, at the latest, he learned that church councils can err. In his published report to his old student friend Oecolampadius, then Cathedral preacher in Augsburg, Melanchthon affirmed: "A council cannot establish any new article of faith."[2]

In September 1519, after exactly one year of theological studies in Wittenberg, Melanchthon earned the degree of "Bachelor of Bible." The theses of his promotion disputation were, at least in part, composed by himself, which was unusual. Three among them are: "It is not necessary for a Catholic to believe any other articles of faith than those to which Scripture is a witness. The authority of councils is below the authority of Scripture. Therefore not to believe in the *character indelebilis*, transubstantiation, and the like is not open to the charge of heresy."[3]

The theses created a stir, and Luther called them "bold but true."[4] What was shocking in Melanchthon's syllogism was not that the Bible is the source of doctrine, and that Scripture is above church councils, but the conclusions he drew from these accepted general truths. He asserted that the two pillars of Catholic piety, the priesthood and the Mass, have no biblical basis and therefore do not have to be believed.

Law and Gospel

For Luther and even more strongly for Melanchthon, the right understanding of the gospel resides in its distinction from the law.

Melanchthon's funeral oration for Luther in the Wittenberg Castle Church[5] paid tribute to Luther's significance for the church. Luther had again brought the gospel to light; he clarified the doctrine of penance; he revealed Paul's teaching of justification by faith; and he explained the distinction of law and gospel, of civil righteousness and the righteousness of the spirit. Further, he taught true prayer and everything that pleases God, in particular the value of civil life, previously less valued than clerical life. He also cleared away human rituals that had stood in the way of the true call of God. Melanchthon judged that Luther's learned achievement existed in his biblical commentaries, but that above all he had translated the Bible into German with such clarity that his translation created more understanding for the reader than most commentaries. Fittingly, he did not mention in his funeral oration that Melanchthon himself had given the impulse for this Bible translation and had worked on it with Luther for more than twenty years.

Melanchthon's appreciation of Luther naturally emphasized what he himself considered important, and thereby provides a compendium of his own theology. He stressed Luther's cultural and religious significance, and the message of the gospel understood as righteousness by faith and consolation of consciences. The systematic theological presupposition for this doctrine of justification, as well as the revalorization of civic life, is the distinction of law and gospel, the dominant principle of Melanchthon's theology and philosophy. He tirelessly sharpened this distinction, especially in his ethical writings. For instance: "To begin with, it is very necessary to distinguish politics from the gospel, and to refute the opinion of the inexperienced who dream that the gospel is nothing else than a political teaching according to which the nations may be regulated."[6]

Luther placed equal weight on this distinction. In his 1521 *Exposition of the Epistles and Gospels*, Luther wrote: "Next to knowledge of the whole of Scripture, the knowledge of the whole of theology depends upon the right knowledge of law and gospel."[7] In Luther's opinion, the highest art in Christendom is the distinction between law and faith, between commandment and gospel.

Melanchthon used two trains of thought in order to grasp exegetically and systematically the dialectic of law and gospel. First, he focused on the gift of the gospel. Paul's Romans was his guide. During his earlier theological studies, he had had to consider the gospel according to the prevailing curriculum dominated by Peter Lombard. This scholastic approach had become intolerable for him, so he replaced it by a presentation of evangelical doctrine in terms of the fundamental concepts "sin, law, and grace," in keeping with Romans. These appear for the first time in his 1521 *Loci* that became his main theological work. He continually improved it in the further editions of 1535 and 1543 as his knowledge advanced. He thereby created the most influential evangelical dogmatics.

In the first edition of 1521, he differentiated the gospel as God's gift from every human achievement. The law cannot be a way to the gospel, and the gospel may not be understood as a super-elevation of the law, but rather as something qualitatively other, to which the person gains no access by natural capabilities, especially by the will.

On this topic, Melanchthon showed himself to be Luther's keenest pupil. In the 1521 *Loci*, with youthful sharpness, he opposed the entire tradition. He saw Christian anthropology in diametrical opposition to philosophy and human reason. He re-interpreted the whole tradition, including Augustine and Bernhard, critiquing their ideas by Scripture because they had also wanted to be right according to human reason. They had dragged philosophy into Christendom; God's good deed became obscured by the profane wisdom of our reason, and thus the godless interpretation of the doctrine of free will has taken over. "Free will," according to the early *Loci*, is completely alien to the Bible and the Holy Spirit. The equally pernicious word "reason" has appeared from Platonic philosophy. For Melanchthon neither *liberum arbitrium* nor *ratio* can describe the person. According to Melanchthon, the definition of *liberum arbitrium* as the agreement of the will with knowledge is not a given. Rather as in a state where the tyrant sets aside the conclusion of the senate, so in persons the will despises the advice of reason because it is ruled by the emotions. But an emotion is never overcome by reason but only by a stronger emotion: "*affectus affectu vincitur.*"[8]

The freedom of the will challenges not only Christian anthropology but also divine predestination: "Since all things that happen, happen necessarily according to divine predestination, our will has no liberty."[9] Later in the same but completely reworked place in the *Loci*, he wrote: "One may not confuse disputation over divine predestination with the question of free will."[10] Nevertheless, already in 1521, Melan-chthon did not challenge a certain freedom in external things. His point here is that God is not revealed in external works but in the inner movements of the heart.

Free Will

The distinction of law and gospel presented the systematic foundation for clarification of the function of the human will. The context for this clarification included the misunderstanding of the evangelical message as resentment against higher education, antinomism, and libertinism by many followers and opponents of the Reformation as well as the Luther–Erasmus conflict on free will. Melanchthon regretted most deeply the conflict between Erasmus and Luther. He himself found a solution that did not separate him from Luther and was nevertheless recognized by Erasmus. While he knew this question was finally not solvable, he published his own position in his 1527 Commentary on Colossians.[11]

For Melanchthon the question of free will is not concerned with free choice in external things but rather with justification and sanctification. Scripture clearly testi-fies that the human will does not have the freedom to bring forth Christian or spiritual righteousness, for these exist not just in civil works but in the new life. For this, the Holy Spirit is necessary. But Melanchthon did not stop with this reformat-ory demarcation from every type of Pelagianism. He added what the human will is for: civil righteousness, the second table of the Decalogue. One can fulfill the law in its external sense without the Holy Spirit; God wills thereby that humankind be ruled by laws and authorities. The problem of theodicy still remains. If God maintains the creation but people nevertheless sin in all their civil acts, then God appears to be the origin of sin. Melanchthon's solution is that God maintains and directs nature according to its essence, whereas he has given humankind its own reason and freedom of choice. I think this is a good theological statement. The alternative would be double predestination.

Melanchthon did not imagine he provided a rational solution to the theodicy problem. His final word on this question is thus prayer for God's support, for spiritual knowledge and the guidance of the Spirit.

In the *Visitation Instructions* of 1528, authorized by Luther's Foreword, Melanchthon wrote:

> Man has in his own power a freedom of the will to do or not to do external works, regulated by law and punishment. There are good works he can do and there is a secular goodness he can achieve through a power of his own which he has and receives from God for this purpose.... He must have a certain freedom and choice to refuse evil and to do good. God also requires such external or secular righteousness.... But this freedom is hindered by the devil.[12]

This accorded with the sense of Erasmus and also was never disputed by Luther. However, for Melanchthon this is only the one side he had to emphasize because it had been pushed into the background, even by himself. The other side is, however, not thereby called into question. Thus he continued: "On the other hand, man cannot by his own power purify his heart and bring forth divine gifts, such as true repentance of sins, a true, as over against an artificial fear of God, true faith, sincere love, chastity, a spirit without vengefulness, true long-suffering, longing prayer, not to be miserly, etc."[13] With this dialectic he proved himself to be a genuine student of Luther. But it is so formulated that Erasmus could also agree. Melanchthon "transcended" the conflict over the freedom of the will.

This teaching received official acceptance by the *Augsburg Confession*. Article 18 begins: "It is also taught among us that man possesses some measure of free will which enables him to live an outwardly honorable life and to make choices among the things that reason comprehends. But without the grace, help, and activity of the Holy Spirit man is not capable of making himself acceptable to God."[14]

Melanchthon maintained this doctrine in his 1535 and 1543 revisions of the *Loci*. Many Lutherans, namely Nicholas von Amsdorf and Konrad Cordatus, were critical of it, but not, however, Luther himself. That Luther highly praised Melanchthon's *Loci* in its first edition with its polemic against Aristotle, philosophy, and free will in his tract against Erasmus is not surprising. But Luther also praised the new revision of 1535, of which Cordatus wrote that it displeased him as much as it pleased Erasmus. In a table conversation in the winter of 1542/43, Luther recommended students read above all else the Bible and Melanchthon's *Loci*. "There is no book under the sun in which the whole of theology is so completely presented as in the *Loci Communes*.... No better book has been written after the Holy Scriptures than Philip's."[15] On August 1, 1537, at the time when Melanchthon was being accused of errors by Cordatus and others, Luther wrote on the table with chalk: "Substance and words – Philip. Words without substance – Erasmus. Substance without words – Luther. Neither substance nor words – Karlstadt."[16]

Culture and Ethics

After the gospel was clearly described in its independence from every human achievement and activity, the task remained, in a second train of thought, to explore the human realm, its capabilities and responsibilities. This was urgently necessary because the message of Christian freedom was being misunderstood, by students as well as peasants, as freedom from all earthly constraints and responsibilities.

Luther and Melanchthon were not innocent of this, for in their fight against ideological opponents they had said and written opinions that could be misunderstood or were falsely understood. The dominant influence of Aristotelian philosophy upon theology had to be removed. Yet the theological criticism of Aristotle also ruined his reputation in the Arts Faculty, which was not intended. This was not easily understood by the students. They now no longer wanted to learn any grammar and logic, but rather to study the burning issues of salvation. They streamed into the newly offered courses on biblical writings. The lectures on scholastic logic, the basis of the curriculum, were less and less attended. The pressure for religious fare was so strong that the academic foundations – grammar, logic, and rhetoric – were neglected. As a consequence, because the students did not have the stipulated prerequisites, no graduations or examinations could be held in the Philosophy Faculty. This development was not limited to Wittenberg; it was painfully observed elsewhere. From Erfurt, the famous poet and humanist, Helius Eobanus Hessus, anxiously addressed Luther and Melanchthon with his concern that the Wittenberg theology was eroding academics and that the Germans would thereby become worse barbarians than they were before. In their response of March 29, 1523, which was immediately published by Eobanus under the title "That Humanistic Studies Are Most Necessary for the Future of Theology and May Not be Neglected," Luther and Melanchthon reported on the counter-measures they were already taking.

Shortly before this, Melanchthon had given his programmatic address "That the Linguistic Arts are Absolutely Essential for Every Kind of Study," the so-called *Encomium eloquentiae*. The humanistic fields are necessary because the ability to speak well and the discernment of the Spirit are essentially connected. He sharply turned against those who challenged that knowledge of the *artes dicendi* is useful for the treatment of theological writings. If the humanistic sciences are no longer learned, the same thing will occur as in the previous centuries of scholasticism, where the ignorance of this literature will undermine the foundations of everything. It pleased God to speak to us in our language, therefore no one who is inexperienced in the linguistic arts can properly judge the divine speech. Just as God exhibited mercy and gave the gospel, so he restored classical literature to support discussion of the gospel. Melanchthon understood Renaissance humanism as a God-given means – a second miracle of Pentecost – to assist the Reformation. Nevertheless, intellectual efforts cannot fathom the Holy. There are areas of the Holy that are glimpsed only because God reveals them, and Christ is known to us only through the Holy Spirit.

In August 1527 Melanchthon lectured on the Nichomachean Ethics. What is astonishing is not that he promoted ethics but that he ventured into Aristotle. Instruction in ethics was already anchored in the 1526 curriculum, however it was in relation to Cicero, whose name was never so loaded as was Aristotle's. Already in 1523, the year of his rectorship and the beginning of reformatory-humanistic curriculum reform, he had, together with Luther, defined the systematic place of the whole of philosophy in relation to theology on the basis of the distinction of law and gospel.

Philosophy is a duty of the church and ethics is a part of the law in the theological sense. Melanchthon began his 1546 *Commentary on Ethics*: "The determination of the relationship of moral philosophy to God's law and gospel is beneficial and illustrates the methods of teaching. Namely, one has to observe the distinction of law and gospel, and know that ethics is that part of the divine law which deals with civil morality."[17] The church needs philosophy because without cultural formation, piety also perishes, as one learns from history and is to be feared in the present. The church needs education, not only in grammar but all the disciplines of the Philosophical Faculty. For the root of all evil is an ignorant theology. It tosses everything together, clarifies nothing correctly, mixes up what should be distinguished, and pulls apart what belongs together. Melanchthon promoted philosophy as a theologian, not theology as a philosopher.

If the church and thereby every theologian needs philosophy, then only the best is good enough. According to Melanchthon, there is no better philosopher than Aristotle. All other philosophical schools represent something or other absurd – apathy and fate in the Stoics, atheism and atomism in epicureanism, scepticism in the Academy. However, Melanchthon was no dogmatic Aristotelian, but rather expressly represented an eclecticism. In his lectures he commented on Aristotle's writings on ethics, politics, and physics; and he published commentaries and created his own textbook in the style of one at the height of the Aristotelianism of the time.

For Melanchthon, as for Luther, the distinction of law and gospel remains the focus of fundamental significance. The law may not become a way of salvation; the gospel may not become a law. But both are God's means of relating to humankind. The law of God, also called the moral law (*lex moralis*), is the eternal wisdom and righteousness in the will of God, the distinction of good and evil. It is revealed to men in the creation and therefore is often repeated in the church. The demand of perfect obedience cannot be produced as a consequence of original sin, and due to sin the knowledge of the will of God is also clouded. The ethical knowledge remaining from the creation is also named the natural law or natural right. In content it is identical with the eternal moral law that is revealed in classical brevity in the Decalogue, understood as a cipher for fundamental ethical norms which form the basis for peaceful coexistence among fallen humanity. This is the first of three functions of the one law, the so-called political use (*usus politicus*). Political ethics, clearly distinguished from the gospel and with no significance for salvation, belongs here. Thus it can be broadly developed, with Luther's complete agreement, in dependence upon Aristotle. At the beginning of his textbook on ethics, Melanchthon sharpened even more the distinction between law and gospel. "Moral philosophy is that part of the divine law that provides principles for external actions."[18] The legal system given by

God through Moses to the people of Israel is also characterized as law. It exists in three parts: moral law, ceremonial law, and legal regulations. Only the first part is binding on everyone, even if some of the legal regulations, in particular marriage law, have general validity. The laws of the state have to conform to the natural law. Then they serve the obedience which can and must be enforced by state means of compulsion. Outer conformity is sufficient to facilitate its goal of enabling life together. The law of God, however, demands inner agreement and perfect obedience. No one can achieve this. The law therefore is excluded as a way of salvation. To be sure, Melanchthon presents the civil function, the *usus politicus*, in connection with the gospel insofar as through learning the gospel, a certain readiness for the works of the Holy Spirit can arise.

The second function of the divine law and its main theological goal is, for Melanchthon as well as for Luther, to uncover the sins that accuse and condemn. Here in Melanchthon's system, law and gospel are connected. The judging function of the law (later called the *usus theologicus* or *elenchticus*) comes to full effect by a work of the Holy Spirit, that occurs through the proclamation of the gospel as the preaching of repentance and forgiveness of sins. True, salutary repentance with trust in the forgiveness of sins is thus no work of the law, but rather of the gospel; here again is a clear distinction of the two ways God relates to humankind. Justification, the salvation of sinners by God's forgiveness, is completely independent of every kind of condition or human achievement. It is a judge's verdict by God. Thus the certainty of salvation is guaranteed.

But ethical renewal must begin at once as a necessary consequence. The justified are instructed in a new way to be obedient to God's will. This is the third function of the law. With this deepened knowledge a more extensive fulfillment of the will of God may be bound, but this is not the deciding thing, for the justified also can and will continue to sin; what renews him or her is repentance. The so-called third use of the law is not a higher morality for Christians. There is no particular Christian ethic, no double morality for Christian and non-Christian, but rather the one eternal will of God that can be differently known and followed. This corresponds to the New Testament parenesis itself nourished with pre- and extra-Christian ethics.

Thanks to this clear distinction of law and gospel, where they remain functionally related to each other, the civil laws or the political order are not called into question by the gospel. The world cannot be ruled by the gospel. The Creator has given the law for that purpose. This presupposes that the order of the state belongs to the natural law, and thus is not contrary to the divine law. There is no place in either Melanchthon's or Luther's theology for an autonomous national law (*Volksnomos*). If the state laws disregard the divine law, then Acts 5:29 is valid. The right to resist extends for Melanchthon – in extreme cases – to preventative war and to the murder of tyrants.

The Formulation of the Doctrine of Justification

The distinction of law and gospel forms the foundation not only for ethics but also for the doctrine of justification. Melanchthon took great pains to attain a formulation that would satisfy him (and many others). Luther did not complete an intermittently planned monograph on justification because he was so openly pleased with Melanchthon's work.

In the first years of the Reformation what was evangelically preached far and wide varied, and must not have always agreed with Luther's teaching. There was no doctrinal norm, and there was no agreement on what effected the gospel and what was to be understood under justification. For Osiander it included human renewal, and he could feel confirmed in this conviction by Luther's early expressions. In this perspective, Melanchthon missed the certainty of salvation. He eventually understood justification, strictly speaking, "forensically," as God's judgment. How that relates to the repentant sinner, and what the justified has to do, must nevertheless be explained.

During his visitation journeys, Melanchthon encountered the interpretation that good works are superfluous, indeed, detrimental, because salvation is given by grace through faith without works. The reproach of Catholics that Luther's teaching corrupted morality was in this case not without grounds. Melanchthon proceeded energetically against this opinion, and urged pastors to preach not only the forgiveness of sins but also to discuss penance as its presupposition. Because Jesus charged his disciples to preach repentance and the forgiveness of sins (Lk. 22), Melanchthon defined the preaching of the gospel as not only the proclamation of forgiveness but also as the preaching of repentance. This did not remain without criticism and, even today, has not always been understood, because one thinks of repentance as a function of the law. According to Melanchthon, the law indeed demands good actions that to a certain degree can be done, but he recognized and noted the import of this demand: one can never expect perfection, and moreover is frightened and feels remorse. This is a work of the Holy Spirit set in motion through the exhorting word of the preaching of the gospel. The demand of the law complies with repentance, and remorse and forgiveness are thus within one another worked by the Holy Spirit. Here the law in its theological function and the gospel are systematically theologically interconnected.

The struggle for a satisfying formulation of the doctrine of justification is nowhere more descriptively to be studied than in the origins of the *Apology* to the *Augsburg Confession*. Melanchthon repeatedly formulated the doctrine of justification in his *Apology*, even replacing already printed pages at the last minute. In September 1531, the final version of the *Apology*, the so-called "Octave Edition," appeared in which Melanchthon was satisfied with the doctrine of justification. It was reprinted nearly forty times, and in 1580 included in the *Book of Concord*. In 1584, it was replaced by the first version of April 1531 on the basis of a formalistic honoring of the "editio-princeps." Thus the text authorized by Melanchthon, to this day, is not in the prominent edition of the Lutheran Confessional writings.[19] Melanchthon's further confessional improvements of this doctrine appeared in the 1540 *Variata* of the *Augsburg Confession* and in the 1551 *Confessio Saxonica*.

The Understanding of the Lord's Supper

Overall we have established major agreement between Luther and Melanchthon. Now we come finally to the doctrine of the Lord's Supper, and here this agreement no longer holds. Melanchthon's understanding of this doctrine went through major changes during which religious concerns and political motives were closely interwoven.

In 1521, the Day of St. Michael and All Angels, September 29 – a day Melanchthon had always honored and even celebrated with a poem – fell on a Sunday. On this day, together with some students, Melanchthon received the Lord's Supper in both kinds in the town church. It is not known which priest officiated, or whether this took place during the main worship service or in one of the still numerous private masses held at that time. In any case, it was the first evangelical celebration of the Lord's Supper in Wittenberg. At the time Luther was at the Wartburg. Melanchthon had translated one of Luther's demands into practice.

During the Lord's Supper controversy of the 1520s, Melanchthon remained firmly on Luther's side. Nevertheless, his theological rejection of the Zwinglians also had a political component. He did not in any way want to enter an alliance with such enemies of the empire. His historical dogmatic certainty that the Lutheran doctrine of the Lord's Supper agreed with the church fathers was shaken by his learned friend of student days, the Basel Reformer, Oecolampadius, a partisan of Zwingli's. His dislike of the Strasbourgers was overcome by the tireless unionist Martin Bucer. They worked together on the doctrinal formula that imposed the Lutheran concern for Christ's Real Presence in the sacrament without confining this faith in the bread and wine, and also affirmed its reception by the unbelieving. Briefly stated: *cum pane* instead of *in pane*. Luther accepted this in the 1536 Wittenberg Concord, and Melanchthon accordingly revised the *Augsburg Confession*.

Thereafter, however, Melanchthon was not able to discuss this theme openly with Luther. Luther had indeed through the Wittenberg Concord recognized as Christian Melanchthon's formulation of the active presence of the entire Christ with the bread and wine in the celebration of the Lord's Supper. But he himself further believed the reception of the body and blood of Christ is not only *with* but *in* these elements. Melanchthon occasionally spoke about this with Luther and the other Wittenberg theologians, but the question was not resolved. Yet, in 1542, the elevation was abolished in Wittenberg. Already in 1538, Prince Philip of Hesse, who stood theologically close to Bucer, had wondered about seeing the elevation of the elements during his visit to Wittenberg. Other Reformers, namely Amsdorf in Magdeburg and Osiander in Nuremberg, generally were not pleased with the Concord. They also were not among its signatories. Melanchthon avoided every discussion with them.

When Melanchthon was with Bucer in Bonn in 1543 at the invitation of the archbishop of Cologne, Hermann von Wied, in order to work on a reformatory church order, Luther responded to an inquiry from Italian Protestants about the understanding of the Lord's Supper. Melanchthon would rather have done this himself in the sense of the Concord because he disapproved of Luther's interpretation.

On August 31, 1543, when Melanchthon was home from Bonn, Luther wrote a letter thanking the Zurich publisher Christoph Froschauer for an edition of the Bible and included a polemic against the Swiss theologians. The scandal reached crisis proportions. Melanchthon sought to smooth things over. He wrote to Bucer on November 4 that he was exerting himself for good relations with the Upper Germans and Swiss, and that one should overlook with silence Luther's customary coarseness.

There were new troubles in January 1544 in relation to Bucer's letter to Philip of Hesse that provided, with respect to the approaching Imperial Diet, a comprehensive evaluation of the situation and criticized Luther's polemics against George of Saxony, Albrecht of Mainz, and Heinrich of Wolfenbüttel. Luther became so angry about this, reported Melanchthon, that he said that had he, Melanchthon, been at the Diet he would not have returned home. In spite of this, he wrote a reply that Luther approved.

In spite of the tensions between the two great Wittenbergers their fruitful cooperative work was not adversely affected. This also holds for the only event that appears to have endangered their functional and personal harmony. In July 1544, Luther's friend Amsdorf, who at that time resided in Zeitz as the evangelical bishop of Naumburg, sharply criticized the "Cologne Reformation Proposal" penned by Melanchthon and Bucer which had been in print since the beginning of November 1543. Apparently Luther had not read the text up to this point. But now he scared the completely surprised Melanchthon with an abusive attack upon Bucer. At this time, Luther was also working on a book on the Lord's Supper. Melanchthon did not have the freedom to express himself openly to Luther, but rather reported his distress and apprehensions to his friends abroad, and inquired about the possibility of finding another teaching position. Apparently this was a consciously inserted effort for leverage because the Electoral Saxon Court may have made it clear that it simply could not let its most diligent professor leave. The matter came to nothing. When Luther's *Short Confession on the Blessed Sacrament Against the Fanatics* appeared at the end of September it turned out that it attacked neither Melanchthon nor Bucer, but only the Swiss, who indeed had not agreed to the Wittenberg Concord on the sacrament.

Melanchthon set forth his mature understanding of the sacraments in his theological testament, the dispute with the Bavarian Inquisition. Sacraments are signs instituted by God of his promise of grace. According to this definition, there are only two sacraments: baptism and the Lord's Supper. Absolution could possibly be included. Faith is required of adults; thus the sacraments do not work automatically. Because they are actions instituted by God, nothing has a sacramental character outside the instituted actions. To pray to the bread in the Corpus Christi procession is just as much idolatry as if someone carried around baptismal water and claimed the Holy Spirit were in it.

The words of institution do not speak of a sacrifice but only of reception, of eating and drinking, and of their effect. Paul also speaks of the return of Christ with the promise that the church shall not perish till then. The celebration of the sacrament is the center of the congregation's assembly whereby the remembrance of the death of Christ includes the entire teaching of the Son of God, his deeds, forgiveness of sins, faith, and finally prayer and thanksgiving.

One brings to this an attitude of repentance and should remember that the almighty Son of the eternal Father, identical in nature to God, has taken on our nature, has appeased the wrath of the Father, and made us members of himself. He is truly and essentially present, giving himself and his benefits in the fellowship of his body and blood, and wills that we believe that by his death he has truly merited for us the forgiveness of sins and righteousness, and that he is resurrected and lives, and makes us his members, and will truly be effective in us. When one considers this, then one becomes enthusiastic about faith, prayer, and thanksgiving. This is the designated use the Reformation churches preserve.

The True Church

Melanchthon tirelessly advocated communication with those of differing opinions insofar as a common basis was recognizable. He could do this because he was not of the opinion that he knew what was right in advance, but hoped to find the truth in conversation with well-intentioned scholars. He was thereby able to approach partners so different in perspective, that he fell under suspicion of giving up essential positions of Lutheran theology. From his perspective that was clearly not the case. He knew precisely the limits that could not be passed without surrendering what he summarized in the concept "Evangelium." At least partially, he together with Bucer was successful in the settlement of the sacramental controversy, and he resolved the problem of the freedom of the will for many in an acceptable manner. Nevertheless, all the efforts for agreement with the Imperial-Roman party failed. At the Diets and religious colloquies in Augsburg (1530), Worms (1540 and 1557), and Regensburg (1541), he negotiated on behalf of his Electoral Princes for settlement of the ecclesiastical conflicts. The best result he attained was with the wiser head of the opposition, Luther's old opponent Eck. With him he was able to achieve a formulation of the doctrine of justification in which both parties could find their basic religious concerns. However, this was only *one* chapter, even if a central one. But in the questions of the sacraments, the Mass, and the office of ministry there were no agreements, and the political principals themselves were not really interested. Melanchthon dismissed the one-sided decrees of the Council of Trent from 1545 and those of the victorious Emperor in the Augsburg Interim of 1548. To many Protestants he was not decisive enough, and they discredited him. Nevertheless, what really troubled him in his final years were not the disputes but rather the truth which doctrine represented in the church. Spontaneously he fought the Antitrinitarians and Separatists, and constantly the followers of the papacy, who claimed to represent the true church.

For Melanchthon the church in this life is the flock of those who receive the gospel and rightly use the sacraments. Here the Son of God is truly effective through the ministry of the gospel and renews many by the voice of the gospel and the Holy Spirit, and makes them heirs of eternal life. In this flock are many elect and others, who are not holy, but nevertheless agree with true doctrine. This is what is meant by the parable of the weeds among the wheat (Mt. 13:24–30). This church is holy only from the vital part here named. The sanctified members are called living members of the church, the others, insofar as they have correct doctrine, but are not holy, are dead members. The holy members could also have errors, if only they do not destroy the foundation. Thus many of the Apostles dreamed of a political lordship or desired to maintain the Jewish ceremonial law. Even the esteemed church fathers could express themselves very awkwardly. "But the saints are quick to learn and yield if one says the right thing."[20] With Paul, one should accept the weak. But whoever publicly defends idols or falsifies an article of faith forsakes the foundation. This is what the papists do with the adoration of the bread in the Corpus Christi procession, the selling of masses, prayer to the dead, destruction of the doctrine of faith, receiving in vain forgiveness and redemption. If such blasphemers rule in the church, they are in no case members of the church, not even dead members, but a curse.

There are three necessary and complete signs by which one recognizes the church: the pure confession of the doctrine of the gospel, the use of the sacraments in agreement with their institution, and the ministry of the gospel in free obedience. Worldly structures of governance in the church, the estate of bishops, the primacy of the bishop of Rome, the episcopal succession, the identity of rites, all these are not signs of the church as the opponents emphasize. Rather, one has to keep one's distance from the Roman bishops, just as the Apostles kept their distance from the Levitical priesthood, even though their office was once instituted by God.

The true church is also visible in this life, but in a different way than the papal kingdom. The flock of those who at the time of Jesus kept their distance from the ruling Pharisees and Sadducees was visible. The persecution of the saints shows that the church is visible. Service to the gospel is public and visible. The church is thus neither a Platonic idea nor a mystery religion. Melanchthon emphasized that the reformatory parishes are churches of God in which there are many saints, but which also include the weak and many rotten members. He contested, however, that the papacy and its adherents were God's church because they defend idolatry and are blasphemers of God and murderers. Before its time there were many saints who taught rightly, as may be seen from their writings. Sometimes there were only a few, but God has always maintained a true church. Its administration is monarchical if one looks to its head, Christ, but with respect to the teachers and hearers it is aristocratic, like a university.

The identification of Roman and Catholic is to be rejected. The claim of the papacy was never universally accepted. The confession of the reformatory community agrees with the Catholic church, namely with the Apostolic, Nicene, and Athanasian confessions, and with the proven ancient authors. The faith that recognizes these texts is not supported by the authority of the church but rather by the clear Word of God. Nevertheless the teaching of the Catholic church is devoutly heard, and the witnesses of the pure ancient church serve the strengthening in faith. Outside the Catholic church there is no salvation, but there certainly is outside the papal church. The unity of the Catholic church exists in the foundation of faith, not in external forms.

Councils are not free from errors, and if their conclusions contradict the divine commands and articles of faith, as is the case with the Council of Trent, they must be rebuked. For Paul's statement remains valid: "Whoever teaches another gospel is to be cursed." On the other hand, the church needs courts, and there were many synods that have provided useful conclusions. In the controversies of the present, a true church court would be necessary. However, the gospel of the eternal Father and God's law valid for everyone cannot be changed by any synod, for the Word of God remains in eternity. Also, a council has no authority or judging power. In the worldly arena there are final courts with executive power. Not so in the church. Here a decision is valid, not with respect to the authority of the synod, but because the Word of God creates conviction. The decisions of a pious synod are also always substantiated from the biblical sources. Because error is possible, the interpretations of the whole church are to be heard and critically compared with the source of the faith.

Melanchthon the Man

From the time he was 21, Melanchthon lived in Wittenberg. The Saxon University became his home. To be sure, there were times he groaned under its bonds. But he accepted none of the opportunities to leave. On the contrary, after the Schmalkald War it was he who worked so that the university would reopen and be financially supported by the new territorial lord. So he was and remained a professor in a small town. It was his daily work to instruct students and to write books. This he did amply and happily. An extensive correspondence and the visits of numerous scholars and students bound him to the whole of Europe. In addition, he had to take on all the tasks in politics and church which made his life so dramatic and fascinating, but which often led to months-long absences from Wittenberg. At 23 he married Katharina Krapp, daughter of a town council family. They had four children.

Melanchthon saw the meaning of life in the knowledge of God and – inferred from this – in the cultivation of human community. Theology was the means of his thinking, but it was always bound up with responsibility for those who were assigned to him. His sense for human community and the responsibility due to it was strongly impressed on him and led him continually to take on responsibilities that were not welcome to him and that broke up his studies.

Daily prayer was the source of his mental and spiritual health, and helped him in all the difficult situations of his life. In his theological system, prayer next to doctrine was the second pillar of the church. That one should adore rather than investigate the mysteries of God, he had already written in his 1521 *Loci Communes Rerum Theologicarum*. As he expounded the doctrines of the Trinity and the God-man, Jesus Christ, his expositions ended in the form of prayers. That prayer for him remained no theory is witnessed numerous times in the casual remarks in his correspondence.

Exactly as a systematic theologian, Melanchthon remained conscious that he did not know so many things. He hoped and believed that after death, in conversation with his friends, with the prophets and Apostles, at times with Christ himself, he would experience all that on earth had remained hidden to him. The kingdom of heaven was to him like an ideal university.

In April 1560, the 63-year-old took ill on a journey of service to Leipzig; he did not recover. On the evening of April 19, 1560, he passed away peacefully. On April 21 he was buried in the choir of the Wittenberg Castle Church, next to Luther.

His last note on a scrap of paper listed the reasons why one need not fear death: "You escape sins. You will be freed from all the strains and fury of the theologians. You will enter the light to contemplate God and God's Son. You will learn every wonderful secret which in this life you could not understand: why we are so created, how we are, and wherein the union of the two natures in Christ exist."[21]

Notes

1 See Heinz Scheible, "Luther and Melanchthon," *LQ* 4/3 (Autumn 1990), 317–39.
2 *MBW* 59.5 = *MBW*.T 1, 139.136–7.
3 Charles Leander Hill, trans., E. E. Flack and L. J. Satre, eds., *Melanchthon: Selected Writings* (Minneapolis: Augsburg, 1962), 18 (theses 16–18).
4 *WA Br* 1, 514.33 (to Staupitz, October 3, 1519).
5 *CR* 11, 726–34 Nr. 89.
6 *CR* 16, 417.
7 *WA* 7:502, 34f.
8 *Loci Communes Theologici*, trans. Lowell Satre and Wilhelm Pauck in Wilhelm Pauck, ed., *Melanchthon and Bucer*, Library of Christian Classics, vol. 19 (Philadelphia: Westminster Press, 1969), 27.
9 *Loci Communes Theologici*, 24.
10 *MSA* 2/1, 237.1 f.
11 See Timothy Wengert, *Human Freedom, Christian Righteousness: Philip Melanchthon's Exegetical Dispute with Erasmus of Rotterdam* (New York: Oxford University Press, 1998).
12 *LW* 40:301–2.
13 *LW* 40:302.
14 Tappert, 39.
15 *LW* 54:440.
16 *LW* 54:245.
17 *CR* 16, 277 f.
18 *MSA* 3, 157.7–9.
19 For a discussion of these editions, and the reintroduction of the Octavo text in contemporary editions of the Lutheran Confession, see Charles P. Arand, "The Texts of the Apology of the Augsburg Confession," *LQ* 12 (Winter 1998), 461–84 and Christian Peters, *Apologia Confessionis Augustanae. Untersuchungen zur Textgeschichte einer lutherischen Bekenntnisschrift (1530–1584)* (Stuttgart: Calwer, 1997).
20 *MSA* 6, 286.10–11.
21 *CR* 9, 1098 Nr. 6977 = *MBW* 8, 470 Nr. 9299.

Bibliography

Primary Sources

Beyer, Michael, Stefan Rhein, and Günther Wartenberg, eds., *Melanchthon Deutsch*, 2 vols., Leipzig: Evangelische Verlagsanstalt, 1997.
Corpus Reformatorum. Philippi Melanchthonis opera quae supersunt omnia, ed. Karl Gottlieb Bretschneider and Heinrich Ernst Bindseil, 28 vols. Halle: Schwetschke & Son, 1834–60.
Hill, Charles Leander, trans., *Melanchthon: Selected Writings*, eds. E. E. Flack and L. J Satre, Minneapolis: Augsburg, 1962.
Loci Communes Theologici, trans. Lowell Satre in Wilhelm Pauck, eds., *Melanchthon and Bucer*, Library of Christian Classics, vol. 19, Philadelphia: Westminster Press, 1969.
Melanchthons Briefwechsel: Kritische und kommentierte Gesamtausgabe. Regesten by Heinz Scheible and Walter Thüringer, 10 vols. to date. *Texte* by Richard Wetzel, 3 vols. to date. Stuttgart and Bad Cannstatt: Frommann and Holzboog, 1977–.
Stupperich, Robert, ed., *Melanchthons Werke in Auswahl*, 7 vols., Gütersloh: Mohn, 1951–75.
Philip Melanchthon, Orations on Philosophy and Education, ed. Sachiko Kusukawa, trans. Christine F. Salazar, Cambridge Texts in the History of Philosophy, Cambridge: Cambridge University Press, 1999.

Secondary Sources

Bellucci, Dino, *Science de la Nature et Réformation. La physique au service de la Réforme dans l'enseignement de Philippe Mélanchthon*, Rome: Vivere, 1998.
Frank, Günter, ed., *Der Theologe Melanchthon*, Sigmaringen: Jan Thorbecke, 2000.
Kusukawa, Sachiko, *The Transformation of Natural Philosophy. The Case of Philip Melanchthon*, Cambridge: Cambridge University Press, 1995.
LQ 12/4 (Winter 1998), entire issue devoted to Melanchthon.
Maag, Karin, ed., *Melanchthon in Europe: His Work and Influence Beyond Wittenberg*, Grand Rapids: Baker Books, 1999.
Scheible, Heinz, "Luther and Melanchthon," *LQ* 4/3 (Autumn 1990), 317–39.
——, *Melanchthon. Eine Biographie*, Munich: C. H. Beck'sche, 1997. Includes bibliography up to 1997.

——, *Philipp Melanchthon. Leben und Werk in Bildern. Sa vie et son oeuvre en images. Life and Work in Pictures*, Karlsruhe: Landesbildstelle Baden, 1998.

——, "Die Reform von Schule und Universität in der Reformationszeit," *LuJ* 66 (1999), 237–62.

——, "Die Unterscheidung von Gesetz und Evangelium. Ein zentrales Motiv in theologischer Ethik und Praktischer Theologie am Beispiel Melanchthons" in Wilhelm Gräb et al., ed., *Christentum und Spätmoderne. Ein internationaler Diskurs über Praktische Theologie und Ethik,* Stuttgart: Kohlhammer, 2000, 93–100.

Wengert, Timothy, "The Day Philip Melanchthon Got Mad," *LQ* 5 (Winter 1991), 419–33.

——, "Philip Melanchthon's 1522 Annotations on Romans and the Lutheran Origins of Rhetorical Criticism" in Richard A. Muller and John L. Thompson, ed., *Biblical Interpretation in the Era of the Reformation. Essays Presented to David C. Steinmetz in Honor of His Sixtieth Birthday,* Grand Rapids: Eerdmans, 1996, 118–40.

——, *Law and Gospel. Philip Melanchthon's Debate with John Agricola of Eisleben over Poenitentia,* Grand Rapids: Eerdmans, 1997.

——, "The Scope and Contents of Philip Melanchthon's Opera Omnia, Wittenberg, 1562–1564," *ARG* 88 (1997), 57–76.

——, *Human Freedom, Christian Righteousness. Philip Melanchthon's Exegetical Dispute with Erasmus of Rotterdam,* New York: Oxford University Press, 1998.

——, "Philip Melanchthon's Patristic Exegesis" in David C. Steinmetz, ed., *Die Patristik in der Bibelexegesis des 16. Jahrhunderts,* Wiesbaden: Harrassowitz, 1999, 115–34.

Matthias Flacius (1520–1575)

Oliver K. Olson

At his death, only days before being banished from Frankfurt am Main, Matthias Flacius was "the most hated man in Germany."[1] Part of the reason was prejudice. He was a Slav, *a non-German*. His credentials, however, should have given him a rank in the history of thought "directly beside Erasmus and Melanchthon."[2] Indeed, according to Ignaz Döllinger, he was superior to most theologians of his time, Melanchthon included.[3] One standard reference work calls him "one of the greatest scholars of his time."[4] Yet since his death he has been largely neglected, perhaps out of distaste. The academy prefers tranquil figures like Erasmus of Rotterdam to polemicists like Flacius, especially – to quote his Croatian biographer – one who was "totally fire and flame."

Flacius, moreover, provoked detractors on both sides of the confessional divide. For those who opposed the Reformation, Flacius, as the most articulate defender of Luther's legacy, was a lightning rod. "The most abominable monster," a French reference work judges, "that the earth has produced."[5] "Seldom," wrote the Jesuit James Brodrick, sounding the same note, "was there a man whose life was mastered so much by a dark and mad conviction."[6] Among many in his own camp, he aroused equally bitter opposition. The Lutheran poet Johann Major, whose whole career was devoted to the vilification of Flacius, wrote that he was the kind of ass, which, if the Lord Jesus had ridden him on Palm Sunday, would have bucked him off. Flacius's offense was the (correct!) charge that, by subtly pursuing his own theological system, Philipp Melanchthon had departed from Luther's theology. That critique led to Melanchthon's demotion: the undisputed leader of the Reformation after the death of Luther was reduced to being merely the chief of the Philippist party.

Others, however, think well of him. He is given high honors in his native land, although his reputation there, oddly enough, has little to do with his theological teaching. "Flacius's work, also in more recent times, must be counted among the obligatory texts of Croatian *Geistesgeschichte*, through which the self-understanding of the Croatian people as a cultural community is constituted, interpreted, and thereby further developed."[7]

Independently from each other, at least three non-Croatian historians – and for the sake of brevity let them represent his many admirers elsewhere – chose for him no lesser laudation than words from the Letter to the Hebrews. "A man of faith, one from that cloud of witnesses of whom the world was not worthy."[8]

Chances are that an inquiry into the life of the extraordinary man able to provoke such contrary judgments would be a useful exercise.[9]

Life

Matthias Flacius was born Matija Vlacic in 1520, in Albona (now Labin), a hill town on the Adriatic in Istria, not far from Trieste, then in Venetian territory. His father was Andreas Vlacic, a small landowner; his mother a member of the patrician family of the Luciani. In the humanist fashion, he Latinized his Croatian name, and adopted the cognomen, "Illyricus," from Illyria, the Roman province.

Soon after it began, the Reformation movement was present in his province, Istria. "Molti luterani" were reported in his home town, Albona. No lesser Istrian personages had enlisted in Luther's cause than Peter Paul Vergerio, bishop of Flacius's native diocese of Pola, and his brother, Giovanni Vergerio, bishop of Capo d'Istria. All of Istria, it was foreseen, was on the way to reformation. The Inquisition, however, soon swung into action. Peter Paul was forced to flee to North Germany and Giovanni died under suspicion of being poisoned. The religious persecution also affected Flacius directly. One of the many Reformation martyrs among the South Slavs, most of them forgotten, was his mother's cousin, Baldo Lupetino, Franciscan Provincial in Venice. Young Flacius, then, was among the survivors of the once-thriving Reformation community in Istria and in Venice. Important for understanding his passionate defense of the Reformation is that after years of imprisonment for preaching justification by faith, Baldo, whom he called his mentor, was done to death by order of the Inquisition by drowning in the Lagoon.

After the death of his father, Flacius's elementary education was overseen by an uncle, his guardian. He was instructed by a tutor, Franciscus Ascerius of Milan. Flacius's success later at the University of Jena as teacher of several of the leaders of the literary "Slavic Springtime" suggests that he had learned Cyrillic and Glagolitic as a child – a promising theme for Slavic research. He continued his education at the San Marco school in Venice under Giambattista Cipelli, a friend of Erasmus, known as Egnazio. The curriculum of his school had been put together for training editors of ancient manuscripts by members of the "Academy" of Aldus Manutius, the celebrated publisher of Latin and Greek classics. True to his training, Flacius made collecting, editing, and selling manuscripts and books his lifelong occupation. Were his identification with the Reformation less obvious, his career could be considered part of the Venetian High Renaissance.

His commitment to the Lutheran movement, however, caused him to redirect the passion for collecting manuscripts he had contracted in Venice. Whereas Aldus collected classical, Flacius collected medieval manuscripts, most of them relevant, in one way or another, in vindicating the Reformation. Among them are several of those declared "cimelia" (treasures) of the library at Wolfenbüttel in Germany: an eighth-century *Capitulare ecclesiasticum*, the *Capitulare de Villis* from the court of Charlemagne, and an eleventh-century Graduale from Minden.[10] The eleventh-century Rescript against Lanfranc of Bec by Berengar of Tours, later famously discovered in the Wolfenbüttel library by the philosopher, Lessing, is also one of those treasures, as well as the celebrated music manuscript, W1, a record of early polyphony from the School of Notre Dame. Among the first editions he published from other manuscripts are texts of Sulpicius Severus, Fredegar, Firmicus Maternus, and Otfrid of Weissenburg.

His most important liturgical publication was published to correct the fundament-alist claims made by Coadjutor Bishop Michael Helding of Mainz. In a sermon during the 1547 "armored" Diet of Augsburg, following the emperor's defeat of the Schmalkald League, Helding confidently announced that the text of the Latin Mass had been written by the apostles themselves, and that the liturgy had remained totally unchanged through the centuries. The most persuasive of the extended series of variant texts that Flacius published in response was a bizarre text from an eleventh-century mass order (since called, after him, "Missa Illyrica").[11]

Having completed his schooling, Flacius determined to study theology. Since it seemed to him that that specialty was limited to monks, he was willing to join the Franciscan order and to enroll at either the universities of Padua or Bologna. Under the influence of Fra Baldo, however, he decided instead to study at the University of Wittenberg. It was there, according to Baldo, that Martin Luther had "brought the gospel to honor again."

As a student at Wittenberg he underwent a religious crisis not unlike Luther's own. He reported being despondent about evil in the world to the point that he considered suicide. Under the pastoral care of Luther himself, however, and after public prayers at St. Mary's Church, he recovered. One result was that his doctrine tended to be centered on forgiveness of sins. Some historians think that his theological perspective was less abstract, therefore, than that of his later rival, Melanchthon. His reporting of his spiritual crisis was the immediate cause of the first work of modern Flacius research, an 1844 lecture by Professor August Twesten of Berlin, who like his predecessor, Friedrich Schleiermacher, was interested in religious experiences.[12]

Flacius's linguistic skill earned him an appointment as professor of Hebrew at the University of Wittenberg. But, after the Lutheran princes were defeated in the Schmalkald War of 1545–6, Emperor Charles V imposed a religious law on the Lutheran territories, the Romanizing "Augsburg Interim." Flacius then became the central figure in a resistance movement. He resigned his professorship in Witten-berg, and took up residence in Magdeburg, a city that had not been occupied by the victorious imperial army. Because of the torrent of publications produced there by Flacius and his fellow "exiles of Christ," Nicholas Gallus and Nicholas von Amsdorf, Magdeburg – in contrast to the imperial government – came to be known among Lutherans as "Our Lord God's Chancery."

One argument that arose out of resistance to the new religious law was the Adiaphora Controversy. "Adiaphora" is a term from stoic philosophy, meaning "indifferent matters." Flacius's famous statement during that controversy, later quoted in Article X of the *Formula of Concord*, is "*in casu confessionis et scandali, nihil est adiaphoron*" ("in the situation in which a confession is required or which causes scandal, nothing is an indifferent matter"). The basic issue, often misunderstood, was not primarily what liturgical ceremonies were permissible, but whether the government had the authority to decide what they should be. The controversy, put another way, is whether the church ought to be a state church. Addressing himself to the crisis, Melanchthon advised the authorities to avoid the "danger of confession" and to submit to the Imperial Interim law by separating private beliefs from public stance.

Flacius, who required a clear confession, whatever the danger, countered: "In secular matters one must be obedient [to the government], but not in spiritual matters."[13] That meant that the church had authority independent of the state. He denied that Melanchthon was "so wise as to manage word and the fire that Christ sent with it from the gospel." An effective propagandist, he made the white vestment, the "surplice," a symbol of the resistance against a state church. Pastors should not wear the surplice, he argued, *because the secular government required it.*

The same conflict spread to England as the Vestments Controversy when the Puritans opposed wearing the surplice. For them, Flacius's argument was axiomatic.[14] Anglicans were willing to recognize the right of the government to determine the adiaphora – of which the surplice was the most visible – just as Melanchthon had done in Germany. But, unlike the Lutherans (who were free to don the surplice again when the pressure was off), the Puritans added the argument that nothing should be done or used in the church except what is mentioned in the Bible.

Flacius's identification of a *casus confessionis* was rediscovered in 1940 at Union Theological Seminary in New York by Hans Christoph von Hase, who was seeking a principle around which the *Kirchenkampf* against National Socialism could be organized.[15] In Flacius's own time, the publicistic campaign at Magdeburg incited the "Princes' Revolt" of 1552 against Charles V. The success of that operation under the leadership of Elector Moritz of Saxony effectively reversed the military verdict of the imperial victory of 1547. The resulting Treaty of Passau and the 1555 *Peace of Augsburg* granted Protestant civil rights and guaranteed the survival of Luther's cause. For his role in influencing these events, Flacius has been credited with saving the Reformation.

Although he was a layman, Flacius was called in 1557 to be superintendent of the church in Ernestine Saxony and professor at the University of Jena. There he took up his polemics – "sour work" he called it – this time against Luther's creative rivals. "Everyone," he commented, "wants to overcome Dr. Luther's teaching and hereby win his spurs." According to Andreas Osiander, for instance, after fifteen hundred years, Christ's blood had dried up. Historical information about it was "colder than ice." Justification, therefore, comes about, not by reckoning, as Luther taught, but by the indwelling in the human heart by God himself. "Although sin lives in the flesh," Osiander explained, "it is like a drop against a whole pure sea."[16] Against him, Flacius defended "forensic" justification, that is, that on the basis of Christ's work, righteousness is *reckoned* to sinners.

Influenced by the mystical tradition, Caspar von Schwenckfeld, too, challenged Luther's teaching. In his case, he denied the physical "means of grace" – the Bible and the sacraments. He talked instead about "a living, internal scripture, written by God's finger."[17] Against him, Flacius defended the Schmalkald Articles: "Whatever is attributed to the Spirit apart from such word and sacrament is of the devil."

He combined his case against Osiander and Schwenckfeld, whom he dismissed as *Schwärmer* (enthusiasts, ravers), with critiques of other contemporary rivals of Luther in a *Book of Confutations*, for a short time an official text in Ernestine Saxony.

The confrontation between representatives of the churches of the Hanseatic cities of Germany and Melanchthon, the Coswig talks of 1557, is emphasized less in narratives of the Late Reformation than its historical significance merits. Having brought together church leaders from the leading Hanseatic cities, Flacius almost succeeded in resolving the controversies left over from the Interim crisis. As a formula of concord, he proposed the *Magdeburg Confession* of 1550.[18] Melanchthon, however, was adamant on the matter of free will in salvation and about assigning the "adiaphora" to the government. He thereby prolonged the period of controversy by twenty years. Because of Melanchthon's great historical influence, it is not inappropriate to ask what influence his defense of free will had on the origins of the Enlightenment, and what influence his stance on the "adiaphora" may have had on the origins of the absolutist political tradition in Germany. Both of those matters, as well as the other "Philippist" controversies, at any rate, dealt with important theological matters, and cannot be explained as simple conflicts of personality.[19]

During his time at Jena, while he still enjoyed the support of Duke Johann Friedrich the Middler, Flacius was able to frustrate the attempt at theological compromise at the imperial religious conference at Worms in 1557. But in a 1560 academic colloquy in Weimar, Flacius disputed university colleagues who were in league with Melanchthon. One result of that colloquy was that Flacius lost the favor of the duke, for whom theological distinctions hardly mattered. After a bitter confrontation, involving also the freedom of the church from the state, he lost his professorship and was forced to flee.

He found a refuge in Regensburg, where his friend and associate, Nicholas Gallus, was superintendent and the unofficial bishop of the Lutherans in Austria. Together with Gallus, he became involved in the failed attempt by Lutheran nobles at a 1563 *Landtag* in Ingolstadt to have the *Magdeburg Confession* adopted officially in Bavaria. Trying to strengthen the Reformation in the south of Europe, he attempted unsuccessfully to found a school in Austria and a university in Regensburg. At the end of his Regensburg period, in an audience with Emperor Maximilian II, he presented a work on political science, *On the Transfer of Empire*, that argued against the papal claim of universal political authority.

With the approval of Prince William of Orange he was called next as consultant to organize the "Martinists" in Antwerp. In 1566, the "Wonderjaar," during which the Dutch Revolt began,[20] he prepared a liturgical agenda and a doctrinal Confession. Since it was based on the principle that congregations may ordain their own pastors, expressed by Luther in his 1523 letter to the Bohemians, Flacius's order has been called the original Lutheran order.[21] That "congregational-synodical" order, which spread to Amsterdam and New Amsterdam, was foundational in the Lutheran Church in the New World.[22]

One important – and seldom understood – reason for his unpopularity, and for the unfounded charge of a "Flacian heresy," was his campaign against the state's domination of the church. Powerful German princes – the same grandees who sponsored the 1577 *Formula of Concord* – firmly rejected Flacius's position. Flacius managed to elude efforts by agents of Elector August of Saxony to arrest him. Having failed to arrest him, the Elector then actively worked to destroy his reputation, accusing him of a "new papacy." August's charge is preserved at Coburg Castle, in a caricature of Flacius pursuing a mitre on the shaft of the "Flacius cannon." What the Elector was unable to do directly he accomplished by diplomatic pressure: Flacius was hunted down "like a baited boar."[23] After a stay at Strasbourg, he died in 1575 at Frankfurt am Main. A controversial figure, he was denied a Christian funeral.

Legacy

Whereas Aldus collected the classics, Flacius, having embraced the Reformation, turned Europe upside down searching for medieval manuscripts. As an answer to the reproach that the Reformation was a break with the Catholic tradition of the church, he published texts from his researches in a *Catalog of Witnesses to the Truth*. He was confident that such historical records demonstrated that Luther's reform was faithful to the Catholic tradition. According to his "remnant" argument, derived from 1 Kings 19:18 and Romans 11:4, there had always been a few faithful to the authentic tradition of the church. Catholicity, consequently, must be traced through the *successio doctrinae* rather than in the *successio personarum* of the "historical episcopate."

Characteristic is his entry on the Eastern churches. They "never recognized the primacy of the pope, have never approved purgatory, private masses, so-called vigils for the dead, indulgences, communion in one kind, the necessity of clerical celibacy, the veneration of statues and other similar things. Rather they have always resisted and still resist today such ungodliness."[24] It was the Church of Rome that had introduced novelties.

One can avoid anachronism at this point by remembering that in the early sixteenth century no comprehensive church history existed. What passed for the memory of the church in those days was dependent on works like the fanciful *Golden Legend* of Jakob of Voragine. It is due to Flacius's efforts that for the first time since Eusebius (c.260–c.340) that such a history became available, and that for the first time ecclesiastical history was subjected to scientific investigation. Not yet fully investigated is the influence of the *Catalogus* on the Book of Martyrs of John Foxe in England and the extent of his copying from it. In refuting his historical publications, Flacius's opponents, too, felt compelled to imitate his method and make use of original sources. He gets credit, consequently, for revolutionizing the writing of church history. Flacius "founded church history in its modern phase."[25]

A witness, for instance, of the teaching of justification by grace before Luther was John Tauler (d. 1361):

> Johannes Tauler, a German preacher, was active two hundred years ago. He taught quite correctly on justification by grace, namely because he so emphasized that man must be free from all creation and from himself. Here is no doubt, as is seen from his many sermons, that he has that power to teach that godly people, not depending

on any human assistance, must place their entire trust only in God, depend only on God, and seek everything from him by faith alone. He strongly minimized the merit of human works and traditions, and was a very sharp enemy of all superstition, carefully commending only God's mercy.[26]

The prognostication of Hildegard of Bingen (1098–1179), he wrote, pointed to the Reformation:

> At that time the mitre of apostolic honor will be divided, because in apostolic circles no faith will be found. Therefore, people will despise the dignity of that name and acquire other men as leaders and archbishops, so that the apostolic father [*papa*] will hardly have Rome and a few neighboring places under his mitre at that time, because of the diminishment of his honor. He will come to that partly by the outbreak of wars and partly by general council and with the consent of both ordained and lay people. Then justice will stand in its proper place.[27]

He opposed the secular power of the papacy, citing the history of the quarrel between the pope and Emperor Ludwig the Bavarian (d. 1347):

> Ludwig the Bavarian, who acquired imperial authority in the year 1314, was excommunicated and dethroned by the pope, because immediately after his election, before the pope commanded it, he deemed to assume the imperial title. He was even proscribed and condemned as a schismatic and heretic by the pope. Throughout the thirty-three years of his reign, he had many struggles with the three popes, including wars with the rebels in his kingdom, which the pope with his bishops initiated against the emperor in order to acquire his kingdom.[28]

Flacius conceived and organized (but did not write) a longer historical work, the "Magdeburg Centuries," a multi-volume collection of primary sources.[29] It was organized for easy use in polemics, by sections of one hundred years each. Since that series, the word "century" in modern languages no longer means a hundred of anything, as it once did, but exclusively a hundred years.

In his *Clavis Scripturae Sacrae*, that grateful pastors called the "golden key," Flacius founded the discipline of hermeneutics – the art of interpreting texts. In that publication, according to the philosopher Wilhelm Dilthey, he delivered "the kernel of a modern theory of the process of explanation [of written texts] of the greatest importance for the firm foundation of philosophical-historical knowledge."

> [It was the] first important work of this kind, and perhaps the most profound. Here for the first time the essential rules for interpretation which had already been worked out were connected with a systematic doctrine, and this was done under the postulate that a universally valid comprehension was to be reached through the orderly and systematic application of such rules.[30]

H.-G. Gadamer agrees: "The first important work of this kind [of hermeneutics] was the Clavis of Flacius."[31]

An "important turning-point in the history of literature"[32] was the *Clavis* Rule about preferring the literal sense to metaphor: "Let the reader be content with understanding the simple and genuine sense of Holy Scripture . . . and not seek shadows or pursue allegorical dreams or anagogies, unless the allegory is obvious or the literal sense is either unprofitable or absurd."

> It is a basic Christian confession that all scripture bears testimony to Jesus Christ. In this sense, there is a single, unified voice in scripture. When the church Fathers and Reformers spoke of the 'scope' of scripture, they were addressing the kerygmatic content of the Bible which the interpreter of the Bible was urged always to keep clearly in sight in order to comprehend the true nature of the biblical witness. Matthias Flacius stood firmly within this exegetical tradition when he admonished the readers of scripture to direct their attention first of all to the perspective, goal and intention of the entire writing.[33]

Another *Clavis* rule was that all biblical interpretation was to be subjected to the "analogy of faith," which is roughly equivalent to the recently developed notion of "kerygma." "Let all understanding and explanation of scripture be an analogy of faith, which is a kind of norm or boundary of sound faith." Flacius's authority was Romans 12:6: "Having gifts that differ according to the grace given to us, let us use them: if prophecy, in proportion [*kata ten analogian*] to our faith." Adherence to an "analogy of faith" is based on Flacius's confidence in the authority of the biblical canon. Flacius's confidence was shared latterly by Hans-Georg Gadamer: "In the meanwhile we have become more receptive through the critique of historical theology carried on during the last half-century, which has culminated in the working out of the concept of kerygma, to the hermeneutical legitimacy of the canon and therefore for the hermeneutical legitimacy of Flacius's dogmatic interest."[34]

Although Flacius was personally unknown in Austria, his influence lasted longer there than elsewhere. The nobility was almost wholly Lutheran, and, in opposition to syncretism, agreed with Flacius. Although in 1556 the heir to the imperial throne, Archduke Maximilian, had been expected to announce his conversion to Lutheranism, he had second thoughts – but nevertheless supported the *Centuries* initiative.

Doctrine

There is substantial opinion that Flacius's combative publications led to the triumph of Luther over Melanchthon in the *Formula of Concord* of 1577, as well as contributing much to the precision of the tradition of theological dogmatics. In the unstable post-Lutheran years, according to Gustav Frank, his polemics served the church well as a "principle of stability."[35] The *Formula* agrees, for instance, with him in his opposition to synergism (human cooperation with God in salvation), a teaching advocated by Melanchthon and Johann Pfeffinger; with his position against Melanchthon that repentance is produced by the law, and not by the gospel; and with his arguments against Andreas Osiander that justification comes about by God's indwelling.

Article I, however, rejects his statement that "original sin is man's substance." In a colloquy at Weimar in 1562, to oppose the arguments of his opponent, Johan Strigel, who used Aristotle's terms, "substance" and "accidence," Flacius rejected the term "accidence" for original sin, and to eliminate any modicum of free will, chose to speak of it as "substance." For that, he has been accused of a "Flacian heresy." But according to the eminent historian of doctrine, Reinhold Seeberg, "Flacius was no heretic."[36] Karl Barth stated that Flacius's opponents no longer understood Luther. "That he could be execrated by his Lutheran contemporaries because of this thesis," Barth wrote, "shows how little Luther's most important insights were understood even within his own Church, and how thoroughly they had been forgotten only two decades after his death."[37]

Some, apparently, *chose* not to understand. "But so that they could still struggle against him," writes Ignaz Döllinger. "They drew consequences from his statements that he emphatically denied."[38] The men who later, as serving the princes, prepared the 1577 *Formula of Concord* that finally brought the controversies to an end, considered themselves obligated for political reasons, "at all costs to put Flacius in the wrong."[39]

Article X, which employs the stoic category, "adiaphora," specifies that "We believe, teach, and confess that in time of persecution, when a clear-cut confession of faith is demanded of us, we dare not yield to the enemies in such indifferent things...." Had the formulators learned from Flacius to write, "we dare not yield to the government," the *Formula of Concord* would have been a clear guide for the church's struggle against National Socialism. The question, of course, is whether a more candid statement would have fostered concord in the sixteenth century. Although Flacius and his followers believed that unity could be achieved by an independent synod, perhaps the only realistic possibility – the agreement reached in 1577 – was concord based on princely support.

Despite the virtues of the *Formula of Concord* in asserting Luther's doctrine against its rivals, Flacius's party bitterly rejected it because it was sponsored by princes. Flacius's party, thus, is historically significant not least because of its resistance against the rise of political absolutism. Discovering Flacius, writes Jörg Baur, is to take leave of "the legend of a passive Lutheranism, submissive to the state."[40] An index of how thoroughly that party was defeated, however, is the disappearance of Flacius's term, "Samaritanism," or the subordination of church to the state. Universally used, instead, is the Calvinist term, "Erastianism." For those engaged in rethinking history, however – and able to overcome distaste for "theological bickering" – Flacius's career gives promise of uncovering a fascinating variant tradition, a tradition that – had it succeeded – might have led Germany in a different direction.

It is gratifying that researchers these days are discovering and investigating historical figures of the second rank. It should be a matter of special gratification to recognize that one of those long consigned to a secondary place has been underestimated. A fair survey of his record and his influence will confirm the verdict that, together with such personages of the Reformation period as Luther, Melanchthon, and Erasmus, Matthias Flacius Illyricus deserves a place in the first rank.

Notes

1 Pontien Polman, "Flacius Illyricus, Historien de l'Eglise," *Revue d'histoire ecclésiastique* 27 (1931), 69.

2 Johannes Ficker and Otto Winckelmann, *Handschriftenproben des sechzehnten Jahrhunderts* (Strassburg: Karl J. Tuebner, 1905), II:95.

3 Johann Joseph Ignaz von Döllinger, *Die Reformation. Ihre innere Entwicklung und ihre Wirkung im Umfange des Lutherischen Bekenntnisses,* 2 vols. (Arnheim: Josue Witz, 1853/4), I:407; II:233.

4 Adolf Herte, "Matthias Flacius," *Lexikon für Theologie und Kirche,* 2nd ed. (1932), IV:27.

5 H.-M Féret, "Centuries de Magdebourg," *Catholicisme Hier – Aujourd'hui – Demain,* III (Paris: Letrouzeyet Ané, 1949), 815.

6 James Brodrick, *Petrus Canisius, 1521–1597,* II (Vienna: Herder, 1950), 373.

7 Franjo Zenko, "Flacius-Rezeption in Kroatien als ideologisierende Vermittlung mit dem gegenwärtigen Leben" in Josip Matesic, ed., *Matthias Flacius Illyricus – Leben & Werk* (Munich: Südsteuropa-Gesellschaft, 1993), 171.

8 Eduard Böhl, *Beiträge zur Geschichte der Reformation in Österreich* (Jena: Gustav Fischer, 1902), 106. Gottlob von Polenz, *Geschichte der französischen Calvinismus,* III (Gotha: Friedrich Andreas Perthes, 1860), 78; Christian Friedrich Kling, "Flacius," *Realencyklopädie für Protestantische Theologie und Kirche,* 1st ed. (Stuttgart and Hamburg, 1855), III:415.

9 I have attempted that task, up to the year 1557, in *Matthias Flacius and the Survival of Luther's Reform,* scheduled for publication by the Herzog August Bibliothek at Wolfenbüttel in 2001. See my "Matthias Flacius," *TRE* 11: 206–14.

10 *Wolfenbüttler Cimelien* (Weinheim, VCH, Acta Humaniora, 1989), 37, 59, 97, 103, 173.

11 Oliver K. Olson, "Flacius Illyricus als Liturgiker," *Jahrbuch für Liturgik und hymnologie* XIII (1947), 45–69.

12 August Twesten, *Matthias Flacius Illyricus, eine Vorlesung. Mit autobiographischen Beilagen und einer Abhandlung über Melanchthons Verhalten zum Interim von Hermann Rössel* (Berlin: Bethge, 1844).

13 *Eine Schrift wider ein recht heidnisch ja epicurish Buch* (Magdeburg: Christian Rödinger, 1549), Biiij.

14 *The Fortresse of Fathers,* 1566. Btr-cv. Leonard J. Trinterud, *Elizabethan Puritanism* (New York: Oxford University Press, 1971), 82.

15 Hans Christoph von Hase, *Die Gestalt der Kirche Luthers. Der Casus Confessionis im Kampf des Matthias Flacius gegen das Interim von 1548* (Göttingen: Vandenhoeck & Ruprecht, 1940).

16 Andreas Osiander, *Von dem Einigen Mittler Jhesu Christo und Rechtfertigung des Glaubens. Bekenntnus* (Königsberg, 1551), 332.

17 *CS* 12: 461.

18 Oliver K. Olson, "Theology of Revolution: Magdeburg 1550–1551," *SCJ* 3 (1972), 50–79.

19 Clyde Leonhard Manschreck, "A Critical Examination and Appraisal of the Adiaphoristic Controversy in the Life of Philip Melanchthon" (dissertation, Yale University, 1948), 105.

20 Oliver K. Olson, "The Rise and Fall of the Antwerp Martinists," *LQ* 1/1 (Spring 1987), 98–119.

21 Paul Estié, *Het Plaatselijk Bestuur van de Nederlandse Lutherse Gemeenten. Ontstaan I (1987) en Ontwikkeling in de Jaren 1566 tot 1686* (Amsterdam: Rodopi, 1987), 13.

22 W. J. Kooiman, "Die Amsterdamer Kirchenordnung in ihrer Auswirkung auf die luthersichen Kirchenordnungen in den Vereinigten Staaten Americas, *Evangelische Theologie* 16 (1956), 225–38.

23 Johannes Jannsen, *Geschichte des deutschen Volkes seit dem Ausgang des Mittelalters* (Freiburg im Breisgau: Herder'sche Verlagsbuchhandlung, 1878–94), VIII:182.

24 *Catalogus Testium Veritatis qui ante nostram aetatem reclamarunt Papae* (Basel: Oporinus, 1556) 13; 2nd ed. (Strassburg, 1562), 5.

25 Harry Elmer Barnes, *A History of Historical Writing,* 2nd. rev. ed. (New York: Dover, 1962), 124.

26 *Catalogus* [1556] 869–71; [1562] 507–8.

27 *Catalogus* [1556] 652; [1562] 391. See Joseph L. Baird and Radd K. Ehrman, eds., *The Letters of Hildegard of Bingen* (New York: Oxford University Press, 1994).

28 *Catalogus* [1556] 814; [1562] 480.

29 Ronald Diener, "The Magdeburg Centuries. A Bibliothecal and Historiographical Analysis" (dissertation, Harvard Divinity School, 1978).

30 Wilhelm Dilthey, "The Rise of Hermeneutics," trans. Frederick James, *New Literary History: A Journal of Theory and Interpretation* III (1972), 238.

31 Hans-Georg Gadamer, "Die Universalität des hermeneutischen Problems," *Philosophisches Jahrbuch* LXXIII (1966), 215.

32 Sigmund von Lempicki, *Geschichte der deutschen Literaturwissenschaft bis zum Ende des 18. Jahrhunderts* (Göttingen: Vandenhoeck & Ruprecht, 1968), 85.

33 Brevard S. Childs, *Biblical Theology of the Old and New Testaments. Theological Reflection on the Christian Bible* (Minneapolis: Fortress Press, 1993), 725.

34 Hans-Georg Gadamer, *Rhetorik und Hermeneutik* (Göttingen: Vandenhoeck & Ruprecht, 1976), 4.

35 Gustav Frank, "Matthias Flacius und seine Zeit," review of Wilhelm Preger's biography of the same name, in *Protestantiche Kirchenzeitung für das evangelische Deutschland* (1859), 771–6.

36 Reinhold Seeberg, *Lehrbuch der Dogmengeschichte* IV (Darmstadt: Wissenschaftliche Buchgesellschaft, 1975), 115.

37 Karl Barth, *Church Dogmatics* III/2 (Edinburgh: T. & T. Clark, 1960), 27.

38 Döllinger, *Die Reformation.*

39 Otto Ritschl, *Geschichte des Protestantismus* (Leipzig: Hinrichs, 1908–27), II:453.

40 Jörg Bauer, "Flacius – Radikale Theologie" in *Matthias Flacius Illyricus, 1575–1975* (Regensburg: Lassleben, 1975), 40.

Bibliography

Besides the references in the notes, see the following works by Oliver K. Olson:

Matthias Flacius and the Survival of Luther's Reform, Wolfenbüttel: Herzog August Bibliothek, 2000.

"Matthias Flacius Illyricus, 1520–1575" in Jill Raitt, ed., *Shapers of Religious Traditions in Germany, Switzerland, and Poland, 1560–1600*, New Haven: Yale University Press, 1981, 1–17.

Argula von Grumbach (c.1490–c.1564)

Peter Matheson

Lay theology was different. Even before the Reformation began, movements such as the Devotio Moderna were suggesting the need for a new style of theology: a synthesis of personal discipleship, pastoral care, and the teaching office. Humanists challenged the monopoly of theology by the universities and the religious orders, championed the *via rhetorica*, a literary rather than a philosophical approach, and set Scripture and the early church at the center of the scene. Both provoked "territorial" disputes by impinging on the turf of the traditional exponents of theology. The Reformation went still further in redrawing the boundaries for theology: its primary themes, its criteria, its methods, its intended audience, to some extent at least, its rationale. We are coming to see today that the study of theology has to deal not only with shifts in its content but in its discourse and its interactivity.

As the reforming movement gathered momentum, lay people had already begun to raise the *cui bono* question: Whom does the current pattern and "output" of theological studies benefit? Is it training the intelligent and committed pastors which civic and rural communities alike require? Is it tackling the issues which ordinary people have to resolve in their day-to-day living: work, communal bonding, family life, the great life crises of illness, marriage, and death, the joys and perplexities of parenthood, relations with their neighbors?

When such issues were adequately addressed, most lay people tended to be content to leave theological matters to the clergy, who had tradition on their side, time to write, access to libraries, a monastic or university training behind them. There is little evidence of egalitarianism. Popular as it was, the doctrine of the priesthood of all believers did not mean for most lay Protestants that Jack was as good as his master. They wanted a biblical theology based on divine revelation, not on arbitrary human norms, and so they recognized the need for specialist scholars in the biblical languages. In fact the new Protestant academies and faculties were soon to exercise a magisterium, a teaching office, not too dissimilar from that of the episcopate in the old church.

Yet civic disputations and princely plans made it clear that the new breed of theologians was answerable not only to God and Scripture but to the whole people of God. People had always thought their own thoughts about sermons and preachers.

A significant minority now had vernacular copies of Scripture to check on the line taken. The exciting new medium of the pamphlet offered lay people a window into theological debate, and for an adventurous few a platform to explore issues, especially of a more contextual nature, on which they believed they were the experts.

The absolute authority of the school theologian – always more myth than reality in any case – was being replaced, or at least complemented, by a meritocratic and accountable patriarchalism. Where, however, did this leave women? On what, if anything, were they the experts? Where did it leave those with no access to the higher schools of learning or the higher reaches of power? The humanists and reformers may have used the literary fiction of the learned peasant, such as Karsthans, to refute the elitism of the old theology, but what would happen if women and "peasants" left the field of virtual reality and actually moved into the public square?

Argula von Grumbach is probably the most sensational example of such an intervention. Hitherto totally quite unknown, she was propelled into prominence in the autumn of 1523 by a most unlikely constellation of events. The University of Ingolstadt organized a show trial against a young student, Arsacius Seehofer. On pain of death, he was forced to deny his new evangelical beliefs. Perplexed by the failure of any men to speak out against this, and outraged by the spectacle of Arsacius swearing by the gospel to deny that same gospel, she issued an extraordinary challenge. She would engage in public debate about the legitimacy of such coercive action with the Ingolstadt Faculty, which included the redoubtable Dr. Eck.[1] She happened to be a member of the prominent von Stauff family, which had never shunned a confrontation. She was well educated and well connected. She happened also to have links with the growing evangelical movement in Würzburg and Nuremberg, and had been in correspondence with the Wittenberg theologians.[2]

Nevertheless, this intervention by a woman, a mother of four, was totally unprecedented. It raised quite new questions about the role of theology and about the nature of leadership in a reformed church. She suggested that the debate be conducted in German and that Holy Scripture be the sole norm by which the debate would be judged. She envisaged a secular body as the judges: the princes of Bavaria and the "whole community."

She had been surprised into speech. The logic of events then pushed her into ever more radical measures. Her letter, unsurprisingly, was not answered or even acknowledged. Repressive measures lumbered into action. In the context of the times, however, it was no longer possible to smother her submission by silence or suppression. Her biblically grounded challenge began to circulate, and then, with the assistance of friends in Nuremberg, was printed with a fiery preface which hailed her intervention as the birth sign of a new age, and put her in the apostolic succession of other notable women in biblical and patristic times. She had become a "star" for the nativity of the Bavarian reform movement. Within a year another fourteen editions of the original letter were published; and seven more pamphlets flowed from her pen. It has been estimated that some 29,000 copies of her writings circulated in the crucial years, 1523–4. Clearly this rapturous reception indicates that the legitimacy of her intervention was not only recognized, but seen as betokening a new style of theologizing. She was feted as the real expert in Scripture, and in much else besides. Ironically this point was made by the dramatic woodcut on three of the editions of her letter to the university which portrays her in her skirts, bible in hand, taking on the bemused Ingolstadt theologians, whose tomes litter the ground. As a symbolic glove indicates, a challenge about the very nature of theology had been thrown down. Judith and Holofernes lived again![3]

Luther and other leaders of reform were quick to appreciate her courage and confessional importance, but did not think of her as a theologian.[4] Others ranked her in the prophetic tradition of Deborah and Hannah, the women around Jesus, the daughters of Philip.[5] Yet until very recent times she has been absent from the historiography of the Reformation. With the notable exception of Silke Halbach's recent monograph, the question of her possible contribution to the overall theological achievement of the Reformation has not even been raised.

It will be important, in redressing this balance, not to go to the other extreme. Her public theological engagement through the medium of print, though not her advocacy of the Reformation, ceased in 1524. Unlike Katharina Schütz Zell, her contribution to Reformation theology was an episodic one.

It was also limited in its scope. As a lay theologian she had a good general education, and a sharp, analytical mind. She had a formidable understanding of Scripture based on her own passionate and intelligent engagement with it. She could deploy some knowledge of the Reformers' writings, particularly evident in her understanding of the Word of God and in her ecclesiology. It is conceivable that as a young woman in the Munich court she met Johann Staupitz. But she was unschooled in mystical or patristic theology, apart from the incidental knowledge she would have picked up from Jerome's prefaces to the biblical books in the Koberger edition of the Bible, probably the one she possessed. She had no training in philosophy and no knowledge of the biblical languages. She was restricted to the traditional literary forms available to women: the letter and the poem. She wrote occasional pieces, responses to particular events or crises. The entire corpus of her work, quantitatively, would fit within the covers of one of Luther's larger writings. Beset by a sea of problems after 1524, she lacked the facilities, the leisure, and the opportunity to develop her theological interests in any systematic way. She came up against a cultural brick wall. The window of opportunity for her to engage in theology had never been very open, and it soon slammed shut. Part of the reason why her writing terminated when it did may well be that she had said all she had to say. It does her no service to ignore this.

This said, her writings are remarkable. We have to rub our eyes with utter astonishment at her achievement in developing a rounded and consistent theology, unmistakably hers, bricks out of veritable straw. Surprised into speech, she produced a language all her own, a new hermeneutic of Scripture, a passionate vision of a new church and a just society, a new style of leadership.[6] Her writings offer us a precious insight into how articulate lay people, in this case an impoverished member of the nobility, sought to read Scripture in the light of their times, and to exegete their times in the light of Scripture. She speaks as a woman. Her approach to Scripture, her theological priorities and perspectives, and her passionate ethical engagement reflect, inter alia, her experience as a daughter, as a mother of four children, as a wife, as a woman very much in charge of her own household. She reflects from a woman's standpoint on prating preachers, boorish princes, oppressive husbands.

Her work poses, therefore, some fascinating questions: How did she find her way about Scripture? What was its center for her? Did she see herself as having a leadership role? What was her understanding of righteousness, of sin, of the church? What was her vision of a Christian society? To what extent did she share the anticlericalism and the apocalyptic mind-set of the day? How does her writing "mirror" her courageous and in many ways impossibly difficult life?

There are some larger questions, too: How does her work complement that of the male reformers? To put it slightly differently: how does incorporating her work within the total picture change our view of their perspectives, discourse, and achievements? Together with the writings of Katharina Schütz Zell and others, does she to some extent anticipate the views of Marie de Dentière, and even of modern feminist theologians?[7] What is the lasting significance of her theology?

Argula von Grumbach saw herself as a biblical theologian. Indeed, for her, there was no other kind of theology. Philosophy and canon law, Aristotle and the decretals, as she put it, were futile and hostile to the Word of God. Her writings are studded with biblical quotations. Some sections of her letters are virtual catenae of citations.

I have identified 130 quotations from the Hebrew Bible in her writings.[8] She cites the Psalms 22 times, which is no surprise, given their devotional use. The prophetic books of Isaiah, Jeremiah, and Ezekiel are prominent, but the Pentateuch hardly appears. Despite the strongly apocalyptic flavor of her work there is only one reference to Daniel, and none to Revelation. Of the 194 New Testament quotations no less than 62 come from her favorite Gospel, Matthew, with 31 from John, Luther's Master Gospel, and 21 from Luke. Mark is little used. Not counting a few citations from Ephesians and the Pastorals, there are 42 from Paul and 7 from 1 Peter. The heart of her theology appears to beat in the Gospels and the prophetic books of the Hebrew Bible.

How did she operate, theologically? As a laywoman caught up by the recovery of Scripture, she apparently sat herself down and simply worked her way through the Testaments. "I have always wanted to find out the truth," as she put it. She saw herself as "studying" Scripture systematically, allowing one text to interpret another, in classic Lutheran mode: "Ah, but what a joy it is when the Spirit of God teaches us and gives us understanding, flitting from one text to the next."[9] She read in a context of prayer: "As I prayed God for more understanding, Scripture's words came to me winging."[10]

She had no commentaries to hand, but was guided by the German writings of Luther, Karlstadt, and others, having an extensive collection of their writings, ordered from a list provided by Spalatin in Wittenberg. The way in which she draws on different books of Scripture to illustrate particular points suggests that she had thoroughly interiorized the Bible.[11] She had her favorite books, her canon within the canon, and commuted at ease between the prophetic and apostolic writings. Her exegesis, too, was a highly existential one. She continually related the biblical texts to the contemporary situation and her own personal position.

She does not see herself as a "scholar,"[12] but her willingness to pit herself against the formidable Ingolstadt "scholars" suggests a robust confidence in her ability to "read Scripture straight,"[13] to sustain a biblically based argument. This gave one, she believed, access to the mind and will of God. Christians are called to be the mouth for the mouth of God.[14] This claim goes some way to explain her self-confidence in entering the theological arena.

Her hermeneutic of Scripture was one of affection, of affinity, of a perceived identity between the biblical witness and the situation of the lowly folk, including other women, she sees herself as representing. If she were to perish because of persecution, a hundred other women would appear in her place.[15]

It is impossible to overlook the elation that courses through her writings. She had been born into exceptional times. With the advent of the Reformation, "the word of God, that salvation which was to be prepared, is revealed."[16] True theology is a theology of the Word. Unlike human wisdom, with its prattle or babble, every word of God is true, as Deuteronomy 4:2 and Proverbs 30:6 tell us. It is sufficient in itself. It alone offers us access to God's will. It is the only source of our salvation. We can neither add nor subtract anything from Scripture; as she puts it, we are forbidden to "tear it to bits."[17] She cites the Psalmist on the happiness that flows from following the discipline of the law of God in this way.[18]

In a transient world, the Word of God endures forever. This Lutheran theme recurs again and again.[19] The Word is a fiery shield. If we stand by it we, too, will be "stood by," unshakeable.[20] Although she avoids allegory, the Word is not to be understood legalistically or literalistically. It is a fruitful, creative, life-giving force, like the rain from heaven, which, in the language of Isaiah, will never return empty.[21] She seizes on this theme of life, of birth and rebirth, again and again. The whole healing and teaching mission of Jesus is summed up as the promise of life.[22] Both in creation and in salvation God is revealed as the generous life-giver, in blatant contradistinction to the greedy papal institutions and canon law systems, which suck life from us.[23]

One of Argula's favorite images is the fountain of life, the living waters of Jeremiah 2, the gratuitous well of Isaiah 55.[24] John 1:3, characterizing God as the source of all life, is quoted in the context of God's "Yes which excludes any No." This genial paraphrasing of 2 Corinthians 1:17ff. expresses rather beautifully her sense of the overwhelmingly affirming and energizing nature of the Christian message. Jesus' dialogue with the Samaritan woman at the well in John 4 epitomizes the way in which God meets our deepest "thirsts."[25] The whole of human life, from Adam and Eve's first breath to the consummation of all things in Christ at the end of time, stands under God's "Yes" to us. Here, as elsewhere, Matthean, Johannine, and Pauline themes are woven intricately together in her discourse. The scriptural image of light is, if anything, even more important than that of life. Her first pamphlet, which reached a remarkable 14 editions, begins with John 12:46: "I have come as light into the world."[26] She emphasizes both the inclusiveness of God's light, which is not restricted to the clergy or the scholar, and its gratuity. Her little writing to Prince Johann is devoted to "walking in the light," recognizing Christ as the true light. She emphasizes in this letter to a prince that it is to the humble that light comes; Scripture is God's gift to the lowly.[27] In all her writings, published and unpublished, she describes herself as *demütig*, humble. God's light is for all people; yet it is hidden from "the world."[28] God has made foolish the wisdom of the world.[29]

The apocalyptic note is ever present in Argula's writing, even in her reading of John: "He who holds me in contempt and rejects my word will find he has one who judges him." Those who one would expect to see the light fail to do so, and vice versa.[30] What appears to be "women's chitchat" is in fact the word of God, for God has turned everything upside down.[31] Those who have something to hide always shun the light – a reference to the anonymous author of the poem that besmirched her intelligence and reputation in 1524.[32] Evildoers hate the light![33] Like the Pharisees, who exclude all who recognize Jesus from the synagogue, they want to excommunicate the young student Seehofer for his defense of the gospel.[34]

She reads the whole of Scripture as a deadly struggle between life and death, light and darkness. The struggle for life and light moves seamlessly into that for freedom from tyranny and arbitrariness.[35] She underlines the conflictual dimensions of John 16.[36] Threatened with death herself, she notes that Jesus had faced the same violence. If, however, you settle theology with coercion, that would make the hangman the best theologian; it will, in any case be self-defeating.[37]

This concern for the freedom of the gospel provoked her to enter the public square. For when the Word of God is entrusted to us, we cannot keep it to ourselves. We have to speak out from the rooftops, irrespective of risk or whom we are addressing, lest we sin against the Holy Spirit.[38] No chapter in Scripture is cited so often as Matthew 10. If we are ashamed to confess Christ, he will be ashamed of us.[39] Responsible stewardship of a life-giving message is yoked to eschatological urgency. We have to expect opposition. A disciple is not above his master. The hate Luther and his followers are encountering is predictable for anyone acquainted with the Bible.[40] The images of fire, of the hammer which shatters rock, convey something of the searing, irresistible force of the Word, which the prophets Isaiah, Jeremiah, and Ezekiel knew so well. Like fire, or a shattering hammer, it sweeps aside everything in its way, and will inevitably excite rage and persecution.

Thus the same Word which is a source of life and light and freedom, of living water, to those who espouse it, becomes a rod, a murder weapon, to those who forsake it, resist it. Argula quotes Hosea: God will pounce on them, kill them, hew them down.[41] The context for such words is the contumely and threats of violence and death which the evangelicals, including her, had encountered for championing, as she saw it, the cause of Scripture.

God's Word is not addressed to individuals only. "Land, land, hear the Word of God," she cries out with Jeremiah.[42] The confessional mode flows into the prophetic one. The Word of God should rule all aspects of life.[43] It is deplorable, she tells her censorious uncle, that "I have yet to meet anyone, either in the clerical or the secular realm" who set aside time to study Scripture to ascertain God's will for church and country.[44] At times, Argula's language becomes poignant as she paints the terrible corporate consequences for a land like Bavaria, when it resists the message of the gospel. Writing in the wake of the imperial city of Regensburg's decision to proscribe Lutheran views, she warns that it will be stricken with plague after plague, as Pharoah and ancient Egypt were.[45] The souls entrusted to the magistrates have been bought "with the costly rose-red blood of the Lord Jesus," and cannot be abandoned for prudential reasons.[46] As was the case with disobedient Israel, it will be the weak and the innocent who will bear the brunt of the suffering. Children will die at their mother's breast.[47] Murder and cannibalism will break out, family feuds and parricide.[48] Fathers will eat their sons; sons their fathers. Mothers will cook their own children and offer them for a meal.[49] For when God's Word is resisted, all morality, order, and humanity will disappear. This apocalyptic language reflects the social reality of a Germany about to slide into the terrors of the Peasants' War and to some extent her own grim reality, as many of her family and even her own husband turned against her. "But where the word of God is concerned neither Pope, Emperor nor Princes . . . have any jurisdiction."[50] Or husband, either, she might have added.[51]

She lays much of the blame for the catastrophe at the feet of the clergy, bishops, monks and nuns.[52] As with so many of her contemporaries, anticlericalism was a strong feature of her thought. Her language lambasting clerical robbery of the poor, hypocritical chastity, false prophecies, and immunity from punishment is typical of the time.[53] The incessant emphasis on their greed may seem at first sight rather moralistic, but this laywoman has a sharp eye for the way in which truth issues and power issues are inseparable. A proper exercise of the pastoral, teaching, and preaching ministry requires moral integrity. Approvingly, she quotes Paul about those who "peddle" the truth.[54] Because of their bondage to materialism those who should lead have become false prophets, falling into the pit themselves and dragging others down with them.[55] Her main concern is theological: They "hypocritically market God's word like some cheap trinket."[56] "His sole command is that we preach and bring his holy word to speech."[57]

But the clergy have neglected this primary mark of the church. To defend their interests they have become tyrannical and violent. They should be servants, but have put themselves above the law, even above God, being a burden to others, not treating them as they themselves would wish to be treated.[58] Argula combines the prophetic critique of Isaiah and Jeremiah with the evangelists' polemic against the Pharisees.[59] God's wrath is against those who resist the gospel, the stupid or lazy shepherds, the preachers who do not preach. God's Word is the cornerstone of Zion, but it will become a stone of stumbling to those who abuse power, the sharp-tongued church leaders who spit out venom like snakes.[60] We need not fear them. They can destroy the body, but we need only fear God, who can destroy soul and body in hell.[61] God's vengeance will put the "foaming rage" of the persecutors in the shade.[62]

This is a counter-cultural theology, aware of the scandal of the Word to the power and wisdom of this world. We are not called to follow tradition or the fickle winds of convention.[63] "The Lord says: 'I am the way the truth, and the life.' John 14. He does not say: 'I am what is customary.' "[64] As a woman it was particularly scandalous for her to challenge the gatekeepers of theology and morality, but she had to rise above her natural inhibitions. "I speak as Paul did."[65] "I consider that God has presented us to be like the dregs of the earth, deserving death, a spectacular mirror (*Schauspiegel*) to all the world."[66] The little writing to the Regensburg Council, the source of the last quotation, is the most apocalyptic in tone of all her works. The devil roams abroad, in the form of ravening wolves who imperil the souls of believers and invite divine judgment on the whole city.[67] She draws on Matthew 24, with its references to Daniel, and warns of persecution and conflict ahead and the imminence of the coming of the Lord. But the Psalms, the prophets, the Gospels, especially John, are all read apocalyptically. All her writings breathe this mingled exhilaration and awe at the overturning of normal patterns of leadership in church and state as God's Word runs free. The very stones cry out![68] Light against darkness, truth against lies, life against death. The lucrative masses for the dead remind her of the sacrifices to Baal. Jeremiah's dramatic image of the burning-pot, flaring out at midnight, much favored in contemporary art, sums up the crisis-ridden scenario that clamors for immediate redemption.[69]

Argula von Grumbach's theology of the Word vividly reflects her own experience as a layperson and a woman of powerlessness, of conflict, persecution, and violence; it reflects, too, her hatred of arbitrary coercion, hole-and-corner justice, the suppression of debate, all that she calls tyranny. By God's grace, she will not hold her peace, "though it cost me my neck a thousand times."[70] God would revenge the sufferings of his servants. Christ, the Rock, will crush all his enemies.[71] Human curses and condemnations will turn into God's blessings.[72]

The godly will receive all they need to sustain them, if their trust in God is resolute. John 13's emphasis on love and gentleness as the trademark of the Christian is impressively evident: "Let us fight chivalrously against the enemies of God. . . . We must not hit out with weapons, but love our neighbour. . . ." "It is a joy to me to be reviled for the sake of the holy gospel."[73] The confidence of the Psalmist has become existential reality for her.[74]

> For Christ says: "Those who believe in me
> From judgement will be fully free
> And pass from death to life with me."
> John's Gospel, Chapters Three and Five,
> Describes all this, or so I find.[75]

The apocalyptic and anticlerical dimensions to her thought, therefore, are only the flip side to an overwhelmingly positive theology. This is seen in her ecclesiology. Her view of the church is an inclusive one, drawing heavily on Jeremiah, Joel, the Gospels, Paul. The word "all" keeps recurring. Under God's new covenant all are taught by God.[76] Constituted by the Word, and led by the Spirit, all the people of God are called to discipleship and empowered by the Spirit to exercise their talents fully. She uses the proud term "Christian" to express this in the title of her first writing. "What Christian could keep silence in this situation?," she exhorts her uncle, referring to the need for a prophetic voice in church and society.[77] The basic commission to witness to Christ, in word and action, is given to all by baptism. There is a mutuality to this covenant. God will speak up for us only if we recognize him.[78] Unless we are prepared to speak out, and to speak up for Christ, we are no Christians, even if baptized a thousand times over.[79]

Argula's debt here to Luther's doctrine of the priesthood of all believers is evident, but so is her different accent. Being a child of God, through baptism, subverts not only traditional status distinctions but those of gender as well. She relishes references to the "little sheep" who know the shepherd's voice.[80] Women, peasants, humble folk can all be called to speak out prophetically without respect of persons. "I am not under constraint to obey any one at all, for I vowed at baptism to believe in God, to confess him, and to renounce the Devil and all his illusions."[81] It was Judith whom God called upon to instruct the faltering priests and elders that God is the Lord of history.[82]

This is not, of course, the language of women's rights, but of responsibilities and obligations. To be a Christian is to resist all that opposes the Word of God.[83] Her pastoral concern for the "lost sheep" of Jeremiah 50:6 led her to teach and perhaps preach, and certainly to work tirelessly throughout her life for the renewal of the church. The founding of the little Lutheran church at Zeilitzheim is attributed to her, for example. Nor is the new role of women to be confined to the ecclesiastical realm. God can put princes, too, "under the feet of women," when they misuse their authority.[84]

The Spirit is no respecter of persons. The early disciples were simple folk, fishermen like John. Jesus gathered women around him. The prophets, the evangelists, and Paul all testify that "peasants or women" are not excluded.[85] Initially, Argula had doubted, on the basis of 1 Timothy 2, whether she, a woman, should speak out on such theological matters. However, as she looked at Scripture – Isaiah, Jeremiah, Ezekiel, the Psalms, Joel, and above all Matthew 10 – it became clear to her that, as Jesus says in Luke 10:21, God hides things from the wise and reveals them to the little ones.[86] In extraordinary times God acts in extraordinary ways, through Deborah, and Jael, and Judith, even through Balaam's ass.[87] In her own defense she reminds the theologians of Ingolstadt that Christ, our only teacher, "was not ashamed to preach to Mary Magdalene, and to the young woman at the well," and that the great Early Church scholar, Jerome, devoted himself to teaching Blesilla, Paula, and Eustochium.[88] "Which doctor has made a greater vow in baptism than I have?"[89] The humility so important to her personal piety should not debar her, or other women, from exercising their God-given talents. Quite the contrary, it is to the humble that God speaks with special clarity.[90] While the Pharisees, representing the clergy, spoil everything with their sour dough, the parable of the kingdom of heaven has a woman putting in the good yeast and leavening the whole lump.[91]

The church needs its scholars and preachers, but they are there to serve and to teach, to administer the sacraments, and to give pastoral care, not to dominate. "No person should be held in more respect than a good preacher, schooled in God's Spirit and not in a literalistic way."[92] They are not priests, however, but ministers. She takes for granted the obsoleteness of the papacy, episcopacy, and monastic orders. The church is no longer to be seen institutionally, and certainly not hierarchically, but eschatologically. The real Temple of the Lord is people.[93] The church has a prophetic role to play in society, and has to challenge magistrates and princes to critique existing structures in law, education, and family relationships, and work towards a biblical goal of moral integrity and justice.[94]

She insists, therefore, that this inclusive, outward-looking, prophetic church is also to be a biblical one. Its sole head is Christ, and its sole guideline is Scripture.[95] Canon law, the decretals, philosophy, with their dreams and lies, their purely human conceits, are all worse than useless.[96] More surprising, perhaps, is her emphasis on the Spirit.[97] The Spirit is the church's "schoolmaster."[98] Unless God's Spirit dwells within us, we can achieve nothing. We are all poor and weak, and without the Holy Spirit we cannot even pray, or be led to the truth. It is God's Spirit alone that tests our inward being and unites us to God. The Lord is Spirit.[99] Following the Gospel of John she insists that it is the Spirit that gives life: "My words are spirit and life."[100]

Her first writing, to the University of Ingolstadt, had dealt with the question of authority in the church, her second, to the Bavarian princes, with the reform issues facing church and society. Her letters to the Ingolstadt and Regensburg councils call upon them to distance themselves from the clergy and make the spiritual welfare of their subjects their main concern. Her address to her uncle, Adam von Thering, tackles the issue of her right to speak out, and the need to defy persecution. But it is perhaps in her long poem, her last writing, that she sets out most clearly her vision for a new theology and a new church. She is conscious of speaking *with* David, *with* Jeremiah, *with* Paul.[101] In human terms she may only be a foolish woman, but the promises that Christ will stand by his own are always before her eyes.[102] Where Scripture speaks of a thousand fleeing from one, she is that one![103] As for her four children, God, who clothes the lilies, and feeds Elijah with the birds of the air, would take care of them.[104]

Her own religious experiences shine through such asseverations. She herself has been reborn by Christ's word,[105] tested by the Spirit, blessed as she waits on God, but also attacked and reviled, in person, in print, and from the pulpit.[106] Her sense of solidarity with the prophets and the apostles, in exaltation and in distress, is a profound one, and so the question of the relationship of her theology to the Reformers is far from simple. Halbach has suggested that it is on the whole derivative from Luther's, differing only in nuances.[107] It is clear from her writings, however, that she sees Luther primarily as a quite genial translator of Scripture, as one whose books are only a guide to Scripture for others, including herself. "I was baptized in the name of Christ; it is him I confess and not Luther."[108] She had, of course, tactical reasons for understating her debt to such a notorious heretic. However, there seems no reason to doubt her emphatic and theologically based denial that she is a "Lutheran." It is the Word of God alone, not Luther's words, which must rule. All mortals, including Luther, are liars and sinners. Christ is the true rock on which she stands.[109]

My own impression is that Argula's main debt to Luther is in her understanding of the Word of God and the church. Luther's central concerns about justification by faith, on the other hand, do not appear to be central. One would not expect technical formulations on Christology and the Trinity in a layperson's work, but I cannot recall a single Trinitarian formula in Argula's work. She shows no awareness of the Lutheran polarity of law and gospel. Her understanding of Christian society may be closer to a Reformed view than to that of Luther. She had to work her own way toward an understanding of women's role in the church, one that owed little to Luther. It is very interesting that she attempted to mediate between the Wittenberg and Reformed theologians on the vexed issue of the Eucharist at the Diet of Augsburg in 1530.[110] She may have felt herself bound to neither camp.

In her grateful, but critical reception of Luther, therefore, Argula von Grumbach may stand for many other lay people. The themes most prominent in her writings: the defense of Christian freedom, the victory of light over darkness, the authority of Scripture, and the call for a just society are precisely those which struck the strongest chord in the communal reformation of the early 1520s.

I suspect that she understands righteousness and sin rather differently from Luther.[111] In regard to sin it has to be remembered that she had suffered personally from the hysterical anxieties about women's sexuality. Her fiercest opponents, such as the Ingolstadt Professor Hauer, branded her, and other women followers of Luther, as typical daughters of Eve; she was a "heretical bitch," defiling the honor of the Virgin Mary.[112] Unlike Luther, Argula von Grumbach never had a good word to say about Mary. She had a different ideal of womanhood from the traditional image of Mary propounded by Hauer, and was highly critical of ideals of chastity.[113]

The libelous poem directed against her by "Johann of Landshut" had even suggested she was sexually obsessed by the young student she was defending. "Are you in heat, perhaps/For this eighteen-year-old chap?"[114] Women who did not know their place represented a threat not only to society but to all order and morality. Just being a woman put one's salvation under threat.

Argula von Grumbach openly acknowledged that we are all sinners: "I can do nothing but sin." She seems to have accepted Luther's anthropology.[115] The whole weight of her analysis of sin shifts, however, away from individual to social sin and to the need for corporate righteousness. It is the structures of church life, of monastic life, of the universities, of a wildly expensive legal system, of the social mores of the nobility, and the political priorities of the princes that are the main concern for her. She is fiercely critical of the secular rulers of Germany, quoting Isaiah 3:14 about the elders and princes grinding down the face of the poor. She also cited Hosea 8:4, "they were princes, but I do not recognize them as such," in relation to the unimpressive conduct of the Imperial Diet at Nuremberg. The authorities "curse, kill and rage away, devoid of all knowledge and grounding in Scripture."[116] The coercive repression of the church authorities infuriates her. "The sweat of the poor is being used in the service of the devil," she told Duke Wilhelm. The inveterate "busyness" of the male world of the rulers, which never had time for scriptural reflection, is compared with Jesus' commendation of Mary for the one thing needful; as it is, their ignorance allows the clergy to lead them around "like monkeys on a chain."[117]

She is outraged, as a woman, at the gluttony and drunkenness at the Imperial Parliament. How could sensible decisions for the good of the nation be made by such a body? Sin was the abuse of privilege and power, whether in the bedroom, the princely court, or the pulpit. The epidemic of sin which society faces comes not from female licentiousness but from the corporate male world. Women were the victims: "There is no way out, whatever a woman does. . . ."[118]

The graciousness with which she personally responded to the vicious attacks on her, her advocacy of reason, education, and courtesy, no doubt mirror her own understanding, on the other hand, of God's graciousness to us. She likes, as Luther does, to talk of God's "friendliness." Certainly she reiterates again and again that we have to turn the other cheek. "We must not hit out with weapons, but love our neighbor, and keep peace with one another."[119] Grace becomes earthed in daily life.

Hers is as unmistakably a layperson's and a woman's theology as it is a biblical one. There is an ongoing dialectical relationship between her self-understanding and her reading of Scripture. As she came to see Paul's admonitions to women in the context of the whole of Scripture she was able to see a new prophetic role for herself. And this in turn enabled her to approach Scripture in a different way. There is a costly consistency between her words, her exegesis, and her actions.

The cognitive dissonance which followed the calamity of the Peasants' War, and the collapse of her reforming hopes for Bavaria, led to her revising one of the weak features of her theology, its overblown apocalyptic hopes. From now on we hear no more melodramatic threats about God showering plagues upon the opponents of the Reformation. Instead she quietly sets about working at the local level, building up networks of friends, fostering evangelical worship, forging alliances between home, church, and school.[120] She sought to develop new contours of lay spirituality that offered an alternative to the indolence, illiteracy, drunkenness, and brutality that had characterized the life of the lesser nobility. Her confidence in God's providence enabled her to endure personal tragedy and transcend the apparent collapse of her reforming dreams.

For centuries now her reforming activity and her theology have been ignored. Ludwig Rabus published many of her writings and honored her as a confessor of the faith in the second half of the sixteenth century.[121] The Pietist Rieger hailed her zeal for the faith in the eighteenth century.[122] Theodore Kolde's articles on her work as a reformer at the beginning of the century are still of value. But not until Silke Halbach wrote her fine monograph in 1991 did Argula begin to edge her way into the male-dominated and confessionally structured historiography of the Reformation in Germany. We are without a critical German edition of her writings.[123] It would appear, after five centuries, that she is still having difficulty in finding a hearing.

Notes

1 Not surprisingly, one of her favorite texts was Matthew 10:19: "When they hand you over, do not worry about how you are to speak. . . ; for what you are to say will be given to you at that time." *AvG*, 90, 175.

2 Much of the history of her life remains uncertain; see *AvG* and Silke Halbach, *Argula von Grumbach als Verfasserin reformatorischer Flugschriften*, Europäische Hochschulschriften Reihe XXIII Theologie, Vol. 468 (Frankfurt am Main: Peter Lang, 1992).

3 Editor's note: The story of Judith's decapitation of the Assyrian general Holofernes is in the apocryphal book Judith, 13:6–9.

4 On Luther's correspondence with and about her, and on the reception of her work generally, see *AvG*, 21–5, 47–55.

5 Among early supporters were later radicals such as Balthasar Hubmaier and Sebastian Lotzer, but also Johann Eberlin von Günzburg and Andreas Osiander, the Nuremberg Reformer.

6 I have attempted to characterize her language and imaginative reach in *The Rhetoric of the Reformation* (Edinburgh: T. & T. Clark, 1998), 131–8.

7 We cannot explore here the growing volume of literature on the role of women in the Reformation, but see Merry E. Wiesner, *Women and Gender in Early Modern Europe* (New York: Cambridge University Press, 1993). See also "Marie de Dentière's Use of Scripture in her Theology of History" in Mark S. Burrows and Paul Rorem, eds., *Biblical Hermeneutics in Historical Perspective* (Grand Rapids: Eerdmans, 1991), 225–42.

8 These are conservative figures, based on explicit references.

9 *AvG*, 86.

10 *AvG*, 179.

11 Her citations are generally from memory, often condensing or conflating texts. Halbach, *Argula von Grumbach*, 196–200.

12 *AvG*, 185.

13 *AvG*, 176, paraphrasing Joel 2:28–32: "Your sons and daughters, servants, maids/ Will prophesy; read Scripture straight."

14 She cites the prophets: "The word which I say to you, proclaim to them from my mouth." Is. 59:21; Jer. 1:9. *AvG*, 81.

15 *AvG*, 120.

16 *AvG*, 127.

17 *AvG*, 80f., 180; Dt. 12:32 is also cited.

18 Ps. 94:12; *AvG*, 179.

19 *AvG*, 40, 88, 143.

20 *AvG*, 132, quoting Is. 51.

21 *AvG*, 148; Halbach, *Argula von Grumbach* (201), believes that the Word, in Lutheran manner, is explicitly identified with Christ; it does appear to be personalized – it can be "oppressed," for example. *AvG*, 182. However, caution is in place about reading it in explicitly Christological terms.

22 *AvG*, 88; Mt. 4:23f.

23 Jn. 6:40; *AvG*, 88.

24 *AvG*, 90, 148, 158.

25 *AvG*, 88.

26 *AvG*, 75.

27 *AvG*, 87, 126.

28 *AvG*, 125f, 158; Jn. 1:9–12.

29 1 Cor. 1:20; *AvG*, 156.

30 Jn. 1:11f.; 9:39; 12:48; *AvG*, 87, 143, 158.

31 *AvG*, 90.

32 Jn. 3:19; *AvG*, 174.

33 Jn. 7:7; *AvG*, 101.

34 Jn. 9:22; *AvG*, 119.

35 Peter Matheson, "Breaking the Silence: Women, Censorship, and the Reformation," *SCJ* 27/1 (1996), 97–109.

36 *AvG*, 84.

37 *AvG*, 84.

38 *AvG*, 76.

39 Mt. 10 is cited 17 times; the central verse Mt. 10:32, 5 times; *AvG*, 75, 103, 118, 121, 127, 156.

40 *AvG*, 75, 81, 101; Jer. 1:9; Ez. 33:7ff.; Mt. 10:24.

41 Hos. 6:5; Hos. 13 quoted in *AvG*, 77f.; cf. 158, 190.

42 Jer. 22; *AvG*, 88.

43 *AvG*, 82, 101.

44 *AvG*, 146.

45 Dt. 10:17; Ps. 145:3.

46 *AvG*, 157.

47 *AvG*, 105 quoting 2 Chr. 36:17–21.

48 Mt. 10:21, 34, 37; *AvG*, 145.

49 *AvG*, 104.

50 *AvG*, 76.

51 *AvG*, 145, 192. The phrase "persecuting and crucifying Christ anew" is used in her letter to Frederick the Wise of the oppression of evangelicals by "pagan," presumably Catholic, princes. *AvG*, 132.

52 Three of the daughters of her uncle, Hieronymus von Stauff, had left their nunneries in Regensburg.

53 *AvG*, 105–8, 111.

54 *AvG*, 181f.; 2 Cor. 2:17.

55 *AvG*, 106, 144; Mt. 7:15. Her reading of Mt. 15.14 is interesting, focussing on the greed of the clergy.

56 *AvG*, 181.

57 This is her gloss on Jesus' commission to his disciples: Mt. 10:5–11. *AvG*, 180.

58 *AvG*, 108, 145, quoting Mt. 20:26ff. and Mt. 7:12, respectively.

59 Is. 8:14f; 34:3; Ps. 109:6–11; Is. 30; Ps. 140:3; Mt. 23:33. *AvG*, 78, 105, 107.

60 Is. 30:9f; Jer. 6:10–21; 1 Pt. 2:6–8. *AvG*, 121, 144, 188f.

61 Mt. 10:28ff; quoted four times; what does make her tremble is the misuse of power by church authorities to stymie the spread of the gospel. *AvG*, 76.

62 *AvG*,194.

63 *AvG*, 156ff.; Eph. 4:14.

64 *AvG*, 157.

65 Gal. 1:10; *AvG*, 143.

66 *AvG*, 158f.; 1 Cor. 4:9.

67 *AvG*, 154, 156; 1 Pt. 5:8f.

68 *AvG*, 158, 182.

69 *AvG*, 134, 191. *Aquilo*, the north, is translated by Koberger and other late fifteenth-century German translations as "midnight;" Ps. 106:28; Jer. 1:11,13.

70 *AvG*, 103, quoting Mt. 10:39.

71 *AvG*, 132f., citing Dan. 2:35, 45 and 1 Pt. 2:6; Thomas Müntzer also used this theme of Christ as the living stone in his Sermon to the Princes. See CTM, 234.

72 Ps. 110:17f., 28; *AvG*, 190.

73 *AvG*, 158, 121, quoting the beatitude in Mt. 5:11; in her poem she cites the parallel in Lk. 6 and also 1 Pt. 4:13–14; *AvG*, 194.

74 Ps. 3:6; 37:25; 68:2; *AvG*, 78, 109, 190.

75 *AvG*, 193.

76 Jer. 31:33; Is. 54:12; *AvG*, 80, 178f.

77 *AvG*, 146.

78 *AvG*, 145.

79 *AvG*, 143.

80 Jn. 1:11f.; 10:4f.

81 *AvG*, 142.

82 Two entire pages of her poem develop this theme from Judith 8. *AvG*, 183f. It is illuminating that at one imperial diet after another,

most notably at the Diet of Augsburg, Argula von Grumbach took it upon herself to exhort the Protestant princes in person to remain steadfast, emphasizing that God is in control; God had never slept on the job yet, a reference to Ps. 121:5. See Justas Jonas's letter to Luther of August 6: *WA Br* 5, 536.

83 *AvG*, 118.

84 Is. 3:12; *AvG*, 133f.

85 *AvG*, 176–9.

86 *AvG*, 79f. It is interesting that she omits the criticisms of the "daughters of the people" when citing Ez. 13:17; *AvG*, 78.

87 *AvG*, 182–5.

88 *AvG*, 88.

89 *AvG*, 142.

90 The rhetoric of deference which women writers had to affect does not mean that her humility was not genuine; on the many-layered nature of the concept of humility see Ursula Hess, "Oratrix humilis. Die Frau als Briefpartnerin von Humanisten, am Beispiel der Caritas Pirckheimer" in F. Worstbrock, ed., *Der Brief im Zeitalter der Renaissance* (Weinheim: Verlag Chemie, 1983), 196f.

91 *AvG*, 122, 144; Mt. 13:33; 16:6.

92 *AvG*. 105f.; "Der in Gottes Geist/und nit im Buchstaben gelehrt ist."

93 1 Cor. 3:16; *AvG*, 178.

94 Note the use of the apocalyptic language of Mt. 24 in addressing the Regensburg council. *AvG*, 154f.

95 *AvG*, 118, citing Eph. 4:15.

96 Ez. 13:19; *AvG*, 78,105.

97 It would be worth looking for possible verbal echoes of Karlstadt's writings in her work.

98 *AvG*, 118; an interesting variation on Galatians 3! Schoolmasters played a key role in her educational plans for her children and for society as a whole.

99 Note the remarkable long section on the inspiration of the Holy Spirit in her poem to "Johann of Landshut." *AvG*, 176–8.

100 Jn. 6:63; *AvG*, 76.

101 She understands herself "als reformatorische Prophetin." Halbach, *Argula von Grumbach*, 217.

102 *AvG*, 103, 141.

103 *AvG*, 109, 119, 190.

104 Mt. 6:26–30 appears to be conflated with 1 Kgs. 17:6.

105 *AvG*, 187.

106 *AvG*, 118, 187, 191; Is. 30:18.

107 Halbach, *Argula von Grumbach*, 220.

108 *AvG*, 101, 102, 105, 144f., 148, 189.

109 *AvG*, 89.

110 She arranged a meeting between Bucer and a reluctant Melanchthon at Augsburg in 1530. See the draft letter by Bucer in Stadtarchiv Strassburg, AA 425a, cited by Walther Köhler, *Der Streit über das Abendmahl* (Gütersloh, 1953), 222.

111 I have explored this issue more fully in "A Reformation for Women? Sin, Grace and Gender in the Writings of Argula von Grumbach," *Scottish Journal of Theology* 49/1 (1996): 39–56.

112 Theodor Kolde suggests that Argula von Grumbach's third letter to the city council of Ingolstadt was a response to this furious attack. See his "Arsacius Seehofer und Argula von Grumbach," *Beiträge zur bayerischen Kirchengeschichte* 11(1905), 99f.

113 *Drei christlich predig vom//Salve regina/dem Eva//ngeli vnnd heyligen//schrift ge//mess.* Ingolstadt, 1523(?).

114 *AvG*, 167.

115 Prov. 20:9; Rom. 14:23; *AvG*, 142, 149.

116 *AvG*, 106, 146, 148.

117 *AvG*, 83, 108, 192; she cites Lk. 10:42.

118 *AvG*, 147.

119 *AvG*, 158.

120 Her personal papers offer abundant information on this; some preliminary gleanings from them are to be found in Peter Matheson, *The Imaginative World of the Reformation* (Edinburgh: T. & T. Clark, 2000), 102–18; they show conclusively that Russell's reductionist view of her as a cunning propagandist, who "deliberately overstated, feigned naivety, and manipulated," is without foundation. See Paul Russell, *Lay Theology in the Reformation* (Cambridge: Cambridge University Press, 1986), 208.

121 Ludovicus Rabus, *Historien der Märtyrern*. Ander theil. Strassburg, 1572.

122 M. Georg Cunrad Rieger, *Das Leben Argulae von Grumbach, gebohrner von Stauffen. Als Einer Jüngerin Jesu, Zeugin der Warheit und Freundin Lutheri, samt eingemengter Nachricht von Arsatio Seehofern*. Stuttgart, 1737.

123 The original pamphlets are reproduced in the microfiche series, *Flugschriften des frühen 16 Jahrhunderts*, ed. Hans-Joachim Köhler, Hildegard Hebenstreit-Wilfert, and Christoph Weismann (Zug, 1978ff.).

Bibliography

Halbach, Silke, *Argula von Grumbach als Verfasserin reformatorischer Flugschriften*, Europäische Hochschulschriften Reihe XXIII Theologie, Vol. 468, Frankfurt am Main: Peter Lang, 1992.

Matheson, Peter, *Argula von Grumbach. A Woman's Voice in the Reformation*. Edinburgh: T. & T. Clark, 1995 (Cited as *AvG*).

——, "A Reformation for Women? Sin, Grace and Gender in the Writings of Argula von Grumbach," *Scottish Journal of Theology* 49/1 (1996), 39–56.

——, *The Imaginative World of the Reformation*. Edinburgh: T. & T. Clark, 2000.

Urbanus Rhegius (1489–1541)

Scott Hendrix

cha*p*ter 7

Urbanus Rhegius was a remarkable theologian of the German Reformation who deserves to be counted among the major Lutheran reformers. His career is a case study in the process of reform. Trained as a humanist in south German intellectual circles, Rhegius studied for the priesthood under Luther's opponents before he became a follower of Luther. As a young urban preacher in Augsburg during the turbulent 1520s, Rhegius faced all the early challenges of the burgeoning Protestant movement. He wrote about serfdom as the Revolution of 1525 began, and he confronted the strong Anabaptist community in Augsburg. Advocating the marriage of clergy, Rhegius himself wed a prominent Augsburg woman in the same month that Luther was married in Wittenberg. He also became a contested figure in the sacramental controversy which divided followers of Luther and Zwingli. In 1530 Rhegius joined the cadre of Lutheran theologians who helped Melanchthon draft the *Augsburg Confession*.

As a mature reformer in northern Germany during the last decade of his life, Rhegius helped to consolidate the Reformation in a much larger, mostly rural area. As superintendent of the church in Lower Saxony, he wrote catechisms, exegetical studies, polemical tracts, church orders, and pastoral treatises. He was personally involved in the process of installing the Reformation in towns like Hanover and Lüneburg. Rhegius was thus a major contributor to the course of confessionalization which made that area Lutheran, and he was hailed by Luther as bishop of Lower Saxony.[1]

During his years in the north, Rhegius certainly thought of himself as Lutheran, although he never set foot in Wittenberg. He was a great admirer of Luther, stopping to see him at the Coburg in 1530 and calling him a theologian without equal for the entire world.[2] At the Diet of Schmalkald in 1537 Rhegius not only worked together with Melanchthon and the other theologians present, but he also signed both Luther's *Schmalkald Articles* and Melanchthon's *Treatise on the Power and Primacy of the Pope*. Although Rhegius felt connected to the Wittenbergers and saw himself as part of their movement,[3] he fashioned a theology which bore the imprint of his own experience. Never occupying an academic chair but always active as a pastor on the front line of the Reformation, Rhegius developed a version of Lutheran theology which emphasized its pastoral and confessional character but still left room for Protestant unity.

This theology is contained in a collection of over ninety manuscripts and more than one hundred and forty printed works, as counted by Liebmann in the only reliable modern bibliography of Rhegius's corpus.[4] Some of the printed works became quite popular and appeared in numerous editions and translations. His defense of Protestant theology against the charge that it was a new and thus heretical teaching (*Nova Doctrina* 1526) appeared in eight editions, including English and Spanish versions. His treatise for the consolation of the sick and dying (*Seelenärtznei* 1529) was a bestseller in its day. It was published in ninety editions and appeared in ten languages. A manual for young preachers, designed by Rhegius to help them explain the evangelical message clearly and accurately (*Formula quaedam caute* 1535), was frequently reprinted in Latin and German and translated into Polish and Swedish. After his death in Celle in 1541, the German and Latin works of Rhegius were collected by his son Ernest and published in two large volumes in Nuremberg in 1562. In all these formats the works of Rhegius continued to exercise influence after his death, but so few of them were published or translated that his theology remains little known.

The Young Scholar (1508–1521)

As a young man, Rhegius acquired a reputation as a scholar who corresponded with other humanists such as Erasmus of Rotterdam, Michael Hummelberg, and Joachim Vadian. He studied the liberal arts and theology at four universities: Freiburg (1508–12), Ingolstadt (1512–18), Tübingen (1519), and Basel (1520). In Freiburg, he met two men who would later become vigorous opponents of Luther and his own adversaries: John Eck, whom he admired and followed to Ingolstadt, and John Faber, with whom Rhegius lived in Constance in 1519 and who later became Bishop of Vienna. In Ingolstadt, Rhegius attached himself to the humanist sodality of John Aventinus and delivered lectures on works by Franciscus Philelphus and Jacques Lefèvre d'Etaples. At Ingolstadt he also earned the master's degree and received from Emperor Maximilian the title of poet laureate. Like many humanists the young scholar, who was born Urban Rieger in Langenargen on Lake Constance, now began to use the Latinized form of his name.[5]

From 1508 to 1520 Rhegius also acquired the tools and resources that would mark his theological and reforming work in the years to come. He was well trained in scholastic theology by Eck, and he put that training to good use in later disputes, even against Eck himself. His humanist education endowed him with a thorough knowledge of Greek and Hebrew, and he became so well acquainted with the Bible and the church fathers that he was able to cite them copiously in his works. While preparing for his ordination in Constance in 1519, Rhegius produced his earliest theological texts. First, he wrote a book on the dignity of the priesthood and then, as he observed the poor quality of many ordinands, he revised a textbook of pastoral care and issued it as a manual for priests in the diocese of Constance. The son of a priest himself, Rhegius was especially concerned about the quality and preparation of clergy. Even later, as a Protestant pastor, he devoted much of his energy to the training of clergy, both supervising their ministries and writing doctrinal and biblical studies for their edification. In 1520, Rhegius the scholar-priest completed his formal education by fulfilling in Basel the requirements for a doctorate in theology.[6]

Convert to Luther (1521–1522)

Now that he possessed the necessary credentials, Rhegius was able to accept a call to become the cathedral preacher in Augsburg. When he arrived in this city in late 1520, the trial of Martin Luther was nearing its climax, and one of his first duties was to read from the pulpit the papal bull, *Exsurge domine*, which threatened Luther with excommunication. The bull was unpopular with members of the cathedral chapter and Rhegius apparently had his own doubts about it, but he did his duty nonetheless. It was not long, however, before he was speaking and writing publicly in favor of Luther. In a pseudonymous pamphlet from the summer of 1521, Rhegius argued that the papal bull itself, and not Luther's writings, presented the real threat to the church.[7] By that time he had already alarmed the cathedral canons by preaching a sermon against indulgences.[8] In good evangelical fashion, Rhegius proclaimed that the only true indulgence was grace issuing from the cross of Christ and received in faith.[9] As he continued to preach on evangelical themes, Rhegius requested a leave of absence from Augsburg that ended with his replacement as cathedral preacher in 1522. By this time Rhegius had become a follower of Luther, and his evangelical preaching at Hall in Tirol led to his removal from that position as well in 1523.

The twelve pamphlets published by Rhegius during 1521 and 1522 included three pseudonymous works in support of Luther. The subtitle of his attack on *Exsurge domine* not only proposed to defend Luther but also posed a challenge that would occupy Rhegius for much of his ministry: "One ascribes to Luther things which he does not say or does not say exactly that way. For there are few scholars who understand him correctly, not to mention the common folk. He bases [his teaching] on the holy scripture – the prophets, evangelists, and apostles – according to their correct meaning, but his opponents are stuck in human opinions."[10] In several pamphlets that appeared later during his career, Rhegius strove to defend Luther and to clarify what he taught by refuting misunderstandings and distortions and by offering numerous citations from Scripture in support of the evangelical message.

In this first attempt, Rhegius demonstrated that he was acquainted with at least thirteen of Luther's writings[11] and that he was able to explain and defend Luther's teaching on a wide range of topics: sacraments and the Mass, confession, purgatory, indulgences, veneration of the saints, faith and works, free will, and the church.[12] Rhegius argued that Luther acted "like a good pastor" and was moved "by Christian indignation" when he offered the *Ninety-five Theses* for debate, because he saw how the indulgence preachers paid no attention to the gospel and spread lies among the people.[13] He also refuted the charge that Luther was against the priesthood. On the contrary, said Rhegius, Luther was attacking only the Roman hierarchy and its parasites, not pious priests, who would be a lot better off without the others. Luther's only target was abuse of the priestly office because he was really trying to portray the true dignity of the priesthood.[14] Rhegius was obviously impressed by the biblical basis of Luther's teaching and by its pastoral effect. No doctor in hundreds of years, he wrote, had with more profitable diligence caused consciences to be reconciled and cleansed than Doctor Luther.[15]

Preacher in Augsburg (1523–1530)

In 1523, Rhegius began to preach in the Carmelite Church of St. Anna at the invitation of the city council. That same year he also published two summaries of evangelical theology in Augsburg: *A Short Explanation of Some Common Points of Scripture,*[16] which discussed 48 topics in the manner of *loci communes*, and *The Twelve Articles of Our Christian Faith with Reference to the Scripture on Which They Are Based,*[17] an exposition of the Apostles' Creed. After he settled in Augsburg in 1524, he also preached for a while at St. Moritz at the behest of the Fuggers, who were the patrons of that pulpit. For most of his time in Augsburg, however, Rhegius preached at St. Anna where, in the beginning, he also held popular lectures on the Pauline epistles. In 1525 Rhegius dramatically demonstrated his adherence to the evangelical movement and its theology. On the Friday after Corpus Christi he was married to Anna Weisbrucker by his colleague at St. Anna and the former prior of its Carmelite monastery, Johann Frosch, at whose own wedding Rhegius had presided three months earlier. Then, on the Christmas following, the two pastors administered the Sacrament of the altar in both kinds for the first time formally and publicly in Augsburg. It was reported that the communicants actually touched the elements and that private confession was not required ahead of time.[18]

The period that Rhegius spent as a pastor in Augsburg coincided with the rapid expansion and diversification of the evangelical movement. The reform in Wittenberg had taken a conservative turn after Luther resumed its leadership at the expense of Andrew Karlstadt. The multiple challenges from the peasants, the Anabaptists, and Zwingli were still to come. In Augsburg, where Luther had disciples like Rhegius and his colleagues, the challenges were especially sharp, because the city refused to commit itself to one religious party and the popular preacher at St. Moritz, Michael Keller, was an avid supporter of Zwingli. In this unsettled milieu, Rhegius, whom the council viewed as the leader of the clergy, had to decide what kind of theology and practice he would advocate and seek to install. As a consequence, he began to develop the accents of his own theology even as he continued to explain and defend the evangelical movement as a whole.

In response to the peasants, Rhegius actually departed little from the position of Luther. In fact, his pamphlet on the subject of serfdom[19] was recommended by Luther to those who wanted to know more about the topic than he said in response to the 12 articles of the peasants in Swabia.[20] Rhegius was one of the earliest theologians to comment in print on the escalation of the revolt; this happened after his sermon on Romans 13 in February 1525 led to accusations that he had turned against the common people. In response to those accusations, he attempted to explain the nature of Christian freedom and define the duties of rulers and subjects. In effect, Rhegius drew a sharp distinction between the temporal and the spiritual kingdoms. Arguing that serfdom was an external matter which belonged to the kingdom of the world, he maintained that Christians could live as serfs without undermining their freedom as Christians. That freedom was based on faith and belonged to the spiritual kingdom which alone determined their relationship to God. Although Rhegius admonished the authorities to treat their subjects with love, which he named the guideline for Christians in all relationships, he nevertheless advocated the practice of love and justice within the prevailing structures and not as a political program to change them.[21] Authorities were obliged to work for the good of their subjects and the latter were obliged to obey and not to rebel against them.

While the experience of Rhegius with the Revolution of 1525 was mainly a literary one, he was more personally involved with the Anabaptist community, which remained unmolested by the city council until 1527. In this benign environment the community had grown apace, attracting adherents and radical leaders from outside the city like Ludwig Hätzer, Hans Denck, Balthasar Hubmaier, and Hans Hut. Rhegius crossed swords with all of these, or tried to. When Hätzer arrived in Augsburg from Zurich in 1525, he became a spokesperson for the earliest radicals in the city, calling for strict moral conduct and the sharing of goods. After Hätzer criticized one of his sermons, Rhegius challenged him to a disputation, but Hätzer failed to show up and the council evicted him from the city.[22] In 1526 Denck was baptized in Augsburg, perhaps by Hubmaier, and was actively teaching and publishing there. The conflict with Rhegius was caused by Denck's advocacy of universal salvation, which implied that even the devil would be saved. Invited to a public debate before the council, Denck chose to leave the city in secret beforehand.[23] Rhegius also reports one encounter with Balthasar Hubmaier, whom he had known in Freiburg and Ingolstadt and whom he held mainly responsible for the errant theology of the Augsburg Anabaptists. Rhegius reported to John Eck, with whom both had studied, that he tried to change Hubmaier's mind but failed.[24] Finally, Hut, who was baptized by Denck at Pentecost 1526, stopped in Augsburg for brief periods before he was arrested in late 1527 and interrogated by Rhegius and the other preachers.

In the meantime, Anabaptists in Augsburg were producing local leaders and meeting in private according to their conviction that the new evangelical church was a simple fellowship of brothers and sisters bound to give evidence of their improved Christian life.[25] Then, in August 1527, the so-called Martyrs' Synod drew Hut, Denck, and other radicals back to Augsburg to coordinate a mission of Anabaptist apostles. At this meeting Hut and Denck settled a controversy between them over the second coming of Christ. Hut had prophesied that Christ would return three or four years after the end of the revolution, but he agreed to preach this message only to those who wanted to hear it. A copy of this agreement carried by Hut and other apostles was later published with a critique by Rhegius.[26] In September, the council began to break up meetings and to make arrests, and at this point Rhegius became involved again. The people who were apprehended had to swear not to attend any more Anabaptist meetings, and those who would not take the oath had to leave the city. Those who remained, along with Hut and three other leaders, were forced to meet with the preachers, including Rhegius, who tried to convince them to recant their views and to resume their place in the evangelical churches. Many of the Anabaptists eventually complied, but Hut was overcome by smoke in his cell and died in December.

In connection with these events, Rhegius published three works against the Anabaptists in 1527 and 1528. The last of these was his commentary on Hut's account of his agreement with Denck.[27] Rhegius accused Hut of hiding the date of the Last Judgment, which he pretended to know, from ordinary Christians, when instead he ought to reveal it so that everyone could prepare for the end. Rhegius also believed he was living in the last days of the world, but he contended that no date had been revealed and that all Christians should await that day in confidence bestowed by their faith in Christ. In addition, Rhegius charged that Hut distorted the faith by insisting that the first duty of Christians was to follow the life and example of Christ. That, he said, was to make Christianity a religion of external works and to promote a new kind of "monkery." Less than a year earlier, in his *Necessary Warning to all Faithful Christians against the New Baptizing Order* (1527),[28] Rhegius had accused the Anabaptists of trying to create communities of perfect Christians like the monastic orders before them and of claiming that other people in Augsburg had failed to show any improvement after having heard the gospel from preachers like Rhegius. In reply, Rhegius alleged that the Anabaptists could not tolerate any weakness among Christians and he reminded them that the church was a mixed body in which God's children were dispersed among a crowd of unbelievers.[29] Rhegius was not the only theologian to tar the Anabaptists with the brush of monasticism, but he made this argument more elaborately than many others. Behind this argument lay his concern that Anabaptists were undermining the Reformation of society as a whole and that they threatened to turn the good news of freedom in Christ into a new bondage of legalism and perfectionism.

Rhegius's stance in the controversy between Zwingli and Luther has been the object of considerable analysis. Gerhard Uhlhorn argued that Rhegius's early theology was thoroughly Lutheran but that he was unclear about the necessity of the Sacrament and thus allowed a Zwinglian view of the Lord's Supper, which he never fully adopted, to lodge itself briefly in his theology.[30] In response to Uhlhorn, Otto Seitz contended that the so-called Lutheran views of the early Rhegius were generically evangelical and that Rhegius exalted Scripture as a formal principle of theology more strictly than did Luther. Together with his high opinion of Jerome and Erasmus, this adherence to Scripture reflected his humanist values and placed him nearer to Zwingli than to Luther.[31] Consequently, his sympathy for the Zwinglian view of the Supper in 1526 did not require a theological conversion from Luther and that sympathy was not a foreign body in his teaching. In Seitz's opinion, Rhegius genuinely shared Zwingli's view of the Supper until he was forced by the radicals to take a more mediating stance.[32]

Both Uhlhorn and Seitz treated the views of Zwingli and Luther as the only sides of the controversy and tried to fit Rhegius into their reconstruction of it.[33] It seems clear, however, that Rhegius was trying to avoid such categorization altogether. True, his tendency to exalt both Luther and Zwingli has encouraged the attempt to place him in the camp of one reformer or the other. The evidence, however, suggests that Rhegius appreciated the concerns which lay behind the assertions of both sides.

His rebuttal of Karlstadt, the first pamphlet issued against the former Wittenberger (1524),[34] indicates that Rhegius, like Luther, placed a high value on the external means of grace. Christians needed to cling to external signs, like bread and wine, which themselves contained and signified spiritual things. At the same time, Rhegius also realized with Zwingli that emphasizing a physical presence of Christ in the elements could promote popular superstitions connected with transubstantiation. Rhegius may have shied away from that emphasis after the publication in Augsburg of Eck's book on the sacrifice of the Mass intensified Catholic pressure on the evangelical movement.[35] In his *Nova doctrina*, Rhegius polemicized against the Mass as a repetitive sacrifice and stressed that faith was the true eating and drinking of Christ through which forgiveness for all sin was received.[36] The bodily presence of Christ was not an issue for Rhegius in *Nova Doctrina*; it was more important to take a decisive evangelical stand against Rome than to choose between Luther and Zwingli.

That stance remained his priority during the last three years in Augsburg. Rhegius never did take a public stand for Luther or Zwingli but sought instead a position that was consistent with his respect for both Reformers and beneficial to the movement as a whole. In 1528 he wrote that the peaceful leadership of the church was his only goal.[37] That goal led to his involvement in a statement on the Lord's Supper that might be acceptable to Lutheran and Zwinglian preachers alike;[38] it also moved him to concentrate on teaching laypeople the importance of preparing properly for the Sacrament.[39] Although his encounter with the Anabaptists may have moved Rhegius closer to Luther,[40] in Augsburg Rhegius was not thinking in terms of installing a Lutheran instead of a Zwinglian Reformation. He wanted to assure the survival of an evangelical movement that would withstand the challenge from Catholics on the right and from Anabaptists on the left. For that reason he was dismayed when he learned that Augsburg did not join the protest against the declaration of the Diet at Speyer in 1529, and he expressed that dismay to Philip of Hesse, whose efforts at Protestant unity he supported with enthusiasm.[41]

Confessional Theologian (1530–1531)

In 1530 and 1531, several events besides his alleged "initiation" at the Coburg[42] prompted Rhegius to adopt a more self-consciously Lutheran theological stance. The submission of the *Augsburg Confession* and its gradual acceptance as the basis of a distinct Lutheran coalition was soon to make Rhegius, like many others, part of this new confessional movement. Rhegius was present at the final editorial meeting of princes and theologians on June 23, 1530. Before that meeting, he persuaded Philip of Hesse, with whom he had formed a good relationship, to sign the *Confession*. Although the Marburg Colloquy, which Rhegius was unable to attend, had failed to bring agreement on the presence of Christ between Luther and Zwingli, Rhegius promised Philip that he would support further efforts to reach that goal.[43] Rhegius did help to arrange negotiations between Philip Melanchthon and Martin Bucer in Augsburg, and in August, 1530, Rhegius carried letters from both theologians to Luther at the Coburg along with theses on the Sacrament which each had formulated. When Luther rejected this attempt at a compromise, however, Rhegius took the side of Luther without giving up hope for the kind of concord that was eventually reached at Wittenberg in 1536.

During the negotiations that were held after the *Confession* was presented, Rhegius had been a firm supporter of Melanchthon. He recalled their strategy in a memorandum which he prepared for a colloquy in 1539, commenting that in 1530 the papists, as he called them, had been more conciliatory than they were at present.[44] He and Melanchthon had decided they would accept an agreement if the Catholic side conceded the following: the prophetic and apostolic doctrine which the evangelical side said it could not surrender without denying Christ and, in external matters, the marriage of priests and monks, the evangelical Mass, and reception of both elements in the Lord's Supper. In return, recalled Rhegius, the Protestants would submit to the episcopal jurisdiction for which the Catholics fought so strenuously and which he and Melanchthon thought would help to contain both sacramentarians and Anabaptists.

The final event that moved Rhegius in a more Lutheran direction was his acceptance of the invitation from Duke Ernest of Lüneburg, whom he met at the Diet, to take over the consolidation of the Reformation in his North German territory. Together with his brother Francis, Duke Ernest had signed the *Augsburg Confession* and his unwavering support for it earned him the sobriquet "Ernest the Confessor." In Lüneburg the *Augsburg Confession* gradually became a standard of faith and practice that would guide the work of Rhegius.[45] In late 1530, Rhegius and his household moved to Celle near Hanover. Unlike his position in Augsburg as one preacher among others in a town with no official Protestant allegiance, Rhegius now became the superintendent of a clergy spread across a large territory whose princes were prominent leaders in the Lutheran movement.

Hellmut Zschoch has clarified what it means to call Rhegius a confessional theologian at the end of his Augsburg years.[46] He did not become so Lutheran that he despaired of the Protestant unity which he had worked so hard to maintain in Augsburg. The essence of Reformation theology was for him the doctrine of justification, and this doctrine was the dividing line between the genuine evangelical substance of Christianity and what was unevangelical and thus not genuinely Christian. Intra-Protestant differences over the Lord's Supper were less important to him than the preservation of that central Reformation insight which defined both the new life in faith and the new evangelical churches he would now supervise. For him the confessional divide lay between Protestant and Catholic and not between Reformed and Lutheran, although Rhegius certainly identified with the Lutheran majority in northern Germany, where he now headed.

Superintendent in Northern Germany (1531–1541)

To build up the Protestant churches around his new home, Rhegius focused on two tasks: first, to bring the Reformation to those areas and communities that were still Catholic and, second, to train a skilled corps of clergy that would present the evangelical message clearly and convince people to make changes which were called for by the gospel. These tasks shaped his mature theology in complementary ways.

In both cases he had to advance a polemical theology which demonstrated why Catholic theology was wrong and why Protestant theology was the correct reading of Scripture. This project required Rhegius, as it had in Augsburg, to offer ample citations from Scripture and the church fathers as proof that the new Protestant theology was in fact the authentic old faith of early Christianity. In this missionary situation, as it were, Rhegius continued to focus on those points which divided Protestants from Catholics and not on intra-Protestant issues. There were a few exceptions, such as his rejection of the Anabaptist chiliasm at Münster. But on the whole, even when he was instructing young pastors how to preach the evangelical message clearly and wisely, he focussed on the common core of Reformation themes related to justification by faith.

The homiletical manual composed by Rhegius for those pastors is the best illustration of how his theology was shaped by the tasks now facing him. Rhegius entitled it bluntly: *How to Speak Cautiously and without Giving Offense about the Chief Articles of Christian Doctrine* (1535). He had heard so many one-sided distortions of the evangelical message, he claimed, that he wrote up and published some notes that he used as a guide for preaching Protestant themes in a full and balanced way. The fact that it became his second most popular work indicates that it was not enough for university professors to expound upon the new theology in their lectures and commentaries, but that scholar-pastors like Rhegius had to provide handbooks that would tell young preachers how to proclaim and practice it. He treated those topics which were easily misunderstood by new Protestants because they dealt with changes in thinking and practice that needed to be made in evangelical parishes. The topics were: repentance, faith, good works, merit, the Mass, law, free will, predestination, Christian freedom, authority, how everyone is taught by God, satisfaction, virginity, confession, human regulations, fasting, prayer, invoking the saints, images, rituals, and burial. The scope of this treatise was typical of Rhegius's writings, and its content reveals much about the shape and the style of his mature thought.

Most of all, Rhegius was concerned that faith not be misunderstood as a stance that eliminates the need for either repentance or good works. In the case of repentance, he cited here and elsewhere in his writings a portion of the last words of Jesus in the gospel of Luke (24:47): "that repentance and forgiveness of sins is to be proclaimed in his name to all nations, beginning from Jerusalem." Forgiveness of sins always has to be preceded by repentance, argued Rhegius on the basis of this verse. "People who do not first acknowledge their own manifold sin and also believe the pure grace of God in Christ our Lord, without any pretending at all, remain stuck in their sins and impenitence and are certainly not Christians, even if they are able to speak and write profusely about the gospel."[47] On the necessity of preaching repentance Rhegius was in agreement with the position of Luther and Melanchthon against John Agricola in the first so-called antinomian controversy in Wittenberg (1527–8). It is uncertain how directly he was acquainted with that conflict, but he had definitely read the *Instruction of the Visitors*, composed by the two Wittenbergers for the visitations in Saxony, which also invoked Luke 24:47 for the necessity of repentance.[48]

Rhegius was equally concerned to show that justification by faith did not mean Christians should avoid good works. On this point he shared the frustration of many

Protestant clergy, who found that parishioners heard their sermons against works righteousness as a do-nothing message. This emphasis on good works as well as repentance was, in the judgment of Hans-Walter Krumwiede, typical of Rhegius's theology and gave the Lutheran tradition of Lower Saxony an emphasis which differed from the Wittenberg theology. Krumwiede believed that Rhegius, by refusing to systematize Luther's theology, allowed its paradoxical elements to stand side by side in preaching, just as they coexisted in the Christian life.[49] A similar opinion was held by Hans-Emil Weber, who declared that Rhegius was less interested in true doctrine than he was in righteous living.[50] The emphasis which Rhegius placed on the necessity of good works may well have established a theological direction for the Lower Saxon churches that would later be followed at Helmstedt by Georg Calixt.[51] Nevertheless, this ethical accent was less of a systematic decision to allow paradoxes to stand than it was a consequence of his effort to head off a shallow appropriation of the evangelical message.

While Rhegius was not interested in true doctrine as a comprehensive systematic theology which he, like Luther, never wrote, he was very much concerned to demonstrate that Protestant doctrine was true in the sense that it conformed to Scripture and the early church fathers. Rhegius himself knew both biblical languages and exhibited a special fondness for Hebrew. He urged pastors to read a chapter from the Old Testament in Hebrew every day and to compare the Hebrew text with the Greek version. In the numerous exegetical works that came from his pen, one can find two principles at work.[52] The apostolic principle sought agreement between the Testaments, using the New Testament to interpret the Old and the Old Testament to confirm the New. A striking example is the enormous catalog of messianic prophecies from the Old Testament which Rhegius identified as "the things concerning himself in all the Scriptures" that Jesus taught the disciples on the road to Emmaus.[53] The catechetical principle sought the support of early Christian doctrine for the evangelical interpretation of Scripture. Rhegius argued that a proper understanding of Scripture was not to be found outside the Catholic church, meaning the doctrine of the ecumenical creeds and the early Fathers. Rhegius had learned the typical humanist's appreciation for the church fathers, but he was forced to study them more intensively in Augsburg in order to rebut Eck's arguments for the Mass as a sacrifice.[54] That study eventually produced a thick topical compendium of citations from the church fathers and later theologians which he consulted frequently. After his death it was published by his admirer and translator, Johannes Freder.[55]

The collection of messianic prophecies also served another piece of Rhegius's theological agenda. Along with many Protestant reformers, Rhegius hoped for the conversion of European Jews to Christianity now that the evangelical heart of the faith had been recovered and made available to them. Like Luther, he was disappointed that such a conversion did not take place, but he engaged in dialogue with rabbis nonetheless. At the Diet of Augsburg in 1530, Rhegius debated the exegesis of Isaiah 53 and Daniel 7 with a rabbi from Prague. During the debate he gave evidence that he had studied rabbinic exegesis and was acquainted with Jewish anti-Christian apologetic. The messianic prophecies collected and published by him not only served to answer that apologetic but also to prepare him and other theologians for debates with Jewish scholars. Although his conversations with such scholars in Hanover and

Braunschweig failed to change any minds, Rhegius did intercede for a rabbi and the Jewish community in Braunschweig in 1539 and 1540.[56] In letters to the city council he asked that a certain Rabbi Samuel be allowed to live in the town where he was already teaching Hebrew. He then asked the Lutheran clergy to give up their anti-Jewish stance and to support a policy of keeping the Jewish community in Braunschweig. Rhegius argued for toleration because he still hoped that Jews would be converted to Christianity if they were instructed and treated properly. On this issue he was notably less hostile than many of his colleagues.

Rhegius's treatment of other theological topics was also influenced by the challenges of the 1530s. He commented on the sacraments, for example, mainly in polemical contexts, defending the reception of both elements against Catholics in Lüneburg and infant baptism against the Münsterites. As arguments for infant baptism Rhegius offered both its parallel to circumcision in the Jewish people and the need of children as well as adults to be reborn out of sin and to receive the grace of the Holy Spirit.[57] In the town of Lüneburg, which Rhegius visited on three occasions in 1531 and 1532 in order to establish the Reformation, he engaged in two controversies over the Lord's Supper. In one he strongly rejected, as he had done in Augsburg, the Mass as a sacrifice, and in the other he defended the distribution of both elements to the laity.[58] In neither case did Rhegius emphasize the real bodily presence of Christ in the elements, focussing instead on the Eucharist as thanksgiving for the all-sufficient sacrifice of Christ on the cross and its power to forgive sin and to strengthen faith. In one of his catechisms, however, he did define the Lord's Supper clearly as "the true body and blood of our Lord Jesus Christ, under the bread and wine, instituted by Christ himself, so that Christians may eat and drink it in remembrance of Christ, announcing his death until he comes."[59]

Since Catholics were his main polemical target during these years, the nature of the true church also emerged as a prominent theme. The church order that he wrote for the city of Hanover in 1536 was more like an ecclesiological treatise than a code of liturgy and administration. In it Rhegius defined the true church as "the spiritual assembly of the children of God or faithful in Christ throughout the world, out of Jews and gentiles, in one faith, hope, and love of the Spirit, which Christ gathers, sanctifies, and upholds through his word, . . ."[60] Rhegius argued that this true church was now represented in the evangelical churches which had defined themselves by the *Augsburg Confession* of 1530. As the decade proceeded, he gave up on reconciliation with Rome and eventually denied to the Catholic party the name of church. When they recalled the statement of Augustine that he would not have believed the gospel unless the church had taught him, Rhegius replied that the Word still took precedence over the church. The latter only testifies to the Word through which it was brought into being in the first place, and cannot change that Word, much as a messenger, who receives a message directly from a prince, afterwards testifies that it is the prince's command without thinking he can change it.[61] His conviction that Christians were living at the end of the world and that the Antichrist was afoot also prompted Rhegius to draw this sharp distinction between the true and false churches. It was necessary to know where true Christendom was to be found, he said, "especially now in the last days . . . when everybody wants to be the Christian church even when they live worse than Turks and pagans."[62]

Influential Reformer

It is difficult to assess the influence of Rhegius with precision, but it was certainly greater than the modern awareness of him suggests. Viewed as a major Lutheran reformer, he was responsible for the spread and establishment of the Wittenberg Reformation in Lower Saxony. Rhegius was more than a Lutheran reformer, however. He saw himself primarily as an evangelical pastor and theologian whose main goal was to establish the Protestant Reformation wherever he was at work. In Augsburg that meant ensuring the survival of a diverse evangelical movement in a city that was not yet committed to it. In the 1530s it meant expanding and protecting the existence of Protestantism in the north, primarily against Catholic resistance at the local and imperial levels. Rhegius's theology was Lutheran, but the practical nature of his reforming work on behalf of Protestant unity and expansion bestowed on that theology some features which would be seen as less typically Lutheran when Protestant unity in Germany deteriorated after the 1540s. Some of his works did leave traces of their popularity. The *Formulae quaedam caute* became part of two normative theological collections of Lower Saxony,[63] and in 1580 his "useful writings," along with the those of Melanchthon, Brenz, and Bugenhagen, were recommended in the prefaces to the *Formula* and *Book of Concord*.[64] Some of his writings were reissued in many editions and translated into other European languages. Most important of all, perhaps, the theology of Rhegius demonstrates how it is possible to be ecumenically open and confessionally aware at the same time, and how that combination both arises from, and contributes to, effective Christian ministry.

Notes

1 *WA* 53:399.

2 *Iudicium D. Urbani Rhegii de D. Martino Luthero*, printed at the end of *Loci theologici e patribus et scholasticis neotericisque collecti per D. Urbanum Rhegium*, ed. Johann Freder (Frankfurt: Peter Brubach, 1545), 251v–252r.

3 Scott Hendrix, "Die Bedeutung des Urbanus Rhegius für die Ausbreitung der Wittenberger Reformation" in Michael Beyer and Günther Wartenberg, eds., *Humanismus und Wittenberger Reformation* (Leipzig: Evangelische Verlagsanstalt, 1996), 53–72.

4 Maximilian Liebmann, *Urbanus Rhegius und die Anfänge der Reformation: Beiträge zu seinem Leben, seiner Lehre und seinem Wirken bis zum Augsburger Reichstag von 1530 mit einer Bibliographie seiner Schriften* (Münster: Aschendorff, 1980), 319–434. This bibliography contains some of the letters of Rhegius but no complete list or critical edition of his correspondence has been published.

5 Liebmann, *Urbanus Rhegius*, 76–7.

6 Ibid., 108–11.

7 *Anzaygung dasz die Romisch Bull mercklichen schaden in gewissin manicher menschen gebracht hab und nit doctor Luthers leer durch Henricum Phoeniceum von Roschach* (Augsburg: Sigmund Grimm, 1521).

8 *Ain Sermon von dem hochwirdigen sacrament des Altars gepredigt durch Doctor Urbanum Regium* (Augsburg: Silvan Otmar, 1521).

9 Liebmann, *Urbanus Rhegius*, 144.

10 *Anzaygung dasz die Romisch Bull*, Ai.

11 Liebmann, *Urbanus Rhegius*, 149–50.

12 Ibid., 151–2.

13 *Anzaygung dasz die Romisch Bull*, Aiii.

14 Ibid., Aiv^v.

15 Ibid., Aii^v.

16 *Ain kurtze erklärung ettlicher leüffiger puncten aim yeden Christen nutz vnd not zu rechtem verstand der hailigen geschryfft zu dienst* (Augsburg: Sigmund Grimm, Simprecht Ruff, & Philipp Ulhart, 1523).

17 *Die zwolff artickel unsers Christlichen glaubens mit anzaigung der hailigen geschrifft darinn sie gegründt seind* (Augsburg: Sigmund Grimm, 1523).

18 Liebmann, *Urbanus Rhegius*, 196–7.

19 *Von leibaygenschafft oder knechthait wie sich Herren vnnd aygen leüt Christlich halten sollend Bericht auss gotlichem Rechten* (Augsburg: Heinrich Steiner, 1525); reprinted in Adolf Laube and H. W. Seiffert, eds., *Flugschriften der Bauernkriegszeit*, 2nd ed. (Berlin: Akademie Verlag, 1978), 242–60.

20 Luther, *Ermahnung zum Frieden*, WA 18:327. Cf. *LW* 46:39.

21 Hellmut Zschoch, *Reformatorische Existenz und konfessionelle Identität* (Tübingen: Mohr [Siebeck], 1995), 109–20. Robert Kolb, "The Theologians and the Peasants: Conservative Evangelical Reactions to the German Peasants' Revolt," *ARG* 69 (1978), 103–31.

22 Zschoch, *Reformatorische Existenz*, 220.

23 Ibid., 223–4.

24 Ibid., 224–7.

25 Friedwart Uhland, "Täufertum und Obrigkeit in Augsburg im 16. Jahrhundert" (Ph.D. dissertation, University of Tübingen, 1972).

26 *Ein sendbrieff Hans huthen etwa ains furnemen Uorsteers im widertauffer ordenn. Uerantwortet durch Urbanum Rhegium* (Augsburg: Alexander Weissenhorn, 1528), reprinted without the commentary of Rhegius in Adolf Laube, ed., *Flugschriften vom Bauernkrieg zum Täuferreich (1526–1535)*, 2 vols. (Berlin: Akademie Verlag, 1992), 1:858–61.

27 See n. 26. In 1528 Rhegius also published with a rebuttal two anonymous open letters directed at the Anabaptist community in Augsburg: *Zwen wunderseltzam sendbrieff zweyer Widertauffer an ire Rotten gen Augspurg gesandt. Verantwurtung aller irrthum diser obgenanten brieff durch Vrbanum Rhegium* (Augsburg: Alexander Weissenhorn, 1528). The two letters are reprinted in Laube, ed., *Flugschriften vom Bauernkrieg zum Täuferreich*, 1:832–57.

28 *Wider den newen Taufforden Notwendige Warnung an alle Christgleubigen Durch die diener des Euangelij zu Augspurg* (Augsburg: Heinrich Steiner, 1527); reprinted in Laube, ed., *Flugschriften vom Bauernkrieg zum Täuferreich*, 2:1167–248.

29 Laube, ed., *Flugschriften vom Bauernkrieg zum Täuferreich*, 2:1186, 10–17; 1188, 37–1189, 1.

30 Gerhard Uhlhorn, *Urbanus Rhegius: Leben und ausgewählte Schriften* (Elberfeld: R. L. Friderichs, 1861), 85, 103–4.

31 Otto Seitz, *Die Theologie des Urbanus Rhegius speziell sein Verhältnis zu Luther und zu Zwingli* (Gotha: F. A. Perthes, 1898), 27–8, 39–40, 45–6.

32 Ibid., 91, 96.

33 Zschoch, *Reformatorische Existenz*, 165–9.

34 *Wider den newen irrsal Doctor Andres von Carlstadt des Sacraments halb warnung* (Augsburg: Sigmund Grimm & Simprecht Ruff, 1524).

35 Letter of Rhegius to Ambrosius and Thomas Blaurer, June 14, 1526, in Traugott Schiess, ed., *Briefwechsel der Brüder Ambrosius und Thomas Blaurer 1509–1548*, vol. 1 (Freiburg: F. E. Fehsenfeld, 1908), 134.

36 *Nova Doctrina per Urbanum Rhegium* (Augsburg: Sigmund Grimm, Simprecht Ruff, & Philipp Ulhart, 1526), C2ᵛ.

37 Letter of Rhegius to Ambrosius Blaurer, December 21, 1528, in *Briefwechsel der Brüder Blaurer*, 1:175.

38 *Verainigung der ewangelischen praedicanten zu Augspurg* (April 15, 1527) in *CR* 96:136–7 (No. 619: Beilage).

39 *Prob zu des herrn nachtmal für die eynfeltigen Durch Urbanum Rhegium* (Augsburg: Heinrich Steiner, 1528).

40 Zschoch, *Reformatorische Existenz*, 312.

41 Letter of Rhegius to Philip of Hesse, April 30, 1529, in Hessisches Staatsarchiv Marburg, PA 1429, fol. 3r f. Zschoch, *Reformatorische Existenz*, 5: "He [Rhegius] was with the greatest intensity a theologian of 'evangelical unity.'"

42 Uhlhorn, *Urbanus Rhegius*, 160: "The day at Coburg was like an initiation [Weihe] that Rhegius took with him into his new sphere of activity."

43 Letter of Rhegius to Luther, May 21, 1530, in *WA Br* 5:334, 11–25.

44 *Iudicium Urbani Regii de doctorum conventu Norebergae habendo* (1539), in *Opera Urbani Regii latine edita* (Nuremberg: Johann vom Berg & Ulrich Neuber, 1562), Part III, IXᵛ.

45 Scott Hendrix, "Urbanus Rhegius and the Augsburg Confession," *SCJ* 11 (1980), 63–74.

46 Zschoch, *Reformatorische Existenz*, 4–5.

47 *Wie man fürsichtiglich und ohne Ärgerniss reden soll von den fürnemesten Artickeln Christlicher Lehre (Formulae quaedam caute et citra scandalum loquendi)*, ed. Alfred Uckeley (Leipzig: A. Deichert'sche Verlagsbuchh. Nachf. [Georg Böhme], 1908), 44–5.

48 *Unterricht der Visitatoren*, in *WA* 26:202. Cf. *LW* 40:274.

49 Hans-Walter Krumwiede, "Vom reformator-ischen Glauben Luthers zur Orthodoxie: Theologische Bemerkungen zu Bugenhagens Braunschweiger Kirchenordnung und zu Urbanus Rhegius' formulae quaedam caute et citra scandalum loquendi," *Jahrbuch der Gesellschaft für niedersächsische Kirchengeschichte* 53 (1955), 46.

50 Hans Emil Weber, *Reformation, Orthodoxie und Rationalismus*, I: *Von der Reformation zur Orthodoxie* (Gütersloh: C. Bertelsmann, 1937), 193–4.

51 Inge Mager, "Reformatorische Theologie und Reformationsverständnis an der Universität Helmstedt im 16. und 17. Jahrhundert," *Jahrbuch der Gesellschaft für niedersächsische Kirchengeschichte* 74 (1976): 31.

52 Scott Hendrix, "The Use of Scripture in Establishing Protestantism: The Case of Urbanus Rhegius" in David C. Steinmetz, ed., *The Bible in the Sixteenth Century* (Durham, NC and London: Duke University Press, 1990), 41–9.

53 Rhegius, *Dialogus von der schönen predigt die Christus Luc. 24. von Jerusalem bis gen Emaus de zweien jüngern am Ostertag aus Mose und allen propheten gethan hat* (Wittenberg: Josef Klug, 1537).

54 Scott Hendrix, "Validating the Reformation: The Use of the Church Fathers by Urbanus Rhegius" in W. Brandmüller, H. Immenkötter, and E. Iserloh, eds., *Ecclesia Militans: Studien zur Konzilien- und Reformationsgeschichte*, 2 vols. (Paderborn: Schöningh, 1988), 2:281–305.

55 *Loci theologici e patribus et scholasticis neotericisque collecti per D. Urbanum Rhegium* (Frankfurt: Peter Brubach, 1545).

56 Scott Hendrix, "Toleration of the Jews in the German Reformation: Urbanus Rhegius and Braunschweig 1535–1540," *ARG* 81 (1990), 189–215.

57 *Widderlegung der Münsterischen newen Valentinianer und Donatisten bekentnus* (1535) in Robert Stupperich, ed., *Schriften von evangelischer Seite gegen die Täufer* (Münster: Aschendorff, 1983), 127–32.

58 Dieter Fabricius, *Die theologischen Kontroversen in Lüneburg im Zusammenhang mit der Einführung der Reformation* (Lüneburg: Museumsverein für das Fürstentum Lüneburg, 1988), 114–77, 152–5.

59 *Catechismus minor puerorum, generoso puero Ottoni Furster, dicatus* (Wittenberg: Johannes Luft, 1535), I^v.

60 *Kirchenordnung der statt Hannofer durch D. Urbanus Regium* (Magdeburg: Michael Lotter, 1536) in Emil Sehling, ed., *Die evangelischen Kirchenordnungen des XVI. Jahrhunderts*, VI/1/2 (Tübingen: Mohr [Siebeck], 1957), 945.

61 *Verantwortung dreyer gegenwurff der Papisten zu Braunswig* (Wittenberg: Josef Klug, 1536), Eiv.

62 *Der xv. Psalm Davids ausgelegt durch Dr. Urbanum Rhegium* (Magdeburg: Michael Lotther, 1537), Bi.

63 *The corpus doctrinae Wilhelminum* (1576) for the duchy of Lüneburg and the *corpus doctrinae Julium* (1576) for the duchy of Braunschweig-Wolfenbüttel. Hans-Walter Krumwiede, "Gesetz und Evangelium: Zur Begrifflichkeit reformatorischer Theologie in niedersächsischen Lehrschriften" in Walter Blankenburg et al., eds., *Kerygma und Melos: Christhard Mahrenholz 70 Jahre* (Kassel: Bärenreiter Verlag, 1970), 518–32.

64 *Die Bekenntnisschriften der evangelisch-lutherischen Kirche*, 6th ed. (Göttingen: Vandenhoeck & Ruprecht, 1967), 10.20–5, 752.22–7. See Robert Kolb and Timothy J. Wengert, eds., *The Book of Concord: The Confessions of the Evangelical Lutheran Church* (Minneapolis: Fortress Press, 2000).

Bibliography

Primary Sources

Jacobs, Charles M., "Sources for Lutheran History II: Sixteenth Century Preaching," *Lutheran Church Quarterly* (July 1928), 350–61. English translation of the preface to *Formulae quaedam caute* (1535).

Opera Urbani Regii latine edita cum eius vita ac prefatione Ernesti Regii, Nuremberg: Johann vom Berg & Ulrich Neuber, 1562.

Seelenärtzney für die gesunden und kranken zu disen gefärlichen zeyten (1529), in Gunther Franz, *Huberinus – Rhegius – Holbein: bibliographische und druckgeschichtliche Untersuchung der verbreitesten Trost- und Erbauungsschriften des 16. Jahrhunderts*, Nieuwkoop: De Graaf, 1973, 241–60.

Urbani Regii Weylandt Superintendenten im Fürstenthumb Lüneburg Deutsche Bücher unnd Schrifften, Nuremberg: Johann vom Berg & Ulrich Neuber, 1562.

Wie man fürsichtiglich und ohne Ärgerniss reden soll von den fürnemesten Artickeln Christlicher Lehre (Formulae quaedam caute et citra scandalum loquendi), ed. Alfred Uckeley, Leipzig: A. Deichert'sche Verlagsbuchh. Nachf. (Georg Böhme), 1908.

Secondary Sources

Fabricius, Dieter, *Die theologischen Kontroversen in Lüneburg im Zusammenhang mit der Einführung der Reformation*, Lüneburg: Museumsverein für das Fürstentum Lüneburg, 1988.

Gerecke, Richard, "Studien zu Urbanus Rhegius' kirchenregimentlicher Tätigkeit in Norddeutschland, Teil 1: Konzil und Religionsgespräche," *Jahrbuch der Gesellschaft für niedersächsische Kirchengeschichte* 74 (1976), 131–77.

——, "Studien zu Urbanus Rhegius' kirchenregimentlicher Tätigkeit in Norddeutschland, Teil 2: Die Neuordnung des Kirchenwesens in Lüneburg," *Jahrbuch der Gesellschaft für niedersächsische Kirchengeschichte* 77 (1979): 25–95.

——, "Studien zu Urbanus Rhegius' kirchenregimentlicher Tätigkeit in Norddeutschland, Teil 3: Urbanus Rhegius als Superintendent in Lüneburg (1532–1533)" in *Reformation vor 450 Jahren: eine Lüneburgische Gedenkschrift*, Lüneburg: Museumsverein für das Fürstentum Lüneburg, 1980, 71–93.

Hampton, Douglas B., "Urbanus Rhegius and the Spread of the German Reformation". Ph.D. dissertation, Ohio State University, 1973.

Hendrix, Scott, "Rhegius, Urbanus (1489–1541)" in *TRE* 29:155–7.

——, "Rhegius, Urbanus" in *OER* 3:429–30.

——, "Urbanus Rhegius and the Augsburg Confession," *SCJ* 11/3 (1980), 63–74.

——, "Validating the Reformation: The Use of the Church Fathers by Urbanus Rhegius" in W. Brandmüller, H. Immenkötter, and E. Iserloh, eds., *Ecclesia Militans: Studien zur Konzilien- und Reformationsgeschichte*, 2 vols., Paderborn: Schöningh, 1988, 2:281–305.

——, "Toleration of the Jews in the German Reformation: Urbanus Rhegius and Braunschweig 1535–1540," *ARG* 81 (1990), 189–215.

——, "The Use of Scripture in Establishing Protestantism: The Case of Urbanus Rhegius" in David C. Steinmetz, ed., *The Bible in the Sixteenth Century*, Durham, NC and London: Duke University Press, 1990, 36–49, 202–9.

——, "Die Bedeutung des Urbanus Rhegius für die Ausbreitung der Wittenberger Reformation" in Michael Beyer and Günther Wartenberg, eds., *Humanismus und Wittenberger Reformation*, Leipzig: Evangelische Verlagsanstalt, 1996, 53–72.

Krumwiede, Hans-Walter, "Vom reformatorischen Glauben Luthers zur Orthodoxie: Theologische Bemerkungen zu Bugenhagens Braunschweiger Kirchenordnung und zu Urbanus Rhegius' formulae quaedam caute et citra scandalum loquendi," *Jahrbuch der Gesellschaft für niedersächsische Kirchengeschichte* 53 (1955): 33–48.

Liebmann, Maximilian, *Urbanus Rhegius und die Anfänge der Reformation: Beiträge zu seinem Leben, seiner Lehre und seinem Wirken bis zum Augsburger Reichstag von 1530 mit einer Bibliographie seiner Schriften*, Münster: Aschendorff, 1980.

Seitz, Otto, *Die Theologie des Urbanus Rhegius speziell sein Verhältnis zu Luther und zu Zwingli*, Gotha: F. A. Perthes, 1898.

Uhlhorn, Gerhard, *Urbanus Rhegius: Leben und ausgewählte Schriften*, Elberfeld: R. L. Friderichs, 1861.

Wrede, Adolf, *Die Einführung der Reformation im Lüneburgischen durch Herzog Ernst den Bekenner*, Göttingen: Druck der Dieterich'schen Univ. Buchdruckerei, 1887.

Zschoch, Hellmut, *Reformatorische Existenz und konfessionelle Identität: Urbanus Rhegius als evangelischer Theologe in den Jahren 1520 bis 1530*, Tübingen: Mohr (Siebeck), 1995.

Johannes Brenz (1499–1570)

Hermann Ehmer

Like many of the reformers of Southwest Germany, Johannes Brenz was the son of an imperial city.[1] He was born on June 24, 1499 in Weil der Stadt, a half-day's journey west of Stuttgart, the capital of the Duchy of Württemberg, where Brenz was active in his last two decades. Brenz's parents were Martin Hess and Katharina née Hennig. The Hess family bore the cognomen Brenz, which in the generation of Johannes Brenz became the family name. The father's occupation is unknown. But he was for a long time *Schultheiss* (presiding officer) of the court in Weil, and to hold that honorable office he had to have been a man of considerable means. He was, moreover, able to provide three of his sons with a university education.

Little is known of Brenz's private life. We know he attended the Latin school in Weil and then in 1510 transferred to the school in Heidelberg, where he may have become acquainted with Philip Melanchthon, who studied in Heidelberg from 1509 to 1512. In 1511 Brenz was sent to the school in Vaihingen an der Enz, closer to his native city. On October 13, 1514 he matriculated at the University of Heidelberg, where he pursued the arts curriculum, earning his BA in 1516 and his MA in October 1518, before devoting himself to theology.

Brenz's studies were influenced by the Heidelberg humanism founded by Rudolf Agricola. Pursuing the humanist ideal of the *vir trilinguis*, Brenz studied Greek and Hebrew as well as Latin. In 1517 he assisted Johannes Oecolampadius in the preparation of the index for Erasmus's edition of Jerome. The best evidence of the humanistic orientation of Brenz as a student, however, is his handwriting, a clear humanist italic that changed little in the succeeding decades.

Conversion and Reforming Career

Due to Luther's *Heidelberg Disputation* (1518), Brenz's studies – and the course of his life – were given a new direction. In the disputation Luther demonstrated that justification, salvation, and life are received from God alone. On the following day, Martin Bucer, accompanied by Brenz, visited Luther to discuss these matters further.

This was the beginning of a lifelong relationship between Luther and Brenz and, at the same time, the event that turned Brenz into a future reformer.

In 1520 Brenz became a vicar at the Church of the Holy Spirit in Heidelberg and was thereby entitled to teach at the university. In addition to his lectures in the Faculty of Arts, Brenz eventually began – doubtless inspired by what Luther had said in the disputation – to lecture on the books of the Bible as well. This activity got him into difficulties, though these had no lasting effect because in the fall of 1522 he was called to be preacher at St. Michael's Church in Schwäbisch Hall.

An imperial city, Schwäbisch Hall was considerably larger and, on account of its production of salt, economically much more important than Weil. The preaching position at St. Michael's, the chief city church, was one of the few clerical posts provided by the city council. In 1508 the council acquired the patronage over the pastoral position to which Johann Isenmann, Brenz's fellow-student in Heidelberg, was called in 1523. Though pastor, and thus Brenz's superior as preacher, Isenmann had to live with the fact that Brenz played the more important role. It is thus remarkable that the collaboration of the two men evidently produced no friction whatever.

In 1523, after reaching canonical age, Brenz took holy orders. The first of his reform sermons to survive in print dates from St. James's Day (July 25) of the same year: the *Sermon on the Saints*,[2] in which he passionately denounced the traditional cult of the saints. By means of such sermons Brenz set to work to transform the consciousness of his congregation. Actual reforms were inaugurated only later and gradually. A local chronicler describes 1524 as the year in which the Reformation began, as priests began to be taxed and were forbidden to keep concubines that they were not willing to marry. In this year, too, the Franciscans surrendered their cloister – the only one in the city – to the city council, which then guaranteed their subsistence.

Already in these early years Brenz's influence spread beyond the bounds of Schwäbisch Hall. This was evident at the beginning of the Sacramentarian Controversy, which divided the Reformation into Lutheran and Zwinglian camps. Oecolampadius, now a pastor in Basel, shared Zwingli's symbolical interpretation of the Lord's Supper. In September 1525 he published an interpretation of the words of institution of the Lord's Supper under the title *De genuina verborum Domini: Hoc est corpus meum iuxta vetustissimos authores expositione liber*. In the afterword to this work, in which the argument was based chiefly on citations from the church fathers, Oecolampadius addressed himself to the brethren who were preaching Christ "throughout Swabia," and solicited their opinion. He had in mind the clergy around Brenz in Schwäbisch Hall, Heilbronn, and in the vicinity, most of whom he knew personally from their time together as students in Heidelberg. But the brethren in Swabia took issue with Oecolampadius in a work titled *Syngramma Suevicum*.[3] Brenz must be seen as the principal author, but 13 other preachers accepted responsibility for it by affixing their signatures to it at a conference in Schwäbisch Hall on October 21, 1525. The *Syngramma* rejected the Swiss interpretation of the Lord's Supper and defended that of Luther, who was greatly pleased with his Swabian colleagues for their support.

Before further ecclesiastical changes could be undertaken in Schwäbisch Hall the Peasants' War of 1525 intervened. As elsewhere in the region, the subjects in Hall's rural territory were restless in the winter of 1524/25. At the beginning of April

1525, the city was threatened by a band of local peasants. With Brenz's encouragement, the council decided to resist and assembled an armed troop. A few cannon shots from this municipal contingent were enough to cause the surprised peasants to panic and disperse. A few weeks later, after the general defeat of the insurgents, the authorities in Hall exacted the complete subjection of the peasants in their territory. The leaders of the "rebels" were punished.

Brenz expressed himself several times on the issue of the Peasants' Revolt. Because he viewed government as God's ordinance, he condemned any form of rebellion against it, even if it were guilty of injustice. But following the Peasants' War, he called for mild treatment of the peasants and declared that the governing authorities bore a share of the blame for the uprising.[4] In so doing, he implicitly but clearly criticized Luther's harsh polemic against the peasants.

Further reform measures could only be undertaken in Hall in the wake of the recess of the Diet of Speyer of 1526, which left it to the imperial estates to conduct themselves in ecclesiastical matters in the way each believed itself able to justify itself before God and the emperor. Accordingly, at the end of 1526 or the beginning of 1527, Brenz submitted to the Hall city council the outline of a church order. The starting point of church order is worship, with the congregation formed by preaching, baptism, and the Lord's Supper. Brenz made a series of practical recommendations for the order of worship as well as for the closely related question of church holidays. To secure adherence to the order, a board comprising several honorable persons from the citizenry in addition to the pastors and preachers was to be established.

Brenz's draft church order also dealt with the question of providing for the poor by the establishment of a common chest. In addition, Brenz drew the attention of the council to the need for qualified pastors in the rural congregations and recommended that, where possible, the council should purchase the patronage rights of "foreign" governments or individuals so that it could appoint evangelical pastors.

In a supplement to his draft church order, Brenz made recommendations for the reorganization of the schools in Schwäbisch Hall. He aimed at cost-free school attendance and recommended that the learning of a trade be combined with attendance at school. He also favored a connection of the German school with the Latin school, and he called for the instruction of girls.

It is not clear how many of these proposals were put into effect. But it is certain that on Christmas Day 1526 Brenz and his congregation celebrated the Lord's Supper in both kinds for the first time. In certain other Hall churches Mass was celebrated until 1534, when the city council forbade it. Unfortunately, one cannot say which of Brenz's recommendations concerning schools went into effect. But his efforts for the education and instruction of children and young people are reflected in the catechism for Hall that dates from 1527/8 and, with its question-and-answer form, was intended for use in schools. The Latin school was reorganized in 1527, but no connection of it with the German school was undertaken.

Brenz soon established relations with the neighboring Margravate of Brandenburg and the Imperial City of Nuremberg. Margrave George of Brandenburg, who had come to power in 1527, held strongly evangelical views and in 1528 instituted a visitation for the purpose of the ecclesiastical reformation of his principality. In the process it became clear that the cooperation of Brandenburg's immediate neighbor

Nuremberg, whose possessions overlapped those of the margrave, would be advantageous. From Nuremberg's point of view, this meant that starting in 1528/9 its reformation, hitherto confined within the city walls, could be extended to its rural territory with the cooperation of the margrave's officials and theologians. As a result of this common effort, both Nuremberg and Brandenburg joined in the protestation of the evangelical estates at the Diet of Speyer in 1529 and were signatories to the *Augsburg Confession* of 1530.

Brenz was brought in as theological adviser to the margrave when Nuremberg and Brandenburg decided to prepare a church order that would be promulgated jointly in both territories. Due to frequent political changes, work on the common church order was several times interrupted. But in 1533 it was at last possible to publish the order in Nuremberg and introduce it in both Nuremberg and Brandenburg. The Brandenburg–Nuremberg Church Order[5] became the model for many other territories, and through his participation in the preparation of it Brenz acquired experience that would later, both in the years after 1534 and in those after 1550, stand him in good stead in Württemberg.

Through his connection with Brandenburg, Brenz's sphere of activity was substantially enlarged. Margrave George thought very highly of him. When Landgrave Philip of Hesse, eager to achieve a settlement of the Sacramentarian Controversy between Luther and Zwingli, arranged for a colloquy between the most renowned representatives of both sides, Brenz too was invited. Most of what we know about the course of the Marburg Colloquy of October 1529, at which it proved impossible to end the disagreements over the Lord's Supper, comes from reports written by Brenz.[6]

Brenz's participation in the Marburg Colloquy marked his conclusive entry into the circle of the most important Reformation theologians. At the invitation of Margrave George, Brenz attended the Diet of Augsburg in 1530, where he worked closely with Philip Melanchthon. They had to revise the confession of faith that the Saxon delegation had brought to the Diet so as to make it suitable for presentation to the emperor in the name of as many Protestant estates as possible. In the decisive days of the Diet, when it was a question not only of the theological problem of formulating a confession but also of the political problem of Philip of Hesse's plans for an armed alliance of the evangelical estates, Melanchthon and Brenz had an anxious time of it. Despite the threatening situation, Melanchthon and Brenz opposed an alliance with the Swiss so long as doctrinal unity with them remained impossible.

Following the submission to the emperor of the Catholic "Confutation" of the evangelical confession there were negotiations in committees seeking compromise. Brenz, along with Melanchthon, Erhard Schnepf, and others were chosen to represent the evangelical side in these negotiations. Like Melanchthon, Brenz was prepared to make certain concessions, but evangelical doctrine had to be defended at all costs. If this were guaranteed, then one could accept certain other things, as for example the right of the bishops to govern the church. This position earned Brenz and Melanchthon a good deal of criticism from within the evangelical camp.

The negotiations, however, were fruitless, and the recess of the Diet reaffirmed the Edict of Worms (1521), that had forbidden Luther's teaching. The evangelically-minded imperial estates now had to decide whether to follow the will of the emperor or the dictates of their conscience. After his return from Augsburg, Brenz himself gave expression to his personal decision to break with the old church by marrying Margareta Gräter, the widow of the Hall city councilman Hans Wetzel.

A new field of activity opened for Brenz after 1534, the year in which Duke Ulrich of Württemberg, who in 1519 had been expelled from his territory, reconquered it with the help of Landgrave Philip of Hesse. Determined to introduce the Reformation into Württemberg, Ulrich called Erhard Schnepf from Marburg and Ambrosius Blarer from Constance to be his leading theologians. Then, in July 1535, he summoned Brenz from Schwäbisch Hall to help with the preparation of a new church order. It was not only Brenz's recommendations, however, that were incorporated into the order, which went into effect in the spring of 1536. The form of worship prescribed in the order was the kind of simple preaching service favored by the Swiss, not the German Mass that had been introduced in Schwäbisch Hall.

In connection with the preparation of the new church order the question of a catechism was raised. As a result, the catechism by Brenz that in 1535 had been published in Schwäbisch Hall under the title *Fragstück des christlichen Glaubens für die Jugend* was now introduced into Württemberg as well. Brenz's catechism subsequently became – next to Luther's – the most widely disseminated book for evangelical instruction and has, albeit with many changes, survived into the present day.

Brenz also participated in the creation of a marriage ordinance for the Duchy of Württemberg. The essential features, at least, of the Württemberg marriage ordinance of 1535/36 correspond to Brenz's ideas on the subject. For the enforcement of the newly created ecclesiastical ordinances in Württemberg Brenz recommended an annual visitation of the churches. Such visitations in fact took place in Württemberg in the succeeding period, though not in the systematic way that Brenz had recommended.

The reformation of the University of Tübingen, particularly the development of an evangelical Faculty of Theology, produced serious difficulties. It was therefore necessary for Duke Ulrich to ask the Hall City Council to lend him the services of Brenz for this purpose. For one year, from the beginning of April, 1537 until the spring of 1538, Brenz resided in Tübingen as a teacher at the university. Together with Joachim Camerarius, a lifelong friend, Brenz was also ducal commissioner for the reform of the university, which found its temporary conclusion in the new university statutes of 1537.

Meanwhile, Brenz continued to participate in religious policy-making at the highest level. In February, 1537 he took part in the Diet of the Schmalkald League, where the delegates had to discuss whether the Protestants should participate in the council summoned by Pope Paul III to Mantua. It was at this Diet that Luther's *Schmalkald Articles*, in which the essential points of evangelical doctrine were defined, were formally adopted.

Ever since 1521 imperial diets had dealt with the religious question. In the attempt to have the issues settled by experts, the emperor arranged a religious colloquy that took place in Hagenau in Alsace in June 1540. Along with Bucer, Schnepf, and Osiander, Brenz was among the theologians invited to the colloquy. In October 1540 the colloquy was continued in Worms and then adjourned until the Diet that was to take place in Regensburg in the spring of 1541. Brenz was also summoned to this colloquy, which in the end made no progress toward a solution of the questions in dispute. Finally, there was a religious colloquy in Regensburg in January 1546, in which Brenz once again participated. But this one too exhausted itself in procedural disputes and negotiations were broken off.

From the beginning of the 1546 Regensburg Colloquy there were rumors that the emperor was preparing for a military showdown with the Protestants. War preparations on both sides led to the Schmalkald War, which within a few months brought significant changes, not only for Protestantism in Southwest Germany but also for Brenz himself. The Protestants fared badly in the war, and on December 16, 1546, Charles V made his triumphal entry into Hall at the head of his troops. During the war Brenz had spoken and written against the emperor's policies but remained in the city until marauding soldiers threatened him and drove him from his house. On the following day a Spanish bishop appeared, ordered Brenz's desk broken open, and took possession of his letters and sermons. The content of these papers, "distorted and magnified," was reported to the emperor, with the result that Brenz was forced to flee Schwäbisch Hall because of the fear of imperial reprisals on the city. Brenz went into hiding several miles from the city but two weeks later was able to return and resume his duties.

After his final defeat of the Protestant forces in the spring of 1547, the emperor decided to undertake a settlement of the religious problem at the Imperial Diet that was to meet in Augsburg in the spring of 1548. He demanded of the imperial estates either that they return to the Catholic faith or that they submit to the "Interim." This was a temporary church order that was to remain valid pending a definitive settlement by a council and that conceded to Protestants only communion in both kinds and the right of priests to marry. In all the theological questions that had been in dispute – for example, the doctrine of justification – Catholic positions were prescribed. Brenz refused to accept the Interim. Together with Isenmann, he wrote a memorandum for the city council in which he refuted the teachings in the Interim point by point. But the council, threatened with the quartering of the emperor's Spanish troops in the city, accepted the Interim. A copy of Brenz's memorandum found its way to the imperial court, whence came a demand for the surrender of the author. On June 24, 1548, his birthday, Brenz narrowly escaped capture by precipitous flight. The imperial city was not able to protect him from the emperor. Brenz finally had to send his family back to Hall, commending them to the protection of the council. His sick wife died shortly thereafter, while he was forced to find refuge elsewhere.

Brenz made his way to Württemberg in the hope that Duke Ulrich, out of gratitude for his earlier services, would help him. At first Ulrich arranged for Brenz to be hidden in the remote fortress of Hohenwittlingen near Urach in the Swabian Upland. For this reason, Brenz, in his letters in which he had to use pseudonyms for the people mentioned, honored the duke by referring to him as Obadiah (1 Kgs. 18:4). Knowing that Brenz was constantly receiving calls to other posts – Magdeburg, Prussia, Denmark, and England – Ulrich obtained Brenz's pledge to enter his service as soon as circumstances might permit. As a consequence, Brenz subsequently turned down all these calls.

Not safe in Württemberg because of the Spanish occupation, Brenz was sent via Strasbourg to the Württemberg territory of Montbéliard in Burgundy, and thence to Basel, where he spent the winter of 1548/9. During 1549, Brenz led an unstable existence underground, during which he was probably in Württemberg several times. His publications in this period appeared pseudonymously. At last he and his children were assigned a residence in the Württemberg fortress of Hornberg, near Calw. Here he bore the title of prefect, though it was obvious that he was not leading the life of such an official. In this period Brenz was married again, to Katharina Isenmann, a niece of his Hall colleague.

Duke Ulrich died in November 1550 and was succeeded by his son Duke Christopher, who also took Brenz into his service. The emperor had demanded that the imperial estates send delegations to the newly opened council in Trent. In preparation, Brenz wrote the *Confessio Virtembergica*, a confession intended to be in harmony with the *Augsburg Confession* of 1530, while at the same time taking account of the new situation. In this confession Brenz's aim, in contrast to that in his Hall memorandum against the Interim, was not to define the evangelical faith in sharp contrast to Catholicism but rather to emphasize the common roots of both in the Bible and in the writings of the church fathers.

Following difficult negotiations, a Württemberg delegation was sent to Trent, where on January 24, 1552, the confession was presented to the council. Although he still had to be concerned for his own safety – the Interim was still in effect – Brenz was the head of the theological delegation which, in the spring of 1552, traveled to Trent to take responsibility for the confession and, if necessary, to defend it. But the Württemberg theologians, joined by two theologians from Strasbourg, were never heard by the council. When rumors of war reached Trent, many of the council fathers departed. In the end, Brenz and his Württemberg delegation also returned home.

Thus the Council of Trent never addressed itself to the content of the Württemberg Confession. The Spanish Dominican, Pedro de Soto, professor at the newly founded University of Dillingen, after some considerable delay, finally did so in a rejoinder published in 1555. His criticism dealt chiefly with the doctrine of justification, to which he opposed the Catholic doctrine of merit. Overarching Soto's argument was his conviction that the papal church was the only true church. Following Brenz's answer to Soto and Soto's answer to that, four Württemberg theologians wrote a defense of the Württemberg Confession that was published in 1561.

Further developments in the Empire, namely Maurice of Saxony's successful uprising against the emperor in the spring and summer of 1552 and the subsequent conclusion of the Treaty of Passau, led to the abrogation of the Interim in Württemberg. This made it possible for Brenz to assume public office once more. In 1553 he was appointed Provost of the Stuttgart Collegiate Church. The title was a survival of the pre-Reformation constitution of the Collegiate Church and was now intended to designate Brenz as the highest-ranking clergyman and theologian in the duchy.

In Stuttgart, the Collegiate Church, the residence of the Provost, the ducal palace, and the princely chancellery were all in immediate proximity of one another. This circumstance no doubt contributed to the close relationship of trust that bound Duke Christopher and Brenz to one another. Their trusting relationship made it possible for them together to complete the reorganization of the Württemberg church within a few years. This is all the more remarkable, given that other comprehensive reforms – e.g., the revision of the law code and the standardization of weights and measures – were implemented in the same period. The ecclesiastical reorganization reached its completion with the Great Church Order, a compendium of all the reform measures of the previous decade, assembled and revised under Brenz's supervision and published in 1559.

Even in the period during which Brenz had to supervise the task of ecclesiastical reorganization, he continued to think of himself, as he did throughout his life, primarily as a preacher. He preached at both the Sunday and the weekday services in the Collegiate Church. The weekday sermons were normally devoted to the systematic exposition of a biblical book, which explains Brenz's large output of exegetical works: the sermons were developed into Latin commentaries that cover nearly all the books of the Bible.[7] Only in 1568 did Brenz, on grounds of age, request and receive release from his duties as a preacher.

Brenz also took part in Duke Christopher's diplomatic attempts to support the Reformation in the Empire and in Europe. Not only did he go to the Council of Trent, he also attended the Colloquy of Worms in 1557 and took part in the Diet of Princes in Frankfurt in 1558. In 1562 he accompanied Duke Christopher to Saverne in Alsace for a meeting with the Guise brothers, in the attempt to mediate in the French religious wars then getting under way. In 1564 he took part in the colloquy in Maulbronn in which an attempt was made to persuade Elector Frederick III of the Palatinate, who had turned Calvinist, to return to Lutheranism. In this last instance, however, the spokesman for the Württemberg delegation was Jakob Andreae (professor in Tübingen), a sign that the younger generation was beginning to assume control.

At the end of 1568 Duke Christopher died, to Brenz's immense sorrow. A year later, Brenz himself suffered a stroke from which he never recovered. On September 11, 1570, he succumbed to a fever, after having had his "spiritual testament" (confession of faith and admonitions to his successors) read out to the assembled pastors of Stuttgart and after receiving the Lord's Supper. He was the last surviving member of the first generation of Lutheran reformers. He was survived by no fewer than 13 children from his two marriages. While the last one to bear the name Brenz died in Schwäbisch Hall at the end of the seventeenth century, his direct descendants are today without number. Among them are the philosopher Hegel and the theologian Dietrich Bonhoeffer, as well as the recent president of the German Federal Republic, Richard von Weizsäcker.

A Theology of the Word

At his own request, Brenz was buried in the Stuttgart Collegiate Church, beneath the pulpit from which he had preached for almost two decades. From that day to this, every preacher who mounts the pulpit in the Collegiate Church has to walk over Brenz's gravestone. Brenz intended this as a reminder that the Word of God was to be understood as the center of his theology. He left no single, comprehensive statement of that theology but, over the span of his career, he responded to individual inquiries and demands with a series of works in which he elaborated his central theme of reformation centered on God's Word. The starting point of Brenz's reform theology was the encounter with Luther in Heidelberg in 1518, on the basis of which he began his independent development of the ideas acquired from Luther. Fundamental here is the new relationship between man and God that Luther defined in the Heidelberg Disputation, namely that man is wholly dependent on God and his grace. This grace manifests itself in the creative Word of God, which is identical with Christ and brings about the salvation of humankind. This happens by means of the preaching of the Word, which mediates the forgiveness of sins and effects justification. This is the basis of all of Brenz's activity as a reformer. From it sprang his criticism of church practice, of church officials, and of worship and the administration of the sacraments. From this same basis, moreover, came the conviction that, once the truth has been recognized, there can be no retreat from it. Hence the brusque rejection of the Interim, which nevertheless did not prevent Brenz, in the *Confessio Virtembergica*, from attempting to explore areas of agreement with Catholic theology to the extent that he could without abandoning the fundamentals of his own faith.

The theology of the Word is also determinative for Brenz's doctrine of the Lord's Supper and his position in the sacramentarian controversy. At first, Brenz, like Bucer and Oecolampadius, adhered to a spiritualizing view of the Lord's Supper influenced by Augustine. According to this view, Christ and his gifts are made present in faith by means of the remembrance of him. In the process, faith is strengthened by the *signum visibile* of the distribution of the bread and wine, and the presence of Christ is made known by the prayer and thanksgiving of the congregation. This view was undermined for Brenz by the symbolic interpretation of 1 Corinthians 10:3–4 that Oecolampadius used in his 1525 treatise on the Lord's Supper. By its arbitrary preference for a symbolic rather than a literal reading of the text, Oecolampadius's interpretation implicitly called into question the meaning of the entire Word of God, on which faith is dependent. Thus in the *Syngramma*, Oecolampadius's tropological interpretation of the words of institution was rejected, despite his attempt to support this interpretation by citing the church fathers. According to the *Syngramma*, the words of institution spoken over the bread and wine are the Word of Christ that effects the presence of His Body and Blood. The Lord's Supper is, therefore, the actual presence of the gift of salvation, not a symbol of fellowship.

Subsequently, Brenz developed even further his doctrine of the Word as means of grace and its relationship to the Sacrament. In the *Syngramma*, the Real Presence was not yet Christologically grounded. Before that could happen, Brenz had to develop his Christology further. Important for him in this connection was the incarnation of Christ, his assumption of human nature, by means of which the faithful are able to partake of the gifts of Christ. For this reason the human nature of Christ also partakes of the omnipotence and majesty of God, and Christ is God even according to his human nature, even though this was at first hidden and became apparent only after the Ascension.

Christology thus became a central theme in Brenz's later years. His articulation of the doctrine of the two natures as the personal union of the man Jesus with God sprang, however, not from a speculative interest but was rooted in his soteriology. The issue at stake in Christology is the saving act of Jesus, the incarnation of the Word as the redemption of humankind. The development of Brenz's Christology – or his doctrine of the ubiquity of Christ's body, as his opponents called it – was influenced by his conversation in 1556 with Jan Laski (Johannes à Lasco), the pastor of an exile congregation in Frankfurt, and the composition of the 1559 Apology of the *Confessio Virtembergica* against Soto. The occasion of a binding formulation of the Doctrine of the Personal Union was a case that arose among the Württemberg pastors, in connection with which the Stuttgart *Confession On the Lord's Supper* was promulgated in 1559 and made obligatory in the duchy. This confession, however, led to a break with Melanchthon and a cooling of the friendship between him and Brenz.

In three works of 1561/2 directed at his opponents in the reformed camp, Peter Martyr Vermigli and Heinrich Bullinger, Brenz developed his Christology even further.[8] Here it was a question of discerning Christ in order to believe in him properly, because salvation depends on doing so. The emphasis on the personal union of Jesus with God rather than simply on the doctrine of the two natures is further evidence of Brenz's soteriological interest. The *communicatio idiomatum*, the communication of attributes, is the actual communication of Christ's divinity and humanity to one another, the new definition of the relationship between God and man. In his Christology Brenz thus attempted to capture the process of salvation set forth in Scripture in a philosophically grounded definition. In so doing, however, the placement of the *communicatio idiomatum* in the center of his doctrine produced certain difficulties, as for example in the question of how one can conceive of God's participation in suffering.

Naturally, the doctrine of justification also played an important role in Brenz's theology. The justification of the sinner that emanates from God is effected by Christ and received by faith. Justification is not only a matter of being declared righteous in a forensic sense but also of the gift of the Spirit as well. In 1531 Brenz corresponded with Luther and Melanchthon on the doctrine of justification. The two Wittenbergers pointed out that Brenz, following Augustine, still linked justification to a fulfilling of the law out of faith. Brenz then developed his doctrine of justification further, primarily in his commentary on Romans (1538/9)[9] and in the *Confessio Virtembergica*. The question of justification was at the center of the so-called Osiandrian controversy in Prussia in 1551–7, in which Brenz, who knew Osiander from the latter's earlier days as the leading reformer in Nuremberg, tried to mediate. It proved impossible to calm the dispute from Württemberg, largely because the great distance made communication difficult and also because Brenz could not accede to the repeated entreaties of Duke Albert to come to Prussia.

Political Philosophy

Closely connected to Brenz's theology and activity as a reformer was his political philosophy. Axiomatic for him was the identity of the political commonwealth with the community of Christians. Here Brenz essentially followed Luther's "Doctrine of the Two Kingdoms," according to which secular government is an ordinance of God that checks the chaos that is the result of sin. The chief duty of government is the promotion of the common good and of peace. The duty to maintain peace is imposed on it by divine command. Brenz developed the conception of Christian government as an instrument of God's will, responsible to provide for the observance of God's commandments and for the spiritual welfare of its subjects.

His conception of government was thoroughly patriarchal. Subjects have the duty of obedience; rebellion against divinely established secular government constitutes rebellion against God himself. The only possible form of opposition against unjust religious persecution is passive resistance, which includes the duty to endure patiently the penalties imposed. Christians must also fulfill the unjust demands of secular government, for they have been forbidden to resist evil. Zealous, earnest prayer is the most effective means against an unjust government. For Brenz there was thus no right of resistance. But in the extremity of the Interim he was nevertheless able, on the basis of Old Testament models, to imagine a charismatically legitimated resistance.

A preacher, however, has the duty to measure government against the standard laid down in the Word of God. Despite the distinction between spiritual government and secular government, the spiritual and secular spheres overlap widely in Brenz's view. It is not simply a question of the salvation of private individuals, for God's punishments befall not only the individual sinner but also the whole community. From this Brenz derived the preachers' right and duty to criticize their governments, something that he did quite often. Such was the case following the Peasants' War, the origins of which he attributed in large measure to government misrule. So also the conduct of the government of Schwäbisch Hall with respect to the Speyer Protest of 1529 and the recess of the Diet of Augsburg in 1530, which he characterized as denial of Christ. But his criticisms never led to serious disagreements, because he always pointed the way to change and improvement. Thus his advice was frequently sought on political and legal questions. Before and during the Peasants' War, for example, he wrote letters and memoranda stating his views on the issues that had arisen.

In his memoranda on specific legal questions Brenz sought, with theology as his starting point, to demonstrate the harmony between the Word of God and secular law. His comments reveal his familiarity with the legal literature. He drew upon imperial (i.e., Roman) law with the Bible as the standard for a Christian interpretation of the law. Where the two agreed, imperial law had to be acknowledged as God's ordinance and thus binding on everyone. In a case like the polygamy of the Old Testament patriarchs, Brenz sided with imperial laws and declared polygamy an exception. Because canon law played an insignificant role in Brenz's thinking, he avoided citing it directly.

Criminal law and its enforcement are justified by the duty of government to maintain peace and order. The goal of legal penalties imposed for a crime is the intimidation of those who might be tempted to imitate it, not the punishment of the deed itself. The latter is God's business. Whenever it serves the cause of improvement and the common peace to do so, punishments can be reduced or, in certain cases, even increased. In all its judgments, however, government should be motivated by the principles of mildness and benevolence.

Theological and juridical considerations came together in the question of the treatment of Anabaptists, who practiced a strict division between world and church and believed that Christians should remain aloof from secular government. The question of how to deal with Anabaptists was the subject of controversy. Brenz first addressed the subject in a memorandum written in 1528 in response to a request from Nuremberg for his opinion on the question of whether Anabaptism is punishable by death.[10] At issue was the validity of a section of the *Corpus Iuris Civilis*, originally aimed at the Donatists and imposing the death penalty on rebaptizers. An imperial mandate had just revived that provision of ancient imperial law and applied it to the Anabaptists. Here again Brenz proceeded on the basis of the Doctrine of the Two Kingdoms and distinguished between spiritual and secular offences. Spiritual offences like doctrinal error and heresy can only be overcome by preaching. If one employs secular penalties against heretics, one merely confirms them in their error. At most one can banish them from the territory. As for the article of the *Corpus Iuris Civilis* that mandated the death penalty, Brenz got around it in a rather willful manner by proposing that it had been aimed at secular crimes no longer known that had somehow become associated with the spiritual crime of rebaptism. Brenz saw the Anabaptists not as rebels, but as simple people with doctrines based on a misunderstanding of certain passages of Scripture, peace-loving and blameless in their conduct.

The memorandum just summarized is not an early example of religious tolerance. Brenz was not out to achieve the toleration of Anabaptist congregations but to prevent the punishment of heresy by death. In this he differed from Melanchthon and Luther. Brenz's only concern was public peace, which he believed would be undermined by the inevitable discord resulting from disunity in the preaching of doctrine. Individual Anabaptists could remain in the territory as long as they remained passive. But Brenz was decisive in his opposition to Anabaptist preaching and the formation of Anabaptist congregations, with imprisonment and banishment as the maximum penalties. Brenz remained true to these principles throughout his life, especially his opposition to the death penalty. He championed them not only in Schwäbisch Hall – where Anabaptists posed no problem until 1544/5 – but also later in Württemberg. For this reason, and despite Brenz's refusal to grant Anabaptists toleration in the modern sense, his memorandum of 1528 has a place in the history of the idea of tolerance. In 1558 Sebastian Castellio, an early champion of religious toleration, incorporated it into his book *De Haereticis an sint persequendi*[11] and praised Brenz as a man who had saved the lives of countless men and women. Rightly so, for in Württemberg no Anabaptist was ever executed.

Brenz dealt in much the same way with the question of witchcraft that arose during his years in Stuttgart. He argued that misfortune happens with God's permission, and that the devil and his allies cause misfortune or at least create the illusion that they can do so. To be sure, he did not absolutely reject the notion that alliance with the devil could be a crime worthy of death. The physician Johann Weyer, one of the earliest opponents of the belief in witches, reproached Brenz for this in correspondence with him in the years 1565/6. Weyer nevertheless printed Brenz's *Sermon on Hail* (1565), which dealt with the question of witches, in his *De praestigiis daemonum*, because Brenz admonished governments to deal cautiously with accusations of witchcraft and to prefer pastoral or medical care to courts and torture as the appropriate treatment for accused individuals. Brenz thereby inaugurated in Württemberg a tradition of sober consideration of the question of witches. Although there were subsequently witch trials and condemnations, there were never any of the great waves of trials that were elsewhere characteristic of the persecution of witches.

Theological and juridical questions were also closely connected in the area of marriage and family law, traditionally the reserve of the church and its courts. In 1529, after having written a number of memoranda and opinions on the question of marriage law, Brenz published a book on the subject, *Wie in Eesachen . . . nach Göttlichen billichen rechten christenlich zu handeln sey.*[12] The principal points dealt with the consent of parents to a marriage, the question of divorce, the remarriage of divorced persons, and the appropriate penalty for adultery.

Legacy

In addition to becoming one of the most important theologians of the Reformation period, Brenz also emerged as the most important church organizer (alongside Johann Bugenhagen) among the Lutheran reformers. He not only participated in the preparation of the church order of 1533 for Brandenburg and Nuremberg and that of 1536 for Württemberg but was also the principal influence on the church order of 1543 for Schwäbisch Hall. Most important, however, was his participation in the reorganization of the church in Württemberg in the years 1553–9. The Great Church Order published in 1559 included, in addition to the *Confessio Virtembergica* of 1552, the ordinances – some of them issued earlier but now revised – regulating worship, marriage, schools, social welfare, and church government.

Because the texts of the laws included in the Great Church Order were undoubtedly the product of discussions among a group of experts on law, theology, and administration, Brenz's precise share in the process of ecclesiastical reorganization is difficult to assess. But it is clear that it was Brenz's ideas that came to fruition in the ordinances. This is true, for example, with respect to schools, especially in the case of the cloister schools. Following the Religious Peace of Augsburg in 1555, it was possible to reform the once-more vacated monasteries that had been given back to their respective orders during the Interim. The Cloister Ordinance issued in 1556 was clearly Brenz's work, since it took up again a scheme he had devised in 1529 for returning monasteries to their original purpose by turning them into schools. Thus the 13 cloister schools were established in which future pastors and theologians were prepared for their university studies in the Tübingen Stipendium (which still exists today, under the name Evangelisches Stift). The Stipendium, which had been founded in 1536, was thus provided with a reliable source of qualified students. All those students assigned places in the cloister schools and the Stipendium were given full scholarships. The fact that in the year of their foundation Brenz visited some of the cloister schools several times shows without doubt that he regarded them as his own creation.

The second field in which it is obvious that Brenz's ideas were realized is that of church organization and administration. The Württemberg church was given a hierarchical structure in which the local pastors were subordinate to district superintendents, and the superintendents in turn were subordinate to one of four general superintendents. The superintendents were to visit every parish in their district twice a year – initially it was to have been four times a year – and submit reports of their findings to their general superintendent. The central governing body of the church, the consistory, comprised a "spiritual bench" of theologians and a "secular bench" of jurists. Twice a year – initially four times – the members of the consistory and the four general superintendents were to meet in Stuttgart in the so-called *Synodus* to deliberate on the contents of the visitation reports and to decide on appropriate measures. The key feature of the system of ecclesiastical administration was thus the process of visitation. It gave to the church a significantly more efficient administration than the one that ran the state, particularly since the attempt to duplicate this system of visitation in the secular administration failed completely.

It is clear that Brenz's patriarchal conception of government was decisive for this hierarchically structured church devoid of presbytery or synod (in the customary sense of that term). The obligation to promote and protect the Word of God was imposed upon the government. Denied the right to choose their own pastors, congregations were conceded only a limited right of rejection in the process of appointing pastors. Even church discipline was centralized; an attempt by the young Jakob Andreae, initially supported by Duke Christopher, to assign to congregations the right to exclude public sinners from the Sacrament, was firmly rebuffed by Brenz, who had assigned that right to the *Synodus*.

Brenz's long-term legacy to Württemberg was, first of all, the establishment of a biblically oriented theology that expressed itself in a high esteem for preaching. Just as important was his catechism, which captured the faith of many generations in memorable words. The demand for knowledge of the content of the catechism became a fundamental element in the educational system. This indicates that Brenz's influence spread well beyond the ecclesiastical sphere. On the basis of Brenz's model of monastic reform that replaced the abbots by evangelical theologian-schoolteachers, Duke Christopher modernized the late-medieval system of estates in Württemberg by making these evangelical "prelates" the successors of the abbots as the first estate in the territorial Diet. In 1565 the Diet demanded from the duke permanent recognition of the territory's Lutheran faith and church organization. Only when urged to do so by Brenz did Duke Christopher agree to this demand. The recess of the Diet incorporating this agreement acquired constitutional status and thus entrenched the intimate association of church and state that was personified in the prelates. Thereafter Lutheran faith and the constitutional authority of the estates reinforced one another to such a degree that the system survived intact until the end of the Holy Roman Empire in 1806.

Brenz's long-term significance beyond Württemberg was based in part on his exegetical work, which was long esteemed in many places. Moreover, it is owing to Brenz that the theology of the Württemberg church had such significance and weight in the early period of Lutheran Orthodoxy. Standard in that orthodoxy were not only his formulation of the doctrine of the Personal Union but also his system of church order and government, which became a much imitated model. The Württemberg consistorial system of church government was adopted in the Neuburg Palatinate in 1553, in the Margravate of Baden and the Electoral Palatinate in 1556, and in Electoral Saxony in 1573. Many imperial cities adopted the same system. This spread of the Württemberg model was only possible, however, because an efficient educational system had been established which made it possible – at least until the Thirty Years' War – to export theologians. Foremost among these theologians was

Jakob Andreae who, apart from his efforts in behalf of the *Formula of Concord*, functioned as an expert on matters of church order in numerous territories where he either introduced the Reformation or helped organize an already established church. In either case he introduced the Württemberg system of church government.

Far more influential than Brenz's bible commentaries and system of ecclesiastical administration, however, was his catechism. It was published in and distributed from numerous European locations: from Königsberg and Brest in the east to London and Amsterdam in the west, from Hamburg and Lübeck in the north to Basel and Mont-béliard in the south. Already in the sixteenth century Brenz's catechism, his explanation of the catechism, and other writings were translated not only into Latin but also into French, English, Dutch, Danish, Polish, Czech, and Italian. An adaptation of Brenz's catechism was the first book published in the Slovenian language. His catechism played the same pioneering role in the nineteenth century when, as part of Christian missionary activity, it was translated into a number of African and Asian languages. It thus became – exactly as in Germany in the sixteenth century – both a textbook of instruction in the Christian faith and an exercise book for the spread of literacy.

Notes

1 Editor's note: There were some sixty-five "free imperial cities" (*Reichstädte*) that were "self-governing" under the aegis of the emperor. For an introduction to the topic of the imperial cities and the Reformation, see Miriam U. Chrisman, "Cities in the Reformation" in William S. Maltby, ed., *Reformation Europe: A Guide to Research II* (St. Louis: Center for Reformation Research, 1992), 105–27, and Peter G. Wallace, "Cities" OER 1:354–60.

2 Martin Brecht et al., eds., *Johannes Brenz Werke. Eine Studienausgabe*, 5 vols. (Tübingen: J. C. B. Mohr, 1970ff.), 1:4–15.

3 Brecht, *Brenz Werke, Frühschriften* 1:222–78.

4 Ibid., 1:180–92.

5 Editor's note: The order is in Emil Sehling, ed., *Die evangelischen Kirchenordnungen des XVI. Jahrhunderts* (repr. Tübingen: J. C. B. Mohr, 1961), 11/1:140–205.

6 Brecht, *Brenz Werke, Frühschriften* 2:401–28.

7 Cf., e.g., on Daniel: Brecht, *Brenz Werke, Schriftauslegungen* 1.

8 Brecht, *Brenz Werke, Die christologischen Schriften*, Teil 1.

9 Brecht, *Brenz Werke, Schriftauslegungen* 2: 1–455.

10 Brecht, *Brenz Werke, Frühschriften* 2:472–98.

11 Roland Bainton, ed. and trans., *Concerning Heretics* (1935, repr. New York: Octagon, 1965).

12 Brecht, *Brenz Werke, Frühschriften* 2:253–96.

Bibliography

Primary Sources

Brecht, Martin and Hermann Ehmer, eds., *Confessio Virtembergica. Das Württembergische Bekenntnis 1552*, Holzgerlingen: Hänssler Verlag, 1999.

——, and Gerhard Schäfer, eds., *Johannes Brenz Werke. Eine Studienausgabe*, 5 vols. to date, Tübingen: J. C. B. Mohr (Siebeck), 1970ff.

Operum reverendi et clarissimi theologi D. Ioannis Brentii . . ., 8 vols., Tübingen: Georg Gruppenbach, 1576–90.

Pressel, Theodor, ed., *Anecdota Brentiana. Ungedruckte Briefe und Bedenken von Johannes Brenz*, Tübingen: J. J. Heckenhauer, 1868.

Secondary Sources

Brandy, Hans Christian, *Die späte Christologie des Johannes Brenz*, Tübingen: J. C. B. Mohr (Siebeck), 1991.

Brecht, Martin, *Die frühe Theologie des Johannes Brenz*, Tübingen: J. C. B. Mohr (Siebeck), 1966.

Estes, James Martin, *Christian Magistrate and State Church. The Reforming Career of Johannes Brenz*, Toronto: University of Toronto Press, 1982.

Fehle, Isabella, ed., *Johannes Brenz 1499–1570. Prediger – Reformator – Politiker*, Schwäbisch Hall: Hällisch-Fränkisches Museum, 1999.

Hartmann, Julius and Karl Jäger, *Johannes Brenz. Nach gedruckten und ungedruckten Quellen*, 2 vols., Hamburg: F. A. Perthes, 1840/2.

Köhler, Walther, *Bibliographia Brentiana. Bibliographisches Verzeichnis der gedruckten und ungedruckten Schriften und Briefe des Reformators Johannes Brenz*, Berlin: C. A. Schwetschke & Son, 1904.

Weismann, Christoph, *Die Katechismen des Johannes Brenz*, 2 vols., New York: De Gruyter, 1990–.

Martin Chemnitz
(1522–1586)

Robert Kolb

Son of a merchant and clothmaker of Treuenbrietzen in Brandenburg, Martin Chemnitz suffered the death of his father before his eleventh birthday. The heavy hand of an older brother prevented him from continuing his schooling. Finally, through the efforts of a local schoolmaster and his mother, he left behind the clothmaker's trade and was able briefly to attend primary school in Wittenberg (1536), later renewing his formal education in Magdeburg (1539–42). Unable to afford university study, he taught for a year in Calbe an der Saale before matriculating at the University of Frankfurt an der Oder, drawn there by a relative, Georg Sabinus, who was also Philip Melanchthon's son-in-law. His money ran out after a year, but after 18 months, his earnings from teaching and serving as a tax official enabled him to return to Wittenberg in 1545.

There Chemnitz made immediate contact with Melanchthon, who guided his new disciple into the study of mathematics and fostered his interest in astrology. During his year in Wittenberg Chemnitz attended Luther's lectures, heard him preach, and experienced the old Reformer's last public academic disputation; he later regretted not paying more attention to the man whose writings would decisively shape his theology. Financial exigencies drove the young student back to work, teaching in Nienburg an der Saale, where again he not only taught but learned, through an intensive reading program. The theologian Chemnitz was largely self-taught.

The turmoil of the Schmalkald War (1546–7) impelled Chemnitz to join Sabinus in Königsberg, where he gained another teaching position. Fleeing the city during an outbreak of the plague, he found himself forced to read what was at hand: Luther's postils and Peter Lombard's *Sentences*. Luther deepened his understanding of the biblical message, and Lombard fired his interest in patristics. He dedicated himself to the study of the ancient church fathers as ducal librarian in the service of Duke Albrecht of Prussia (1550–3); the duke also treasured his astrological skills. Guided by the advice he had sought from Melanchthon regarding his growing interest in theology, he assessed his readings in Scripture and the Fathers on the basis of the Wittenbergers' hermeneutical principle of the distinction of law and gospel. This principle served as the organizing axiom for all his biblical interpretation.

The Development of Chemnitz's Doctrine of Justification

Chemnitz's rapidly expanding knowledge of Wittenberg thought and his sensitivity to its biblical foundations set him on a collision course with Andreas Osiander, the favorite of his prince. As a preacher in Nuremberg, Osiander converted Albrecht to the Reformation in 1525. When imperial troops enforced the Augsburg Interim in Nuremberg (1548), Osiander was forced into exile and found refuge in Königsberg, where the duke provided him with a parish and a position on the university theological faculty. Osiander's initial education had consisted largely of studies in the Cabbala, and its Neoplatonic presuppositions determined the way he absorbed Luther's teaching.

Along with Osiander's university colleague, Melchior Isinder, Chemnitz quickly noticed that the doctrine of justification Osiander was proclaiming differed significantly from Luther's and Melanchthon's. Osiander's ontological presuppositions led him to assert that God would be a liar if human righteousness rested only on his Word, a "forensic" regard for the sinner not based upon some ontological reality within the fallen human creature. Therefore, he held that Christ bestows human righteousness on believers by placing his divine righteousness within them through faith, that reconciliation between God and fallen human creatures takes place through the uniting of Christ's divine righteousness with the believer. Neither the work of the incarnate Christ nor the pronouncement of his Word of forgiveness had great significance in Osiander's system. Chemnitz recognized that Osiander had failed to grasp the incarnational nature of Luther's thought, both in regard to the work of Christ (which atoned for sin through suffering execution under God's law, and which renewed life through his resurrection) and in regard to the power of the gospel (which in oral, written, and sacramental form accomplishes what God wills when it forgives sin and bestows life and salvation). On the basis of his philological study of the Old Testament concept of God's Word Chemnitz advanced Luther's understanding of God's Word as that which establishes and effects reality, both as the Incarnate Word and as the several forms of the means of grace, in preaching, absolution, and the sacraments.

Chemnitz and Isinder won to their side a pastor in the city, who had initially tried to mediate the dispute with Osiander, Joachim Mörlin. Also a refugee, exiled from Göttingen because of the Augsburg Interim, Mörlin had studied under Luther and Melanchthon in the 1530s and was associated with those Wittenberg graduates who interpreted Luther's teaching in more radical fashion (whom scholars later labeled "Gnesio-Lutherans"). Mörlin's good will toward Osiander diminished as the two exchanged views, for Mörlin also came to see the fundamental difference between what he had learned from Luther and what Osiander was propagating regarding the justification of sinners. Mörlin's outspoken public criticism of the duke's favorite and of Albrecht himself earned Mörlin another exile in February 1553. Chemnitz left Prussia two months later.

Leadership in the Church of Braunschweig

Chemnitz returned to Wittenberg for a year and a half. There he was welcomed into Melanchthon's inner circle, listened to his Preceptor's lectures, traveled with him to a critical meeting of evangelical princes in Naumburg (May 1554), became a member of the arts faculty, and was chosen as one of three (with David Chytraeus and Tilemann Hesshus) who had the privilege of offering lectures on Melanchthon's dogmatics textbook *Loci communes*. Only very reluctantly did the professor let his student leave the university at the end of 1554 to accept a call from the city of Braunschweig, where Mörlin had become ecclesiastical superintendent after leaving Prussia. Chemnitz's instructor, colleague, and pastor in Wittenberg, Johannes Bugenhagen, ordained him on November 25, 1554. Melanchthon and Chemnitz had formed a friendship which the student reflected in his own positions and method, even though their relationship later fell under stress because, in the later 1550s, Chemnitz stood ever more clearly on the side of his Preceptor's critics.

The Braunschweig city council called Chemnitz to be Mörlin's coadjutor; among other duties the continuing education program for the city's clergy became his responsibility. He fulfilled it initially with two or three lectures each week on Melanchthon's *Loci*. After his death his successor Polycarp Leyser edited this commentary on Melanchthon's work, and Chemnitz's *Loci* became a foundational text for the theology of Lutheran Orthodoxy.

Braunschweig's ministerium was active in an association of Lower Saxon city ministeria; the intellectual gifts of Mörlin and Chemnitz made them leaders in that group. In January 1557 they led a Lower Saxon delegation in conducting mediation between Melanchthon, with his colleagues in Wittenberg, and a group of former students headquartered in Magdeburg, led by Matthias Flacius Illyricus, who were criticizing their Preceptor and those around him for their compromising stance following the defeat of the Protestant Schmalkald League by Roman Catholic armies under Emperor Charles V (1547). The Wittenberg faculty had contributed to formulating a policy proposal, never officially adopted and only partially implemented, which tried to stave off papal–imperial invasion of Electoral Saxony. The attacks on this so-called "Leipzig Interim" had led to disputes on other issues, including two propositions advanced by Electoral Saxon theologians: "good works are necessary for salvation" (Georg Major) and "the human will gives its consent to God's grace in conversion" (Johann Pfeffinger). Magdeburg representatives accompanied the Lower Saxon theologians to Coswig in January 1557, Chemnitz was placed in Wittenberg with Melanchthon and his colleagues, and Mörlin carried messages between the two groups. Flacius's demands for clarity in rejecting Wittenberg positions (demands Chemnitz supported) and Melanchthon's bitterness over what he considered betrayal by Flacius and his comrades prevented the negotiations from succeeding.

In August 1557 Chemnitz accompanied Mörlin to Worms to serve as one of two secretaries for the evangelical negotiators in a colloquy called by Emperor Ferdinand between adherents of the *Augsburg Confession* and the papal party. The ducal Saxon delegation, with instructions written by Flacius, supported by Mörlin and Erasmus Sarcerius of Mansfeld, insisted on clarification of issues which were dividing the evangelicals before, they believed, forthright discussions with the Roman Catholics could take place. The clarification failed to materialize, and the departure of the "Gnesio-Lutherans" ended the colloquy. There Chemnitz came to know the other evangelical secretary at these talks, Jakob Andreae of Württemberg, with whose life his own became intertwined.

The Development of Chemnitz's Theology of the Lord's Supper and Christology

At this time tensions in the Lower Saxon city of Bremen between two pastors, Albert Hardenberg and Johann Timann, over the Lord's Supper commanded the concern of the other ministeria in the area. Hardenberg, a close friend of Melanchthon, held the sacramental position of Martin Bucer and avoided expressions with which Luther defined the presence of Christ's body and blood in the sacrament. Timann affirmed with Luther that Christ's words of institution should be literally interpreted – the argument repeated by most North German Lutherans – and that the communication of attributes between the two natures of Christ helped explain how such a bodily presence in bread and wine is possible – an argument neglected by most followers of Luther, apart from Andreae and his mentor in Württemberg, Johannes Brenz. Mörlin and Chemnitz supported Timann; Melanchthon supported Hardenberg.

The matter came to a head in 1561 when Hardenberg was deprived of his office by Bremen officials. Chemnitz criticized Hardenberg's position in his *Anatomy of The Propositions of Albert Hardenberg on the Lord's Supper*.[1] The Lower Saxon ministeria, meeting in Lüneburg in July, affirmed Chemnitz's position as summarized by Mörlin in the Lüneburg *Articles of Faith*. The "Braunschweig theology" which Mörlin and his coadjutor represented had come to dominate Lutheran thought in North Germany. Shortly thereafter Chemnitz published his *Repetition of the Salutary Teaching on the True Presence of the Lord's Body and Blood in the Supper*,[2] which became a standard for Gnesio-Lutheran argument regarding the sacrament. Here Chemnitz exhibited a characteristic of his method that he would continue to practice his entire life. Unlike some of his comrades and some opponents, he strove to state fairly the opinions of the latter, and to deal with their concerns rather than with his own fears about where their opinions might lead. With careful exegetical examination of relevant biblical passages (Mt. 26:26–8, Mk. 14:22–5, Lk. 22:19–20, 1 Cor. 10:16–17, 11:23–6, 27, 29) and extensive patristic citation, Chemnitz argued that Christ's body and blood are truly present in the bread and wine of the Supper, to be received through the mouths of both worthy and unworthy recipients. He grounded his position on the literal interpretation of Christ's words of institution. The sole basis for his position was the authority of God's Word, as Jesus had spoken it in those words. Faith cannot speculate on the basis of what God's almighty power might accomplish but can only adhere to what God has said in Scripture. Conjecture regarding God's power or Christological arguments based upon the communication of attributes between Christ's natures could do no more than offer plausible bases of support for the teaching that God gives of the body and blood of Christ in the Sacrament. The words of Christ, "This is my body," alone establish that teaching, Chemnitz believed.

Luther's Christological doctrine became an ever more important issue in Wittenberg circles in the 1560s. Melanchthon labeled Chemnitz's Lower Saxon Gnesio-Lutheran friend Joachim Westphal, pastor in Hamburg, a "bread worshiper" because he defended the presence of Christ's Body and Blood in the bread and wine of the Supper, and particularly because he held the "new dogma" of the communication of attributes which departed from Melanchthon's teaching. That "new dogma" was intended to reiterate Luther's belief that within the indissoluble person of Christ, the divine and human natures share their characteristics in such a way that concretely the human nature within that person exercises the characteristics of the divine nature, even though it always remains completely distinct from the divine nature, retains its own characteristics, and never possesses divine characteristics as its own.[3] Brenz and Andreae, representing the church in Württemberg, defended their unique formulation of this teaching in their polemic with neighboring Calvinists, particularly in the colloquy of Maulbronn (1564). Their Palatine opponents labeled them "ubiquitists" because they taught that the human nature not only shares the divine nature's characteristics of omnipotence and omniscience but also that of omnipresence (ubiquity); Melanchthon's heirs in Wittenberg privately attacked the Württembergers. Chemnitz found their position relied too much on philosophical argument and deduction. He himself preferred to say that Christ's human nature, bound in the one person to his divine nature, could be present in whatever form God ordained wherever and whenever God willed (multivolipresence). In correspondence in the mid-1560s Andreae and Chemnitz worked toward a common understanding of Christology, never quite reaching accord but recognizing that they held essentially the same view.

As Chemnitz composed a formal treatment of the subject, he solicited comments on an early draft from Andreae as well as from his friend in Rostock, David Chytraeus, and North German Gnesio-Lutherans including Tilemann Hesshus and Johannes Wigand. The work appeared in 1570, *On the Two Natures in Christ*.[4] Composed in the same style as his treatment of the Lord's Supper, its massive biblical argument, framed with patristic citations, set forth his interpretation of Scriptural teaching on the Incarnation and analyzed ancient heresies and contemporary opposing views. Chemnitz's view lay closer to Luther's than that of Brenz, for Chemnitz taught that the communication of attributes so united divine and human natures that where God is, Jesus is, but he regarded this truth as the presupposition that makes Christ's presence in the Supper possible, not that which can be proven to be its basis. Nonetheless, he recognized the critical connection between Christ's presence in the Supper and the Incarnation.

Chemnitz's most critical contribution to Lutheran Christology was his formulation of the three "genera" of the communication of attributes. The way in which Christ's two natures share their characteristics can first be described with the *genus idiomaticum*, according to which the "essential properties of each nature . . . are not communicated in such a way that they come into being in or through the union and become the properties of the other nature, but rather are communicated to the person."[5] The characteristics of each nature are characteristics of the one person of Christ, without ceasing to be characteristics of that nature and without becoming characteristics that belong to the other nature. The second genus, the *genus apotelesmaticum,* asserted that in his redemptive actions the characteristics of each nature are the characteristics of the one person of Christ. These two explanations encountered almost no objections from other Lutheran theologians. However, Chemnitz's third genus, the *genus maiestaticum,* did. It taught that the characteristics of the divine nature are shared with the human nature, even though they never belong to the human nature as such. That means that concretely, within the personal union of the natures, the human nature exercises divine characteristics, not by virtue of possessing them but rather by virtue of being inseparably united to the divine nature, in that union which is the one person Jesus Christ. His incarnation makes possible for Jesus things that no other human being can be or do, because he shares divine characteristics as a human being in one single person, who is God and this particular human creature. In his ascension both natures of Christ also received the almighty power designated with the biblical expression, "the right hand of God."

Chemnitz's book aroused embittered hostility from the Wittenberg faculty, for its members believed that this "Judas brother" was betraying Melanchthon's legacy. He certainly was opposing their interpretation of it, and that became clear when they issued a catechism for secondary schools in early 1571. From several quarters came protests against its presentation on Christ's presence in the sacraments and on the communication of attributes; Chemnitz himself wrote one from the ministerium of the city of Braunschweig.[6] At the end of 1571 the Lower Saxon ministeria accepted his Christological teaching as their own in the *Repetition of the Common Christian Confession . . . Against the Sacramentarian Teaching,*[7] which he himself had drafted.

Chemnitz's Critique of the Council of Trent

Not only issues raised within Lutheran circles engaged Chemnitz. In 1562 he responded to early Jesuit attacks against evangelical reform, in his *Analytical Description and Delineation of Jesuit Theology.*[8] Soon thereafter he began his most ambitious work, his *Examination of the Council of Trent,*[9] which appeared in four volumes between 1565 and 1573. It carefully analyzed all the canons and decrees of the Council of Trent, presenting not only its errors in doctrine but also Lutheran teaching on the subjects the Council had treated. Chemnitz's formidable command of the church fathers was employed to put his own biblical interpretation in the context of the teaching of the early church. He analyzed the text of Trent's decisions in the context of both late medieval scholastic theology and contemporary Roman Catholic theology, particularly that of Jacob Payva de Andrada, a Portuguese Jesuit, but also the Dutch bishop William Lindanus, the Dutch theologian Albert Pighius, and the Polish bishop Stanislaus Hosius.

Trent had begun with the question of authority in the church, specifically the relationship between Scripture and tradition. Chemnitz anchored all teaching in Scripture, for its dignity and authority rested on God's "institut[ing] and command[ing] the plan of comprehending the heavenly doctrine in writing" and upon his initiating, dedicating, and consecrating it by writing the words of the Decalog himself (Ex. 34:1). God caused the "true, genuine, and pure voice of the heavenly doctrine" to be committed to writing in the prophetic books. Because the Holy

Spirit inspired it, Scripture is the Word of God. Therefore, "the sacred Scripture is the canon, norm, rule, foundation, and pillar of our whole faith, so that whatever is to be accepted under this title and name, that it is the doctrine of Christ and of the apostles, must be proved and confirmed from the Scripture." Against his opponents he defended the sufficiency and clarity of Scripture, affirming that it contains all that God wants his people to know of himself and his will and that the eyes of faith can comprehend its truth clearly.[10]

Though Scripture serves as the sole ultimate authority for the church's teaching, Chemnitz treasured the tradition of Christian teaching and analyzed that concept in eight categories. The first seven were different forms of handing down and expressing biblical teaching; the eighth consisted of "traditions which pertain both to faith and morals and which cannot be proved with any testimony of Scriptures." When the church of Rome attempts to impose such "traditions" upon believers as authoritative, it establishes its own will above that of God, Chemnitz argued.[11] As highly as he valued the testimonies of the Fathers, he held that every tradition from them had credibility and authority for public teaching only if it could be demonstrated as in accord with Scripture.

Although he commented on all of Trent's official pronouncements, the heart of Chemnitz's critique lay in his evaluation of its decrees related to the doctrine of justification. Presuming that God created human beings with powers "in the whole heart, the complete will, in all members of the body and capacities of the soul" that were "entirely whole and perfect for the knowledge and love of God and thereafter of the neighbor," Chemnitz taught that any deviation from that perfect trust and obedience is sin, even the concupiscence which remains in believers after baptism.[12] His doctrine of sin laid the basis for excluding any human contribution to that which constitutes human righteousness in God's sight.

In discussing the critical question of the freedom of the will Chemnitz recognized the psychological activity of thinking and willing involved in conversion, but he insisted that the will is moved by the Holy Spirit, without preparing itself in any way for its turning from evil to God. The sinful will can outwardly keep God's laws to a greater or lesser extent, but until the Holy Spirit changes its disposition, it opposes God's lordship and refuses to trust in him.

Chemnitz believed that the key issue on which the Roman church erred was the doctrine of what makes sinners righteous in God's sight, the doctrine of justification. He identified the critical point of controversy: what it is that causes God to receive sinners into grace, or what it is that faith apprehends when it trusts in the forgiveness of sins. His fundamental answer to that question is expressed in his definition of justification: "absolution from sins, the remission of sins, through imputation of the righteousness of Christ, through adoption and inheritance of eternal life, and that only for the sake of Christ, who is apprehended by faith." This definition did not deny that renewal of new obedience, love, and good works flow naturally from the disposition of this trust in God's reconciling gift of new life in Christ.[13] But Chemnitz took great pains to distinguish that renewal from God's justifying act that restores sinners to innocence and righteousness in his sight.

The *Examination* provides a refined linguistic analysis of the Greek and Hebrew words for "to justify," with copious biblical citations and also, in the case of the

Greek, references from classical literature. On the basis of ancient Latin usage he rejected the interpretation of the verb as making righteous through the infusion of the quality of righteousness, as his opponents taught. Instead, he noted that "to justify" has two meanings: "to judge or to pronounce something just," and to inflict judicial punishment. With Luther's understanding of the Word of God as the creative agent which fashions all reality, Chemnitz taught that, on the basis of Christ's suffering the punishment of sin, i.e., death, God's Word of absolution justifies as a re-creative act of God. God makes sinners into saints through the power of the gospel for the sake of Christ's suffering, death, and resurrection.[14]

This Word of the promise of new life creates and is grasped by trust. "Faith is the means, or instrument, through which we seek, apprehend, receive, and apply to ourselves from the Word of the Gospel the mercy of God, who remits sins and accepts us to life eternal for the sake of his Son, the Mediator."[15] Chemnitz presumed Luther's distinction between the "active righteousness" of good works in relationships between human beings, which even unbelievers could do outwardly ("civic righteousness"), and the passive righteousness of receiving God's gift of love and the status of being his child, which he bestows through his grace and favor apart from every human activity. On this basis Chemnitz explained with quotations from Scripture and the Fathers that the biblical concept of faith is that trust which embraces the whole human life, the disposition of reliance on and confidence in God which dedicates all of life to God. No human work can bring forth faith or create the relationship with God. God alone can create this relationship with his children.

Chemnitz defended his view with an extensive study of the biblical writers' use of the "exclusive particles," those words which indicate that God alone is responsible for salvation, apart from any role for human performance or merit. His examination of the exclusive particles, "grace," and "gratis," "apart from the law," "apart from works," and related usage of the concepts of imputation, remission of sins, and faith assembled scriptural support for his doctrine of justification through faith in Christ alone.[16]

The *Examination*'s critique of Trent's sacramental theology employed massive biblical and historical citation to repudiate all divergences from what Chemnitz believed God willed for the church's use of the "means of grace," the Word in its oral, written, and sacramental forms. He believed that God's Word is efficacious in incorporating God's chosen children into the household of faith, forgiving their sins, and bestowing life and salvation upon them.[17] The *Examination* codified the Lutheran critique of Roman Catholic theology and served the conduct of further polemic against Rome in subsequent centuries.

Formulating Lutheran Concord

As Chemnitz was engaged in his defense of Lutheran teaching against Roman Catholicism, he was also exercising leadership in new ways. Four years earlier, Mörlin had been called back to Prussia. Duke Albrecht sought Chemnitz's return as well, but the Braunschweig city council placed him in Mörlin's office as superintendent of the church, insisting it could not lose them both. Chemnitz's contribution to the system of church government in the city in 1563 helped prepare him to assist Mörlin in drafting a new constitution and standard of doctrine for Prussia (*Corpus doctrinae Prutenicum*), and that experience paved the way for his work on the new church order for the duchy of Braunschweig-Wolfenbüttel. When that principality became Lutheran, in mid-1568, as Duke Julius succeeded his arch-Roman Catholic father, Heinrich, Chemnitz became the duke's chief theological advisor, director of the introduction of the Reformation in his lands. With Andreae he fashioned a constitution for Julius's church in 1569; in 1576 he constructed collections of confessional documents (called a *Corpus doctrinae*) for Braunschweig-Wolfenbüttel and Braunschweig-Lüneburg.

In 1569 Chemnitz also created an important tool for introducing the Reformation in Julius's lands, an examination for pastors that served in fact as a basic doctrinal textbook. This work, *The Chief Parts of Christian Teaching*,[18] subsequently revised and reissued a number of times, was patterned after Melanchthon's *Examination of Those to be Ordained* of 1552, and it referred its readers to Melanchthon's coverage of certain topics. Once again using copious biblical citations, Chemnitz led pastors through the fundamental topics regarding their own office and their teaching with questions which not only taught them what to think but how to think about and to use the Scriptures for their parishioners. In this little volume the pastor's concern for pastoral care, for the proper admonition and comfort of the sinner-saints of the congregation, is clearly and skillfully expressed and conveyed to priests converted by ducal decree to their new faith.

Julius also borrowed Andreae for two years from his cousin, Duke Christoph of Württemberg, to assist in introducing the Reformation into his lands and, in 1570, obtained the services of Nikolaus Selnecker from August of Saxony as well. Though the relationships forged in these days did contribute to theological rapprochement among the three a few years later, suspicion and friction marked their relationships during the time of their initial teamwork.

Andreae had come north in 1568 with a twofold commission from his duke, who had been trying to restore Lutheran unity since 1553. Not only was he to help institute the Reformation of Julius's duchy. He was also to promote Lutheran unity by visiting cities and princely courts with five brief statements designed to cover the differences of the Gnesio-Lutherans and their "Philippist" opponents. But Chemnitz sought unity on a different basis than did Andreae. Andreae's "Five Articles" appealed above all to lay leaders, especially the princes, with short, positive summaries vaguely enough worded to paper over and paste together what Andreae believed were significantly different positions on the issues of adiaphora, freedom of the will, the necessity of good works for salvation, and the Lord's Supper. Without the condemnations of false teaching and false teachers and without the explicit development of proper teaching that the Gnesio-Lutherans demanded, his approach had only a negative effect in their circles, and Chemnitz opposed it. For he believed that the Lutherans of varying opinions shared fundamentally the same view of most issues, and he believed that the task of bringing unity required explicit and detailed examination of all sides of the disputed questions dividing Luther's and Melanchthon's followers.

Therefore, when Andreae tried to create the appearance of unity at a special synod of Lutheran governments at Zerbst (May 1570), he elicited Chemnitz's criticism. He encountered outright rejection, however, from the Wittenberg faculty, which now openly dismissed his "ubiquitous" doctrine of the communication of attributes. Andreae returned to Württemberg in disappointment. Lutheran harmony in teaching seemed elusive if not impossible to create. That, seven years later, two-thirds of the Lutheran churches of Germany found concord rested in part on Andreae's diplomatic persistence, in part on Chemnitz's theological skill.

The internal situation of German Lutheranism appeared grim at the beginning of the 1570s. It seemed impossible to dream of Lutheran concord because of the collapse of the Altenburg Colloquy between ducal Saxon Gnesio-Lutheran theologians and their Philippist counterparts from electoral Saxony (1569), the emergence of a public Philippist counterattack against both Gnesio-Lutheran and Swabian opponents (1570–1), and the intensification of the dispute over Christology and the Lord's Supper between the Electoral Saxons and almost all other Lutheran theologians during 1571. But Andreae dared to dream, and in 1573 he authored a little book in sermon form, *Six Sermons on the Divisions Among the Theologians of the Augsburg Confession*.[19] Still directed at a lay audience, with argumentation drawn largely from the Catechism, he turned sharply in the Gnesio-Lutheran direction. He rejected the most radical of their positions, Flacius's doctrine that original sin is the essence of the sinner, a position that most of his Gnesio-Lutheran comrades (including Chemnitz) had also rejected. Andreae did join them in condemning false teaching and false teachers, above all the Wittenberg theologians, in the text or marginal notations of his sermons. He developed his positive exposition of Lutheran teaching in detail. He appealed to theologians as well as princes for support.

Chemnitz was one of those to whom he turned. With David Chytraeus, Chemnitz first requested that Andreae hand the task over to his fellow theologians in Württemberg and have them compose articles of concord that would formulate solutions to the disputes at a higher level of theological discourse. Andreae obliged the second request but ignored the first. Alone he drafted the "Swabian Concord." Chemnitz and Chytraeus circulated this text in the course of 1574 to their associates throughout northern Germany and themselves revised Andreae's efforts into the "Swabian Saxon Concord." By 1575 that text was ready to be used in a strikingly altered political situation.

Elector August of Saxony had discovered in early 1574 that his leading theologians, aided by key secular advisors, were promoting a spiritualized view of Christ's presence in the Lord's Supper. Raised by parents who had risked much to support Luther, sensitive to the charge that divergence from the *Augsburg Confession*'s doctrine of the Lord's Supper could place his government outside the legal protection of the Religious Peace of Augsburg, August, driven by a sense of betrayal, exiled or jailed the leaders of what was called a "crypto-Calvinist" plot.[20] He also enlisted Selnecker and other Philippists in his ministerium who were not supportive of their colleagues' spiritualizing direction to return the teaching and practice of his lands to the old Wittenberg tradition of Luther and Melanchthon. The elector also called Andreae from Württemberg, gaining a five-year commitment for assistance in that process from him and his prince. August's remaining theologians supported his desire to use their own need for a program of doctrinal clarification as an occasion for Lutheran concord in general. Against Andreae's wishes, Chemnitz was drawn into the deliberations, along with three other outside theologians, David Chytraeus and two representatives from Brandenburg, Andreas Musculus and Christoph Körner.

When the expanded electoral Saxon committee met at Torgau in May 1576, Chemnitz provided theological leadership for combining the *Swabian Saxon Concord* with another document composed by theologians from Württemberg, Baden, and Henneberg in the previous January, the *Maulbronn Formula*. After this *Torgau Book* had been circulated to ministeria throughout Germany and their critiques had been gathered, Chemnitz, along with Andreae, Chytraeus, Selnecker, Musculus, and Körner, refined the text at Bergen Abbey in May 1577, and produced the *Solid Declaration* of the *Formula of Concord*. In almost all of its 12 articles on the disputed topics that had been dividing Lutherans, Chemnitz's careful crafting addressed Philippist concerns while affirming the teaching of the main body of Gnesio-Lutherans. Thus Chemnitz created a document of reconciliation that indeed served to produce the concord that had so long eluded his church.

Chemnitz's influence appears, for instance, in the Formula's article on justification, both in his draft of its critique of Roman Catholic teaching and in the rejection of Osiander's doctrine composed by Andreae. Chemnitz's finely tuned analyses of the disputed issues regarding the Lord's Supper and the person of Christ guided his colleagues' solutions to these issues. He crafted the Formula's treatment of good works, as a necessary result of God's gift of faith but in no way a contributing factor to salvation, thereby meeting concerns for the moral performance of believers but also preserving the clarity of Luther's teaching on salvation by grace through faith.

His skill at addressing the agendas of both sides in controversy is seen also in his formulation of the *Formula*'s approach to the topic of God's choosing of those who would come to faith. Many of Luther's disciples had avoided his conclusions regarding eternal election in his *On the Bondage of the Will*, focussing instead on the later Melanchthon's concern for human responsibility and the activity of the will. Chemnitz followed Luther's guidelines for thinking about God's unconditioned choosing of his people before the foundation of the world (Eph. 1:3–14) in his Genesis lectures (chapter 26), anchoring the use of this teaching in the proper distinction of law and gospel and in the use of the means of grace. Chemnitz distinguished God's foreknowledge of what would happen among fallen human creatures from God's creative and merciful choice of those to whom he would give the gift of faith, his election. Election is only an expression of the gospel of Jesus Christ, and therefore predestination to damnation is impossible, he argued. Believers need not worry about whether they are elect or not, for the means of grace, the promise of the gospel in preaching and absolution, in baptism and the Lord's Supper, give them the assurance that nothing can separate them from God's love in Christ (Rom. 8:28–39).[21]

Chemnitz contributed decisively not only to the composition of the content but also to the process leading to the publication of the *Solid Declaration*, along with Andreae's summary of it, the Epitome, in the *Formula of Concord* within a collection of confessions called the *Book of Concord*. During the three years between the composition of the *Formula of Concord* and the publication of the *Book of Concord* on June 25, 1580, he worked together with Andreae and others to win acceptance for the settlement. The two of them journeyed to Heidelberg to convince the Calvinist Elector Friedrich's Lutheran son and successor Ludwig to support their *Concord*, with success, drawing the Palatinate to the cause of concord.

In the midst of the process of using the *Book of Concord* to effect concord, Chemnitz suffered one significant disappointment. In 1578 Duke Julius had his three sons submit to Roman Catholic consecration in order to win the right for them to assume possession of ecclesiastical territories in order to expand the power of his house. With the confessional courage and prophetic defiance of erring governing officials which had cost a number of his Gnesio-Lutheran friends their positions, Chemnitz sharply criticized this move, and his friendship with Julius collapsed. The duke deprived his theological counselor of his appointments in the ducal government (although he remained superintendent of the church in the city of Braunschweig). Julius continued to mount objections to the *Concord* and to attempts to defend it in which Chemnitz participated. Efforts to bring Julius's government back into the *Concord* failed at the colloquy in Quedlinberg in early 1583, where Chemnitz and others met with Julius's representatives.

The *Formula of Concord* elicited immediate reactions, both from Flacius's disciples who opposed its condemnation of his doctrine of original sin, and from Philippists and Calvinists who disapproved its articles on the Lord's Supper and Christology. The elector of Brandenburg asked Chemnitz to meet with Selnecker from Saxony and Timotheus Kirchner from the Palatinate to refute these attacks. In 1581 they began work on four lengthy essays which were combined into the *Apology of the Book of Concord* (1583).[22]

Afflicted with failing memory and increasing physical ills, Chemnitz resigned his office on September 9, 1584. He died on April 8, 1586. His successor Polycarp Leyser supervised the posthumous publication of his commentary on Melanchthon's *Loci* and his postil.[23] Johann Gerhard completed his harmony of the Gospels.[24]

Often designated "the second Martin" because his reformulation of Luther's theology in his major works and the *Formula of Concord* conveyed the chief elements of the Reformer's thought to subsequent generations, Chemnitz must also be regarded as one major interpreter of Melanchthon's thought. Chemnitz's theology combined his synthesis of the concerns and emphases of the two Wittenberg colleagues with viewpoints of contemporaries and his own study of Scripture and the Fathers; his thought significantly shaped the direction and form of Lutheran Orthodox theology for a century and a half. His works were made available in the nineteenth and twentieth centuries because they are regarded as important expressions of Reformation theology.

Notes

1 *Anatome propositionum Alberti Hardenbergii de coena Domini* . . . (Eisleben: Gaubisch, 1561).

2 *Repetitio sanae doctrinae de vera praesentia corporis et sanguinis Domini in coena* (Leipzig, Vögelin, 1561), rev. ed. 1570, under the title *Fundamenta sanae doctrinae de vera et substantialti praesentia, exhibitione, et sumptione corporis et sanguinis Domini in Coena* (Jena, 1571).

3 Editor's note: On the *communicatio idiomatum* see Johann Anselm Steiger, "The *communicatio idiomatum* as the Axle and

Motor of Luther's Theology," *LQ* 14/2 (Summer 2000), 125–58.

4 *De duabus naturis in Christo. De hypostatica earum unione: de communicatione Idiomatum* . . . (Jena: Richtzenhan, 1570; 2nd ed. Leipzig: Rhamba, 1578).

5 Ibid., 178.

6 *Bedencken Der Theologen zu braunschweigk, von dem Newen Wittenbergischen Catechismo* . . . (Jena: Richtzenhan, 1571).

7 *Wiederholte Christliche Gemeine Confession vnd Erklerung: Wie in den Sechsischen Kirchen* . . . *wieder die Sacramentierer gelehret wirdt* (Wolfenbüttel: Horn, 1571).

8 *Theologiae Iesvvitarvm praecipva capita* (Leipzig: Vögelin, 1562).

9 *Examen decretorum concilii Tridentini*, 4 vols. (Frankfurt and Main: Feyerabend, 1566–73).

10 Martin Chemnitz, *Examination of the Council of Trent*, trans. Fred Kramer, 4 vols. (St Louis: Concordia, 1971–86), 1:53, 55, 101.

11 Ibid., 1:272, 272–307.

12 Ibid., 1:323, 311–74.

13 Ibid., 1:468, 467.

14 Ibid., 1:470–1, 457–544.

15 Ibid., 1:565; cf. 547–611.

16 Ibid., 1:582–5.

17 Ibid., 2:69–89. The entire second volume of the *Examination* treats sacramental issues; the third and fourth a variety of practices, including clerical celibacy, purgatory, invocation of the saints, images, indulgences, fasting, and festivals.

18 *Die fürnemsten Heuptstu[e]ck der Christlichen Lehre* . . . (Wolfenbüttel: Horn, 1569).

19 *Sechs Christlicher Predig Von den Spaltungen so sich zwischen den Theologen Augspurgischer Confession von Anno 1548. biss auff diss 1573. Jar nach vnnd nach erhaben. . . .*, trans. in Robert Kolb, *Andreae and the Formula of Concord* (St. Louis: Concordia, 1973).

20 It must be noted that the Wittenberg faculty members were representing their own understanding of Melanchthon's views of the Lord's Supper and Christology. Because they tried to conceal the spiritualizing direction of their theology, they may be labeled "crypto-" but their commitment to Melanchthon's theology justifies their being called "crypto-Philippist" since, in spite of their contacts with Swiss Reformed theologians, Calvin's actual influence on their thought was minimal. That Chemnitz and others interpreted Melanchthon differently than the Wittenberg theologians does not mean that the latter were not trying to be faithful to their common preceptor as they developed their differing views.

21 On election, see FC XI: *The Book of Concord, The Confessions of the Evangelical Lutheran Church*, ed. Robert Kolb and Timothy J. Wengert (Minneapolis: Fortress Press, 2000), 640–56.

22 *Apologia, Oder Verantwortung dess Christlichen ConcordienBuchs* . . . (Heidelberg: Spies, 1583).

23 *Loci theologici* . . . (Frankfurt am Main: Spies, 1591); *Postilla Oder Ausslegung der Euangelien* . . . (Magdeburg: Franck, 1594).

24 *Harmoniae . . . Evangelicae à M. Chemnitio inchoatae . . . libri quinque* (Jena, 1622).

Bibliography

Primary Sources

Chemnitz, Martin, *Examination of the Council of Trent*, trans. Fred Kramer, 4 vols., St. Louis: Concordia, 1971–86.
——, *Loci Theologici*, trans. J. A. O. Preus, 2 vols., St. Louis: Concordia, 1989.
——, *The Lord's Supper*, trans. J. A. O. Preus, St. Louis: Concordia, 1979.
——, *Ministry, Word, and Sacraments, an Enchiridion*, trans. Luther Poellot, St. Louis: Concordia, 1981.
——, *The Two Natures in Christ*, trans. J. A. O. Preus, St. Louis: Concordia, 1971.

Secondary Sources

Dingel, Irene, *Concordia controversa, Die öffentlichen Diskussionen um das lutherische Konkordienwerk am Ende des 16. Jahrhunderts*, Gütersloh: Gütersloher Verlagshaus, 1996.
Ebel, Jobst, "Die Herkunft des Konzeptes der Konkordienformel, Die Funktionen der fünf Verfasser neben Andreae beim Zustandekommen der Formel," *Zeitschrift für Kirchengeschichte* 91 (1980), 245–7.
——, *Wort und Geist bei den Verfassern der Konkordienformel*, Munich: Kaiser, 1981.

Green, Lowell C., "Three Causes of Conversion in Philipp Melanchthon, Martin Chemnitz, David Chytraeus, and the 'Formula of Concord,'" *LuJ* 47 (1980), 89–114.

Hägglund, Bengt, "'Majestas hominis Christi,' Wie hat Martin Chemnitz die Christologie Luthers gedeutet?," *LuJ* 47 (1980), 71–88.

Johansson, Torbjörn, *Reformationens huvudfrågor och arvet från Augustinus, En studie i Martin Chemnitz' Augustinusreception*, Göteborg: Församlingsförlaget, 1999.

Jünke, W. A., ed., *Der zweite Martin der Lutherischen Kirche*, Braunschweig: Ev.-Luth. Stadtkirchenverband, 1986.

Kaufmann, Thomas, "Martin Chemnitz (1522–1586), Zur Wirkungsgeschichte der theologischen Loci" in Heinz Scheible, ed., *Melanchthon in seinen Schülern*, Wiesbaden: Harrassowitz, 1997, 183–253.

Klug, Eugene F., *From Luther to Chemnitz on Scripture and the Word*, Grand Rapids: Eerdmans, 1971.

Mahlmann, Theodor, *Das neue Dogma der lutherischen Christologie*, Gütersloh: Gütersloher Verlagshaus, 1969.

Martens, Gottfried, *Die Rechtfertigung des Sünders – Rettungshandeln Gottes oder historisches Interpretament?*, Göttingen: Vandenhoeck & Ruprecht, 1992.

Oftestad, Bernd Torvild, "'Historia' und 'Utilitas'. Methodologische Aspekte der Abendmahlstheologie bei Martin Chemnitz," *Archiv für Reformationsgeschichte* 77 (1986), 186–225.

——, "Lehre, die das Herz bewegt. Das Predigtparadigma bei Martin Chemnitz," *Archiv für Reformationsgeschichte* 80 (1989), 125–53.

Preus, J. A. O. *The Second Martin, The Life and Theology of Martin Chemnitz*, St. Louis: Concordia, 1994.

Reformed Theologians

part 3

Huldrych Zwingli (1484–1531)

Gregory J. Miller

Although the importance of Huldrych (Ulrich) Zwingli in the opening scenes of the Protestant Reformation has never been contested, only in the last few decades has there been widespread interest in his life and teachings in and of themselves. Zwingli's reputation suffered the triple negative of being castigated by Luther as a tool of the devil, being overshadowed by John Calvin in Upper Germany and Switzerland, and, perhaps most damaging of all, dying an untimely and violent death on the battlefield of Kappel. "Zwinglianism" came to be identified not with any positive theological or liturgical construction but with a denial of the presence of Christ in the Eucharist.[1] In many surveys of the Reformation, Zwingli appears primarily in contrast to Luther: more a humanist than a theologian, lacking true spiritual depth, and advocating a disastrous admixture of politics and religion. His most important role was understood to be his opposition to Luther at the Colloquy of Marburg (1529) and thus his responsibility, at least indirectly, for the splintering of Protestantism. Only in Zurich was a rearguard action fought to preserve the independent importance of Zwingli.

The combination of two factors in twentieth-century scholarship encouraged a renewed study of Zwingli and an appreciation of his unique contributions. As scholarship on the Reformation became disentangled from confessional history, Zwingli could be investigated without serving as a foil to other reformers. Also, the important work of Bernd Moeller drew attention to Zwingli and the unique aspects of the Protestant Reformation in the Free Imperial cities.[2] As a result, there have been important reinterpretations of Zwingli and a flurry of scholarship concerning him since the 1950s.[3]

The Background of Zwingli's Reformation Activity

Zwingli was born on January 1, 1484, in the Toggenburg, an alpine region of Switzerland under the joint jurisdiction of the alliance of Swiss cantons. His parents were well-to-do peasants who were leaders in the local government and had connections with the organization of the church. Zwingli was a dedicated patriot who loved the Swiss land and people. His earliest extant writing, the patriotic poem *The Ox* (1510), extolled the industrious Swiss and urged self-sufficiency and independence. Zwingli's dedication to his fatherland was an important factor throughout his life, influencing the early development of his humanism, the motivation of his reforming activities, and the conduct of the Zurich reform.

Zwingli attended the University of Vienna, where he was significantly influenced by the humanism of Conrad Celtis and others. He completed his Bachelor (1504) and Master (1506) of Arts at the University of Basel, where he received theological instruction according to the *via antiqua* of Thomas Aquinas. When he was 22 Zwingli was ordained a priest by the bishop of Constance. His first position, the parish priest of Glarus, was not insignificant. His experience as chaplain of the Glarus mercenary contingent in the Italian campaigns of 1513 and 1515 instilled within him a deep sense of the immorality of the mercenary trade and a conviction that the wrath of God would be poured out upon the Swiss if they persisted in this sinful activity. Zwingli's support of the papacy and his public opposition to mercenary service for France led to his departure from Glarus for the position of people's priest at nearby Einsiedeln. In his two years at Einsiedeln (1516–18) he immersed himself in the Greek New Testament and preached to the large crowds of pilgrims that gathered at its famous shrine of the Black Virgin.

In 1518 the city government of Zurich and the canons of the Great Minster called Zwingli to be people's priest. Zurich was a significant city (with a population of around five thousand) which directly controlled a sizable area of northern Switzerland. Despite some opposition to his appointment, the guilds of Zurich supported him as an advocate of their own resistance to an alliance with France and as a proponent of humanism. In addition, he was already a recognized preacher and one of the best Greek scholars north of the Alps. When Zwingli began his preaching responsibilities on January 1, 1519, he declared that he would break from the tradition of using the lectionary texts and instead preach "only the Scriptures."

By 1522, preaching "only the Scriptures" in Zurich emboldened some of his listeners to abandon the Lenten tradition of abstinence from meat. Although Zwingli did not himself participate in the "affair of the sausages," he defended the actions of the fast-breakers. Tensions between Zwingli's *sola scriptura* preaching and traditional religious practices continued to mount. The Zurich Town Council sought to avert unrest and to establish its own control over religious life in the canton through the First Zurich Disputation (January 1523). The meeting concluded that the Scriptures alone, not obedience to the ecclesiastical hierarchy, were to be the measure of orthodoxy. Zwingli's preaching was validated and the town council effectively declared its independence in religious matters from the bishop of Constance. Further action resulted in the permission of priests to marry (including Zwingli himself in April 1524), the removal of religious images (June 1524), the disbanding of the leading Zurich monastery (October 1524), and the abolition of the Mass (April 1525).

While Zwingli was concerned with a thorough reform in Zurich, he was also eager to see the reform established throughout Switzerland and beyond. This led him to consider a wide variety of diplomatic alliances for the sake of the defense of the faith. In this context Zwingli sought the confidence of the Lutheran prince, Philip of Hesse.

To achieve a unified front of reform in opposition to the Hapsburgs, Philip recognized that a symbolic union would need to take place between Luther and Zwingli. Instead, the Colloquy of Marburg (October 1–4, 1529) simply brought into sharp relief the serious differences between them.

After Marburg, Zwingli was more compelled than ever to secure reform through political means. Attempts were made to win over France and even Venice to a defensive alliance. With the reluctant help of Bern, conflict was initiated with the Catholic Swiss cantons to force the issue of the free preaching of Scripture. The Second Kappel War found Zurich indecisive and ill prepared. Among the Zurichers killed in the battle were 25 clergy, including Zwingli. Zwingli's death did not end the reform in Switzerland or entirely discredit his work. Under the leadership of his successor, Heinrich Bullinger, the Zwinglian heritage was preserved and Zurich remained an important center for the European Reformation.

Zwingli as Theologian

Without essential reservations, Zwingli should be considered a traditional scholastic theologian with a common Catholic understanding of piety and the priesthood during the early portion of his ministry. Although the *via antiqua*, with its emphasis on the supreme and absolute doctrine of God, was an important influence, scholasticism and humanism cannot be regarded as mutually exclusive opposites.[4] From the earliest of Zwingli's extant writings there is a humanist element. Zwingli corresponded with humanist friends and sprinkled his writings with classical allusions. Erasmus was a significant influence. Zwingli owned more of Erasmus's writings than any other contemporary author, commented on them favorably in the margins, and expressed deep admiration for the scholar in correspondence.

The humanistic influences on Zwingli were important but not exclusive. Zwingli himself stated that in around 1516 he had turned from an intensive study of theology and philosophy to Scripture in its original languages.[5] By 1522 he no longer acknowledged the authority of the pope and the hierarchy of the church.[6] In this turn to the authority of Scripture, Luther had a significant influence on Zwingli. This influence was not theological, but as a model of heroism. Zwingli accused Erasmus of being reluctant to face consequences; Luther, on the other hand, was a "Hercules" at the Leipzig Disputation because he stood for truth regardless of the consequences.[7] As Zwingli read Luther's writings he saw in them confirmation of his own conclusions.[8]

Several key themes are evident throughout his writings: Christ and salvation, Spirit and Word, Sacrament and sign, the church, and the state and magistrate.[9]

Christ and Salvation

According to an autobiographical comment, a poem by Erasmus, *Expostulatio Jesu cum homine*, led Zwingli to a Christological emphasis that would remain distinctive of his theology. Salvation is through Christ alone: "I do not need the presence of any bishop or priest to ensure my forgiveness; for Christ himself did this once and for all in the most wonderful way in giving his body as a sacrifice for us and shedding his blood."[10] When Christ has done everything for us, "Why do we seek help in the creature?"[11]

The humanity of Christ is essential, but Zwingli's emphasis is clearly on the divinity which saves us and in which we are to put our trust. Zwingli was concerned that Luther was limiting God by confining him to Christ and enclosing him within the humanity of Christ. For Zwingli, there should be no adoration of Christ's humanity; the earthly life of Christ is primarily an example.[12]

Zwingli is no exception to the Reformed theologians' concern to assert and defend the absolute sovereignty of God. "[A]ll things are so done and disposed by the providence of God that nothing takes place without His will or command."[13] A sense of humankind as vessel in the hands of the potter is a theme of the poem he wrote after surviving a deadly encounter with the plague (the *Pestlied* of 1519), and throughout his letters.[14] An emphasis on sovereignty does not lead to resignation but rather to an active, trusting submission to the will of God.[15]

Zwingli asserts that salvation comes through Christ alone as a result of God's free election of individuals, regardless of the individual's actual knowledge of Christ. Therefore, it is possible for a gentile to be a Christian without even knowing anything about Christ.[16] It is in this context that specific gentiles such as Hercules and Socrates are mentioned in his vision of heaven.[17] At first blush this may seem to be evidence of a Renaissance universalism through proper moral choices accomplished by human free will. For Zwingli, however, it is a testimony to the absolute freedom of God. Ultimately, no outward means at all are necessary for salvation, including sacraments, church, Scripture, or even knowledge of Christ. Rather there is complete freedom of the Spirit to draw men unto salvation wherever they may be.[18] This aspect of Zwingli's thought was developed by his successor in the teaching office of the *Prophezei*, Theodor Bibliander. Bibliander considered himself a genuine follower of Zwingli in his interest in Islam and his desire for missionary work among the Muslims.[19]

The Spirit and the Word

The freedom of the Spirit in Zwingli's soteriology highlights the critical role that the Holy Spirit has throughout his theology.[20] Few Bible verses are quoted more frequently than John 3:8: "the wind blows where it chooses." For Zwingli the Spirit of God cannot be limited to either the Bible or the sacraments, for "in this way the liberty of the divine spirit which distributes itself to individuals as it will, that is, to whom it will, when it will, where it will, would be bound."[21]

The Spirit is particularly important for Zwingli in relation to the Word of God. Zwingli distinguished the "outer Word" (the Scripture heard without the Spirit) from the "inner Word" (the Word of God heard truly). "Even if you hear the gospel of Jesus Christ from an apostle you will not follow it unless the heavenly father teaches and draws you by his Spirit. . . . You must be *theodidacti*, that is, taught of God, not of men."[22] The anointing of the Holy Spirit frees the interpreter from the need of any teacher.[23] This inner word comes with a self-validating, existential assurance. "I know for certain that God teaches me, for I know this by experience."[24] Concerning how others could know that he was divinely enlightened, he simply stated: "The God who enlightens him [the Spirit-led exegete] will enable you [the listener] to perceive that what he says is of God."[25]

At times it appears that the Spirit is more important than the Word, and Luther strongly criticized Zwingli for divorcing the Spirit and the Word to the denigration of the latter. However, Zwingli does link the two.

> The shepherd must learn the Word of God only from the Holy Scriptures of the Bible. But it is vain for him to learn the letter, unless God draws his heart, so that he places trust in the Word, and does not wrest it according to his own desires, but gives it free rein, in keeping with its divine inspiration.[26]

Fidelity to Scripture serves as an indicator or measure of the true presence of the Spirit. Scripture restrains personal interpretation; Spirit and Scripture are never contrary.[27]

In *The Clarity and Certainty of the Word of God* (1522) Zwingli outlines the basics of his exegesis. Although analogy is a permissible exegetical method, the Word of God always has a "true and natural sense."[28] Context and comparison are the keys to understanding. Picking out verses without regard to their contexts is like breaking off a flower and trying to plant it in a garden. The proper interpretation of Scripture will always humble the exalted and exalt the lowly, help the poor but oppose those who trust in themselves, and not seek its own gain.[29]

The centrality of the Bible is evident in all essential aspects of the Zwinglian reform, in preaching, disputations, and in the educational institution created to train the Zurich clergy, the *Prophezei*. Scripture is to be the ultimate judge in the community as it was in the First Disputation, where large folios of the Scriptures in Latin, Hebrew, and Greek symbolically replaced the suzerain bishop as arbiter. Zwingli optimistically believed that true reform would occur, despite all adversity, if just the Scripture were permitted to be freely preached.

Sacrament and Sign

Not all of Zwingli's listeners came to perceive he was led by the Holy Spirit. Controversies concerning baptism and the Eucharist sharpened and refined his positions and clearly differentiated him from other advocates of reform.

A necessary foundation for a correct understanding of Zwingli's teaching on baptism and the Eucharist is his view on sacrament in general. Zwingli accepted Augustine's definition that a sacrament is "a sign of a sacred thing."[30] The etymology of the term *sacramentum* as a Roman military oath of allegiance described sacraments as signs "by which a man proves to the church that either he aims to be, or is, a soldier of Christ, and which informs the whole church rather than yourself of your faith."[31]

In his treatment of sacrament, a dichotomy between inward and outward is evident. He rejected the view that what is done outwardly in the sacrament causes inward change. A sacrament does not make present what it signifies, but it shows and attests that what it signifies is there. It is the sign of a grace that has been given, but not the instrument of that grace.

Faith does not need the sacraments or any sign. Salvation through Christ is not limited to Word and sacrament any more than it is historically limited to Israel.[32] "In the end Word and sacrament guarantee nothing. They are not automatically effective or effective for all because the Spirit blows where he wills, and you cannot make him blow simply by your act of preaching or baptizing or offering the sacramental bread."[33] The Spirit does not need the sacraments, although the sacraments need the Spirit.

It cannot be overstated how strongly Zwingli feared the seduction of the sign. It was a subtle and yet serious temptation for people to be drawn to the (physical) sign rather than to the salvific, spiritual reality. According to Zwingli we cannot learn Christ from any image or sacramental sign, for they affect only the senses. All we can learn about Christ from images is that He was handsome. It does not save us to know that He was crucified unless we understand that He was crucified for us. The Spirit teaches this inwardly without need of signs or images.[34]

Zwingli accused the Anabaptists of sacramentalism and legalism because they made being a Christian depend on the manner or fact of baptism.[35] For Zwingli, election precedes faith and in fact creates it. Therefore the Anabaptists reverse the divinely instituted order by requiring faith before inclusion in the church.[36] Since election is known only to God, Zwingli forbade any anticipation or attempted restriction according to external human standards. Baptism, as with all outward things, cannot save, but is a covenant sign or pledge.[37] It is not a pledge to sinlessness, but to amend one's life and follow Christ. Baptism is a pledging of oneself and a pledge to bring up one's children under the covenant.[38]

As in *A Reply to Hubmaier* (1525), the primary basis of his support of infant baptism is the essential unity of Old and New Testaments in a single covenant. Baptism should be given to infants because they are God's people. They should receive it as children because baptism replaces circumcision. Adult baptism breaks the unity of the church by excluding children.[39] Although there is no explicit reference to infant baptism in the New Testament, Zwingli believes that it was more likely than not practiced by the Apostles. He uses the analogy that just because the New Testament does not mention women receiving the Lord's Supper does not mean that they were not served during the time of the Apostles.

Zwingli is best known for his doctrine of the Eucharist. A key to understanding Zwingli's doctrine of the Eucharist, as in other aspects of his thought, is the dichotomy between inward and outward. From his earliest writings on the subject, the key verse is also Erasmus's theme, John 6:63: "It is the spirit that gives life; the flesh is useless."[40] For Zwingli it is clear: "To eat Christ physically does not help to give life."[41] "Everything rests on faith."[42] To eat is to believe.

It was also important for Zwingli that the distinction between the two natures of Christ be maintained. Christ's physical body must be in some particular place in heaven by reason of its character as a real body. Therefore Christ cannot be physically present in the Eucharist because He cannot be physically present in more than one place at one time.[43]

Beginning in 1524 he held a symbolic view of Jesus' words "this is my body" in which "is" was interpreted as "signifies."[44] A series of biblical tropes are given to demonstrate the propriety of this exegesis. A particularly important analogy for him is the Passover. "Every Jew knew very well the meaning of 'this is the Passover'; they knew that the lamb was not the Passover, but was a testimony to, or a memento of, the Passover."[45] The fact that he taught that the bread remained common bread did not detract from its significance. Using examples of a bride's flowers and a king's signet ring as flowers or common gold made significant by their use, "the usage and worthiness of the Last Supper give it [the bread] greater value – but it is still no different from any other bread."[46]

The famous conflict with Luther at the Marburg Colloquy did not create the division between the two reformers, but revealed how deep and significant it was. For both men essential issues were at stake and personal contexts made rapprochement difficult. Luther saw the denial of Christ's real presence in the Eucharist as an attack of the devil. Zwingli could not hold that the Eucharist was necessary for salvation without thereby denying his understanding of Christ and salvation.[47] For Luther the Eucharist is God's concrete offer of the gospel. For Zwingli the Eucharist is a community celebration of thanksgiving for the gospel. Both saw in the other a threat to their life's work as a reformer of the church and minister of the gospel. Both saw in the other a denial of the God-given means of salvation, a serious misunderstanding of the nature of Christ, and an erroneous handling of the Word of God.[48]

To state that Zwingli merely taught a doctrine of the "real absence" of Christ is to ignore the more positive articulations of his teaching. Eucharistic elements are signs pointing to liberation and salvation. Yet the Lord's Supper is more than a mere looking back, since the relationship between the remembering subject and the remembered creates a kind of "presence" in the heart.[49] Zwingli taught that Communion is given so that Christians may be united with one another, may testify that they are one body, and may pledge together to live the life of Christ.[50] Through the Eucharist the community becomes manifest as the people of God.[51] This unity was visibly represented in Zurich from Easter 1525 onward through the abolition of the Mass and its replacement by a service of clarity and austere simplicity. Organ music and singing disappeared, wooden patens and cups replaced the metal eucharistic implements, and the congregation sat at tables as for a meal.[52]

The Church

In his early controversies with Roman Catholics Zwingli's fundamental concern was to distinguish the true church from the hierarchical or institutional church. Christ's headship is set in opposition to the pope. The church is not just where the Word is preached, but where there is both Word and Spirit, where people adhere to the Word and live for Christ.[53]

Zwingli considered the greatest danger of the Anabaptists to be their sectarian ecclesiology. "[I]t is just as I have said from the very first. The root of the trouble is that the Anabaptists will not recognize any Christians except themselves or any church except their own."[54] The entire community must test whether something is of the Spirit.[55] "For if every blockhead who had a novel or strange opinion were allowed to gather a sect around him, divisions and sects would become so numerous that the Christian body which we now build up with such difficulty would be broken in pieces in every individual congregation."[56]

Zwingli's doctrine of the church includes a strong emphasis on the role of a well-trained ministry. He was himself a noted preacher and considered the task of the public proclamation of the Word of God to be *the* essential task of the clergy.[57] Zwingli actually preferred the term "prophet," although prophet, evangelist, pastor, and teacher all had the same fundamental meaning for him. The preacher has an indispensable role in the life of the community: to make known God's will. In Zwingli's biblical commentaries there is a strong expression of the social or political dimensions of the prophet's preaching. "If a prophet looks to the glory of God, if he looks to justice, peace and the public good, it is certain he is a true prophet, one sent by God. If he looks to anything else, he is false."[58]

The absolutely essential tool for the prophet's task is the knowledge of the Scriptures in their original languages. One of Zwingli's most significant contributions to the Reformation is his founding of the *Prophezei*, a theological school where the learned prophet could receive training in biblical languages and in the scriptural text. The intensity and rigor of the *Prophezei* is impressive. A part of each day except Friday and Sunday was devoted to detailed bible study. Select students and the clergy of Zurich gathered for prayer and then, in a serial manner, the reading of the scriptural passage for the day in Hebrew or Greek, followed by a grammatical and exegetical lecture in Latin.[59] Lectures were frequently copied verbatim and circulated to clergy throughout the canton.

The State and the Magistrate

Zwingli's idea of reform went beyond liturgical innovation to include an entire transformation of society based on the law of God. For Zwingli, real Christian living means keeping the law of God and following the example of Christ. "Whoever does not alter his life day by day after he has been restored in Christ, is mocking the name of Christ, and makes it contemptible and shameful in the sight of unbelievers."[60] The law is still in force because it is based in the nature of God.[61] Zwingli considered the greatest danger in carrying out reform to be lack of social–moral renewal. This would bring on the wrath of God and the death of the civil order.[62]

In the Christian state, both prophet and magistrate have essential functions. "For as man cannot exist except as composed of both body and soul . . . so the church cannot exist without the civil government."[63] "I know that the magistrate, when properly appointed, is God's agent no less than the prophet. For just as the prophet is a minister of heavenly wisdom and goodness when he expounds the faith and brings error to light, so too the magistrate is a minister of goodness and justice."[64] Government comes from God and is his servant; to disobey it is to disobey God.[65]

Zwingli found the distinction between divine and human righteousness a valuable tool in understanding the relationship between Christianity and society.[66] Divine righteousness is internal and is perfect in Christ. Human righteousness (synonymous with the term "government") is external and imperfect, but still necessary.[67] God directs the history of humanity with consummate power and skill toward the time when human and divine righteousness will grow into unity. It is therefore the task of all believers to advance the Reformation with all their might in the certain knowledge of God's support and of victory. Zwingli's political theology starts from this principle, which in turn makes *Realpolitik* the execution of God's righteous justice, trusting to God's omnipotence.[68]

Zwingli was committed to a state-run church. The clergy are to be subject to external, human righteousness with the exception of the necessary freedom for the proclamation of the Word of God and "so far as they [the magistrates] do not order what is contrary to God."[69] Even excommunication is by the magistrate. The minister is only to admonish.[70]

The Influence and Significance of Zwingli

Zwingli's public preaching, numerous publications (nearly ninety works), and extensive correspondence exercised considerable influence among contemporaries. His message spoke especially to the urban middling and lower classes, perhaps because his radical rejection of the Mass, images, and holy objects may have seemed an unambiguous break with the old church and its priests.[71]

Through the incorporation of elements of his thought in the work of Bullinger and Calvin, Zwingli continued to assert a significant influence after his death. While his personal influence was more local, "Zwinglianism" had a larger geographical impact. Calvin explicitly rejected some aspects of Zwingli's doctrine, including his view of the Eucharist and of the relationship between church and state. However, Calvin reacted positively to key aspects of Zwingli's theology, including his doctrines of law, penance, and the coordination of faith and works. While it may not be correct to refer to a dependence of Calvin on Zwingli, "Calvinism is inconceivable without the Zurich Reformation."[72] Zwingli's influence extended beyond the Continent to England and Scotland, specifically on Tyndale, Latimer, and Coverdale. The prophesying form was used in many places throughout Europe and became a staple of Puritan ministerial education.[73] Even when it is not explicit, Zwingli's influence is foundational to the Reformed tradition.[74]

Zwingli was open to Truth wherever it might be found. He was the first Protestant to construct a theology based on the *via antiqua* and Anselm's *fides quaerens intellectum*.[75] He was able to combine the individualism of the Erasmian humanist ideal with the concept of community life and discovered a means by which Renaissance humanistic education could be integrated into a biblical, Christian faith.[76] Not to be underestimated is the importance of Zwingli in the history of the Eucharist, in particular the role that the eucharistic controversies played in the early history of Protestantism. Millions of Christians around the globe refer to Zwingli as the articulator of their view of the sacraments. The Zwinglian reform is also significant for its commitment to biblicism, especially in the emphasis on the concept of the covenant.[77] In relation to this should be mentioned Zwingli's educational institution, the *Prophezei*, with its close connection between biblical languages and preaching.

Zwingli's reform is significant also because of its social and political aspects. Not only did one need to turn away from the idols in one's heart; they should be destroyed as well.[78] Without an outward expression of the inward transformation one could not speak of a genuine reform. "His aim was to build a Christian society, a society ordering its life according to God's word, in which preacher and prince (or in his case the council) were both servants of God."[79] Zwingli's pioneer work as an urban reformer shaped the life of one of Europe's most significant cities (and all of Switzerland with it). His concept of the *respublica christiana* inspired several European states and through them "influenced directly many political, social, and economic developments of the modern world."[80] In the evaluation of Gottfried Locher, Zwingli is the most conscious reformer of all the early Protestants. His aim was not only the reformation of the faith or of the church, or even of the personal Christian life, but rather of the whole life of Christendom.[81] There is no question of the impact this ever-expanding outward view of the reform has had upon the history of Christianity.

Notes

1 When most churchmen of the later sixteenth century were accused of or claimed to be "Zwinglian" it was because of their identification with a symbolic or memorial view of the elements of the Lord's Supper. See Gottfried W. Locher, *Zwingli's Thought: New Perspectives* (Leiden: E. J. Brill, 1981), 340–78.

2 Bernd Moeller, *Imperial Cities and the Reformation: Three Essays*, trans. and eds. H. C. Erik Midelfort and Mark U. Edwards, Jr. (Durham, NC: Labyrinth Press), 1982.

3 For example, works in the bibliography by W. P. Stephens, G. R. Potter, Ulrich Gäbler, J. V. Pollet, and Gottfried W. Locher.

4 Ulrich Gäbler, *Huldrych Zwingli: His Life and Work*, trans. Ruth L. Gritsch (Philadelphia: Fortress Press, 1986), 37.

5 *Of the Clarity and Certainty of the Word of God*, Z 1:379; 2: 44–5. Also, G. W. Bromiley, ed., *Zwingli and Bullinger* (Philadelphia: Westminster Press, 1953), 91.

6 Gäbler, *Zwingli*, 49, 87.

7 Locher, *Perspectives*, 53.

8 "Zwingli became a reformer through the Bible and Augustine not through Luther's teaching." Gottfried W. Locher, *Zwingli und die Schweizerische Reformation* (Göttingen: Vandenhoeck & Ruprecht, 1982), 18.

9 His most important summaries of his theology are: *An Exposition of the Articles* (1523), *A Short Christian Introduction* (1523), *A Commentary on the True and False Religion* (1525), and *An Account of the Faith* (1530).

10 Z 1:285–6. Also, Samuel Macauley Jackson, et al., eds., *The Latin Works of Huldreich Zwingli* (New York: Heidelberg Press, 1912), 1:240.

11 Z 2:217.

12 Zwingli had an orthodox understanding of Christ but held to an unusually sharp distinction between the divine and the human. W. P. Stephens, *The Theology of Huldrych Zwingli* (Oxford: Clarendon Press, 1986), 113.

13 Z 3:842–4. Also, Jackson, *Latin*, 1:271–4.

14 W. P. Stephens, *Zwingli: An Introduction to His Thought* (Oxford: Clarendon Press, 1992), 46.

15 "If misfortune and sickness come, think always – God is casting you aside just as a locksmith rejects a worn-out tool. Maybe God will take you up again for this purpose; if not, you must not take it amiss but submit yourself patiently to his will. If we rightly understood God's providence in these matters our conscience would enjoy tranquility, peace, joy and rest all the more." Potter, *Huldrych Zwingli*, 82.

16 "[E]t ethnicus, si piam mentem domi foveat, Christianus sit, etiamsi Christum ignoret." Z 9:459.

17 *An Exposition of the Faith*, in Bromiley, *Zwingli*, 275–6.

18 Stephens, *Theology*, 126.

19 Büsser calls this an "incipient universalism" in the theology of the Zurich Reformation and an openness to other world religions. Fritz Büsser, "The Spirituality of Zwingli and Bullinger in the Reformation of Zurich" in Jill Raitt, ed., *Christian Spirituality: High Middle Ages and Reformation* (New York: Crossroad, 1987), 304.

20 Locher makes a distinction between "spiritualism" and the "pneumatological character" of Zwingli's theology. Gottfried W. Locher, *Die Zwinglische Reformation im Rahmen der europäischen Kirchengeschichte* (Göttingen: Vandenhoeck & Ruprecht, 1979), 208ff.

21 *Commentary on the True and False Religion*, Z 3:761. "It is clear, then, that we are rendered faithful only by that word which the heavenly father proclaims in our hearts, by which also he illumines us so that we understand, and draws us so that we follow." Z 3:752. Also Jackson, *Latin*, 3:183, 376.

22 *On the Clarity and Certainty of the Word of God*, in Bromiley, *Zwingli*, 79.

23 *Clarity*, in Bromiley, *Zwingli*, 82–3.

24 *Clarity*, Z 1: 379; Bromiley, *Zwingli*, 90. For Zwingli understanding scripture was less an adhesion to an extrinsic, revealed truth but rather an experience of divine grace through an intimate and personal revelation by the Spirit. J. V. Pollet, *Huldrych Zwingli: Biographie et Theologie* (Geneva: Labor et Fides, 1988), 90–1.

25 *Clarity*, in Bromiley, *Zwingli*, 93.

26 *The Shepherd*, Z 3: 22.

27 Locher, *Perspectives*, 180. "The Word is mediated through written documents, but it has its character and effectiveness as Word only in so far as it is directed and applied by the Holy Spirit." Bromiley, *Zwingli*, 55.

28 *Clarity*, in Bromiley, *Zwingli*, 86–7.

29 *Clarity*, in Bromiley, *Zwingli*, 93–5.

30 Locher, *Perspectives*, 217.

31 *Commentary*, in Jackson, *Latin*, 1:184.

32 Zwingli to Ambrosius Blarer (May 4, 1528), Z 9:459.

33 Stephens, *Introduction*, 65.

34 Stephens, *Theology*, 174.

35 Locher, *Perspectives*, 219.

36 Gäbler, *Zwingli*, 129. One of the primary arguments used by the Anabaptists was that the word order of Mt. 28 placed discipleship before baptism. Zwingli responded that baptism was not instituted in Mt. 28, but that Christian baptism was the same as John's baptism. *On Baptism*, in Bromiley, *Zwingli*, 161.

37 *On Baptism*, in Bromiley, *Zwingli*, 146.

38 Col. 2:10–12 is specifically quoted in this context.

39 Stephens, *Theology*, 206–9.

40 Other texts cited to support his position include 2 Cor. 5:6, Heb. 1:13, Jn.1:18, and 1 Cor. 10.

41 *On the Lord's Supper*, in Bromiley, *Zwingli*, 201.

42 Potter, *Huldrych Zwingli*, 94–8. Zwingli found important Patristic support for his emphasis on faith in Augustine's statement, "What need of teeth and stomach? Believe and you have eaten. For to believe in him is to partake of the bread and wine. He who believes on him feeds on him." *Lord's Supper*, in Bromiley, *Zwingli*, 197.

43 *Lord's Supper*, in Bromiley, *Zwingli*, 220–1.

44 *Lord's Supper*, in Bromiley, *Zwingli*, 223–4.

45 *Lord's Supper*, in Bromiley, *Zwingli*, 228.

46 Potter, *Huldrych Zwingli*, 82–3.

47 Stephens, *Theology*, 255.

48 Locher, *Zwingli*, 67; Stephens, *Theology*, 178–9.

49 Gäbler, *Zwingli*, 134.

50 Stephen, *Introduction*, 94ff.; Locher, *Perspectives*, 221.

51 At the point in Zwingli's reformed liturgy where the elements traditionally were held to become the Body and Blood of Christ, Zwingli referred instead to the congregation.

52 The sermon became the focal point even of the liturgy of the Lord's Supper. The Eucharist was reduced in frequency to three times per year. Gäbler, *Zwingli*, 106.

53 "This universal church is the communion of all godly, believing Christians. . . . For if he has all confidence, hope, and comfort in God through Jesus Christ, he is in the church, i.e., in the communion of the saints." Quoted in Fritz Büsser, "Zwingli und die Kirche: Überlegungen zur Aktualität von Zwinglis Ekklesiologie," *Zwingliana* (16:3), 186–200.

54 *On Baptism*, in Bromiley, *Zwingli*, 152.

55 Potter, *Huldrych Zwingli*, 43.

56 Quoted in Stephens, *Theology*, 266.

57 His 1525 publication, *The Ministry*, was a defense of paid clergy with the redefinition of the clergy as preacher.

58 Quoted in Stephens, *Theology*, 307. In reference to Zwingli's conception of this office Moeller writes,

> The Christian State was to find detailed instructions for a life of the Spirit in Holy Scripture. Such a state was characterized not only by a general Christian orientation but by direct obedience to the orders of God. To receive these orders, however, it was necessary to have a judge to interpret scripture. Thus the keystone of the whole edifice appears in the figure of the prophet, the man who possesses full powers to proclaim God's will to the community and who in the last analysis guarantees the prosperity of the State. This was the figure of Zwingli himself. (Moeller, *Imperial Cities*, 78)

59 Potter, *Zwingli*, 221–4.

60 *The Shepherd*, Z 3:19.

61 Stephens, *Theology*, 166–7.

62 Gäbler, *Zwingli*, 80. Zwingli scholars have affirmed that the social dimensions of the Zwinglian reformation are due in significant part to the urban setting and Zwingli's connection to the medieval ideal of the Christian city. E.g., Büsser, "Spirituality", 312–14.

63 Jackson, *Latin*, 2:263.

64 *Exposition of the Faith*, in Potter, *Huldrych Zwingli*, 124.

65 In an important letter to Ambrose Blarer (May 4, 1528) Zwingli stated in opposition to Luther that the Kingdom of God is not only internal but is external, and therefore the magistrate was essential. "Those exercising rule are not simply ordained by God, they are also servants of God. Indeed they occupy God's place in the world, so that in the Old Testament they were even called gods. God exercises his rule through them and, it is he who wields the sword that they bear in his name." Quoted in Stephens, *Theology*, 298. According to Ozment, the devotion Zwingli had to civic unity in the tradition of medieval corporatism should not be underestimated. Steven Ozment, *The Age of Reform, 1250–1550* (New Haven: Yale University Press, 1980), 330.

66 Zwingli's view of society was shaped by his urban context, especially by the strong presence of the guilds in Zurich. He preached a brotherly love where life was characterized by mutual obligation. For Zwingli, brotherly love became the sign of God's presence in a Christian and also signified the presence of God in the whole community. Lee Palmer Wandel, "Brothers and Neighbors: The Language of Community in Zwingli's Preaching," *Zwingliana* (17:5), 373.

67 Stephens, *Introduction*, 123ff.

68 Heiko A. Oberman, *The Reformation: Roots and Ramifications*, trans. Andrew Colin Grow (Grand Rapids: Eerdmans, 1994), 193.

69 *Exposition of the 39th Article*, Z 2:323; E. J. Furcha and H. Wayne Pipkin, eds. and

trans., *Huldrych Zwingli Writings*, 2 vols. (Allison Park, PA: Pickwick, 1984), 1:263.

70 Robert C. Walton, "Zwingli: Founding Father of the Reformed Churches" in Richard L. DeMolen, ed., *Leaders of the Reformation* (Selinsgrove, PA: Susquehanna University Press, 1984), 85–6. An important example of this transfer of authority is represented by the Domestic Relations court established in May 1525. A committee of four secular officials and three clergy were appointed to supervise Zurich marriages and to adjudicate domestic conflicts. Although this began with authority only concerning marriage, it was later expanded to supervise morals in Zurich in general. Gäbler, *Zwingli*, 103.

71 Berndt Hamm, "The Urban Reformation in the Holy Roman Empire" in Thomas A. Brady, Jr., Heiko A. Oberman, and James D. Tracy, eds., *Handbook of European History, 1400–1600* (Grand Rapids: Eerdmans, 1995), 2:214–15.

72 Gäbler, *Zwingli*, 159. See also Bromiley, *Zwingli*, 183–4; Walton, "Zwingli", 85.

73 Locher, *Perspectives*, 340ff.

74 For example, the similarity of language in the *Heidelberg Catechism* (1563) and in Zwingli is so striking that one "is bound to conclude that the latter had a direct influence on the former." Locher, *Perspectives*, 201.

75 Pollet, *Zwingli: Biographie et Theologie*, 88.

76 Locher, *Perspectives*, 254; Pollet, *Zwingli: Biographie et Theologie*, 82.

77 Locher, *Perspectives*, 29.

78 Carlos Eire, *War Against the Idols: The Reformation of Worship from Erasmus to Calvin* (Cambridge: Cambridge University Press, 1986), 85. See also Lee Palmer Wandel, *Voracious Idols & Violent Hands. Iconoclasm in Reformation Zurich, Strasbourg, and Basel* (Cambridge: Cambridge University Press, 1995).

79 Stephens, *Introduction*, 145.

80 Büsser, "Spirituality", 312.

81 Locher, *Perspectives*, 4.

Bibliography

Primary Sources

Bromiley, G. W., ed., *Zwingli and Bullinger*, The Library of Christian Classics, Vol. 24, Philadelphia: Westminster Press, 1953.

Egli, Emil et al., eds., *Huldreich Zwinglis Sämtliche Werke*, 13 vols., Berlin et al.: Schwetschke & Son et al., 1905–.

Furcha, E. J. and H. Wayne Pipkin, eds. and trans., *Huldrych Zwingli: Writings*, 2 vols., Allison Park, PA: Pickwick, 1984.

Jackson, Samuel Macauley, *Ulrich Zwingli: Selected Works*, Philadelphia: University of Pennsylvania Press, 1972.

——, et al., eds., *The Latin Works of Huldreich Zwingli*, 3 vols., New York, London, and

Philadelphia: Heidelberg Press, 1912, 1922, 1929.

Potter, G. R., *Huldrych Zwingli*. Documents in Modern History, New York: St. Martin's Press, 1977.

Secondary Sources

Büsser, Fritz, "The Spirituality of Zwingli and Bullinger in the Reformation of Zurich" in Jill Raitt, ed., *Christian Spirituality: High Middle Ages and Reformation*, New York: Crossroad, 1987, 300–17.

Courvoisier, Jacques, *Zwingli: A Reformed Theologian*, Richmond, VA: John Knox Press, 1963.

Eire, Carlos, *War Against the Idols: The Reformation of Worship from Erasmus to Calvin*, Cambridge: Cambridge University Press, 1986.

Furcha, E. J. and H. Wayne Pipkin, *Prophet, Pastor, Protestant: The Work of Huldrych Zwingli After Five Hundred Years*, Allison Park, PA: Pickwick Publications, 1984.

Gäbler, Ulrich, *Huldrych Zwingli: His Life and Work*, trans. Ruth C. L. Gritsch. Philadelphia: Fortress Press, 1986.

Locher, Gottfried W., *Die Zwinglische Reformation im Rahmen der europäischen Kirchengeschichte*, Göttingen: Vandenhoeck & Ruprecht, 1979.

——, *Zwingli's Thought: New Perspectives*, Leiden: E. J. Brill, 1981.

——, *Zwingli und die Schweizerische Reformation*. Göttingen: Vandenhoeck & Ruprecht, 1982.

Moeller, Bernd, *Imperial Cities and the Reformation: Three Essays*, trans. and ed. H. C. Erik Midelfort and Mark U. Edwards, Jr. Durham, NC: Labyrinth Press, 1982.

Pollet, J. V., *Huldrych Zwingli: Biographie et Theologie*, Geneva: Labor et Fides, 1988.

——, *Huldrych Zwingli et le Zwinglianisme*, Paris: Librairie Philosophique J. Vrin, 1988.

Potter, G. R., *Zwingli*, Cambridge: Cambridge University Press, 1976.

Stephens, W. P., *The Theology of Huldrych Zwingli*, Oxford: Clarendon Press, 1986.

——, *Zwingli: An Introduction to His Thought*, Oxford: Clarendon Press, 1992.

Walton, Robert C., "Zwingli: Founding Father of the Reformed Churches" in Richard L. DeMolen, ed., *Leaders of the Reformation*, Selinsgrove, PA: Susquehanna University Press, 1984, 69–98.

Walton, Robert C., *Zwingli's Theocracy*, Toronto: University of Toronto Press, 1967.

ch**a**
pter

11

Heinrich Bullinger
(1504–1575)

Bruce Gordon

Until recently it has been customary for any discussion of the life and work of Heinrich Bullinger to begin with a clarion call for a reassessment of this unjustly neglected figure. The time for such worthy admonitions has now passed, for the scholarship of the last quarter of the twentieth century has yielded a general consensus that the leader of the Zurich church from 1532 until 1575 was of seminal importance to both the European Reformation and the development of the Reformed tradition. What has proved less easy to determine, in the absence of critical editions of his major works, has been the precise character of his thought. Although there were key concepts around which Bullinger created his theological vision, it is not easy to speak of him as a systematic theologian, for the essence of his work lay in his life as a servant of the church. What interested Bullinger above all else was the practical application of Scripture in the life of the church; he primarily regarded himself as a preacher and pastor, charged with bringing the Word of God into the community, and with guiding people in living the Christian life. The church was everything for Bullinger; he believed passionately in its catholicity and he revered the authority of its ancient fathers. His thought on spirituality, liturgy, devotion, the sacraments and the priesthood was suffused with a sense of tradition and continuity.

Bullinger was a competent theologian, well trained and lucid, whose writings were essentially syncretistic in the sense that he sought to draw upon tradition to produce answers directly relevant to the church. One finds in his work shades of meaning important in tracing the history of a doctrinal point, but the sum of these nuances does not really add up to a distinctive theological position, and this, when he is set alongside Calvin, has been one reason for his relative obscurity. Bullinger's genius resided in his grasp of tradition: he used patristic and medieval theology extensively but critically. In both his theology and ecclesiology he retained older forms of argument, office, and worship but revised their content in light of Reformed theology. At heart he was a priest and his theological writings invariably stressed the pastoral implications of biblical teaching. During his 44 years as chief minister in Zurich his obligations were legion: he presided over more than one hundred urban and rural parishes; he sought to maintain the precarious balance between ecclesiastical and political authority;

and he served as one of the leading figures of international Protestantism in Europe. By nature diffident and scholarly, he rarely travelled and his instincts were cautious; without doubt the passing years brought disappointments and some bitterness. In the end, Bullinger was more inclined to find hope in the pages of the Book of Revelation than in surveying the situation of Christ's church in the world.

To understand Heinrich Bullinger we need to be aware of those forces, visible and invisible, that shaped his life and work. Every day that he served as chief minister Bullinger had to attend to the fragile relationship between the church and political authority in Zurich. The very existence of the Reformed church in Zurich depended on the magistrates' trust in Heinrich Bullinger. The catastrophic collapse of the church following Zwingli's death in October 1531 had persuaded the anxious political masters in Zurich that the Reformation principles of the freedom of the gospel and the preaching of the Word were inimical to their authority. In their eyes the connection between the Reformation and increased secular control over the church, so much part of its selling point, was a clerical hoax. The church, the changed mood dictated, had to be controlled, placed firmly under the hand of the magistrates. Yet Bullinger, even as he began negotiations to take the office of chief minister in Zurich in 1531, would not accept the subjugation of God's Word to temporal interests. He was, however, shrewd enough to recognize that the survival of the Reformed church lay in the hands of men whose primary interests were not spiritual. He grasped the necessity of compromise, but he wanted that compromise to work for the benefit of the church. The church would retain its spiritual independence insofar as the magistrates would trust Bullinger to keep a weather eye on the clergy and laity. This precarious polity was a crucial part of Zwingli's legacy; the uncomfortable marriage between spiritual and political authorities, so despised by the radical critics, was essentially held together by men of charismatic personality. Without Bullinger's acumen and tact, the Reformed church would not have survived the two decades after Zwingli's violent end. Bullinger did, however, have to pay a price. He was not to air his complaints against the Zurich magistrates in public; rather, he would work behind the scenes and closed doors, to resolve matters and make key decisions. Success was not guaranteed: Bullinger waged a bitter and largely unsuccessful campaign to hold the magistrates to their promise to use the secularized goods of the church for poor relief and the maintenance of the fabric of parish communities. The Reformed church under Bullinger made few public decisions. The sensitivity of its position in Zurich and the fragility of Zurich's place in the Swiss Confederation required the utmost circumspection.

Bullinger did not wear Zwingli's mantle lightly, and nor could he have. The well-known scrap between Zwingli and Luther over the Lord's Supper had resulted in a defeat for Zurich. The Zwinglians had been effectively branded "fanatics" by Luther and his circle, and their highly sophisticated teachings on the Eucharist had been reduced, in the eyes of most contemporaries, to a notion of bare memorialism. Following the exclusion of the Zwinglians from the religious discussions within the empire after the Diet of Augsburg, the rising tide of Lutheran influence in the Swiss Confederation, and the emergence of John Calvin in Geneva, the Zurich position on the sacraments was regarded as far too extreme to form the basis for any negotiations toward Protestant unity. The Zwinglians, including Bullinger, never forgave Luther for his treatment of Zwingli, and hostility to all that emerged from the Lutheran churches in Germany became a hallmark of Bullinger's Zurich. It was crucial to the Zurichers that Zwingli's memory be defended against his detractors, and Bullinger was obliged in public to remain close to the teachings of his predecessor, even if there were subtle distinctions and differences. The reality for Bullinger remained that Zwingli was so controversial that the mere mention of his name could lead to conflict. Whatever mediating positions were taken, Zwingli's theology had been publicly rejected by Wittenberg and Geneva, and through the years of painful conflict and polemic Bullinger alone had the status to hold together critics and disciples for the sake of a wider Protestant community. This required constant firefighting and Bullinger got burnt. A notable consequence of these conflicts was that he could never publish his *History of the Reformation* during his lifetime, for to have allowed such a favourable account of Zwingli's life to be printed would certainly have destroyed with one stroke any possibility of reconciliation within the Protestant world.

Bullinger's Works

Bullinger was a prolific writer and the flow of works from the press of his colleague and friend Christoph Froschauer did not ebb. Fundamental to the understanding of Bullinger's thought are his commentaries on almost every book of the Bible. The provenance of most of these commentaries was the pulpit. Bullinger's industry is indicated by even a brief list of his major works: *Preaching and Synodal Ordinance* (1532), *On the Only and Eternal Covenant* (1534), *The Old Faith* (1537), *Orthodox Statement on both of the two Natures in Christ* (1534), *On the Authority of Holy Scripture* (1538), *On the Origin of Errors* (1539), *On Christian Marriage* (1540), *A True Confession* (1545), *Sermonum Decades* (1549–51), *The Christian Religion* (1556), *Commentary on the Revelation of John* (1557), *Against the Anabaptists* (1560), *On Councils* (1561), *Second Helvetic Confession* (1566).

Almost all of Bullinger's work arose either from his preaching and exegetical work in Zurich or in response to particular challenges, such as attacks from the Anabaptists and Lutherans or the advent of the Council of Trent. In reading through this enormous corpus of writing one can agree with the judgment of Edward Dowey:

> The practicality of Bullinger's teaching is twofold: negatively it is wholly non-speculative in intent, and positively his thought lives wholly within and on behalf of the historical and daily life of the church. There is no private virtuoso theology in Bullinger, and no theological or spiritual soliloquy. This feature is of special significance to the ad hoc character of most of his writing, and the rhetorical determination of appropriate writing style and organisation of his material.[1]

In addition to the theological works and scriptural commentaries, Bullinger also wrote a number of pastoral and devotional texts. These, for the most part, have received less attention, but they offer a window on how far Bullinger the pastor was prepared to bend orthodox religion in order to meet the vexing pastoral issues of primary concern to the people in the parish churches.[2] They remind us that one must read across the range of Bullinger's work to gain a sense of the mental world of this man.

The Bible and Its Interpretation

All of Bullinger's writings served one purpose: they were to elucidate Holy Scripture. Bullinger was a teacher who employed an array of rhetorical tools to provide the reader with a comprehensive study guide to the Bible, which he envisaged sitting open next to his work. The vernacular and Latin Bibles produced in Zurich were handsomely appointed with chapter summaries and cross-references to ensure that God's Word was appropriately interpreted. Similarly, Bullinger buttressed his texts with vast numbers of scriptural references to guide the untrained mind through difficult passages, and the prolixity of his writings was grounded in good pedagogical theory.

For Bullinger the goal of biblical exegesis was clarity and simplicity. Where Calvin looked for doctrinal exactitude, Bullinger deployed his humanist scholarship to articulate God's message to humanity. Scripture, according to Bullinger, should not be laden with complex interpretations, but rather the exegete should be sensitive to the rhetorical nature of God's Word. Jerome, Chrysostom, and Augustine were Bullinger's guides in the art of biblical interpretation, and Bullinger, in contrast to Zwingli, remained gracious in his acknowledgment of his debt to Erasmus and his grammatical analysis.[3] As Joel E. Kok pointed out in his study of Bullinger's 1533 commentary on Romans, the "stated purpose for his commentary, the promotion of humble piety among ordinary believers, echoes Erasmus's well-known desire that farmers, weavers, and 'even the lowliest women read the gospel and the Pauline Epistles'."[4] Bullinger's critique of obscurantism in interpretation and his desire to make the Word of God accessible to all reflected the dominant strand of spirituality in Zurich in the period following Zwingli. Bullinger's mentor and colleague through the difficult decade of the 1530s was Leo Jud, who had begun his career as a reformer translating Erasmus's *Paraphrases* into Alemanic as a means of preparing the simple folk for the pure Word of God, which was thought too strong without commentary. The culmination of the exegetical exercises conducted in the Grossmünster, now known as the *Prophezei*, was the sermon to the people in the vernacular in which the fruits of humanist scholarship were to be made relevant to ordinary Christians. This was the ethos of the Zurich Reformation and it was Bullinger's most cherished goal.

Preacher and Bishop

One of the most arresting aspects of Bullinger's writings is the sheer volume of his surviving sermons. Among those that were printed, the *Decades* are the most well known, but they form but the tip of the iceberg. The 1972 bibliographical work of J. Staedtke allows us a sense of Bullinger's fecundity, but even this is not the full story.[5] The work of Fritz Büsser has brought to light the number of Bullinger's unprinted sermons in the Zentralbibliothek in Zurich. On the basis of the surviving sermons or sermon outlines, together with Bullinger's own record of his preaching in his *Diarium*, it has been reckoned that the people of Zurich heard him from the Grossmünster pulpit between 7,000 and 7,500 times.[6] He preached on all the books of the Bible and, following the principle of *lectio continua*, he made his way through all the verses, genealogies and all. For instance he commenced his Sunday sermons on Romans in the autumn of 1549 and finished that epistle sometime in February 1553. We know that from 1546 Bullinger preached three times a week (Friday, Sunday, and Monday), and for each of those days he followed a different book of the Bible. His biblical commentaries came from his preaching series. Yet one must not overlook the collaborative nature of learning in Zurich; every day Bullinger and Rudolf Gwalther would attend the lectures of Theodor Bibliander on the Old Testament, and their notes from these lectures survive.

The preaching of the Word of God was very much at the center of Bullinger's understanding of the role of the parish minister. His view of the parochial ministry, however, owed much to the late medieval reforms of the conciliar period. He believed that every parish should have a resident minister who, by his moral rectitude, provided an example to the people, and whose learning brought knowledge of God's laws and Christ's teachings. Bullinger was extremely clerical in his perspective, for the minister was not only to watch over the people admonishing them when necessary, but he also bore responsibility for their actions. There is a clear sense of the mediating role for the parish clergy in Bullinger's church.[7]

The Zurich church was hierarchical with Bullinger wholly in control. With the Burgermeister he headed the synod of the church, a disciplinary and pedagogical institution, to which all the ministers were summoned twice a year.[8] Bullinger also sat on the all-powerful body known as the *Examinatorskonvent*, which not only directed the education of prospective ministers but recommended to the Council which candidates should be placed in which parish. The recommendations were never rejected and all were written in Bullinger's hand.[9] For four decades no aspect of the Zurich church fell outside his purview.

God and Divine Election

The core of Bullinger's theology found beautiful expression in his *Christian Religion* (1557), in which he articulated his belief that God had revealed his true nature to humanity in Scripture. This divine nature is the creative and sustaining force of all that is, for Scripture shows that God is in relationship with the created order, and that relationship takes the form of a covenant of grace. The terms of this covenant are that God has provided in Christ salvation from sin and punishment, but that humanity must respond in obedience to God's laws.[10] Human activity is emphasized by Bullinger, but not to the extent that God is dependent upon the human response to his free gift of grace. Grace comes from God's unfathomable goodness and love, and it is grace which brings about the justification of individual Christians.

The center of this covenantal relationship between God and humanity was Christ, who fully embraced both natures, divine and human, and was the fulfillment of God's intervention in human history.[11] As Richard A. Muller has written,

> Bullinger here draws together the themes of covenant and the imputation of right-eousness . . . here we see the promise of God grounded in the propitiatory work of

Christ's righteousness and, as demonstrated later in the lengthy discussion of Christ's satisfaction, the profound historical, indeed *heilsgeschichtlich* thrust of Bullinger's presentation. His concern is with the historical manifestation of God's saving will.[12]

It was through this view of God's sovereignty that Bullinger was forced upon the subject of predestination, a topic, it is clear, that he eagerly tried to avoid. The central thrust of the attack on Calvin's doctrine of predestination, which drove the debate in the 1540s and 1550s, was its implication that God is the author of evil. Bullinger did not hold with Calvin's position on double predestination, but, as with other doctrinal points, he was content that their disagreement remain private in order to preserve a united Reformed front.[13] Bullinger dealt with this objection by relying upon the traditional argument of "divine permission" in which God did not impel anyone to commit evil but simply permitted what he himself found repugnant.[14] In his *On God's Providence*, Bullinger wrote:

> Furthermore, predestination, preordination, or predetermination – that is the ordination of all things to a certain end by God from eternity. However, the Lord has primarily destined every man, and this is his holy and just counsel, his just decree. Now the election of God from eternity is that he truly elects some to life, others to destruction. The cause of election and predestination is nothing other than the good and just will of God, undeserved in the salvation of the elect, yet deserved in the damnation and rejection of the reprobate.[15]

Bullinger regarded predestination as a comforting doctrine, for he primarily spoke of it in terms of faith and unbelief. Salvation was assured to those who believed, while perdition awaited those who rejected God. The rejection of God was not, according to Bullinger, because God has preordained it, but rather because men and women had turned their backs on him. Bullinger's treatment of predestination must be seen in light of the massive quantity of pastoral literature produced in Zurich by himself and his colleagues, in which at every moment the saving God was emphasized. Bullinger's teaching on justification and sanctification, in which the medieval sacramental language of the indwelling of God was appropriated and given a Protestant turn, underscored the lengths to which Bullinger went to stress the presence of God, and the comfort which that presence afforded in the face of a hostile world. Bullinger, in his work on predestination, rejected the idea that the elect were few, and referred to God as a "lover of man" who desired the salvation of all.[16] Bullinger's pastoral tone is found in the statement "As a matter of fact, we prefer to insist upon these universal promises and to have a good hope for all." Thus the gospel was to be brought to all.

Faith, Justification and Sanctification

What is striking about Bullinger's understanding of salvation is the manner in which he brought together justification and sanctification with regard to the Christian life. Justifying faith sanctifies the believer not only because the person responds with gratitude to the gift of God, but because through that gift the human person is infused with Christ. Mark Burrows has persuasively argued that Bullinger drew upon a rich tradition of medieval Augustinian thought in which the infusion of grace into the individual was at the same time the infusion of God himself.[17] This extraordinarily intimate understanding of justification and sanctification emphasized the closeness of God without having to resort to material forms of mediation, such as the sacraments. The union between God and the believer in Christ was a union of persons, not substance. This allowed Bullinger to reject the materialism of the Roman sacramental system while embracing the Reformation ideal of faith alone. God justifies and sanctifies at once, though the two acts are distinguished in that the believer's assurance begins with the former and is confirmed by the latter. As Burrows has written:

> The certainty of our salvation thus depends on our faith alone, which as we have seen he understands as the very presence of God through the Holy Spirit: in short, Bullinger's emphasis is that faith necessarily assures us because it is not merely descriptive of some extrinsic relationship, but rather itself arises from God's indwelling presence. He is not at the moment at all concerned with the circularity of this pastoral argument: no faith, no assurance; no assurance, no faith.[18]

Faith is the indwelling of God in the person and sanctification, according to Bullinger, is the regeneration of that person. This regeneration is not physical, but rather the transformation of the mind and heart. He speaks of justification in terms of "adoption," the beginning point for a lifelong struggle in which no Christian will ever fully be freed of the "old self." Regeneration is not to a life of perfection, but is a "process of faithfulness" in which the Christian has restored within him or herself the image of God. The connection between Bullinger's doctrine of sanctification and the parish church lay in the reformer's understanding of the journey of faithfulness in terms of growth in obedience. The Christian life is one of obedience to earthly and divine powers and the role of the church and its discipline, therefore, was to guide the faithful in their service to God. This is a classic example of how Bullinger used the old language of Christian life, in which one grew in righteousness, and revised it in order that righteousness was replaced by obedience as the human dynamic.

The key to Bullinger's understanding of the Christian life is its utter interiority. The righteousness of Christ is something outside the individual which is infused through the gracious gift of grace. The faith of the individual which responds to this justifying act is not merely a response to an external act of God, but is rather an effervescent expression of the indwelling Christ. This parallelism of the internal and external Christ, as found in the mature writings of Bullinger, was part of his delicate resolution of the powerful dualism of Zwinglian thought. Whereas Zwingli had famously placed the external and internal (i.e., flesh and spirit) as countervailing forces, Bullinger moved toward portraying them as parallel. We shall encounter this again in his eucharistic theology.

What Bullinger achieved in his discussion of justification and sanctification was an effective means of speaking of God's intimacy with humanity. God was present in the believer through the infusion of Christ. The echoes of the *Devotio moderna* and of medieval Augustinianism in Bullinger's thought were clear; the indwelling of God restoring the image of God in the believer through the life of faithfulness was the assurance required by every man and woman. Bullinger wanted to claim the tradition with its profound pastoral implications, while freeing it from any connection to material objects.

The Lord's Supper

The origins of Bullinger's thought on the sacraments have been much debated, but there is a general consensus that his inspiration came from the tradition of the *Devotio moderna*, the writings of Luther, Zwingli, and Erasmus. Paul Rorem has suggested that in 1524 the young Bullinger may have influenced the older Zwingli in his belief, derived from the work of Wesel Gansfort, that the Lord's Supper was not merely a symbolic commemoration in which the emphasis was upon the actions of the congregation in bearing witness to their faith, but was in fact an act of Christ.[19] There was in Bullinger a delicate balance between the role of the faithful, who commemorated Christ in thanksgiving and remembrance, and that of Christ himself, the once-offered sacrifice who through his death and resurrection brought the faithful into union with God. His living presence in the community alone gave force to the actions of the people, who ultimately were the passive recipients of his grace.

The Lord's Supper, Bullinger argued, was an analogy provided by God for the benefit of feeble human nature, in which the reality of Christ's sacrifice was visibly represented in the form of the bread and wine. This was not merely some form of clerical play-acting for the benefit of forgetful parishioners; Bullinger's instincts always led him to emphasize the divine action above the human, for salvation stems from nothing other than God's grace. Bullinger would never allow that the sacraments could be understood as instruments of God's grace, for that would suggest that the human response was integral to God's plan for salvation. There were two premises to which Bullinger was seriously allergic: first, that God's grace could in any manner be attached to material forms; second, that there is any trace of human cooperation in salvation. In the *Decades* Bullinger wrote:

> Now in the Lord's Supper the bread and wine represent the very body and blood of Christ. The reason for this is that just as bread nourishes and strengthens a man, and gives him the ability to labour, so the body of Christ eaten in faith feeds and satisfies the soul of man and readies the whole man to the duties of godliness. As wine is the drink for the thirsty and makes the hearts of men merry, so the blood of our Lord Jesus Christ, drunk in faith, quenches the thirst of the burning conscience and fills the hearts of the faithful with unspeakable joy.[20]

Even through the delicate negotiations leading to the 1549 *Consensus Tigurinus*, in which Bullinger and John Calvin reached an agreement on the Lord's Supper – largely by leaving crucial differences off the page – Bullinger never accepted Calvin's language of the sacraments as instruments or vehicles of God's grace.[21] He simply could not allow that the external forms were necessary to the inner reception of God's gift of grace. Having said that, however, in Bullinger's most mature statement of his eucharistic theology, the *Helvetic Confession* of 1566 (which had first been drafted as a personal confession of faith in 1561), he seems to have at least moved somewhat toward Calvin's view. Rorem has persuasively suggested that Bullinger allowed the outer sacramental reality and the inner spiritual reality to be simultaneous.[22] We find this expressed in the *Confession*:

> And this is outwardly represented unto us by the minister in the sacrament, after the visible manner, and, as it were, laid before our eyes to be seen, which is inwardly in the soul invisibly performed by the Holy Spirit. Outwardly bread is offered by the minister . . . and meanwhile inwardly by the working of Christ through the Holy Spirit, they receive also the flesh and blood of the Lord, and do feed on them unto eternal life.[23]

The Catholicity of the Church

For Bullinger the bishop, pastor, theologian, and historian it was absolutely imperative to prove that the Reformed church of the sixteenth century was the true church in continuity with the ancient church. The first sign of membership in this true church was the acceptance of the whole biblical canon, for Scripture in its entirety was the only true witness to the beliefs of the earliest church.[24] Bullinger believed that the subsequent ages of the church could not be uncoupled from the Apostolic age, for they stood in continuity with it insofar as their traditions and interpretations were consonant with the witness of the Bible. Tradition, for Bullinger, was an essential part of the church, for it was the record of its witness to the truth of the gospel through the generations.

> But here we do not repudiate or hold in contempt in the least the disputations and scriptural expositions of the Blessed Fathers, and antistes or doctors of the ancient church, as for example Irenaeus, Origen, Chrysostom, Ambrose, Jerome, Augustine, and others like these, as long as both their exposition and their conclusions depart in nothing from those apostolic rules [of faith].[25]

For Bullinger the fathers of the church were his great heroes; he closely identified with the orthodox figures of the early church in their struggles against doctrinal opponents. For example, Bullinger consciously modelled his enormous history and refutation of Anabaptism, *Der Widertöufferen Ursprung*, on Irenaeus's *Against the Heresies*.[26] Despite Bullinger's rejection of any independent authority for the church fathers, their interpretations of Scripture were for him the accepted standard, and he saw himself as a defender of their legacy. Thus, for this leading figure of the Reformed tradition, the boundaries between tradition and biblical authority were anything but clearly marked.

The link with the ancient church was through the covenant in which God's promises required Christians to live according to his laws. It was within this context that Bullinger understood the continuity of the Reformed church with antiquity:

> The Evangelical Church of Christ does not cling on to words superstitiously and captiously, neglecting the holy and genuine sense: to that end it received openly all

symbols which by other and more abundent words, nevertheless in conclusions changing nothing nor containing anything different, were formulated by holy or orthodox fathers in councils. Therefore it receives and venerates the Nicene Creed, the Creed of the Blessed Athanasius, the Second or Constantinian Creed, and all other good definitions of the true faith which agree with these.[27]

This meant above all for Bullinger the acceptance of ancient formulations of Trinitarian theology and pronouncements on Christ's two natures.

Christ, for Bullinger, stood at the center of history and therefore the reformer's understanding of Catholicity focussed on the churches and their relationship to the Son of God. Garcia Archilla has pointed out that Bullinger tended to reduce all heresies to heresies of Christology, for his view of history was the Augustinian struggle of the city of God against the city of flesh. For Bullinger there was no more certain foundation for the belief that the Reformed churches stood in continuity with the patristic church than their absolute adherence to Chalcedonian Christology. To depart one jot from this was to begin the descent into heresy, and this is where he saw his most vexing division with the Lutherans.

If Christology was one foundation of catholicity, persecution was the witness for the existence of the True Church, for the history of the church could be written in terms of its persecutions. Bullinger believed that only the orthodox were persecuted. Persecution is a sign of the church because it comes from God, who tests his people in order that they should remain vigilant and pure. The persecutors, being responsible for their actions, will be punished by God and the faithful will emerge strengthened, chastened, and readied for eternity. Such a view parallels Bullinger's views on plague, which he similarly interpreted as the scourge of God upon the faithful to remind them of their covenantal obligation – obedience to his laws.

Bullinger used a number of different themes when speaking of the history of the church. Essentially the true tradition of the church was its witness to the apostolic faith, but depending upon the theological or rhetorical point he wished to make Bullinger might stress this continuity in terms of biblical interpretation, church councils (*De Conciliis*), or persecution. None of these precluded the others, rather each underscored Bullinger's concept of the God who acts in human history; a concept grounded in his reading of the Book of Revelation. Bullinger viewed medieval church history in terms of the rise of the papal monarchy as an agent of the devil and its struggle against the legitimate councils of the church, which represented the true authority of the Body of Christ. The papacy was a persecuting force in the tradition of the pagan emperors, and those who suffered under its lash were, therefore, witnesses to the truth. Bullinger wrote in his *Persecution. Concerning the long and difficult persecution of the Holy Christian Church* (printed in 1578):

> From here, as from the right main source, flows out the harsh papal persecutions of the Christian Church. For whoever does not put up with the monarchy of the Pope and the spiritual plot which they call the *consensus totius ecclesiae*, and does not declare all things according to the right teaching of the canonists and theologians, they kick out with the full troops and they have, with the help of the Pope and worldly arms, decried as heretics such among many, and persecuted and oppressed them.[28]

It was also of the greatest importance to Bullinger that he was able to demonstrate that the Reformed church did not constitute heresy as defined by imperial law. The first edition of the *Decades* (1549) was prefaced with an array of confessional documents: the creeds of Nicaea, Constantinople, Ephesus, Chalcedon, the first and fourth councils of Toledo, the declaration of faith of Irenaeus, Tertullian's rule of faith, the creeds of Athanasius and Pope Damasus, and the anti-heresy edict of Emperor Gratian (380). These documents, for Bullinger, embodied the ancient verity of the Christian religion, a received body of truth not open to examination or speculation. As Mark Taplin has written: "When Bullinger chose not to probe the more abstruse articles of doctrine, it was because such speculation was unlikely to contribute to the edification of ordinary believers, rather than because he had ceased to regard those tenets as fundamental: Bullinger's preferred option was simply to take the doctrinal formularies of the early Church as read."[29]

Bullinger as Historian

Bullinger was a passionate historian, and a good one. From the early 1520s he began to collect historical material. His first effort was the *Annales Coenobii Capellani*, a history of the religious house at Kappel, embracing both its historical development as well as the history of its construction. The work was one of the first building histories to be written in Swiss lands. This first work was soon followed by others: *A History of the Counts of Habsburg*, *A Chronicle of the Bishops of Constance*, and *A History of the Monastery of Einsiedeln*. In the 1530s the first of his major historical works appeared, his *Swiss Chronicle*, which was a collection of documents along with the *Testimonium veterum*, the oral history of the Swiss people that Bullinger wished to commit to paper.[30] In addition, Bullinger prepared his *A Short History of the Old Zurich War*, a work that would form the basis for Johannes Stumpf's *Swiss Chronicle* of 1548. Bullinger's relentless pursuit of historical documents, combined with his encyclopaedic knowledge of the sources, bore fruit in his mature work, the *History of the Reformation 1519–1532*, which he wrote in two manuscript volumes. This history of the Reformation was the second part of his larger work, *History of the Venerable Swiss Confederation*, which was an account of the Swiss from antiquity to 1516. In 1574 Bullinger produced another version in his *History of the City of Zurich*. In fact all of Bullinger's histories focussed on Zurich, and it was for this reason that the *History of the Reformation* remained unpublished until the nineteenth century. Neither the Calvinists nor the Lutherans were in any mood to hear Zwingli eulogized.

Bullinger was an excellent storyteller and he knew how to construct a narrative filled with men and women who lived, breathed, fought, believed, and committed acts of mendacity. Ever the student of human behavior, he was fascinated by why people acted and believed in the manner they did, and like his contemporary Sebastian Münster, Bullinger rejoiced in the details of life and filled his history with episodes and piquant moments which allow the reader into the world of the protagonists. Nevertheless, the hand of providence is everywhere evident in his history; the Augustinian idea of a struggle between good and evil in history guided Bullinger's pen. He was deeply confessional, loyal to Zwingli and the Reformation cause, and deeply hostile to Zurich's traditional enemies; villains are harshly judged and Catholics rarely appear in a positive light. Bullinger was not a man who easily hated, but his total abhorrence of the military rises from the written page; he had lost a son on a battlefield in France and could, therefore, match Zwingli's elegant loathing of mercenary service, which both men saw as destroying the fabric of rural communities and corrupting urban politics. Bullinger the historian was deeply reflective, and when writing of the past he ruminated on the failings of the Reformation: the Ittinger iconoclasm, the execution of Konrad Grebel, and the spat between Zurich and Berne following the First Kappel War were for him symptomatic of a movement which at times had lost its way. Bullinger was not, however, inclined to cast aspersions on the character of either persons or states. After his long years of labor in the service of unity between the Swiss Reformed churches there were few secrets not known to Bullinger, and he was uniquely positioned to record his age, but in both his history writing and his correspondence judicious silences were his trademark.

Conclusion

The ongoing publication of the correspondence of Heinrich Bullinger, which runs to about twelve thousand letters, has revealed to us what readers of his works have long known, that the head of the Zurich church was a highly sophisticated man, who, from his perch on the Limmat, had a better grasp than any other of the complexities of the European Reformation. He was pastor, teacher, and confidant to men and women from England to Hungary, and he stood by those verities which for him were lucidly articulated in Scripture and mediated through the church. Perhaps more than any other figure of his day, Bullinger was responsible for finding a *modus vivendi* in which the evangelical principles of *sola scriptura* and *sola fide* could be reconciled with the necessity of tradition and functioning church offices in the world. It is not in Bullinger that we find the groundbreaking formulations of Reformed thought, but it is to this quiet, gentle man that we must turn when we wonder why that tradition survived at all.

Notes

1 Edward A. Dowey, "Heinrich Bullinger's Theology: Thematic, Comprehensive, Schematic" in John H. Leith, ed., *Calvin Studies V* (Davidson, NC: Davidson College, 1990), 43.

2 See Hans Ulrich Bächtold, "Gegen den Hunger beten. Heinrich Bullinger, Zürich und die Einführung des Gemeinen Gebetes im Jahre 1571" in Hans Ulrich Bächtold, Rainer Henrich, and Kurt Jakob Rüetschi, eds., *Vom Beten, vom Verketzern, vom Predigen. Beiträge zum Zeitalter Heinrich Bullingers und Rudolf Gwalthers* (Zug: Achius, 1999), 9–44; Bruce Gordon, "Malevolent ghosts and ministering angels: apparitions and pastoral care in the Swiss Reformation" in Bruce Gordon and Peter Marshall, eds., *The Place of the Dead. Death and Remembrance in Late Medieval and Early Modern Europe* (Cambridge, Cambridge University Press, 2000), 87–109; Bruce Gordon, "'God killed Saul': Heinrich Bullinger and Jacob Ruef on the power of the Devil" in Kathryn A. Edwards, ed., *Werewolves, Witches and Wandering Spirits* (Kirksville: Thomas Jefferson University Press, forthcoming).

3 Joel E. Kok, "Heinrich Bullinger's Exegetical Method: The Model for Calvin?" in Richard

A. Muller and John L. Thompson, eds., *Biblical Interpretation in the Era of the Reformation* (Grand Rapids: Eerdmans, 1996), 245. In the same volume see John B. Payne, "Erasmus's influence on Zwingli and Bullinger in the Exegesis of Matthew 11:28–30," esp. 78–80.

4   Kok, "Heinrich Bullinger's Exegetical Method," 245.

5   J. Staedtke, *H. Bullinger. Bibliographie. Beschreibendes Verzeichnis der gedruckten Werke von Heinrich Bullinger*, 2 vols. (Zurich: Theologischer Verlag Zurich, 1972).

6   Fritz Büsser, "Bullinger – Der Prediger" in his *Wurzeln der Reformation in Zurich* (Leiden: E. J. Brill, 1985), 143.

7   On Bullinger's understanding of ministry, see Pamela Biel, *Doorkeepers at the House of Righteousness. Heinrich Bullinger and the Zurich Clergy 1535–1575* (Berne: Peter Lang, 1991).

8   On the synod and administration of the rural church see Bruce Gordon, *Clerical Discipline and the Rural Reformation. The Synod in Zurich, 1532–1580* (Berne: Peter Lang, 1992).

9   Hans Ulrich Bächtold, *Heinrich Bullinger vor dem Rat: Zur Gestaltung und Verwaltung des Zürcher Staatswesens in den Jahren 1531 bis 1575* (Berne: Peter Lang, 1982).

10 See Charles McCoy and J. Wayne Baker, *Fountainhead of Federalism: Heinrich Bullinger and the Covenantal Tradition; With a Translation of De testimento seu foedere Dei unico et aeterno 1534 and a Bibliography on Federal Theology and Political Philosophy* (Louisville: Westminster/John Knox, 1991).

11 The key work on this subject is J. Wayne Baker, *Heinrich Bullinger and the Covenant: The Other Reformed Tradition* (Athens, OH: Ohio University Press, 1980).

12 Richard A. Muller, *Christ and the Decree. Christology and Predestination in Reformed Theology from Calvin to Perkins* (Grand Rapids: Baker Book House, 1986), 41.

13 Bruce Gordon, "Calvin and the Swiss Reformed Churches" in Andrew Pettegree, Alastair Duke,

and Gillian Lewis, eds., *Calvinism in Europe 1540–1620* (Cambridge: Cambridge University Press, 1994), 82–99.

14 Cornelis P. Venema, "Heinrich Bullinger's Correspondence on Calvin's Doctrine of Predestination, 1551–1553," *SCJ* 17 (1986), 444.

15 Quoted in Venema, "Heinrich Bullinger's Correspondence," 445.

16 Venema, "Heinrich Bullinger's Correspondence," 446.

17 Mark S. Burrows, "'Christus intra nos Vivens' The Peculiar Genius of Bullinger's Doctrine of Sanctification," *ZKG* 98 (1987), 56.

18 Burrows, "'Christus intra nos Vivens'," 61.

19 Paul Rorem, *Calvin and Bullinger on the Lord's Supper* (Bramcote, Nottingham: Grove Books, 1989), 14.

20 *The Decades of Henry Bullinger, Minister of the Church of Zurich*, ed. for the Parker Society by T. Harding, 4 vols. (Cambridge: Cambridge University Press, 1849–52), IV, ch. 7, 329.

21 Timothy George, "John Calvin and the Agreement of Zurich (1549)" in Timothy George, ed., *John Calvin and the Church: A Prism of Reform* (Louisville: Westminster John Knox, 1990), 42–58.

22 Rorem, *Calvin and Bullinger*, 53–4.

23 John H. Leith, ed., *Creeds of the Church* (Oxford: Basil Blackwell, 1973), 170–1.

24 Aurelio A. Garcia Archilla, *The Theology of History and Apologetic Historiography in Heinrich Bullinger. Truth in History* (San Francisco: Mellen Research University Press, 1992), 168–72.

25 Archilla, *The Theology of History*, 174.

26 Mark Taplin, "The Italian Reformers and the Zurich Church, c.1540–1620" (Ph.D. thesis: University of St. Andrews, 1999), 43.

27 Archilla, *The Theology of History*, 174.

28 Archilla, *The Theology of History*, 189.

29 Taplin, *Italian Reformers*, 42–3.

30 Richard Feller and Edgar Bonjour, *Geschichtsschreibung der Schweiz*, 2 vols. (Basel and Stuttgart: Benno Schwabe, 1962), I:190.

Bibliography

Bullinger's Works in Print

Heinrich Bullinger, *Briefwechsel*, ed. Ulrich Gäbler et al., Zurich: Theologischer Verlag Zürich, 1973–. Currently being edited by Hans Ulrich Bächtold, Rainer Henrich, and Kurt Jakob Rüetschi.

All of Bullinger's printed works are available on microfiche: Fritz Büsser, ed., *Bullinger and the Swiss Urban Reformation on Microfiche*, Leiden: Interdocumentation Co.

The Decades of Henry Bullinger, Minister of the Church of Zurich, ed. for the Parker Society by

T. Harding, 4 vols., Cambridge: Cambridge University Press, 1849–52.

The Zurich Letters, ed. for the Parker Society by Hastings Robinson, 2 vols., Cambridge: Parker Society, 1842–5.

Secondary Sources

Bächtold, Hans Ulrich, *Heinrich Bullinger vor dem Rat: Zur Gestaltung und Verwaltung des Zürcher Staatswesens in den Jahren 1531 bis 1575*, Berne: Peter Lang, 1982.

Baker, J. Wayne, *Heinrich Bullinger and the Covenant: The Other Reformed Tradition*, Athens, OH: Ohio University Press, 1980.

Biel, Pamela, *Doorkeepers at the House of Righteous: Heinrich Bullinger and the Zurich Clergy*, Berne: Peter Lang, 1991.

Burrows, Mark S., "'Christus intra nos Vivens' The Peculiar Genius of Bullinger's Doctrine of Sanctification," *Zeitschrift für Kirchengeschichte* 98 (1987), 47–69.

Büsser, Fritz, *Wurzeln der Reformation in Zürich: Zum 500. Geburtstag des Reformators Huldrych Zwingli*, Leiden: E. J. Brill, 1985.

Fast, Heinold, *Heinrich Bullinger und die Täufer: Ein Beitrag zur Historiographie und Theologie im 16. Jahrhundert*, Weierhof: Mennonitischer Geschichtsverein e.V., 1959.

Gäbler, U. and Herkenrath, E., eds., *Heinrich Bullinger 1504–1575. Gesammelte Aufsätze zum 400. Todestag*, 2 vols., Zurich: Theologischer Verlag, 1975.

Gordon, Bruce, *Clerical Discipline and the Rural Reformation. The Synod in Zurich, 1532–1580*, Berne: Peter Lang, 1992.

Hollweg, Walter, *Heinrich Bullingers Hausbuch: Eine Untersuchung über die Anfänge der reformierten Predigtliteratur*, Neukirchen: Verlag der Buchhandlung des Erziehungsvereins Neukirchen Kreis Moers, 1956.

Maag, Karin, *Seminary or University?: The Genevan Academy and Reformed Higher Education, 1560–1620*, Aldershot: Ashgate, 1995.

Staedtke, Joachim, *Die Theologie der jungen Bullinger*, Zurich: Zwingli Verlag, 1962.

John Calvin (1509–1564)

Randall C. Zachman

Calvin is best understood as a participant in two distinct but related movements of restoration in the sixteenth century: the restoration of arts and letters by the recovery of classical literature, and the restoration of the church by the recovery of the genuine meaning of Scripture. Calvin used the gifts of teaching and interpretation developed as a student of classical texts to restore both the doctrine and genuine interpretation of Scripture to the teachers, pastors, and ordinary Christians of the church of his day. He hoped to renew the knowledge of God in Jesus Christ through the Holy Spirit, not only in name, but in the experience of power, so that the faithful might know God as the author and fountain of every good thing, and be united to God in eternal life.

Calvin's Relationship with Other Reformers

Calvin was initially educated in Noyon in the home of Charles de Hangest, a local aristocrat, and then at the Collège de Montaigue at the University of Paris, where he studied with one of the finest Latinists there, Mathurin Cordier, who awakened in Calvin a love for refined Ciceronian Latin. Calvin then pursued the study of law at the request of his father, first at Orléans, and then at Bourges. While at Orléans, Calvin studied classical Greek with the German Hellenist Melchior Wolmar, who reinforced Calvin's love of classical arts and letters. Indeed, Calvin may have ruined his health by studying both law and literature during this time. After his father's death in 1531, Calvin directed the whole of his attention to the study of classical literature, at the newly founded College of Royal Readers in Paris. There Calvin came under the influence of the two great philologists of his day, Guillaume Budé and Desiderius Erasmus.[1] Calvin learned from them the importance of establishing reliable critical editions of Greek and Latin texts, and of interpreting these texts in light of their literary, linguistic, and cultural contexts, so that their genuine meaning would emerge from that context. He first applied this method to Seneca's treatise *De Clementia*, in a work published at his own expense in April 1532. Calvin's clear preference for Budé over Erasmus is evident in his reference to Budé as "the first ornament and pillar in literature, on account of whom our France today claims for itself the palm of learning."[2] Erasmus, on the other hand, is referred to as "the second glory and darling of literature,"[3] who missed certain things in Seneca's treatise even though he published two works on it. Calvin's deference to the learning and erudition of Budé, and critical independence over against Erasmus continued throughout his life. After Calvin restored Seneca to his rightful place in the reading of the most learned in the world of letters, he turned to restoring Scripture to its rightful place in the reading of the unlearned in the church.

Calvin first appears to have come to an appreciation of the writings of Luther in 1533–4, during which time he most likely experienced his "sudden conversion to teachableness."[4] Calvin addressed him as "the very excellent pastor of the Christian Church, my much respected father."[5] It is quite likely that Calvin viewed Luther as his father in the faith, i.e., as the one who brought him to faith in the gospel, most likely through his own reading of Luther's 1520 treatises, *The Freedom of a Christian* and *The Babylonian Captivity of the Christian Church*.[6] Calvin had the highest praise for the role of Luther in restoring the church of his day, viewing him as an apostle raised up miraculously by God to free the church from the papacy. "Concerning Luther there is no reason . . . to be in any doubt when . . . we openly bear witness that we consider him a distinguished apostle of Christ whose labour and ministry have done most in these times to bring back the purity of the gospel."[7] Because of Luther's role in restoring the gospel, Calvin was willing to acknowledge that the evangelical churches were in fact founded on his ministry, as the divine restoration of apostolic doctrine. "God raised up Luther and others, who held forth a torch to light us into the way of salvation, and on whose ministry our churches are founded and built."[8] Calvin was firmly convinced by Luther's claim that justification by faith alone apart from works was the turning point of the controversy with Rome, and that such faith could only be created and sustained by the preaching of the gospel of the free grace and mercy of God in Jesus Christ, through the power of the Holy Spirit. Calvin also agreed with Luther, over against Zwingli, that the sacraments are signs appended to the gospel to aid and strengthen faith.[9]

Calvin began to have a more complicated relationship with Luther after the latter's attack on Heinrich Bullinger in 1544. Calvin was quite critical of Luther's temper and pride, exacerbated by the fact that he surrounded himself with flatterers who would not point out his shortcomings.[10] Calvin claimed that the vehemence and tenacity that made Luther such an effective opponent of the papacy became his greatest liability when directed against fellow preachers of the gospel.[11] Calvin was also critical of Luther's method of interpreting Scripture. As early as 1540, he wrote to Pierre Viret concerning Luther's commentary on Isaiah: "Luther is not so particular as to propriety of expression or the historical accuracy; he is satisfied when he can draw from it some fruitful doctrine."[12] After Luther's death, Calvin criticized Luther's exegesis more publicly, often noting in his Genesis Commentary Luther's "groundless speculations" on the text. When other followers of Luther took strong exception to these critical comments, Calvin responded, "If I was not permitted at any point to depart from the opinion of Luther, it was utterly ridiculous of me to undertake the office of interpretation (*munus interpretandi*)."[13] By demonstrating his own independence from Luther, Calvin challenged the subservient attitude to Luther he saw in others, which he thought undermined Luther's own efforts to restore the preaching of the gospel and the interpretation of Scripture in the church of his day. Calvin was willing to give Luther the pride of place in the restoration of the church in his day, but he was not willing to let Luther be the dominant individual in the newly restored church.[14]

After his sudden conversion to teachableness, Calvin went first into internal exile within France, and then moved to the city of Basel in the years 1535–6. While he was in Basel, Calvin came into contact with the teaching and exegesis of the Swiss Reformers, especially John Oecolampadius and Ulrich Zwingli. Oecolampadius had been the Reformer of Basel until his death in 1531, and was deeply admired by Calvin for the depth of his learning and for his skill as a biblical interpreter.[15] While in Basel, Calvin also read Zwingli's 1525 *Commentary on True and False Religion*.[16] Calvin was persuaded by Zwingli's claim that the true body of Christ is in heaven, where it will remain until he comes again in glory. He was also persuaded by Zwingli's claim that the Roman doctrine of *ex opere operato* bound the efficacy of the sacraments too much with the ministry of the church, and not with the free mercy of God in Christ through the Holy Spirit. Calvin also seems to have been decisively influenced by Zwingli's description of God as the freely self-giving fountain of every good thing, both as Creator and as Redeemer. However, Calvin throughout his life was highly critical of the way Zwingli divorced the sacraments from the self-offer of Christ, making them empty signs (*nuda signa*). He was also critical of Zwingli's disorderly method of teaching, and of his exegesis, which wandered too far from the text.[17] Calvin throughout his life demonstrated more respect for Oecolampadius than for Zwingli, viewing Oecolampadius as the more learned, moderate, sober, and diligent of the two reformers.[18]

Calvin's sudden conversion to the gospel preached by Luther, Zwingli, and Oecolampadius meant that he felt called to teach the same gospel. Calvin's goal now was to restore the reading of Scripture for everyone in the church, especially those whom he called "the unlearned," i.e., those with no knowledge of or training in Greek, Hebrew, or Latin. This initially meant producing catechetical works for the unlearned, such as the 1536 edition of the *Institutes*. However, Calvin did not feel called to public ministry, but rather to a life of quiet scholarship in retirement. It was Guillaume Farel who presented to Calvin the call of God to the public ministry of teaching and preaching the gospel, when Farel summoned Calvin to help in the restoration of the church in Geneva, under the threat of God's wrath were he to refuse this call.[19] When Calvin accepted this call, first as teacher of Scripture, then as pastor in the newly restored church of Geneva, he had neither training nor aptitude as a public teacher or pastor. Calvin was therefore initiated into his public ministry both by Farel, and by his colleague from the Pays-de-Vaud, Pierre Viret. Calvin was deeply impressed by the prophetic fire and tenacity of Farel, but was also aware that this could lead him to become over-ardent and vehement, making those already opposed to him into hardened enemies.[20] Calvin was equally impressed by the calm moderation of Pierre Viret, who manifested not only quiet self-control even when angry, but even a sense of humor most appreciated by the citizens of Geneva.[21] Throughout the rest of his ministry, Calvin seems to have attempted, with varying degrees of success, to wed the prophetic zeal and tenacity of Farel (reminiscent of Luther) with the moderation and self-control of Viret (reminiscent of Bucer and Melanchthon). He consistently referred to Farel and Viret as his "most amiable and excellent brothers," and appears to have forged very close and lifelong bonds of genuine friendship with each, sharing with them his inmost concerns, hopes, and fears.

After the expulsion of Calvin and Farel from Geneva in 1538, Calvin thought he was no longer suited for the ministry, and that he should instead pursue the quiet life of scholarship from which he had been diverted by Farel in 1536. However, the Strasbourg reformer, Martin Bucer, refused to let Calvin go back into hiding, comparing him to Jonah in his desire to flee from his calling from God to be a teacher and pastor in the church.[22] Calvin came to Strasbourg deeply conscious of his failings as a pastor and teacher in the church, and sought to learn how to become more effective in these offices. Calvin learned the most about the office of ministry from Bucer, whom he termed "that most distinguished minister of Christ."[23] Calvin addressed Bucer as "my much honored father in the Lord," and acknowledged himself to be subject to Bucer's authority. "Admonish, chastise, and exercise all the powers of a father over a son."[24] It may be that Calvin viewed Bucer as his father in the ministry, even as he viewed Luther as his father in the doctrine of salvation. Calvin learned from Bucer how to order the polity and worship of the church, especially with the fourfold office of teacher, pastor, elder, and deacon, and how to order the community via discipline, which Calvin came to describe as the sinews of the body of Christ. Calvin also developed a deep appreciation for Bucer's skill as an interpreter of Scripture, demonstrating his great depth of learning and attention to context.[25] Calvin called Bucer "that most faithful teacher of the church (*fidelissimus ecclesiae doctor*)," and praised his commentaries on Romans and the Psalms in particular.[26]

If Bucer was a decisive influence on Calvin's effectiveness as a pastor and interpreter of Scripture, Johann Sturm and Philip Melanchthon were equally influential on Calvin's development as a teacher. Calvin's call to teach Scripture at Sturm's new Academy in Strasbourg not only refined his abilities as an interpreter of Scripture (his Romans commentary appeared in 1539), but also gave him a vision of how to train and educate a new generation of pastors in the newly restored church. Calvin's deep appreciation for Sturm's work in Strasbourg bore fruit twenty years later in the opening of the Geneva Academy in 1559, which had as its primary task the training of future pastors for ministry in Geneva and in France.[27] Calvin also used his time in Strasbourg to redesign the purpose and method of his *Institutes*, under the influence of Melanchthon's 1535 *Loci Communes*. The impact of Melanchthon on Calvin was reinforced by the personal meetings they had at the colloquies of Worms (1540/1) and Ratisbon (1541), which Calvin attended as part of the Strasbourg contingent, leading to an epistolary friendship that would last until Melanchthon's death in 1560.[28]

If Bucer was to Calvin the most distinguished minister of Christ, Melanchthon was to him the "most illustrious light and distinguished teacher (*doctor*) of the church."[29] Calvin had great respect for Melanchthon's as an interpreter of Scripture, based as it was on his great learning in both biblical and classical literature.[30] Calvin was especially impressed by the clear, orderly, and simple plan of teaching that Melanchthon followed in his major theological handbook, the *Loci Communes*. In a dedication written for Melanchthon, Calvin says: "you are pleased by an unembellished and frank clarity which, without any concealment, sets a subject before the eyes and explains it. This quality of yours has often stirred in me great admiration, just because it is so rarely found."[31] Calvin sought from 1539 onward to bring that same clarity to his own *Institutes*, being finally content with the clarity of the order of its topics in the 1559 edition.[32] Like Melanchthon, Calvin understood the office of the teacher to involve guiding future ministers of the church by setting forth the major topics to be sought in their reading of Scripture, so that they might teach this doctrine to their congregations. However, Calvin thought the teacher of godly doctrine not only led the pious and teachable by the hand to show them what they should seek in Scripture, but also contended in hand-to-hand combat with the ungodly enemies of pious doctrine. He found this combative zeal lacking in Melanchthon, and he became increasingly critical of his friend for having a pliant and weak manner of teaching, a tendency Calvin also saw in his friend Martin Bucer.[33]

Both Bucer and Melanchthon were committed to the efforts undertaken in the sixteenth century to heal the rifts created by the Reformation, both between the evangelicals and the church of Rome, and among the evangelicals themselves. Calvin was suspicious of attempts to seek an accord with Rome, as he viewed the papacy as being in principle opposed to reform. However, Bucer and Melanchthon made Calvin aware of the need to address the question of the catholicity of evangelical doctrine, and its continuity with the previous tradition, in light of the charges of innovation and schism leveled by Rome against the evangelicals. The 1543 edition of the *Institutes* directly addressed these questions, reflecting the enduring influence of Bucer and Melanchthon. Calvin was more enthusiastic about their efforts to unite the divided evangelicals, especially over the question of the Lord's Supper. Calvin accepted the *Wittenberg Concord* of 1536, drafted by Melanchthon and signed by Luther, Melanchthon, and Bucer, which united the churches of Wittenberg and Strasbourg. He signed the 1540 *Augsburg Confession* that included the terms of the *Concord* in the article on the Supper, i.e., that the body of Christ is both exhibited and presented in the bread and wine. Calvin was convinced (perhaps wrongly) that he and Melanchthon were of one mind concerning the Supper, and that it was therefore possible to reach a union between Wittenberg, Strasbourg, Geneva, and Zurich. For such an agreement to succeed, however, Calvin would need to bring Heinrich Bullinger and the pastors of Zurich from their adherence to Zwingli's position to one that reflected the *Wittenberg Concord* and the 1540 *Augsburg Confession*.[34]

Calvin had deep respect for Heinrich Bullinger as his senior pastor in the evangelical churches of the Swiss regions. He consistently referred to him in his letters as his "respected and learned brother." Bullinger was renowned for his learning, both of Scripture and of the Fathers, having been brought to the evangelical side by comparing the writings of Luther with those of the Fathers, and finding Luther to be more catholic than Rome.[35] Calvin sought the counsel of Bullinger in matters regarding the church of Geneva, beginning with the convulsions in Geneva leading to the expulsion of Calvin and Farel in 1538.[36] However, Calvin was aware that the one area in which Geneva and Zurich were not of one mind was the meaning of the Lord's Supper. At the urging of Farel, Calvin went to Zurich (itself a sign of deference to the greater authority of the church there), in order to initiate talks designed to reach an agreement on the Supper, which finally came to fruition in the

Zurich Consensus of 1549, published in 1551. This ecumenical achievement, demonstrating an irenic side of Calvin's nature not often noted, was clouded by the harsh attacks on it by the Lutherans Joachim Westphal and Tilemann Hesshusius, both of whom rejected the claim made by Calvin that the *Zurich Consensus* reflected the teaching of the *Augsburg Confession*. Calvin himself describes this period of his life as one of the most bitter, made all the more painful by the utter silence of Philip Melanchthon on the dispute, perhaps indicating his own problems with the *Consensus*.[37] However, Bullinger never wavered in his adherence to the consensus reached with Calvin, as is reflected in the *Second Helvetic Confession*, written by Bullinger as a statement of his faith two years after the death of Calvin.

The picture that emerges of Calvin from his association with other reformers of his day is significantly different from the popular picture of Calvin as an intolerant dogmatist. Calvin was first of all a highly learned person, trained and skilled in the interpretation of Hebrew, Greek, and Latin texts, deeply committed to the recovery of letters brought about by the labors of Guillaume Budé and Desiderius Erasmus. Calvin was also a teacher of the gospel of Jesus Christ, whose teaching was founded on the ministry and teaching of his "father" in faith, the "apostle of Christ," Martin Luther. However, like Zwingli and Oecolampadius, Calvin was not only concerned with the Roman denial of justification by faith alone, but was also dismayed by the superstitious Roman worship of the signs of spiritual realities instead of the spiritual realities themselves. To Calvin, worship was to lift our minds and hearts to heaven, not to confine them to earth. Calvin was called to the public ministry of teacher and pastor by the prophetic Guillaume Farel, and supported in it by the moderate and self-controlled Pierre Viret. Calvin was called back to the ministry by his "father," Martin Bucer, who advanced his training both as pastor and as interpreter of Scripture. Calvin was decisively shaped as a teacher by Johann Sturm and especially by Philip Melanchthon, whose method of teaching via *loci communes* Calvin followed in every edition of the *Institutes* from 1539 to 1559. Finally, in large part under the influence of Bucer and Melanchthon, Calvin was profoundly committed to the cause of ecumenical unity among the evangelicals, even though his hopes in this regard were in large part frustrated. In sum, Calvin saw himself as both a teacher and pastor, called to restore the preaching of the gospel to the church of Christ, by restoring the right way to read Scripture both to pastors and to unlearned laity, in the company of other learned and godly teachers and pastors.[38]

Calvin's Restoration of the Right Worship of God

Calvin was convinced that the Roman Church had led the Catholic Church into captivity and ruin by teaching and preaching doctrines not drawn from the genuine sense of Scripture, and by preventing the reading of Scripture for ordinary, unlearned Christians. He therefore dedicated his life to restoring the teaching and preaching of the doctrine drawn from Scripture by teachers and pastors, so that pastors might guide ordinary Christians in their own reading of Scripture. By the time Calvin left Strasbourg, he had developed the framework to accomplish these goals. From 1539 on, he developed a program of instruction for future pastors of the church consisting of successive editions of the *Institutes* and a series of biblical commentaries, beginning with Romans in 1539 and culminating with the unfinished lectures on Ezekiel in 1564. The *Institutes*, following the *loci communes* method of Philip Melanchthon, were designed to set forth in a clear, orderly, and persuasive way the topics to be sought in the reading of Scripture, so that such reading might bear fruit. The commentaries were designed to give a contextual reading of Scripture so that the mind of the biblical author might be revealed by the context, and so that fruitful but general doctrine might be drawn from the genuine sense of Scripture.

Once trained to draw their teaching from Scripture by the *Institutes* and commentaries, pastors were then to teach the sum of topics found in Scripture to the young people of their congregations by means of the *Catechism* of 1545. After the sum of godly doctrine had been taught, pastors were then to preach contextually from Scripture, following the same method of *lectio continua* followed by Calvin in the commentaries. The pastors were not only to draw general doctrine from Scripture, but to apply it to the lives of the members of their congregations, both in public sermons and in private exhortations and admonitions. Once instructed by the pastors in the *Catechism* and sermons, the members of the congregation, women, men, and children, were to read Scripture for themselves, so that they might confirm that what the pastor taught them was drawn from Scripture, and teach one another as they had been taught.[39] Calvin thus envisioned the church as a school in which all are students as well as teachers, being instructed by God through Christ by the doctrine of the Holy Spirit set forth in Scripture.[40] Since this model assumes that every Christian will be literate, and hence able to read Scripture, the completion of the school of Christ in Geneva only came with the inauguration of the Geneva Academy in 1559.

The goal of reading Scripture under the guidance of godly, learned interpreters was for Calvin the restoration of the proper worship of God the Creator, that he thought the Roman Church had corrupted. The Roman Church, following the dictum of Gregory the Great (d. 604), had taught that images, and not Scripture, are the books of the unlearned. In spite of the repeated warnings by the prophets that images teach falsehood, Christians under the Roman Church were led to the superstitious worship of a carnally imagined deity, culminating in the worship of the bread of the Lord's Supper as if it were the eternal Son of God himself. The carnal and superstitious worship of God in turn fostered all manner of hypocrisy. Consequently, God cannot be worshiped in sincerity and truth from the inmost affection of the heart, but rather hypocritically and deceitfully by means of a vast and impressive array of human ceremonies, all meant to conceal the fact that we are fleeing from God while appearing to approach God.

In order to restore the true worship of God, Calvin sought first of all to distinguish the true God, the Creator of heaven and earth, from the false gods and idols taught by Rome. He did this not by rejecting images altogether, but by pointing the godly from the dead images of superstition to the living images created by God, in which the invisible God becomes somewhat visible. Calvin taught that the universe itself was such a living image of God, setting before the eyes of all, learned and unlearned, the self-representation of God meant to lead us to the true knowledge of God. In the works that God does all around us, and even within us, the powers of God are set forth as if in a painting.[41] When these powers are rightly contemplated and considered by us, they should lift our minds and hearts up to God, who is their source.[42] "Then, by these benefits shed like dew from heaven upon us, we are led as by rivulets to the spring itself."[43] The living image of God in the universe therefore represents to us God as the author and fountain of every good thing.[44] Thus we are led to trust in God, call on God for everything we lack, thank God for everything we have received, and obey God from the inmost affection of the heart, in order to be drawn to and united with God in eternal life.

However, given Adam's fall into sin, we can no longer come to the true know-ledge of God by means of the self-manifestation of God in the universe. In particular, our blindness keeps us from judging rightly about the works of God that we see, and our ingratitude keeps us from acknowledging God to be the source of the benefits we enjoy. For true knowledge of the Creator, we must use the spectacles God has provided for us in Scripture to contemplate the works of God, and we must be inwardly illumined by the internal testimony of the Holy Spirit so that we profit from the spectacles of Scripture. When we view the works of God through the spectacles of Scripture, we learn that "nothing is set down there that cannot be beheld in his creatures. Indeed, with experience as our teacher we find God just as he declares himself in his Word."[45] In particular, Scripture sets forth God's infinite and spiritual essence, but of three persons in the one essence, who provided all things for us before we were created, and continues to provide for us with special and tender care.

However, the fall into sin has not only brought about our inability rightly to view the living image of God in the universe without the teaching and illumination of the Holy Spirit, but it has also brought about a change in the self-manifestation of God in the universe itself. For since we are sinners, the universe manifests the curse of God due to our sin, and the wrath of God against us as sinners, as much as it does the blessing of God towards us as creatures. "This curse, while it seizes and over-whelms innocent creatures through our fault, must overwhelm our souls with des-pair."[46] To know God as the author and fountain of every good thing, we must be directed to a new living image of God, one that not only manifests the benefits God wishes to lavish upon us, but that also takes away our sin and the curse and wrath upon us. The preaching of the gospel directs us to this new image of God set forth in Christ crucified, and we must turn to contemplate this living image of God if we hope to know and worship God aright.[47]

The cross of Christ reveals that God has placed on his Son, and the Son has taken on himself, our sin and guilt. Christ has therefore taken on himself our curse and death, including our eternal damnation under the wrath of God, which he suffered in his soul as he died on the cross.[48] The resurrection of Christ, on the other hand, and especially his ascension to the right hand of the Father in heaven, reveal that God has laid up with Christ everything that we lack, so that we may seek it in him alone. In place of the sin that Christ has taken upon himself, God gives us the righteousness of Christ's obedience. In the place of the death he suffered on our behalf, God gives us eternal life. In place of the curse and wrath of God, we are given in Christ the blessing and mercy of God. Calvin locates the reception of these blessings of God by Christ in the ascension; following Peter's sermon in Acts, Christ received the promised Holy Spirit when he ascended to God.

In order for us to have access to the benefits bestowed on Christ on our behalf, Christ must offer himself to us to be received and enjoyed by us. According to Calvin, he does this by manifesting himself and his benefits to us in the living image of the gospel.[49] The goal of the gospel is to lead us to union with Christ himself, so that we might draw from him all that he has been given for us, and he might take on himself all that we have that prevents us from having access to God.

> Yet more: we experience such participation in him that . . . while we are sinners, he is our righteousness; while we are unclean, he is our purity; . . . while we still bear about with us the body of death, he is yet our life. In brief, because all his things are ours and we have all things in him, in us there is nothing.[50]

Our faith should seek to unite us with Christ himself, for by union with him we are freed of all that alienates us from God, and given all that we lack by which to unite us to God. However, when we are united to Christ himself by faith, we cannot help but experience the power of all of his benefits, especially that which Calvin called the twofold grace of Christ (*duplex gratia Christi*), consisting of repentance and justification.[51] Calvin described repentance as our participation in the death and resurrection of Christ, putting sin to death within us and creating newness of life, whereby we are renewed in the image of God. Such renewal really does mean that God can begin to recognize us as children of God, and we can begin to discern a harmony between our lives and the righteousness of God set forth in God's law. However, the vestiges of sin always remain in the repentant, which even when not consented to are still mortal in God's sight. Thus those engrafted in Christ continually need to be forgiven even as they are continually being regenerated in Christ.[52] Because the faithful cannot participate in Christ without experiencing the force and benefit of all his blessings, they cannot be renewed without being forgiven, nor can they be forgiven without, at the same time, being renewed. Thus the Roman claim that the faithful no longer need to be forgiven, and the distorted evangelical claim that the faithful are not called to holiness of life and good works, are equally false on these grounds.

Calvin's vision of the Christian life grows out of the experience of regeneration brought about by participation in Christ. Calvin's ethics were not so much casuistic prescriptions regarding specific actions in particular situations, but rather the setting forth of the plan or method for the conduct of life (*ratio vitae formandae*) gathered from the whole of Scripture. He consistently contrasted the Christian conduct of life with the pattern of life set forth by classical philosophers such as Plato, Cicero, and Seneca. Calvin finds two such plans in Scripture, the law of God revealed through Moses and rightly interpreted by Christ; and the pattern of Christ's life itself, to which believers are conformed by participation in him. The Ten Commandments set forth the pattern to which our lives must conform if they are to express the image of God. "For God has so depicted his character in the law that if any man carries out in deeds whatever is enjoined there, he will express the image of God, as it were, in his own life."[53] The faithful, by participation in Christ, are renewed in the image of God, so that their lives do express the image of God by their conformity with the righteousness of God in the law.[54]

Since Christ is the living image of God who alone conforms us to the image of God by our participation in him, the ultimate image the godly are to express in their lives is that of Christ crucified. "For we have been adopted as sons by the Lord with this one condition: that our life express (*repraesentet*) Christ, the bond of our adoption."[55] If our lives are to represent Christ himself, then the ultimate pattern of our lives will be self-denial and complete self-surrender to the guidance of God through the Holy Spirit, which is the real meaning of the Sabbath, according to Calvin.[56] In contrast to the philosophers who bid us rule our lives by reason alone, Calvin claimed that "Christian philosophy bids reason give way to, submit and subject itself to, the Holy Spirit so that the man himself may no longer live but hear Christ living and reigning within him [Gal. 2:20]."[57] Thus the form of the Christian life is ultimately born of the same source as faith, i.e., the gospel. In agreement with Erasmus, Calvin claims that the gospel must find a seat and resting place in the inmost affection of the heart, and "must enter our heart and pass into our daily living, and so transform us into itself that it may not be unfruitful for us."[58]

Calvin was well aware that the faith that unites us to Christ is always weak and under assault in this life, both from persecution from the world and from doubts within our minds and hearts. Moreover, the gospel portrays spiritual blessings to us that we can neither see nor feel. In order to provide aids to strengthen and support our faith, God has created the ministry of the church, that by its teaching, preaching, discipline, and especially its administration of the sacraments, our faith might not fail. "First of all, he instituted sacraments, which we who have experienced them feel to be highly useful aids to foster and to strengthen faith."[59] The sacraments are especially effective aids of faith because they portray the self-presentation of Christ in the gospel in ways that we who are earthly can see and contemplate. "Here our merciful Lord . . . condescends to lead us to himself even by these earthly elements, and to set before us in the flesh a mirror of spiritual blessings."[60]

The sacrament of baptism portrays our adoption into the family of God, and especially the twofold grace of repentance and forgiveness that God gives to his children in Christ. The Sacrament of the Holy Supper of the Lord portrays our union with the flesh of Christ, from which we draw all we need in order to unite us to God in eternal life.[61] Since we cannot perceive our union with Christ in this life, the Supper portrays this to us in a way that confirms our faith. "In this Sacrament we have such full witness of all these things that we must certainly consider them as if Christ here present were himself set before our eyes and touched by our hands."[62] However, the faithful are to remember that Christ is not in fact here, but is in heaven, to which he calls us by the Supper. Hence when we see the pledge and offer of his body and blood in the Supper, we must immediately bring to mind the analogy between the bodily food of bread and wine and the spiritual food of Christ's body and blood; we must rise from the temporal to the spiritual by means of an anagogical elevation; we must seek Christ not in the Sacrament, but in heaven, through the power of the Holy Spirit, who unites us to him even though he is no longer with us on earth. Calvin was especially concerned with two errors he saw in his day: seeking Christ in the symbol that represents and offers him (as in the Roman adoration of the eucharistic host), and thinking that we feed on the Body and Blood of Christ with our mouths, and not with our souls. He thought that he was in fundamental agreement with Luther by maintaining, against Zwingli and with the *Wittenberg Concord,* that the signs of bread and wine truly represent and present the body and blood of Christ. However, his rejection of the oral eating of the Body and Blood of Christ prevented the followers of Luther from seeing him as a kindred spirit, even though Luther himself knew of Calvin's position and did not attack it.

The Holy Supper of the Lord is at the very heart of Calvin's understanding of Christian life in the church, for it sets before us and offers us the very flesh of Christ in which the Father has placed every good thing that we lack. All that is meant to flow to us from the Father, the author and fountain of every good thing, through the eternal Son of God, by means of the Holy Spirit, is to be sought in the flesh of Christ alone. "In like manner, the flesh of Christ is like a rich and inexhaustible fountain that pours into us the life springing forth from the Godhead into itself. Now who does not see that communion of Christ's flesh and blood is necessary for all who aspire to heavenly life?"[63] To be a Christian means to participate in this body by the power of the Holy Spirit, in company with all whom God has engrafted into Christ. Christ offers us himself and all his benefits in the preaching of the gospel and the administration of the sacraments, so that we might feel and experience the power of his life in us, and be transformed into the image of his life in our lives. The entire ministry of the church is meant to facilitate the experience of the power of the flesh of Christ in the lives of the godly, so that they may be united with Christ unto eternal life.

Notes

1 T. H. L. Parker, *Calvin's New Testament Commentaries,* 2nd ed. (Louisville, KY: Westminster/ John Knox Press, 1993), 164–88.

2 *CO* 5:54, cited in Parker, *Commentaries,* 188.

3 John Calvin, *Calvin's Commentary on Seneca's De Clementia,* trans. Ford Lewis Battles and André Malan Hugo (Leiden: E. J. Brill, 1969), 7.

4 *CO* 31:21; *Calvin: Commentaries,* trans. Joseph Haroutunian (Philadelphia: Westminster Press, 1958), 52. See B. A. Gerrish, "The Pathfinder: Calvin's Image of Martin Luther" in *The Old Protestantism and the New: Essays on the Reformation Heritage* (Edinburgh: T. & T. Clark, 1982), 27–48.

5 Calvin to Martin Luther, January 21, 1545, *CO* 12:7; *The Letters of John Calvin,* trans. Jules Bonnet, 4 vols. (New York, Burt Franklin, 1972), 1:440.

6 The last two sections of the 1536 *Institutes* directly echo these two treatises, whereas the first section directly echoes Luther's *Small*

Catechism. See Alexandre Ganoczy, *The Young Calvin,* trans. David Foxgrover and Wade Provo (Philadelphia: Westminster Press, 1987), 137–45.

7 John Calvin, *The Bondage and Liberation of the Will, CO* 6:250; trans. A. N. S. Lane (Grand Rapids: Baker Books, 1996), 28.

8 John Calvin, *The Necessity of Reforming the Church* (1543), *CO* 6:459; *Calvin: Theological Treatises,* trans. J. K. S. Reid (Philadelphia: Westminster Press, 1954), 185.

9 For a detailed comparison of Luther and Calvin on the nature of faith, see Randall C. Zachman, *The Assurance of Faith: Conscience in the Theology of Martin Luther and John Calvin* (Minneapolis: Fortress Press, 1993).

10 "Flatterers have done him much mischief, since he is naturally too prone to be over-indulgent to himself" (Calvin to Heinrich Bullinger, November 25, 1544, *CO* 11:774; *Letters,* 1:433).

11 Ibid.

12 *CO* 11:36; *Letters,* 1:188.

13 Calvin to Francis Burkhardt, February 27, 1555, *CO* 15:454.

14 Calvin to Philip Melanchthon, June 28, 1545, *CO* 12:99; *Letters*, 1:467.

15 "No one, as I think, has hitherto more diligently applied himself to this pursuit than Oecolampadius, who has not always, however, reached the full scope or meaning" (Calvin to Viret, May 19, 1540, *CO* 11:36; *Letters*, 1:188.

16 Ganoczy, *The Young Calvin*, 90–102, 151–8.

17 Calvin to Viret, May 19, 1540, *CO* 11:36; *Letters*, 1:188.

18 Calvin does note, however, that the memory of both Zwingli and Oecolampadius "ought to be held in honorable esteem by all the godly" (Calvin to Melanchthon, January 21, 1545, *CO* 12:11; *Letters*, 1:437–8).

19 "But William Farel forced me to stay in Geneva not so much by advice or urging as by command, which had the power of God's hand laid violently upon me from heaven" (*CO* 31:23; *Calvin: Commentaries*, 53).

20 Calvin to Martin Bucer, October 15, 1541, *CO* 11:296; *Letters*, 1:290. See David N. Wiley, "Calvin's Friendship with Guillaume Farel" in *Calvin and His Contemporaries: Calvin Studies Society Papers 1995, 1997* (Grand Rapids: CRC Product Services, 1998), 187–204.

21 Robert D. Linder, "Brothers in Christ: Pierre Viret and John Calvin As Soul Mates and Co-Laborers in the Work of the Reformation" in Wiley, *Calvin and His Contemporaries*, 134–58.

22 "Terrified by the example of Jonah, which he had set before me, I continued the work of teaching" (*CO* 31:25; *Calvin: Commentaries*, 54).

23 Ibid.

24 Calvin to Martin Bucer, October 15, 1541, *CO* 11:296; *Letters*, 1:294–5.

25 Calvin to Heinrich Bullinger, March 12, 1539, *Letters*, 1:114.

26 "It is to his special credit that no one in our time has been more precise and diligent in interpreting Scripture than he" ("John Calvin to Simon Grynaeus," *Ioannis Calvini Commentarius in Epistolam Pauli ad Romanos*, ed. T. H. L. Parker (Leiden: E. J. Brill, 1981), 2, lines 53–9; henceforth *Romans* 5.53–9; *Calvin's New Testament Commentaries*, ed. David W. Torrance and Thomas F. Torrance (Grand Rapids: Eerdmans, 1959–72), Vol. 8, p. 2, henceforth *CNTC* 8:2. This assessment of Bucer is echoed many years later, when Calvin

praises his singular erudition, diligence, and faithfulness in the preface to his Psalms commentary of 1557 (*CO* 31:16).

27 Karin Maag, *Seminary or University? The Genevan Academy and Reformed Higher Education, 1560–1620* (Aldershot: Ashgate, 1995).

28 Timothy Wengert, "'We Will Feast Together in Heaven Forever': The Epistolary Friendship of John Calvin and Philip Melanchthon" in Karin Maag, ed., *Melanchthon in Europe* (Grand Rapids: Baker Books, 1999), 19–44.

29 Calvin to Philip Melanchthon, December 13, 1558, *CO* 17:384–6; *Letters*, 3:484.

30 Calvin speaks of Melanchthon in glowing terms as "Master Philip, who excels in genius and learning, and is happily versed in the studies of history" (Comm. Dan. 9:25, *CO* 41:176). See also "Calvin to Grynaeus", *Romans* 2.45–7; *CNTC* 8:2.

31 *The Bondage and Liberation of the Will*, 3; *CO* 6:229–30.

32 For the influence of Melanchthon on Calvin's *Institutes*, see Richard A. Muller, *The Unaccommodated Calvin: Studies in the Foundation of a Theological Tradition* (New York: Oxford University Press, 2000).

33 Calvin to Melanchthon, September 10, 1555, *CO* 16:738; *Letters*, 3:337. See Randall C. Zachman, "Restoring Access to the Fountain: Melanchthon and Calvin on the Task of Evangelical Theology" in Wiley, *Calvin and His Contemporaries*, 205–28. About both Melanchthon and Bucer, Calvin says that "in their method of proceeding they accommodate themselves too much to the time" (Calvin to Farel, May 11, 1541, *CO* 11:217; *Letters*, 1:263).

34 One can see his interest in reaching such an agreement early during his stay in Strasbourg, when he wrote his *Short Treatise on the Holy Supper of our Lord and only Saviour Jesus Christ, 1539, CO* 5:429–60; *Calvin: Theological Treatises*, trans. J. K. S. Reid (Philadelphia: Westminster Press, 1954), 140–66.

35 Parker, *New Testament*, 72.

36 Calvin to Bullinger, February 21, 1538, *CO* 10:153–4; *Letters*, 1:65–7.

37 *CO* 31:33; *Calvin: Commentaries*, 56–7.

38 William Bouwsma rightly notes the combination of the contextual reading of Scripture in Calvin's work as interpreter of Scripture, learned from the work of Budé, Erasmus, and later Bucer, and the concern for the order of right teaching in his work as a teacher

of godly doctrine, learned in large part from Melanchthon. However, Bouwsma mistakenly reads these two tasks as reflective of a deep conflict in Calvin's personality, representing two mutually exclusive ways he attempted to cope with his profound anxiety. Bouwsma's thesis regarding the anxiety of Calvin is pure speculation on his part. His discernment of these two aspects of Calvin is properly to be understood in light of Calvin's vocations as teacher of godly doctrine (*Institutes*), interpreter of Scripture (commentaries), and pastor (*Catechism* and sermons). As noted above, Calvin did attempt to combine prophetic zeal (Luther, Farel) with godly moderation (Viret, Bucer, Melanchthon), but in light of his fulfillment of his vocation, not in an attempt to cope with deep-seated anxiety. William J. Bouwsma, *John Calvin: A Sixteenth Century Portrait* (New York and Oxford: Oxford University Press, 1988).

39 See Randall C. Zachman, "'Do You Understand What You Are Reading?' Calvin's Guidance for the Reading of Scripture," *Scottish Journal of Theology* (forthcoming).

40 Comm. 1 Cor. 14:31, *CO* 49:530; *CNTC* 9:303.

41 *Inst.* I.v.10, *Institutio Christianae religionis, 1559, OS* III. 54.19–21; *Calvin: Institutes of the Christian Religion*, ed. John T. McNeill

and trans. Ford Lewis Battles (Philadelphia: Westminster Press, 1960), 1:63.

42 *Inst.* I.v.9, *OS* 3:53.14–16; (1:62).
43 *Inst.* I.i.1, *OS* 3:31.15–16; (1:36).
44 B. A. Gerrish has done more than any other Calvin scholar to turn our attention to Calvin's description of God as the author and fountain of every good thing. See his *Grace and Gratitude: The Eucharistic Theology of John Calvin* (Minneapolis: Fortress Press, 1993).
45 *Inst.* I.x.2, *OS* 3:86, 27–30; (1:98).
46 *Inst.* II.vi.1, *OS* 3:320, 15–18; (1:341).
47 *Inst.* II.vi.1, *OS* 3:320, 33–6; (1:341).
48 *Inst.* II.xvi.10, *OS* 3:495, 12–15; (1:517).
49 *Inst.* III.ii.6, *OS* 4:13, 15–19; (1:548).
50 *Inst.* III.xv.5, *OS* 4:244, 19–28; (1:793).
51 *Inst.* III.iii.1, *OS* 4:55, 2–6; (1:592).
52 *Inst.* III.xi.16, *OS* 4:200, 17–23; (1:746).
53 *Inst.* II.viii.51, *OS* 4:390, 15–20; (1:415).
54 *Inst.* III.vi.1, *OS* 4:146, 14–17; (1:684).
55 *Inst.* III.vi.3, *OS* 4:148, 23–6; (1:686–7).
56 *Inst.* II.viii.29, *OS* 3:372, 10–15; (1:396).
57 *Inst.* III.vii.1, *OS* 4:152, 2–5; (1:690).
58 *Inst.* III.vi.4, *OS* 4:149, 30–2; (1:688).
59 *Inst.* IV.i.1, *OS* 5:1, 18–21; (2:1012).
60 *Inst.* IV.xiv.3, *OS* 5:260, 23–9; (2:1278).
61 *Inst.* IV.xvii.2, *OS* 5:343, 21–4; (2:1362).
62 *Inst.* IV.xvii.3, *OS* 5:344, 7–10; (2:1362).
63 *Inst.* IV.xvii.9, *OS* 5:350, 38–351, 1–4; (2:1369).

Bibliography

Primary Sources

Ioannis Calvini opera quae supersunt omnia, ed. Wilhelm Baum, Edward Cunitz, and Eduard Reuss, Brunswick: A. Schwetschke & Son (M. Bruhn), 1863–1900.
Ioannis Calvini opera selecta, ed. Peter Barth, Wilhelm Niesel, and Dora Scheuner, Munich: Chr. Kaiser, 1926–52.
Calvin: Institutes of the Christian Religion, ed. John T. McNeill, trans. Ford Lewis Battles, Philadelphia: Westminster Press, 1960.
Calvin: Theological Treatises, trans. J. K. S. Reid, Philadelphia: Westminster Press, 1954.
Calvin's Commentary on Seneca's De Clementia, trans. Ford Lewis Battles and André Malan Hugo, Leiden: E. J. Brill, 1969.
Calvin's New Testament Commentaries, ed. David W. Torrance and Thomas F. Torrance, Grand Rapids: Eerdmans, 1959–72.

The Commentaries of John Calvin on the Old Testament, Edinburgh: Calvin Translation Society, 1843–8.
Institutes, 1536 Edition, trans. and ann. Ford Lewis Battles, Grand Rapids: Eerdmans, 1986.
Supplementa Calviniana: sermons inedits, Neukirchener: Neukirchener Verlag, 1961–.
Tracts and Treatises, trans. Henry Beveridge, Edinburgh: Calvin Translation Society, 1849.

Secondary Sources

Doumergue, Emile, *Jean Calvin, les hommes et les choses de son temps*, Lausanne: G. Bridel, 1899–1927.
Dowey, Edward A., *The Knowledge of God in Calvin's Theology*, expanded ed., Grand Rapids: Eerdmans, 1994.
Engel, Mary Potter, *John Calvin's Perspectival Anthropology*, Atlanta, GA: Scholars Press, 1987.

Ganoczy, Alexandre, *The Young Calvin*, trans. David Foxgrover and Wade Provo, Philadelphia: Westminster Press, 1987.

Gerrish, B. A., *Grace and Gratitude: The Eucharistic Theology of John Calvin*, Minneapolis: Fortress Press, 1993.

Haas, Guenther, *The Concept of Equity in Calvin's Ethics*, Waterloo, Ont.: Wilfred Laurier Press, 1997.

Hoepfl, Harro, *The Christian Polity of John Calvin*, New York: Cambridge University Press, 1982.

McNeill, John T., *The History and Character of Calvinism*, New York: Oxford University Press, 1967.

Millet, Olivier, *Calvin et la dynamique de la parole*, Geneva: Slatkin, 1992.

Muller, Richard A., *The Unaccommodated Calvin: Studies in the Foundation of a Theological Tradition*, New York: Oxford University Press, 2000.

Naphy, William G., *Calvin and the Consolidation of the Genevan Reformation*, Manchester, NH: Manchester University Press, 1994.

Parker, T. H. L., *John Calvin: A Biography*, Philadelphia: Westminster Press, 1975.

Steinmetz, David, *Calvin in Context*, New York: Oxford University Press, 1995.

Walker, Williston, *John Calvin, the Organizer of Reformed Protestantism, 1509–1564*, New York: Putnam, 1906.

Wallace, Ronald, *Calvin's Doctrine of Word and Sacrament*, Edinburgh: Oliver & Boyd, 1953.

Wendel, François, *Calvin: Origins and Development of His Religious Thought*, trans. Philip Mairet, Durham, NC: Labyrinth Press, 1987.

Zachman, Randall C., *The Assurance of Faith: Conscience in the Theology of Martin Luther and John Calvin*, Minneapolis: Fortress Press, 1993.

Peter Martyr Vermigli (1499–1562)

Frank A. James III

John Calvin called Peter Martyr Vermigli "the miracle of Italy."[1] Theodore Beza, no less effusive, described Vermigli as a "phoenix born from the ashes of Savonarola."[2] Other contemporaries were less appreciative of Vermigli's character and talents. William Tresham, a canon of Christ Church, vice-chancellor of Oxford University, and Vermigli's main opponent at the Oxford disputation in 1549, described Vermigli as a "pseudomartyr" and "a doting old man, subverted, impudent, and famous master of errors who fled from Germany for the sake of lust and adultery."[3] Neither was the new Regius Professor of Divinity popular with the townspeople of Oxford, since most retained their allegiance to Catholic teachings. Broken windows and insulting remarks demonstrated that this foreign Protestant divine was a long way from easy acceptance in his adopted homeland.[4]

Despite such hostile attitudes, Vermigli's books went through 110 separate printings in the century following his death in 1562.[5] He made his mark primarily as a biblical commentator, but also as an important theologian of the Reformed branch of Protestantism. The commentaries published during his lifetime were on 1 Corinthians, Romans, and Judges. However, a number of his lectures on biblical books were published posthumously as commentaries on Genesis, Lamentations, 1 and 2 Samuel, and 1 and 2 Kings. Vermigli also wrote theological treatises, most notably on the Eucharist. His *Defensio* against Steven Gardiner, a lengthy tome of impressive erudition, was "incontestably the weightiest single treatise on the Eucharist of the entire Reformation."[6] Vermigli's commentaries contained some of his most important theological writings in the form of *loci* or theological essays, which were in fact substantial theological treatises. Two of his most important theological *loci*, on the doctrines of justification and predestination, are in his Romans commentary of 1558.

While his main theological preoccupations tended to concentrate on predestination, justification, and the Eucharist, Vermigli's theological interests extended to treatises on clerical celibacy and the two natures of Christ. Vermigli's most influential writing was the *Loci Communes*, a posthumous compilation of various *loci* from his biblical commentaries. The compilation by Robert Masson, a French pastor in

London, was deliberately calibrated to coincide with the organizational structure of Calvin's *Institutes*. Reciprocally, the first Latin edition of the *Institutes* to appear in England, the Vautrollier edition of 1576, was keyed to Vermigli's *Loci Communes*. This pattern of coordination between Calvin and Vermigli reflected the prevailing conviction that two of the most important Reformed theologians of this period were in significant theological agreement. This arrangement is splendidly maintained in John T. McNeill's modern edition of the Institutes. Although widely acknowledged as one of the leading theologians of his day, repeated exiles obscured his memory, until rediscovered by doctoral students at British universities in the mid-twentieth century.

A Peripatetic Life

Born in Florence on September 8, 1499, little is known of Vermigli's early years except his abiding affection for the Bible. In his inaugural speech at Zurich in 1556, Vermigli recalled: "From an early age when I was still living in Italy, I decided to pursue this one thing above the other human arts and studies – that I should learn and teach primarily the divine scriptures."[7] Following this conviction, against the wishes of his father, Vermigli joined the Lateran Congregation of Canons Regular of St. Augustine in 1514. Academically precocious, he was sent to study at the University of Padua, then one of the most famous universities in the world. At Padua he lived a dual intellectual existence. On the one hand, he was inundated with the ideas of Aristotle in the theology faculty; on the other hand, he imbibed Renaissance humanism at his monastery, S. Giovanni di Verdara. His study at Padua culminated in ordination and a doctorate in theology (1526). But he encountered more than ideas at Padua. He also acquired a proclivity for action, for among his Paduan friends were Pietro Bembo, Reginald Pole, and Marcantonio Flaminio – all future leaders of the abortive Italian reform movement.[8]

During the Italian phase of his career he was well known as a distinguished young theologian and eloquent preacher.[9] An active reformist within the Catholic Church, he served as consultant to the famous *Consilium de emendanda ecclesia* (Council on the reform of the church) in 1537 and Cardinal Contarini appointed him to a delegation to engage in dialogue with the Protestants at the Colloquy of Worms in 1540. At Spoleto, Naples, and especially Lucca, he actively pursued a reformist agenda. So successful were his reforms in Lucca that the ire of papal conservatives was stirred to resolute reaction. Philip McNair provides compelling evidence that the reconstitution of the Roman Inquisition was directly connected to Vermigli's reforming efforts in Lucca.[10]

Vermigli's critical theological transformation was initiated during his Neapolitan abbacy (1537–40) by the Spanish reformist, Juan de Valdés. In the Valdésian circle in Naples he encountered the Italian reform movement, first read Protestant literature, and embraced the pivotal doctrine of justification by faith alone.[11] His theological reorientation manifested itself during his priorate in Lucca, where he established "the first and last reformed theological college in pre-Tridentine Italy."[12] With Martyr as his mentor, Girolamo Zanchi was introduced to the works of Bucer, Melanchthon, Bullinger, and Calvin.[13]

With the reinstitution of the Roman Inquisition under the iron hand of Cardinal Carafa, whose advocacy for moral reform gave way to repression of suspected heretics within the church, Vermigli experienced a personal crisis of conscience.[14] In the summer of 1542, he was ordered to appear before a Chapter Extraordinary of the Lateran Congregation of the Canons Regular of St. Augustine in Genoa. Warned by highly placed friends, he found himself on the horns of a dilemma: would he flee his homeland for the sake of the Protestant gospel, or would he hold his tongue and conform to the authority of a church he no longer respected? Weighing the consequences, he forsook Italy for a life in exile.

Almost immediately, he was catapulted into prominence as a biblical scholar and Protestant theologian. In October 1542 Vermigli succeeded Wolfgang Capito as professor of Divinity in Strasbourg and forged a close personal alliance with the Alsatian Reformer, Martin Bucer. So valuable was he to Bucer, that Johann Sturm stated that the veteran Reformer made no decisions without first consulting with his Italian colleague.[15] As a teacher, Vermigli was judged by all "to surpass" Bucer.[16]

After five productive years in Strasbourg, Archbishop Thomas Cranmer invited Vermigli to England to help inculcate a generation of Anglican priests with Protestant theology. Appointed Regius Professor of Divinity at Oxford University, his nearly six years in England were among the most fruitful of his career. He single-handedly upheld Protestant eucharistic teaching at the famous Oxford Disputation of 1549; counseled Bishop John Hooper in the Vestarian controversy in 1550; assisted Thomas Cranmer in the promulgation of the 1548 Prayer Book and its 1552 revision; helped formulate the *Forty-two Articles of Religion* in 1553; and played a pivotal role in writing the *Reformatio Legum Ecclesiasticarum* from 1551 to 1553. Vermigli's name would no doubt have been better remembered today if his sojourn in England had not been cut short by Mary Tudor's accession to the throne in 1553.

After expulsion from England, Vermigli returned to Strasbourg. But the atmosphere there in this city, once hospitable, had become contentious. Bucer was dead (1551), and the Lutheran faction, under the leadership of Johann Marbach, was in the ascendancy. Vermigli's letters to Calvin and Bullinger within days of his arrival in Strasbourg indicate he anticipated Lutheran opposition to his sacramental theology.[17] The Lutherans objected to Vermigli's reappointment because they judged he had departed from the *Augsburg Confession*. Besides the matter of the Eucharist, Vermigli's doctrine of predestination also became a bone of contention. The troubles in Strasbourg soon led Vermigli to accept the invitation of Bullinger to succeed the recently deceased Konrad Pellikan at Zurich in 1556. On July 13, 1556, Vermigli, accompanied by his English disciple John Jewel, departed for Zurich, where he was once again welcomed. If Vermigli thought Zurich a refuge from the storm, he was mistaken. Soon after his arrival, he became embroiled in yet another controversy.

The focal point of the controversy was his doctrine of predestination. Bullinger had been quite moderate and cautious in his formulations, preferring a doctrine of single predestination.[18] A few years earlier, Bullinger had provided only lackluster support for Calvin in the Bolsec affair and had also refused to sign the *Consensus Genevensis*, which contained the strong Calvinian view of predestination.[19] Although not an advocate of double predestination like Vermigli, Bullinger was tolerant of his Italian colleague. Theodore Bibliander, Bullinger's colleague at Zurich, was not.[20]

Vermigli had always desired to avoid unwarranted controversy.[21] Thus he took great pains to praise Bibliander upon his arrival in Zurich, and tactfully published his own commentary on Romans in Basel rather than Zurich. However, even if Bullinger could count on Vermigli's good nature, he still had to contend with Bibliander's brooding hostility. The desire for peace went unrequited. Vermigli began lecturing on 1 Samuel on August 24, 1556, and, by June 1557, Bibliander had begun openly to attack Vermigli's doctrine of predestination.[22] The ensuing controversy became so intense that Bibliander challenged Vermigli to a duel with a double-edged axe.[23] Eventually, Bibliander was dismissed from his duties as professor in February 1560. Vermigli's victory in the Bibliander affair "marks an important stage in Zurich's adhesion to a full Reformed teaching on grace and predestination."[24]

The Zurich years (1556–62), although not entirely tranquil, were productive. Vermigli's lectures on Romans (1558) and Judges (1561) were published, along with his massive *Defensio Doctrinae veteris & Apostolicae de sacrosancto Eucharistiae Sacramento . . . adversus Stephani Gardineri* (1559), opposing the eucharistic theology of Stephen Gardiner, bishop of Winchester. With Theodore Beza, he attended the Colloquy of Poissy (1561) where he conversed with the queen mother, Catherine de'Medici, in her native Italian and tried to win her to the Protestant side. Edmund Grindal, bishop of London, spoke of Vermigli's important role at Poissy to Sir William Cecil, saying: "I am of the judgement that no man alive is more fit than Peter Martyr for such a conference . . . for he is better versed in old doctors, councils and ecclesiastical histories than any Romish doctor of Christendom."[25]

Vermigli was successful in the eyes of at least one Catholic bishop present at the Colloquy of Poissy. Antonio Caracciolo, bishop of Troyes (France), was so impressed with Vermigli that he converted to Protestantism and attempted to bring his whole diocese into the Reformed camp. He was the first bishop in the history of the French Reformed Church.[26] Vermigli lived out his final days in Zurich, where he died on November 12, 1562, attended by his fellow Italian refugee Bernardino Ochino and his closest friends and colleagues, Heinrich Bullinger and Josiah Simler.

Theological Loci: Justification

One of the notable features of Vermigli's theological outlook (and early Reformed Protestantism in general) was the pastoral orientation of its understanding of the doctrine of justification. Justification was the "head, fountain and summit of all piety."[27] Vermigli's most extensive treatment of justification is in the locus at the end of the eleventh chapter of his Romans commentary. He also devoted considerable space to the topic of justification in a locus at the end of chapter one of his lectures on 1 Corinthians (1548–9), and more briefly in his lectures on Genesis (15:6).[28] Two reasons explain the rationale for placing his most extensive treatment of justification in his commentary on Romans. First, he believes this doctrine is taught most explicitly in this epistle. Indeed, at the very beginning of the *locus*, he asserts that justification is the "scope and aim of all that Paul has said so far."[29] But second, he was fulfilling his mandate from Archbishop Cranmer to advance the cause of the Reformation in England.

Vermigli developed his doctrine of justification under three propositions: good works do not justify, faith justifies, and faith alone justifies.[30] From the outset, Vermigli set his jaw against the perceived Pelagianism of the Catholic Church. For an Augustinian like Vermigli, whose most basic theological presupposition was that all humanity after Adam's fall is a *massa perditionis* (a mass of perdition), Pelagianism was intolerable. Crucial for understanding Vermigli is the fact that the whole edifice of his doctrine of justification is built upon the foundation of an intensive Augustinian anthropology.[31] For him, this was not simply a clash between individual theologians, but of theological systems.

In many respects, Vermigli provides a conventional Protestant understanding of justification. It is obvious from the opening section of his *locus* that justification in the strict sense is a legal pronouncement of God. He specifically employs the legal term "forensic" to describe this judicial proceeding.[32] Justification, then, belongs to the legal domain and, as such, addresses the theological problem of the legal guilt inherited by all Adam's progeny and how it is that a righteous divine judge reaches a verdict of "not guilty."

If justification is fundamentally a legal or forensic matter, then the question of how the guilty sinner is legally absolved of the deserved punishment comes to the fore. To describe this divine judicial proceeding, he employs the concept of imputation.[33] In general, he sees two movements of imputation. First, when the divine verdict is rendered, it will not be on the basis of the sinner himself, but on the basis of the imputed righteousness of Christ that he is judged.[34] Second, Vermigli also speaks of the non-imputation of sins, by which he means that sins are not counted against the sinner because they have been imputed or transferred to Christ. "He (Christ) justifies those whom he takes to himself and bears their iniquities."[35]

Double imputation brings a double legal benefit – acquittal and the right to eternal life.[36] Because Christ has taken their sins and transferred his righteousness to them, sinners are pronounced forgiven, hence justified. The second benefit is entrance into a new relationship with the divine judge.[37] The "chief and principal part" of forgiveness of our sins is "that we are received into the favor of God."[38] This acceptance into the favor of God is particularly identified with adoption, which also has a legal connotation.[39] With the idea of adoption, Vermigli's understanding of justification is not merely forensic, it also entails a "relational" component.[40]

It is significant that his forensic understanding of imputation necessarily requires an extrinsic view of justification. The act in which Christ's righteousness is imputed to an elect sinner only has reference to his legal status. Such an act is external to the sinner and does not itself bring inner renewal. The imputed righteousness of Christ, technically speaking, does not penetrate and transform the soul of the sinner as is required in the Catholic notion of *gratia inhaerens*, but remains external to the sinner. Justification, then, in the forensic sense, is not *iustitia in nobis* but a *iustitia extra nos*.[41]

An intriguing issue, first raised by John Patrick Donnelly, is that Vermigli never actually employs the distinctively Protestant phrase *simul iustus et peccator*.[42] However, upon closer examination, the idea (if not the terminology) is clearly present in the *locus*. This should not seem strange, in view of the fact that neither does Calvin employ the phrase in the definitive 1559 edition of the *Institutes*, yet he unmistakably embraces the idea.[43] It is difficult to avoid the idea of *simul iustus et peccator* when he writes: "'to justify' means to ascribe righteousness to one by judgment or declaration [and] does not make him righteous in reality."[44] Vermigli's intensive Augustinian anthropology, with its stress on the radical impact of sin on all humanity (including infants), presses him to conclude that even the Christian is both fully a sinner in himself and fully righteous in Christ.

What is unusual in Vermigli's understanding of forensic justification is the inclusion of regeneration and sanctification under the rubric of justification. Like his friend and mentor, Martin Bucer, Vermigli espouses a threefold justification that includes three distinguishable but inseparable components: regeneration, justification, and sanctification. This threefold character of justification is found already in his Strasbourg exposition of Genesis (1543),[45] as well as his 1548 lectures on 1 Corinthians in Oxford. In his Romans *locus*, he makes structural modifications but retains the threefold idea.[46]

The relationship between regeneration and forensic justification is particularly crucial for determining whether one is a Catholic or a Protestant. McGrath has argued that "the notional distinction between *iustificatio* and *regeneratio* provides one of the best *differentiae* between Catholic and Protestant understandings of justification."[47] It is precisely because Vermigli places regeneration in such close proximity to forensic justification that Klaus Sturm has characterized him as a "*Reformkatholik.*"[48]

Although forensic justification is Vermigli's primary understanding, there is a further consideration that necessarily accompanies any full and proper biblical understanding of justification. He argues that God confers righteousness upon humanity in two general ways, by "producing righteousness in men" and by "imputing righteousness in us." Regarding the former (internal righteousness), Vermigli sees two manifestations. First, God produces this internal righteousness "by his Spirit" who "refashions and wholly renews" a person. This also restores "the power of their minds and delivers their faculties from much of their natural corruption." Hence, through the working of the Holy Spirit, an internal righteousness is produced in an individual. It is clear that he has regeneration in view, that is, the initial point at which God begins to bring about redemption in the life of an individual. "This is the righteousness which first clings and adheres to our minds by the blessing of God through Christ."[49] Characteristically, he places forensic justification in close proximity to regeneration.[50]

The second manifestation of this divinely conferred internal righteousness necessarily follows regeneration and forensic justification and has to do with subsequent "good and holy works." Toward the end of the *locus*, he cites Augustine with approval when he speaks of a "righteousness which adheres to us." But immediately, he clarifies that "here we do not treat that justification which is by imputation, but that which we attain after regeneration."[51] According to Vermigli, regeneration creates a habit (*habitus*) or predisposition, which inclines a person "to live honestly and uprightly."[52] This second manifestation of divinely conferred internal righteousness is nothing other than sanctification, the lifelong process by which the Christian progressively grows in holiness and obedience.

It would seem, then, that Vermigli embraces both a narrow and a more strict forensic understanding of justification, as well as a broader moral understanding, which stresses the necessary relationship between forensic justification and its accompanying benefits of regeneration and sanctification. These blessings cannot be separated, neither can they be distinguished. When speaking of justification in the strict or proper sense, he has in view only the divine acquittal and its basis.[53] The righteousness by which one is forensically justified, then, "does not adhere to our souls, but is imputed by God."[54] But when speaking more broadly of justification, he considers both the cause and the effect of the divine acquittal. Forensic justification, based on the imputed righteousness of Christ alone, is necessarily preceded by the regenerative work of the Holy Spirit, who then produces sanctification or moral transformation in the sinner.

He still retains the crucial distinctives of a Protestant understanding of justification – original sin, a dynamic view of faith, forensic justification based exclusively on the imputed righteousness of Christ and *simul iustus et peccator*. But his particular conception of justification includes both regeneration and sanctification under the general meaning of justification. Justification, properly speaking, is forensic, but he is not content to speak of forensic justification alone. It is noteworthy that the biblical text which provides a segue to his *locus* on justification (1 Cor. 1:30) not only speaks of Christ as our righteousness (forensic justification), but also of Christ as our sanctification.[55] In Vermigli's mind, one cannot properly deal with the immense problem of original sin by considering only the legal dimension; one must also deal with the moral implications. Adam's fall, according to Vermigli, brought legal guilt, spiritual death, and moral corruption and the redemptive work of Christ countered each of these three effects, bringing forensic justification, regeneration, and sanctification into close accord.

Vermigli certainly saw himself as a Protestant and as an opponent of Catholicism, but early Protestant conceptions of justification were more fluid and nuanced than is generally understood.[56] He does indeed differ from Luther by placing the principle of "distinct but separate" at the forefront of his formulation rather than stressing the discontinuity of justification and sanctification as expressed in the phrase *simul iustus et peccator*. It is, however, essentially the same doctrine with different stresses.

While his formulation differs from Luther, Vermigli is generally in accord with other Protestant theologians of his day, such as Bucer, Oecolampadius, Zwingli, and later Melanchthon. Vermigli's own distinctive juxtaposition of justification, regeneration, and sanctification especially resonates with Martin Bucer. There is little doubt that those years with Bucer in Strasbourg (1542–7) go a long way to explain his conception of justification.[57] Vermigli's three-tiered justification is a virtual replica of the threefold justification of Bucer. To be sure, there remain Augustinian currents, which often overlap with Bucer's own understanding, and there is evidence of a measure of theological independence. It does seem that in the early years of his Oxford sojourn Bucer's Protestant insights into this doctrine increasingly govern Vermigli's appropriation of the Augustinian soteriological perspective.

Predestination

Vermigli did not make predestination the centerpiece of his theological system. But like Calvin, he was repeatedly called on to defend it and thus he became one of the principal apologists for a Reformed doctrine of predestination. He championed it against Johann Marbach in Strasbourg and against Theodore Bibliander in Zurich.

Protestants claimed to have recovered Augustine's view on the matter. There is truth to this claim, and yet it would appear that the Reformers went beyond Augustine's own doctrine of predestination, at least with regard to the extensive treatment given to reprobation. Vermigli, too, was deeply inspired by Augustine, but in fact surpassed his mentor in his understanding of predestination. Vermigli's intensification of Augustine began at the University of Padua, where he first read and appreciated the robust predestinarianism of Gregory of Rimini (d. 1358), "the first Augustinian of Augustine."[58] Reading Gregory at the formative stages of his theological training, Vermigli encountered one of the most vigorous double predestinarians of the late medieval period.

Gregory took Augustine's doctrine of predestination to its logical extreme, and is credited with having given birth to a late medieval "academic Augustinianism" committed to the pursuit of and obedience to the genuine theology of Augustine. He initiated a concerted effort in the fourteenth century to recover the whole corpus of Augustine's works and to develop a systematic exploration of his entire thought. Thus, one can speak of an "Augustinian renaissance" which some have designated the *schola Augustiniana moderna*.[59] This new and intensified Augustinianism developed a ferociously anti-Pelagian theology of grace, including a vigorous doctrine of double predestination. Although more than a century separates these two theologians, there are remarkable parallels between the views of Gregory and Vermigli.

Vermigli's most vigorous exposition of this doctrine occurs in an extended locus from his commentary on Romans, where he, much like Gregory, develops the doctrine in a causal complex. On the matter of election (which he equated with predestination), God's will in eternity was seen to be the exclusive cause. Vermigli follows Augustine's anthropology in thinking of all humanity as a *massa perditionis*, doomed to eternal condemnation unless God intervenes. Divine election is construed as the rescue of the doomed sinner, who can do nothing to aid in his own deliverance. After being elected from the mass of fallen sinners in eternity past, prompted by the Holy Spirit and granted the gift of faith, the elect embrace Christ in time and thus inherit eternal life. In sum, Vermigli, like Gregory before him, taught what has been called, unconditional election.

Vermigli did not shy away from the difficult matter of reprobation. There are two important features that underscore his view of reprobation. First, he understood it as a passive expression of the sovereign will of God. Although the will of God is absolutely free, God wields it passively in reprobation. By passive willing, Vermigli intends readers to understand something more than mere divine permission, but less than an active willing. God does not sit back and simply permit matters to take their course. Rather, God orchestrates events without coercion in order to produce his predetermined salvific result. To reprobate is characteristically described as "not to have mercy" or "passing over." Yet Vermigli does not want to conjure up visions of a dispassionate deity arbitrarily hurling helpless victims into a lake of fire. His view of reprobation is more nuanced. It portrays God as actively rescuing some sinners, but deliberately and mysteriously bypassing others, knowing full well the inevitable consequence.

A second major feature of Vermigli's view of reprobation is the distinction between reprobation and condemnation. Reprobation, God's decision not to have mercy, has a non-temporal referent and cause in the inscrutable sovereign will of God. Condemnation, on the other hand, has a temporal referent, where causality lies within the matrix of original and actual sins. For Vermigli, "sins are the cause of damnation but not the cause of reprobation."[60] God's role in condemnation is confined to the intention and execution of the general principle that sins are to be punished. Condemnation, however, is the expression of divine justice. The true cause of condemnation is found in sinful individuals, but the true cause of reprobation lies in the unfathomable purpose of God.

Vermigli's doctrine of unequivocal double predestination differs from other reformers such as Zwingli.[61] The latter advocates a strict symmetrical double predestination, but Vermigli envisages an asymmetrical version of this doctrine. According to Vermigli, God does not deal with the elect in precisely the same way he does with the non-elect. For the elect, God is not only the ultimate eternal cause for the attainment of eternal life, but by granting the gift of faith through the Holy Spirit, he is also the temporal cause of the reward of eternal life. That parallel is not sustained when one considers reprobation and condemnation. Although the ultimate eternal cause of election and rejection is precisely the same (the inscrutable will of God), the cause for condemnation does not correspond to the cause for eternal blessing. Those who are finally condemned can blame only themselves and their sins.

Vermigli's adoption of double predestination, apparently inspired by Gregory, illustrates the threads of soteriological continuity between late medieval and Reformation thought emphasized by Heiko Oberman. In 1974, Heiko Oberman proffered a controversial thesis, in which he argued that Luther's revolutionary theology was derived in some sense from Gregory of Rimini and the *schola Augustiniana moderna*.[62] Many scholars judged that Oberman's research was stimulating but circumstantial. Some were persuaded, but most preferred to await further evidence. In 1986, Alister McGrath, following Oberman's lead and building on the Reuter thesis, explored the question of whether Calvin had come under the influence of Gregory.[63] McGrath concluded that while there were a number of provocative theological parallels, there was no documentary evidence that Calvin had actually read Gregory. Vermigli provides a much more fruitful line of inquiry. The fact that he read and approved the writings of Gregory of Rimini at the formative stage of his theological development make Vermigli an especially enticing medium for inquiring into Gregorian influence on Reformed theology.

A comparison of Vermigli's doctrine and that of Gregory reveal an extraordinary degree of compatibility. Linguistic and conceptual parallels abound. Time and again, the same issues are isolated and resolved with the same theological conclusions, often employing the same terms, and always based on the twin sources of Scripture and Augustine. Despite differences in historical circumstances and in degree of treatment, there is an extraordinary degree of continuity between the two Italian Augustinians. Thus, it would appear that Vermigli was an heir to Gregory's late medieval intensification of Augustine's doctrine of predestination. Others may also have contributed to his basic understanding, but the essential doctrine, it seems, comes from Gregory.[64]

Sacramental Theology

It has been argued that, along with Calvin, Vermigli pioneered the distinctively Reformed understanding of the Eucharist.[65] Calvin himself seemed to endorse such a view. In his response to the Lutheran Tilemann Heshusius, Calvin asserted that Vermigli provided the definitive Reformed understanding of the Lord's Supper: "The whole has been crowned by Peter Martyr, who has left nothing to be desired."[66] In what must have been a rarity, even one of the Catholic adversaries at the Colloquy of Poissy, Claude d'Espence, echoed Calvin's sentiments by lauding Vermigli's extraordinary erudition regarding the sacraments: "There is no man of our time who so amply and with such erudition has written about the sacraments."[67] This is no small praise for one who had apostatized twenty years earlier in a hail of Catholic invective.

Even before he fled Italy, Vermigli had already acquired a Protestant doctrine of the Eucharist. Indeed, Simler informs us that he celebrated the Lord's Supper in a Protestant manner in Pisa during his flight from Italy.[68] It is generally assumed that by 1542, he had rejected quintessential Catholic ideas such as transubstantiation, the corporeal presence of Christ in the elements, and the repeated sacrifice of Christ in the Mass. Whatever his convictions in Italy, by the time he arrived in Strasbourg, his own sacramental theology resonated especially with Calvin and Bucer.

Like Augustine, Vermigli defined a sacrament as "a visible sign of an invisible grace."[69] He further distinguished between the *sacramentum* and the *res sacramenti*, the sign (bread and wine) and the thing signified (Body and Blood of Christ).[70] The *sacramentum* or sacramental elements are far more than mere memorials or bare signs. For Vermigli, the bread and wine must be understood as signs of a profound reality – the reality of Christ's presence. Without confusing the *sacramentum* with the *res sacramenti*, he nevertheless wanted to stress that the Body of Christ in heaven is intimately related to the sacramental elements on earth. He argued that just as God's promises are united to his words of Scripture, so also is Christ united to the bread and wine. To be sure, Christ's presence in the elements is spiritual (*per significationem*) rather than physical in nature, but no less real.[71]

When Christians partake of the Sacrament, they receive the Body of Christ, not corporeally but spiritually.[72] This spiritual realization occurs through the internal working of Holy Spirit who grants the gift of faith.[73] Vermigli, much like Bucer and Calvin, places particular stress on the vital role of the Holy Spirit in the Sacrament. He insisted that when three components coalesce – the words of institution, the exercise of faith, and the internal work of the Spirit – these signs become something altogether different.[74] While the signs are not miraculously transformed into the literal Body and Blood of Christ, they do truly become the Sacrament of the Lord's Body and thereby function as instruments of spiritual nourishment for the Christian.[75]

The overarching concept that governs the whole of Vermigli's sacramental theology is the notion of union with Christ.[76] Vermigli delineates three kinds of union with Christ. The first is based on the incarnation and Christ's identification with humanity.[77] The second is a progressive or growing communion between the believer and Christ that brings sanctification.[78] The third level of union is what Vermigli calls the mystical communion.[79] The latter is the most intimate of relationships in which the believer is joined spiritually to Christ's body. This deep mystical communion with Christ spiritually transforms the believer when he or she partakes of the Lord's Supper. This is the goal of the sacramental rite.

Vermigli is adamant that the Sacrament is fundamentally about what God gives to the believer, not what the believer gives to God. This is fundamental to his eucharistic theology, for it underscores the central notion that both the means (Word of God, Christian faith, and the Holy Spirit) as well as the end (mystical communion) find their origin in God alone.[80]

In sum, Vermigli understands a sacrament to be a gift of God to his people. Christ is himself the gift who is given by means of the Sacrament, faith, and the secret working of the Holy Spirit. The fruit of this gift is mystical union with Christ. Through this theological construction, Vermigli was able to negotiate the doctrinally treacherous waters occupied by his opponents by addressing his theology to the central concerns underlying their misapprehensions. He could unhesitatingly affirm with Catholics and Lutherans the very real nature of Christ's Body and Blood in the sacramental elements, although he differed as to how this took place. And he could affirm the concerns of Zwingli, Bullinger, and Calvin that the presence of Christ was spiritual not physical, while rejecting any suggestion that the bread and wine were merely signs. Vermigli was convinced that his configuration of the Eucharist was supported by Scripture, affirmed by the Fathers, and honors the dignity of the Sacrament.

Conclusion

One of the more helpful results of recent research has been the growing recognition that the origins of Reformed theology do not derive exclusively or even primarily from John Calvin, but rather from the collaboration of like-minded theologians, including (besides Calvin) Heinrich Bullinger, Peter Martyr Vermigli, and Martin Bucer.[81] Vermigli's role in the development of Reformed theology underscores that there was no single inaugurator for the whole of Reformed tradition. Thus, to understand Vermigli's doctrine is ultimately to gain a better insight into the theological origins of the Reformed branch of Protestantism.

Surely one of the more ironic twists in the Reformation period is that Vermigli proves to be an important vehicle for a deeper understanding of the Reformation itself, as well as an important means for elucidating subsequent theological developments within the English and continental Reformed traditions. Indeed, one may prophesy that as a more accurate portrait of this "miracle of Italy" appears, a greater appreciation of his theological contributions will inevitably emerge.

Notes

1 Cited in Joseph C. McLelland, *The Visible Words of God: An Exposition of the Sacramental Theology of Peter Martyr Vermigli 1500–1562* (Edinburgh: Oliver & Boyd, 1957), 1.

2 Theodore Beza, *Icones, id est Verae Imaginis virorum doctrina simul et pietate illustrium* (Geneva: C. Froschauer, 1580), 2.

3 John Strype, *Memorials . . . of . . . Thomas Cranmer* (Oxford: Ecclesiastical Historical Society, 1848–54), 3:xlv.

4 Jennifer Loach, "Reformation Controversies" in T. H. Aston, gen. ed., *The History of the University of Oxford*, vol. 3, *The Collegiate University*, ed. James McConica (Oxford: Oxford University Press, 1986), 374.

5 John Patrick Donnelly, *Calvinism and Scholasticism in Vermigli's Doctrine of Man and Grace* (Leiden: E. J. Brill, 1976), 171. See also Donnelly in collaboration with Robert M. Kingdon and Marvin W. Anderson, eds., *A Bibliography of the Works of Peter Martyr Vermigli*, Sixteenth Century Essays & Studies 13 (Kirksville, MO: Sixteenth Century Journal Publishers, 1990).

6 Philip McNair, "Biographical Introduction" in Joseph C. McLelland, ed., *Early Writings: Creed, Scripture and Church*, The Peter Martyr Library 1 (Kirksville, MO: Sixteenth Century Journal Publishers, 1994), 12.

7 Peter Martyr Vermigli, *Loci Communes . . .* (London: Thomas Vautrollerius, 1583), 1062. English translation in John Patrick Donnelly, ed. and trans., *Life, Letters and Sermons*, The Peter Martyr Library 5 (Kirksville, MO: Thomas Jefferson University Press, 1999), 322.

8 See Salvatore Caponetto, trans. Anne C. and John Tedeschi, *The Protestant Reformation in Sixteenth-Century Italy* (Kirksville, MO: Truman State University Press, 1999).

9 Philip M. J. McNair, *Peter Martyr in Italy: An Anatomy of Apostasy* (Oxford: Clarendon Press, 1967), 192. The records of his own Augustinian order, in April 1540, characterized him as "an exceptional preacher." These records are in the Biblioteca Classense in Ravenna, Italy.

10 McNair, *Peter Martyr in Italy*, 127–79, 197–9, 206–38, 249–50. See Elisabeth Gleason, *Gasparo Contarini: Venice, Rome and Reform* Berkeley: University of California Press, 1993), 129–57, and Caponetto, *The Protestant Reformation in Sixteenth-Century Italy*, 277–80, 327–31.

11 Charles Schmidt, *Peter Martyr Vermigli, Leben und ausgewählte Schriften nach handschriftlichen und gleichzeitigen Quellen* (Elberfeld: R. L. Friderichs, 1858), 20, deduces that it was Valdés who provided writings from Bucer and Zwingli to Vermigli.

12 McNair, *Peter Martyr in Italy*, 221.

13 Joseph N. Tylenda, "Girolamo Zanchi and John Calvin: A Study in Discipleship as Seen Through Their Correspondence," *CTJ* 10 (1975), 104. In an undated letter to Calvin, Zanchi invokes Peter Martyr as a witness to his deep affection for the Genevan reformer. See Zanchi's *Opera Theologica* (Geneva: Stephanus Gamonetus, 1605–13), vol. 2, *Liber Epistolarum*, 331, cited by John Farthing, "*Praeceptor Carissimus*: Images of Peter Martyr in Zanchi's Correspondence" (paper presented at the Sixteenth Century Studies Conference, St. Louis, M., October 28–31, 1999), 25.

14 McNair, *Peter Martyr in Italy*, 239–68. Vermigli was not alone in his apostasy. The vicar general of the Capuchins, Bernardino Ochino, also fled the Inquisition with Vermigli's encouragement. See Karl Benrath, trans. H. Zimmern, *Bernardino Ochino of Siena: A Contribution Towards the History of the Reformation* (New York: Robert Carter & Bros., 1877), 105ff.

15 Letter from Sturm to Marbach in Zanchi, *Opera Theologica*, vol. 2, *Liber Epistolarum*, 163.

16 Simler, *Oratio*, 4. The English translation is found in J. Patrick Donnelly, ed. and trans., *Life, Letters and Sermons*, 29. Likewise, Zacharias Ursinus, in a letter (March 10, 1561) to Abel Birkenhahn, praises Vermigli's writing as clearer than Zwingli or Oecolampadius: see Eerdmann Sturm, "Brief des Heidelberger Theologen Zacharias Ursinus aus Wittenberg und Zurich (1560/1)," *Heidelberger Jahrbucher* 14 (1970), 90–1. Even Catholic detractors, such as Cornelius Schulting, argue that Vermigli was clearer and more learned than Calvin. See Schulting's *Bibliotheca catholica et orthodoxae, contra summam totius theologiae Calviniae in Institutionibus I. Calvini et Locis Communibus Petri Martyris, breviter comprehensae* (Cologne, 1602), 1:1.

17 *Original Letters Relative to the English Reformation, 1531–1558*, ed. Hastings Robinson for the Parker Society (Cambridge: Cambridge University Press, 1846–7), 2:505.

18 J. Wayne Baker, *Heinrich Bullinger and the Covenant: The Other Reformed Tradition* (Athens: Ohio State University Press, 1980), 27–47. See also Peter Walser, *Die Prädestination bei Heinrich Bullinger im Zusammmenhang mit seiner Gotteslehre* (Zurich: Theologischer Verlag Zurich, 1957), 9–22.

19 The *Consensus Genevensis*, otherwise known as *De aeterna Praedestinatione*, was approved by the Genevan Syndics but never accepted by the other Swiss churches. Philip Schaff, *History of the Christian Church* (New York: Scribner's Sons, 1910; repr. Grand Rapids: Eerdmans, 1976), vol. 8, *Modern Christianity: The Swiss Reformation*, 210–11, 619.

20 Theodore Bibliander, professor of Old Testament at Zurich, had long been an opponent of Calvin, but had restrained himself from public attack. Bibliander held to a view of predestination much like that of Erasmus. Schmidt, *Leben*, 215.

21 Despite their differences, neither Bullinger nor Vermigli wanted to make predestination a subject of controversy. One gets a sense of their mutual reluctance to quarrel over predestination in two letters exchanged in late 1553. See *Original Letters* 2:506 and Alexander Schweizer, *Die Protestantischen Zentraldogmen in Ihrer Entwicklung Innerhalb Der Reformierten Kirche* (Zurich, 1853), 1:275.

22 See Marvin W. Anderson, *Peter Martyr Vermigli: A Reformer in Exile (1542–1562)* (Nieuwkoop: De Graaf, 1975), 380 and Joseph C. McLelland, "Reformed Doctrine of Predestination according to Peter Martyr," *Scottish Journal of Theology* 8 (1955), 266.

23 Joachim Staedtke, "Der Züricher Prädestinationsstreit von 1560," *Zwingliana* 9 (1953), 536–46; Schmidt, *Leben*, 218.

24 Donnelly, *Calvinism and Scholasticism*, 183.

25 *The Remains of Edmund Grindal, D.D.*, ed. William Nicholson for the Parker Society (Cambridge: Cambridge University Press, 1843), 244–5. I have modernized the English slightly to make it clearer.

26 Vermigli letter to Beza, November 6, 1561, in F. Aubert, H. Meylan, et al., eds., *Correspondance de Theodore de Bèze* (Geneva: Librairie Droz, 1960–), 3:209. See also McLelland, *The Visible Words of God*, 64; Schmidt, *Leben*, 272–3; and Donnelly, *Calvinism and Scholasticism*, 173–4.

27 Peter Martyr Vermigli, *In Epistolam S. Pauli Apostoli ad Romanos commentarij doctissimi* . . .

(Basel: P. Perna, 1558), 521. Calvin refers to justification as the "sum of all piety." See Alister McGrath, *Iustitia Dei: A History of the Christian Doctrine of Justification* (Cambridge: Cambridge University Press, 1986), 2:36.

28 Klaus Sturm, *Die Theologie Peter Martyr Vermiglis während seines ersten Aufenthalts in Strassburg 1542–1547* (Neukirchen: Neukirchener Verlag, 1971), 58–70 looks at the locus on justification in Vermigli's Genesis commentary.

29 Vermigli, *Romanos*, 517.

30 Vermigli, *Romanos*, 520.

31 See Frank A. James, III, *Peter Martyr Vermigli and Predestination: The Augustinian Heritage of an Italian Reformer* (Oxford: Clarendon Press, 1998), pp. 245ff.

32 Vermigli, *Romanos*, 517.

33 Vermigli, *Romanos*, 517. McGrath, *Iustitia Dei*, 2:31–2, has argued that this legal term "imputation" has its origins in Erasmus's *Novum instrumentum omne* of 1516 where he replaced the term "*reputatum*" of the Vulgate translation of Romans 4:5 with "*imputatum*."

34 Vermigli, *Romanos*, 565.

35 Vermigli, *Romanos*, 553.

36 Vermigli, *Romanos*, 558.

37 Vermigli, *In selectissimam D. Pauli Priorem ad Corinth. Epistolam Commentarij* (Zurich: C. Froschauer, 1579), fols. 16r and 18v.

38 Vermigli, *Romanos*, 558.

39 Vermigli, *Romanos*, 525. He writes: ". . . there is no doubt that justification [brings] . . . the favor of God by which men are received into grace, adopted as his children and made heirs of eternal life."

40 McGrath, *Iustitia Dei*, 1:33.

41 McGrath, *Iustitia Dei*, 2:20.

42 Donnelly, *Calvinism and Scholasticism*, 154. "Martyr never uses Luther's phrase *simul iustus et peccator*, not only because its paradoxical expression is foreign to his mentality, but also because it does not square with his understanding of justification by faith alone."

43 *Calvin, Institutes of the Christian Religion*, III.14.9 (in John T. McNeill ed., trans. Ford Lewis Battles, Philadelphia: Westminster Press, 1954, I:776).

44 Vermigli, *Romanos*, 517: ". . . *ut iustificare est iudicio ac existimatione iustitiam alicui tribuere, non autem reipsa efficere ut sit iustus.*"

45 James, *Peter Martyr Vermigli and Predestination*, 49.

46 Vermigli, *Romanos*, 79.

47 McGrath, *Iustitia Dei*, 2:186: "the essential feature of the Reformation doctrines of justification is that a deliberate and systematic distinction is made between justification and regeneration."

48 Sturm, *Die Theologie Peter Martyr*, 69.

49 Vermigli, *Romanos*, 517.

50 Vermigli, *Romanos*, 552.

51 Vermigli, *Romanos*, 578.

52 Vermigli, *Romanos*, 517.

53 Vermigli, *Romanos*, 548. He states: "we say justification [forensic] cannot consist in that righteousness and renewal by which we are recreated by God, since our corruption renders it imperfect so that we are not able to stand before the judgment of Christ."

54 Vermigli, *Romanos*, 522.

55 Vermigli, *Corinthios*, 28v.

56 Vermigli, *Romanos*, 546–8.

57 W. P. Stephens, *The Holy Spirit in the Theology of Martin Bucer* (Cambridge: Cambridge University Press, 1970), 48–70.

58 Damasus Trapp, "Augustinian Theology of the Fourteenth Century," *Augustiniana* 6 (1956), 181.

59 Heiko A. Oberman, *Masters of the Reformation: The Emergence of a New Intellectual Climate in Europe*, trans. D. Martin (Cambridge, MA: Harvard University Press, 1981), 70–1.

60 Vermigli, *Romanos*, 414.

61 James, *Peter Martyr Vermigli and Predestination*, 191–222.

62 Heiko Oberman, "Headwaters of the Reformation" in H. Oberman, ed., *Luther and the Dawn of the Modern Era* (Leiden: E. J. Brill, 1974), 40–88.

63 A. E. McGrath, "John Calvin and Late Medieval Thought: A Study in Late Medieval Influence upon Calvin's Theological Development," *ARG* 77 (1986), 58–78. See Karl Reuter, *Das Grundverständnis der Theologie Calvins* (Neukirchen, 1963) and his *Von Scholaren bis zum jungen Reformator: Studien zum Werdegang Johannes Calvins* (Neukirchen, 1981).

64 James, *Peter Martyr Vermigli and Predestination*, 106–50.

65 McLelland, *Visible Words of God*, 279ff.

66 John Calvin, "Clear Explanation of Sound Doctrine concerning the True Partaking of the Flesh and Blood of Christ in the Holy Supper, in order to dissipate the mists of Tileman Heshusius" in Henry Beveridge, ed., *Selected Works of John Calvin: Tracts and Letters* (Grand Rapids: Baker Book House, repr., 1983), 2:535.

67 A. Vacant, E. Mangenot, and E. Amann, eds., *Dictionnaire de la théologie catholique* (Paris, 1899–1950), 15: col. 2696. Cited by Salvatore Corda, *Veritas Sacramenti: A Study in Vermigli's Doctrine of the Lord's Supper*. Zürcher Beiträge zur Reformationsgeschichte 6 (Zurich: Theologischer Verlag Zurich, 1975), 9.

68 *Oratio*, 6: Simler states: ". . . Coenam Domini Christiano ritu celebravit," which almost certainly refers to the Protestant rite. See McNair, *Peter Martyr in Italy*, 25–6; and McLelland, *Visible Words*, 271.

69 Vermigli, *Tractatio de sacramento Eucharisti habita in celeberrima universitate Oxoniensi* . . . (London: R. Wolf, 1583), 22.

70 Vermigli, *Corinthios*, fol., 300v. Cf. Corda, *Veritas Sacramenti*, 101–3.

71 Vermigli, *Corinthios*, fols. 299r, 301v, 429r, 430r.

72 Vermigli, *Corinthios*, fol. 242r.

73 Vermigli, *Corinthios*, fol. 305v.

74 Vermigli, *Corinthios*, fol. 339r.

75 Vermigli, *Corinthios*, fols. 302v–303r.

76 McLelland, *Visible Words of God*, 142.

77 *Loci Communes. Ex variis ipsius Authoris libris in unum volumen collecti, & quatuor classes distributi*. . . . (London: Thomas Vautrollerius, 1576), 1092. See Vermigli's letter to Calvin (March 8, 1555) in *The Life, Early Letters and Eucharistic Writings of Peter Martyr*, ed. J. C. McLelland and G. Duffield (Appleford, Abingdon, Oxford: Sutton Courtenay Press, 1989), 343–8.

78 Vermigli, *Corinthios*, fols. 302v, 303r.

79 Vermigli, *Corinthios*, fols. 258v–259r.

80 Vermigli, *Corinthios*, fol. 339r.

81 Richard A. Muller, *Christ and the Decree: Christology and Predestination in Reformed Theology from Calvin to Perkins* (Durham, NC: Duke University Press, 1988), 39. Donnelly, *Calvinism and Scholasticism*, 2, states that Reformed theology derived from a "group of like-minded thinkers and scholars whose theologies developed along parallel lines during roughly the same period." He includes such persons as Beza, Viret, Farel, and Myconius.

Bibliography

Primary Sources

Vermigli's writings are being edited and published in the *Peter Martyr Library*, 5 vols. to date, Kirksville: Sixteenth Century Publishers, 1994–.

J. C. McLelland and G. E. Duffield, eds., *Early Letters and Eucharistic Writings of Peter Martyr*, Appleton, Abingdon, Oxford: Sutton Courtenay Press, 1989.

Secondary Sources

Anderson, Marvin W., *Peter Martyr Vermigli: A Reformer in Exile (1542–1562): A Chronology of Biblical Writings in England and Europe*, Nieukoop: De Graaf, 1975.

——, "Rhetoric and Reality: Peter Martyr and the English Reformation," *SCJ* 19 (1988), 451–69.

Corda, Salvatore. *Veritas Sacramenti: A Study in Vermigli's Doctrine of the Lord's Supper*, Zurich: Theologischer Verlag, 1975.

Donnelly, John Patrick. *Calvinism and Scholasticism in Vermigli's Doctrine of Man and Grace*, Leiden: E. J. Brill, 1976.

——, F. A. James, and J. C. McLelland, eds., *The Peter Martyr Reader*, Kirksville: Thomas Jefferson University Press, 1999.

——, in collaboration with Robert M. Kingdon and Marvin W. Anderson, eds., *A Bibliography of the Works of Peter Martyr Vermigli*, Sixteenth Century Essays & Studies 13, Kirksville, MO: Sixteenth Century Journal Publishers, 1990.

James, Frank A., III, "A Late Medieval Parallel in Reformation Thought: *Gemina Praedestinatio* in Gregory of Rimini and Peter Martyr Vermigli" in Heiko A. Oberman and Frank A. James III, eds., *Via Augustini: Augustine in the Later Middle Ages, Renaissance and Reformation*, Leiden: E. J. Brill, 1991, 157–88.

——, *Peter Martyr Vermigli and Predestination: The Augustinian Inheritance of an Italian Reformer*, Oxford: Clarendon Press, 1998.

——, "Peter Martyr Vermigli: At the Crossroads of Late Medieval Scholasticism, Christian Humanism and Resurgent Augustinianism" in Carl R. Truman and R. S. Clark, eds., *Protestant Scholasticism: Essays in Reassessment*. Carlisle, Cumbria: Paternoster Press, 1999, 62–78.

——, "Peter Martyr and the Reformed Doctrine of Justification," *Princeton Theological Review* (October 1999), 15–20.

Kingdon, Robert M., *The Political Thought of Peter Martyr Vermigli: Selected Texts and Commentary*, Geneva: Droz, 1980.

McLelland, Joseph C., *The Visible Words of God: An Exposition of the Sacramental Theology of Peter Martyr Vermigli 1500–1562*, Edinburgh: Oliver & Boyd, 1957.

——, ed., *Peter Martyr Vermigli and Italian Reform*, Waterloo, Ont.: Wilfrid Laurier University Press, 1980.

McNair, Philip M. J., *Peter Martyr in Italy: An Anatomy of Apostasy*, Oxford: Clarendon Press, 1967.

Sturm, Klaus, *Die Theologie Peter Martyr Vermiglis während seines ersten Aufenthalts in Strassburg 1542–1547*, Neukirchen: Neukirchener Verlag, 1971.

Theodore Beza (1519–1605)

Richard A. Muller

Calvin's follower and successor, Theodore Beza, was, without doubt, one of the several most influential Reformed leaders and teachers in the second half of the sixteenth century.[1] Once his importance has been noted, however, there remains a fair amount of disagreement over the character of his contribution to the post-Reformation history of Calvinism, specifically to the rise of Reformed orthodoxy. Beza's Reformed contemporaries thought highly of him as an exegete, teacher, and defender of the Reformation. His personal confession of faith was used as the basis of the *Hungarian Confession* of 1562,[2] and he was one of several theologians who developed the 1580/1 *Harmony of the Reformed Confessions*[3] in response to the Lutheran *Formula of Concord*. Since, moreover, he remained a major intellectual force in the Genevan Academy until the final decade of his life, his influence was felt by several generations of Reformed teachers and pastors.

Beza was, certainly, both gifted and personally suitable for the role he played in Geneva following the death of Calvin. He was a fine scholar, particularly adept at classical languages, and well able to play a major role as teacher and exegete in the Academy. In particular, his work on the text of the New Testament received the accolades of his contemporaries. He also possessed refined organizational and leadership abilities; in addition to his teaching, he oversaw ecclesiastical discipline in Geneva and served as president of the Company of Pastors until 1580.[4] In the field of theological formulation and debate, moreover, Beza evidenced considerable skills. He was adept at definition and debate, equally talented in offering basic expositions of doctrine for teaching in the church and in defending Reformed doctrines – notably Christology, predestination, and the Lord's Supper – in detail.

Where there is credit, however, there is also blame. Beza has also, quite frequently, been identified as the developer of an extreme predestinarianism out of accord with Calvin's doctrine and as the primary source of a form of scholastic orthodoxy different in substance as well as in form from the theology of the Reformation.[5] Indeed, it is Beza's doctrine of predestination and, in particular, the form that it took in his *Tabula praedestinationis* or *Summa totius christianismi* of 1555 that has been the focus of a claim of significant discontinuity between Beza's thought and

Calvin's and, beyond that, between later "Calvinism" and the Reformation.[6] Given the date of the treatise, the fact that Beza consulted with Calvin in some detail over its contents, as well as the brevity and limited pastoral scope of the *Tabula*, this thesis is somewhat remarkable.[7] What is more, it has been disputed by a series of scholars. Jean Barnaud, for one, argued that Beza's *Confession de la foi* offered a doctrine of predestination "much more moderate" than Calvin's, inasmuch as it presented "the teaching of Saint Paul, without drawing the extreme consequences" associated by many with Calvin's thought.[8] Commenting on the same document, Michel Réveillaud observed that Beza's favorite "refrain" is the identification of "Jesus Christ alone" as the foundation of Christian assurance and not the doctrine of the divine decrees.[9] In order to introduce and assess Beza's contribution to the Reformed faith, therefore, some effort must be made not only to survey his life and work but also to clarify his role in the rise of Reformed orthodoxy, particularly with a view to his place in the development of the doctrine of predestination and of the large-scale dogmatics of scholastic orthodoxy.[10]

Life and Work

Theodore Beza was born on June 24, 1519, at Vezelay, in Burgundy, a child of the lesser nobility. His father, Pierre de Bèze, served as governor of the district. His uncle Nicholas was a member of the Parlement of Paris and his uncle Claude was abbot of a Cistercian monastery. Beza's earliest education was in Paris, under the care of his uncle Nicholas. In December 1528 Beza was sent for further study to Orléans, where he was placed in the care of Melchior Wolmar, a humanist scholar.[11] In 1530, Wolmar left Orléans for Bourges at the invitation of Marguerite d'Angoulême – and Beza went with him. Not only did Beza receive from Wolmar the foundation of philological and literary skills, he also was introduced, at Orléans, into a circle of reformist scholars that included the young John Calvin. It was also at Bourges, after reading Bullinger's *De origine erroris* (1528), that Beza became sympathetic to the Reformation, although it would be years before he became actively engaged in the reform of the church.[12]

When Wolmar left France for the relative safety of Germany in 1535, Beza remained behind to enter the university of Orléans as a law student. Beza's interest in classical language and literature continued unabated, but he did complete his law degree in 1539 and moved to Paris where, presumably, given his family connections, he could take up the practice of law. Yet, at this point in his life, Beza turned away from nearly all serious pursuits and became a member of the Paris literary elite. Given his income from ecclesiastical benefices and the likelihood that he would succeed his uncle to the Parlement of Paris, Beza did not need to exercise his legal skills. He also became secretly engaged to Claudine Denosse. Details concerning this phase of Beza's life are few; Geizendorf refers to the decade between Beza's legal studies and his arrival in Geneva in October 1548 as a "parenthesis."[13]

Two events occurred in 1548 that marked turning points in Beza's life: a book of his Latin poems was published, assuring him some reputation as a literary figure – and, shortly after the book appeared, Beza fell gravely ill. The latter experience turned him away from his somewhat dissolute existence and appears to have rekindled his interest in the reform of the church. Quite abruptly, Beza gave up his ecclesiastical income and left for Geneva. Once there, he identified with the Protestant cause, married Claudine (who had been living with him as his mistress), and turned his literary skills toward the task of reform.

It is important to note that, at this time, Beza had no theological training; he was a lawyer and a skilled humanist, but the turn toward theology is evident in his literary output. The latter ability led to his appointment as professor of Greek at Lausanne in November of 1550. There he finished work on a religious drama, *Abraham sacrifiant*, the theme of which was faith and the difference between the Protestant and Roman Catholic understandings of the doctrine.[14] While at Lausanne, Beza also completed his *Alphabetum Graecum* (1554), in which he analyzed the language of the New Testament,[15] published his *De haereticis a civili magistratu puniendis* (1554),[16] the *Tabula praedestinationis* (1555),[17] and completed the initial version of the *Annotationes in Novum Testamentum* (1556).[18] Each of these works was of considerable significance for understanding Beza's development. The work on New Testament Greek indicates Beza's humanistic leanings – a feature of his work that would remain prominent throughout his life. The treatise on the punishment of heretics defended Calvin's policies in Geneva against Sebastian Castellio, in particular, the execution of Servetus. The third work, probably intended as a defense of Calvin's views in the aftermath of the Bolsec controversy, demonstrates Beza's adherence to the doctrine of double predestination. The last marks the beginning of Beza's eminent career as exegete, translator, and interpreter of the New Testament.

In 1557, Beza engaged in a series of diplomatic missions with theological overtones, presaging his later efforts as a major representative of the Reformed faith in significant colloquies with the Lutherans and Roman Catholics. The first of these missions was undertaken with William Farel to organize support for the Waldensians, who were being ruthlessly persecuted by the French. Beza journeyed to Berne, Zurich, Basel, Schaffhausen, Strasbourg, Montbéliard, Baden, and Göppingen. Later in the same year, Beza went to Strasbourg and to Worms in order to convince the German cities and princes to protest persecution of the Huguenots in France. Each of these efforts had major theological overtones. In the course of his first journey, Beza's pleas for the Waldenses led to discussion of their doctrine of the Lord's Supper and to an attempt by Beza and Farel to create an understanding between the Reformed and the Lutherans. Their brief *Göppingen Confession* proved quite acceptable to the Strasbourg theologians and the Lutherans, but was opposed by Bullinger as a movement away from the *Consensus tigurinus* of 1549.[19] During his mission to Worms, Beza raised the issue of a union of the Reformed and Lutheran churches, and was again opposed by Bullinger as well as by the Bernese.

Doubtless these varied efforts, theological, exegetical, and diplomatic, demonstrated Beza's abilities to Calvin as well as indicating Beza's close theological agreement with Calvin's views. In any case, Beza was invited in 1558 to accept the position of professor of Greek in the Genevan Academy. The appointment marks not only Beza's transfer of residence to Geneva but also the beginning of his work as the primary assistant and, ultimately, the successor of Calvin. Beza's work included, among other duties, the continuation of debate with adversaries of Calvin's theology after the point that Calvin ceased publication on a particular issue. This pattern began as early as 1555, when Beza produced his *Tabula praedestinationis* in the wake of the Bolsec controversy and debates with Berne over the relationship of predestination to Christian preaching and teaching. This pattern would continue with a treatise on predestination against Sebastian Castellio and in Calvin's final eucharistic controversy with the Lutherans. Beza, in short, was primed to become the chief defender of the Genevan line of Reformed theology in Calvin's later years.

Beza's literary and theological efforts also continued, with substantial result. In 1558, he published his highly influential *Confession de la foy*[20] with a view toward explaining his Protestant faith to his father. Once published, however, it secured a wide audience as an able statement of the Reformed faith. It was rapidly translated into Latin, English, Dutch, and Italian.[21] In addition, the confession was adopted by the Synod of Tarczal in 1562 as the *Compendium doctrinae christianae, quam omnes Pastores et Ministri ecclesiarum Dei in tota Ungaria et Transsylvania*, becoming one of the official confessional documents of the Hungarian Reformed churches. This use of Beza's confession is certainly a sign of his increasing eminence in Reformed circles.

Beza's importance was also felt at the Colloquy of Poissy (1561), where he represented the Reformed churches of France and Switzerland in dialogue with French Roman Catholics. Nothing was resolved, but Beza had clearly become one of the leaders of the Reformed. A decade later, Beza presided over the French National Synod at La Rochelle (April 1571). His influence here can be detected in the retention of Calvinian language of the substantial presence of Christ in the Lord's Supper and in the rejection of "sacramentarian" denials of presence in the wording of the *Gallican Confession* then ratified by the Synod.

After Calvin's death, Beza assumed Calvin's role as the primary teacher of theology in the Genevan Academy, leader and moderator of the Company of Pastors, and advisor to the Huguenots in France. He continued to defend the Genevan position in polemics, responding to the last of Calvin's eucharistic adversaries, Tilemann Hesshusius and Joachim Westphal, and continuing the debate with Johannes Brenz, Nicolaus Selnecker, and Jakob Andreä.[22]

The decade following 1570 was an era of considerable literary activity on Beza's part. He devoted considerable energy to the edition of his major theological essays in the three volumes of his *Tractationes theologicae*, which appeared between 1570 and 1582. In addition, he also wrote his expanded catechesis, the two-part *Quaestionum & responsionum christianarum libellus*, during this time.[23] It proved to be one of his most popular and widely disseminated works; part one was printed nine times during Beza's lifetime (1570, 1571, 1577, 1578, 1580, 1583, 1584, 1587, and 1601) and part two five times (1576, 1577, 1581, 1587, and 1600) in Geneva alone. The work was also translated in to English, French, German, and Dutch.[24] As in the case of the *Tabula praedestinationis*, Beza's purpose here was basic instruction, and he offered little by way of what might be called speculative elaboration. In the *Quaestionum & responsionum*, moreover, there is no attempt at all on Beza's part to link formally the doctrines of God and the decrees and, in fact, Beza places providence and predestination together, fairly late in his exposition, echoing the model of Calvin's 1539 *Institutes*.

The *Quaestionum & responsionum* was followed by a short catechism in 1575.[25] During this time, Beza also published a volume of his more weighty theological correspondence[26] and wrote treatises on moral, ceremonial, and political law and on the marks of the true church.[27] In the latter work he further developed the view, which had already taken root in the *Belgic Confession*, that proper ecclesiastical discipline, as well as true preaching of the Word and the right administration of the sacraments, was a mark of the church.

In the wake of the St. Bartholomew's Day massacre (1572), Beza saw fit to release his treatise on the right of the magistrates – in French, and published anonymously at Lyon.[28] So inflammatory was the work that the town council of Geneva had voted against its publication in Beza's own home. In brief, the treatise moves beyond the more cautious statements of Calvin that an oppressed people ought to have resource and relief through the magistrates to the more pointed doctrine that the magistrates have the duty to resist tyranny, including the tyrannical rule of a legitimately enthroned monarch. Beza does not extend this right, however, to the general populace; they are enjoined only to refuse obedience to commands that are contrary to the divine law and, at the same time, to obey the divine law, even when commanded to ignore it by an unrighteous ruler.

In the following decade, Beza engaged in considerable exegetical work; expanding his *Annotationes*, originally published in 1556, in a series of new editions (1582, 1589, and 1598). Beza presented a Greek text of the New Testament based on the best manuscripts he could find, paralleled by his own Latin translation and by the Vulgate. He then provided a brief marginal annotation and a lengthier annotation on each verse in which he raised philological issues in dialogue with the Vulgate, Erasmus, Calvin, and other translators, and finally drew out theological conclusions. Given the wide use of the *Annotationes* both in Beza's own time and in the seventeenth century, together with the use of Beza's Greek text both by Stephanus in Geneva and by Elzevir in Leiden (in what became known as the *Textus receptus*), this was certainly Beza's most influential work.[29] Beza also published a commentary on Job together with a paraphrase of Ecclesiastes,[30] and sermons on selected Psalms, Ecclesiastes, and the Song of Songs.[31]

Beza also continued to participate in colloquies and dialogues with Roman Catholics and Lutherans, the most notable of these being the Montbéliard Colloquy of 1586. Here, at the request of the Duke of Württemberg, Beza addressed the question of Christian union with representatives of the Lutheran churches, the most prominent of whom were Jakob Andreä and Lucas Osiander. Beza was accompanied by Antonius Faius of Geneva and Abraham Musculus of Berne. The parties began by expressing their agreement on the ancient faith of the church as found in the Nicene and Chalcedonian formulae. Following this ecumenical agreement, however, they were unable to reach any consensus on the communication of proper qualities in the Person of Christ, the mode of Christ's presence in the Lord's Supper, predestination, images and ceremonies in churches, and the necessity of baptism.

So extensive was the disagreement that controversy continued after the Colloquy in the attempt to produce a transcript of it. Each side claimed to have emerged as the victor in debate. The Lutherans went so far as to publish their own version of the Colloquy, demonstrating the orthodoxy of their position against the Reformed.

Beza responded with a Reformed response to the Lutheran "acts," indicating the superiority of the Reformed position.[32] In a continuation of the controversy, Beza participated in a debate before the magistrates at Berne leading to the censure of Samuel Huber. Huber had objected to the doctrine of predestination offered as Reformed by Beza and Musculus at Montbéliard and defended in the Reformed version of the acts of the Colloquy.

It was about this time that Beza's advancing age began to sap his energies. By 1594 he commented that his hands trembled and that writing had become difficult, and in 1595 he asked that a second chair in theology be instituted at the Academy in order to relieve him of some of his teaching duties. The chair was held briefly by Conrad Vorstius, and offered unsuccessfully to Amandus Polanus. Finally, in 1599, Beza retired fully and his chair was turned over to Antonius Faius – a theologian not remembered for his intellect! – with the second chair being filled by the very promising Jean Diodati, the professor of Hebrew.[33]

Beza's physical decline was marked from the beginning of 1601. Attendance at the meetings of the Company of Pastors became difficult and irregular. By 1605, Beza was largely confined to his home; he was so weak toward the beginning of October in that year that the Company of Pastors arranged for a daily visitation. On the evening of October 12, sensing the end approaching, Faius read to Beza from Psalm 130 and Perrot offered the text of Romans 5, "being justified by faith, we have peace through our Lord Jesus Christ." Faius and Perrot remained with Beza through the night and as the bell of St. Pierre struck eight o'clock on the morning of October 13, 1605, Beza breathed his last.[34]

Beza and the Reformed Tradition

The mature work of the extraordinarily long-lived Theodore Beza covered nearly the entire half-century during which Protestantism developed from a Reform movement in the early phase of its confessional and doctrinal codification into a well-defined and institutionalized orthodoxy. Beza's own work contributed much to this development, particularly in the areas of exegetical definition and polemical defense, but it is also true that the development of Protestant orthodoxy can hardly be explained as primarily due to Beza's efforts. His theology underwent an elaboration and formal development that was as much the product as the cause of the institutionalization or confessionalization of Protestantism. It is certainly a mistake, therefore, to interpret his early writings, notably the *Tabula* and the *Confessio*, as breathing the air of Protestant scholasticism. Rather, they are clearly products of the first confessional phase of the Reformed faith and reflect the level of confessional formulation of that era. Beza's *Confessio*, as already indicated, itself became an integral part of the Reformed confessional movement of the mid-sixteenth century, while the *Tabula* belongs to a particular controversy of that era, specifically over the ways in which the doctrine of predestination can be preached and taught with pastoral concern.[35] Similarly, Beza's *Annotationes in Novum Testamentum* is not "scholastic" in style or method. One can, however, argue that Beza's basic efforts at definition – whether confessional, controversial, or exegetical – did lend themselves to the task of concise and definitive doctrinal definition, a task at the heart of the academic and doctrinal enterprise of confessional Protestantism. This task was also furthered by Beza's method of teaching in the Academy, where the results of exegesis and of attempts at doctrinal definition were consistently brought to bear on the shaping of classroom disputations, the basic methodological device of scholastic instruction. This movement from "Scripture to disputation" belonged to the rise of Protestant scholasticism.[36]

This more cautious way of associating Beza with the rise of Protestant scholasticism serves to underscore the point that Beza did not work to produce a "predestinarian system." Predestinarianism is not to be associated with the scholastic enterprise as such – any more than the development of covenantal thought should be understood as a product of humanism. Scholasticism, whether that of the Reformed in the late sixteenth century or that of Bonaventure and Aquinas in the mid-thirteenth, is primarily a method associated with the university or academy classroom; it is not a particular understanding of doctrines or a particular set of theological and philosophical conclusions.[37] Beza's efforts in the classroom increasingly took scholastic form, and his later writings, including those on predestination, manifest an increasing sense of technique and attention to the theological tradition (including the writings of the medieval scholastics). But the point remains: the scholastic forms used by Beza did not cause doctrinal change but rather were a method used to defend and elaborate an already existent confessional orthodoxy. And, in Beza's case, his approaches were also steeped in the methods of humanism – he retained his interest in and emphasis on philological training throughout his career.

A comment is necessary here concerning Beza's famous *Tabula praedestinationis* or *Summa totius christianismi*, the document usually placed at the center of arguments concerning Beza's predestinarianism. Beza published the chart of the divine decree and its effects together with a brief explanatory treatise in 1555, at the close of the Bolsec controversy, at a time when Bolsec was living in Berne and several of the Berne clergy sympathized with his denunciation of the doctrine of predestination. The chart and treatise are concerned to line out the causality of the decree and then to offer a pastoral explanation. Both the genre and the date of the work militate against its use as a framework for understanding Beza's entire thought, much less all of later Reformed theology. Calvin still lived and the treatise does not propose a system of doctrine. In addition, in the larger context of Beza's thought, in which other Christian doctrines are given due place, much time is devoted to exegesis and pastoral concerns, and works on the topics of theology in confessional and catechetical form do not parallel the causal model of the *Tabula*. Beza hardly appears as the systematizer of the Reformed faith around a particular doctrinal point.[38]

If Beza was not the inventor of Reformed scholasticism, he was certainly one of the eminent teachers of the era of orthodoxy, who left his mark on several generations of students. Indeed, contrary to the impression given by much of the older scholarship on Reformed orthodoxy, Beza appears to have been a balanced teacher whose approach in the classroom produced able but highly varied students, none taught merely to reproduce a particular line of thought. In addition, Beza supported his students with enthusiastic recommendations as they pursued their careers – including such later dissidents as Arminius, Uitenbogaert, and Vorstius. These characteristics of his teaching led one nineteenth-century scholar to hypothesize a near-bifurcation of the Bezan personality: here was a staunch defender of Calvinistic orthodoxy and an advocate of academic freedom as well![39] Although there is no reason to split Beza's personality or divide his allegiance, it remains clear that he was able to couple orthodoxy with academic breadth, as evidenced by the published theses debated under Beza and his colleague, Faius, in 1586.[40] A similar conclusion appears from examination of the *Harmony of the Reformed Confessions* produced under Beza's auspices in 1580; it is not only infralapsarian, it uses the *Second Helvetic Confession* for its basic confessional position.[41]

The portrait of Beza is also incomplete when he is studied only as a formal theologian and exegete, while his efforts as a preacher are neglected. Here too, he sought to follow his mentor and became a significant voice in the Genevan pulpit. In later life he published several volumes of meditations and sermons both on Old Testament and New Testament themes. Beza's choice of Old Testament themes – at least for publication – led him to a selection of Psalms, the Song of Songs, and Ecclesiastes.[42] In each of these series of homilies, as in his commentary on Job, Beza manifests an interest in the Christian life. He preaches on God's providence as the underlying source of security and trust and, therefore, as a foundation of Christian conduct, particularly of the exercise of the virtues. When preaching on the Song of Songs, Beza draws on the traditional understanding of the text as an allegory of Christ's love for the church for the sake of directing Christians away from concentration on self toward a focus on Christ and Christ's work. Beza's New Testament preaching is exemplified in two published volumes of homilies, one on the passion and death, the other on the resurrection of Christ.[43] Beza's emphasis here is on the person of Christ and, by way of the divine–human person, on the life and nature of human beings as the subject of redemption. Although the doctrine of predestination is evident in the sermons, Beza quite pointedly (as adumbrated in the *Tabula*) emphasizes the life of repentance and faith.[44]

Conclusion

An inventory of Beza's major writings and of his activities as teacher and defender of the Reformed faith in the late sixteenth century offers strong evidence of his major role in the continuance of Reformed theology and, specifically, in the rise of a Reformed orthodoxy between 1550 and 1605. This role, however, was not that of a systematic theologian, but rather of a teacher, exegete, and defender of the faith. Beza produced nothing of the scope of Calvin's *Institutes*, Hyperius's *Methodus theologiae*, Ursinus's *Explicationes catecheticae* and *Loci communes*, Zanchi's major treatises, *De natura Dei* and *De tribus Elohim*, or of Lambert Daneau's *Christianae isagoges*, all systematic or dogmatic works written between 1560 and 1580. Beza's impact was not as dogmatic systematizer. He was neither the chief exponent of scholastic Protestantism in his day, nor did he engineer a system of theology based on a speculative view of the doctrine of the divine essence, the doctrine of the divine will, or the doctrine of predestination. Neither can his work be associated with the rise of rationalism. He was, however, a major teacher and defender of Reformed dogmatics and a significant exegete who consistently maintained the teaching of the Reformation in forms of late-sixteenth-century discourse.

Notes

1 The best biography of Beza is still Paul F. Geizendorf, *Théodore de Bèze* (Geneva: Alexandre Jullien, 1949); also see also Henri Clavier, *Théodore de Bèze; un aperçu de sa vie aventureuse, de ses travaux, de sa personalité* (Cahors: A. Coueslant, 1960), and the brief study in David Steinmetz, *Reformers in the Wings* (Philadelphia: Fortress Press, 1971), 162–71. Beza's academic influence is traced in Herman De Vries, *Genève: Pépiniere du Calvinisme Hollandaise*, 2 vols. (Fribourg: Fragnière Frères and The Hague: Nijhoff, 1918–24).

2 *Compendium doctrinae christianae, quam omnes Pastores et Ministri ecclesiarum Dei in tota Ungaria et Transsylvania, quae incorruptum Iesu Christi Evangelium amplexae sunt, docent ac profitentur* was adopted by the Synod of Tarczal in 1562 and ratified, in the following year, by the Synod of Torda (in *BSRK*, 376–449), based on Theodore Beza, *Confessio christianae fidei* (Geneva, 1558).

3 *Harmonia confessionum fidei, orthodoxarum & reformatarum Ecclesiarum* (Geneva, 1581); *An Harmony of the Confessions of the Faith of the Christian and Reformed Churches* (Cambridge, 1586); also, *The Harmony of Protestant Confessions: Exhibiting the Faith of the Churches of Christ, Reformed after the Pure and Holy doctrine of the Gospel, throughout Europe*, trans. Peter Hall (London: Petrus Santandreanus, 1842).

4 See *Registres de la Compagnie des Pasteurs de Genève*, vol. III: 1565–74, ed. Olivier Fatio and Olivier Labarthe; vol. IV: 1575–82, ed. Olivier Labarthe and Bernard Lescaze; vol. V: 1583–8, ed. Olivier Labarthe and Micheline Tripet (Geneva: Droz, 1969–76), passim; and see Eugène Choisy, *L'État Chrétien Calviniste à Genève au Temps de Théodore de Bèze* (Geneva: Eggiman and Paris: Fischbacher, 1909), 5–11, 172–8.

5 See Ernst Bizer, *Frühorthodoxie und Rationalismus* (Zürich: EVZ-Verlag, 1963), 6–11; Charles S. McCoy, "Johannes Cocceius: Federal Theologian," *Scottish Journal of Theology*, 16 (1963), 354, 364–9; R. T. Kendall, *Calvin and English Calvinism to 1649* (Oxford: Oxford University Press, 1979), and idem, "The Puritan Modification of Calvin's Theology" in W. Stanford Reid, ed., *John Calvin: His Influence in the Western World* (Grand Rapids: Zondervan, 1982), 197–214.

6 Thus, Johannes Dantine, "Das christologische Problem in Rahmen der Prädestinationslehre von Theodor Beza," in *ZKG*, 78 (1966), 81–96; idem, "Les Tabelles sur la doctrine de la prédestination par Théodore de Bèze," *Revue de théologie et de philosophie*, 16 (1966), 365–7; Basil Hall, "Calvin Against the Calvinists" in Gervase Duffield, ed., *John Calvin* (Appleford: Sutton Courtnay Press, 1966), 19–37. For further bibliography and a critique of these essays and of the problem of "central dogmas," see Richard A. Muller, "Calvin and the Calvinists: Assessing Continuities and Discontinuities Between the Reformation and Orthodoxy, Part I," *CTJ* 30/2 (November 1995), 345–75; "Part II," *CTJ* 31/1 (April 1996), 125–60.

7 See further, Richard A. Muller, *Christ and the Decree: Christology and Predestination in Reformed Theology from Calvin to Perkins* (Durham, NC: Labyrinth Press, 1986; paperback edition, Grand Rapids: Baker Book House, 1988), 79–96; and idem, "The Use and Abuse of a Document: Beza's *Tabula praedestinationis*, the Bolsec Controversy, and the Origins of Reformed Orthodoxy" in Carl Trueman and Scott Clark, eds., *Protestant Scholasticism: Essays in Reappraisal* (Carlisle: Paternoster Press, 1999), 33–61.

8 Jean Barnaud, "La confession de foi de Théodore de Bèze," *Bulletin de la Société de l'Histoire Protestant Français*, 48 (1899), 625.

9 Michel Réveillaud, "Introduction" in Beza, *Confession de foi, La Revue Réformée*, VI/23–4 (March and April 1955): 5.

10 Beza's contribution to the development of Reformed orthodoxy is examined in Walter

Kickel, *Vernunft und Offenbarung bei Theodor Beza* (Neukirchen: Neukirchener Verlag, 1967); John S. Bray, *Theodore Beza's Doctrine of Predestination* (Nieuwkoop: De Graaf, 1975); Tadataka Maruyama, *The Ecclesiology of Theodore Beza: The Reform of the True Church* (Geneva: Droz, 1978); Jill Raitt, *The Eucharistic Theology of Theodore Beza: Development of the Reformed Doctrine* (Chambersburg, PA: American Academy of Religion, 1972), idem, "The Person of the Mediator: Calvin's Christology and Beza's Fidelity," *Occasional Papers of the Society for Reformation Research*, I (December 1977), 53–80; Ian McPhee, "Conserver or Transformer of Calvin's Theology? A Study of the Origins and Development of Theodore Beza's Thought, 1550–1570" (Ph.D. dissertation, University of Cambridge, 1979); and Cornelis van Sliedregt, *Calvijns opvolger Theodorus Beza, zijn verkiezingsleer en zijn belijdenis van de drieënige God* (Leiden: Groen, 1996).

11 Geizendorf, *Théodore de Bèze*, 10.

12 See Beza to Bullinger, August 18, 1568, in *Correspondance de Théodore de Bèze*, coll. Hippolyte Aubert, ed. Fernand Aubert, Henri Meylan, Alain Dufour, et al. (Geneva: Droz, 1960–), IX:121 with Hippolyte Aubert, "La conversion de Théodore de Bèze à la Réforme: Théodore de Bèze et sa famille d'après des extraits de la correspondence de Bèze," *Bulletin de la Société de l'Histoire Protestant Français*, 52 (1904), 534–6.

13 Geizendorf, *Théodore de Bèze*, 13.

14 Theodore Beza, *Abraham sacrifiant* (Geneva, 1550); trans. *A Tragedie of Abrahams Sacrifice* (London, 1577); critical edition, ed. Keith Cameron, Kathleen Hall, and Francis Higman (Geneva: Droz, 1967).

15 Theodore Beza, *Alphabetum Graecum. Addita sunt Theodori Bezae scholia, in quibus Germana Graecae linguae pronunciatione differitur* (Geneva, 1554).

16 Theodore Beza, *De haereticis a civili magistratu puniendis* (Geneva, 1554); also found in Theodore Beza, *Tractationes theologicae*, 3 vols. (Geneva, 1582), 85–169.

17 Theodore Beza, *Summa totius christianismi, sive descriptio & distributio causarum salutis electorum & exitii reproborum, ex sacris literis collecta* (Geneva, 1555); also in *Tractationes theologicae*, 3 vols. (Geneva, 1570–82), I:170–205; trans. *A Briefe Declaration of the Chiefe Poyntes of the Christian Religion* (London,

1575); also *The Treasure of Trueth . . . with a Briefe Summe of the Comfortable Doctrine of God his Providence, comprised in 38 Short Aphorismes* (London, c.1576).

18 The *Novum D. N. Jesu Christi Testamentum, latine jam olim a vetere interprete, nunc denuo a Theodoro Beza versum: cum eiusdem annotationibus, in quibus ratio interpretationis redditur* (Geneva, 1556) were reissued with some revision in 1582.

19 On the *Consensus tigurinus*, see Paul Rorem, "Calvin and Bullinger on the Lord's Supper," *LQ* 2 (1988): 155–84, 357–89. On Beza's early eucharistic views, see Raitt, *Eucharistic Theology*, 3–6.

20 Theodore Beza, *Confession de la foy chrestienne, faite par Theodore de Besze, contenant la confirmation d'icelle, et la refutation des superstitions contraires* (Geneva, 1558; quatriesme edition, revue sur la Latine, & augmentée avec un Abregé d'icelle: Geneva, 1561); translated as *A Briefe and Pithie Summe of the Christian Faith, made in the Forme of a Confession, with a confutation of all such superstitious errours, as are contrary thereunto*, translated out of the Frenche by R. F. (London, 1565).

21 Frédéric Gardy and Alain Dufour, eds., *Bibliographie des oeuvres théologiques, littéraires, historiques et juridiques de Théodore de Bèze* (Geneva: Droz, 1960), 60–78; also note J. Barnaud, "La confession de foi de Théodore de Bèze," *Bulletin de la Société de l'Histoire Protestant Français*, 48 (1899), 632–3.

22 Notably, Theodore Beza, *Adversus sacramentariorum errorum pro vera Christi praesentia in coena Domini, homiliae duae* (Geneva, 1574) and *De hypostatica duarum in Christo naturarum unione* (Geneva, 1579).

23 *Quaestionum et responsionum christianarum libellus, in quo praecipua Christianae religionis capita kat' epitome proponuntur* (Geneva, 1570), translated as *A Booke of Christian Questions and Answers* (London, 1572); and *Quaestionum et responsionum christianarum libellus pars altera, quae est de sacramentis* (Geneva, 1576), translated as *The Other Parte of Christian Questions and answeres, which is Concerning the Sacraments* (London, 1580).

24 Gardy, *Bibliographie de Théodore de Bèze*, pp. 148–57; cf. Alfred W. Pollard and G. R. Redgrave, *A Short Title Catalogue of Books Printed in England, Scotland, and Ireland . . . 1475–1640* (London: B. Quaritch, 1926), s.v. "Beza."

25 *Petit catéchisme* (Geneva, 1575), translated as *A Little Catechisme* (London, 1578).

26 *Epistolarum theologicarum Theodori Bezae Vezelii, liber unus* (Geneva, 1573).

27 *Lex Dei, moralis, ceremonialis, et politica*, Geneva, 1577; and *De veris et visibilis Ecclesiae catholicae notis, tractatio* (Geneva, 1578), translated as *A Discourse of the True and Visible Markes of the Catholique Church* (London, 1582, 1623).

28 *Du droit des magistrats sur leurs sujets* (Lyons, 1574); critical ed., with an intro. by Robert M. Kingdon (Geneva: Droz, 1970).

29 Beza's textual work is described in great detail in Irena Backus, *The Reformed Roots of the English New Testament: The Influence of Theodore Beza on the English New Testament* (Pittsburgh: Pickwick Press, 1980).

30 Theodore Beza, *Iobus. Theodore Bezae partim commentariis partim paraphrasi illustratus. Cui additus est Ecclesiastes, paraphrasticè explicata* (Geneva and London, 1589), translated as *Iob Expounded partly in a commentary, partly in a paraphrase [with] Ecclesiastes, with a paraphrase* (Cambridge, c.1589).

31 Theodore Beza, *Chrestiennes méditations sur huict psaumes du prophète David* (Geneva, 1582), translated as *The Psalmes of David, truly Opened and Explained by Paraphrasis* (London, 1590); *Sermons sur le Cantique des Cantiques* (Geneva, 1586), translated as *Maister Bezaes Sermons upon the Three First Chapters of the Canticle of Canticles* (Oxford, 1587); and *Sermons sur Ecclésiaste* (Geneva, 1588). On Beza's reading of the Psalms and Job, see Jill Raitt, "Beza, Guide for the Faithful Life," *Scottish Journal of Theology*, 39/1 (1986), 83–107.

32 *Acta colloquii Montis Belligartensis* (Tübingen, 1586).

33 Geizendorf, *Théodore de Bèze*, 395–6.

34 Geizendorf, *Théodore de Bèze*, 424–5; see the accounts in Henry Martyn Baird, *Theodore Beza* (New York: G. P. Putnam's Sons, 1899), 350 and Heinrich Heppe, *Theodore Beza* (Elberfeld: R. L. Fridericks, 1861), 316–17.

35 On this point, see Muller, "Use and Abuse of a Document," 50–5.

36 See Pierre Fraenkel, *De l'Ecriture à la dispute: le cas de l'Académie de Genève sous Théodore de Bèze*, Cahiers de la Revue de théologie et de philosophie, 1 (Lausanne: Revue de théologie et de philosophie, 1977); Luc Perrotet, "Chapter 9 of the Epistle to the Hebrews as Presented in an Unpublished Course of Lectures by Theodore Beza," *Journal of Medieval and Renaissance Studies* 14/1 (1984), 89–96.

37 See Muller, "Calvin and the Calvinists," I:360–73 and II:126–9, 131–2, 159–60, with idem, *Scholasticism and Orthodoxy in the Reformed Tradition: An Attempt at Definition* (Grand Rapids: Calvin Theological Seminary, 1995), 8–19.

38 See further, Muller, *Christ and the Decree*, 80–96; and idem, "Use and Abuse of a Document," 33–61.

39 De Vries, *Genève Pépinière*, I:212–20.

40 *Theses theologicae in schola Genevensi ab aliquot sacrarum literarum studiosus sub DD. Theod. Beza & Antonio Fayo ss. theologiae professoribus propositae & disputatae* (Geneva, 1586), translated as *Propositions and Principles of Divinitie Propounded and Disputed in the University of Geneva under M. Theod. Beza and M. Anthonie Faius* (Edinburgh, 1595). Note especially the theses on predestination, which are distinctly infralapsarian.

41 On these collateral points, see Richard A. Muller, *God, Creation and Providence in the Thought of Jacob Arminius: Sources and Directions of Scholastic Protestantism in the Era of Early Orthodoxy* (Grand Rapids: Baker Book House, 1991), 19–20.

42 Theodore Beza, *Chrestiennes méditations sur huict psaumes du prophète David* (Geneva, 1582), translated as *The Psalmes of David, truly Opened and Explained by Paraphrasis* (London, 1590); *Sermons sur le Cantique des Cantiques* (Geneva, 1586), translated as *Maister Bezaes Sermons upon the Three First Chapters of the Canticle of Canticles* (Oxford, 1587); and *Sermons sur Ecclésiaste* (Geneva, 1588).

43 Theodore Beza, *Sermons sur l'histoire de la passion et sepultre de nostre Seigneur Iesus Christ* (Geneva, 1592) and *Sermons sur l'histoire de la résurrection de nostre Seigneur Iesus Christ* (Geneva, 1593).

44 See Armand Duckert, *Théodore de Bèze: Prédicateur* (Geneva, 1891); see the similar conclusions in Raitt, "Beza, Guide for the Faithful Life," 103–7.

Richard A. Muller

Bibliography

Primary Sources

Frédéric Gardy and Alain Dufour, eds., *Bibliographie des oeuvres théologiques, littéraires, historiques et juridiques de Théodore de Bèze*, Geneva: Droz, 1960. See also the endnotes.

Secondary Sources

Backus, Irena, *The Reformed Roots of the English New Testament: The Influence of Theodore Beza on the English New Testament*, Pittsburgh: Pickwick Press, 1980.

Bray, John S., *Theodore Beza's Doctrine of Predestination*, Nieuwkoop: De Graaf, 1975.

Nugent, Donald, *Ecumenism in the Age of the Reformation: The Colloquy of Poissy*. Cambridge, MA: Harvard University Press, 1974.

Raitt, Jill, *The Eucharistic Theology of Theodore Beza: Development of the Reformed Doctrine*, Chambersburg, PA: American Academy of Religion, 1972.

——, "Theodore Beza, 1519–1605" in Jill Raitt, ed., *Shapers of Religious Traditions in Germany, Switzerland, and Poland, 1560–1600*, New Haven: Yale University Press, 1981, 89–104.

——, *The Colloquy of Montbéliard: Religion and Politics in the Sixteenth Century*, New York: Oxford University Press, 1993.

224

Katharina Schütz Zell
(1498–1562)

Elsie Anne McKee

ch**a**
pter

15

Katharina Schütz Zell was one of the outstanding lay theologians of the first-generation Protestant movement.[1] Her thought and her life form an indivisible whole, and thus it is appropriate first to outline her active faith as she lived and taught it, and then to sketch the major tenets of her theology along with its distinctive personal characteristics.

Katharina Schütz Zell: Pastor and Theologian

The daughter of a comfortably established Strasbourg citizen and craftsman, Katharina received a good vernacular education, though she never learned more than a few words of Latin. Strasbourg was served by great penitential preachers like Geiler von Kaysersberg and Jakob Wimpfeling, and the Schütz family imbibed a vigorous moral training. The young Katharina was intensely devout from childhood, and at the age of ten she dedicated herself to God to be what she would later call "a church mother." In her teens, this meant a holy life of celibacy, and participation in the sacraments and good works, living in her own home.[2] However, like her older contemporary Martin Luther, she gradually came to realize that none of her unceasing religious activities could assure her of a sense of God's grace, and she came ever nearer to despair. Then in 1521 Matthew Zell, the new parish priest at the cathedral, began to preach in a "Lutheran" style, and Katharina found her peace in "the gospel." This experience remolded her understanding of the way to salvation and the nature of the holy life, and transformed the shape of her religious vocation.

Her new vision of God's will appeared as a call to be "a fisher of people" alongside the clergy.[3] To put her convictions into practice and encourage others to follow the gospel for their salvation, she married Matthew Zell on December 3, 1523. She thus became one of the first women of good reputation to seal her commitment to the biblical faith by breaking canon law to marry a priest. Together with Matthew for 24 years, and then as a widow until her death, Katharina continued the work of a "mother of the church" in the light of her new understanding of how

God willed to be served. Over time, the passionately committed and tireless witness for the gospel wrote and spoke as well as acted out her faith. She knew many of the leading religious figures of her day, and was always willing to learn from them. However, she also studied Scripture for herself and maintained a considerable independence, respecting other teachers but never afraid to think for herself, and was always ready to respond to any human need, spiritual or material.

The Zells' marriage was a partnership in ministry. Matthew was the first and always the most popular Strasbourg Reformer, a man of the people, a fiery preacher, a pastor with an open heart and home. Katharina was certainly among the most remarkable of the women who established the new religious vocation of "pastor's wife," but she herself saw her role as that of fellow worker with the (male) reformers. Others might not be entirely pleased about this, but Matthew apparently came to regard her as his partner and colleague in pastoral and teaching ministries, as well as the more traditional feminine tasks of welcoming refugees and caring for the sick and destitute.[4]

The Zells offered hospitality to high and low, rich and poor, citizen and stranger. They welcomed followers of Luther, Zwingli, Schwenckfeld, and the "poor Baptist brethren," and even included Roman Catholic neighbors. The first three leaders and their disciples might see themselves as very different, but the Zells greeted them all as sharing the common faith of the gospel. While clearly recognizing that the Anabaptists differed on secondary matters, especially ecclesiology, the Zells still welcomed these frequently persecuted, sometimes deluded souls because they also had broken with Rome for the gospel of Christ as sole Savior.[5] The Zells even received those who remained loyal to Rome, but Katharina as well as Matthew felt compelled not only to preach against their errors but also to argue theology with them, to teach them the fallacy of trusting in the Mass, the saints, or their own merits. Open-hearted did not mean empty-headed, but both Zells were always more ready to see what Christians held in common than what divided them, while demarcating very firmly the difference between those who followed Christ alone and those who still divided their trust between Christ and other saviors.[6]

Over the years Schütz Zell became acquainted with most of the German-speaking leaders of the Reform, many in person, and the rest through their published writings and private correspondence.[7] Luther was the most significant figure for both Zells, and they made a long journey in 1538 to meet him and his Katherine, and a number of his close associates, including Philip Melanchthon and Nicolas Amsdorf. Johannes Brenz was one of Matthew's colleagues whom Katharina knew only through correspondence. Despite Luther's central influence, regional traditions linked Strasbourg more closely with South Germany and Switzerland than with Wittenberg. In 1529 Ulrich Zwingli and Johannes Oecolampadius stayed with the Zells on their way to the Marburg Colloquy, and after Matthew's death Katharina made a visit to Switzerland to see their Alsatian colleague Conrad Pellican, also meeting Heinrich Bullinger and Oswald Myconius, and other wanderers like John Hooper. Sometime Strasbourg residents Wolfgang Musculus, Peter and Katherine Martyr, and especially the Blaurer family in Constance, particularly Ambrose and Margaret, were other partners in Reform. Schütz Zell also met foreign Reformers in Strasbourg. Some, like the young Calvin, she scarcely knew, since they had no common language; others, like Urbanus

Rhegius and especially Caspar Schwenckfeld, became close acquaintances. Naturally, however, the Strasbourg church leaders were the Zells' closest colleagues, friends, and sometimes critics: Wolfgang and Agnes Capito, Martin and Elisabeth Bucer, Caspar and Margaret Hedio, Wibrandis Rosenblatt, and the families of Conrad Hubert, Diobald Schwarz, and Paul Fagius.

Influences may go in several directions; the effect of the great figures on Schütz Zell is clear, but it was also possible for Schütz Zell to have an effect on them. Together Matthew and Katharina offered hospitality to many leading figures, and her role was not simply that of cook; she frequently took an active part in the theological table talk. Matthew was evidently quite willing to share his ministerial activities with his wife, and those who came to his table were apparently expected to allow Katharina a voice, at least to pose questions and probably also to express her own convictions. Sometimes duty conflicted with pleasure, as when in 1540 the cook and lay theologian set up a dinner party for participants of the religious colloquy at Hagenau (30 guests from all over Germany!) but had to miss it herself because she needed to nurse the ailing Rhegius.[8]

Both Zells, influenced by the biblical models of Martha and the Good Samaritan, were extremely concerned to serve "unimportant people," whether in their home or the wider community; no one was too insignificant to receive their attention. Thus, alongside illustrious friends and guests, there were the simple and the strangers. These people included religious refugees, like the men of Kentzingen who appeared on the parsonage doorstep in July 1524, or Dr. Mantel and his four children who came from Baden in 1528 (and spent the winter with the Zells!), or destitute people fleeing the Augsburg Interim (1548) whom Katharina took in after Matthew's death. Even Bucer and Fagius, exiled and in hiding, spent their final days in Strasbourg with her.[9] Some poor students or orphaned relatives lived with the Zells for years; other guests were victims of plague or war, needy widows and apprentices, the sick and the dying. Both Zells also spent much time counseling and comforting, reproving and instructing, serving the troubled souls and tender consciences of men, women, and children confused by the religious conflicts or depressed by grief or fearful in face of death. This pastoral work was normally done in person, in the homes of Strasbourg and the surrounding villages. However, both Zells, but especially Katharina, also exercised this ministry by writing to those she could not visit, and sometimes publishing her words of consolation and encouragement, exhortation and rebuke.

Early in 1548 Matthew Zell died. Katharina carried on their joint work and her own lifelong dedication to God's service, alone, until her death on September 5, 1562. But the situation had changed in a number of ways. The loss of Matthew was Katharina's greatest personal sorrow. It also meant that she was gradually distanced from her unofficial official role of leadership in the Strasbourg church by Zell's successor Ludwig Rabus and his colleagues. Nonetheless, to the end of her life not a few Strasbourgers continued to treat Katharina Schütz Zell as their pastor. A second, more global, change was the effect on the religious and political scene of the Augsburg Interim and the increasingly strict Lutheran confessional stance of the Strasbourg clergy. Like many laity but with greater energy and theological ability, Schütz Zell resisted the narrowing and more rigid creedal patterns of the 1550s. She believed the faith taught by Luther, Zell, Zwingli, and their colleagues in the 1520s was true and saving, and that those who elaborated and refined it were in danger of losing it, of replanting the old weeds that the first reformers had dug out.[10] Despite growing ill health and family responsibilities, Schütz Zell continued to receive refugees, care for the sick, counsel troubled people, and teach her faith. In addition, though, now she also had to defend her understanding of the gospel, shaped by the struggles of the 1520s, to a second generation of Protestants who had never known what it meant to bear the burden of earning their own salvation.

Most of Schütz Zell's strictly theological writing dates from the 1550s when she felt compelled to explain the early teachers and their work to their forgetful heirs. The content is in fact largely unchanged from the Protestantism being preached and published in the early 1520s. The character of a lay theologian's appropriation of the gospel message is preserved in her work. Her articulate presentation and defense of the teaching that had changed her understanding of Christian salvation and vocation makes a rich contribution to the picture of what the new Protestant faith meant to "ordinary Christians," and what it became in their minds, hearts, and lives.

Katharina Schütz Zell's remarkable corpus of writings provides a comprehensive expression of her theology, its central affirmations and pastoral orientation, her piety and her polemic.[11] These writings were produced over the course of 34 years, an unusually long publishing career for a lay person. Each writing was prompted by specific pastoral and theological concerns. The range of genres is impressive, as are the biblical coherence, the historical accuracy, and the sometimes sharp humor; Schütz Zell wielded a lively pen with confidence and considerable fluency. Before giving a synoptic summary of the very consistent theology found in the wide range of her writings, it is appropriate to identify and characterize the individual texts.

Shortly after her marriage Katharina, using her family name of Schütz, began to write in defense of the gospel and for the sake of encouraging its hearers. Her first known text was a letter to Strasbourg's bishop in February 1524 affirming the biblical truth of clerical marriage and attacking human traditions of clerical celibacy. The city government forbade the publication of this "hot letter" and Schütz Zell at first desisted. Later she concluded that the simple citizens of Strasbourg and its neighboring regions were being led away from the gospel by calumnies against the morality of married priests, Matthew Zell in particular. She felt compelled to defend the truth of the gospel and to refute attacks on biblical faith in order to save both the deceived and the deceivers. Her *Apologia for Matthew Zell* (c. September 1524) incorporated the polemic of her earlier letter and pastoral care, along with a marvelous defense of lay speech.[12] In fact, this *Apologia* was the second of Schütz Zell's writings to be published, having been preceded in July 1524 by a letter of pastoral consolation addressed *To the Women of Kentzingen*, to encourage them in their witness for their faith, despite the loss of their husbands (refugees in Strasbourg at the time). The letter's biblical imagery conveyed a rich picture of the worth of Christian suffering for the gospel and comfort for the women, but also a real admiration for their role as witnesses – "preachers!" – of the faith.[13]

Within ten years Katharina Zell (now using her married name) was again writing and teaching for a larger community. In 1532 she produced a thoughtful exposition of the Lord's Prayer for two women of Speyer whose anxiety over their religious state had come to her ears and whom she felt obliged to help as best she could. The preface includes some rather intriguing maternal imagery for Christ. This text apparently circulated in manuscript form until 1558.[14] However, in 1534 she felt compelled to take a more public role in the reform of piety in Strasbourg, specifically because she was clearly aware of the lack of devotional material to replace the medieval prayers addressed to the saints. She republished a hymnal of the Bohemian Brethren in four small fascicles priced to suit children and the poor. A didactic preface encouraged "lay preaching" of the faith by the singing and teaching of these biblical hymns. These pages combined one of Schütz Zell's most stark arguments contrasting right and wrong with her clearest and most attractive expression of the priesthood of believers and the role of women, children, and laity generally in educating their households and neighbors in the faith.[15]

The crisis years of the late 1540s were the context of some of Schütz Zell's most unusual public and most painful private writings. At Matthew Zell's funeral in January 1548 Martin Bucer preached to the gathered assembly in German and Latin. Katharina then stood up to speak to Matthew's weeping parishioners, recounting his ministry and death, repeating his teaching and exhorting his flock to follow his faith. Katharina's sermon expressed her own personal sorrow but, in face of the impending Interim, she subordinated her grief to her deep pastoral concern for the people she had served alongside Matthew for so many years. This text was not printed but continued to be copied and spread by her friends.[16] In private, her grief had a more penitential and painful expression as she worked her way through the Psalms, meditating and paraphrasing. Most of these personal notebooks disappeared without a trace, but in 1558 she made a selection of the Psalm texts (51 and 130) to share with other troubled souls seeking evidence of God's mercy in the midst of pain.[17]

Through the years Schütz Zell had corresponded with many reformers; the letter format was a common pattern of theological discourse. In 1543–5 she had unsuccessfully attempted to reconcile Schwenckfeld with Lutherans (in the person of Brenz) and Zwinglians (through Pellican and others).[18] In the 1550s she continued her epistolary efforts to bring differing followers of the gospel into accord, or at least to mutual tolerance. Her main opponent was Ludwig Rabus, her former foster son and Matthew's successor, but she also carried on a remarkable argument with Schwenckfeld and his Strasbourg disciples. While the argument with Rabus is well known, the evidence for the little-known conflict with Schwenckfeld is found in perhaps the single most intriguing piece of Schütz Zell's literary corpus,[19] the only extant letter from her to Schwenckfeld (all the other known texts are his to her). Dated October 19, 1553, this small treatise combined a courteous but blunt personal letter of friendly reproach with a defense of her religious integrity and independence vis-à-vis not only Strasbourg's Lutheran clergy but also against the possessive and intolerant demands of the city's Schwenckfelders. Effectively, Schütz Zell demonstrated her friendship and appreciation for Schwenckfeld as a colleague(!) of Luther, Zwingli, and Zell, from whom she was as glad to learn as she did from them. However, she also clearly but politely declared her independence; she will no more be his party follower than belong to the party of Rabus. Schütz Zell expounded her religious position with particular attention to the relationship between Christ as sole Savior (grace alone) and the human instruments that God uses to proclaim the gospel, and what respect is due to each. She explicitly rejected special or continuing inspiration; she "never saw, much less received, a single feather of the Holy Spirit"[20] – the Bible alone is authoritative.

Best known among Schütz Zell's writings is the epistolary controversy with Rabus. The latter was among the most outspoken Strasbourg adherents of the strict inter-pretation of the *Augsburg Confession* and all things Lutheran, and he was attacking from the pulpit not only Roman Catholics but also Schwenckfeld, then Zwingli and other Swiss, as well as Anabaptists.[21] To Matthew's widow, Rabus's polemic against fellow followers of the gospel was reprehensible, and she attempted to argue with him in private (c.1553–5) and then by personal letters (beginning in December 1555). Rabus was having none of this, and when late in 1556 he left Strasbourg to become the superintendent of the church at Ulm, departing secretly and without permission from Strasbourg's council, Schütz Zell took him to task in another long letter (March 1557). Rabus's rude response, calling her apostate, heretic, inspired by the devil, Schwenckfelder, Zwinglian, Anabaptist, and more, produced what for him must have been an unexpected and certainly an unwelcome effect. After some reflection, Schütz Zell decided that it was her duty to the truth, the first Reformers, and the people Rabus had served, to bring the whole matter to the church (Mt. 18:17).[22] In December 1557 she published their correspondence, with a long historical and theological refutation of his accusations. The text is not only a personal testimony but also an amazingly full and notably accurate history of the early Reformation in Strasbourg and beyond. Her *Letter to the City of Strasbourg* was reprinted in 1753 by a Swiss historian in a collection detailing the Swiss Reformation.[23]

Schütz Zell's final publication was a collection of devotional texts, some old, some new: *The Miserere Psalm, . . . and Lord's Prayer . . . for Sir Felix Armbruster* appeared in July 1558.[24] Along with her exposition of the Lord's Prayer from 1532 and a few of her personal meditations on the Psalms (from the late 1540s), she presented a most poignant and attractive pastoral letter to Sir Felix, expressing in mature fashion the consolations of the faith for those troubled in conscience because of the sufferings of this sinful and afflicted life.

Katharina Schütz Zell's literary corpus is diverse in genre, but the theology that it expresses is remarkably coherent and consistent from beginning to end, permeated by Scripture. It reflects the thought of an articulate, intelligent, confident, and responsible Christian.

Katharina Schütz Zell's Theology

It is helpful to begin a discussion of Katharina Schütz Zell's theology with a brief explanation of why she may be considered a Reformed theologian.

Schütz Zell's life as a Protestant spanned the most decisive years of the movement, from the early years of Luther's new preaching until the confessionalization process of the second half of the century was well underway. Her theology, however, forged in the fires of the 1520s, did not develop significantly. Thus as the world changed around her, Schütz Zell's position came to seem heretical to some members of the second generation. She had known and in some cases worked with most of the

German-speaking leaders of the first generation, virtually all of whom respected her as a devout and charitable follower of the gospel, even when they found her outspokenness rather trying and her generosity to those with whom they disagreed a kind of soft-headedness. Second-generation Protestants, though, often considered Schütz Zell a disciple of Schwenckfeld, and Rabus even called her an apostate because she did not adhere strictly to the *Augsburg Confession*. Schwenckfeld and his Strasbourg circle also claimed her, though some of them found her as unsatisfactory a follower as did the Lutherans, that is, she would not follow.

Schütz Zell herself refused any party designation. She defended Schwenckfeld as a faithful adherent of the gospel, a man of the first generation who (along with Zwingli, Oecolampadius, and others) was being unfairly attacked by other Protestants. However, on significant issues, such as the nature of religious authority, she clearly distanced herself from the spiritualist position; and she rejected the objective character of sacramental grace as expressed by the Lutherans. Although she has usually been regarded as a Schwenckfelder, in fact she is appropriately understood as a lay Protestant most closely identified with the Reformed tradition. Her thought can best be described as a biblical Protestantism, with a Reformed orientation in ecclesiology (ministry, sacraments, and church discipline) and ethics, nuanced by a lay Christian's distinctive focus on the importance of the priesthood of believers.[25]

The whole of Schütz Zell's theology was shaped by the classical Reformation watchwords: Christ alone, faith and grace alone, Scripture alone, and their corollary, the priesthood of believers. She explicitly identified the gospel with the affirmation of Christ as sole Savior, i.e., no works righteousness, no objective (mechanical) efficacy of the sacraments, no invocation of the saints; sin is unbelief, lack of trust in Christ. When she described the faith of the first-generation Protestants which she shared, she said they "all preached, taught, wrote, and confessed in writing and speaking, that Christ is the true Son of God and the sole savior, redeemer, and sanctification of human beings, against all false teaching which would give that [honor, power] to works, creatures, or elements."[26]

The basis of all religious authority is the Bible, through which the Holy Spirit spoke. This is to be read with intelligence and the aid of the best interpreters (i.e., the Reformers' early writings), although each Christian is responsible for her or his own study and judgment, not rote recitation or mindless parroting of the clergy. Schütz Zell rejected unequivocally all forms of scholasticism, including Protestant philosophical elaborations, as well as both Roman Catholic tradition and spiritualist reliance on continuing revelation. The Bible is the sole source of religious knowledge, and every Christian is responsible for learning and practicing, and then for teaching, the biblical faith.[27]

Schütz Zell understood that learning the faith is a corporate as well as a personal activity, and her ecclesiology is essentially Protestant with Reformed nuances. Unlike the Anabaptists, she was perfectly willing to have an established church, with civil authorities involved in calling clergy as well as ordering practical affairs. She had a great respect for the ordained or learned ministry of the church (she commonly called them *Gelerten*, which has a slight but useful ambiguity), as long as the clergy taught only the Bible. This meant preaching only biblical content; such preaching must refute the errors of trust in human traditions or individual revelations, but not attack fellow followers of the gospel over differences of opinion on secondary matters. In her exposition of the Lord's Prayer, Schütz Zell described a good pastor as she prayed for daily bread:

> Dear Father, give us also wise, faithful preachers, who are faithful stewards: who do not preach the inclinations of their own hearts but proclaim Your Word opened to us out of Your mouth through Jesus Christ, and who spread forth the appropriate food in the right time. . . . Grant them peace in themselves and unity with each other, and a common understanding of Your truth.[28]

The disunity among theologians was particularly acute on the doctrine of the sacraments.

Schütz Zell seems to have considered the precise definition of the sacraments a secondary issue, so long as one did not return to the old errors of trusting a mechanical grace and the eucharistic elements rather than Christ. She maintained a strong polemic against emergency baptism and trust in the objective rite, which she described as a form of unbelief, and she criticized sharply the unbiblical ceremonies which had traditionally accompanied the act and which Rabus was reintroducing. Emergency baptism was also a pastoral problem, since the fate of unbaptized babies was a particular concern for women, as Schütz Zell knew very well. Her primary critique focused on Catholic views of baptism, but there is no evidence that she ever questioned the appropriateness and value of baptism as an ecclesiastical rite or of infant baptism in particular.[29]

With regard to the Lord's Supper the situation was quite similar: a vigorous polemic against Roman errors, especially as readopted by second-generation Protestants, combined with a positive interpretation somewhat like that of Zwingli (or rather, the Luther of the 1520 treatises), with perhaps echoes of Bucer. In the same text that describes the petition for daily bread, Schütz Zell prayed for fellowship with Christ in the Supper:

> Grant . . . that we also may be worthy to come together to hold the memorial of Your love and the obedience of Jesus Christ, to break the bread and to drink the cup of thanksgiving, to be fed in His remembrance, that it may be the fellowship of the body and blood of Jesus Christ for the forgiveness of our sins, in the communion of the saints; and thus to hold a living memorial of His death and to proclaim it until He comes again, there [in the Supper] truly to confess that His body is there given and broken for us and the record of our sins against us is wiped out and hung on the cross.[30]

The following passage emphasizes the connection between the Supper, self-dedication, and love of the neighbor:

> [Thus] we will also be kindled in burning love and hold the living memorial and communion in Jesus Christ with our fellow believers, and also willingly give ourselves to obedience to the cross, to suffer all things with Christ: abuse, exile, poverty, and death. Also as Christ there gave Himself for us and set His soul to death for us, so

also we may offer ourselves for all people and brothers, Your disciples our brothers and sisters, in their accidents, exile, poverty, sickness, and all need, to stand by them, counsel and help them out of sin, poverty, exile, and all affliction, with our goods, honor, body, and life. . . .[31]

The lay theologian had a clear sense of sacramental fellowship, but she did not consider the variations among Lutheran or Zwinglian (or Schwenckfelder) views of the sacraments sufficient grounds for breaking the bond of love and fellowship, much less persecuting others.

Schütz Zell had considerable appreciation for a life that manifested faith in practice in both personal and corporate spheres. She admired the moral strictness of the "Baptists" and advocated and modeled an austere lifestyle of firm self-discipline, including a sharp criticism of worldliness and self-indulgence of any kind. Like others in Strasbourg, the Zells also valued church discipline, applying it mostly to ethical matters but also considering it appropriate for issues of doctrine. Schütz Zell herself faithfully followed the procedure of Matthew 18:15–18 in her dealings with Rabus, addressing him first repeatedly in private and then in the presence of a mutual friend, before she finally felt obliged to take the matter "to the church" (Mt. 18:17). The sturdy lay reformer also expected this adherence to Christ's teaching from others.[32]

For both of the Zells but perhaps especially for Katharina, the role of love for the neighbor – defined according to the parable of the Good Samaritan – was a major theological tenet, set alongside the central Reformation affirmations. The lay reformer never seems to have seen any contradiction between biblical law and gospel, only between human laws and traditions and the gospel. The insistence on Christ–faith–grace alone, and the commandment to love and serve her neighbor as herself, naturally went together. The gospel must not be sacrificed; it is worth breaking fellowship with Rome over unbiblical teaching. However, differences of understanding on the sacraments or church order are worth arguing about but not sufficient reason to break fellowship. And even those with whom one does not have fellowship should not be persecuted; they deserve the love of Good Samaritans.[33]

There were some distinctive characteristics of Schütz Zell's theology, especially as regards the responsibilities of Christians as witnesses for the truth. Three strands in her thought can be distinguished. One has to do with the qualifications for and practice of public teaching, a second concerns the task of non-official leaders in rebuking ordained clergy, and a third develops a rather convincing biblical argument for the duty of any Christian to defend the truth by speaking out.

Every Christian is obligated to teach the gospel as well as she or he can; the criterion for being able to teach is biblical knowledge (and its practice). It is thus quite logical that Schütz Zell supported a learned ministry for the public preaching of the gospel. While recognizing that this is usually an ordained office, and that St. Paul restricted ordination to men, the lay woman reformer believed that the principal qualification for ministry is knowledge and faithful practice. Thus she could support public teaching by women and other laity if they were properly learned in Scripture. Biblical knowledge is not based on a university education and philosophy:

however, it definitely involves a learned content and not mere parroting of Scripture; it presupposes a study of the Bible informed by the best interpreters and a spirit of faith and humility. The aged widow Anna of Acts 2:36–8, who welcomed the infant Jesus and proclaimed God's kingdom, was Schütz Zell's key biblical example. Her thinking on this subject was essentially that of the Protestant Reform movement, rejecting human traditions and personal inspiration in favor of biblical content read through Protestant spectacles. She differed from other Protestants in her view of how learning may be acquired (a university education and Latin are not necessary) and thus who may be candidates for this office. She was too biblical, however, to disregard the Pauline strictures on women's roles (e.g., 1 Cor. 14:34), and thus she did not argue for the ordination of women.[34]

Preaching by lay Christians became a more precise or situational obligation if the ordained clergy failed to carry out their duty. Like other early Protestants, Schütz Zell believed firmly that when clergy do not do their proper task they may and should be rebuked by those not officially ordained. For the Strasbourg lay theologian, this rebuke did not involve additional religious content but focussed essentially on recalling the leaders to their appointed duties. Her biblical examples included Judith's reprimand of the elders of Israel (Jth. 7:29ff, 8:11ff) and Balaam's ass (Nm. 22), and once, Christ's words about the stones crying out (Lk. 19:40), although the last instance seems the least favored, apparently because stones are inanimate.[35]

Schütz Zell's third and most distinctive contribution to the debates about public speaking by Christians was in fact the first to appear and the most universal in application. It also weaves together her understanding the biblical "gospel" and the love of the neighbor in a fascinating way. For this creative lay theologian, every Christian who hears the biblical truth being contradicted or slandered is obligated to defend the truth and set the record straight, as a confession of faith and act of love for the neighbor. Defending the truth is necessary to honor God's teaching in the Bible and to clear one's conscience of the charge of participating in lies. One must not put stumbling blocks before the simple (Lk. 17:1–2), but must make sure they have access to the Word and thus to faith (Rom. 10:17). On the basis of Christ's example (Jn. 18:22–3) one must speak out, at the price of suffering, in order not to support falsehood by silence. Speaking out is an expression of love for one's neighbors (Lv. 19:18). It is love for the deceived, telling them the truth so that they may know it and be saved; it is love for the deceivers: love tells them their falsehood so that they may have the opportunity to repent.[36]

The three clearly distinct though related theories about the Christian obligation to witness for the gospel truth, along with her insistence on locating that witness squarely in the midst of ordinary life, are the most vivid evidence for Schütz Zell's characteristic views as a lay theologian. It is helpful to note a corollary, the way she thinks about the relationship of women and men and about feminine imagery. In simplest fashion, it can be said that she does not appear to privilege men or women in the gospel; all are held to an equal accountability and praised in similar fashion for Christian faith and practice. Unlike some women pamphleteers, Schütz Zell never used any self-deprecating language (except in rare irony). She seems to have had a strong sense of confidence in her own voice as a knowledgeable Christian teacher, a confidence which made her unselfconscious in addressing men as well as women and children. While many of her biblical examples are women, she also likened herself – and occasionally other women – to male figures in Scripture. On occasion she also appropriated maternal imagery for Christ and sometimes for the male clergy. For Schütz Zell, there are ranks in the Christian community but these are primarily spiritual ranks: greater and lesser knowledge and faithful practice of the biblical gospel, not male or female, noble or commoner. The priesthood of believers does not mean that everyone is identical but that everyone is called to the same confession and shares the same obligations.[37]

Conclusion

Katharina Schütz Zell was an unusual Reformation theologian. Clearly very biblical, and Protestant in her biblicism, she affirmed the central *solus/solae*. Within those bounds, however, she was a very inclusive thinker, distrusting the importance accorded to increasingly fine theological distinctions such as the nature of Christ's presence in the Lord's Supper.[38] She was able to define her own stance and recognize some major differences among her fellow Protestants, but she did not consider disagreement on secondary issues such as church order worth breaking the bond of peace. Doctrinal theology was vitally important; to uphold the teaching of justification by Christ and faith alone it was plainly worth breaking with Rome. Christian ethical theology and practice were also vitally important; love of the neighbor and generosity to fellow followers of the gospel were equally worth defending, even at the expense of arguments with "the dear Luther" and being ostracized by the second generation.

No individualist but a strong individual, the lay reformer Katharina Schütz Zell learned gladly, but she also made theology her own and gave it a distinctive expression when she in turn taught others, men as well as women and children. Though her influence was more restricted than that of most of the well-known male reformers, the Strasbourg lay woman certainly taught and wrote more than many ordained preachers of her day. Her work provides one of the best illustrations of how the gospel was creatively appropriated and expressed in the lives of intelligent and dedicated lay Christians. Her theology also expresses a freshness and vivid excitement that convey even today something of the wonder and liberation, the power and appeal of the gospel preaching in the 1520s.

> Since I was ten years old I have been a church mother, a supporter of pulpit and school. . . . Since however my distress about the kingdom of heaven grew great, and in all my hard works, worship, and great pain of body, from all the clergy I could not find or achieve any comfort or certainty of the love and grace of God, I became weak and sick to death in soul and body. . . . Then God had mercy on us and many people, He awakened and sent out by tongue and writings the dear and now blessed Dr. Martin Luther, who described the Lord Jesus Christ for me and others in such

a lovely way that I thought I had been drawn up out of the depths of the earth, yes, out of grim bitter hell, into the sweet lovely kingdom of heaven. So that I thought of the word which the Lord Christ said to Peter: "I will make you a fisher of people. . . ."[39]

Notes

1   The major source for this article is Elsie Anne McKee, *Katharina Schütz Zell: Volume One: The Life and Thought of a Sixteenth-Century Reformer* (Leiden: E. J. Brill, 1999), hereafter cited as *KSZ: Life and Thought*. The source for some specific references is Elsie Anne McKee, *Katharina Schütz Zell: Volume Two: The Writings, A Critical Edition* (Leiden: E. J. Brill, 1999), hereafter cited as *KSZ: Writings*, with abbreviated titles of individual works. This theologian is usually known as Katharine Zell, under which name she published in later life. In Strasbourg, according to early modern custom, she was often known as Katharina Schütz, under which name she published for a time, even after her marriage. To distinguish her from her husband Matthew Zell and to honor the two ways she was known in her own day, I have adopted "Schütz Zell" as a surname for the adult Reformer.

2   For her self-understanding as "church mother" see *KSZ: Life and Thought*, 465ff. For childhood and conversion, see ibid., chs. 1–2.

3   For the designation "fisher of people" (Lk. 5:10), see *KSZ: Life and Thought*, 440. For life with Zell, see ibid., chs. 3–4.

4   There were several titles which KSZ claimed or considered attributed to her by others; she saw herself as "fellow worker" with the first Strasbourg Reformers, and said that Zell had called her his "wedded companion" (in the gospel), "mother to the poor and exiled," and (most impressive) "assistant minister" (*Helffer*). See *KSZ: Life and Thought*, 441ff. for Zell's names; 451ff. for "fellow worker."

5   See *KSZ: Life and Thought*, 318ff.

6   See *KSZ: Life and Thought*, 77; KSZ invited the genial Roman Catholic Jacques von Gottesheim to dinner in order to argue theology with him!

7   See *KSZ: Life and Thought*, 288ff. for her learning from the Reformers, 453ff. for her views of them and theirs of her; see also index of proper names.

8   For her participation in conversation, see *KSZ: Writings, Ein Brieff*, 170:22ff., 275:11ff.; example of Hagenau, see *KSZ: Life and Thought*, 105f.

9   See *KSZ: Life and Thought*, 324, 254f., 318ff.; 56f., 77f., 135f.

10   See *KSZ: Life and Thought*, 130ff.; for image of weeds replanted, see *KSZ: Writings, Ein Brieff*, 192:22–193:3.

11   See *KSZ: Writings*. For the circumstances surrounding each publication see the individual introductions; for KSZ's literary style, see *KSZ: Life and Thought*, 337ff.

12   See *KSZ: Writings*, 15ff. Full title: *Entschuldigung Katharina Schützinn/für M. Matthes Zellen/jren Eegemahel/der ein Pfarrher und dyener ist im wort Gottes zuo Strassburg. Von wegen grosser lügen uff jn erdiecht* [Strasbourg, 1524]. Designated *Entschuldigung*.

13   See *KSZ: Writings*, 1ff. Full title: *Den leydenden Christglaubigen weyberen der gmein zuo Kentzigen minen mitschwestern in Christo Jesu zuo handen* [Strasbourg, July 1524]. Second ed., November 1524 at Augsburg, the only one of KSZ's texts republished in her lifetime.

14   Published in text designated *Den Psalmen*, see below, n. 24.

15   See *KSZ: Writings*, 55ff. Full title of the first fascicle: *Von Christo Jesu unserem säligmacher/einer Menschwerdung/Geburt/Beschneidung/etc. etlich Christliche und trostliche Lobgsäng/auss einem vast herrlichen Gsangbuoch gezogen/Von welchem inn der Vorred weiter anzeygt würdt.* Strasbourg, 1534–6 [preface signed 1534, last fascicles published 1536]. For analysis and translation of preface, see Elsie Anne McKee, *Reforming Popular Piety in Sixteenth-Century Strasbourg: Katharina Schütz Zell and Her Hymnbook*, Studies in Reformed Theology and History 2:4 (Princeton: Princeton Theological Seminary, 1994).

16   See *KSZ: Writings*, 65ff. Full title: *Klag red und ermahnung Catharina Zellin zum volk*

bey dem grab m: Matheus Zellen pfarer zum münster zu Strassburg/dess frommen mannss/ bey und über seinen todten leib. Den 11. january 1548.

17 Published in *Den Psalmen*, see below, n. 24.

18 See *KSZ: Life and Thought*, 109ff.

19 See *KSZ: Writings*, 115ff. Designated *1553 Letter*.

20 See *KSZ: Writings, 1553 Letter*, 127:21–128:1.

21 See *KSZ: Writings*, 155ff. Full title: *Ein Brieff an die gantze Burgerschafft der Statt Strassburg/ von Katharina Zellin/dessen jetz säligen Matthei Zellen/dess alten und ersten Predigers des Evangelij diser Statt/nachgelassne Ehefraw/Betreffend Herr Ludwigen Rabus/jetz ein Prediger der Statt Ulm/sampt zweyen brieffen jr und sein/ die mag mengklich lesen und urtheilen on gunst und hasss/sonder allein der war heit warnemen. Dabey auch ein sanffte antwort/auff jeden Artickel/seines brieffs* [Strasbourg], 1557. Designated *Ein Brieff*. [Editor's note: For Rabus see Robert Kolb, *For All the Saints: Changing Perceptions of Martyrdom and Saint-hood in the Lutheran Reformation* (Macon: Mercer University Press, 1987).]

22 Argument explained in *KSZ: Life and Thought*, 400ff.

23 J. C. Füsslin, *Briefwechsel Frauen Catharina Zellin von Strassburg und Herrn Ludwig Rabus, Superintendenten zu Ulm*, in *Beyträge zur Erläuterung der Kirchen-Reformations-Geschichte des Schweitzerlandes*, 5. Theil. (Zürich, 1753), 151–354. Füsslin alters the order of the letters, omits the connecting material between them, changes the orthography, and makes a few errors of transcription.

24 See *KSZ: Writings*, 305ff. Full title: *Den Psalmen Miserere/mit dem Khünig David bedacht/ gebettet/und paraphrasirt von Katharina Zellin M. Matthei Zellen seligen nachgelassne Ehefraw/ sampt dem Vatter unser mit seiner erklärung/ zuogeschickt dem Christlichen mann Juncker Felix Armbruster/zum trost in seiner krankheit/ und andern angefochtenen hertzen und Concientzen/der sünd halben betrüebt &c. in truck lassen kommen* [Strasbourg, 1558]. Designated *Den Psalmen*.

25 See *KSZ: Life and Thought*, ch. 9 (biblical knowledge), ch. 10 (central Protestant doctrines), ch. 11 (practical theology–piety).

26 *KSZ: Writings, Ein Brieff*, 269:19–23. For discussion of *solus/solae* see *KSZ: Life and Thought*, 266ff.

27 See *KSZ: Life and Thought*, ch. 9, especially 233ff. on the nature of religious knowledge.

28 *KSZ: Writings, Den Psalmen*, 354:29–34, 355:10–12. For discussion of ministry, see *KSZ: Life and Thought*, 280ff.

29 For baptism, see *KSZ: Life and Thought*, 278f.

30 *KSZ: Writings, Den Psalmen*, 356:27–357:4. For discussion of Lord's Supper see *KSZ: Life and Thought*, 275ff.

31 *KSZ: Writings, Den Psalmen*, 357:4–14.

32 See *KSZ: Life and Thought*, 284ff., 335f., 400ff., 472.

33 See *KSZ: Life and Thought*, 318ff.

34 See *KSZ: Life and Thought*, 407ff. It is notable that KSZ's argument for women preaching is not based on the typical biblical texts such as Gal. 3:28 and Jl. 2:28/Acts 2:17. Especially the last pair is foreign to her way of thinking, and is used only once as a counter to 1 Cor. 14:34 without in fact being the grounds for KSZ's own argument. Her use of prooftexts confirms the lay theologian's unusual position in rejecting special inspiration as a religious authority.

35 See *KSZ: Life and Thought*, 403ff.

36 See *KSZ: Life and Thought*, 398ff. This argument is first and most clearly put forward in the *Entschuldigung* in 1524, but another version of the same theory is the basis for her publication of the correspondence with Rabus in *Ein Brieff* in 1557.

37 For an overview of KSZ's understanding of women in the Christian faith and feminine imagery for Christ, see *KSZ: Life and Thought*, 377ff.

38 She probably did not understand such philosophical issues as whether or not Christ was a creature, points which divided Schwenckfeld from most Protestants, but she also did not regard philosophy as important; the language of scripture was sufficient. See *KSZ: Life and Thought*, 109ff.

39 *KSZ: Writings, Ein Brieff*, 170:20–2, 170:27–171:5, 15–22.

Bibliography

Primary Source

McKee, Elsie Anne, *Katharina Schütz Zell: Volume Two: The Writings, A Critical Edition*. Studies in Medieval and Reformation Thought 69, 2, Leiden: E. J. Brill, 1999. [A selection of English translations is in process.]

Secondary Sources

Jung, Martin, "Katharina Zell geb. Schütz (1497/98–1562): Eine 'Laientheologin' der Reformationszeit?," *Zeitschrift für Kirchengeschichte* 107/2 (1996), 145–78.

McKee, Elsie Anne, *Reforming Popular Piety in Sixteenth-Century Strasbourg: Katharina Schütz Zell and Her Hymnbook*, Studies in Reformed Theology and History 2:4, Princeton: Princeton Theological Seminary, 1994.

——, *Katharina Schütz Zell: Volume One: The Life and Thought of a Sixteenth-Century Reformer*, Studies in Medieval and Reformation Thought 69, 1, Leiden: E. J. Brill, 1999.

Wolff, Anne, "Le recueil de cantiques de Catherine Zell, 1534–1536," 2 vols., Mémoire de Maîtrise, Université des Sciences Humaines de Strasbourg, Institut d'Etudes Allemandes, 1986.

Thomas Cranmer (1489–1556)

Peter Newman Brooks

In a neglected exchange between Norfolk and Suffolk found in Act III, Scene 2 of the *Famous History of the Life of King Henry VIII*, William Shakespeare offered Cranmer historiography a rare gem:

> *Norfolk*: This same Cranmer's
> A worthy fellow, and hath ta'en much pain
> In the King's business.
> *Suffolk*: He has; and we shall see him
> For it an archbishop.

No mere allusion of late sixteenth-century drama, the bard's insight, because it effectively summarized the primate's loyalty to the Tudor crown, has endured. Even in the wake of the quincentenary (1989), the scholar-diplomat Henry secured to serve him at Canterbury, and the churchman who survived court faction to stand as godfather to Edward VI and remain England's chief pastor is still remembered more as a faithful flunkey than for any theological prowess.

It has taken almost five centuries for church historians to begin to appreciate sixteenth-century reformations as a three-dimensional world.[1] For much of that time *odium theologicum* had shrouded a wide-ranging period and full cast of otherwise colorful characters. Cranmer illustrates the point well, and up to the middle of the last century was invariably regarded as a shameful, pathetic figure whose political ambition obliged him to yield to the every whim of Henry VIII. Had the wretched archbishop been numbered among Holbein's famous spectrum of sensitive Tudor subjects, the primate's very portrait would no doubt have been interpreted as that of a sycophant, a cowardly prelate cringing at shadows and fearful lest the headsman's axe should some day fall his way. In this context, Shakespeare's play can be remarkably instructive. First there is focus on Wolsey's abuse, and then on Cranmer's use, of royal authority. The Cardinal's "*Ego et Rex meus*" (III.ii) certainly highlights the contrast with Cranmer's:

It is my duty
To attend your highness' pleasure. (V.i)

It is precisely the detailed exercise of such duty and deference to "the godly prince" that explains Cranmer and provides keys historians must use to unlock and make sense of the Tudor primate's life and work in a crowded, controversial career. The theological development of the man has a particular fascination. This is not only because such ideological progress runs in parallel with Cranmer's rise and fall from power; but also for an almost staged progression in spiritual pilgrimage unique among divines who embraced the so-called "new religion." From his grounding in what Ralph Morice famously termed "the grossest kynd of sophistry" to his ultimate embrace of the advanced views held by "Protestants" forwarding a radical "evangelical" cause, Thomas Cranmer thus provides every scope as frustrating as it is fruitful.

At Cambridge – in addition to the traditional grounding in logic – Cranmer's studies included the classics as well as an introduction to philosophy, a subject he evidently valued more than Luther, to judge from extensive *marginalia* on Scotist material David Selwyn lists in an accession of his early theology library.[2] Proceeding Bachelor of Arts in 1511, the young Jesus College scholar had still some way to go before being able to read theology as a postgraduate discipline. Instead the university's revised curriculum introduced him to mathematics and music before, the residence qualification fulfilled, he became Master of Arts in 1515. The tragic interlude of his first marriage then postponed *Magister* Cranmer's introduction to theology still further. But once welcomed back to a fellowship at Jesus College, he found himself well placed to study the scriptures in depth when the statutes of that new foundation (1496) gave the "queen of the sciences" priority over canon law as the rival postgraduate discipline.

Made priest on the title of his fellowship, the 1520s saw Cranmer living the life of a don in holy orders, and although open to the latest fashions in Early Modern learning, there seems no reason to suppose an approved preacher of the university dabbled in heresy. Rather does such status suggest orthodoxy and acceptance by the establishment. Erasmian philology certainly encouraged his biblical studies, but as Diarmaid MacCulloch has argued from the evidence of more *marginalia* – this time Cranmer's notes on the refutation of Martin Luther set out by Fisher in his *Confutatio* (1523) – he is better viewed as a "papalist" than one who showed sympathy for those who debated the new opinions in the inner bar parlor of Foxe's White Horse hostelry.[3] At such an early date it was in any case likely that members of such a semi-heretical cell discussed the latest satire of Erasmus and not Lutheran doctrine at all.

Accordingly, at his genesis Cranmer was, in MacCulloch's comprehensive phrase, "a secular priest and academic of a conventionally traditional, if humanist, cast of mind."[4] Basic biblical scholarship secured his recognition as divinity examiner in the Schools; and his respect for Erasmus related more to philological emphases – that scholarly trek back to, and interpretation of, scriptural texts – than any root-and-branch repudiation of the *via dialectica*. Nor did this approach to learning leave him. For if Luther, in his classic controversy with Erasmus on the human will, urged *propositio, oppositio, solutio* in the hallowed approach of medieval debate, Cranmer was later to do likewise in the *cause célèbre* over the Eucharist, and in the fateful

1554 disputation at Oxford.[5] Old habits die hard, and the probability is, in these misty fenland Cambridge days, Dr. Thomas Cranmer, albeit as open-minded as any academic has to be, was a very conservative don indeed.

To the historian, the next stage in Cranmer's career – a progress itself inextricably intertwined with the developing theology of the man – registers almost more as fiction than fact. For by any standards this was extraordinary for the way regular academic routines were quite suddenly changed for the largely unpredictable crises of court life. Headhunted by Wolsey's talent scouts, a range of rising Cambridge stars were lured from the fens to found Cardinal College, Oxford, just as others, including Cranmer, found their way into the diplomatic service. Stephen Ryle's spectacular discovery of the two earliest letters that survive from Cranmer's pen provided evidence MacCulloch has used to effect in a biographical breakthrough constituting the principal advance of his recent, monumental study.[6] For the present purpose such details unquestionably infringe the offside rule, however much they also serve to explain how, when the king's "privy matter" had discredited Wolsey to dominate English diplomacy, such a loyal servant was already within the royal orbit.

Returning to Cambridge at midsummer, Cranmer, according to MacCulloch, busied himself with a twofold task. For if he gave priority to his responsibilities as University examiner, from 1527 he was increasingly drawn into the king's "Great Matter," working away "as an advocate of the royal case."[7] Wolsey's failure to secure papal support would soon lead to royal repudiation of Roman legalism; and at the same time that anxious supporters sought new counsel that might console their king, Stephen Gardiner and Edward Foxe chanced to meet Cranmer at Waltham. Plague had prompted the cautious Jesus College don to stay there with the Cressy family as tutor to their boys, and at dinner the idea of canvassing university opinion was discussed. Where canon law had failed, could theology succeed? Cranmer clearly deemed it worth a bid; and on return from such a secluded summer seminar, Gardiner and Foxe drew their Cambridge colleague into the royal web. By the fall, Cranmer had met Henry again, and was soon engaged in full-time research to afford the royal cause every possible academic support. Much grist to the mill here was the way Cranmer noted that certain findings of early Councils of the church stood opposed to papal authority, a realization that in its turn warmed him more to patristic authority than to medieval philosophy and legalism.

From a London base at Durham Place, Cranmer was now very much the protegé of the Boleyns, and it was with the entourage of Thomas Boleyn, earl of Wiltshire (from 1529) that he returned to mainland Europe in 1530. If the plan was to gain imperial favor – Charles V was to be crowned by the pope at Bologna – Clement VII effectively thwarted this by forbidding Henry VIII to take a new queen, and then summoned the English king to Rome to answer for himself. And to Rome Cranmer went, briefed both to monitor developments, as well as to recruit further university opinion for the cause. On August 4, 1530, clearly desirous of an outcome determined by debate and conscience rather than by influence and "retainers," Clement sanctioned inquiry into the Tudor dilemma. For the Curia was evidently aware of the scandalous way bribes were influencing opinion at Bologna, Ferrara, and Padua! Cranmer returned to London towards the end of October, his principal objective frustrated. Even so, his diplomatic experience had been enlarged, and like Luther before him he had gained firsthand knowledge of papal procedures. How logical then, that, as a key part of his research into the royal cause, Cranmer began to collect canon law *catena* focussed on supremacy claims of particular relevance to the age-old issue of *regnum versus sacerdotium* and to do so in a way which, in summary at least, favored royal opposition to papal claims.[8] A parallel task saw Cranmer delving into Scripture and the early fathers in search of opinion favorable to the king. Although but a team member in such an undertaking, he had already begun to distance himself from Roman doctrine, a development eagerly noted by the visiting Basel reformer Grynaeus when he reported back to Strasbourg where Bucer was "consistently sympathetic with the problems of Henrician England."[9]

From this background, Cranmer emerged (in January 1532) for further European service proceeding on embassy to the court of Charles V. In March the emperor was at Regensburg, and that summer the Diet moved to Nuremberg, an imperial city which had declared for Luther. There Pastor Osiander, in marked contrast to Dr Martinus of Wittenberg, had written a tract favorable to Henry VIII's dilemma over the "divorce." *En passant*, too, the good pastor recorded that Cranmer had visited his home "conversing on much in earnest, yet with wisdom and inspiration, concerning Christian faith and true religion."[10] The Nuremberg visit certainly afforded Cranmer firsthand experience of both the faith and practice of the new "Protestant" religion. That such Lutheranism made a real impression is evident also from a bold flouting of western canon law when, that summer, Cranmer chose to marry Margarethe, Osiander's wife's niece, the pastor in all probability officiating at their nuptials. Clerical status denied Roman priests this right, and such a solemn slip made two points of practical theology clear. First, Cranmer's genuine conviction that scriptural support could trump canon-law prohibition; and secondly that he already valued a new biblical theology and found himself opposed to any enforcement of clerical celibacy. For its focus on papal prohibitions and their rejection, Cranmer's apéritif to the main course of a revised theological understanding is unique. But when Rome no longer posed a threat – particularly after the Tudor monarch had secured bulls for one who, on the death of William Warham, became in a very special sense Henry's archbishop (1533) – Cranmer had every opportunity to immerse himself in the new theology his skills would use to bring gradual reform to the English church.

Any attempt to chart Cranmer's development in the mid-1530s will always be clouded with confusion. It is tempting to draw an analogy between his flirtation with Margarethe, and with the scriptural fundamentals according to Luther discussed with Osiander as he prepared for matrimony at Nuremberg. For he would have valued Luther's teaching both for its biblical base, and for the fact that Wittenberg had adopted an anti-papal stance. Yet it is unlikely that Cranmer underwent any kind of Damascene conversion in these years. Rather was he molded by events which in their turn influenced his developing theology. As primate of all England he clearly had reservations about papal supremacy from the start, at his consecration qualifying the traditional canonical oath to Rome with another in language giving clear priority to God's law and homage to the King:

> I, Thomas Cranmer, renounce and utterly forsake all such clauses, words, sentences, and grants, which I have of the pope's holiness in his bulls of the archbishoprick of

Canterbury, that in any manner was, is, or may be hurtful, or prejudicial to your highness, your heirs, successors, estate, or dignity royal: knowledging myself to take and hold the said archbishoprick immediately, and only, of your highness, and of none other.[11]

Raised to Canterbury when Elton's "revolution in Tudor government" was proceeding apace, Cranmer was obliged to show loyalty in full measure! With amazing deference he thus begged leave "to proceed to the examination, final determination, and judgement in the said great cause, touching Your Highness" (Henry, having secretly married Anne Boleyn, was now in a hurry); and likewise succumbed to royal supremacy over the English church. Not that it was any longer deemed heresy to criticize papal authority, for a final Act of what historians now term the "Reformation Parliament" extinguished the pontiff's sway and reduced all popes to the ranks as mere "bishops of Rome." The constitutional changes that subjected two provinces of the medieval western church to the supremacy of the king in Parliament likewise gave Thomas Cromwell sway (as vicar-general or vice-gerent) to challenge archiepiscopal authority at every level. Nor did Cranmer object to such reordering, for when Gardiner sniped at his superior in 1535, the archbishop at once informed Cromwell that "my style . . . '*Totius Angliae Primas*' [was] to the derogation and prejudice of the king's high power and authority, being supreme head of the church."[12] In short, the newly consecrated primate set no more store by the style and title of his office than he did "by paring of an apple, farther than it shall be to the setting forth of God's word and will."[13] For him it was now fundamental for genuine bishops to be termed *apostolos Jesu Christi*, a conviction that gave greater weight to the claims of pastoral ministry than to any grandiose ranking traditionally linked to their prelacy. For a theologian, this was entirely compatible with the Pauline doctrine of the godly prince (so recently revived by the tract on temporal authority, *Von weltlicher Oberkeit*, that Luther had written in 1523), an ideology echoing the tune called by Tudor doctrines of supremacy. It was certainly the case that Cranmer analyzed such basics from his grasp of Scripture and the judgments of the Councils and Fathers of the early church. Yet how far was he able to urge his private belief and commitment on clerical colleagues, let alone on the supreme head who, now rid of the papal albatross, was determined that his English church should continue in orthodoxy and uphold traditional Catholic doctrine? Without due caution such a personal dilemma for the primate must rapidly assume the proportions of a Gilbertian "how-de-do," to become not only "a state of things" but the "pretty mess" of *Mikado*!

The European background to the isolation of Henry's English church has long intrigued historians. Hitherto much has been made of the way Tudor diplomacy, in awe of the formidable power bloc posed by the emperor, France, and Rome itself, began to flirt with the Schmalkald League as if to seek support from German and Scandinavian states Lutheran in solidarity. But the latest research makes much of the fact that "a third element in Continental evangelicalism at this time began to make itself felt within England."[14] This influence came from the South German (or "Upper Rhineland") and Swiss Reformations where theologians such as Bucer, Sturm, and Capito in Strasbourg, Grynaeus and Oecolampadius in Basel, Zwingli and Bullinger in Zurich, and von Watt (Vadianus) in St. Gall had all moved beyond Luther's obdurate conservatism, particularly in matters sacramental. United by their concern to forward and widen the cause of Reformation, such theologians actively sought to influence the English situation. But loyal to the godly prince as a primate fully involved in the high affairs of Henry's state, Cranmer rarely revealed his hand. And when he did, conflicting signals were registered in his correspondence. If the "moderate Catholic humanism"[15] of the 1520s was now clearly behind him, despite a written admission in a letter to von Watt (1537) that he had seen "almost everything written . . . by Oecolampad. or Zwingli," Cranmer insisted on the need to be choosy and make intelligent judgments in theology.[16] And it comes as no surprise that he fell back on the "authority of the ancient doctors and first writers in the Church of Christ."[17] A year earlier, a first-fruits formulary of the faith of Henry's church – the Ten Articles of 1536 – fell in behind Luther's understanding for its focus on the three gospel sacraments. In 1537, the *Bishops' Book* also gave priority to Christ's own institution over any rites derived from hallowed ecclesiastical tradition. No wonder, with penance in mind, R. W. Dixon would not rule out "a secret infusion of Lutheranism" in the Formulary.[18] Above all, this was the time – MacCulloch thinks "certainly . . . no later than 1538" – when Cranmer set about compiling his massive *Commonplaces*, immersing himself not only in patristic cullings, but also in the late-night final controversies of reformation in Europe. Such *catena*, collected with the aid of chaplain secretaries from many a banned book sent across by Osiander, could counter or enhance the new theology and concentrate a developing mind on fundamentals.[19]

If, many years ago, the present writer made a bid to interpret a range of eucharistic material in these *Commonplaces*, more recent research by a perceptive pupil, this time focussed on penance, has both strengthened earlier findings and forwarded frontiers to take in new areas of fascination. Not only has Ashley Null redirected attention to the overall significance of justification in this context to urge that the "crucial issue of the Reformation – indeed of Christianity itself – was how sins are forgiven,"[20] but he has also shown how in the mid-1540s Cranmer's Protestant probings reached a new stage in certainty and repudiated reactionary arguments in the *King's Book* (1543). For if that Formulary redefined sacramental ideas to make them at least patient of "the new religion" in reforming passages of the *Bishops' Book* – in particular the argument that good works could enhance and ornament saving faith and in some measure qualify salvation as God's free gift to needy sinners – Cranmer used both Paul and Augustine to spotlight the uniqueness of a conversion experience altogether distinct from traditional sacramental practice in the day-to-day routines of church life. In short, from this time the *sola gratia*, *sola fide* principle was as central to the archbishop's own theological understanding as it had already become to those committed to reformation on the European mainland. In time such private convictions would be upheld in public, respect for Henry's traditionalism alone holding Cranmer back. Nor was such deference to his king demeaning, if only because in microcosm that very deference itself reflected the archbishop's higher loyalty to Almighty God.

In the 1540s there were occasions when Cranmer appeared to be "an almost powerless puppet,"[21] and but for the confidence of the king, the primate could scarcely have survived, let alone succeeded in any *grand dessein* for reformation of the English church. In lighter vein, it was as if his renowned equestrian expertise gave Cranmer the skill to ride Tudor court faction through threatening years when charged as "the greatest heretic in Kent." Be that as it may, much had been achieved, the archbishop's *Preface* to the so-called *Great Bible* (first set out in the second impression of 1540) indicated his commitment to reformation with all possible clarity. When informed of Cromwell's success in securing the publication of Holy Scripture in the English vernacular, the archbishop rejoiced, and in a letter to the vice-gerent assured Cromwell that the news had given him "more pleasure . . . than if you had given me a thousand pound."[22] Commending the Scriptures in language intended to make the widest appeal, Cranmer emphasized that fact that "this book . . . is the word of God, the most precious jewel, and most holy relic that remaineth upon earth."[23] Such words served not only to preface the *Great Bible,* but also proclaimed the scriptural base of Cranmer's life and work in liturgical revision, eucharistic debate and the pastoral priorities which denote the final stage of the archbishop's development as a theologian of sixteenth-century reform.

Charitable supposition remains an essential characteristic of effective, meaningful liturgy, and this has ever been so since the earliest days of Christendom. It is also the case that liturgical advance has rarely resulted from the composition of services for Christian worship *de novo*; to the contrary, such advance has invariably built on past strengths. Granted what may be termed the need for gradualism, therefore, it can be difficult to discern doctrinal change in liturgy, and the inexperienced should be wary. Past luminaries who have charted the quicksands at the mouth of a great estuary reaching way out into the sea of western – and for some even eastern – tradition, include F. E. Brightman (sometime fellow of Magdalen College, Oxford) and the inimitable Edward Craddock Ratcliff (sometime Regius professor of divinity, and fellow of St. John's College, Cambridge). Both scholars stressed the futility of crediting Cranmer with much original composition, and Brightman in particular illustrated the point in a key two-volume source work with parallel columns which indicate the derivation of Prayer Book material from the widest range of rites.[24] That Cranmer had a real feeling for liturgy is beyond dispute, however difficult it remains to name all the written sources that supplied such inspiration.

In the nineteenth century, E. C. Burbidge hoped to find the answer by searching through what remained of the archbishop's considerable library. David Selwyn has continued the task, but despite almost a lifetime's dedication tracking down difficult sources, he has recorded "no great advance on Burbidge's findings in 1892" in "a mere handful of liturgical books."[25] Whatever sources Cranmer used, in terms of theological insight there can be no doubting the use he made of Scripture and the church fathers as he worked, in and out of drafting committees, to set out gospel services in the vernacular.

Tilting at the saints of the *Processionale,* a first glimpse of Cranmer's skill in this respect was the Litany of 1544. If Edward's accession and Somerset's support offered greater scope, the archbishop remained remarkably cautious, and the interim *Order of Communion* (1548) merely "afforded the Mass an English inset of Confession, absolution," some "comfortable words" from Scripture, a prayer of "humble access" and communion in both kinds (wafer-bread and wine) or what F. E. Brightman termed "an English supplement to the Latin missal."[26]

Enforced by Parliament's Act of Uniformity, new services in a *Book of Common Prayer* prescribed for English people, "and in Wales, at Calais, and the marches of the same," the religion established at law by Whitsun 1549. Its principal rite was "The Supper of the Lorde and holy Communion" – a liturgy of profound significance in any theological context. For if traditional reference appended something of a subtitle for worshippers to note that their Eucharist was "commonly called the masse," serious consideration soon revealed a very different approach to that sacrament. So although the *Sarum Missal* and a number of other sources undergirded the "holy Communion" with old forms to give an appearance of an English *Canon Missae*, "the guiding principle governing Cranmer's composition was unquestionably his determination both to emphasize the eucharist as a memorial of Christ's sacrifice for sin, and to express his understanding of a scriptural 'sacrifice of laud and praise'."[27]

In short, the service Cranmer had piloted through committee to achieve publication as "Common Prayer" was, by Sarum standards, a marked advance. When the old Canon offered prayer so to bless the oblation that it became the Lord's Body and Blood, the new form chose instead an affirmation of the unique nature and perfection of the sacrifice offered once for all on Calvary:

> O God heavenly Father, which of thy tender mercy didst give Thine only Son Jesu Christ, to suffer death upon the cross for our Redemption, who made there (by his one oblation, once offered) a full, perfect, and sufficient sacrifice, oblation and satisfaction for the sins of the whole world, and didst institute, and in his holy Gospel command us to celebrate, a perpetual memory of that his precious death, until his coming again.[28]

When "consecration" came – and in his invited "censure" Martin Bucer took grave exception to the very idea[29] – it took place with the priest's recital of the biblical narrative of institution, the service once again stressing the Sacrament as a memorial. And for those who chose to question such an interpretation, categoric reference in a rubric was there to silence doubt. The 1549 instruction thus prohibited "any elevation, and shewing the Sacrament to the people," and in effect not only took propitiatory sacrifice and transubstantiation out of focus, but strove completely to remove both concepts. In its staple service, Edward VI's church had thus absorbed new theology. In a teaching ministry he intended should substitute an understanding of the sacrament centered on hearing the word of God for seeing salvation in the sacrifice of the altar, Cranmer wrote (between 1550 and 1551) first his *Defence*, and then his *Answer* to Stephen Gardiner in a determined bid to expound the faith and explain its implications for the liturgy. As MacCulloch has argued, this was a wise and highly relevant move "all the more necessary because of the failure of his efforts to do so in the 1548 *Catechism*," a stopgap work of Lutheran origin and real-presence language no longer acceptable, granted the new alignment with the reforms in Switzerland and South Germany.

In five books – which dealt in turn with what he held to be Christ's own intention for the "true use of his sacrament," "the errors of transubstantiation," "the manner how Christ is present in his holy Supper," "of the eating and drinking," and of "the oblation and sacrifice of our Saviour Christ" – Cranmer's *Defence* thus set out his eucharistic theology. And an autumnal reference at his Oxford trial (September 1555) that the work was "made seven years before" (or about the time of the celebrated debate on the sacrament in the House of Lords [December 1548]), affords "proof . . . that both Prayer Books were written with the same theological agenda behind them."[30]

As a theologian, Cranmer cannot compare with leading luminaries of Reformation such as Calvin or Bucer, let alone with Martin Luther. Yet his grasp of justification by only faith – that *sine qua non* of the whole sixteenth-century crisis – provided the *Defence* with resilient *raison d'être*. For although that substantial work amounted to root-and-branch refutation of what the archbishop held to be erroneous Roman doctrines enshrined in the late-medieval Mass, the Eucharist was not discussed in isolation but carefully related to Christian proclamation as a whole. If scriptural principles laid firm foundations, patristic consensus frequently furnished the coping stones of profound respect for genuine church tradition. Characteristic of this enthusiasm, the *Defence* thus itemized various "old authors" on a select scale of approval suggested by the proximity of their writings to "Christ's time," and who, for that reason, "might best know the truth."[31] Such zeal for patristic inheritance also embraced new-found respect for Oecolampadius of Basel, whose work the primate had found decidedly unconvincing when it had been urged upon him by von Watt (Vadianus) in 1537. And there can be little doubt of the debt Cranmer owed Oecolampadius's skill in turning patristic passages – citations customarily used to support traditional baptismal and eucharistic doctrines – against Gardiner and other "papist opponents."[32]

In midsummer 1547, Edward VI's new regime under Protector Somerset had published twelve *Homilies*. Intended for the use of a largely non-preaching clergy "until the King's pleasure be further known," the *Book* included three set pieces from Cranmer's eloquent pen. Focussed respectively on "Salvation," "True, Lively and Christian Faith," and "Good Works," these clearly indicated the archbishop's theological commitment.[33] A reformation classic of its kind, Cranmer's "Homily of Salvation" is clarity itself in its grasp of Christ's atonement. After careful journeying through Pauline and patristic foothills, the theological argument attains great heights with prose which itself peaks to extend a summit experience to congregation and reader alike. For: "Whereas we were condemned . . . [God] hath given his own natural Son . . . to be incarnated, and to take our mortal nature upon him . . . to suffer . . . death for our offences, to the intent to justify us and restore us to life everlasting."

Cranmer has thus probed the "mystery of redemption," a Pauline focus (Rom. 3) explaining how the ransomed Christ "fulfilled the law . . . perfectly." At one with the apostle, he is clear that "only a true and lively faith," itself "the gift of God" can justify man. This is his *feste Burg*, the faith "holy scripture teacheth" as "the strong rock and foundation of Christian religion." And characteristically the archbishop adds that it is also the "doctrine all old and ancient authors of Christ's Church do approve."[34] The teaching on good works and baptism is just as lucid. For if in terms of "faith, hope, charity, repentance, dread and fear of God," such be "far too weak and insufficient and upright to deserve remission of . . . sins, and . . . justification," once forgiven, the faithful "are most bounden to serve God in doing good deeds commanded . . . in . . . holy scripture" throughout their lives. Baptism thus remits "original sin" and "all actual sin committed" thereafter if, that is, "we truly repent, and convert unfeignedly to him again."[35] Observing such ground rules in his other homilies, Cranmer provided his flock with something of a theological paradox. In the "Short Declaration of True, Lively, and Christian Faith," much was made of good works, just as the main emphasis in his "Sermon of Good Works" brought a fine focus to bear on faith. On form as chief pastor, the archbishop made abundantly clear his contempt for the "dead faith which bringeth forth no good works."[36] Yet as theological argument unfolded in his third homily, Cranmer resorted to Augustine, whose commentary on Psalm 31 provided the primate with the perfect order of priority that none "reckon upon his good works before his faith." In such a context too he set out a notable, yet little known, ascription:

> Honour be to God, who did put light in the heart of his faithful and true minister of famous memory, King Henry the eighth, and gave him the knowledge of his word, and an earnest affection to seek his glory, and to put away all such superstitious and pharisaical sects by anti-christ invented, and set up against the true word of God.[37]

Historians have hitherto assumed that once Somerset settled into power the quickening Protestant pace of his Edwardine regime was assured, and the latest research partly confirms such a scenario, with due emphasis on the Council's determination to pursue reformation policies. In lively narrative, MacCulloch's *Tudor Church Militant* details the way church ornaments – the statuary of rood lofts, patron saints and images, as well as stone altars, monstrances, plate, and the widest range of artifacts related to the miracle of the Mass and its sacrificial emphasis – were methodically confiscated or destroyed. In so many respects this was new lamps for old, wall painting being exchanged for whitewash superimposed with painted commandments and texts that transformed church interiors into "a giant scrapbook of scripture" for the catechism of worshippers.[38]

Such practical concerns the Council considered central to home affairs; and at a time when the nation's politics virtually revolved around theology, it might be assumed that a green light at last gave Cranmer the go-ahead to pursue pastoral policies appropriate to strengthening basic structures for ongoing reformation. In fact, the very assumption is something of a half-truth. MacCulloch's unusually distinguished set of Birkbeck Lectures (Trinity College, Cambridge, 1998) posed "the question of priorities between national and international reformation."[39] So however personally pledged to a theology of church reform, Cranmer was still obliged to use due caution when the politics of court faction (in, for example, the ambitions and rivalries of Somerset and Warwick and their supporters) could be out of step with such convictions.

Most scholars are now agreed that the developing theology of Thomas Cranmer had ripened into a Reformation maturity by 1546 or 1547. Accordingly, it had been his carefully considered aim that, in its basic liturgiology, the 1549 Prayer Book should convey fundamental Reformation doctrine. In short, despite minor modifications which resulted from the critique invited from Bucer in *Censura*, as well as changes made when the political situation allowed revision, the architect of the *Book of Common Prayer* did not move his ground between 1548 and 1552. Like the leaders of many a successful revolution, Cranmer made the best possible use of the traditional forms and language he inherited; he showed genius in the way he adapted them to suit changes that, if ongoing, were largely imperceptible until explained. For all was planned by a chief pastor whose sensitivity sought to provide a new piety for his people. A sentence from his *Answer* to the carping Gardiner made the point: "This the husbandman at his plough, the weaver at his loom, and the wife at her rock can remember, and give thanks to God for the same."[40]

Yet just as the *Book of Common Prayer* (1549) had to await clarification until the 1552 revision appeared, political uncertainties again imposed a delay of some six months before the Prayer Book approved by Parliament that spring came into use. In such a context, MacCulloch's judgment that "examination of Cranmer's career reveals how repeatedly ends justified means . . . so that he could cut legal corners to get the result he wanted, and even turn the prose of his enemies inside out in his liturgical work, to redeploy it in the service of the revolution," as a point of view, has at least a ring of truth about it.[41]

Following England's dramatic repudiation of papal authority in the 1530s, and policy moves progressively aimed to avoid isolation in Europe, much diplomatic flirtation took place with Lutheran princes opposed to the emperor and to states allied to Rome. But with Henrician traditionalism never really in tune with Wittenberg theology, the future lay with wider European contacts. With wavering uncertainty a thing of the past, early links with South German and Swiss City States were well established when Edward ascended the Tudor throne. A. G. Dickens was well aware of this foreign influence, and in a chapter of his classic study *The English Reformation* devoted to Somerset, wrote that "Before Henry's death there began a gradual infiltration . . . of Protestant concepts more advanced than those of Luther."[42] This may be termed the South German–Swiss Connection for the priority Dickens gave Bucer and Bullinger compared with his reference to Calvin as "merely one of the greater stars among the Protestant galaxy."[43] But it should be recalled that the Protestant patriarch who was profoundly influenced by Bucer during his Strasbourg sojourn himself at least indirectly influenced Cranmer in the matter of the Eucharist. In this respect, Wittenberg was replaced by Strasbourg, Zurich, and Geneva, all of them significant planets to the satellite moon of Canterbury. Ever the keen observer, Dickens found "ample evidence of Calvinist doctrinal emphases" in "the writings of several English divines." The latest findings afford sharper focus, and MacCulloch – himself indebted to Gordon's work on the Swiss Reformed Church – has emphasized the significance of the 1549 Zurich agreement (*Consensus Tigurinus*).[44] A vital rapprochement between the extreme views of those aligned to Luther and Zwingli and their "Supper-strife," this brought a second-generation sanity to the great Marburg eucharistic divide.

At this time too, shifts in the primitive balance of European power politics played their part. For having defeated the Schmalkald League at Mühlberg, the emperor had imposed a reactionary truce on his Protestant subjects by the Augsburg Interim (May 1548). If a measure of toleration thus allowed the authorities to tolerate marriage of clergy and grant communion in both kinds, the Mass was restored and the six remaining sacraments were to be upheld with traditional ceremonial. Preferring the manna of a wilderness journey and exile to any such reversal of Reformation principle and practice in such an about-turn, Bucer left Strasbourg for England. And because he did so, the mantle of European leadership fell to the Swiss, in particular to Bullinger and Calvin. While he lived, Bucer was a revered first-generation Reformer welcomed to England as very much the grand old man of a *cause célèbre*. Sensitive to Luther as well as to more radical Swiss doctrine, he proved something of a sounding-board to his archiepiscopal host in the revision of the first Prayer Book. But recent research suggests this to have been more deference than discipleship in a Cranmer who, his Lutheran phase behind him, already had more sympathy with Peter Martyr and advancing Swiss theology in the matter of the sacrament. Edward's regime may have displayed "fervent Protestant internationalism" but was at least prepared to delay this publication of a formulary of the faith (this time the Forty-two Articles) until 1553 "mainly because of the Archbishop's hopes for some greater international action."[45]

In our ecumenical era, such openness may find respect. But in Tudor times it was highly dangerous and so quite remarkable that Cranmer managed to survive as long as he did before Mary took her revenge. Portrayed by many as blown about with every wind of doctrine, the primate certainly made sure that he kept abreast of developing theologies in a unique period of change and crisis, just as he was "always to be found at the centre of government action until the chill descended in his relations with Northumberland in 1552."[46] In the middle of the twentieth century, G. W. Bromiley argued the case for *Thomas Cranmer Theologian*. If his assessment has merit, when viewed alongside the religious genius of Martin Luther, or contrasted with the scholarly brilliance of John Calvin, the conscientious Tudor divine, despite real liturgical understanding and evident pastoral gifts, does not compare. Even so, such a crowded life span with its staged development away from, and disagreement with what he termed "the papistical church," is full of fascination. And as long as the Muse inspires, Clio's disciples will afford Cranmer either passionate support or vehement criticism. An irony it may be, but in his case *via media Anglicana* was far from reality!

Notes

1 See the excellent Gunning Lectures given by Peter Matheson before Edinburgh's Divinity Faculty, now published as *The Imaginative World of the Reformation* (Edinburgh: T. & T. Clark, 2000).

2 David G. Selwyn, *The Library of Thomas Cranmer* (Oxford Bibliographical Society, 1996), 28–9. It is not possible to identify these MS notes. Ashley Null, in a Cambridge Ph.D. thesis entitled "Thomas Cranmer's Doctrine of Repentance" (1994), suggests that they date from Cranmer's "days as a graduate theological student," while Diarmaid MacCulloch takes the point, an *en passant* observation in his *magnum opus* (*Thomas Cranmer: A Life* [New Haven: Yale University Press, 1996], 20)

hinting that the neat, abbreviated hand "seems to be an early version of his [viz. Cranmer's] hand." Selwyn, however, argues that "on balance, the hand would seem to be that of a reader older than Thomas Cranmer would have been at the time" (28).

3 MacCulloch, *Thomas Cranmer*, 26–7.

4 MacCulloch, *Thomas Cranmer*, 33.

5 See especially, *An Answer unto a crafty and sophistical cavillation devised by Stephen Gardiner, 1551.*

6 See MacCulloch, *Thomas Cranmer*, 33f.

7 MacCulloch, *Thomas Cranmer*, 43.

8 The Lambeth collection (MS 1107) and summary (MS 1107ff. 76–80), as indeed the summary in Corpus Christi College, Cambridge

(MS 340), almost certainly date from this time (1531), so MacCulloch is correct in his claim, somewhat feebly contested in Paul Ayris and David Selwyn, *Thomas Cranmer: Churchman & Scholar* (Woodbridge, England, and Rochester, NY: Boydell Press, 1993), 317 that, with secretarial aid, these canon law commonplaces predate Cranmer's consecration as archbishop.

9   MacCulloch, *Thomas Cranmer*, 66.
10 Andreas Osiander, *Werke: Gesamtausgabe*, ed. Gerhard Müller (Gütersloh, 1975–85), 6:248.
11 Cranmer's oath to the king for his temporalities is quoted in P. N. Brooks, *Cranmer in Context* (Minneapolis: Fortress Press, 1989), 31.
12 J. E. Cox, ed., *Miscellaneous Writings and Letters of Thomas Cranmer* (Cambridge, for the Parker Society, 1846), 304. Cited below as P. S. *Cranmer* II.
13 P.S. *Cranmer* II, 305.
14 MacCulloch, *Thomas Cranmer*, 173.
15 Ibid., 179.
16 Hastings Robinson, ed., *Original Letters relative to the English Reformation* (Cambridge, for the Parker Society, 1846), 13.
17 Ibid., 14.
18 Richard W. Dixon, *History of the Church of England from the Abolition of the Roman Jurisdiction*, 2nd ed., revised in 6 vols. (Oxford: Oxford University Press, 1891–1902), 1:415.
19 Oh that the missing Commonplace text listed in the *tabula* as "18. Osiander" would come to light! See CCB MS. Royal 7 B. XI. fol. 5 r.
20 A. Null, "Cranmer's Doctrine of Repentance" (Ph.D. thesis, University of Cambridge, 1994, soon to appear in the series of Oxford Theological Monographs), 2.
21 MacCulloch, *Thomas Cranmer*, 237.
22 P.S. *Cranmer* II, 345–6.
23 P.S. *Cranmer* II, 122.
24 F. E. Brightman, *The English Rite, being a Synopsis of the Sources and Revisions of the Book of Common Prayer*, 2nd ed., revised in 2 vols. (London: Rivingtons, 1921). The recent study by C. Frederick Barbee and Paul F. M. Zahl, eds., *The Collects of Thomas Cranmer* (Grand Rapids: Eerdmans, 1999), ix is also of value here for the editors' appreciation that "the vast majority of the Prayer Book Collects are in fact pre-Reformation."
25 Selwyn, *Thomas Cranmer*, xcii and xcv.
26 Peter Newman Brooks, *Cranmer in Context* (Minneapolis: Fortress Press, 1989), 53.

27 Peter Newman Brooks, *Thomas Cranmer's Doctrine of the Eucharist*, 2nd ed. (Basingstoke: Macmillan, 1992), 73.
28 J. Ketley, ed., *Liturgies of Edward VI* (Cambridge, for the Parker Society, 1844), 88.
29 Martin Bucer, *Censura* in E. C. Whitaker, ed., *Martin Bucer and the Book of Common Prayer* (Alcuin Club edition, 1974), 55: "*Pracatio ista, pro tali panis, & vini in Mensa Domini, benedictione, atque sanctificatione, non est mandata a Domino: et ad retinendas, confirmandasque horrendas impietates ab Anti-christis detorquetur*" [viz. "is twisted"!].
30 MacCulloch, *Thomas Cranmer*, 463. See Brooks, *Thomas Cranmer's Doctrine of the Eucharist*, 77–8 and 107–10.
31 Thomas Cranmer, *Defence of the True and Catholic Doctrine of the Lord's Supper*, ed. C. H. H. Wright (1907), 45, 46, 47, 49, 51 and 55. See J. E. Cox, ed., *Writings and Disputations of Archbishop Cranmer relative to the Sacrament of the Lord's Supper* (Cambridge, for the Parker Society, 1844). So P.S. *Cranmer* I.
32 Brooks, *Thomas Cranmer's Doctrine of the Eucharist*, 3f.; see 90 for ref. to CCCC MS 102. See also the interesting article by K. J. Walsh, "Cranmer and the Fathers," *Journal of Religious History* 11/2 (1980), 227–47.
33 Text in P.S. *Cranmer* II, 128–49.
34 Ibid., 131.
35 Ibid., 132. Note here phrasing reminiscent of the General Confession prefacing the *Book of Common Prayer* Order for Morning and Evening Prayer.
36 Ibid., 135.
37 Ibid., 148.
38 MacCulloch, *Tudor Church Militant. Edward VI and the Protestant Reformation* (London: Allen Lane, 1999), 159.
39 Ibid., 99.
40 *Answer* in P.S. *Cranmer* I, 328.
41 MacCulloch, *Tudor Church Militant*, 104.
42 A. G. Dickens, *The English Reformation*, 2nd ed. (University Park: Pennsylvania State University Press, 1989), p. 222.
43 Ibid., 225.
44 Bruce Gordon, "Calvin and the Swiss Reformed Churches" in A. Pettegree, A. Duke, and G. Lewis, eds., *Calvinism in Europe, 1540–1620* (Cambridge: Cambridge University Press, 1994), 64f.
45 MacCulloch, *Tudor Church Militant*, 79, 101.
46 Ibid., 104.

Bibliography

Primary Sources

Most primary sources are no longer in print, but good libraries will have the two Parker Society volumes edited by J. E. Cox: Vol. I, *On the Lord's Supper* (Cambridge, 1844) and Vol. II, *Miscellaneous Writings and Letters of Thomas Cranmer* (Cambridge, 1846). The Parker Society also published the *Liturgies of Edward VI*, edited by J. Ketley (Cambridge, 1844), an indispensable volume containing the *Books of Common Prayer*. Peter Newman Brooks, *Cranmer in Context* (Minneapolis: Fortress Press, 1989) is still available, and provides a handy anthology of select sources for students.

Secondary Sources

Among significant sources in print the works of Diarmaid MacCulloch stand alone and are to be recommended for their rare distinction: *Thomas Cranmer: A Life* (New Haven: Yale University Press, 1996) and *Tudor Church Militant. Edward VI and the Protestant Reformation* (London: Allen Lane, 1999).

Richard Hooker (1554–1600)

Daniel F. Eppley

The traditional view of Richard Hooker that continues to be widely asserted identifies him as one who has "contributed mightily to what has been called in recent times the Anglican tradition."[1] His influence is based primarily on his great opus, *Of the Lawes of Ecclesiasticall Politie*, a defense in eight books of the Elizabethan church against so-called "Puritan" detractors, who argued that the church was only partially reformed and needed to be purged of remaining "popish" superstitions. The first four books were published in 1593, the fifth in 1597. While it appears that the final three books were substantially complete before Hooker's death,[2] the completed forms have not survived. Drafts of these books were published after Hooker's death, the sixth and eighth books in 1648 and the seventh in 1662. Additionally, several of Hooker's sermons and tracts have survived.

While Hooker has traditionally been portrayed as a detached, scholastically inclined theorist of the "Anglican middle way" between the Reformed churches and the Roman Church, recent studies have added depth and breadth to our image of Hooker and have called into question long-held assumptions. We are beginning to appreciate Hooker the polemicist, humanist rhetorician, and Reformed theologian.[3] The current study will focus on two aspects of Hooker's work that have recently been brought to the fore. First, Hooker will be considered as a polemicist among whose primary aims was the defense of the Elizabethan church as established by law.[4] Second, Hooker will be presented as a theologian holding decidedly Reformed views on issues such as justification and the sacraments.[5]

Hooker addressed the *Lawes* to "*them that seek (as they term it) the reformation of Laws, and orders Ecclesiastical, in the Church of ENGLAND.*" His goal was to win their conscientious obedience to these laws.[6] Because such an effort entailed especially showing these ardently Calvinist detractors that worship in the Elizabethan church was an effective means to salvation, it is well to begin with Hooker's views on justification and salvation. Hooker's most detailed consideration of these points was not in the *Lawes*, but rather in sermons and other writings.

Hooker based his ideas on justification on a typically Calvinist rejection of the notion that humans could do anything at all to earn salvation. "[T]he little fruit which we have in holiness it is God knows corrupt and unsound, we put no confidence at all in it . . . The best things that we do have somewhat in them to be pardoned, how then can we do anything meritorious and worthy to be rewarded?"[7] Because of sin, any person who would be justified had to gain this not by works but rather by the redemption that Christ wrought through his suffering and death. The person who was redeemed by Christ's sacrifice was indeed righteous, and the righteousness of a Christian was of three kinds. "There is a glorifying righteousness of men in the world to come, and there is a justifying and a sanctifying righteousness here. *The righteousness, wherewith we shall be clothed* in the world to come, is both perfect and inherent: that whereby we are justified is perfect but not inherent, that whereby we are sanctified, inherent but not perfect."[8]

The key to salvation was justifying righteousness alone, and this was attained solely through faith. "Christ has merited righteousness for as many as are *found in him*. In him God finds us if we be faithful for by faith we are incorporated into him." The faithful person,

> even the man who in himself is impious, full of iniquity, full of sin, him being found in Christ through faith, and having his sin in hatred through repentance, him God beholds with a gracious eye, puts away his sin by not imputing it . . . and accepts him in Jesus Christ as perfectly righteous as if he had fulfilled all that is commanded him in the law.[9]

Sanctifying righteousness, by contrast, was the actual righteousness of those who were redeemed by Christ. While nothing a human being could do was meritorious or efficacious toward salvation, Hooker recognized sanctifying righteousness and its fruit, good works, as a necessary accompaniment to justifying righteousness. Thus, "none shall see God but such as seek peace and holiness though not as a cause of their salvation yet as a way through which they must walk that will be saved."[10] Both types of righteousness were freely given gifts of God, "the one by accepting us for righteous in Christ, the other by working Christian righteousness in us."[11] Salvation was thus by grace, not excluding good works as a necessary consequence but fully excluding merit.[12]

In speaking of salvific faith, Hooker meant not only an objective identification of Christ as Savior but also a subjective recognition that the salvation wrought by Christ applied to oneself.[13] Such an affirmation "is far above the reach of human reason," and consequently "cannot otherwise than by the spirit of the Almighty be conceived." Thus "our life is Christ by the hearing of the gospel apprehended as a Saviour and assented unto by the power of the Holy Ghost."[14] In the *Lawes* Hooker confirmed that "belief [in the truths of Christianity] is the gift of God,"[15] and he noted the predestinarian corollary that God's free choice was solely responsible for separating the saved from the damned.[16]

Hooker's fullest discussion of predestination came in his answer to "A Christian Letter," an attack on the orthodoxy of the *Lawes* published in 1599. In his response, Hooker argued that God's original purpose in creating humanity was ultimately to bring each individual to salvation through the voluntary observation of God's will.[17] In actuality, however, "*[o]ut of the liberty wherewith God by creation endued reasonable creatures*, angels and men, there ensued sin through their own voluntary choice of evil, neither by the appointment of God, nor yet without his permission."[18] The entrance of sin "awakened [God's] justice, which otherwise might have slept,"[19] and consequently "from God, as it were by a secondary kind of will there grows now destruction and death, although otherwise the will of his voluntary inclination towards man would effect the contrary."[20] Thus the punishment of some was not a part of God's original intent in creation, and it was a mistake to say that God predestined some to condemnation otherwise than foreseeing sin as the cause of damnation, "forasmuch as it [reprobation] presupposes in man a just and deserved cause leading him who is most holy thereunto."[21]

While Hooker emphasized sin as the cause of reprobation, this need not be taken as implying that he based predestination on divine foreknowledge of particular sins in persons excluded from salvation or particular virtues in the elect.[22] Rather, it seems that when Hooker spoke of foreknown sin as the cause of damnation he was referring to the "sentence of death and condemnation [that] might most justly have passed over *all*," from which God "voluntarily and freely" pardoned *some*, not to the cause of God's damning particular individuals.[23] Responding to "A Christian Letter" Hooker cited Augustine against an understanding of predestination based on divine foreknowledge, and he noted that God knew that Peter would be saved "before" God knew that Peter would have the merits through which he was to be saved.[24] This need not be considered an alteration of Hooker's original position. Already in 1586 he emphasized that election involved absolutely nothing predisposing God to favor the elect, "no more than the clay when the potter appoints it to be framed for an honorable use, nay not so much, for the matter whereupon the craftsman works he chooses, being moved with the fitness which is in it to serve his turn: in us no such thing."[25] Summarizing his position on predestination in terms similar to the Lambeth Articles, Hooker asserted:

> 1. That God has predestinated certain men, not all men. 2. That the cause moving him hereunto was not the foresight of any virtue in us at all. 3. That to him the number of his elect is definitely known. 4. That it cannot be but their sins must condemn them to whom the purpose of his saving mercy doth not extend. 5. That to God's foreknown elect, the final continuance of grace is given. 6. That inward grace whereby to be saved, is deservedly not given unto all men. 7. That no man comes to Christ whom God by the inward grace of his Spirit draws not. 8. And that it is not in every, no not in any man's own mere ability, freedom, and power to be saved, no man's salvation being possible without grace.[26]

Consistent with his assertion that God sanctified those he would save as well as justifying them, Hooker noted that predestination did not exclude the need for godliness in Christians. "God is no favourer of sloth and therefore there can be no such absolute decree touching man's salvation as on our part includes no necessity of care and travail, but shall certainly take effect, whether we ourselves do wake or sleep."[27] Although the elect were eternally with God "according to that intent and purpose whereby we were chosen to be made his, ... [o]ur being in Christ by eternal foreknowledge saves us not without our actual and real adoption into the fellowship of his Saints in this present world."[28] Chief among the means by which

Christians were thus adopted was "not only the Word, but [also] the sacraments, both having generative force and virtue."[29]

The first prerequisite for salvation was participation in the Word of God. "For the instruction therefore of all sorts of men to eternal life it is necessary, that the sacred and saving truth of God be openly published unto them;"[30] the Word was "the instrument which God has purposely framed, thereby to work the knowledge of salvation in the hearts of men . . ."[31] This was not to deny the need for grace and the Holy Spirit's guidance, but merely to stress that "the Word of God outwardly administered (his spirit inwardly concurring therewith) converts, edifies, and saves souls."[32] Hooker included under the concept of the salvific "Word" not only the Scriptures, but also prayer, because of the crucial role prayer played in the life of the church.[33] "Between the throne of God in heaven and his Church upon earth here militant if it be so that angels have their continual intercourse, where should we find the same more verified than in these two spiritual exercises, the one '*Doctrine*', and the other '*Prayer*'?"[34] Just as God addressed the Christian community through the teaching of doctrine, so the community addressed God through prayer. Public prayers were of special value both for their greater dignity and efficacy as compared to private prayers and for their power to arouse "zeal and devotion to God" in participants.[35]

In addition to the Word, the sacraments were also central in bringing Christians to salvation. Hooker recognized two valid sacraments: baptism, in which Christians "have laid the foundation and attained the first beginning of a new life," and the Eucharist, supplying Christians with "their nourishment and food prescribed for *continuance* of life in them."[36] Like sharing in the Word, reception of the sacraments was virtually essential for salvation. While God's grace alone was salvific, the sacraments were necessary because "[n]either is it *ordinarily* his will to bestow the grace of sacraments on any, but by the sacraments."[37] Hooker rejected the notion that the sacraments were mere signs or teaching instruments, asserting instead that they served a "more excellent and heavenly use . . . first as marks whereby to know when God imparts the vital or saving grace of Christ unto all that are capable thereof, and secondly as means conditional which God requires in them unto whom he imparts grace."[38] "This is therefore the necessity of sacraments. That saving grace which Christ originally is or has for the general good of the whole Church, by sacraments he severally derives into every member thereof."[39] Hooker rejected, however, the idea that the sacraments themselves bestowed grace, a point that he clarified in his response to "A Christian Letter." "Sacraments," he explained, "are signs effectual, they are the instruments of God, whereby to bestow grace, howbeit grace not proceeding from the visible sign, but from his invisible power."[40]

On the controversial topic of Christ's presence in the Eucharist, Hooker sought a position that all Reformed Protestants could accept. He began by considering the union of Christ's human and divine natures. "[F]orasmuch as there is no union of God with man without that mean between both which is both, it seems requisite that we first consider how God is in Christ, then how Christ is in us, and how the sacraments do serve to make us partakers of Christ."[41] Hooker began his discussion of the union of the divine and human in Christ with the reminder that "[i]t is not in man's ability either to express perfectly or conceive the manner how this was brought to pass."[42] He then put forward a Chalcedonian vision of Christ's divine and human natures as forever inseparable yet neither mingled, confused, nor changed by the union.[43] More precisely, Christ's human nature did change, but not to the extent that it ceased to be a fully human nature. It became rather a perfected human nature, including a perfecting of Christ's bodily human nature after his resurrection.[44]

This discussion raised an essential issue with regard to the Eucharist – did the perfection of Christ's bodily human nature include the power of omnipresence?[45] Hooker's initial response was that "we hold it . . . a most infallible truth that Christ as man is not every where present,"[46] but he immediately qualified this. "There are those which think it as infallibly true that Christ is every where present as man. Which peradventure in some sense may be well enough granted." Since the divine nature of Christ, as divine, was necessarily omnipresent, so also his "human substance . . . which cannot have in itself universal presence has it *after a sort* by being *no where severed* from that which every where is present. . . . Else should the Word be in part or somewhere God only and not man which is impossible." Thus "*only* [the] *conjunction*" of Christ's "manhood" was omnipresent, its "actual *position* restrained and tied to a certain place. Yet presence *by way of conjunction* is in some sort presence."[47]

Regarding Christ's presence in the Eucharist in particular, Hooker emphasized the key points on which all agreed. Christians were, he claimed, "grown (for ought I can see) on all sides at the length to a general agreement, concerning that which alone is material, namely the *real participation* of Christ and of life in his body and blood *by means of this sacrament*." Given this general consensus, Hooker wondered why there remained contention over the sacrament "when there remains now no controversy saving only about the subject *where* Christ is? Yea even in this point no side denies but that the *soul of man* is the receptacle of Christ's presence."[48] Stressing that what really mattered was the point on which all agreed – that "[t]he real presence of Christ's most blessed body and blood is not therefore to be sought for in the sacrament, but in the worthy receiver of the sacrament"[49] – he called on all sides to leave off disputes concerning whether or in what manner Christ's body and blood were present in the elements before their reception by the Christian.[50] Overall, Hooker championed a real mystical presence of Christ in the Eucharist and proffered an exposition of Christ's words "this is my body" that was truly Christian and could be accepted by all:

> "*This hallowed food, through concurrence of divine power, is in verity and truth, unto faithful receivers, instrumentally a cause of that mystical participation, whereby as I make myself wholly theirs, so I give them in hand an actual possession of all such saving grace as my sacrificed body can yield, and as their souls do presently need, this is 'to them and in them' my body.*"[51]

As a polemicist trying to win the conscientious obedience of English Puritans to church laws, Hooker sought to present the worship of the Elizabethan church as consistent with his Reformed views regarding salvation and the sacraments. Consequently in the fifth book of the *Lawes* he constantly descended to detailed discussions to demonstrate that the established church was an effective conduit of divine grace, and that legally prescribed liturgical practices and conventions truly fostered the salvation of souls. In this manner he sought to allay Puritan concerns that the English church was tainted with superstition and an ineffective vehicle of salvation.

While a large part of Hooker's effort was devoted to the defense of the worship and ceremonies of the Elizabethan church, as the title of his *magnum opus* indicates, he also focussed on defending the institutional structures by which the ceremonies and orders of the church were established. This aspect of Hooker's apologetic touches on several important themes including his ecclesiology, legal theory, and political theory. The justified and sanctified elect of God formed, for Hooker, the "Church of Christ which we properly term his body mystical." This was the church invisible, of which Christ alone was the head and concerning which "our Lord and Saviour hath promised, *I give unto them eternal life, and they shall never perish.*"[52] Membership in this church was clearly known to God but could not be discerned with certainty by mortals.[53] There was also a second church, the visible church whose members were unified "by reason of that *one Lord* whose servants they all profess themselves, that *one Faith* which they all acknowledge, that *one Baptism* wherewith they are all initiated."[54]

One particularly important difference between the visible and invisible churches was the fact that the visible church was a species of human society. Hooker asserted that the universal community of Christians was "divided into a number of distinct societies, every one of which is termed a Church within itself. In this sense the Church is always a visible society of men," and like all human societies, the church could not function or even survive without harmony and order among community members.[55] Furthermore, while all societies required peace to endure, in the church the need for concord also rested on a divine mandate. The Christian God was a God of peace, unity, and order, and thus a church divided by strife was offensive to God.[56] As a society of people brought together in the name of the God of peace and harmony, the visible church needed structure and guidance both to serve as an effective vehicle to salvation, and so that internal order could be maintained.

The most important source of guidance for the church was, naturally, the will of God. Hooker agreed with his Puritan opponents that God's will was to be obeyed in all aspects of ecclesiastical life, but he disagreed with their further assertion that the Bible was the only means by which God's will was made known. "For as they rightly maintain, that God must be glorified in all things, and that the actions of men cannot tend unto his glory unless they be framed after his law: So it is their error to think that the only law which God has appointed unto men in that behalf is the sacred Scripture."[57] This should not, of course, be taken as implying that Hooker denied the need for laws revealed by God in the Scriptures to lead fallen humanity to salvation. The ultimate end of human beings was union with God, to which end the only means that nature taught was the performance of good works.[58] Since, however, no person could ever attain salvation in this way, God provided "a way which is supernatural, a way which could never have entered into the heart of man as once to conceive or imagine, if God himself had not revealed it extraordinarily."[59] The Scriptures were a perfect guide in things essential to salvation, and consequently the visible church was eternally bound by scriptural dictates regarding "matters of faith, and in general matters necessary unto salvation." Other aspects of church life, by contrast, were not ordered by scriptural precepts and thus with regard to such matters there was room for flexibility and diversity among churches.[60] Rather than looking to the Scriptures to order such matters, one must look to other laws under which God had placed humanity, in particular (1) the natural law that could be discerned by human reason and (2) human laws.

Regarding the former of these (hereafter referred to as the "law of nature") Hooker stated:

> Law rational therefore, which men commonly use to call the law of nature, meaning thereby the law which human nature knows itself in reason universally bound unto, which also for that cause may be termed most fitly the law of reason: this law, I say, comprehends all those things which men by the light of their natural understanding do evidently know, or at leastwise may know, to be beseeming or unbeseeming, virtuous or vicious, good or evil for them to do.[61]

This law even enabled pagans to "learn in many things what the will of God is,"[62] and was essential for Christians as well because the sufficiency of Scripture as a guide to salvation was not absolute but presupposed knowledge of the natural law.[63] "It suffices therefore that [the law of] nature and Scripture do serve in such full sort, that they both jointly and not severally either of them be so complete, that unto everlasting felicity we need not the knowledge of any thing more than these two, may easily furnish our minds with on all sides."[64]

The divine law and the law of nature alone did not, however, meet all the needs of the church. Even when both of these laws were taken into account there were vast tracts of Christian life that comprised things indifferent, "adiaphora," that God neither forbade nor commanded. A key aspect of Hooker's defense was to limit things essential for salvation and then claim for the church authorities power over matters of adiaphora. Hooker circumscribed the essentials of the faith by claiming that *"things absolutely unto all men's salvation necessary, either to be held or denied, either to be done or avoided . . . are not only set down, but also plainly set down in Scripture: so that he which hears or reads may, without any great difficulty, understand."*[65] Because of the clarity of God's teachings regarding essentials of belief and practice, dispute regarding God's will in a particular matter was itself strong evidence that the matter in question did not concern something necessary for salvation. This limitation of essentials left a wide array of non-essential aspects of church life, including the ordering of ceremonies associated with Christian worship, the establishment of holy days, the institutional ordering of the church, and generally "whatsoever does by way of formality and circumstance concern any public action of the Church."[66] Most importantly, all of the criticisms raised against the Elizabethan church by Puritan detractors were identified as concerning indifferent matters.[67]

Because of the existence of this vast realm of adiaphora, the needs of the church were not entirely filled by the directives revealed in Scripture and the law of nature. Where standards of conduct were left undefined, life in society, even a society like the visible church, inevitably gave rise to contention and confusion, and thus there was need for additional laws framed by human wisdom and enforced by human agents to maintain peace and order.[68]

> The law of nature and the law of God are sufficient for declaration in both what belongs unto each man separately as his soul is the spouse of *Christ*, yea so sufficient that they plainly and fully show whatsoever God requires by way of necessary introduction

> unto the state of everlasting bliss. But as a man lives joined with others in common society and belongs unto the outward politique body of the *Church* . . . [n]o man doubts but that for matters of action and practice in the affairs of God, for the manner of divine service, for order in Ecclesiastical proceedings about the regiment of the *Church* there may be oftentimes cause very urgent to have laws made.[69]

The removal of human laws from the governance of the church would lead to "the utter confusion of [the] Church," and thereby "would peradventure leave neither face nor memory of Church to continue long in the world."[70]

The need for human laws in the church made manifest the need for an institutional structure to create and enforce those laws. Hooker thus demonstrated the necessity of polity, but not the need for any particular type of polity; it still remained for him to demonstrate that "unto [a] Civil Prince or Governour there may be given such power of Ecclesiastical Dominion as by the Laws of this Land belongs unto the Supreme Regent thereof."[71] To address this issue Hooker turned to a consideration of the locus of authority rightly empowered to formulate the laws governing societies. "[T]he lawful power of making laws to command whole politique societies of men belongs," he claimed, "properly unto the same entire societies," and since the visible church was also a society, "the true original subject of power also to make church laws is the whole entire body of that church for which they are made."[72] The authorization of the community as a whole to formulate laws did not, however, mean that every community member had personally to consent to each law. Rather, one's assent to a law could be given in one's place by representatives "[a]s in parliaments, councils, and the like assemblies," and one was subject to laws and rulers if their authority was based on appointment by one's ancestors.[73]

To demonstrate that the monarch was the rightful head of the church in England Hooker then showed that in England the community that authorized the prince to exercise civil dominion was identical with the community that authorized the prince to exercise ecclesiastical dominion. Crucial to this effort was his very inclusive definition of the membership of the visible church. "[B]ecause the *only object* which separates ours from other religions is *Jesus Christ*," Hooker reasoned, we should consider all "*them which call upon the name of our Lord Jesus Christ to be his Church.* . . . That which separates therefore *utterly*, that which cuts off *clean* from the visible Church of Christ is plain Apostasy . . ."[74] On this basis schismatics, heretics, and all manner of evildoers were recognized as members of the church as long as they continued to profess the lordship of Christ. "Albeit . . . heresies and crimes . . . exclude quite and clean from that salvation which belongs unto the mystical body of Christ; yea, they also make a separation from the visible sound Church of Christ; altogether from the visible Church neither the one nor the other does sever."[75]

Recalling the breadth with which he defined church membership, Hooker pointed out that in England the church and the state were essentially identical in terms of membership.[76] On this basis he asserted that it was entirely appropriate that this community (as both church and state) determined who had authority over religious as well as civil affairs. Authority over "the making of *Ecclesiastical* laws" the community had granted to representatives who spoke for the entire church: the Parliament (speaking for the laity), along with the Convocation (speaking for the clergy).[77] As leading members of Parliament English princes had unique authority generally termed "spiritual dominion or supreme power in Ecclesiastical affairs and causes," which meant "that within their own precincts and territories they have authority and power to command even in matter of *Christian Religion*, and that there is no higher, nor greater, that can in those causes over-command them."[78] Royal authority entailed not only the "power of maintaining laws made for the *Church* regiment and of causing them to be observed . . . [but also] principality of power in making them."[79] Consequently, "no *Ecclesiastical* law [was to] be made in a *Christian Commonwealth* without consent as well of the laity [in Parliament] as of the clergy [in Convocation] but least of all without consent of the highest power [the prince]."[80]

Thus by explaining their necessity and showing that they had been properly established, Hooker legitimated the human laws ordering the Elizabethan church. His argument assumed that the human laws ordering the church either reinforced dictates of higher laws or ordered matters of adiaphora, and it is in this vein that references to the unconditional obedience due to church laws are to be taken. In matters determined by the law of nature or the divine law, however, obedience to the human laws that ordered the church was conditioned by prior obedience to the divine law or the natural law.[81] Human laws "must be made according to the general laws of nature, and without contradiction unto any positive law in scripture. Otherwise they are ill made," and inherently unworthy of obedience.[82] Because the authority of church laws was absolute only over matters of adiaphora, to secure order in the church Hooker needed to address the issue of determining which matters were adiaphora and which were not. An aspect of Hooker's thought that has not been sufficiently appreciated is the fact that he addressed this issue in such a way as to render essentially all resistance against the laws of the Elizabethan church illegitimate.

Notwithstanding the importance of other laws, Hooker, as much as his Puritan opponents, recognized the divinely inspired Scripture as the ultimate standard of truth for Christians. "For many inducements besides Scripture [e.g., natural law or human laws] may lead me to that, which if Scripture be against, they all give place and are of no value; yet otherwise are strong and effectual to persuade."[83] In religious affairs, "what the Scripture plainly delivers, to that the first place both of credit and obedience is due; the next whereunto is whatsoever any man can necessarily conclude by force of reason; after these" and *only* after these, "the voice of the Church succeeds."[84] Because of the primacy that he afforded to Scripture, Hooker's efforts to ensure that essentials were properly distinguished from matters of adiaphora centered on ensuring that the Bible was properly interpreted.

> For although Scripture be of God, and therefore the proof which is taken from thence must needs be of all other most invincible; yet this strength it has not, unless it avouch the self same thing for which it is brought. . . . But for the most part, even such as are readiest to cite for one thing five hundred sentences of Holy Scripture; what warrant have they, that any one of them means the thing for which it is alleged?[85]

Hooker agreed with the Puritans that the key to a proper interpretation of Scripture was the aid of the Holy Spirit, but he emphasized that not all claims to the guidance of the Holy Spirit were to be accepted as valid. "Dearly beloved *says S. John*, Give not credit unto every Spirit." This warning was given because it was often not clear whether persuasions thought to be of divine inspiration really *"have been wrought by the Holy Ghost, and not by the* fraud *of that evil Spirit which is even in his illusions strong."*[86] Thus, one had to consider "how the testimony of the Spirit may be discerned, by what means it may be known, lest men think that the Spirit of God testifies those things which the spirit of error suggests."[87]

True testimony of the Holy Spirit could be recognized by sure signs. On rare occasions (such as the apostles) the Spirit enlightened people by special revelation, but such inspiration was always unambiguously validated by a concomitant special power to perform miracles. The far more common means by which the Spirit guided people was by empowering their reason to discern the will of God. Christians confronted with a claim to supernatural insight were thus to believe the claimant only if it could be demonstrated that the Spirit was behind the pronouncements by means of miraculous signs or by sound rational arguments.[88] The Puritans produced no miraculous signs, and thus *"the soundness of [their] reasons . . . must declare their opinions . . . to have been wrought by the Holy Ghost."*[89]

In this manner Hooker claimed that in all but the most extraordinary circumstances reason, empowered by the Holy Spirit, was the highest standard to which Christians should turn when interpreting the Bible. "[A]lbeit the Spirit lead us into all truth and direct us in all goodness, yet because these workings of the Spirit in us are so privy and secret, we therefore stand on a plainer ground, when we gather by reason from the quality of things believed or done, that the Spirit of God has directed us in both."[90] This was not to detract from Scripture; "we do not add reason as a supplement of any maim or defect [in Scripture], but as a necessary instrument, without which we could not reap by the Scripture's perfection, that fruit and benefit which it yields."[91] "That which by right exposition builds up Christian faith, being misconstrued breeds error: between true and false construction, the difference reason must show."[92] By this standard Puritan dissent was invalid, because according to the standard of reason, "the error and insufficiency of their arguments does make . . . against them a strong presumption, that God has not moved their hearts to think such things, as he has not enabled them to prove."[93]

Thus Puritan opposition in particular was answered, but to secure order in the church something needed to be done to curb the subjectivism surrounding what was "reasonable." Hooker himself noted that all too often people were "apt to believe upon very slender warrant and to imagine infallible truth where scarce any probable show appears."[94] Consequently, to restore peace and order in the church, there was need for English subjects to submit *"unto some definitive sentence"* as the standard of a reasonable interpretation of the Bible.[95]

Hooker directed those who would discover the dictates of reason to begin with his discussion of the means by which human reason determined the standards of the natural law regarding good and evil. "[O]f discerning goodness there are but these two ways; the one the knowledge of the [first principle] causes whereby it is such, and the other the observation of those signs and tokens, which being annexed always unto goodness, argue that where they are found, there also goodness is. . . ." While the former of these was the most certain, it was "so hard that all shun it," especially "considering how the case does stand with this present age full of tongue and weak for brain."[96] In such circumstances, the best course of action was for community members to look for the signs of proper use of reason, "[t]he most certain" of which was "if the general persuasion of all men do so account it."[97]

This highlights another important aspect of Hooker's assertion that Parliament, including the prince as its leading member, spoke for the entire realm. While not strictly infallible, community-wide assent was the most certain sign available of concurrence with the dictates of right reason; since prince and Parliament spoke for the entire community of England, their determinations could be assumed to be in accord with the dictates of reason.[98] Hooker furthermore argued that deference was rightly given to the consensus of the wise and learned in determining the dictates of reason, even in matters of religion; in England, it was the Convocation that spoke on behalf of those learned in matters of religion.[99]

His identification of the crown, Parliament, and Convocation as the voice of reason in matters of religion enabled Hooker to safeguard order in the church by pointing to these authorities as the surest guides for distinguishing between reasonable and unreasonable interpretations of Scripture. To legitimate disobedience to church laws, arguments drawn from the Bible had to be strong enough to convince all who heard them;[100] certainly such arguments would win over those learned and wise persons who spoke on behalf of the English church. Consequently, unless an individual could produce arguments "grounded upon such manifest and clear proof, that *they in whose hands it is to alter them* [church laws] may likewise infallibly even in heart and conscience judge them so; . . . to urge alteration [of church laws] is to trouble and disturb without necessity."[101] Because he identified reason as the standard of biblical interpretation and the church authorities as the voice of reason, Hooker was able to secure obedience to church laws by claiming that the same people who made church laws authoritatively determined when opposition to such laws was licit!

By addressing the issue of biblical interpretation Hooker rendered illegitimate private opposition to church laws based on prior obedience to the will of God. The individual Christian was allowed to seek God's will as revealed in the Bible, but conclusions reached in this way were always to be brought to the bar of the crown in Parliament with Convocation. When an individual's interpretation of the divine will was contrary to a law of the church, the interpreter was to appeal to the proper authorities to alter the law in question. If the dissenter could not convince church authorities to accept his or her understanding of God's will, then he or she must assume that the spirit of error, not the Holy Spirit, had planted the idea in question and abandon it. After all, "*in litigious and controversed causes . . . the will of God is to have* [dissenters] *do whatsoever the sentence of judicial and final decision shall determine, yea though it seem in their private opinion to swerve utterly from that which is right.*"[102] In the *Lawes* Hooker not only claimed for crown, Parliament, and Convocation the authority to formulate church laws but also defended them against wanton disobedience of the church laws that they had framed.

It is impossible to do justice to the richness of Hooker's thought in such a brief survey; at best the present reflections can hope to give a taste of Hooker's thought and to encourage more detailed study. This chapter has focussed primarily on the *Lawes* because of the tremendous influence of this work, while also taking into account aspects of Hooker's thought revealed and clarified in earlier and later tracts. In the *Lawes* Hooker, revealed in other writings to be a moderate Calvinist, sought to convince English Puritans of the legitimacy of the Elizabethan church. To carry this out Hooker both defended the consistency of church laws with orthodox Protestant theology and also defended the legitimacy of the polity of the church, the means by which these laws were established. Finally, he safeguarded church leaders against resistance (although not against reform) by outlining a rationalist approach to biblical interpretation, and then identifying church leaders themselves as the highest standard of sound reason in the realm. Study of Hooker's works, while perhaps not revealing the mild-mannered detached philosopher that earlier hagiography would lead one to expect, does reveal a serious and thorough scholar defending a church that he considered an effective vehicle of salvation, and a vision of public order that he felt was based on divine mandate.

Notes

1 John Booty, *Reflections on the Theology of Richard Hooker: An Elizabethan Addresses Modern Anglicanism* (Sewanee: University of the South Press, 1998), 3; see also Philip Secor, *Richard Hooker: Prophet of Anglicanism* (Toronto: Anglican Book Centre, 1999), xviii–xix; Nigel Atkinson, *Richard Hooker and the Authority of Scripture, Tradition and Reason: Reformed Theologian of the Church of England?* (Carlisle: Paternoster Press, 1997), ix–xii.

2 Secor, *Richard Hooker*, 308, 320; Hill, *RHCCC*, 4–6 (see Bibliography).

3 See McGrade, *RHCCC*, xi–xxii; Hill, *RHCCC*, 3–20.

4 This is by now a widely accepted, although not unanimous, interpretation of Hooker's work. The *locus classicus* is W. D. J. Cargill Thompson's "The Philosopher of the 'Politic Society': Richard Hooker as a Political Thinker" in W. Speed Hill, ed., *Studies in Richard Hooker: Essays Preliminary to an Edition of his Works* (Cleveland: Case Western Reserve University Press, 1972), 3–76; for recent examples of concurring opinions see William Haugaard, *FLE* 6:72–80; Lee Gibbs, *FLE*, 6:81–6; M. E. C. Perrott, "Richard Hooker and the Problem of Authority in the Elizabethan Church," *JEH* 49/1 (January 1998), 29–60.

5 The reformed character of Hooker's thought is supported by studies such as W. J. Torrance Kirby's *The Theology of Richard Hooker in the Context of the Magisterial Reformation*

(Princeton: Princeton Theological Seminary, 2000), *Richard Hooker's Doctrine of the Royal Supremacy* (Leiden: E. J. Brill, 1990), and "Richard Hooker's Theory of Natural Law in the Context of Reformation Theology," *SCJ* 30/3 (Fall 1999), 681–703; Atkinson's *Richard Hooker*; and Bryan Spinks's *Two Faces of Elizabethan Anglican Theology: Sacraments and Salvation in the Thought of William Perkins and Richard Hooker* (Lanham: Scarecrow Press, 1999), 93–158. Unfortunately space will not allow for discussion of Hooker as a humanist and rhetorician in the present context. For discussion of these aspects of Hooker's thought and leading references see P. E. Forte, *FLE*, 5:674–82; P. G. Stanwood, "Richard Hooker's Discourse and the Deception of Posterity" in Neil Rhodes, ed., *English Renaissance Prose: History, Language, and Politics* (Tempe: Medieval and Renaissance Texts and Studies, 1997), 75–90; and the articles by William Bouwsma, R. J. Schoeck, Brian Vickers, and Charles Watterson Davis in *RHCCC*.

6 *Lawes*, Preface.title; Preface.1.3; Preface.7.1. (Citations of the *Lawes* will use the traditional book and chapter divisions; references to Hooker's other works will cite volume and page in *FLE*. Hooker's italics. Texts partially modernized.)

7 *FLE*, 5:116; see also *FLE*, 4:103; *FLE*, 5:50, 105–6, 312–13; *Lawes*, I.11.5.

8 *FLE*, 5:109.

9 *FLE*, 5:112–13; see also *FLE*, 5:50–1.

10 *FLE*, 5:128.
11 *FLE*, 5:129.
12 *FLE*, 5:160–1.
13 *FLE*, 5:136–7.
14 *FLE*, 5:138.
15 *Lawes*, V.63.1.
16 *Lawes*, V.49.1–2.
17 *FLE*, 4:134–6.
18 *FLE*, 4:136; see 135–7.
19 *FLE*, 4:139.
20 *FLE*, 4:145; see also *Lawes*, V.49.3.
21 *FLE*, 4:146; see also *FLE*, 5:253.
22 See Peter Lake, *Anglicans and Puritans? Presbyterian and English Conformist Thought from Whitgift to Hooker* (London: Unwin Hyman, 1988), 184–6, 190–7.
23 *FLE*, 4:152, emphasis added.
24 *FLE*, 4:85, 148–9, 153.
25 *FLE*, 5:152–3.
26 *FLE*, 4:167.
27 *FLE*, 4:167; see also *FLE*, 5:152–3, 253.
28 *Lawes*, V.56.7.
29 *Lawes*, V.50.1.
30 *Lawes*, V.18.1.
31 *Lawes*, V.21.3.
32 *Lawes*, V.21.5.
33 *Lawes*, V.50.1.
34 *Lawes*, V.23.1.
35 *Lawes*, V.24.1–2; V.25.1–2.
36 *Lawes*, V.67.1.
37 *Lawes*, V.57.4.
38 *Lawes*, V.57.1, 3.
39 *Lawes*, V.57.5.
40 *FLE*, 4:119.
41 *Lawes*, V.50.3.
42 *Lawes*, V.52.1.
43 *Lawes*, V.52.4–V.53.3.
44 *Lawes*, V.54.5–8.
45 *Lawes*, V.54.9.
46 *Lawes*, V.55.7; see V.55.4–6.
47 *Lawes*, V.55.7.
48 *Lawes*, V.67.2.
49 *Lawes*, V.67.6.
50 *Lawes*, V.67.4, 12.
51 *Lawes*, V.67.12.
52 *Lawes*, III.1.2.
53 *Lawes*, III.1.2–3.
54 *Lawes*, III.1.3; see also III.1.4–6.
55 *Lawes*, III.1.14.
56 *Lawes*, Preface.6.3; Preface.6.6; Preface.9.4; V.10.1.
57 *Lawes*, I.16.5; see the first and second books generally, especially I.15.4; I.16.7; II.1.2–4; II.8.5–7.
58 *Lawes*, I.11.2–5.
59 *Lawes*, I.11.5; see I.11.5–6; I.14.3.
60 *Lawes*, III.2.2; see also Preface.4.4; II.2.1; IV.2.3–4; V.4.3; VII.5.8.
61 *Lawes*, I.8.9; see I.8.3–9. Regarding Hooker's naming of this law, see Lee Gibbs, *FLE*, 6:102–3.
62 *Lawes*, I.8.3.
63 *Lawes*, I.14.1.
64 *Lawes*, I.14.5.
65 *Lawes*, Preface.3.2; see also III.10.7; V.21.3.
66 *Lawes*, III.11.20; see III.7.4; III.10.7; V.65.3–5; V.71.7.
67 *Lawes*, III.1.1; V.4.3.
68 *Lawes*, I.10.1–11; III.11.14.
69 *Lawes*, VIII.6.4.
70 *Lawes*, II.7.1; V.10.1.
71 *Lawes*, VIII.title.
72 *Lawes*, I.10.8; VIII.6.1.
73 *Lawes*, I.10.8.
74 *Lawes*, V.68.6; see also III.1.4–11.
75 *Lawes*, III.1.13; see III.1.7–13; V.68.6.
76 *Lawes*, VIII.1.2.
77 *Lawes*, VIII.6.1, 10–11.
78 *Lawes*, VIII.2.1.
79 *Lawes*, VIII.6.13–14. For other powers entailed in this headship, see *Lawes*, VIII.5.1–2; VIII.7.1–5; VIII.8.1–7.
80 *Lawes*, VIII.6.7. It has been noted that this vision of the governance of the church included a larger role for Parliament and Convocation than was typical of conformist thought or, perhaps, than would have been appreciated by the monarch. Secor, 313–14; Lake, 208–12. This may reflect Hooker's "intention to transform the Elizabethan political establishment in the course of justifying it." A. S. McGrade, *FLE*, 6:378; see also *FLE*, 6:366–70.
81 See *Lawes*, II.7.6; III.9.3; IV.14.6; V.8.2–5.
82 *Lawes*, III.9.2.
83 *Lawes*, II.5.7.
84 *Lawes*, V.8.2.
85 *Lawes*, II.7.9.
86 *Lawes*, Preface.3.10.
87 *Lawes*, III.8.15.
88 *Lawes*, IV.14.2; V.10.1.
89 *Lawes*, Preface.3.10.
90 *Lawes*, III.8.15.
91 *Lawes*.III.8.10.
92 *Lawes*, III.8.16.
93 *Lawes*, V.10.1.
94 *Lawes*, V.Dedication.5.
95 *Lawes*, Preface.6.3.

96 *Lawes*, I.8.2.
97 *Lawes*, I.8.3.
98 *Lawes*, VII.15.15; VIII.6.11.
99 *Lawes*, II.7.4–6; VIII.6.1, 11–12.
100 *Lawes*, Preface.6.6; V.29.8.
101 *Lawes*, IV.14.2, emphasis added.
102 *Lawes*, Preface.6.3. Hooker did not immunize the Elizabethan church against challenges to the legitimacy of aspects of its doctrine and

worship. In fact it does not appear to have been Hooker's intention to close all doors to possible reform, but rather to ensure that reform was always carried out through the proper channels. See *Lawes*, Preface.5.2. Hooker occasionally implied that there were aspects of the church that even he would like to see reformed. *Lawes*, V.20.10; VII.24.7–16.

Bibliography

Primary Sources

The definitive modern edition of Hooker's works is *The Folger Library Edition of the Works of Richard Hooker*, 7 vols., gen. ed. W. Speed Hill (various publishers: 1977–98), cited as *FLE*. This edition also contains discussions of Hooker's life and thought by leading Hooker scholars.

Secondary Sources

Hill, W. Speed, ed., *Studies in Richard Hooker: Essays Preliminary to an Edition of his Works*, Cleveland: Case Western Reserve University Press, 1972.

McGrade, A. S., ed., *Richard Hooker and the Construction of Christian Community*, Tempe: Medieval and Renaissance Texts and Studies, 1997, cited as *RHCCC*.

Because the above provide excellent bibliographies, the present bibliography includes only works published after 1993.

Atkinson, Nigel, *Richard Hooker and the Authority of Scripture, Tradition and Reason: Reformed*

Theologian of the Church of England?, Carlisle: Paternoster Press, 1997.

Booty, John, *Reflections on the Theology of Richard Hooker: An Elizabethan Addresses Modern Anglicanism*, Sewanee: University of the South Press, 1998.

Kirby, W. J. Torrance, *The Theology of Richard Hooker in the Context of the Magisterial Reformation*, Princeton: Princeton Theological Seminary, 2000.

Perrott, M. E. C., "Richard Hooker and the Problem of Authority in the Elizabethan Church," *JEH* 49/1 (January 1998), 29–60.

Secor, Philip, *Richard Hooker: Prophet of Anglicanism*, Toronto: Anglican Book Centre, 1999.

Spinks, Bryan, *Two Faces of Elizabethan Anglican Theology: Sacraments and Salvation in the Thought of William Perkins and Richard Hooker*, Lanham: Scarecrow Press, 1999.

Stanwood, P. G., "Richard Hooker's Discourse and the Deception of Posterity," in *English Renaissance Prose: History, Language, and Politics*, ed. Neil Rhodes, Tempe: Medieval and Renaissance Texts and Studies, 1997, 75–90.

Roman Catholic Theologians

Thomas de Vio Cajetan (1469–1534)

Jared Wicks, SJ

Cardinal Cajetan's philosophical and theological legacy stirred criticism in the sixteenth century, both in little-known rebuttals by his Italian Dominican brethren and in a censure from the University of Paris. Still his thought was a point of reference both for the Salamancan Thomists of the sixteenth century and for the "neothomists" of Catholic philosophy and theology between the two Vatican Councils of 1870 and 1962–5.

Cajetan demonstrated no little versatility. In the 1490s he marked out foundational positions in metaphysics and logic. He commented on Aristotle amid debate on the cosmos and the human soul in Padua. While a major administrator of the Dominican order from 1501 to 1518, he wrote most of a landmark commentary on the *Summa theologiae* of Aquinas, with accounts of divine providence and human freedom, fallen humankind and grace, the life of virtue and justice, Christology, and sacraments. In ecclesiology, he defended papal primacy against conciliarism in 1511–12 and Luther in 1521. Created cardinal in 1517 by Pope Leo X, he went on diplomatic missions beyond the Alps, which led to his exchange with Luther in October 1518. He composed some forty short works on personal, social, and economic morality, along with a manual for confessors. In his later years, he wrote on issues raised by the Reformation, but mainly labored on a strictly literal commentary on all of Scripture.

As a native of Gaeta (Latin, *Caieta*), Giacomo de Vio felt a bond with St. Thomas, who had been born just 40 kilometers away. Upon entry into the Dominican province of Naples in 1484, de Vio took "Thomas" as his religious name. In 1488 he was assigned to study at his order's faculty in Bologna, then known for fostering ideals of Dominican austerity and dedication to study. In Bologna, the young friar from Gaeta heard about Dominic of Flanders (died 1479), who traced a path de Vio was to follow, by presenting Thomistic metaphysics as the foundation of a sound theology.

The Cajetanian Stream of Thomistic Philosophy

In spring 1491 Friar Thomas went to Padua to complete his studies and begin teaching. During his four years there, he began to be called *Caietanus* or *il Gaetano*, from the city of his birth. In 1493, he was incorporated into the university as an instructor and began lecturing on the *Sentences* of Peter Lombard. Notes from these lectures constitute a bulky commentary, still in manuscript in the Bibliothèque Nationale in Paris. With this course Cajetan inserted himself into the Thomist tradition, often vindicating Aquinas against fourteenth-century opponents like John Duns Scotus and Durandus of Saint-Pourçain, and frequently following the *Defensiones* (1409–33) of Johannes Capreolus.

In 1494 Cajetan was made master of theology by his order and was able to fill the university chair of Thomistic metaphysics in Padua for a year. Naturally he opposed the veteran Scotist chairholder, Antonio Trombetta, OFM. He lectured on Aquinas's treatise *On Being and Essence*, leading to a commentary published in 1496 and reprinted as a standard expression of Thomistic fundamentals during the scholastic revivals of the sixteenth and early twentieth centuries.[1]

Cajetan's philosophical Thomism offers refined dialectic. He argues that the Scotists depart from Aristotelian principles, then regnant in Padua, on being, substance, and universal concepts. Where they exalt God's freedom, even to decree the existence of form without matter, Cajetan holds a meaningful universe with these principles intrinsically ordered and inseparable from each other. Cajetan makes a real distinction between "essence," by which a reality is what-it-is, and "existence," conferring actuality upon a being. Creatures are not identical with the existence given them by the First Cause, while the latter is distinctive in that what-it-is is uncreated actual existence itself, which Thomists found in God's self-revelation as "I am who am" (Ex. 3:14).

Cajetan completed another work, *The Analogy of Names*, in 1498 after leaving Padua.[2] This offers a lucid systematization of scattered remarks by St. Thomas. Cajetan classifies the ways in which concepts and notions, especially those of metaphysics, apply to the realities of which they are predicated. He features the "analogy of proportionality" based on the correlation between the principles constituting being, as between what-it-is and existence, with the latter being ever correlative or proportionate to what-it-is. Cajetan ascribes minimal importance to the "analogy of attribution," basing the relations between beings, for example, to an effective cause which imprints some likeness of itself upon its creations. Analogically, the notions of "being," "truth," and "good" can be applied, based on somewhat similar intrinsic constitutions, to creatures and to God. From this basis our terms for God are not part of a special linguistic universe apart from daily discourse, and are saved from being mere approximations.[3]

Controversy over Aristotle, 1495–1510

Philosophy in Padua featured the study of Aristotle based on the commentaries of the Arab scholar Averroës of Cordova (died 1198). This lens gave Paduan

Artistotelianism a naturalist coloration, prescinding from Christian teachings on creation and providence, human individuality, and the soul's immortality. One exponent of the school, Nicoletto Vernia (1420–99), espoused the eternity of the cosmos, a finite first mover, the existence of a single "agent intellect" for all human beings, and the corruption of the individual soul upon death. Pietro Pomponazzi began teaching in 1488. His courses on Aristotle's *De anima* questioned the possibility of rationally proving the immortality of the human soul. The Scotist Trombetta contested Vernia's denial of the soul's destiny to live on after death. Thus Friar Thomas de Vio began his teaching in an agitated situation of philosophical argument on themes concerning the world and the human person.[4]

Cajetan's response to the Averroist theses came in commentaries on fundamental works by Aristotle, *On Interpretation, Posterior Analytics, The Categories*, and *Metaphysics*. The last-named commentary has not survived, but Cajetan published the others in 1506, adding a work on Porphyry's *Introduction to the Categories* and his own works on being, essence, and analogy. His aim was to vindicate an understanding of Aristotle coherent with the Thomistic vision of reality and thus to show his brethren the first steps toward a sound philosophy.[5]

Cajetan confronted the Averroist reading of Aristotle in *The Infinity of the First Mover*, completed in 1499 and printed in 1510. His argument was constricted by the Aristotelian focus on causes of change in nature, not on existence itself, but he still developed philosophical arguments for the "intensive infinity" of God's power, and even found such a view in Averroes.

To treat Paduan theories of human destiny, the central text was Aristotle's *The Soul*. Cajetan's composition of a commentary was delayed by changes of residence, and by attacks on the Averroists for using inaccurate Latin versions of Aristotle. Humanists competent in Greek saw Paduan philosophical naturalism building on shaky textual foundations. In 1497 the arts faculty of Padua established a chair for teaching Aristotle from his original Greek. Moving with the times, Cajetan's commentary of 1509 works on a new Latin version of *De anima*, which helped him undercut some Averroist positions as not grounded in Aristotle's original text.[6]

Cajetan's fresh access to Aristotle also led him to break with the Thomist tradition of finding Aristotle proving the soul's immortality. Cajetan disengaged an historical Aristotle for whom the human soul would corrupt when it ceased functioning as the substantial form of the body. Aristotle, wise as he was, had chosen a method that left immortality unproven. Cajetan offered other arguments for the soul's potential to exist in separation from the body. The overall symmetry of a wisely created universe makes appropriate a reality intermediate between the angelic pure spirits and the merely sentient animating principles of animal life.

In 1516 Pietro Pomponazzi's *The Immortality of the Soul* rejected any rational proof for human life after death. This brought an accusation of heresy and led to charges of Cajetan's complicity in the gestation of Pomponozzi's position. A Dominican, Bartolomeo Spina, began his 1519 refutation of Pomponozzi with the claim that Cajetan had opened the door to disruption by holding an incompatibility between Aristotelian reasoning on the human person and the tenets of revelation and Catholic doctrine.[7]

Theologian and Dominican Administrator, 1501–1518

Cajetan left Padua in 1495 to lecture in the Dominican priories of northern Italy. In 1497 he became professor of Thomistic theology in Pavia, at the request of the duke of Milan. But in 1499 he was called to Milan mainly to deal with questions of social and economic morality, while continuing on his commentaries on Aristotle. In Pavia he began his commentary on the *Summa theologiae* of St. Thomas, which we will take up in the next section.

Cajetan's work in Milan ended in 1501, with a call to Rome and appointment to the office of procurator general of the Dominican order, which placed him at the side of the master general, with responsibility for the order's dealings with the pope and his associated curial officials.

By tradition, the Dominican procurator preached before the pope and his entourage on the first Sundays of Lent and Advent. From Cajetan five such sermons given before Popes Alexander VI and Julius II are extant.[8] These texts show Cajetan adorning his prose with an elegance lacking in other works. His treatment was doctrinal, on the efficacy of prayer, the marvel of the Incarnation, the cause of evil, human immortality, and the pains suffered in hell by lost souls. His explanations, based on St. Thomas, were rarely technical and brought in common-sense examples. He moved easily from instruction to pleasingly brief exhortations to sincere prayer, devout longing for Christ, and resolute turning-away from dissipation in the busyness of everyday life.

In Milan and during his first years in Rome, Cajetan composed numerous short works on ethical questions and cases requiring the application of moral norms. A set of these, reprinted in his *Opuscula*, treated marital questions. Others were on the seal of confessional secrecy and the obligations of a priest taking a stipend for offering mass for a given intention. In late 1503, a year which had seen two papal elections, Cajetan wrote a position paper on the intrinsic evil of the purchase of pastoral office, which in a papal election was exacerbated by promises of lucrative offices to avaricious electors. Other treatises, much studied by later moralists, treated the just price, exchange banking, moneylending, and licit forms of interest. Cajetan interpreted the prohibition of usury quite strictly, with the effect of broadening areas of licit banking and commercial credit practices. On the Franciscan *montes pietatis*, a form of credit union, he disapproved of their mandatory 6 percent interest on loans, holding that the indigent should pay less. He urged that the *montes* become public institutions of welfare, with expenses covered not from interest but from the revenues of the commune or principality. But the Fifth Lateran Council in 1515 gave the *montes* its approval, including their rates of interest.[9]

In 1507 the Dominican master general died before completing his term, and Cajetan was appointed by the pope as vicar general. In 1508 the general chapter elected him master in his own right and he began a decade in the order's highest office. His decisions amid crises affecting the order lie outside of the scope of this essay. But we note that in October 1508 he had the Spanish friars send men to the New World. Soon some forty Dominicans were in this mission, including two advocates of the rights of the Amerindians, Pedro de Córdoba and Antonio de

Montécino, soon joined by Bartolomé de las Casas, who entered the order in 1522. Informed by his confreres, Cajetan's commentary on the *Summa* includes a pronouncement on the immorality of plunder and wars of subjugation against innocent people. In 1532 he answered questions about pastoral practice in instructing and baptizing the Amerindians and dealing with cases of polygamy.[10]

Cajetan's generalate included marshaling Dominican opposition to the conciliarism that emerged, under French royal sponsorship, against Pope Julius II. When an antipapal council was convoked in Pisa in 1511, Cajetan prepared a refutation of the claim that a general council could sit in judgment on, and even depose, a reigning pope. This work, *A Comparison of the Authority of Pope and Council*, argued that papal superiority over councils was instituted by Christ in words to Peter in Matthew 16 and John 21. After refuting conciliarist arguments, Cajetan did admit that a council was the forum for removing a heretical pope from office, but lesser abuses should be countered by argument, refusal to obey evil laws, and prayer that God deliver his people from an evil shepherd. In Paris, Jacques Almain published a rebuttal, to which Cajetan responded with an *Apologia* in November 1512. With these works Cajetan joined his confrere Juan de Torquemada (1388–1468) and the Jesuit Robert Bellarmine (1542–1621) in laying foundations for the accentuation of papal authority in Catholic ecclesiology in modern times.[11]

But Julius II convoked his own council, Lateran V (1512–17), where Cajetan delivered an oration on papal plenitude of authority and on using this in enacting reform measures.[12] As the council continued under the first Medici pope, Leo X, elected in 1513, it took up the question of immortality and issued *Apostolici regiminis* condemning the notion of the soul's mortality, along with the idea that this followed from philosophical reasoning. A second part mandated philosophers to vindicate Christian teaching and refute arguments against it. When the 130 council members voted, two dissents were recorded, one of which was Cajetan's, against the second part, which for him compromised the distinctiveness of philosophical reflection.

The Commentary on the *Summa* of Aquinas

In Pavia, Milan, and Rome, Cajetan worked on the first complete commentary on the *Summa theologiae* of St. Thomas, published in four volumes between 1508 and 1523. Cajetan is excruciatingly attentive to detail but also expansive in vision, as he locates each article systematically in the *Summa*, traces the steps of argumentation, refutes fourteenth-century adversaries, gives cross-references to other works by Thomas, and at times makes contemporary applications. The commentary was read during the flowering of scholasticism in Salamanca by Vitoria, Domingo de Soto, Cano, Bañez, and their disciples. To serve the Thomist revival promoted by Pope Leo XIII, it was printed with the *Summa* in the stately Leonine edition (vols. IV–XII, 1888–1906).

Cajetan's construal of Aquinas did not escape criticism, both in the sixteenth and twentieth centuries. Francisco de Vitoria could lament Cajetan's subtlety, while Henri de Lubac finds him treating the natural order as practically a self-sufficient sphere to which God adds on a call to salvation in Christ. Gilson called the opening passage of the commentary less an interpretation of Aquinas than a substitution of Cajetan's own notion of the aim and purpose of theology.[13]

But in explaining the *Pars Prima*, completed in 1507, Cajetan did set forth the Thomist doctrine of God by emphasizing the divine influence penetrating the whole universe and all history. God's providential governance is more than foreknowledge, for it entails a causality by which God works in all things, moving and disposing them. Thomas had cited Wisdom 8:1, "She reaches mightily from one end to the other, and she orders all things well," which the Vulgate rendered with wisdom working *fortiter*, disposing everything *suaviter*. God's *suavis dispositio* became a motif for Cajetan, even when he admitted that our understanding cannot grasp how God's mode of causing certainly leaves true contingency in history and freedom in human choices.[14]

While master general of his order, Cajetan completed his commentary on the *Pars Prima Secundae* (printed in 1514), including treatment of fallen humankind and justification. He affirmed the inroads of original sin, which upsets the harmony of human powers and reduces ability to do good, even making sin inevitable if God withholds the aid of grace. Although fallen humans retain considerable abilities, the help of grace is necessary in beginning the passage to justification, but once justified a person has no complete certitude about being reconciled with God. Even though the sacraments of Christ are effective of themselves (*ex opere operato*), their grace can only be received with actual devotion of trust and love. The good works of the justified are meritorious because grace intrinsically orders human actions to eternal life with God, making meaningless the added free "acceptation" by God, taught in the Scotist and Ockhamist schools.

Cajetan worked on the *Pars secunda secundae* during the Fifth Lateran, finishing in 1517. He affirmed papal superiority over general councils and infallibility in doctrinal definitions of the faith. Numerous articles treated moral questions, e.g., the obligation to restore unjustly obtained goods, usury, the obligations consequent on vows, and simony in acquiring church offices. On the sin of plunder (*rapina*), he branded the conquest of lands rightly held by native peoples "highway robbery" (*magna latrocinia*). Such people should encounter exemplary preachers of Christ, not pillaging oppressors. He argued for two reform measures in the church, namely, the constant residence of a bishop in his diocese, and forbidding unreformed religious communities to admit new members, so as to place the non-observant before the dilemma of reform or extinction.

Cajetan's comments on the Second Part offered a Christian ethics, treating moral norms and conscience, the virtues and opposed vices, the law's obligation and graces's empowerment, a whole span of economic questions, and the obligations of justice in society and responsibility in the church. To make this available, Cajetan prepared in dictionary style a *Summula peccatorum*, completed in 1523 and reprinted over twenty-five times in the century that followed.[15]

Cajetan took up the *Pars tertia* in 1517, treating Christology and sacraments. Christ's humanity has a fullness of grace which is the universal principle of all grace given to humans. The passion has universal causal influence, even to effecting our believing reception of grace in faith and love. Christ as living Head joins his members' actions to his own to give them value before God. But in justification and sacramental reception, the heart must move devoutly toward God in faith in Christ's death for the life of the work and, for example, in interior repentance when given absolution from sin. In this volume Cajetan insists on Scripture as the norm in sound theology, for example, in criticizing the Scotist speculation that the Word would become incarnate even if Adam had not sinned. From Scripture we know only that Christ came to save sinners. Cajetan lamented that teachers neglect biblical language to introduce allegories not sanctioned by the inspired text. But Scripture does not answer every question, and so one needs church teaching, for example, on the sacraments as causes, not just symbols, of grace, and on the "conversion" of bread and wine into the eucharistic body and blood of Christ. He urged biblical and ecclesial evidence against popular piety regarding Mary, giving voice to the Dominican aversion to Mary's Immaculate Conception as entering the sphere of teaching by an erratic path of development.[16]

Cajetan concluded his commentary with Question 90, Article 3 of the Third Part of the *Summa*, the point at which Aquinas was interrupted by his death in 1274. To round off his work, Cajetan composed 28 supplementary treatises on penance, indulgences, and marriage, eventually writing *finis* to his monumental project on December 19, 1520.

By late 1520, Cajetan's life had changed. He was made cardinal by Leo X in July 1517 and handed over governance of his order to a vicar in 1518, when he went as papal legate to Augsburg, where he met Luther. By September 1519 he was back in Rome with time for study and writing. Volume four of the *Summa* commentary came out in January 1523, in an edition including other treatises by Cajetan.

Well into the twentieth century, Cajetan was for Catholic theologians a guide to the synthesis of St. Thomas. Readers could find Cajetan more complex than the lucid Aquinas, but he showed them the distinctive traits of Thomism in contrast with Scotist and other positions. His high view of the papacy harmonized with modern Catholic ecclesiology. Although his Marian doctrine was set aside, his soteriology and sacramental theology fitted well with the Council of Trent (1545–63). Thus, the Thomist doctrine of God's creation and saving economy that was widely influential in modern Catholicism was shaped in no small measure by Thomas de Vio Cajetan.

Meeting Luther in Person and in Print, 1518–1521

Cajetan left Rome in May 1518, as the pope's legate to the Diet of the German Empire in Augsburg. On August 5 he called on the assembled estates to give financial backing to Leo X's plan of defense of central Europe against the Turks. The princes and delegates of free cities of the empire balked at levying a tax for this cause and postponed a response until the next diet. By late September the emperor and many princes had left Augsburg. Cajetan was to stay close to Maximillian to solidify his backing of the defensive "crusade," but this changed with the emperor's death on January 12, 1519. Cajetan was then to contact the seven electors to assure that they took account of the pope's interests when they chose the new emperor.

After Cajetan left Rome, a canonical case began against Luther as "suspect of heresy." The papal theologian Sylvester Prierias examined Luther's *Ninety-five Theses*, writing an accusatory *Dialogus* printed in June 1518. On this basis, Luther was summoned to Rome to answer charges. Cajetan received it with Prierias's booklet, so he could inform the Saxon Prince-Elector Friedrich, and send the materials to Luther. In late August, Friedrich petitioned Cajetan to have the case remitted to a German tribunal, which Cajetan agreed to request from Rome. But in Rome a denunciation by Emperor Maximillian escalated the case, by charging that Luther was openly and obstinately spreading heresies. Luther moved from being "suspect" to stand accused, and an August 23 letter from Rome told Cajetan to have Luther arrested. Elector and legate again conferred, with Cajetan gaining Friedrich's cooperation by offering to hear Luther and do everything possible to terminate this threat against the good name of Friedrich's University of Wittenberg. By September, Cajetan had a new commission, calculated to please Friedrich, namely, to examine Luther and judge whether to terminate the case or confirm the heresy charges.[17]

While Luther came to Augsburg, Cajetan studied works by Luther then available, *Explanations of the Ninety-five Theses* and a *Sermon on Penance*. A year before Cajetan had, without realizing it, prepared himself by composing his own treatise on indulgences.[18] In Augsburg, the legate concretized his study in 14 treatises, cast as *quaestiones* in which he first cites Luther's arguments for particular positions, then states a counter-position, after which he offers definitions and arguments to ground the position taken, and finally rebuts Luther's initial arguments.[19] Thus Cajetan knew exactly what he had to say to Luther when they met on October 12, 13, and 14. This meeting of the pope's legate and the Wittenberg professor was a critical moment in Luther's life and the Reformation, but rare are the Luther biographers or Reformation historians who know Cajetan's previous analyses of Luther's positions.

In a treatise completed on September 26, Cajetan concluded that Luther's *Sermon on Penance* and his *Explanations*, Thesis 7, proposed a novel view about how to receive absolution in confession. Luther stressed faith to the point of believing in the efficacy of absolution here and now. The priest's declaration rests on the potent words of Jesus, "Whatever you loose on earth will be loosed in heaven" (Matt. 16:19), and so faith must be assured of the grace imparted through absolution. For Cajetan faith indeed holds that sacraments are efficacious, but faith's certitude does not extend to particular cases in which the recipient may harbor attitudes impeding the reception of God's grace.[20]

Completed on October 7, Cajetan's study of Luther's *Explanations*, Thesis 58, found Luther diverging from Pope Clement VI's fourteenth-century document on indulgences. Luther said that indulgences were granted in virtue of the power to bind or loose conferred on Peter and his successors, whereas Clement VI taught that the accumulated merits of the good done by Christ and his saints were applied by the pope in remitting penances through an indulgence.[21]

Luther, we know, was not swayed by Cajetan's statement of the two alleged errors, and held fast to these positions. In a last-ditch diplomatic effort, Cajetan suspended his demand on faith in absolution and offered to let the case drop if Luther would only declare his adherence to Clement VI's doctrine on the basis of indulgences.[22] But Luther went over Cajetan's head with an appeal to the pope and left Augsburg for Wittenberg.

Cajetan added to his treatises a fifteenth text, on Luther's *Sermon on Excommunication*, which he received in mid-October. Cajetan found Luther treating this church-penalty as only juridical and external, without import in the realm of mutual intercession in the Communion of Saints.[23] Also, to offset the difficulty of applying a papal teaching of 1343 in judging Luther's *Explanations* of 1518, Cajetan prepared a draft text of indulgence teaching and sent it to Rome. It quickly came back as a doctrinal declaration by Leo X on indulgences as effective for those rightly disposed in lessening the punishment they must undergo for sin, by an application from the superabundant satisfaction of Christ and the saints.[24] When Luther saw Leo's document, he dismissed it as not based on Scripture, the Fathers, and the canons, from which one rightly asks the grounds of teaching. One senses that the central argument is the basis and mode of papal teaching in the church.

During most of 1519, Luther's case was overshadowed by the election of a new emperor. Cajetan sought to align the electors with Leo X's opposition to the Hapsburg candidate, Charles of Burgundy, ruler of the Netherlands, Spain, and the Kingdom of Naples. But Charles was elected on June 28, 1519, and this ended Cajetan's diplomatic mission with a further failure beyond those of the crusade proposed at the Diet and the Luther case.

In early 1520 Cajetan worked in Rome on the drafting of the condemnation of Luther's errors, but argued in vain for a select list with exact qualification of the gravity of the error and evidence of the norms being applied. Johann Eck had come to Rome with lists of propositions excerpted from Luther, and these were globally censured, without counter-argument, in the papal bull *Exsurge Domine* (June 15, 1520), threatening Luther with excommunication if he held obstinately to these positions.

In late 1520 Cajetan took up the basis of papal authority, the main issue at the Leipzig Disputation between Luther and Eck in midsummer 1519. Cajetan defended the primacy as an element in the constitution of the church as founded by Christ himself.[25] Cajetan treats the texts of Matthew 16 and John 21 qualifying Peter as "rock," the bearer of the keys, and the shepherd of the sheep. The last chapter surveys Fathers of the Church and councils attesting to reception of the primacy. Like Cajetan's other works of Reformation controversy, this one marshals evidence dispassionately, with no hint of animus against the author whose interpretations he cites and refutes. Shortly afterward, Cajetan responded to a request of Pope Leo to explain the condemnation in *Exsurge* of certain views of Luther, over which some readers were left mystified.[26]

Confronting the Reformation, 1525–1534

After Leo X's death, Cajetan exercised influence in the conclave of January 1522 that elected Adrian, Cardinal Dedel of Utrecht, then regent of Charles V in Spain. The new pope, Adrian VI, sent Cajetan as legate to Hungary, but the mission was cut short by Adrian's death in 1523 and the accession of Pope Clement VII. Under Clement, Cajetan was left free to study and publish the biblical commentaries to be treated in our next section. On occasion, however, he was asked to furnish responses on issues of debate with the Protestant Reformation.

In 1525, Clement VII was alerted to Zwingli's teachings and planned to send a spokesman to Zurich on behalf of normative doctrine on the Eucharist. Cajetan was asked to furnish the envoy with a doctrinal text, and he wrote an *Instruction* with counter-arguments to 12 points in Zwingli's spiritualist interpretation of John 6 and of the words of institution.[27] Cajetan countered with a basic principle of faith, which lays hold of invisible realities precisely in their union with what is visible, which here is the Body of Christ united with the forms of bread and wine. St. Paul offers ample evidence of the presence of the true Body and Blood of Christ. Further, it is wrong to reduce the Supper solely to Communion, for it also signifies the sacrificial death of Christ that is offered spiritually.

Cajetan's thought on the Eucharist found limpid expression in a work of 1531.[28] He had noted the denial of eucharistic sacrifice in the *Augsburg Confession*, Article 24, and Melanchthon's *Judgment on the Mass* (1530). In response, Cajetan offered biblical arguments, making much of Jesus' mandate to *do* the action in commemoration of his giving his "body offered for you." Since Lutherans hold the true presence of Christ's Body and Blood, Cajetan specified that this is the body-offered and the blood-shed, now present "in the mode of an offering."

Other points in the *Augsburg Confession* prompted a short response by Cajetan critical of four Lutheran tenets, namely, that Communion under both forms is an obligation admitting no alternative, that one need not confess all one's serious sins, that it is wrong to perform satisfactory prayers or works after absolution, and that invocation of the saints has no basis in Scripture.[29] But along with the biblical grounding of Catholic practices, Cajetan also explored ways of an accommodation with the Lutheran leadership in matters not of the substance of the faith. A memorandum of 1531 states that clerical marriage and Communion under both forms can be allowed, that different liturgical forms of the Mass can be admitted (providing the Roman Canon is not excluded), and that one need not insist on laws of purely ecclesiastical origin when there is good reason for not observing them.[30]

A final response to Reformation teaching was Cajetan's *Faith and Works*.[31] He had before him Melanchthon's *Apology* of the *Augsburg Confession*, and on faith he reworked his Augsburg treatise (September 26, 1518), adding biblical texts, to distinguish faith in God's revealed word from belief in grace given here and now. On good works, he opposed the charge that ascribing to them meritorious value derogates from the sufficiency of Christ's mediation. Cajetan defines "merit" restrictively as that which God has ordained to found in Christ's members and to reward. Instead of a lack in Christ's mediation, the merits of his members show instead the overflowing value of the work of the Head, by which the members come to act in conformity to Christ.

Cajetan's theological assistance of Clement VII also treated the marriage of King Henry VIII and Catherine of Aragon. By early 1530 numerous opinions had been written for and against the validity of the dispensation of 1503 by which Pope Julius II had freed Henry and Catherine from the canonical impediment resulting from Catherine's previous marriage with Henry's deceased brother Prince Arthur. Cajetan's report took the form of an analysis of the prohibitions of such marriages in Leviticus and Deuteronomy, for which he had help from individuals knowledgeable in Hebrew. His conclusion fully justified the dispensation and the consequent validity of the royal marriage.[32] Four years later, one of Cajetan's last writings was a belated appeal to Henry VIII to reverse the erroneous decision of having his first marriage dissolved.[33]

A Work of Biblical Exposition, 1524–1534

In mid-1524 Cajetan completed his first work of biblical exposition, the *Jentacula Novi Testamenti*, on 64 selected verses which might well need clarification for their apposite use in teaching or preaching.[34] But this was only a prelude. At Easter 1527 Cajetan had the satisfaction of completing three years of labor on his exposition of the Psalms according to their literal sense. It was not easy, since it entailed composing a new Latin translation based on word-by-word oral explanations of the original text by two assistants who knew Hebrew.[35] The preface explains that the centrality of the Psalms in liturgical prayer, as in the divine office, made this a work of formation of Christians. Further, the expositions then circulating treated many Psalm verses according to their "mystical sense," which was not what the inspired author meant to provide. Further, the Vulgate text proved upon examination so inexact that a new Latin version had to be made as the basis of the commentary.

With the commentary on the Psalms, Cajetan began the last great project of his life. He moved on to expound the four Gospels (1527–8), the Pauline corpus (1528–9), Acts and the Catholic Epistles (1529), the Pentateuch (1530), the historical books from Joshua through Nehemiah (1531–2), Job (1533), Proverbs and Qohelet (1534), and, before his death in August 1534, the initial three chapters of Isaiah.[36] After the Psalms, Cajetan offered no further new Latin translations, although he noted numerous faulty renderings in the Vulgate text of John's Gospel and the Epistle to the Romans. His passion for Scripture's literal sense was such that he omitted the Book of Revelation and the Song of Songs from his exegetical project, admitting that their authors' original communicative intentions were beyond his grasp.

Some have said that Cajetan's clashes with Luther showed him the importance of the biblical text in defending the Catholic faith, and thus his final work is thought to be an instrument for anti-Reformation controversy. But this does not stand up in the face of the actual content of the commentaries. References to Lutherans are rare and Cajetan's treatment of texts on Peter's role, bishops, and the Eucharist make no extended effort at proving Catholic tenets. On Matthew 16:18f. he counters excesses regarding papal authority, while what Paul says about prayer in tongues (1 Cor. 14:14) is for Cajetan reason to recommend suppressing Latin in the Mass.

Cajetan's motivations in his Scripture commentaries are first theological, since he holds that God's revelation of everything necessary for salvation is given in what Scripture says according to its literal sense, which we know either by competent interpretation or by a clarificatory church teaching. As for Aquinas, so for Cajetan faith holds what God revealed through the prophets and apostles who speak in Scripture. Second, teachers and preachers of his day need to know the true doctrines of Scripture, both to shape their teaching accordingly and to have a clear norm for introducing reform of Christian life. For example, the literal sense of Matthew 19:9 on adultery and divorce shows that current church practice prohibiting remarriage could in fact change in the light of the exception made by Jesus. Also, New Testament texts on the lifestyle of Jesus' disciples and on the duties of pastors constitute an admonition to present-day religious orders and to the bishops of the church. Thus Cajetan set forth Scripture both to place theology on solid ground and to guide practice in the church.[37]

Cajetan's main authorities on Scripture were St. Jerome and, on the New Testament, Erasmus, even though he at times differs with the annotations of the latter. Jerome provided much information on the *hebraica veritas* of the Scriptures of Israel, but he also instilled in Cajetan a restrictive view of the biblical canon. Thus, Cajetan did not treat the deuterocanonical books of the Old Testament, since he held they were works of edification not admissible in ascertaining the content of faith. In the New Testament, Cajetan qualified the longer ending of Mark as less authoritative than the rest of the Gospel, questioned the authenticity of John 8:1–11, and ranked James with Second and Third John below the Epistles of certain apostolic authorship. On Hebrews, he held doubtful canonicity, and insufficiency by itself to ground an article of faith.

Cajetan's biblical work was naturally appreciated, in its intention if not fully in its execution, by later historical-critical exegetes, beginning with Richard Simon in the late seventeenth century.[38] But the immediate reaction by some was sharply critical, as in polemical writings by Dominicans Ambrosius Catharinus and Melchior Cano against Cajetan's audacity on the canon, his correction of the revered Vulgate, and his views on many passages that diverged from the tradition.[39] Catharinus denounced Cajetan to the Sorbonne, where the theology faculty examined a list of Cajetan's biblical errors in 1532–3. An intervention of the pope headed off a formal condemnation, but the faculty composed and sent to Cajetan a sharp reprimand listing 24 censurable points in his commentaries. The letter circulated and was printed, of all places, in Wittenberg, to publicize this slur on the good name of Luther's judge in 1518.[40]

Thomas de Vio Cajetan, being "a man of many parts," is unfortunately most widely known as the unsuccessful interlocutor of Luther at Augsburg in 1518. His role there was in part diplomatic but also theological. For diplomacy he was not well prepared, whereas his theological competence is beyond question, and is evidenced by his preparation for meeting Luther and his selectivity in addressing precise issues of Luther's teaching. But in biblical studies he was a lonely prophet of things to come, while contributing directly to early modern Catholic theology, in its philosphical foundations, its doctrine, and its ethics, both personal and social.

Notes

1 The work saw sixteenth-century printings and many more in Cajetan's *Opuscula omnia*. After Leo XIII mandated study of St. Thomas, Cajetan's *In de ente et essentia* was appended to the Paris edition of Aquinas's *Quaestiones disputatae* in 1883, and new editions were edited by Michaele de Maria (Rome: Pontificia Officina Typographica, 1907) and Marie-Hyacinte Laurent (Turin: Marietti, 1934). In English: *Commentary on Being and Essence*, trans. Lottie H. Kendzierski and Francis C. Wade (Milwaukee: Marquette University Press, 1964).

2 Like *In de ente et essentia*, *De nominum analogia* appeared often in the sixteenth century by itself and in Cajetan's *Opuscula omnia*. Dominicans at the Angelicum University

brought out editions in 1934 and 1952, while Bruno Pinchard issued a Latin-French edition, with introduction and commentary, *Métaphysique et sémantique. Autour de Cajétan* (Paris: Vrin, 1987). In English: *The Analogy of Names* . . . , trans. Edward A. Bushinski (Pittsburgh: Duquesne University Press, 1953).

3 Modern Thomist criticism has not spared Cajetan's doctrine, e.g., George Klubertanz, *St. Thomas Aquinas on Analogy* (Chicago: Loyola University Press, 1960); Ralph McInerny, "Where Cajetan Went Wrong" in *Aquinas and Analogy* (Washington, DC: Catholic University of America Press, 1996), 3–29. An informed appreciation is Franco Riva, *Analogia e univocità in Tommaso de Vio "Gaetano"* (Milan: Vita e Pensiero, 1995).

4 Antonino Poppi, *Introduzione all'Aristotelismo padovano* (Padua: Antenore, 1970); Charles B. Schmitt, *Aristotle in the Renaissance* (Cambridge: Harvard University Press, 1983); Edward P. Mahoney, "Nicoletto Vernia on the Soul and Immortality" in his edited collection, *Philosophy and Humanism. Essays in Honor of Paul Oskar Kristeller* (Leiden: E. J. Brill, 1976), 144–63; Martin L. Pine, *Pietro Pomponazzi: Radical Philosopher of the Renaissance* (Padua: Antenore, 1986).

5 Reprints appeared in 1575, 1579, and 1587. In modern editions: the exposition of Porphyry, ed. Isnard Marenga (Rome: Angelicum, 1934), and of Aristotle's *Categories*, ed. Marie-Hyacinte Laurent (Rome: Angelicum, 1939). In English: Aristotle, *On Interpretation. Commentary by St. Thomas and Cajetan*, trans. Jean T. Oesterle (Milwaukee: Marquette University Press, 1962).

6 The modern edition is *Commentaria in De Anima Aristotelis*, ed. Ioannes Coquelle, 2 vols. (Rome: Angelicum, 1938–9), on Books I and II and *Commentaria in libros Aristotelis De Anima Liber III*, eds. Guy Picard and Gilles Pelland (Brouges: Desclée, 1965). A perceptive study is Etienne Gilson, "Cajétan et l'humanisme théologique," *Archives d'histoire doctrinelle et littéraire du Moyen Age* 22 (1955), 113–36.

7 B. Spina, *Propugnaculum Aristotelis de immortalitate animae contra Thomam Caietanum* (Venice: 1519). Other Dominican critics of Cajetan have been studied by Michael Tavuzzi, e.g., "Chrysostomus Javelli, O. P. (c.1470–1538), Biobibliographical Essay," *Angelicum* 67 (1990), 457–82; "Valentino

da Camerino, O.P. (1438–1515): Teacher and Critic of Cajetan," *Traditio* 49 (1994), 287–316; "Silvestro da Prierio and the Pomponozzi Affair," *Renaissance and Reformation* 19 (1995), 47–61; "Gaspare di Baldassare da Perugia, O.P. (1465–1531): a Little-known Adversary of Cajetan," *The Thomist* 60 (1996), 595–615; *Prierias. The Life and Works of Silvestro Mazzolini da Prierio, 1456–1527* (Durham, NC: Duke University Press, 1997), 91–104.

8 These texts from 1501–4 appeared in Cajetan's *Opuscula*, with one being translated as "On the Immortality of Minds" (1503) in L. A. Kennedy, ed., *Renaissance Philosophy. New Translations* (The Hague: Mouton, 1973), 46–54. On the sermons of this genre: John W. O'Malley, *Praise and Blame in Renaissance Rome* (Durham, NC: Duke University Press, 1979). More in detail on Cajetan's texts: Jared Wicks, "Thomism between Renaissance and Reformation: the Case of Cajetan," *ARG* 68 (1977), 9–32.

9 These responses were printed in 1511 and edited by N. Zammit, *Opuscula oeconomica-socialia* (Rome: Angelicum, 1934), while a 1501 treatise on the mass stipend is translated in Heiko A. Oberman, ed., *Forerunners of the Reformation* (New York: Holt, Rinehart, & Winston, 1966), 256–64.

10 Alvaro Huerga, "El Cardinal Cayetano ante los problemas teológicos del Neuvo Mundo" in Antonio Piolanti, ed., *S. Tommaso Filosofo* (Vatican City: Liberia Editrice Vaticana, 1995), 305–21.

11 Cajetan's treatises stand first in his *Opuscula*. An edition is V.-M. Jacques Pollet, ed. (Rome: Angelicum, 1936). See Olivier de la Brosse, *Le pape et le concile* (Paris: Cerf, 1965); José A. Dominguez Asensio, "Infalibilidad y potestad magisterial en la polémica anticonciliarista de Cayetano," *Communio* (Seville) 14 (1981), 3–50, 205–26; Ulrich Horst, *Zwischen Konziliarismus und Reformation. Studien zur Ekklesiologie im Dominikanerorden* (Rome: Istituto storico domenicano, 1985); and Katherine Elliot van Liere, "Vittoria, Cajetan, and the Conciliarists," *Journal of the History of Ideas* 58 (1997), 597–616.

12 The oration is in his *Opuscula*. See Nelson H. Minnich, "Concepts of Reform Proposed at the Fifth Lateran Council," *Archivum Historiae Pontificiae* 7 (1969), 163–251, reprinted in *The Fifth Lateran Council (1512–17)* (Aldershot: Variorum, 1993).

13 Saturnino Alvarez Turienzo, "Ambigua recepción de Cayetan en la Universidad de Salamanca 1520–1590" in Bruno Pinchard and Saverio Ricci, eds., *Rationalisme analogique et humanisme théologique. La culture de Thomas de Vio "Il Gaetano"* (Naples: Vivarium, 1993), 325–40, here 331. H. de Lubac, *Le mystère du Surnaturel* (Paris: Cerf, 1965), 26–30, 98–102, 179–208. Gilson, "Cajètan et l'humanisme thèologique," 133. Otto H. Pesch lists 15 discrepancies between Aquinas's theology and modern Thomism created largely by Cajetan: "Thomismus," *Lexikon für Theologie und Kirche*, 2nd ed., 10 (1965), 157–67, here 163–5.

14 This trait in Cajetan's thinking is central in Barbara Hallensleben, *Communicatio. Anthropologie und Gnadenlehre bei Thomas de Vio Cajetan* (Münster: Aschendorff, 1985).

15 For the history of this genre before Cajetan see Pierre Michaud-Quantin, *Sommes de casuistique et manuels de confession au moyen âge* (Louvain: Nauwelaerts, 1962). For subsequent developments see Johann Theiner, *Die Entwicklung der Moraltheologie zur eingenständigen Disziplin* (Regensburg: Pustet, 1970).

16 Cajetan's report to Leo X on the debate over Mary being conceived without original sin, *De conceptione beatae Mariae virginis* (1515), drew many attacks from backers of the Immaculate Conception. See José A. Domínguez Asensio, "Cayetano y las cuestiones de criteriología teológica: El tratado 'De conceptione Beatae Mariae Virginis'," *Communio* (Seville) 16 (1983), 201–34; Ulrich Horst, *Die Diskussion um die Immaculata Conceptio im Dominikanerorden* (Paderborn: Schöningh, 1987), 19–32.

17 Jared Wicks, "Roman Reactions to Luther: the First Year (1518)," *CHR* 69 (1983), 521–62, here 528–39. See also idem., *Cajetan und die Anfänge der Reformation* (Münster: Aschendorff, 1983), 72–80. The relevant texts are now given in Peter Fabisch and Erwin Iserloh, *Dokumente zur Causa Lutheri (1517–1521)* 2 vols. (Münster: Aschendorff, 1988–91), 2:37–185.

18 *Tractatus de indulgentiis* (December 8, 1517) in Fabisch and Iserloh, *Dokumente*, 2:142–68. See Bernhard A. R. Felmberg, *Die Ablasstheologie Kardinal Cajetans (1469–1534)* (Leiden: E. J. Brill, 1998), 72–186.

19 The treatises appeared with the commentary on Part III of the *Summa* (1523) and in the

Opuscula. A Latin-French edition, with introduction and analysis, is Charles Morerod, *Cajetan et Luther en 1518*, 2 vols. (Fribourg: Editions Universitaires, 1994), 1:182–423. I translated six treatises and synopsized eight in *Cajetan Responds. A Reader in Reformation Controversy* (Washington, DC: Catholic University of America Press, 1978), 47–91. See Wicks, "Roman Reactions," 539–49; idem, *Cajetan und die Anfänge*, 80–93; Morerod, *Cajetan et Luther*, 1:145–79; 2:425–96, 517–604; Felmberg, *Ablasstheologie*, 215–345.

20 On Luther's view see Jared Wicks, "*Fides sacramenti – fides specialis*: Luther's Development in 1518," *Gregorianum* 65 (1984), 53–87, reprinted in *Luther's Reform. Studies on Conversion and the Church* (Mainz: von Zabern, 1992), 117–47. Cajetan's text is translated in Wicks, *Cajetan Responds*, 49–55.

21 Translation in Wicks, *Cajetan Responds*, 68–85.

22 Kurt-Victor Selge related this from a letter of Georg Spalatin published in Luther's German works, vol. 9 (Wittenberg, 1560), which Selge cited in the original in "La Chiesa in Lutero" in Massimo Marcocchi, ed., *Martin Lutero* (Milan: Vita e Pensiero, 1984), 13–33, here 31–2.

23 Translation in Wicks, *Cajetan Responds*, 91–8.

24 *Cum postquam* (November 9, 1518), still present in the manual of Catholic magisterial texts: Heinrich Denzinger and Adolph Schönmetzer, ed., *Enchridion Symbolorum Definitionum et Declarationum de rebus fidei et morum*, 33rd ed. (Barcelona: Herder, 1965), 356–7.

25 *De divina institutione pontificatus Romani Pontificis*, printed in Rome, Cologne, and Milan in 1521, in the *Opuscula*, and a critical edition by Friedrich Lauchert (Münster: Aschendorff, 1925), from which translations of six and synopses of eight chapters are in Wicks, *Cajetan Responds*, 105–44. See Wicks, *Cajetan und die Anfänge*, 127–33. Cajetan had before him Luther's 1519 *Resolutio* of the thirteenth thesis of the Leipzig Disputation.

26 *Five Articles of Luther – Justification for their Condemnation*, in Wicks, *Cajetan Responds*, 145–52.

27 Translation in Wicks, *Cajetan Responds*, 153–73, and notes on 282–4 which identify the texts of Zwingli's *Commentary on True and False Religion* (1525) to which Cajetan responded.

28 *De missae sacrificio et de ritu adversus Lutheranos*, printed in octavo editions in Rome and

Paris in 1531 and Cologne in 1532, before going into the *Opuscula*. The Cologne edition was promoted by Erasmus, who admired the reserved but cogent style of Cajetan on Reformation issues. Translation in Wicks, *Cajetan Responds*, 189–200. See Marie-Vincent Leroy, "Une traité de Cajetan sur la messe" in Carlos-Josaphat Pinto de Oliveira, ed., *Ordo Sapientiae et Amoris* (Fribourg: Editions Universitaires, 1993), 469–87.

29 Translation in Wicks, *Cajetan Responds*, 205–17.

30 Ibid., 201–3.

31 Ibid., 219–39.

32 Ibid., 175–88.

33 Ibid., 241–4.

34 After the first edition (Rome 1525), a dozen printings of this offering of "breakfasts" occurred in the following century in Cologne, Paris, Lyons, Venice, and Douai.

35 André F. von Gunten, "Le contribution des 'hebreux' a l'oeuvre exégétique de Cajetan" in Olivier Fatio and Pierre Fraenkel, ed., *Histoire de l'exégése au XVIe siècle* (Geneva: Droz, 1978), 46–83.

36 These were published sporadically during the sixteenth century in Venice, Lyons, and Paris, but were united in five volumes, prepared by the Dominicans of Madrid, published at Lyons in 1639.

37 The best general study to date of Cajetan's biblical work is Michael O'Connor, "Exegesis, Doctrine and Reform in the Biblical Commentaries of Cardinal Cajetan (1469–1534)" (D.Phil. thesis, University of Oxford, 1997), available for reading in the Bodleian Library.

38 *Histoire critique des principaux commentateurs du Nouveau Testament* (Rotterdam: Reinier Leers, 1693), 537–43.

39 Ulrich Horst, "Der Streit um die hl. Schrift zwischen Kardinal Cajetan und Ambrosius Catharinus" in Leo Scheffczyk, ed., *Wahrheit und Verkündigung*, 2 vols. (Munich: Schöningh, 1967), 1:551–77. Cano, *De locis theologicis*, Locus VII, ch. III, nos. 11–13, 31, in Cano, *Opera*, 2 (Rome: Forzani, 1890), 63–5, 73–4.

40 *WA* 60, 114–30. See James K. Farge, ed., *Registre des Procès-verbaux de la Faculté de l'Université de Paris (1524–33)* (Paris: Amateurs des Livres, 1990), 266–7, 276–9, 281–93.

Bibliography

Primary Sources

To our notes on editions and translations of Cajetan's works, we add the reprint, *Opuscula omnia* (Hildesheim: Georg Olms, 1995). The same publisher also lists, without date, a reprint of the five-volume collection of biblical commentaries from the original of Lyons (1639).

Among studies of Cajetan, the 1934 centenary of his death occasioned supplementary volumes of the *Revue Thomiste* and *Rivista di Filosofia neoscholastica*, while *Angelicum* devoted to him vol. 11, no. 4 (1934). A bibliography of studies is given by Eckehart Stöve (cf. below), to which we add the following secondary works.

Secondary Sources

Congar, Yves M.-J., "Bio-Bibliographie de Cajétan," *Revue thomiste* 17 (1934), 4–49. Complete chronological list of the works.

Felmberg, Bernhard, *Die Ablasstheologie Kardinal Cajetans*, Leiden: E. J. Brill, 1998.

Groner, J. F., *Kardinal Cajetan. Eine Gestalt aus der Reformationszeit*, Fribourg: Société Philosophique and Louvain: Nauwelaerts, 1951. Lists all works chronologically.

Hallensleben, Barbara, *Communicatio. Anthropologie und Gnadenlehre bei Thomas de Vio Cajetan*, Münster: Aschendorff, 1985.

Mahoney, Edward P., "Cajetan (Thomas de Vio)" in Edward Craig, ed., *Routledge Encyclopedia of Philosophy* (London and New York: Routledge, 1998), 2:171–5.

Nieden, Marcel, *Organum Deitiatis. Die Christologie des Thomas de Vio Cajetan*, Leiden: E. J. Brill, 1997.

Pinchard, Bruno, and Saverio Ricci, eds., *Rationalisme analogique et humanisme théologique. La culture de Thomas de Vio "Il Gaetano,"* Naples: Vivarium, 1993.

Riva, Franco, *Analogia e univocità in Tommaso de Vio "Gaetano,"* Milan: Vita e Pensiero, 1995.

Stöve, Eckehart, "De Vio, Tommaso," *Dizionario biografico degli Italiani*, 39 (1991), 567–78.

Wicks, Jared, *Cajetan und die Anfänge der Reformation*, Münster: Aschendorff, 1983.

Thomas More
(1477/8–1535)

Ralph Keen

Born in London and marked out early on by his father, a judge, for a career in the law, Thomas More received little or no formal training in theology and was never ordained. Moreover, his sympathies and energy were on the side of the Catholic Church once the Reformation began, and he died defending Roman authority against assertions of royal supremacy. These considerations notwithstanding, More played a vital role in the religious history of England during the Reformation era, one that proves the truth of the adage that England wore its reformation with a difference. Nowhere else in that century do we find a person rising to the highest office in government, only to die by the punishment for treason. Nor did any other writer achieve renown for imaginative narratives in elegant Latin, only to pen reams of vernacular invective. And neither did anyone else turn from clever translations of satiric Greek epigrams to devotional meditations on the agony of Christ in the garden.

More's legacy has been one of the more vociferously contested ones of modern times. Especially since his beatification in 1885 and canonization in 1935, Catholic intellectuals have claimed him as a patron of an array of causes: resistance to tyranny, defense of faith, courage of conscience, and forerunner of modern Catholic statesmen. The more modern More appears, the less he resembles the figure reflected in a vast body of writings and letters. Difficult as it is to discipline the tendency to create legendary narratives for heroic figures, such a task is especially timely in More's case. The Yale edition of his works has been completed, a cycle of revisionist biography and reaction has run its course, and a wave of careful research is underway.[1] The following may serve as a preliminary guide to the religious thought of Thomas More.

In setting More within the context of his age, it is essential to recognize the connections between religious thought and humanism. The movement of Catholic reform in which More occupies a distinguished position must be recognized as a form of religious humanism that discovered the biblical and patristic traditions.[2] Thus it is necessary to regard the Catholic reaction to the Reformation as a phenomenon within the humanist movement, indeed a more complex phenomenon in some ways than the beginnings of the Reformation. As a counter-attack to Protestant charges, the Catholic response addressed the Reformers' challenges on their own terms, and

in so doing presented scriptural and patristic counter-arguments each time the Reformers invoked Scripture and the Fathers. And in the course of this campaign,
Catholic polemicists argued that their method of interpretation was valid, while that
of the Reformers was erroneous and deviant. The strategy demanded legal skills as
well as humanistic ability; and these More provided in abundance.

The Humanist Works

More's earliest works, English poems and some prose pieces, date from the first decade
of the sixteenth century, when More was in his twenties and rising in the legal profession and governmental rank. Translations into Latin from Greek, a number of
epigrams, and some dialogues by Lucian followed. Although he appreciated Lucian
for his moral message, More saw his translations as exercises in language and style.[3]
In some of them he saw himself in competition for elegance with William Lily and
Erasmus.[4] The translations reflect the contemporary concern for a suitable style over
mere linguistic exactitude; and the vernacular compositions are stylistically vigorous,
attempts at capturing in English some of the vitality of the Greek and Latin classics.

More's poetry, both English and Latin, reflects both the solemn and mirthful
sides of his personality.[5] But the mirthful side is tinged with irony, the comical
element often resting on the exposure of a person's pride or ignorance. The solemn
poems accentuate the inevitability of death and the artificiality of social stations:
pauper and potentate are equal in the grave.

> Hic seruus dum uixit, erat, nunc mortuus idem
> Non quam tu Dari magne minora potest.
> ("While he lived, this man was a slave. But now, in death, he wields
> no less power than you, mighty Darius.")[6]

Utopia

Utopia, More's best-known work, is also, not unrelatedly, his most enigmatic.
Ostensibly a description, in dialogue form, of a new and mysterious island just discovered in a European traveler's voyages, the work also offers direct and indirect
critiques of the conventions of European society. The difficulty in discerning More's
actual intention lies in the arrangement of the interlocutors. The traveler's name,
Raphael Hythlodaeus, suggests "weaver of nonsense;" his dialogue partner, "Morus,"
may or may not represent More's own opinion. To complicate matters, *morus* means
fool or idiot; thus the character may be the very opposite of More, a *morus*, or More
himself, using his Latin name.[7] Like Erasmus's *Praise of Folly*, written in More's
house, the author seems to have veiled his own viewpoint in such a way that no
reader can be completely certain whether the veil is a thin or a thick one.[8]

If Utopia, the place, represents More's proposal for the reform of society, this
ideal resembles a cloistered community more that it does secular society. Property is
held in common; activities are rigorously scheduled; social life is regulated; and

worldly values are inverted, with precious commodities being put to base uses, golden chamber pots being the best-known example. The Utopian life is an austere one, one in which natural and contemporary social tendencies are carefully restrained; the work is as scathing in its social criticism as it is constructive of an alternate cultural system.[9]

A more profound work in some respects is More's *History of King Richard III*, a chronicle of the events leading to Tudor sovereignty, in which the character traits of the principal figures are captured as vividly as their deeds. More's depiction of the honorable and the sinister, the dishonorable grasping for power and the noble bearing of authority, point to an awareness of the intangible forces bearing on all human acts. Such attention to character reveals a sensitivity to the darker aspects of psychology, a theme that emerges in force in his religious polemic. As More depicts the various actors in his political drama, it is evident that their inner natures, and not their social rank or political position, provide the true account for their actions.[10]

The works that link More most closely with Erasmian humanism, however, are his epistolary defenses of Erasmus's contributions to scholarship. Despite their differences, these letter-essays are valuable position statements on behalf of the new learning. For example, with various motives agitators in England had opposed the study of Greek, which Erasmus and a few other continental humanists were promoting as the only path to a true understanding of religion. More's letter to the scholars of the University of Oxford, defending Greek against the charges of the self-styled "Trojans," is an appeal by a loyal alumnus, arguing that the Christian tradition cannot be preserved or completely understood without careful knowledge of the Greek tradition and also the Hebrew Bible.[11] Knowledge of Latin sufficient for understanding the Vulgate and a few compendia of patristic sources, although adequate for earlier generations, was no longer enough for the era of humanistic exploration. If Oxford were to remain a center of learning, it would have to defend the study of literature – even against detractors from within.[12]

The recovery of the Greek tradition demanded new methods of study and exposition, and here too the Erasmian initiative encountered stiff opposition from a number of sources.[13] With Edward Lee, More argues ironically, reproaching his acquaintance for criticizing Erasmus after having learned so much from him – implying that Lee's erudition, if superior to More's, is so only because he has drawn more from Erasmus's compilations and compendia, not because he is more versed in the original literature.[14] The English Carthusian John Batmanson, similarly, receives a retort of good-natured irony in More's defense of Erasmus's translation of the *logos* of John 1:1 as *sermo*.[15] Behind the jocular image is a serious point: careful scholarship is a more valuable aid to the faith than uncritical adherence to the received tradition.

More's defenses of humanism are effective rejoinders to the claims of scholasticism. In his letter to the Dutch theologian Martin van Dorp, for example, the advantages of scholasticism in understanding theology are enumerated and weighed, yet found lacking in comparison with the benefits of close study of ancient texts, freed from the artificial restraints of philosophic systems. Such philosophic structures, More claims, are themselves distortions of classical thought, and inadequate frameworks for appreciating ancient texts.[16] As he had claimed in his letter to the Oxford scholars, no person can claim knowledge of a subject without intimate familiarity with it; and with Dorp, too, he contrasts the appearance of knowledge presented by scholastics with the true understanding of men like Erasmus.[17] Amidst the contemptuous dismissals of speculative philosophers and supposedly erudite old clerics who think Augustine wrote the *Sentences* is a powerful statement of the need for reform in theology.[18] More first of all wants to replace scholasticism with "positive" theology, a body of teachings based on ancient texts correctly understood. Only then can the errors that have accumulated over time be corrected, and only then can one appreciate the meaning and pertinence of the New Testament.

The second plank of the Morean reform proposal is linked to the replacement of scholasticism with positive theology, as it calls for limiting the dominance of logic as an analytical tool and emphasizing rhetoric in its stead as a method of theological teaching. For More, the original message of Jesus was rhetorical in nature; its transformation in the work of the apostolic community was similarly an event within the realm of proclamation; and the patristic tradition was in the main a homiletical literature. Thus fidelity to the origins and spirit of the tradition called for attention to rhetoric, both in the reading and the communicating of dogma.[19]

With Erasmus, More shared a strong desire to recover the patristic tradition, favoring the Greek fathers over the Latin. His dogmatic writings fairly bristle with citations from Cyril, Gregory of Nyssa, Gregory of Nazianzen, and other Byzantine theologians; in most cases these authors make their first appearance in English by courtesy of More's pen.[20] With the patristic corpus as well as with the biblical canon, More is unembarrassed by discrepancies and unbowed by the argument that differences among the Fathers undermine their authority for doctrine. To More's mind, the presence of divergent witnesses is a challenge to modern interpreters to weigh, discern, and achieve an understanding that is more correct, aware that absolute correctness is impossible to achieve. We see in this view a preference for ancient over modern, tempered by the humility that after the passage of a millennium or more, access to the intentions of the original authors is anything but immediately accessible. And rhetoric, rather than logic, dominates the realm of probability.

Polemics

In March 1528, Cuthbert Tunstall, bishop of London, commissioned More to refute the *insana dogmata* that were appearing in Germany and making their way, despite bans, into England. More was to write in English, for the benefit of the people, and to act like the stringent asserter of the truth that he had already proved to be in his Latin polemics.[21] This charge marks a turning point in More's work, and it has become the occasion for numerous scholarly debates, some as acrimonious as the polemics they attempt to assess.[22] Beyond question is the fact that More took up the task with energy and a clear sense of purpose. The matter in question is whether the task proved to be More's true calling or a duty only grimly undertaken by a man whose private nature lacked the harshness of religious polemic.

More's work in defense of the faith breaks with the irenicism associated with Erasmus, and moves him decidedly to the reactionary wing of Reformation-era Catholicism.[23] In Latin works against the continental Reformers and in English works directed at his evangelical countrymen, More devotes himself to exposing the errors, logical as well as dogmatic, of Reformation teaching. Like some of his polemical peers on the Continent, More hoped that England could be isolated from the religious turmoil in which Germany was embroiled, and thus strove mightily to combat the encroachment of Protestant ideas on British soil. He was instrumental in placing an embargo on Protestant books from the Continent, a move that resulted in a flood of false imprints and pseudonymous or anonymous tracts.

The claim that More was only a reluctant controversialist is weakened by the record of his Latin polemical writings, begun years before the commission from Tunstall. The 1523 *Responsio ad Lutherum* is a massive denunciation of Luther as a buffoon, a raging madman, a drunkard (*pater potator*), and the like. It is invective at fever pitch, and it continues for 350 pages of Latin text, no minor effort for a royal official who became speaker of the House of Commons in the same year. Far from being a merely rhetorical indulgence on More's part, the *Responsio* contains a substantial critique of the fundamental assumptions of Luther's theology, so far as More knew them in 1523. More's intention is to expose the contradictions and inconsistencies of Luther's thought – not to mention the "blasphemy" that he finds on virtually every page – as the trifles of an ignorant and impious poseur, not worthy of serious attention. As a result, More's critique has itself been dismissed as a mere trifle by an orator unskilled in theology, which cannot be maintained by any serious reader of More's text.[24] And the fact that More issued this work pseudonymously, under the name "William Ross," supposedly supports the contention that this is not the "true" Thomas More.[25]

It was surely, however, the true Thomas More who responded to Johann Bugenhagen in an *Epistola* (c.1526) replying to Bugenhagen's very slight appeal to the English people to embrace evangelical beliefs. As a piece of serious theological polemic, this work ranks with the more carefully crafted works of the most acute continental controversialists.[26] Although the *Epistola* is replete with hostile barbs, these are tied more clearly to an organizing thesis, which is that what the Lutherans call the "gospel" is the antithesis of the gospel as understood by all outside a few evangelical circles. Whereas Bugenhagen rejoices at the prospect that Christians in England are finally beginning to embrace the gospel, More counters that the *text* of the four Gospels has been read and cherished in England for a thousand years already.

> But if you want us to take as gospel those new, destructive, absurd doctrines that Luther, like another Antichrist, recently introduced among the Saxons – those doctrines that you, Karlstadt, Lambert, and Oecolampadius (Luther's cacangelists) foment and scatter throughout the world – if that is what you mean by the gospel, then there is hardly anyone in England who welcomes that gospel of yours. And for that we are very glad indeed.[27]

Too much of More the polemicist shares themes with other aspects of More's work to allow anyone to maintain with conviction that the humanist and the polemicist are mutually exclusive aspects of More's personality – the genial humanist being the genuine More and the polemicist being a subordinate stratum of his personality. That More was a complex figure cannot be denied; but he was not a divided one.

Sovereign church authority, similarly, is part and parcel of More's religious and humanistic program. With the Fathers whose works he assiduously studied, More knew that regulation in matters of faith was impossible without a strong disciplinary infrastructure; and with his continental peers in the struggle against Protestantism he saw the Roman Church as the only institution with effective jurisdiction over such matters. Thus when the lawyer Christopher St. German (c.1460–1540) addressed in a number of works the relation to each other of the temporal and spiritual estates, and granted unprecedented authority to civil institutions, More was ready with counter-arguments.[28] More's defenses of spiritual authority in his 1532 *Apology* and his *Debellation of Salem and Bizance* in the following year dispute St. German's charges of abuse of power within the ecclesiastical system. More refutes, on legal and theological grounds, the claim that secular control of ecclesiastical affairs – heresy trials in particular – was a legitimate corrective to abuses within the church. Anonymous though St. German's treatises were, they were transparently part of the Henrician campaign to gain control of the churches. By answering both works in his own name, More declared his opposition to a king who would, with force rather than argument, ultimately prevail over both More and the English church.

Authority

Although the tone and intention of his contributions to dogmatic debate suggest that More's stance toward the Reformation is that of a reactionary, in fact there is a careful and constructive program in this aspect of More's work. Statesman that he was, he recognized that institutions could benefit from discord so long as agreement on common principles was maintained. In More's view, therefore, the criticism of the church and its teachings was not in itself something to be lamented; the rejection of the foundations on which the church taught was what was destructive. As he had stated in his humanistic defenses, the existence of divergent witnesses, whether to a text or to a doctrine, stimulates further consideration and discernment in the hope of advancing upon predecessors' understanding. The Protestant rejection of tradition as a norm governing the formation of doctrine was for him the abandonment of the very basis for asserting the sole authority of Scripture. Hence we find More telling Johann Bugenhagen that, despite his ignorance of theology, his loyalty to Christianity was too great to lead him to become a Lutheran.[29]

In contrast to the Reformers' assertions that the church is made up of human traditions with no power to bind pious consciences, More states in his *Letter to Bugenhagen* that the church is a divine institution, united by a faith consistent with scriptural revelation and instructed by the Fathers.[30] This is a theme developed at great length in his English works, texts that, in the absence of available theological literature in the vernacular, are ecclesiological treatises for the naive and vulnerable laity. The first and certainly most readable of these is the *Dialogue concerning Heresies*, composed in 1529 as a discussion of the thought of Tyndale and his German masters.[31]

The *Dialogue* is organized in four books as a dialogue between More (the real More this time: he is addressed as "Master Chancellor") and an imaginary "messenger" who has appeared with numerous notions hostile to the old faith. In a jovial manner the two interlocutors, with More taking the lead, assess the source and validity of each critique. The dialogue begins by discussing pilgrimages and veneration of saints and proceeds through arguments about scriptural and ecclesiastical authority to the question of the heretical nature of Luther and his followers. The argument throughout relies more on exposing the contradictions of the heretical positions than on refuting the new ideas with traditional witnesses. More recognized, unlike some of his continental peers, that patristic authority had apparently been diminished to such a point by the Protestants that responses from that canon would not prevail. Furthermore, the educated laity might be less persuaded by an ancient source than a contemporary one. There is a rhetorical advantage in having More, rather than one of the Fathers, speak to the new ideas drifting over from Germany.[32]

At close to half a million words, the most imposing of More's polemical works is *The Confutation of Tyndale's Answer*. This work in nine books is a response to a response: it is an extended counter-attack upon Tyndale's 1531 *Answer* to More's *Dialogue concerning Heresies*.[33] In the *Answer*, Tyndale defended his translation of certain crucial passages of the Bible that More had criticized for their potential to lead believers from the inherited Catholic understanding. Disagreements about the exact meanings of biblical texts evolved into a debate about the roles of the individual and the church in interpreting sacred texts. For Tyndale, as for Luther, from whom he drew the idea, the scriptural text was clear enough to be understood without the mediation of the church or the guidance of the dogmatic tradition. This did not mean, of course, that each person's understanding was valid; its truth rested on conformity with the common understanding of the believing community; but it implied that a reading could deviate, even drastically, from the conventional understanding. This was especially true if the interpretation was grounded on intensive study of the original texts, as Tyndale's translations were.

An argument that may have begun as a disagreement between humanists over the meaning of texts escalated to mutually exclusive positions on theological hermeneutics, the question of authority on which the Reformation turned. For just as the Reformers insisted that the biblical canon was clear and sufficient for faithful understanding, so the Catholics asserted that, however clear it might be, the Bible alone was not sufficient: revelation included tradition as well.

> And fynally thus ye se that Tyndale and suche other as wolde haue vs reiecte and refuse al that god hath taughte hys chirche, but yf yt be proued by scripture: be not onely vnable to proue or defende that heresy / but also do handle the scrypture yt selfe in suche a shamefull wyse, that yf other men whom they reproue dyd not handle yt better, yt had been better to haue left all to gether vnwrytten, and neuer hadde scripture at all. And we muste nedes perceyue that wythout the bylyefe and credence geuen vnto the catholyke chyrche of Cryste we coulde be sure of nothynge, but that as saynte Paule sayth, the chirche is the pyller and strength of the trewthe.[34]

The stance is ideally suited to the humanistic era. In earlier centuries, access to even reasonably reliable Greek texts, as well as the linguistic ability to understand them with any accuracy, were severely limited. A strong doctrine of the Holy Spirit as the guide of the hierarchical church in its magisterial function evolved as a control for the uncertainty inherent in depending on Latin translations of the original Hebrew and Greek. The principle of insufficiency of Scripture was to a large extent determined by the issue of clarity of Scripture: the less clear the text, the greater the need for the guidance of the church.

With the advent of printing and the rediscovery of Greek in the second half of the fifteenth century, the West was able to recover meanings and nuances that had been lost for a millennium. The publication of the great Froben Bible in 1498, the Complutensian Polyglot in 1516, and Erasmus's *Novum Instrumentum* in the same year, along with editions of classical Greek texts that illumined the meaning of certain biblical terms, allowed a Renaissance Hellenist to arrive at a more accurate understanding of the original meaning of the biblical texts than the Vulgate offered. With new certainty one could demonstrate that the Latin tradition had misunderstood a specific term in the Greek. For Reformers like Tyndale, this assurance was tantamount to certainty about the meaning of the original; for More, it was merely about the merits of Jerome's Vulgate.

In More's view, clarity and sufficiency of Scripture were separate issues. One could understand the biblical text accurately but still not have the comprehension necessary for salvation. The authority of the church is still necessary, for revelation is not exhausted by Scripture. Hence a humanist scholar like Tyndale can have even a perfect philological comprehension of the text and still lack full knowledge of the faith. In More's view, confidence that one has achieved complete understanding, and assurance that the content of that understanding is complete, are symptoms of pride and demonstrations of the lack, rather than the possession, of salvific understanding.

Along with the central issue of authority in the vernacular polemics, specific doctrines receive their share of attention. In *The Supplication of Souls* (1529), More responds in a tantalizingly indirect fashion to Simon Fish's denial of the existence of purgatory. In the *Supplication* the souls in purgatory address their surviving family and friends, expressing disbelief that a book should appear that questions the existence of purgatory and encouraging those still living to remember the departed with prayers and alms. Fish, whose 1529 work is titled *A Supplication for the Beggars*, accuses the church of exploiting the idea of purgatory in order to collect memorial donations that would otherwise have gone to the poor. Economic woes had increased the numbers of the poor, just as traffic in indulgences brought new light to the uses and abuses of the doctrine of purgatory. Eliminating the role of purgatory in religious life would, in Fish's view, bring substantial social benefit.

The inevitability of death, so strong a theme in More's humanistic work, allows More here to gain the advantage on Fish's imaginary beggars. Poverty is a real condition experienced by the unfortunate, but death is the fate of all, and so the souls are able to make an appeal to the human condition that the beggars cannot. By presenting purgatory as an unavoidable destiny, More made the invisible realm more pressing than the tangible but avoidable and transient reality of worldly poverty. The effect of More's strategy here is to take Fish's economic and ecclesiastical argument and transform it into a spiritual issue. As such the problem at hand is not the misuse of worldly goods but inattention to otherworldly ones; the available remedy is an increase in piety and a corresponding disregard for property, manifested in continued and increased almsgiving. Such a proposal illustrates the dual nature of More's controversial writing, for he is both defending a traditional practice from attack by Reformers from every corner, as well as identifying spirituality as a value demanding increased attention.[35]

The Eucharist also is ably defended in two of More's tracts from 1532–3, the *Answer to a Poisoned Book* and the *Letter against Frith*. Against the sacramentarian positions held by George Joy and John Frith, according to which the bread and wine in the Sacrament are merely symbolic of the Last Supper, More argued on the basis of John 6 and its patristic commentaries that Christ declared literally that his flesh and blood are present in the Sacrament. Abiding by the principle of favoring a plain meaning over an allegorical one, More asserts that the Johannine passage and other biblical sources for eucharistic teaching make sense when read literally and must therefore be taken at face value. Not to do so, More claims, is to substitute a mere image for Christ.[36] For More, to replace the real with the false in this sacrament is to do the same thing that the Reformers are doing with the church as a whole.

Devotional Works

Given his political career and the zeal with which he defended the Roman Church against enemies foreign and domestic, More's most unusual writings are perhaps his devotional works. From his 1522 essay on *The Last Things* to the books he wrote in the Tower while awaiting execution, More's writings in this vein display a sincerity and a spirituality seldom found in his other works.[37]

When counselor to Henry VIII and undertreasurer of England, More composed a meditation on death and judgment. Awareness of the afterlife is a deterrent to sin; Christ's admonition to keep the final judgment in mind is, as More depicts it, a pre-scription by the divine physician to the ailing human soul.[38] That the human condition is sick is for More self-evident, to whom birth is only the beginning of a process toward death.[39] Tendencies toward each of the seven deadly sins are symptoms of the human condition that can be cured by attention to eschatological realities.

The *Dialogue of Comfort against Tribulation*, written in 1534 when More was a prisoner in the Tower awaiting execution for the sake of his beliefs, represents the full harvest of earlier themes. Like *Utopia* and the *Dialogue concerning Heresies*, it takes the form of a dialogue. Like *The Last Things*, it is a meditation on death and the afterlife. And like the English poems and other humanist works, it reveals the fatuity of this life and a Stoic indifference to worldly appetites. More's own position is veiled, as it is in *Utopia*, by the suggestion of exotic geography, in this case by describing the *Dialogue* as having been written by a Hungarian in Latin, and then translated into French, and thence into English. The interlocutors are a nephew, named Vincent, and his uncle Antony, who resembles More himself.[40]

Although it occupies a prominent place in the tradition of consolation literature, the *Dialogue* bears little resemblance to the classic of the genre, Boethius's *Consolation of Philosophy*. Instead, it seems to have been inspired by the *De consolatione theologiae* of Jean Gerson (1363–1429), an author More knew and used in a number of works.[41] In addition to supporting the impression that More's work is a unified whole, the Paris chancellor's philosophical tendencies may have allowed a more critical and modern perspective on the vagaries of earthly existence than the prison meditations of the "last Roman," Boethius.

The central theme of the *Dialogue* is reliance on God as the only genuine source of consolation in this life. In contrast to the vagaries and pains of human experience, divine consolation presents stability and, in the end, the only form of peace. This is a deeply Augustinian position, especially reminiscent of passages in the *City of God*, a work which, like the *Dialogue*, was written in the wake of the collapse of a world which had seemed most stable and real. As More presents it, being deprived of worldly goods and comforts is a divine gift, an occasion for the pious to focus all the more intently on providence and the divine goodness discernible therein.[42]

Isolated as More was from the outside world, the *Dialogue* is not oblivious to the issues for which he had struggled in his polemical period. Indeed, many of the themes in the controversial writings are present in the *Dialogue*, as concern for the church and protection of the faith were the reason for his imprisonment. For More, reliance upon God for certainty amidst the vicissitudes of life calls for disciplined rejection of the pride being manifested so blatantly by the Reformers. As the church offers the only condition for experiencing true comfort, the Reformers' efforts to undermine its role in the religious practice of the people is nothing less than an obstruction of grace.

The fictional setting of the *Dialogue* may in fact be read as an allegory for the Reformation movement. The Turkish threat to Hungary in the 1520s corresponds, *mutatis mutandis*, to the threat posed by Protestantism to western Christendom, especially England.[43] And just as the Turkish menace to Hungary may be seen as a metaphor for Germany's menace to England, so the individual's tribulations addressed in the dialogue itself serve as a microcosmic image of the tribulations the English church was facing in the early to mid-1530s. In both individual and ecclesiastical cases, complete release from trouble is available only by submission to the will of God as exercised through the church.

More's incarceration was a period of prayer and reflection, and it is from these final years that we have his most moving religious works. In addition to the *Dialogue of Comfort*, More composed treatises on the Passion and eucharistic devotion, a number of "instructions" and prayers, most of them in English, and a Latin meditation on the sadness of Christ in the garden, *De Tristitia Christi*. The *Treatise upon the Passion* is organized around a series of prayers for various pious attitudes.[44] Here too there is a discernible, even dominant, Augustinian strain, marked for example by the opening account of the fall of angels and humans, a narrative evocative of Book 14 of the *City of God*.[45]

The much shorter *Treatise to Receive the Blessed Body* is an exhortation to see the Eucharist as something both "sacramental" and "virtual." Sacramental reception of the Eucharist, in More's view, is when persons "receive his very blessed body into theirs, under the sacramental sign, but they receive not the thing of the sacrament, that is to wit, the virtue and the effect thereof, that is to say, the grace by which they should be lively members incorporate in Christ's holy mystical body."[46] Virtual reception, by contrast, is allowing the Holy Spirit into the believer's soul.[47] For More, spiritual or virtual reception allows conversation with Christ; one can "with devout prayer talk to him, by devout meditation talk with him."[48] A similar sense that the spiritual is the real, and that the material world is a illusion and distraction, governs the pious "instructions" and prayers, some of which have become classics of early modern spirituality.[49] More's piety is one that sees this world as an inverted anticipation of the next, so that the more pain one endures here, the more blessedness one might enjoy in heaven.[50]

Such otherworldliness finds its most poignant expression in *De Tristitia Christi*, in which Christ's meditation in Gethsemane serves as a mirror for More as he contemplates his own impending death. As More states it, Christians of his own day resemble the sleeping companions in the garden, unaware of the coming persecution and unable, in their failure to be vigilant, to avert the betrayal of their divine master.[51] The words are a call for renewed spiritual initiatives as much as for increased polemical efforts, and serve as an apt reflection of the ambivalent More, the staunch opponent of heresy who alternates with the prayerful martyr for whom resistance is only an obstruction to grace.

Conclusion

More's claim to the role of religious reformer has not gone uncontested. The volume and virulence of his controversial writings argue powerfully against his being included in the same category as Bugenhagen, Luther, Tyndale, or any of the other thinkers whose work he attacked. If as a youthful humanist he was Erasmian, as a theological polemicist he was Erasmian no longer; even Erasmus stated as much when he regretted that More had ever entered into theological matters.

The defensive posture notwithstanding, More's importance as a humanist and statesman demands that his religious writings be taken seriously. In part because of his literary grounding and experience at court, and in part also because of the mental subtlety evident in all his writings, More must be regarded as one of the genuinely creative religious thinkers of the first third of the sixteenth century. With a dialectician's precision he sought to expose the faulty reasoning of his opponents, and with a rhetorician's gift for style he presented the traditional teachings of the Roman Church in an agreeable fashion to his fellow Englishmen. With a lawyer's thoroughness he heard the case made by the opposition, and with a defender's zeal refuted it. And in defeat, with no support save that offered by his faith, he penned works of piety with the earnestness of the great Fathers. That he lost all his worldly battles and died the death of his beloved martyrs is both tragic and fitting.[52]

Notes

1 The hagiographical tradition that began with R. W. Chambers (*Thomas More* [Ann Arbor: University of Michigan Press, 1958, orig. London, 1935]) and continued with E. E. Reynolds (*Saint Thomas More* [New York: Kennedy, 1954 and numerous later editions]) was challenged by Richard Marius, *Thomas More* (New York: Knopf, 1984) and G. R. Elton (e.g., "Persecution and Toleration in the English Reformation" in W. J. Shiels, ed., *Persecution and Toleration*, Studies in Church History, 21 [Oxford: Basil Blackwell, 1984], 163–87). A number of responses to revisionist treatments of More have appeared,

perhaps the most influential being Louis L. Martz, *Thomas More: The Search for the Inner Man* (New Haven: Yale University Press, 1990). For attempts to retrieve More's contemporaries' views of him, see, e.g., Hugh Trevor-Roper, "The Image of Thomas More in England 1535–1635" in *La Fortuna dell'Utopia di Thomas More nel dibattito politico Europeo del '500*, Fondazione Luigi Firpo, Quaderni, 2, Florence: Leo S. Olschki, 1996, 5–23, and James K. McConica, "The Recusant Reputation of Thomas More" in *Essential Articles for the Study of Thomas More* (Hamden: Archon Books, 1977), 136–49.

2 On humanists and Scripture see Jerry H. Bentley, *Humanists and Holy Writ: New Testament Scholarship in the Renaissance* (Princeton: Princeton University Press, 1963); Ronald G. Witt, "The Humanist Movement" in Thomas A. Brady, Jr., Heiko A. Oberman, and James D. Tracy, eds., *Handbook of European History 1400–1600* (Leiden: E. J. Brill, 1994–5), 2:93–125 (with a copious bibliography); Alastair Hamilton, "Humanists and the Bible" in Jill Kraye, ed., *The Cambridge Companion to Renaissance Humanism* (Cambridge: Cambridge University Press, 1996), 100–17. More's own place in the humanist tradition is concisely assessed by Charles Trinkaus, "Thomas More and the Humanist Tradition: Martyrdom and Ambiguity" in Charles Trinkaus, *The Scope of Renaissance Humanism* (Ann Arbor: University of Michigan Press, 1983), 422–36.

3 See Craig R. Thompson's introduction to More, *Translations of Lucian*, in *The Complete Works of St. Thomas More*, vol. 3/1 (New Haven: Yale University Press, 1974), xxii–liii.

4 More, *Latin Poems*, in *Complete Works*, vol. 3/2 (New Haven: Yale University Press, 1984); Clarence Miller's discussion of More's and Erasmus's epigrams (38–56) is most helpful.

5 This combination is elucidated by W. A. G. Doyle-Davidson, "The Earlier English Works of Sir Thomas More" in *Essential Articles*, 356–74; see also Alistair Fox, *Thomas More: History and Providence* (New Haven: Yale University Press, 1983), 9–49.

6 Epigram 45, in *Latin Poems*, 126–7.

7 See Germain Marc'hadour, "A Name for All Seasons" in *Essential Articles*, 539–62.

8 Richard Sylvester, "Si Hythlodaeo Credimus" in *Essential Articles*, 290–301.

9 Augustine's *City of God* has long been recognized as a source for *Utopia*; see Martin

R. Raitière, "More's *Utopia* and the *City of God*," *Renaissance Studies* 20 (1973), 144–68; Gerard Wegemer, "The *City of God* in Thomas More's *Utopia*," *Renascence: Essays on Values in Literature* 44 (1992), 115–35; István Bejczy, "More's Utopia: The City of God on Earth?," *Saeculum* 46 (1995), 17–30. One of the classic studies of More's dialogue, J. H. Hexter's *More's Utopia: The Biography of an Idea* (Princeton: Princeton University Press, 1952), sees Plato's *Republic* as the text most prominently in the back of More's mind. Dominic Baker-Smith somewhat more prudently acknowledges both Platonic and Augustinian elements; see *More's Utopia* (New York: HarperCollins Academic, 1991). For provocative observations on the rationality of Utopian life and its relation to Christianity, see Eberhard Jäckel, "Experimentum Rationis: Christentum und Heidentum in der 'Utopia' des Thomas Morus" (Ph.D. dissertation, Albert-Ludwigs-Universität, Freiburg, 1955).

10 See Fox, *Thomas More*, 75–107.

11 *CW* 15:137–41; also Craig W. D'Alton, "The Trojan War of 1518: Melodrama, Politics, and the Rise of Humanism," *SCJ* 28 (1997), 727–38.

12 See the edition by Daniel Kinney at *Complete Works*, 15:133, 135, 145.

13 Erika Rummel, *Erasmus and His Catholic Critics*, 2 vols. (Niewkoop: De Graaf, 1989) is the most thorough investigation of this issue.

14 *CW* 15:161.

15 *CW* 15:236–42.

16 *CW* 15:103.

17 *CW* 15:61.

18 *CW* 15:49, 69.

19 See Daniel Kinney, "More's *Letter to Dorp*: Remapping the Trivium," *Renaissance Quarterly* 34 (1981), 179–210.

20 On some aspects of More's use of the Fathers, see Richard C. Marius, "Thomas More and the Early Church Fathers" in *Essential Articles*, 402–20.

21 *The Correspondence of Sir Thomas More*, ed. Elizabeth Frances Rogers (Princeton: Princeton University Press, 1947), 387–8.

22 The most comprehensive and fair-minded assessment of the debate is Brendan Bradshaw, "The Controversial Thomas More," *JEH* 36 (1985), 535–69.

23 For a careful survey of the polemical writings as a whole see William Dillon, "Sir Thomas More: A Descriptive Analysis and Critical

Assessment of his Controversial Writings of 1528–1533" (Ph.D. dissertation, Union Theological Seminary, New York, 1976).

24 John M. Headley, "Thomas More and Luther's Revolt," *ARG* 60 (1969), 145–59; on the dialogue form of the *Responsio*, see R. R. McCutcheon, "The *Responsio Ad Lutherum*: Thomas More's Inchoate Dialogue with Heresy," *SCJ* 22 (1991), 77–90.

25 For common literary strategies between the *Responsio* and *Utopia*, see Peter Iver Kaufman, "Humanist Spirituality and Ecclesial Reaction: Thomas More's *Monstra*," *CH* 56 (1987), 25–38.

26 In vigor and subtlety of argumentation More's response compares favorably with the only other counter-attack Bugenhagen's letter received, Johannes Cochlaeus's *Responsio ad Bugenhagium* (ed. R. Keen, Nieuwkoop: De Graaf, 1988). For an analysis of More's own letter see Elizabeth F. Rogers, "Sir Thomas More's Letter to Bugenhagen" in *Essential Articles*, 447–54.

27 *CW* 7:14/31–16/4.

28 For background to the controversy see, in addition to the introductions by J. B. Trapp and John Guy in *CW* 9 and 10, John Guy, *Christopher St. German on Chancery and Statute* (London: Selden Society, 1985) and Franklin L. Baumer, "Christopher St. German: The Political Philosophy of a Tudor Lawyer," *American Historical Review* 42 (1937), 631–51.

29 *CW* 7:14–15.

30 *CW* 7:40–3.

31 For close analysis of the work, construed as a dialogue about conversion, see John D. Schaeffer, "Dialogue and Faith in More's Humanism: Voice and Belief in the Structure of the Dialogue Concerning Tyndale" (Ph.D. dissertation, University of St. Louis, 1971).

32 Various aspects of the text are addressed by Dale B. Billingsley, "The Messenger and the Reader in Thomas More's *Dialogue Concerning Heresies*," *Studies in English Literature 1500–1900* 24 (1984), 5–22; and Eiléan Ní Chuilleanáin, "The Debate Between Thomas More and William Tyndale, 1528–33: Ideas on Literature and Religion," *JEH* 39 (1988), 382–411.

33 For some of the dynamics of this work see Janey Hecht, "Limitations of Textuality in Thomas More's *Confutation of Tyndale's Answer*," *SCJ* 26 (1995), 823–8.

34 *Confutation*, Book III, *CW* 8:382–3.

35 See in particular the second book of the *Supplication*, in *CW* 7:170–228.

36 *CW* 7:233–58 and *CW* 11.

37 For sensitive appreciation see Louis L. Martz, "Thomas More: The Tower Works" and Germain Marc'hadour, "Thomas More's Spirituality" in Richard S. Sylvester, ed., *St. Thomas More: Action and Contemplation* (New Haven: Yale University Press, 1972), 59–83, 125–59.

38 *CW* 1:128–9.

39 *CW* 1:149.

40 Judith Paterson Jones, "The Polemical Nature of Thomas More's *A Dialogue of Comfort*" (Ph.D. dissertation, Auburn University, 1975), 47; Howard Rollin Patch, *The Tradition of Boethius: A Study of His Importance in Medieval Culture* (New York: Oxford University Press, 1935), 110.

41 E.g., *CW* 13:51.

42 *CW* 12:65–75; cf. Augustine, *City of God*, I.10.

43 Judith P. Jones, *Polemical Nature*, 44.

44 See, for example, meekness at *CW* 13:11, self-control at 24–5, compassion at 49, 52, pious reception of the Eucharist at 65–6, etc.

45 *CW* 13:4–15; cf. Augustine, *City of God*, 14.10–13; Mary Thecla Schmidt, "S. Augustine's Influence on S. Thomas More's English Works" (Ph.D. dissertation, Yale University, 1943), 175–6.

46 *CW* 13:192/15–20.

47 *CW* 13:194.

48 *CW* 13:201/22–3.

49 See *Thomas More's Prayer Book*, ed. L. L. Martz and R. S. Sylvester (New Haven: Yale University Press, 1969).

50 See *CW* 13:226–7.

51 *CW* 14:359.

52 It is a pleasure to thank Dr. Friedrich Unterweg of the University of Düsseldorf for access to the collection of their remarkable Institute for English Renaissance Studies.

Bibliography

Primary Sources

The Complete Works of St. Thomas More, New Haven and London: Yale University Press, 1963–97. The standard edition.

The Correspondence of Sir Thomas More, ed. Elizabeth Frances Rogers, Princeton: Princeton University Press, 1947.

Thomas More's Prayer Book: A Facsimile Reproduction of the Annotated Pages, ed. L. L. Martz and R. S. Sylvester, New Haven: Yale University Press, 1969.

Utopia: Latin Text and English Translation, ed. G. M. Logan, R. M. Adams, and C. H. Miller, Cambridge: Cambridge University Press, 1995. Corrected text and modern translation of the classic.

The Workes of Sir Thomas More Knyght, sometyme Lorde Chauncellor of England, wrytten by him in the Englysh tonge. 1557, London: Scolar Press, 1978. Reprint edition of the 1557 folio edition of More's English works.

Secondary Sources

Baker-Smith, Dominic, *More's Utopia*, New York: HarperCollins Academic, 1991.

Bradshaw, Brendan, "The Controversial Sir Thomas More," *JEH* 36 (1985), 535–69.

Byron, Brian, *Loyalty in the Spirituality of St. Thomas More*, Bibliotheca Humanistica et Reformatorica, 4, Nieuwkoop: De Graaf, 1972.

Fox, Alistair, *Thomas More: History and Providence*, New Haven and London: Yale University Press, 1983.

Gogan, Brian, *The Common Corps of Christendom: Ecclesiological Themes in the Writings of Sir Thomas More*, Studies in the History of Christian Thought, 26, Leiden: E. J. Brill, 1982.

Hexter, J. H., *More's Utopia: The Biography of an Idea*, Princeton: Princeton University Press, 1952.

Kaufman, Peter Iver, "Humanist Spirituality and Ecclesial Reaction: Thomas More's *Monstra*," *CH* 56 (1987), 25–38.

Logan, George M., *The Meaning of More's Utopia*, Princeton: Princeton University Press, 1983.

Marius, Richard C., *Thomas More: A Biography*, New York: Knopf, 1984; repr. Cambridge: Harvard University Press, 1999.

Martz, Louis L., *Thomas More: The Search for the Inner Man*, New Haven: Yale University Press, 1990.

Sylvester, Richard S., ed., *St. Thomas More: Action and Contemplation*, New Haven: Yale University Press, 1972.

Sylvester, R. S. and G. P. Marc'hadour, eds., *Essential Articles for the Study of Thomas More*, Hamden: Archon Books, 1977.

Ignatius of Loyola (1491?–1556)

John W. O'Malley, SJ

Ignatius of Loyola a theologian? On what grounds? The only book that he wrote entirely on his own was the *Spiritual Exercises*, hardly a work of "theology." His correspondence, though the largest of any single person from the sixteenth century, presents problems with trying to discover in it a theology. The correspondence mainly consists of practical directives and suggestions to members of the newly founded Society of Jesus as to how they might deport themselves in the diverse and sometimes exotic situations in which they found themselves, whether in Paris, Vienna, Lisbon, Brazil, or India, whether as itinerant preachers to peasants in obscure hamlets or as founders of schools in large urban centers.

Moreover, most of the extant correspondence of almost 7,000 letters dates after 1547, when Juan Alfonso de Polanco became Ignatius's secretary.[1] The collaboration between Ignatius and Polanco was so close that it is often difficult to know just what to attribute to Ignatius, what to Polanco. Almost the same can be said of the Jesuit *Constitutions*, which Ignatius agreed to draft when elected superior general of the Society a few months after its formal approval as a religious order by Pope Paul III in September 1540. Although the traditional interpretation that Ignatius himself was the principal inspiration behind the *Constitutions* still stands, much of the wording, arrangement, and many of the details must be attributed to Polanco. Everything was submitted to Ignatius for approval and revision, but, as in any case of such close collaboration, the problem of authorship cannot be solved by facilely assigning contents to Ignatius and form to Polanco. In any case, the *Constitutions* are hardly a work of theology in the conventional sense of that term.

Unlike so many Protestant leaders of the era, Ignatius did not emerge to prominence from an academic career. He was a Spanish noble, an *hidalgo*, who had the chivalric and academically sparse education of his class.[2] As a youth he learned how to dance and duel but not how to parse a Latin verb. He began to study Latin only when he was about thirty-three, in 1524, and was forced to sit in grammar classes with boys young enough to be his sons.

By that time, three years after the beginning of his religious conversion, he had become convinced that he needed more formal education, even a university degree, in order, as he said, "better to help souls." Thus, like so many second-career students in divinity schools today, he had his heart set not on academic but on pastoral goals. In that regard, though not in some others, the education that he received at the universities of Alcalá de Henares and Paris would not change him.

He matriculated at the University of Paris in 1527 and received the Bachelor of Arts degree in 1533, the Master of Arts degree in 1535. During his last two years at Paris, 1533–5, he audited courses in theology at the *studia* of the Dominicans and Franciscans. That was the extent of his formal training in theology. He took no degree in it. By 1534 he had gathered around himself six other students at the university, each of whom he accompanied through a month-long experience of the *Spiritual Exercises*. In that year they as a group determined they would travel to the Holy Land "to help souls," thus presaging the missionary character of the order they would later found. The next year Ignatius left Paris, with the intention of meeting the others within a few months in Venice, whence they would embark on their missionary journey. His departure from Paris marked the end of his academic training. He then and later showed little intrinsic interest in the theological issues that buffeted his age.

He never had any sympathy for "Lutheranism," but there is no evidence that his dislike derived from reading the Reformers, except possibly in the most cursory manner. The famous, or infamous, "Rules for Thinking with the Church," a kind of appendix to the *Spiritual Exercises* composed for the most part while he was still at Paris, the last piece added to the book, reflect that antipathy, but they for the most part are guidelines to pastoral practice, hardly theses for theological debate.[3] Later commentators, Catholic and Protestant alike, have extolled or excoriated them as a specimen of hyper-orthodoxy when in fact they would have been accepted by most sixteenth-century Catholics as mainline.[4] To put them in perspective it helps to recall that although the third rule said "long prayers whether in church or outside" should be praised, Ignatius adamantly opposed such prayers within the Society of Jesus, despite much pressure to the contrary.[5]

As superior general of the order, he encouraged other Jesuits like Diego Laínez and Peter Canisius to refute Lutheran errors, but he never attempted the same himself, surely realizing on some level that he was ill equipped to do so. Perhaps more surprising, he manifested little interest in the great doctrinal debates that took place at the Council of Trent in 1545–7 and 1551–2. When three members of the nascent Society of Jesus were early on appointed official theologians of the Council, Ignatius, though he was in no way responsible for their appointments, was immensely pleased. It was a significant recognition of the Society of Jesus just five years after its founding.

In early 1546 he wrote to these official theologians with advice as to how they should deport themselves. The letter is as important for what it does not say as for what it does say. In it Ignatius exhorted the Jesuits to present their opinions modestly, to carry on their usual preaching, catechizing, and visiting of the sick and poor, and to reflect together each evening as to how their work at Trent was proceeding.[6]

Entirely missing from the letter was any word concerning the issues facing the Council. He looked upon the Jesuits more as mediators among the various factions present there than as proponents of any specific agenda – on either doctrine or reform of the church. Even more surprising, he wrote them a few months later asking whether it might not be to God's greater glory for them to withdraw from the Council and take up some pastoral duties elsewhere. The next year, before the Council adjourned, he actually assigned one of them, Claude Jay, to another post.

Ignatius's most heartfelt interests, we must conclude, lay elsewhere. Although in the last few years of his life he began to raise the religious situation in Germany to a high priority in the Society, "Lutheranism" and many of the issues it entailed were even then only one among many of his concerns. In this he was not unique among Catholics but, I think, broadly symptomatic. Catholicism early on produced its controversialists like Eck and Emser and, much later, Bellarmino and others. But the matter of the controversies was ground chosen and defined by the enemy. It did not seize the imagination and heart of many talented Catholics, whose sights were directed elsewhere. Moreover, in Spain, Portugal, and Italy Protestantism, while perceived as a mortal danger by many churchmen, was in fact a geographically distant reality that directly touched relatively few people.

Many of the most talented and devout Catholics directed their gifts to other enterprises and, even on the theological level, often dealt with issues of little concern to either Protestant theologians or Catholic controversialists. I am thinking, for instance, of missionaries like Bartolomé de las Casas and his defense of Amerindian rights, and of Alessandro Valignano and his wrestling with the relationship between (Europeanized) Christianity and cultures as ancient and refined as those of Japan and China. Even Catholic academic theologians like Francisco de Vitoria, Juan de Mariana, Luís de Molina, Francisco de Toledo, and Leonhard Lessius moved on ground defined for the most part by Catholic concerns and, hence, they fell off the screen of modern historiography, defined as it has been by the Reformation. Today even specialists in sixteenth-century theology do not recognize their names.

Ignatius is in that regard broadly indicative of the great bias that has distorted the approach practically all historians have taken to Catholicism in the sixteenth century.[7] That approach wittingly or unwittingly defined Catholicism in relationship to the Reformation and judged it according to criteria that the long, lively, and methodologically sophisticated historiography of the Reformation had established. Instead of asking what Catholicism was like, that approach perforce asked how Catholicism resisted, resembled, caused, reacted to, was affected by and otherwise related to Luther and Calvin. Only recently have there been signs of change, at least in North American historical writing. The point I am trying to make is that to understand Ignatius, as well as many other Catholics of the early modern era, great effort is required. Many received assumptions and prejudices must be shed if we wish to enter the sixteenth-century Catholic situation on its own terms.

Luther and Loyola – they have been paired for centuries! But we cannot enter the one through the door of the other. At Luther's center, for instance, reigned the doctrine of justification by faith alone. Luther was a theology professor, an academician, and we should not be surprised that a doctrine, that is, an *idea*, was what brought him the freedom and the comfort he had so long sought. He drew the idea from what is in effect a theological treatise, the Epistle to the Romans.

Rather than of a doctrine, Ignatius spoke of ways – ways of praying, ways of discerning God's will, ways of proceeding in ministry. He spoke of life in the Society of Jesus as "a way to God." The base texts for him were the synoptic Gospels, narratives where the ministry of Jesus was described – precisely the texts that figured among the least in Luther's "canon." To a large extent Ignatius's "ways" were a refashioning of the medieval *imitatio Christi*, but now qualified through the radical interiority called for by the *Spiritual Exercises*. By the time he wrote the *Constitutions* those "ways" were further refashioned by certain theological and doctrinal assumptions with which he was able to buttress his delineation of the Jesuit "way to God." These assumptions remain for the most part implicit, however, never appearing at center stage.

Is there, then, any justification for including Ignatius of Loyola in a collection of studies about "theologians"? Everything hinges, of course, on how "theologian" is defined.[8] Ignatius is perhaps best understood as a religious activist, but an activist who reflected on his own experiences and tried to communicate them so that they might be of help to others. It is in that sense that Jerónimo Nadal, the contemporary who perhaps best understood him, called him "a theologian." The passage is worth quoting:

> Here, then, you see the necessity for the course of studies in the Society: to be able to preach and become skilled in those ministries that the Church deems ordered for the help of our neighbor. . . . Here is our father, the theologian. His desires were always to seek how he might better employ himself in the service of God.[9]

In effect Nadal was describing a "theology" whose scope was the practice of ministry. We might therefore call that theology pastoral, that is, providing a theological horizon or a religious vision, more or less coherent, that gave shape and a certain distinctiveness to practices of ministry. Ignatius was interested, therefore, in what used to be called practical divinity. Although "Ignatius the theologian" can perhaps be studied from other perspectives, he will here be studied from this one.[10]

In the *Spiritual Exercises* Ignatius created a road map based on his own interior journey from conventional religious practice to a wholehearted commitment to follow the "way" of Christ, a way culminated in a total surrender to God's love and will. It is important to remember, however, that he kept modifying the text over a 20-year period, up to 1540, in the light of his experience of guiding others through the four "weeks." The text reflects, therefore, not only Ignatius's experience in exploring his own interiority but also his experience in helping others do the same. It is also important to recognize that the *Exercises* themselves became an instrument of ministry for the Jesuits and in effect created a new ministry, the spiritual "retreat."

Ignatius made no significant changes in the *Exercises* after about 1540, which was just the time he and the others were founding the new Society of Jesus. For him more so than for the others, the founding marked the end of his days as a "pilgrim," which is how he liked to describe himself up to that point, and it moved him to a position of great responsibility for the ministries of the new order. Through his insistence on frequent correspondence from the members of the order about their ministries, he made himself into an extraordinary recipient of information from widely divergent cultural and religious situations. He seems to have listened well.

In his office as superior general, he showed many gifts of leadership, but one was outstanding: he recognized and utilized in others talents that complemented his own. When he chose Polanco as his secretary in 1547 he could hardly have made a better choice. Among Polanco's outstanding qualifications was a fine education in both the *studia humanitatis* and Thomistic theology.

At about the same time he began to confide more and more responsibility for directing operations in the field to Nadal. By the beginning of the next decade this young Majorcan had become Ignatius's itinerant troubleshooter to Jesuit communities throughout Europe and his interpreter to them of his pastoral vision.[11] He said of Nadal what he never said of any of his companions from Paris: "he altogether knows my mind."[12] Nadal, like Polanco, also had an excellent education, which included a licentiate in theology from Paris and a doctorate from Avignon.

Among the many decisions that were taken by Ignatius in the early years of the order, none was more dramatic or had a more profound impact than the decision that gradually evolved between about 1547 and 1550 to take the staffing and management of schools as the Jesuit primary ministry. Under it lay a reconciliation with "the world" and with human culture that had long been evolving in him but that for its articulation required the vocabulary and theological justification that Polanco and Nadal could provide. I cannot imagine that Ignatius would have seized so enthusiastically upon the religious potential of the humanistic ideals of education had he not been schooled in them by Polanco and Nadal. These two, I believe, would have had to point out to him how the *pietas* of the humanistic educational scheme correlated with the inculcation of *Christianitas* that was the aim of Jesuit ministry.[13]

It was through interaction with these two men that Ignatius completed his theological education, done in the heat of such practical decisions. Indeed, while it is easy on many levels to differentiate these three voices from each other, on profounder levels they speak almost as one. Polanco and Nadal in fact considered themselves to be nothing more than interpreters of Ignatius, sometimes clarifying, sometimes amplifying on his thoughts and sentiments. I will here feel free to use them occasionally in that way.

What the above implies, of course, is the obvious truth: Ignatius continued to change as he grew older. That truth needs to be stated, however, because it is contrary to the usual image of him, which tends to be static and which, correlatively, takes the *Spiritual Exercises* as the almost unique source against which to test how he is to be understood. But the static image flies not only in the face of common sense but even runs contrary to what Ignatius himself implies in his autobiographical account. Here he indicates how God, like a teacher or parent dealing with a little child, helped him, step by step, in the early years of his conversion to ever more profound understanding of what was happening and to behavior consonant with such enlightenment.[14] There is no reason to believe that the process ended when he became general of the Society.

Indeed, few figures from the sixteenth century manifest even on the most superficial level so many shifts in what we might blandly term lifestyle. At age 13 he left Loyola for Arévalo to be trained as a courtier in the household of Juan Velázquez de Cuéllar, chief treasurer of King Ferdinand. When he was about twenty-six, in 1517, he moved to another court to become a *gentilhombre* to the duke of Nájera, a position that sometimes required taking up arms and participating in military expeditions. (Only in this occasional way can the "soldier saint" be called a soldier!)

During one of these expeditions four years later he was wounded in battle at Pamplona. For the next two years, until 1523, he became almost a hermit at Loyola and Manresa as his conversion experiences began and continued. Then for a year he was quite literally a "pilgrim," begging his way from Barcelona until he reached his goal, Jerusalem. Upon his return he became a student for the next nine years, at Barcelona, Alcalá, Salamanca, and, finally, Paris. From 1535 until 1540 he along with his companions from Paris, who during this period were ordained priests, labored essentially as itinerant preachers or evangelists in northern and central Italy while they awaited passage to the Holy Land. In 1541 he became the chief administrator of the new order, a post at which he remained for the next 15 years until his death in 1556, never leaving Rome or its near environs ever again. As modern jargon would have it: he invented himself many times.

How unlikely, therefore, that he would not change considerably through the radically diverse situations and cultures in which he found himself: the feudal culture of his early years, the scholastic culture of his time at Paris, the more humanistic culture of Renaissance Italy, the increasingly Counter-Reformation culture of Rome during his last years.

Before we look at how Ignatius changed, however, we need to be aware of two fundamental continuities that underlie his development. The first, as I already suggested, was his desire from the very beginning of his conversion to be of "help to souls." Even as he lay on his sickbed at Loyola in 1521 when his conversion experiences were beginning, he sought out members of the household to speak with them "about the things of God . . . and thus brought much profit to their souls," as he later described it.[15] Even during his most eremitical period at Manresa the next year, he similarly "spent time in helping other souls."[16] With the passing of the years "the help of souls" became his leitmotif. The expression or its equivalent appears on practically every page of the 12 huge volumes of his correspondence. This constitutes, without doubt, his theological horizon.

The second was his profound conviction that God was active within his soul, guiding, teaching, and comforting him, and that acting in accord with this reality was the key to happiness in this life and the next. The fundamental principle upon which the *Spiritual Exercises* rest is buried away in the Fifteenth Annotation at the beginning of the book: what it is all about is that "the Creator deal directly with the creature, and the creature directly with his Creator and Lord."[17]

How does this divine impulse from Creator to creature manifest itself, how is it detected and assessed? In the *Exercises* Ignatius gives "rules" to help in this delicate process of discernment.[18] The "rules" derived in the first instance from his own experiences that began in the castle of Loyola when he noted within himself certain "motions" of consolation and desolation, depending on the alternative kinds of future he imagined for himself. The point I want to make is that for him – in his own life, in the whole process of the *Exercises* meant for others, and then later in his life as general of the Society – the ideal for ministers was to act out of their interiority, as tested against what the circumstances seemed to require, not to act out of some rigid adherence to external prescriptions for "what is best."

As general of the Society, he wrote hundreds upon hundreds of letters offering advice as to how Jesuits might deal with the sometimes perplexing pastoral situations in which they found themselves, but he consistently qualified the advice with, equivalently, "unless some other course seems better to you." Even more impressive, the *Constitutions*, which lay down the general principles according to which the Society was to be governed, is riddled with similar escape-clauses. Nadal caught the profound implications of this stance when he said the ministries of the Jesuits were to be done *spiritu, corde, practice*, that is, out of a sense of the Spirit's inner presence and direction (*spiritu*), from the heart and to the hearts of others (*corde*), with a view to what truly is helpful in a given situation (*practice*).[19]

If these are two big continuities, what are the discontinuities, the changes? To some extent they consist in making more explicit, more pervasively operative, and more determinative realities present in his life from the early years of his conversion. He was concerned with "helping souls" on his sickbed at Loyola, as I indicated, but that was an aspect of the experience that he singled out for mention many years after the event, when he had already been superior general of the Society for over a decade.

In the *Spiritual Exercises*, which after the "First Week" consists in three other "weeks" that are for the most part contemplations on the life of Christ, he does not often call attention explicitly to Jesus' ministry. It is true that in the meditation on the banner of Christ, he depicts Christ as choosing disciples to send them throughout the world to spread his sacred message and then recommending to them the "ways" (poverty, humility, etc.) in which this enterprise is to be carried out.[20] It can thus be said that the *Exercises* have a bias toward active ministry. But the bias is muted.

In Ignatius's correspondence, however, most of which dates after 1547, and in the *Constitutions*, substantially composed between 1547 and 1550, ministry is the overriding issue. It is the text and the subtext. The *Constitutions* are all about "the help of souls." This emphasis is of course due in part to the audience to whom these documents are addressed, exclusively Jesuit for the *Constitutions* and largely Jesuit for the correspondence. Nonetheless, the accent has become newly insistent.

The Jesuits liked to emphasize how they differed from the mendicant orders that preceded them. The fact is that they resembled them in a number of ways, to a large extent even in the kinds of ministries in which they engaged, especially in their earliest years before they undertook the schools. Among the ways they differed from them, however, was in the more explicit, forthright, and self-aware statements in their official and unofficial documents that ministry was what they were all about. Yes, they had become members of the Society in the hope of saving their own souls by following their call, but their salvation was worked out precisely through the practice of ministry, through "the help of souls."

Ignatius began with them to forge a new vocabulary for the special approach to ministry they were taking. The most striking instance of this vocabulary was "mission." It comes as a surprise to learn that this term, without which we can today hardly speak about Christianity, was not current in our contemporary sense until the mid-sixteenth century.[21] Instead of missions and missionaries, the traditional expressions were "propagation of the faith" and "journeying to the infidel." Despite the Vulgate's employment of various forms of *mittere* in connection with the early disciples of Jesus, medieval authors used that verb and its derivatives almost exclusively for the "missions" internal to the Trinity.

The Jesuits were among the first to inaugurate the new usage and were the group initially responsible for its spread. In the papal bull that founded the order, substantially written by the Jesuits themselves, both the older "propagation of the faith" and then "mission" are used to designate travel for the sake of ministry. By the time of the *Constitutions*, "mission" has displaced the older terms, and it dominates the Seventh Part, the section devoted to "the distribution of members in the vineyard of the Lord," which some commentators consider the heart of the document.[22]

Talk of the *vita apostolica* had circulated in western Europe since at least the twelfth century, indicating different things to different people depending on just how the life of the early disciples was imagined. Ignatius and companions related it directly to ministry. They were about an "apostolic" ministry, by which they meant a ministry that entailed being sent or being on a journey for the ministry. This is a specification and sharper formulation of the ideal which Nadal succinctly formulated in his summary of the stories of Jesus' original band: "Our vocation is similar to the vocation and training of the apostles; first, we come to know the Society, and then we follow; we are instructed; we receive our commission to be sent [on ministry]; we are sent; we exercise our ministry; we are prepared to die for Christ in fulfilling those ministries."[23]

Among the "apostles" Nadal further specified Paul as the one who best exemplified the Jesuit vocation.[24] He meant to suggest the intense zeal of Paul that knew no limits in the hardship it was willing to undergo, but it also meant going forth and seeking the lost sheep, not waiting for them on the doorstep of a church. It meant being *missionaries.* Nothing was more fundamental to Ignatius's original vision of ministry.

The special "Fourth Vow" that he and the early companions created for Jesuits, often erroneously described as a vow of "loyalty to the pope," was actually a vow "about missions," as the formula of the vow itself clearly states.[25] It was a vow to be a missionary, even though the word "missionary" had in effect not yet been coined. It was a vow that radically distinguished Jesuit ministry from the legislation on ministry enacted at the Council of Trent, which dealt exclusively with keeping local ministers (bishops and priests) in the local situations to minister to Christians in their local parishes.

"The world is our house." This bold statement, drummed into Jesuits again and again by Nadal, captures the radicality of the vision. That house

> is altogether the most ample place and reaches as far as the globe itself. For wherever they can be sent in ministry to bring help to souls, that is the most glorious and longed-for house for these theologians. . . . They consider that they are in their most peaceful and pleasant house when they are constantly on the move, when they travel throughout the earth, when they have no place to call their own. . . . Only let them strive in some small way to imitate Christ Jesus, who had nowhere on which to lay his head and who spent all his years of preaching in journey.[26]

It was in relationship to this ideal that Ignatius elaborated for the Jesuit minister a style of life, a "way," that was a notable break with the traditions that immediately preceded it even for members of religious orders. The symbol for this break was the Jesuits' well-known insistence that, unlike members of all other religious orders, they not sing or recite the Liturgical Hours in common, which, by requiring them to be present in their houses at stated times during the day, would hinder their freedom to minister as need arose. Although that was a decision arrived at by all ten of the founders and cannot be attributed solely to Ignatius, he nonetheless had deeply interiorized it and resisted even popes when he thought it was threatened.

That was only one aspect of his delineation of what we might term a new asceticism for ministers, preachers of the Word, that broke with the implicit or explicit model of the half-starved John the Baptist that pervaded the previous tradition. It in effect qualified as well even the image of the evangelizing Paul as totally spent in ministry and yearning for a martyr's death. There were two stages in his development here. The first began during his days at Manresa, where in the early months he engaged in a fierce battle against his body and his sensuality by depriving himself of food, drink, and sleep, by allowing his fingernails and hair to grow, by going about in rags. Bit by bit he gave up these practices, suggesting in one place that he did so in part because they hindered him in the help of souls.[27] By the time he completed the *Exercises* he had included "Rules with regard to Eating," in which he laid down some rather anal-retentive suggestions about how to avoid overindulgence yet be assured of sufficient intake to preserve one's strength.[28]

The accent on such matters in the *Constitutions* is different. While a certain self-discipline is always assumed for Jesuits, self-care emerges even more strongly as a virtue peculiarly appropriate for them so that they might more effectively minister to others. The essence of the message, repeated again and again, was that, although an "excessive preoccupation with the needs of the body is blameworthy, a proper concern for the preservation of one's health and bodily strength is praiseworthy, and all should exercise it."[29] This is not the language or the practice of late medieval preachers like Bernardine of Siena or Vincent Ferrer, this is not the practice of a later bishop like Carlo Borromeo of Milan, who by his fasts practically starved himself to death at age 42. Diego Laínez, Ignatius's successor as general, quoted him to the effect that until individuals surrendered to God they took delight in penances and dealing roughly with their bodies, but once that point was past, they treated their bodies with reverence as gifts from God.[30]

Discretion and moderation in labors and in all other practical matters had become for him the ideal. Ignatius learned a hard lesson from the toll the austerities he practiced in his early days took on him, but he found justification for the quite different approach of his later years in the Thomistic–Aristotelian synthesis that either he learned at Paris or that Polanco taught him in Rome. *Virtus in medio stat* – virtue, the mean between two extremes, the central principle of Aristotle's and later Aquinas's moral teaching, was fully appropriated by Ignatius. *Mediocridad* was the Spanish word that caught this ideal. Ignatius transformed it into a hermeneutical principle for the interpretation of the *Constitutions* themselves, which "do not lean to extremes of either rigor or laxity."[31]

What I see in Ignatius is an ever more profound reconciliation with "the world." No "theology of the cross" here, in Luther's sense! This reconciliation was adumbrated in the *Exercises* with the final contemplation "On Divine Love,"[32] but it received practical implementation in the *Constitutions* with the advocacy of the use of "human means" in ministry, such as the study of the pagan classics for acquiring the eloquence needed in a preacher.[33] It also received a theological foundation that runs quietly as a leitmotif through the *Constitutions*. That foundation was the scholastic, especially Thomistic axiom, that grace perfects nature.

The Jesuit *Constitutions* are not, certainly, a theological document in the conventional sense. Their originality in their own genre of religious literature, however, has never been appreciated. A product of the collaboration between Ignatius and Polanco, the *Constitutions* differed radically from foundational documents of similar groups, which were little more than collections of ordinances. The *Constitutions*, by contrast, enjoyed a rationalized structure in their organization. This structure was based on the assumption of emotional and psychological development of the Jesuit from the time he entered until he reached full maturity; it manifested a new attention to motivation and general principles; insisted in particular and in general on flexible implementation of their prescriptions; conveyed an all-pervasive orientation toward ministry; and, especially, had an implicit but detectable theological leitmotif. Despite the medieval clutter of details that mark them, they are in the features just mentioned a strikingly modern document.

An important aspect of Ignatius's reconciliation with the world was his increasing faith in stable institutions as effective means for helping souls. This is exemplified most dramatically in his work in founding the Society of Jesus and in saying good-bye to what he called his "pilgrim years" to become the chief administrator in that institution for 15 years until his death. From 1521 until 1540 he was either on the road or leading the rootless life of a student. The founding of the Society, even though there is evidence that he had entertained the idea for some time, can be taken as symptom of a psychological development that prepared the way for the Jesuits undertaking formal schooling as their primary ministry.

In that regard we must keep two facts clearly in mind. First, the ten Jesuits who founded the Society had conceived of an organization consisting primarily of itinerant preachers of the Word, who almost by definition would not remain anywhere very long. They envisaged a pastoral blitz of a few days or weeks as the preferred pattern of ministry. The *Constitutions* indicate that even the "missions" entailed by the Fourth Vow should ordinarily not be longer than three months.[34] That vow can indeed be understood as a vow to travel, the polar opposite of the monk's vow of stability. In the early years, to be on the road was the quintessence of what it meant to be a member of the Society.[35]

Second, graduates of the University of Paris though all ten of the original founders were, they not only did not foresee themselves as schoolteachers but expressly precluded for themselves even teaching the younger members of the Society themselves. Circumstances soon led them to offering some instruction to younger Jesuits, and soon other circumstances led to the founding of the first real Jesuit school in Messina in 1547.

The radical change this decision implied was promoted by Ignatius, who within a year or so became enthusiastic over the potential for good that such schools offered, realizing fully the long-term commitment of personnel that they implied. Ignatius thus drastically qualified the original commitment to "mission" with the reality of resident schoolmasters. Though by no means a humanist himself, he became convinced, probably through Polanco and Nadal, of all that the humanists promised to be accomplished for church and society by means of institutions run according to the *pietas* that was their ideal.

What about Ignatius's relationship to the most long-lived institution of his day, the Catholic Church? Is there anything further to say in this matter, since it is obvious that he was an unquestioning believer in the apostolic authenticity of the papacy and of what he called "the hierarchical church," that is, pope and bishops? On the conscious level he was in these matters altogether in accord with the thinking of mainline canon lawyers, and he surely understood that a task of the Society was to defend the institutions of papacy and episcopacy against Protestant attacks. But was there a deeper aspect of his belief-system that somewhat transcended these conventional categories, at least as we today tend to read them back into the sixteenth century?

Polemicists and apologists alike interpret the Fourth Vow as proof positive of Ignatius taking the papacy as the center of his ecclesiological vision. What they fail to take into account is that the idea for it came out of discussions carried on by all ten of the original founders, with no particular indication that Ignatius was its instigator. While he gives it primacy of place in the Seventh Part of the *Constitutions*, he makes it clear that the general enjoys the same authority as the pope to send members on "missions." In his immense correspondence he almost never refers to the papal aspect of the vow, and he speaks of kings like John III of Portugal as having almost the same moral authority as the pope to deploy Jesuits "in the vineyard of the Lord." In comparison with the claims that have been made about how much the papacy meant to him, he speaks of it surprisingly sparingly.

He speaks even of "the church" with the same sparseness. Although the papal bull of 1550 that confirmed the earlier (1540) approval of the Society defined the order as an institution to "serve the church," Ignatius himself practically never uses the expression.[36] Not serving the church but serving, i.e., "helping," souls is what he and the Society of Jesus are about. They do this "in the vineyard of the Lord," an ecclesiological image that is fuzzy at the edges, for that vineyard extends to where there are not yet any Christians – and certainly no bishops or pope. Was this heritage partly responsible for the reluctance of the Jesuits, who arrived in Japan in 1549, to see a bishop installed there – which did not happen until a half-century had elapsed?[37]

Notes

The numbers given in square brackets refer to the standard paragraph/section numbers used in modern editions of the Jesuit *Constitutions*, the *Spiritual Exercises*, and Ignatius's narrative of his early life, which I will call *Autobiography*. Full details are given in the Bibliography.

1   On Polanco see Clara Englander, *Ignatius von Loyola und Johannes von Polanco: Der Ordensstifter und sein Sekretär* (Regensburg: Pustet, 1956).

2   The most detailed biography is by Ricardo Garcia-Villoslada, *San Ignacio de Loyola: Nueva biografía* (Madrid: Biblioteca de Autores Cristianos, 1986). See also André Ravier, *Ignatius of Loyola and the Founding of the Society of Jesus*, trans. Maura Daly, Joan Daly, and Carson Daly (San Francisco: Ignatius Press, 1987). Valuable for its factual precision is Cándido de Dalmases, *Ignatius of Loyola: Founder of the Jesuits*, trans. Jerome Aixalá (St. Louis: Institute of Jesuit Sources, 1985). We await a truly critical biography.

3   *Spiritual Exercises*, [352–70].

4   For a judicious counter-statement to this tradition, see Marjorie O'Rourke Boyle, "Angels Black and White: Loyola's Spiritual Discernment in Historical Perspective," *Theological Studies*, 44 (1983), 241–57.

5 *Spiritual Exercises*, [355].
6 *Monumenta Ignatiana. Santi Ignatii de Loyola Societatis Iesu fundatoris epistolae et instructiones*, 12 vols. (Madrid: Gabriel López del Horno, 1903–11), 1:386–9; English translation in *Letters of St. Ignatius of Loyola*, trans. William J. Young (Chicago: Loyola University Press, 1959), 93–6.
7 See John W. O'Malley, *Trent and All That: Renaming Catholicism in the Early Modern Era* (Cambridge, MA: Harvard University Press, 2000).
8 See Avery Dulles, "Saint Ignatius and the Jesuit Theological Tradition," *Studies in the Spirituality of Jesuits*, 14/2 (March 1982), 1–3.
9 Jerónimo Nadal, *Monumenta Nadal, Commentarii de Instituto Societatis Iesu* (Rome: Institutum Historicum Societatis Iesu, 1962), 282–5.
10 For a quite different approach, see Juan Luis Segundo, *The Christ of the Ignatian Exercises*, ed. and trans. John Drury (Maryknoll: Orbis Books, 1987).
11 On Nadal, see especially William V. Bangert, *Jerome Nadal (1507–1580): Tracking the First Generation of Jesuits*, ed. Thomas M. McCoog (Chicago: Loyola University Press, 1992) and Miguel Nicolau, *Jerónimo Nadal, I.I. (1507–1580): sus obras y doctrinas espirituales* (Madrid: Consejo Superior de Investigaciones Científicas, 1949).
12 Jerónimo Nadal, *Monumenta Nadal* (MHSI) *Epistolae P. Hieronymi Nadal Societatis Iesu ab anno 1546 ad 1577*, 4 vols. (Madrid: Augustino Avrial, 1898–1905), 1:144.
13 On *pietas*, see John W. O'Malley, "Introduction" in *Collected Works of Erasmus* (Toronto: University of Toronto Press, 1988), 66:ix–xxxix. On *Christianitas*, see John Van Engen, "The Christian Middle Ages as an Historiographical Problem," *American Historical Review*, 91 (1986), 519–52.
14 *Autobiography*, [27].
15 *Autobiography*, [11].

16 *Autobiography*, [26].
17 *Spiritual Exercises*, [15].
18 *Spiritual Exercises*, [313–36].
19 Nadal, *Commentarii*, 227–31. See Nicolau, *Nadal*, 305–13.
20 *Spiritual Exercises*, [143–8].
21 See John W. O'Malley, "Mission and the Early Jesuits," *The Way*, Supplement 79 (Spring 1994), 3–10.
22 *Constitutions*, [603–32].
23 Jerónimo Nadal, *Orationis observationes*, ed. Miguel Nicolau (Rome: Institutum Historicum Societatis Iesu, 1964), no. 379.
24 Nadal, *Orationis observations*, no. 414.
25 *Constitutions*, [527].
26 See John W. O'Malley, "To Travel to Any Part of the World: Jerónimo Nadal and the Jesuit Vocation," *Studies in the Spirituality of Jesuits*, 16/2 (March 1984).
27 *Autobiography*, [29].
28 *Spiritual Exercises*, [210–17].
29 *Constitutions*, [292].
30 See Cándido de Dalmases, "Le esortazioni del P. Laínez sull' 'Examen Constitutionum,'" *Archivum Historicum Societatis Iesu*, 35 (1966), 149–50.
31 *Constitutions*, [822].
32 *Spiritual Exercises*, [230–7].
33 *Constitutions*, [814].
34 *Constitutions*, [615].
35 See Mario Scaduto, "La strada e i primi gesuiti," *Archivum Historicum Societatis Iesu*, 40 (1971), 323–90.
36 See Gabriel Côté, "The 'Helping' Church: An Operative Ecclesiology in the 'Help of Souls' of the Early Society of Jesus" (thesis, Weston Jesuit School of Theology, 1996).
37 See now M. Antoni Üçerler, "Sacred Historiography and its Rhetoric in Sixteenth-Century Japan: An Intertextual Study and Partial Critical Edition of *Principio y progresso de la religión christiana en Jappón [...] (1601–1603)* by *Alessandro Valignano*," 2 vols. (dissertation, University of Oxford, 1998), esp. 1:86–8.

Bibliography

Primary Sources

Ignatius of Loyola, *Monumenta Ignatiana* (four series within the *Monumenta Historica Societatis Iesu*), 23 vols., Madrid and Rome: Institutum Historicum Societatis Iesu, 1903–77.

——, *The Constitutions of the Society of Jesus*, trans. George E. Ganss, St. Louis: Institute of Jesuit Sources, 1970.
——, *Ignatius of Loyola: The Spiritual Exercises and Selected Works*, ed. George E. Ganss, New York: Paulist Press, 1991.

Secondary Sources

Aldama, Antonio M. de, *An Introductory Commentary on the Constitutions*, trans. Aloysius J. Owen, St. Louis: Institute of Jesuit Sources, 1989.

——, *The Formula of the Institute: Notes for a Commentary*, trans. Ignacio Echániz, St. Louis: Institute of Jesuit Sources, 1990.

Dulles, Avery, "Saint Ignatius and the Jesuit Theological Tradition," *Studies in the Spirituality of Jesuits*, 14/2 (March 1982).

O'Malley, John W., *The First Jesuits*, Cambridge, MA: Harvard University Press, 1993.

Rahner, Hugo, *Ignatius the Theologian*, trans. Michael Barry, New York: Herder & Herder, 1968.

Segundo, Juan Luis, "Ignatius Loyola: Trial or Project?" in his *Signs of the Times*, ed. Alfred T. Hennelly, trans. Robert R. Barr, Maryknoll: Orbis Books, 1993, 149–75.

Teresa of Avila (1515–1582)

Gillian T. W. Ahlgren

Teresa of Avila is probably one of history's most beloved mystics and saints. Immortalized by Bernini and diligently read and cited by many, Teresa is currently enjoying yet another season of exposure, this time within the field of practical spirituality.[1] Regardless of their background, most readers find her wit, irony, and wry humor both engaging and disarming. In her classic *Teresa of Avila and the Rhetoric of Femininity* Alison Weber speaks of Teresa's "golden pen," the rhetorical skill critical to her survival as an author,[2] which we might also say was a Midas-like ability to turn the grit of everyday experience into a extraordinary narrative of her sustained dialogue with a very personal, personable God. Yet these qualities of freshness, candor, even her lack of sophistication have kept us from a full appreciation of her theological contributions.[3] Long seen as merely devotional treatises, Teresa's works are now being mined more seriously for their theological content.

In reading Teresa's *Life* or her *Interior Castle*, we are struck by her familiarity with God, her knowledge and conviction – at first somewhat incredulous, later gracious and full of merriment – that she lived in "the consciousness of the presence of God,"[4] a consciousness that grew into a full realization of the divine grounding of her own consciousness. Perhaps this is Teresa's greatest contribution as theologian and writer: to encourage readers to more serious examination and contemplation of subjective realities – their own and others – gradually moving them into an awareness of the divine reality of consciousness itself. In the context of the Reformation period, prioritizing subjective reality is quite typical; yet in moving from the depths of her own subjective reality into expressions of God's subjective reality, dedicating herself to the contemplation of the two realms until gradually their differences have disappeared, Teresa is at once a revolutionary mystic and a quintessential Catholic.

Teresa lived in an era of dramatic religious changes, changes she both observed and participated in. Keenly aware of the religious conflicts of her day, Teresa appears to have had a passionate desire to do apologetic theology. In her *Life*, for example, she describes the effects that a vision of hell had on her, including a keen sadness that the many condemned souls (especially of those Lutherans, because, through their baptism, they are members of the Church) give me, and the great impulse to call souls to spiritual improvement, for it seems clear to me that I would willingly suffer a thousand deaths to liberate one single soul from such great torments. . . . This also makes me desire that, in a matter so important as this, we not be satisfied with doing anything less than everything we might be able to do. Let us not leave anything untried, and please God that He may be served to give us grace to do so.[5]

Counter-Reformation Spain is full of paradoxes that preclude any brief description of its religious climate. In her *Life*, often described as a spiritual autobiography, but also aptly characterized as an apologetic confessional,[6] Teresa notes that she lived in "difficult times" (*tiempos recios*).[7] The growing power of the Spanish Inquisition with its *autos de fe* and Indices of Prohibited Books has suggested to some that Roman Catholic orthodoxy was static, monolithic, and easy to monitor and that Spanish religious life was characterized by extreme forms of institutionalized repression. Without discounting the suffering of many Spanish subjects, inquisitional records challenge notions of orthodoxy – and, indeed, of Spanish Catholicism, indicating many idiosyncrasies and even indicating widespread ignorance of doctrine despite pockets of keen interest in mystical prayer.[8] While many of Spain's important religious figures, including Teresa, Luis de León, Ignatius of Loyola, and even Toledo's archbishop Bartolomé de Carranza (one of Spain's representatives to the Council of Trent), underwent scrutiny by the Inquisition, most religious figures discovered creative ways to impact their church, albeit at times through complex processes of accommodation, negotiation, and even subversion. The prolific reform of religious orders suggests vibrant spiritual growth, yet some forms of spiritual life were flatly rejected.[9]

Perhaps it is safe enough to assert that, over the course of the sixteenth century, Spanish religious life, while always multifaceted, developed two faces. The outward "face" expressed an attitude of conformity to ecclesial expectations, such as the requirements to attend mass, participate in the sacramental life of the church, and confess particular doctrines. For some this *was* religion. For others, religion involved such external practices as well as a deeper exploration of what might lie behind the appearance of religiosity – in other words, the cultivation of desires for deeper meaning, more abiding truths, and a practice of ethics rooted in ideals and aspirations, not just codes of rules. While this was the impetus to reform movements throughout Europe at this time, social-political, and ecclesial developments led, for the most part, in Spain to manifestations of extreme polarity where the mystical and picaresque intertwined, often in unexpected ways.[10]

Teresa herself embodied these paradoxes. She was the granddaughter of a converted Jew who had been condemned to penance by the Inquisitional Tribunal of Toledo. Her family – like most others in this situation – bought forged documents attesting to the "purity" of their blood, and carefully avoided any mention of their heritage.[11] Discovery and exploration of this "other side" of Teresa in the 1950s and 1960s moved the next generation of scholarship into a more sophisticated analysis of her rhetorical style. Consequently, in examining her theological contributions we should be prepared for complexity and multidimensionality in her language (as in all mystical texts), adapting ourselves sensitively to the need for decoding Teresa's prose.[12]

Nowhere is this more apparent than in Teresa's approach to Scripture. As an "unlettered" (i.e., unable to read Latin) woman, Teresa was subject to the prohibitions against reading Scripture in the vernacular. Such prohibitions emerged with a censure of bibles throughout Spain in 1554, an inquisitional edict that generalized an earlier (1551) prohibition of particular editions of the Bible.[13] It was therefore bolder than we might initially appreciate for Teresa to riddle her prose with implicit and explicit references to scriptural texts.[14] She used Scripture metaphorically as a form of invitation into an exploration of one's relationship with God. Increasingly, she began to see a relationship between the words expressed by Jesus and the Word of Christ they manifested. Consequently, she approached Scripture meditatively and sacramentally, seeing it as another form of Eucharist, to be chewed/considered, contemplated, even savored. Commenting specifically on the appearance of the Valdes Index and on the void it created, she writes:

> When they took away many books written in the vernacular, so that they would not be read, I was very sorry, because some of them gave me great pleasure, and I could not read them in Latin. But the Lord said to me, "Don't be distressed; I will give you a living book." I could not understand why that was said to me, because I did not then have visions; but just a few days later I understood it quite well, because I have had so much to think about and ponder in what I saw presently, and the Lord has loved me so much as to teach me in many ways, so that I hardly needed books.[15]

In the absence of words, Teresa looked, often through images, for windows into the reality that might lie behind the words, seeking in prayer a more direct route to revelation. Ironically, then, in a move that perhaps intended to deny Teresa access to expressions of God, the prohibition of scriptural and other words forced her to take her own subjective experience more seriously, to probe it for its potential to allow her access to God. As she does so, she begins to express, in words, the story of her soul, a book which we call the *Life* and which she called *The Book of God's Mercies*. Composing this book was an act of prayer, a practical expression of her complex, intuitive, and experiential understanding of God, out of which emerges an entire theological system that does not reduce quite so easily into the standard categories of systematic theology: Christology, anthropology, ecclesiology, sacraments, soteriology.

The first step in Teresa's exploration of the reality of God is her acknowledgment, theoretically and practically, of the personal, redemptive relationship she has with Christ. No less revolutionary for her than Luther's realization of the redemptive power of grace channeled through faith alone, Teresa describes an experience of conversion before a statue of Christ that crystallized her understanding of the magnitude of Christ's love for humanity that made possible his cruel suffering. In a literal outpouring of compassion – a kind of "suffering with" – Teresa threw herself down before the statue and begged God for the grace not to offend Him through sin again. Her discussion of this scene recalls both the agony of Christ in the Garden of Gethsemane and Augustine's conversion in the garden, described in the *Confessions*.

> My soul was, by now, quite fatigued, and, even though it would have liked to rest, my vicious habits would not allow it to. But it so happened that, one day when I

was entering the oratory, I saw an image that they had brought there to store in preparation for a certain feast that we observed in the convent. It was of Christ sorely wounded and it inspired so much devotion that, just in looking at it, my insides were disturbed to see Him thus, because it represented well what He suffered for us. I felt so deeply how poorly we had appreciated those wounds that my heart seemed to split apart, and I threw myself down next to Him with a great torrent of tears, begging him to fortify me once and for all so that I might not offend him. . . . It seems to me that I said to him then that I would not get up from there until He did what I begged Him. And I am sure that I benefited from this, as I have been improving very much ever since.[16]

Thus, for Teresa, while grace is the initiating impetus for spiritual growth, the response of the individual in terms of his or her care of the soul essentially constitutes the whole of the Christian life. There is a progressive movement toward the perfection of virtue, which she likens to the process of cultivating a garden. The garden metaphor stresses that the soul (here understood as the individual soul and as humanity itself) is created in goodness, with all the potential to flourish, even though its potential is not always recognizable, disguised as it is in humanity's fallen state.

The one who is starting out must realize that she is beginning to create a garden in very infertile soil, which has many weeds, so that the Lord will take delight there. His Majesty will uproot the weeds and will then plant flowers. So let us consider that this [process] is occurring [within us] when a soul decides to be prayerful, and it has already begun to make us of it; so, with the help of God we must, as good gardeners, encourage the plants to grow and be careful to water them, so that they are not lost but rather begin to blossom and give off a great fragrance that will give refreshment to this Lord of ours, and thus He will come often to this garden and delight among its virtues.[17]

Thus, embedded in humanity from its creation is its potential to attract God in such a way as to experience forms of joyful union with God. The soul's task is to receive direct and indirect forms of grace and patiently to find its own water when such forms are not forthcoming. Thus the Christian life consists in constant prayer of many types; the type itself is less important than the Christian's devotion to maintaining prayer in all circumstances.[18]

There are four principal ways of watering the garden; while they are not equal in ease or efficiency, the soul, since it cannot control its circumstances, must be flexible and open to whatever way is most appropriate for it at any given time.[19] The first way, the most laborious for the soul, is to water it by hand with water from a well. The second way uses a form of windmill and aqueducts, signaling more efficiency/proficiency at forms of prayer – this way, Teresa writes, is "less work for us and more water for the garden." The third way is to divert a river or stream; using this natural source of water symbolizes a directional shift in the prayer relationship. The gardener disappears, as grace is no longer mediated, but moves more directly into the soul, and the soul's role is to listen more attentively and respond with care to the insights received in prayer. The fourth way is from rain, the most immediate infusion of grace into the soul. As the soul progresses in prayer, opening itself up more fully to its own growth and its ability to receive more and more grace, its relationship to God and its very selfhood change qualitatively, like the flourishing of a garden.

Sincere dedication to the nurturing and development of one's soul, then, symbolizes both Teresa's anthropology and her characterization of the God–human relationship. There must be sincere dedication and discipline to these nurturing activities, for cultivating the fertility of our souls is the only way we have to show fidelity to God and to be good stewards of God's gifts to us. Here, Teresa is developing the idea of an "asceticism of love," in which we discipline ourselves in fidelity, "doing what is in us as good gardeners,"[20] to be faithful in our prayerful relationship with God, even during times of distress or spiritual aridity.

> Thus I say that is well that we never give up prayer – [even] when our understanding becomes distracted or perturbed – nor ever torment our soul [to do] what it cannot. There are other external things [we can do instead], like works of charity or reading, even though sometimes one is unfit even for this; then let it make use of the body out of love of God, because other times it will make use of the soul to serve Him, and let it engage in holy recreation and conversations, or go to the countryside, as her confessor advises. And in all these matters experience is a great thing; it helps us understand what is appropriate for us, and in all of this God is served.[21]

As Teresa writes earlier in the *Life*, mental prayer is the cultivation of an intimate relationship with God in its myriad of forms, but fundamentally epitomized by "taking many occasions to be in conversation with the One who we know loves us."[22]

For Teresa, progress toward union with God, or the movement toward sanctification, involves a healthy acknowledgement of human limitation in all realms except that of love. This theme is explored in even more detail in *The Interior Castle*, where Teresa discusses explicitly the role of the human will in the movement toward divinely empowered life (or, as she puts it, "supernatural" experience of life).

In *The Interior Castle* Teresa describes seven stages in the rediscovery and recovery of the soul. The soul was created in pristine goodness, "like a diamond or very clear crystal," but which is, in its fallen state, as unrecognizable as a diamond that has fallen into a puddle of mud or a crystal covered over by black cloth. The soul never loses its inherent beauty, but, to actualize its potential toward goodness, the soul must move more consciously toward its divine source, "the shining sun that is in the center of the soul."[23] This entire journey is essentially epistemological – i.e., it involves a growing knowledge of one's self, increasingly understood as an unlimited potential in God. Self-knowledge is directly related to Other-knowledge; Teresa urges her readers toward progress here because "to my way of thinking, we will never come to know ourselves completely if we do not try to know God."[24]

Teresa insists on the importance of self-knowledge, which necessitates a great deal of inner freedom and a dedication to exploration:

> This is very important for whatever soul is practicing prayer, whether a little or a lot: it should not be cornered or bound in any way; let it walk around in all of the rooms [of the castle in its interior] – up, down, and all around. For God has given such great dignity, it should not be stuck for a long time in only one room – oh, unless

it is in that of self-knowledge, which is so necessary in this [process] – see if you can understand me here! Even for those who inhabit the same room as God Himself; for as accomplished as one might be, no other thing is more important, nor can one ever accomplish it completely, as much as one might want to. Humility always works like a bee making honey in the beehive – without it everything is lost. . . .[25]

Thus deeper self-knowledge relative to the knowledge we have of God leads to humility and an understanding of our own limitations. But there is a plateau, a resting place, a moment of decision, represented in the third mansion [of *The Interior Castle*], or stage of growth where we choose either to accept our limitations as humans, thereby containing the growth process within ourselves, or to grow into a deeper capacity to love that moves us closer to the actual nature of God.

This plateau or entry into a process of ontological transformation represents at once the strength of the human will, and its capacity, given humanity's fallen state, to cause spiritual desolation and even violence, or, when located in the cultivation of a desire to love, rooted in humility and reverence, to move us into a divinely enhanced potential for understanding and loving. For Teresa this point of choice is encapsulated in the scriptural verse she introduces at the beginning of the third mansion, "Blessed is the one who fears the Lord."[26] (Here, "fear" is best understood as proper reverence, awe, and wonder, rather than intimidation or a crippling sense of subservience.) Once the soul recognizes and "fears" God, it becomes determined to honor that presence in daily life, and that determination is actually a setting of the will to do the will of God, which it understands as love, growth, and holiness. In mystical theology, this would be known as the union of wills, which must be achieved before any other kind of union with God is possible. Immersing itself ever more deeply in the pursuit of expressing love, it begins to remove all the impediments to loving God and others with a kind of healthy self-abandonment. These impediments are many and varied and can be deeply embedded in the soul. Therefore the process of "purgation," a purging of all impediments to true union with the God of love, a thorough pruning of all the weeds that inhibit the growth of the garden of our soul, is an ongoing task.

When Teresa describes the role of reason in this stage of spiritual development, she suggests that our intellects can themselves become impediments to our movement toward total loving unless we are careful to use them to promote this kind of growth in ourselves. Reason can aid the will in resisting the imperative to prioritize the heart. In other words, reason often facilitates our *choice* to see life experiences and relationships, especially when they disappoint us, as burdens to be complained of, intellectual problems to be solved, or people to be blamed; but, when love informs our reason, we choose to empathize rather than to blame, to listen rather than to judge, to ponder rather than dissect and analyze. Teresa does not discount reason here, even though she says of people in the third mansion, "their reason is very much in control. Love has not yet reached the point of overwhelming reason."[27] "But," she continues, "I should like us to use our reason to make ourselves dissatisfied with this way of serving God, always going step by step, for we'll never finish this journey." Our fears, doubts, and rationalizations immobilize us and keep us stationary; "we don't dare go any further – as if we could reach these [deeper] dwelling places while leaving to others the trouble of treading the path for us."[28] So, she exhorts, "Let's abandon our reason and our fears into God's hands ... we should care only about moving quickly so as to see this Lord." As the soul increases in awe and wonder, furthermore, it begins to experience God's presence in prayer in more profound ways than those to which it has been accustomed. Such "internal favors" strengthen the soul in growth and in all of the changes it has gradually been making in order to become more deeply itself. These favors "come brimming over with love and fortitude by which you can journey with less labor and grow in the practice of works and virtues."[29] So the soul begins actually to experience more joy in its life and takes heart that it will continue to progress toward greater fulfillment.

Once the soul chooses to prioritize love, it engages in a process beyond itself, and, therefore, beyond its control, a process epitomized for Teresa by Psalm 119:32: "you have enlarged my heart." Having the heart enlarged, expanded, dilated, or stretched is the first major step in the mystical (supernatural) mansions once the issue of the will has been resolved in the third mansion. Teresa actually is explicit here: the heart is expanded, but this goes beyond our emotions; by "heart" she means "another part still more interior, as from something deep. I think this must be the center of the soul...."[30] And the context for the stretching process is to place ourselves in circumstances that facilitate our loving response. "[T]he important thing is not to think much but to love much; and so do that which best stirs you to love."[31] In some cases the stretching process is slow; in others it is wrenching and involves sharp pains, even a kind of shattering. The stretching process is the next stage in the metaphor of the garden Teresa introduced in the *Life*, for as we knead the soil of our soul, we can imagine the edges of the heart being slowly massaged, preparing us for what is to come. And this stretching process is possible only if our reason is involved in understanding why it is now time to aspire to a wise heart. This is the place where an urgent desire to know, enough to quiet all of the questions of reason and replace them with an intense thirst for something deeper than immediate answers, merges with awe, resulting in the development of a patient openness to mystery. The awe and reverence cultivated in the third mansion helps us in this process. But this patience will be sorely tested with the introduction of revelatory glimpses of God, experienced in the fifth and sixth mansions.

The role of visions in Teresa's theology is a critical issue, related most importantly to epistemology, but clearly also related to the historical circumstances that prohibited her from reading Scripture in the vernacular. In order to appreciate Teresa's contributions here, we must be careful to understand "vision" correctly. For Teresa, visions referred to God's communications to the soul, expressed sometimes in words and images and sometimes as intuitive understandings of God (i.e., some mediated, others unmediated). Teresa's understanding of visions was not unique, nor was it uncontroversial.[32] It mirrored distinctions made many centuries earlier by Augustine, who prioritized spiritual and intellectual visions over corporeal ones.[33] Helpful in this regard is the language of "insight," in which a mystic has a flash of understanding into or a momentary comprehension of a theological truth.[34] These insights, according to Teresa, are not abstractly intellectual; rather they are accompanied by a sharp increase in desire for greater wisdom, and they are often received in a state of rapture. Emblematic of this is the movement from experiences of revelatory prayer as "consolations" to experiences of revelatory prayer as "delights" with an accompanying loving effect. "God makes in the soul such a great operation [of love] that it is undone with desire."[35] As the soul's capacity for love increases, charity merges with an erotic urge to complete union; recalling language from the Song of Songs, Teresa likens the final three mansions of the interior castle to the stages of dating, betrothal, and marital union. Thus as God reveals more of God's being to the soul, the soul responds with a desire for a deeper, fuller, unitive knowledge of God.[36]

The soul in the sixth mansion is "now wounded with love for its Spouse and strives for more opportunities to be alone and in conformity with its state, to rid itself of everything that can be an obstacle to this solitude."[37] In this stage the soul's desire for union with God is purified, its focus intensifies, burning throughout the soul as a kind of final crucible of loving desire. The yearning for fulfillment is *deep* and powerful; the soul suffers with impatience. The Spanish word *ansias*, from which we get the word "anxiety," reflects the depth of the soul's burning desire for total union for God, a desire that only intensifies with its brief encounters with God throughout these mansions.

At this stage passion has overcome reason, and the soul's heightened sensitivity, which has been increasing since the fourth mansion, moves into a form of self-abandonment, a radical loss of control over its circumstances and even its own identity, which is becoming bound up in the identity of God.

Intensely powerful experiences of God in prayer are contrasted with the profound sense of absence once these experiences end. Teresa describes this dynamic as a ship in a tempest being tossed about by waves. The experiences of God's absence evoke sharp pain within the soul, for which there is no spiritual consolation: its usual remedies – vocal or mental prayer, solitude or company – do not compensate for the intense dissatisfaction it feels at its own ontological incompletion.[38]

The prayer experiences in the sixth mansion contain many locutions (words given to the soul in prayer) and visions (again, here, understood as insights into truth). Having recently defended herself in an intense inquisitorial investigation in Seville,[39] Teresa wrote carefully and thoughtfully about the nature of these visions and developed criteria for authenticating them. The first sign is that the revelation brings with it some embodied communication of the truth of the message. The statement "carries with it power and authority;" it resonates within the soul as ontologically true, not merely an abstraction.[40] It is emotionally true as well as intellectually true. To understand this dimension of truth is to understand things not as simply true or false (objectively) but rather as true, because they have been incarnated and experienced and are therefore *real*, not simply conceptualized and/or demonstrated. Second, in experiencing this truth, the person also experiences a transformative, co-creative moment where God continues to implant new life in the person and the person collaborates in this process by being open to and responding to the new truth/new life as an invitation to deeper life. This transformative process is accompanied by a "great, internal peace."[41] Finally, the third sign is the sense in which an experiential/ essential/ontological truth is "imprinted in the memory" and therefore eternal.[42] Thus this truth is an entryway into a transcendent moment of ascent into the shared space of the mind of God and our mind, an experience in which God's thoughts or ideas are given to us and we participate briefly in that creative process that *is* the mind of God. Revelation of this sort is a critical but momentary (existential) participation in what will be the essential ontological reality of participation in the Trinity in the seventh mansion. Before we are ready to live in the reality of the Trinity residing in the apex of our *intellectus* (by which we mean "soul"), we must have glimpses of this reality to prepare ourselves for it.

One of the greatest hallmarks of Teresa's theology is her affirmation of the possibility of living within the mystery of the Trinity. Here Teresa makes the theoretical framework of Augustine's *On the Trinity*[43] a lived reality, for the union experienced in the seventh mansion is qualitatively different from the moments of union that have preceded it, as Teresa describes:

> Now our good God wants to take away the scales from the eyes of the soul, so that it may see and understand something of the mercy He grants it, although it is in a somewhat foreign way and immersed in that mansion in an intellectual vision: in a certain way of representing the truth, the soul is shown the Most Holy Trinity, with all three persons, accompanied by an inflammation of the soul which enters its spirit in the form of a cloud of great clarity. And the soul understands, with an admirable knowledge of the greatest truth, that these distinct persons are one substance and one power and one knowledge and one God alone. In the same way that we hold by faith the soul now knows this truth, shall we say, by sight, even though this is not seen either by the corporal eyes or the eyes of the soul, because this is no imaginary vision. Here all three Persons communicate with the soul and speak to it, and give her to understand those words that the Evangelist says the Lord spoke: that he and His Father and the Holy Spirit would come to dwell with the soul who loves Him and keeps His commandments.[44]

To speak of being united with the Trinity as the culmination of a process of ontological transformation is also, finally, to come to terms with what it is to be human and how to understand the person of Christ. Teresa is clear and forceful about her position that spiritual progress does not entail disembodiment. Meditation does not move us from immanence to transcendence, and, always in prayer, one does not reflect on the essence of God but rather on the embodied life of Christ, whether in Scripture or as it is being lived out in the present moment. "To be always withdrawn from corporeal things and enkindled in love is the trait of angelic spirits, not of those who live in mortal bodies," she writes, rather tartly.[45] Teresa asserts here that searching for and seeing Christ in life experiences *is* seeing God. The encounter with Christ in the world and the self and the other is a living in the presence of God; indeed, she suggests that this is the only way she has found true and meaningful union.[46] Thus, in Teresa's life and theology we see a radical affirmation of the ontological reality of incarnation.[47]

Teresa's description of the soul's journey toward God might suggest that it is an individual one. This journey is intensely personal and subjective, relying on a person's dedication essentially to re-creating the self, but it is also done within the context of a supportive community – in her case, the small, enclosed monastic communities that were part of her discalced Carmelite reform movement – and within the context of the larger Christian community. Teresa's understanding of the church was largely sacramental and soteriological. Through the sacraments the church offered salvation to the whole of humanity. Teresa's use of the word "heretic" is often not tied to theological orthodoxy, per se, but reflects her concerns over lack of reception of and reverence toward the sacraments, particularly that of the Eucharist. Consistent with a long tradition of female mystical experience, her raptures and experiences of revelatory prayer were often triggered by reception of Communion and thus located in some kind of liturgical act.[48] Probably, for Teresa, this represented best her perspective that prayer fostered the life of the church and, despite the widespread suspicion of mental prayer during her day, it should not be feared but encouraged in all Christians.[49]

With regard to her views as a sacramental theologian, we must call Teresa a very "practical theologian." She dedicates no time to speculation on the nature of the sacraments; rather she sees all seven of them as conveyors of grace as God's love, with a particular emphasis on the Sacrament of Communion. Her strong devotion to the Eucharist reflects her understanding of the Sacrament as the real experience of Christ's sacrificed body. Applying Teresa's description of her conversion before the statue to her understanding of Christ's ongoing sacrifice of himself because of humanity's sinfulness might help us appreciate the feelings of compassion and gratitude provoked in her by such an experience. However, sacramental experience of Christ's Body did not begin and end at the Mass. Teresa's notion of sacrament involved a practical – one could say empirical – exploration of Christ's Real Presence in the words of Scripture and in real-life encounters with others, as well as prayer encounters with Christ. Thus we can say that Teresa both probed and, increasingly, modeled a sacramental approach to self, other, community, and life itself.

Regarding the institutional life of the church, Teresa was by no means blind to the need for reform within the church. Often pointedly (although carefully) critical of the corruption of clerics[50] and of the effects of the Spanish Inquisition on religiosity,[51] she chose to advocate change from within monastic structures, primarily by founding reformed convents. Her career as a writer of mystical texts can and should be seen as an extension of this urge to reform, since her books invited readers into personal and communal transformation. Teresa maintained a strong loyalty to the church, as the mediator of the sacraments and as the most powerful symbol of universal salvation offered in Christ.

At the end of her *Life* Teresa describes her mystical evolution as a complete, ontological transformation, a journey toward loving knowledge in which one eventually becomes engulfed in loving knowledge itself. For Teresa, this lived, living truth is God. And this truth is revealed to the human person in the depths of consciousness. She describes an experience of meditation:

> [M]y soul began to be more enkindled than ever, and there came to me a spiritual rapture of such a kind that I would not know how to describe. I seemed to be plunged into that Majesty of which I have been conscious on other occasions, and to be filled with It. In this Majesty I was given to understand a truth which is the fulfillment of all truths, yet I cannot say how this happened, for I saw nothing.[52]

God, as source of all truths and as Truth itself left particular truths "imprinted" upon her:

> From this Divine Truth, which was represented to me without my knowing what it was or how it came, there remained imprinted upon me one truth in particular . . . It left me filled with a great tenderness, joy and humility. . . . Thus I understood what it is for a soul to walk in truth in the presence of Truth Itself. And what I understood comes down to this: the Lord gave me to understand that he is Truth Itself.[53]

Further reflection on her experience of God as Truth led Teresa to suggest that the ontological reality that is God is no different from the ontological reality of the soul. Thus, at the end of the *Life*, she proposes a metaphor for God that she later uses as the starting point for her more systematic theological reflection in the *Interior Castle*: "Let us say that the Godhead is like a very clear diamond, much larger than the whole world, or a mirror. . . ." And at the outset of the *Interior Castle* she proposes: "Let us consider our soul to be like a castle made up of diamond or very clear crystal, where there are many rooms, just like in heaven there are many mansions. . . ."[54] This critical insight is both the Alpha and Omega of Teresa's theology and her invitation to readers of her life to explore the mystery of God on their own.

Notes

1 During the past several years, several non-academic books on Teresa have appeared, including Tessa Bielecki, *Holy Daring: An Outrageous Gift to Modern Spirituality from Saint Teresa, the Grand Wild Woman of Avila* (Shaftesbury: Element, 1994), Carolyn Humphreys, *From Ash to Fire: A Contemporary Journey through the Interior Castle of Teresa of Avila* (Brooklyn: New City Press, 1995), Dwight H. Judy, *Embracing God: Prayers with Teresa of Avila* (Nashville, TN: Abingdon Press, 1996), and John Kirvan, *Let Nothing Disturb You: A Journey to the Center of the Soul with Teresa of Avila* (South Bend, IN: Ave Maria Press, 1996).

2 See Alison Weber, *Teresa of Avila and the Rhetoric of Femininity* (Princeton: Princeton University Press, 1990), 5–8, 165.

3 In introducing the subject of mystical theology itself Teresa is typically understated. Wanting the reader to move beyond the sentimentality of religious experience into its deeper, onto-logical possibilities, Teresa wrote:

> It sometimes happened to me, when I would put myself at the side of Christ, as

I have said, and even sometimes while I was reading, that I would suddenly have a very deep feeling of the presence of God, such that in no way could I doubt that He was inside me, or I was totally engulfed in Him. This was no form of vision; I believe it is called mystical theology. *Life* 10:1.

See also *Life* 11:5. All citations of Teresian texts are my translation, based on the critical edition by Alberto Barrientos et al., *Obras Completas* (Madrid: Editorial de Espiritualidad, 1984).

4 For a discussion of this term and its meaning as an approach to understanding Christian mysticism, see Bernard McGinn, *The Presence of God* (New York: Crossroad, 1991), 5–8 and Mark McIntosh, *Mystical Theology: The Integrity of Spirituality and Theology* (Oxford: Blackwell, 1998), 30–4.

5 *Life* 32: 6–7. See also *The Way of Perfection* 1:2 and 35:3 and *The Book of the Foundations* 18:5. Teresa's missionary/apologetic orientation is discussed in Gillian T. W. Ahlgren, *Teresa of Avila and the Politics of Sanctity*

(Ithaca, NY: Cornell University Press, 1996), 34–64 and J. Mary Luti, "Teresa of Avila, Maestra Espiritual" (Ph.D. dissertation, Boston College, 1987).

6 See the discussion in Carole Slade, *Teresa of Avila: Author of a Heroic Life* (Berkeley: University of California Press, 1995), xi–xii, 9–38.

7 See *Life* 33:5.

8 See, for example, Sara T. Nalle's assessment of Tridentine catechetical reform in *God in La Mancha: Religious Reform and the People of Cuenca, 1500–1650* (Baltimore: Johns Hopkins University Press, 1992). A wide range of perspectives on the effects and/or influence of the Spanish Inquisition is represented in the following studies: Steven Haliczer, ed., *Inquisition and Society in Early Modern Europe* (London: Croom Helm, 1986), Henry Kamen, *Inquisition and Society in Spain in the Sixteenth and Seventeenth Centuries* (Bloomington: Indiana University Press, 1985), and Henry Kamen, *The Phoenix and the Flame: Catalonia and the Counter Reformation* (New Haven: Yale University Press, 1993).

9 For a study of the challenges faced by hermits and recluses in Spain, see Alain Saint-Saens, *Valets de Dieu, Suppots du Diable: Ermites et Réforme Catholique dans l'Espagne des Habsbourg (1550–1700)*, n.p., n.d. For a more general discussion of challenges faced by women see Gillian T. W. Ahlgren, "Negotiating Sanctity: Holy Women in Sixteenth-Century Spain," *CH* 64/3 (September 1995), 373–88; idem, *Teresa of Avila and the Politics of Sanctity*, 6–66; Mary E. Giles, ed., *Women in the Inquisition: Spain and the New World* (Baltimore: Johns Hopkins University Press, 1999) and Mary Elizabeth Perry, *Gender and Disorder in Early Modern Seville* (Princeton: Princeton University Press, 1990), and Alison Weber, "Demonizing Ecstasy: Alonso de la Fuente and the *Alumbrados* of Extremadura" in Robert Boenig, ed., *The Mystical Gesture: Essays on Medieval and Early Modern Spiritual Culture in Honor of Mary E. Giles* (Burlington, VT: Ashgate, 2000), 141–58.

10 See Carlos M. N. Eire, *From Madrid to Purgatory* (New York: Cambridge University Press, 1995).

11 There is a broad range of speculation about the extent to which Teresa was influenced by Jewish traditions and by any need she might have felt to cover up her origins. See, for example, Teofanes Egido, "La familia judia de Santa Teresa," *Studia Zamorensia* 3 (1982), 449–79; Deirdre Green, *Gold in the Crucible: Teresa of Avila and the Western Mystical Tradition* (Shaftesbury: Element, 1989), 77–119.

12 For helpful approaches to Teresa's rhetoric styles and strategies, see Ahlgren, *Teresa of Avila and the Politics of Sanctity*, 67–84; Slade, *Teresa of Avila: Author of a Heroic Life*; and Weber, *Teresa of Avila and the Rhetoric of Femininity*.

13 See the discussion in Virgilio Pinto Crespo, *Inquisición y control ideológico en la España del siglo XVI* (Madrid: Taurus, 1983), 161–5.

14 Teresa refers to many theological sources more implicitly than explicitly, due, most likely, to the ambiguous status of many mystical and theological texts after the appearance of the Valdes Index of Prohibited Books in 1559. For a discussion of her theological sources, see Ahlgren, *Teresa of Avila and the Politics of Sanctity*, 34–41.

15 *Life* 26:6.

16 *Life* 9:1, 3.

17 *Life* 11:6. Implicit in this garden metaphor is the garden of the Song of Songs as locus for the union of two lovers, along with all the preparations for one another that the two undergo.

18 1 Thes. 5:17–18: "Pray without ceasing. Give thanks in all circumstances, for this is the will of God in Christ Jesus for you." See also Eph. 6:18: "Pray in the spirit at all times in every prayer and supplication; to that end keep alert and always persevere in supplication for all the saints."

19 For what follows, see *Life* 11:7.

20 *Life* 11:9.

21 *Life* 11:16.

22 *Life* 8:5.

23 See *Interior Castle* I:2:2–3.

24 See *Interior Castle* I:2:9.

25 *Interior Castle* I:2:8. Repeating her concerns, Teresa continues in I:2:9: "I don't know if I've left this clear enough, because it is such an important thing for us to know ourselves that I would never want any laxity in it, for as high as you might have soared toward the heavens; while we are on this earth there is nothing more important to us than humility."

26 Ps. 112:1.

27 *Interior Castle* III:2:7.

28 *Interior Castle* III:2:8.

29 *Interior Castle* 3:2:11.
30 *Interior Castle* IV:2:5.
31 *Interior Castle* IV:1:7.
32 For a discussion of problematic elements in Teresa's mystical theology, including the thorny issue of visions, see Ahlgren, *Teresa of Avila and the Politics of Sanctity*, 97–111, 114–44.
33 Augustine's visionary typology is available in book 12 of *De Genesi ad litteram*. As described there, the corporeal vision is perceived by the body and the senses and is the least reliable; the spiritual vision is mediated by a "spiritual image," as in 1 Cor. 15:44; and the intellectual vision takes place wholly within the mind.
34 Bernard McGinn, *The Flowering of Mysticism* (New York: Crossroad, 1998).
35 *Interior Castle* IV:2:4. The use of the word "operation" here is interesting because it connotes the sense of God operating or working in the soul as an *opus* and thus creating or remaking it. The word "undone" (*deshacer*) is another tricky one; many translate it as "dissolve;" I prefer the more literal "undo," because it again reinforces the radical depth of the soul's transformation.
36 See, for example, *Interior Castle* V:1:11.
37 *Interior Castle* VI:1:1. This is akin to the intense, impassioned search of the bride for the bridegroom in Song of Songs 3:1–3.
38 Indeed, the soul's distress is externally noticeable, as she writes, "It goes about with a discontented and ill-tempered mien that is externally very noticeable." *Interior Castle* VI:1:13.
39 For an analysis of this encounter and its aftermath see Ahlgren, *Teresa of Avila and the Politics of Sanctity*, 52–64.
40 See *Interior Castle* VI:3:5.
41 See *Interior Castle* VI:3:6.
42 See *Interior Castle* VI:3:7.
43 See book 14 of Augustine, *On the Trinity*, trans. Edmund Hill (Brooklyn: New City Press, 1991), 370–94.
44 *Interior Castle* VII:1:6. The notion of the scales falling off the eyes contains a possible reference to Acts 9:18 and an implicit reference to 1 Cor. 13:12, "for now we see as through a glass darkly, but then we shall see face to face." The final reference is to Jn. 14:23.
45 *Interior Castle* VI:7:6.
46 See *Interior Castle* VII:7:6.
47 Rowan Williams makes a similar assessment. See Rowan Williams, *Teresa of Avila* (Harrisburg, PA: Morehouse, 1991), 158–63, especially the following passages:

> The paradox of Christian mysticism – at least on Teresa's account – is that there is *no* detached divine absolute with which to take refuge. We may and must detach ourselves from all that keeps us from God: our sin, our fearfulness and false humility, our pride of race or family; but the God with whom we are finally united is the God whose being is directed in love towards the world, which we must then re-enter, equipped to engage with other human beings with something of God's own wholeheartedness because we have been stripped of certain modes of self-protectiveness: of an understanding of our worth or loveableness as resting on prestige, achievement or uniformity. (p.160)

> And so the moving of the centre of meaning that is involved in turning away from external ambiguity to inner clarity is saved from being simply a move into the private sphere by its association with God's journey into creation. The rejection of the world's standards is also a claim on behalf of God's will and ability to penetrate the world and to remake it in self-abandoning love. (p.163)

48 See, for example, *Life* 28:1; for a discussion of the relationship between Eucharist and vision for women, see Caroline Walker Bynum, *Holy Feast and Holy Fast: The Religious Significance of Food to Medieval Women* (Berkeley: University of California Press, 1987).
49 For a discussion of the concerns over mental prayer, see Ahlgren, *Teresa of Avila and the Politics of Sanctity*, 9–15, 21–31, 34–66, 114–44.
50 See, e.g., *Life* 38:23, *Way of Perfection* (Valladolid edition) 35:3, and Letter 133:1.
51 See, e.g., *Way of Perfection* (El Escorial edition) 73:4, 35:4, *Way of Perfection* (Valladolid edition) 21:3; see also discussion in Ahlgren, *Teresa of Avila and the Politics of Sanctity*, 86–97.
52 *Life* 40:1.
53 *Life* 40:3.
54 *Interior Castle* I:1:1.

Bibliography

Primary Sources

Teresa de Jesus, *Obras completas*, trans. Alberto Barrientos et al., Madrid: Editorial de Espiritualidad, 1984.

——, *The Complete Works of Saint Teresa of Jesus*, trans. and ed. E. Allison Peers, New York: Sheed & Ward, 1946.

Secondary Sources

Ahlgren, Gillian T. W. *Teresa of Avila and the Politics of Sanctity*, Ithaca, NY: Cornell University Press, 1996.

Arenal, Electa and Stacey Schlau, *Untold Sisters: Hispanic Nuns in Their Own Works*, trans. Amanda Powell, Albuquerque: University of New Mexico Press, 1989.

Barrientos, Alberto, ed. *Introducción a la lectura de Santa Teresa*, Madrid: Editorial de Espiritualidad, 1978.

Bilinkoff, Jodi, *Avila of Saint Teresa: Religious Reform in a Sixteenth-Century City*, Ithaca, NY: Cornell University Press, 1989.

Eire, Carlos M. N., *From Madrid to Purgatory*, New York: Cambridge University Press, 1995.

Garcia de la Concha, Victor, *El arte literario de Santa Teresa*, Barcelona: Ariel, 1978.

Hamilton, Alistair, *Heresy and Mysticism in Sixteenth-Century Spain*, Toronto: University of Toronto Press, 1992.

Rossi, Rosa, *Teresa de Avila: Biografía de una escritora*, trans. Marieta Gargatagli. Barcelona: ICARIA, 1984.

Slade, Carole, *Teresa of Avila: Author of a Heroic Life*, Berkeley: University of California Press, 1995.

Trueman Dicken, E. W., *The Crucible of Love*, New York: Sheed & Ward, 1963.

Weber, Alison, *Teresa of Avila and the Rhetoric of Femininity*, Princeton: Princeton University Press, 1990.

Williams, Rowan, *Teresa of Avila*, Harrisburg, PA: Morehouse, 1991.

"Radical" Theologians

Andreas Bodenstein von Karlstadt (1486–1541)

Alejandro Zorzin

This fascinating and polemical theologian of the Reformation was born in Karlstadt, a small town on the River Main in the Franconia region of Germany.[1] His academic studies were in Erfurt (1499/1500–3), Cologne (1503–5) and Wittenberg, where in 1510 he received the degree of Doctor of Theology. That same year he was ordained a priest, and the following year he received the position of archdeacon in the collegiate church of All Saints, the ecclesial foundation connected to the residential castle of the Saxon princes in Wittenberg. The position of archdeacon, second place in the clerical hierarchy, included teaching responsibilities in the theology faculty of the new University of Wittenberg, founded in 1502. Along with his tasks as priest and professor, Karlstadt continued the study of law. During a stay in Rome from November 1515 to May 1516, he obtained the doctorate *utriusque iuris*, that is, in both civil and canon laws, from the Sapienza, the University of Rome.

Upon his return to Wittenberg he felt challenged by the innovative theological proposals of his colleague Luther, which he debated in the September 1516 academic disputation for Bartholomäus Bernhardi, *De viribus et voluntate hominis sine gratia*. Although he initially questioned Luther's position, he soon began to study in depth the works of Augustine and thereby became an adherent of the "new theology" of Wittenberg. His support of Luther's position became evident with his publication on April 26, 1517 of 152 Augustinian theses on "nature, law, and grace." Between 1517 and the beginning of 1519, he lectured on Augustine's *De spiritu et litera*. But furthermore his theology also expanded beyond the scholasticism of his initial studies through the important contributions of German mysticism (Tauler and Johann von Staupitz) and Renaissance philosophy (Giovanni Pico della Mirandola and Erasmus).

Around the beginning of 1519 Karlstadt began to spread the new Wittenberg theology of grace through pamphlets written in German. Together with Luther he defended the Wittenberg theology against Johann Eck, professor of theology at Ingolstadt, at the Leipzig Disputation (June 27 to July 15, 1519). In the summer of 1520 Eck included Karlstadt in the Roman bull threatening excommunication, *Exsurge domine*. In response, Karlstadt published a harsh pamphlet in which he demonstrated "by means of Holy Scripture . . . that the holy pope can err, sin, and commit injustices" (October 1520) and thus ended his earlier caution before the Roman See, making public his definite break with the papacy.

During Luther's absence from Wittenberg while secluded in the Wartburg Castle from May 1521 to February 1522 following his condemnation at the Diet of Worms, Kalrstadt joined with Gabriel Zwilling, Philip Melanchthon, Nikolaus von Amsdorf, and Justas Jonas to become one of the driving forces of the "Wittenberg Movement." This group of theologians, in close collaboration with the town council, implemented a series of concrete reforms of the Mass, religious life, and various social aspects of the town. The reforms were condensed and published as "A New Order for the City of Wittenberg" (January 1522) and were intended to convert the town into a model "Christian City" to be imitated by others. However, the transformations provoked opposition from a section of conservative clergy and from the prince elector, who having ultimate political authority over the town did not endorse this demonstration of municipal autonomy. In this context, Karlstadt, disobeying the Prince's prohibition, publicly celebrated an "evangelical" mass on Christmas Day in the Castle Church attended by an enormous crowd of the faithful who, for the first time, were invited to commune under both species. In addition, consonant with his strong criticism of monastic vows and priestly celibacy, Karlstadt married the young Anna von Mochau on January 19, 1522.

Soon after Luther's return in early March, profound divergences appeared between the two Reformers; the university censured Karlstadt's publications, and he began to distance himself from his colleagues and academics. In June 1523 he began pastoral work in the small rural parish of Orlamünde in Thuringia that was incorporated in the prebendary foundation of the Wittenberg Castle Church of which he was archdeacon. There in Orlamünde, between July 1523 and September 1524, he began work as a peasant farmer with the objective of gaining independence from his ecclesiastical income and being able to support his family by manual labor. In this profound change of life he also abandoned his title of doctor, and asked to be called "Brother Andie," expressing his desire to be known as "a new layman." In Orlamünde he initiated a communal model of evangelical reform: celebrating worship in a simple and austere manner, communing the Lord's Supper under both species as a memorial of the liberating death of Christ on the cross, removing images from the church, postponing the baptism of infants, intensifying bible study in open debate with the common people, and emphasizing the great importance and autonomy of the laity in the total life of the church.

However, the offensive that Luther launched in the summer of 1524 against Thomas Müntzer, parish priest in Allstedt, also reverberated against the reform project Karlstadt was leading in the Saale valley. It did not matter that Karlstadt and his Orlamünde parish publicly distanced themselves from the Allstedt defensive alliance against tyrants which they had been invited to join by Müntzer, for Luther included Karlstadt among the "heavenly prophets." On August 22, Luther and Karlstadt had a tense discussion of this charge in the Black Bear Inn in Jena. There Luther challenged him to publish his divergent theological views. As soon as a month later, Karlstadt was expelled from the territory by order of Duke John of Saxony.

Karlstadt then deepened his rupture with Luther by a volley of pamphlets, printed in Basel, which spread and defended his views of the Lord's Supper and rejection of infant baptism.[2] He passed the winter of 1524/5 in the Franconian town of Rothenburg on the Tauber. His detractors implicated him in the peasant rebellions in the area, and Karlstadt ended up a fugitive, unable to gain permission to reside in any territory. At his request, Luther interceded for him before the new prince elector, John, so that he could return to Saxony. In exchange for this asylum, Luther demanded that Karlstadt retract his theological positions and maintain silence about the debates breaking out within the heart of the Reform movement concerning the Real Presence of Christ in the Sacrament of the Lord's Supper.

From mid-1525 until the beginning of 1529 Karlstadt subsisted with his family in the environs of Wittenberg, first as a farmer and then as a peddler. But by the onset of 1529, fed up with tolerating control over all his contacts and movements, he fled Saxony and offered assistance to the lay preacher Melchior Hoffman in a dispute over the Lord's Supper with evangelical theologians in Flensburg, in northern Germany. After passing through Strasbourg, he distanced himself from Hoffman, and with the support of Zwingli he obtained a position as pastor in Zurich. In 1534 Karlstadt moved to Basel where, after a decade away from academe, he returned to teaching in the Faculty of Theology and actively collaborated in its reorganization. At the same time he played a role as a parish priest in Basel's St. Peter's Church. There he died on December 24, 1541, a victim of the plague, contracted while ministering to the sick.

In light of this brief biographical sketch, it is clear that Karlstadt was a competent theologian and jurist who began his militancy as Luther's colleague in Wittenberg at the very beginning of the evangelical cause, the cause he continued during the last decade of his life as professor and priest for the Swiss Reformation in the areas of Zurich and Basel. This makes evident that his theology was not only innovative but sufficiently broad to reach between both poles of the Reformation movement. Furthermore, we need to take into account that besides being an initial co-protagonist in the Reform movement that arose in Wittenberg and his later participation in and support of the Swiss Reformation, Karlstadt was also a significant referent for sectors of the "Radical Reformation."[3] There is no doubt concerning the relevance of his person and theology in those intense, stormy years between the Leipzig Debate (1519) and the Colloquy of Hagenau/Worms (1540/1).[4]

With approximately seventy publications spread between 1517 and 1541 in somewhat more than two hundred editions, Karlstadt was one of the most published and prominent spokespersons of the early Reformation movement. The period of his most prolific publication was between 1519 and 1525, when the volume of his published pamphlets in German, directed to the common man (47 pamphlets in some 125 editions), made him one of the most influential authors next to Luther.[5]

Following the renewal impulse of his colleague Luther, Karlstadt rediscovered the anti-Pelagian theology of Augustine,[6] which he set forth in a series of theses and a Latin text on the dynamics of justification titled *De impii justificatione*, in 1518,[7] that he lectured on in Wittenberg. In his 370 (in reality, 405) theses in defense of Holy Scripture and the Wittenberg theologians, *CCCLXX et apologetica conclusiones pro sacris literis*,[8] he has a section (theses 177–85) that reflects his theological "about-face." Combining the Psalm verse "I am poor and needy, but the Lord takes thought for me" (Ps. 40:17) with the Augustinian paraphrase of Galatians 2:20, *ubi non ego, ibi felicius ego*,[9] Karlstadt anticipated *Gelassenheit* (*abnegatio*) as the structural axis of his theology of grace. At the beginning of 1519 he publicly stated the fundamental opposition between an authentic theologian of the cross and a scholastic theologian of glory.[10] Around this distinction he outlined the first flier of the "Wittenberg circle." Illustrated by Lucas Cranach, it was published in two editions (Latin and German) with brief explanatory captions. Shortly after this Karlstadt enlarged this work into his first major pamphlet in German.[11] These works and his bitter polemic with Johann Eck make clear that his progressive theological dissent from Luther did not revolve around the question of the (initial) justification of the sinner *sola gratia*, but rather with regard to the impact or subsequent effect of renewal which liberating grace can and ought to have on the social and ecclesiastical reality in which justified Christians are immersed. The first frictions between Luther and Karlstadt over this theme of renewal occurred by mid-1520 in relation to the Epistle of James. Luther considered this epistle spurious, whereas Karlstadt held that it was a work of authentic exhortation to evangelical ethics.[12]

Increasingly oriented to the horizon of comprehension of the common laity, Karlstadt took leave from the Latin terminological aspects of theology and began articulating his perception of salvation *sola gratia* in biblical language that highlighted the ecclesial and social consequences of justifying faith. In March 1523 he published an important theological treatise titled *The Manifold, Singular Will of God, The Nature of Sin* in which he called himself "a new layman." There he disagreed with his former Wittenberg colleagues. A key passage summarizes his synthesis of Augustinian theology combined with the mystics' accent on the Christian's following of the suffering of the cross of Christ:

> Where there is true knowledge of God in faith, there the true love and friendship of God are. And where love of God is strong, there too is love of neighbor and orderliness. . . . By the new fruits, we know a new tree; and by the old fruits, we know an old one. A person who is new and is found to be in God's will sprouts with new work. If he was hard before, he becomes soft; if he used to steal [see Eph. 4:17–20],[13] he now works with his hands and earns his bread by his labor. By our fruits we are able to know ourselves and others. Therefore, we must look to what we do. For true knowledge of God and the acceptance of his will break forth and present themselves [in fruits]. . . .[14]

This theme returns in his defense against Luther's attacks in *Against the Heavenly Prophets*. There Karlstadt bluntly set forth the consequences of his dissent from Luther's perspective on Christian liberty:

> (One may examine and see . . .) how it is with one's righteousness, and how the righteousness of the heart is to bring forth works or fruit. It is certainly true that regarding works Scripture does not teach that we are to serve ourselves through them, but others. Nor that we become righteous through them, but merely that we bear external testimony to the power of our righteousness and how it is to show itself when it is true. For a free person does not only stand before God and his conscience, but on earth before the congregation of God.[15]

Luther's double thesis in *The Freedom of a Christian* (1520) sets forth the claim that the Christian can be free in the internal sphere of faith and conscience, accepting simultaneously (in solidarity with the neighbor by love) submission to adverse sociopolitical reality.[16] For Karlstadt this perspective was too one-dimensional; probably because it privileges the free existence of the Christian in the interior sphere or dimension before God (*coram Deo*), while it relegates to a secondary plane the transforming action that free individuals realize in reality or the social order in the midst of others (*coram hominibus*). Karlstadt's brief leadership in the first attempt at ecclesial and social reform during the "Wittenberg Movement" (1521/2) revealed to him that Luther's perspective on "Christian freedom" permitted postponing the "historical emergencies" of the socially weakest and little ones, thereby theologically legitimating the resistance of other "weak ones" who, socially powerful, refuse to modify those aspects of ecclesial and communal reality that the Word of God unmasks as obsolete and corrupt. In biblical terms this posture centers more on the individual than on the whole community, tolerating the *scandalum pusillorum* (Mt. 18: 6ff.) in order to avoid the *scandalum phariseorum* (Mt. 15: 12–14).[17] The abuse of the Mass ought to be eliminated, and it can easily be done without generating conflict or rebellion. In a second report to the prince set forth by the group of theologians engaged in the "Wittenberg Movement," they affirmed that:

> No one ought to consider contemplation in the face of scandal or other objection, in the same way as Christ spoke to the pharisees, so that they were scandalized by his teaching that went against their traditions and human laws, Matthew 15 (:14). "Let them alone, they are blind guides of the blind." "It is necessary to obey God rather than men" Acts 5 (:29).[18]

For Karlstadt as theologian and jurist, the implementation of changes in those ecclesial and socioeconomic aspects that openly contradict the Word and will of God was an inescapable responsibility for the whole Christian community. This was a radical stance that Karlstadt set forth without reservation in his *Whether We Should Go Slowly and Avoid Offending the Weak in Matters Pertaining to God's Will* (1524): "[W]here Christians rule, they are not to look to any magistrate, but are to strike out freely and on their own and throw down whatever is against God even without [previous] preaching."[19]

Karlstadt's radicality was a consequence of a programmatic decision in his reformatory theology. In the fifth thesis of a series of 25 formulated for the academic disputation of Jakob Probst (May 13, 1521), he affirmed: "Preachers always ought to lead the people of God towards the interior things (where the Spirit works) and repeatedly call them away from external things."[20]

That is exactly what Karlstadt sought to put into practice with his proposal *On the Abolition of Images* . . . (1522). In the face of a traditional religious practice that perverted the reconciliation of the common laity from the authentic faith, and distracted and saturated laypersons with the false worship of external objects, the Reformer demanded these objects be eliminated. To Karlstadt, institutional piety had been "thingified," and he desired the removal of images from the churches so that the people might return to the essentials of faith.

I cannot advise anyone who is sick unto death to cling to a carved or painted Crucifix, for the simple reason that these are good for nothing, as I said, and incapable of getting the sick any further than the physical suffering of Christ which is of no avail. As Christ himself says, "The flesh avails nothing," Jn. 6:27. It does not please Paul when you know Christ in the flesh only. He therefore says, "We do not know Christ after the flesh" [2 Cor 5:16]. But those who worship images intend to make the fleshly Christ known to lay persons. This is not good. They prefer to teach how Christ was hanging rather than why he was hanged. They teach of his body, beard, and wounds; but regarding the power of Christ, they do not teach anything. Without the power of Christ, no one will be saved; but without the physical form of Christ, many thousands shall be saved in days to come.[21]

The above passage condenses and anticipates the argument Karlstadt would use to reject the Real Presence of the Body of Christ in the Sacrament of the Lord's Supper. His *Dialogue or Discussion Booklet on the Infamous and Idolatrous Abuse of the Most Blessed Sacrament of Jesus Christ* (1524) reflects his position by means of a dialogue between three persons: Gemser, a cleric; Victus, a learned layman; and Peter, a lay peasant. Peter is the one who finally develops and defends the correct view of the subject.[22] In a similar manner as in his *On the Removal of Images*, Karlstadt set forth his conviction that external splendor and the adoration of the Sacrament distracted the attention of the laity from the essential element of genuine faith, the cross of Christ on Golgotha.[23]

Peter: Although I am prepared to concede that the body of Christ is united with the bread, I would speak deceitfully and wrongly, however, if I were to attach to wafer-thin bread so much power and strength as to be able to forgive our sins and bring us peace. That I grant to the bread, I take away from the suffering of Christ. . . . [N]ote how Paul directs us to know the remembrance of the bitter death of Christ which we recall whenever we think back some fifteen hundred years, even though our knowledge and memory extend beyond time and place. No one should be bound to these anyhow, for they contribute nothing toward the forgiveness of sins.

Through this argument in the autonomy given to him by the Holy Spirit,[24] Peter, the layman, convinces Gemser, the priest, of his error which ends with his admission that "the sacrament is an external thing which cannot save us, nor make us holy, or good, or better, or more just, or free, though we look on it a thousand times."[25]

The option for a style of evangelical life – sober and austere – is another essential element in Karlstadt's proposal that makes it "radical." This option progressively took shape as a distinctive characteristic for some other sectors of the movement and became an extra factor of separation and polemic between the theologians of the "new center" (Luther, Melanchthon, Bugenhagen, Rhegius, et al.) and those of the "critical periphery" (Karlstadt, Müntzer, Hubmaier, Hut). Again, the fundamental theology of this choice of life in holiness is rooted in the mystical conception of the centrality of the bitter cross of Christ for the faith and life of the Christian. In a letter that Karlstadt sent between the middle and end of May 1523 to Duke John of Saxony, he laid the foundation of his decision to assume pastoral work in the parish of Orlamünde. To understand what concerned Karlstadt, it is necessary to bear in mind how clergy within the traditional ecclesiastical system enjoyed a series of benefices and special privileges.[26] The continuation of the old prebendary system extended sufficiently beyond the beginning of the Reform movement initiated in Wittenberg to generate criticism from some supporters.[27] For Karlstadt, this incoherence between critical-theological speech and the manner of life of those who articulated it compromised the authenticity and credibility of the movement. For this reason he decided to move with his family to the parish of Orlamünde in order to work there as a parish priest. It is interesting to observe that the "evangelical asceticism" that Karlstadt tried to live in his "dissident phase" (1523–9) did not attempt to evade the responsibilities, limitations, and risks with all their consequences of an ordinary farmer and family father. At first it was simply a natural "inner-worldly asceticism," that only became the subject of polemic and debate when Luther – bothered by the publication at the end of 1524 of a series of tracts by Karlstadt on the Lord's Supper and baptism – attacked him with the blunt and devastating treatise *Against the Heavenly Prophets* (1524/5). Karlstadt's response was equally blunt:

> What do you think, Luther, would blisters on our hands not be more becoming than gold rings? When some people leave work in order to preach and go idly as a result, I am surprised that they do not read that Christ was a carpenter who did carpentry work [Mk. 6] and that many prophets were simple peasant folk and that it was prophesied, "I am a tiller of the soil." . . . How do you like that, Luther, when you dare write, as I reported, that a preacher may demand and take two hundred guilders a year? . . . Paul says to the elders of Ephesus, "I did not desire any of your silver, gold, or clothing, for you know yourselves that my hands served in providing my necessities." But Dr. Luther not only lines his own bastard nest with silver and gold, etc., but desires the poor man's sweat and blood and extracts it by force. I will write about this some other time.[28]

Now Karlstadt's early radicalism – and its theology of the cross that differed from the mystical-apocalyptic elements of Müntzer, with whom he maintained friendship – rejected any recourse to physical force for its implementation. He ruled out resistance to the reaction of the powerful who violently objected to a communal plan of reform such as that he had tried to lead in Orlamünde in 1523/4. Karlstadt developed the foundation for his position by an exhaustive exegesis of a key biblical passage, Matthew 11:12. In his *Interpretation of this verse: The Kingdom of God suffers violence and the violent take it by force* (July/August 1521),[29] he developed the basis of a biblical theology of non-violence in view of the possible reactions to the changes proposed by the Wittenberg group. He had a realistic eschatological anticipation of the consequences for those who followed the cross of Christ and adhered to his Word. They are of the Kingdom of God and because of that they are persecuted. In this situation – of violence to those who support the Kingdom of God – their only recourse is the Word of God. The Word of God "is the hammer with which they crush their assailants; it is the fire with which they consume their enemies; and it is an angelic support, a strong defense and shield with which Christ puts the devil to flight in the time of temptations."[30]

As a biblical paradigm of the violence that erupts against those who point to Christ "in the same way as did John the Baptist who pointed to Christ with his preaching and forefinger," Karlstadt presents the prophet Zechariah. Zechariah withstood severe critics when he openly reproached the people and their leading politicians ". . . to abandon God in order to serve the carved and portrayed saints, delighting in carved images [see Lk. 11:51]. The violent cannot tolerate criticism and in response – now as then – take stones and assassinate him by order of the king."[31]

Already in July 1521, Karlstadt was aware that this violence against the Kingdom of God is not just exercised by the spiritual authorities but also by laypersons, such as jewelers, painters, and sculptors, as in Acts 19. "There are clear biblical passages that show not just priests and clergy exercising violence against the Kingdom of God, but also the group of the powerful, the majority of whom were laity."[32]

In a certain sense, the brief "Letter from the Community of Orlamünde to the People of Allstedt" on how they have to fight in a Christian manner, published at the end of July 1524, is a testimony that Karlstadt anticipated the radical evangelical non-violence such as that chosen by the "Brotherly Union" at Schleitheim (1527) and later by Menno Simons. The text from his Orlamünde faithful is significant because it ought to suffice to correct the distorted image of Karlstadt and his proposal of radical reform spread by his detractors.

> In brotherly fidelity we do not want to conceal from you that we cannot help you with armed resistance (if we have understood your letter correctly). We have not been commanded to do this, for Christ ordered Peter to sheath his sword [Mt. 26:52] and would not permit him to fight for him, because the time and the hour of his suffering were near. Thus, when the time and the hour arrive that we must suffer for the sake of divine justice, let us not reach for knives and spears and drive out the eternal will of the father with our own violence, for daily we pray [Mt. 6:10], "Thy will be done."[33]

Notes

1 See Ulrich Bubenheimer, "Karlstadt, Andreas Rudolff Bodenstein von (1486–1541)" in *TRE* 17:649–57; idem, "Bodenstein von Karlstadt, Andreas" in *OER* 1:178–80. The major biography of Karlstadt remains that of Hermann Barge, *Andreas Bodenstein von Karlstadt*, 2 vols. (Leipzig: Friedrich Brandstetter, 1905); there is also a new short biography by Volkmar Joestel, *Andreas Bodenstein genannt Karlstadt. Schwärmer und Aufrührer?* (Wittenberg: Drei Kastanien Verlag, 2000).

2 See Alejandro Zorzin, "Karlstadts 'Dialogus vom Tauff der Kinder' in einem anonymen Wormser Druck aus dem Jahr 1527. Ein Beitrag zur Karlstadtbibliographie," *ARG* 79 (1988), 27–57.

3 See Calvin Augustine Pater, *Karlstadt as the Father of the Baptist Movements: The Emergence of Lay Protestantism* (Toronto, Buffalo & London: University of Toronto Press, 1984).

4 An impression that Melanchthon confirmed when in July of 1519 he described Karlstadt as "a good person, of rare erudition and extraordinary culture, as recognized by his writings." Philip Melanchthon, *Studienausgabe* 1:10, 7ff. and Richard Wetzel, "Melanchthon und Karlstadt im Spiegel von Melancththons Briefwechsel" in Sigrid Looss and Markus Matthias, eds., *Andreas Bodenstein von Karlstadt (1486–1541). Ein Theologe der frühen Reformation. Beiträge eines Arbeitsgesprächs vom 24.–25. November 1955 in Wittenberg* (Wittenberg: Drei Kastenien Verlag, 1998), 159–222.

5 Alejandro Zorzin, *Karlstadt als Flugschriftenautor* (Göttingen: Vandenhoeck & Ruprecht, 1990), 79–83.

6 His course on *De spiritu et litera* (1517/18–19).

7 Hans-Joachim Köhler, *Bibliographie der Flugschriften des 16. Jahrhunderts. Teil I: Das*

frühe 16. Jahrhundert (1501–1530). Band 2, *Druckbeschreibungen H-L* (Tübingen: Bibliotheca Academica Verlag, 1992). Microfiches of the original editions. Microfiche No. 1553.

8 Köhler, Microfiche No. 2504.

9 Augustine, *De continentia* 13:29; see Ernst Kähler, ed., *Karlstadt und Augustin. Der Kommentar des Andreas Bodenstein von Karlstadt zu Augustins Schrift De spiritu et litera. Einführung und Text* (Halle: Niemeyer, 1952), 57.

10 Thus in a creative manner, Karlstadt popularized the famous thesis 21 of Luther's *Heidelberg Disputation* of April 1518.

11 For the flier "*Currus*" and "*Wagen*" see Zorzin, nos. 10 and 11; and Köhler, Microfiche No. 2564.

12 See Barge, *Andreas Bodenstein von Karlstadt*, I:197–200.

13 It is clear that by theft, Karlstadt is referring to a type of economic exploitation, for example, that to which the church subjects the simple faithful. In this same work this point is affirmed in another passage: "We have nothing to expect of the devil's procurers except for harm and injury to body and soul. They are not content with scraping, scratching, and robbing us by being spiritual princes who bring much ill fortune and assist in nothing that is right." Edward J. Furcha, trans. and ed., *The Essential Carlstadt: Fifteen tracts by Andreas Bodenstein (Carlstadt) from Karlstadt* (Waterloo, Ont. and Scottdale, PA: Herald Press, 1995), 228.

14 Furcha, *The Essential Carlstadt*, 219–20; Köhler, Microfiche No. 2867 (G4, verso).

15 *Several Main Points of Christian Teaching Regarding Which Dr. Luther Brings Andreas Carlstadt Under Suspicion Through False Accusation and Slander*, 1525. Furcha, *The Essential Carlstadt*, 376.

16 A situation of *simul liber et subiectus* before the political authorities, the magistrates, would be equivalent to the famous reality of *simul iustus et peccator* before God.

17 Ulrich Bubenheimer, "Scandalum et ius divinum: Theologische und rechtstheologische Problem der ersten reformatorischen Innovationem in Wittenberg 1521/22," *Zeitschrift der Savigny-Stiftung fürRechtsgeschichte*, Kan. Abt. 90 (1973), 263–342. Karlstadt developed this theme in his *Whether We Should Go Slowly and Avoid Offending the Weak in Matters Pertaining to God's Will* (1524).

See Köhler, Microfiche No. 128; Furcha, *The Essential Carlstadt*, 247–68.

18 In this second dictum of December 12, 1521, they refuted five arguments by which the prince on October 25 had objected to the manner in which they proceeded to reform the Mass in Wittenberg. See Nikolas Müller, *Die Wittenberger Bewegung 1521 und 1522* (Leipzig, 1911), No. 43; 84–90. Bubenheimer provides an in-depth analysis in his "Scandalum et ius divinum." Karlstadt's radical position is presented in his *Whether We Should Go Slowly.*

19 Erich Hertzsch, ed., *Karlstadts Schriften aus den Jahren 1523–1525*, 2 vols. (Halle: Niemeyer, 1956–7), 1:96; Furcha, *The Essential Carlstadt*, 267.

20 "*Contionatores populum dei semper ad interna trahere (ubi spiritus domini operatur) et crebrius ab externis avocare debent.*" See Hans-Peter Hasse, *Karlstadt und Tauler. Untersuchungen zur Kreuzestheologie* (Gütersloh: Gerd Mohn, 1993), 206.

21 Köhler, Microfiche No. 1175. Furcha, *The Essential Carlstadt*, 108.

22 The linking of Karlstadt (in 1529/30) with the lay preacher and missionary Melchior Hoffman may be interpreted in the light of his admiration for the action of the Spirit in simple persons. It is very probable that Hoffman's turn to apocalyptic (when he entered into contact with the group of prophetic, apocalyptic Anabaptists in Strasbourg) led Karlstadt to distance himself from him.

23 In his tract *Von dem Priesterthum und opffer Christi* (*On the Priesthood and Sacrifice of Christ*) (1523/4), Karlstadt set forth how the devil "by means of many lies" skillfully attains that the priests "make a sacrifice of the bread and wine and thus they do business with much money like Judas with his betrayal; all with the object of building – for their profit and based on this deception – monasteries grander than castles and Cathedral foundations, filling each corner with chapels and devilish houses. . . ." The priests, according to Karlstadt, usuriously acquire money and goods from the daily sacrifice of Christ in the Mass. See Köhler, Microfiche No. 175 (C2 verso to C3 verso).

24 It is in this place where one may sense the understanding that Karlstadt developed (from 1522 on) on revelation by the direct hearing of the voice of God (and not just through the Scriptures). When the priest Gemser questions Peter the layman who teaches this new

perspective on the sacrament of the Lord's Supper, Peter responds: "The one whose voice I hear yet whom I do not see and of whom I do not know how he came to me and how he left me." When Gemser asks: "Who is this?" Peter responds, "Our Father in heaven." See Furcha, *The Essential Carlstadt*, 281. This represents one of the few passages where Karlstadt provides a glimpse of his "doctrine of revelation by direct hearing" – for which Luther disqualified him as a "heavenly prophet." In spite of this, there is a difference between Karlstadt and Müntzer that may seem at first of no considerable importance: that for Müntzer, divine revelation mediated by visions and in dreams is considered as being final. In any case there exists a reference from Marcus Thomae, one of the Zwickau prophets, holding a conversation with Karlstadt at the end of December 1521 in Wittenberg. See Müller, No. 63; 136.

25 Furcha, *The Essential Carlstadt*, 294–5.

26 Karlstadt received an annual income for this charge – as second within the hierarchy of the chapter – of 130 ducats per year. Of this sum, 80 ducats came from the Orlamünde parish, incorporated as a prebend in charge and attended by a vicar, who received about 17 ducats per year.

27 In a letter to Duke John in May 1523 he recognized this:

> For the daily profits, that are the cause of poverty and great want [that I tolerate] I am in the habit to collect and take in Wittenberg, and because in addition I have at my disposal a parish [Orlamünde], from which – being an absentee – I collect a pension, I am criticized with such scorn and insults, that my ears no longer want

to hear it. In particular because it has come to my notice that some respectable and upright persons have come to Wittenberg to criticize me and to inform me that I scandalize exceedingly the servants of God and of Christ of the territory [Saxony] and other regions. Furthermore, they would have me request that I rapidly put an end to the mentioned scandal.

Eduard F. Hase, ed., "Karlstadt in Orlamünde," *Mitteilungen der Geschichts- und Altertums-forschenden Gesellschaft des Osterlandes*, 4/1 (1854): 91. See, for example, the passionate defense that the masterly layman Valentin Ickelsamer began in 1525 of Karlstadt's austere style of life in his work *Complaint of Various Persons of all the Christians who Support Andreas Karlstadt against the Great Injustice and Tyranny on the Part of Luther in Wittenberg*. Köhler, Microfiche No. 2513.

28 *Several Main Points of Christian Teaching Regarding Which Dr. Luther Brings Andreas Carlstadt Under Suspicion Through False Accusation and Slander*, 1525. Köhler, Microfiche No. 1561 (F2, recto/verso); Furcha, *The Essential Carlstadt*, 370–1.

29 See Hasse, *Karlstadt und Tauler*, 153–72.

30 Köhler, Microfiche No. 2995 (C3 verso).

31 Köhler, Microfiche No. 2995 (B4 recto).

32 Köhler, Microfiche No. 2995 (B4 recto).

33 This tract of two pages was printed in Wittenberg by Hans Lufft. The original German text is in Adolf Laube, et al., eds., *Flugschriften der frühen Reformationszeit (1518–1524)*, 2 vols. (Berlin: Akademie der Wissenschaften, 1983), 1:443f. An English translation is in Michael Baylor, ed., *The Radical Reformation* (Cambridge: Cambridge University Press, 1991), 33–4.

Bibliography

Primary Sources

Baylor, Michael, ed., *The Radical Reformation*, Cambridge: Cambridge University Press, 1991.

Furcha, Edward J., trans. and ed., *The Essential Carlstadt. Fifteen Tracts by Andreas Bodenstein (Carlstadt) from Karlstadt*, Waterloo, Ont. and Scottdale, PA: Herald Press, 1995.

Hase, Eduard F., ed., "Karlstadt in Orlamünde," *Mitteilungen der Geschichts- und*

Altertumsforschenden Gesellschaft des Osterlandes 4/1 (1854), 42–125.

Hertzsch, Erich, ed., *Karlstadts Schriften aus den Jahren 1523–1525*, 2 vols., Halle: Niemeyer, 1956/7.

Kähler, Ernst, ed., *Karlstadt und Augustin. Der Kommentar des Andreas Bodenstein von Karlstadt zu Augustins Schrift De Spiritu et litera. Einführung und Text*, Halle: Niemeyer, 1952.

Köhler, Hans-Joachim, *Bibliographie der Flugschriften des 16. Jahrhunderts. Teil I: Das Frühe 16. Jahrhundert (1501–1530). Band 2. Druckbeschreibungen H-L*, Tübingen: Bibliotheca Academica Verlag, 1992. Nos. 1846–1973 are microfiches of the original editions.

Laube, Adolf, et al., eds., *Flugschriften der frühen Reformationszeit (1518–1524)*, 2 vols., Berlin: Akademie der Wissenschaften, 1983.

Müller, Nikolaus, ed., *Die Wittenberger Bewegung 1521 und 1522*, Leipzig, 1911.

Secondary Sources

Bubenheimer, Ulrich, "Karlstadt, Andreas Rudolff Bodenstein von (1486–1541)" in *TRE* 17:649–57.

——, *Consonantia Theologiae et Iurisprudentiae. Andreas Bodenstein von Karlstadt Als Theologe und Jurist zwischen Scholastik und Reformation*, Tübingen: J. C. B. Mohr (Paul Siebeck), 1977.

——, "Andreas Bodenstein genannt Karlstadt (1486–1541)," *Frankische Lebensbilder* 14 (Nuremberg, 1990), 47–64.

——, "Bodenstein von Karlstadt, Andreas" in *OER* 1:178–80.

Hasse, Hans-Peter, *Karlstadt und Tauler. Untersuchungen zur Kreuztheologie*, Gütersloh: Gerd Mohn, 1993.

Kriechbaum, Friedel, *Grundzüge der Theologie Karlstadts. Eine systematische Studie zur Erhellung der Theologie Andreas von Karlstadts (eigentlich Andreas Bodenstein 1480–1541) aus seinen eigenen Schriften Entwickelt*, Hamburg-Bergestedt: Herbert Reich, 1967.

Loos, Sigrid and Markus Matthias, eds., *Andreas Bodenstein von Karlstadt (1486–1541). Ein Theologe der frühen Reformation, Beiträge eines Arbeitsgesprächs vom 24–25. November 1955 in Wittenberg* (Wittenberg: Drei Kastenien Verlag, 1998).

Pater, Calvin Augustine, *Karlstadt as the Father of the Baptist Movements: The Emergence of Lay Protestantism*, Toronto, Buffalo, and London: University of Toronto Press, 1984.

Sider, Ronald J., *Andreas Bodenstein von Karlstadt. The Development of his Thought: 1517–1525*, Leiden: E. J. Brill, 1974.

Zorzin, Alejandro, *Karlstadt als Flugschriftenautor*. Göttingen: Vandenhoeck & Ruprecht, 1990.

Thomas Müntzer (c.1490–1525)

Gottfried Seebass

In a certain sense the twentieth century more than any other was Thomas Müntzer's century. Up to then the academic study of his person and work had been impeded by the long dominant misrepresentations of him by Luther and Melanchthon on the one side, and by the representatives of Anabaptism and mystical spiritualism on the other. Modern research began and prospered between the fronts of the so-called "bourgeois" and Marxist historiographies. Initially their perspectives were not essentially different in that both saw Müntzer as the revolutionary protagonist of the Peasants' War. The "bourgeois" perspective branded him a prophet of murder and a revolutionary in light of his participation in the Peasants' War; the Marxist orientation extolled him for the same reason as a prophet of the aspirations of his time. In the West, the first partially positive views of Müntzer were stimulated by the theology of revolution, various liberation theologies, and the impact of the student revolutions in the 1960s. By the mid-1970s, a differentiated evaluation developed above all in the historiography of the German Democratic Republic, especially among the theologians. Thus even before the fall of the Berlin Wall in 1989, Müntzer research had acquired such an extensive understanding of his theological work and its revolutionary implications that it is correct to speak of a growing *opinio communis* on the historical Müntzer.

Müntzer's Life

Müntzer's extant, authentic writings and correspondence from the scant ten years between 1516 and 1525, along with scattered reports about him, are not sufficient sources for writing a genuine biography. Even the intensive and painstaking research of recent decades has not succeeded in shedding much more than a faint light on the obscurity that covers broad stretches of his life.

His given name of Thomas and his matriculation in Leipzig in 1506 suggest that he could have been born in Stollberg in the Harz around 1489 on December 20 or 21.[1] Ernst Bloch's account in his widely read biography[2] that Müntzer might have grown up in Quedlinburg, the home town of his mother, in a fairly well-to-do family that had connections to the upper classes in other cities of the northern Harz region, is nothing but a legend. We certainly know nothing more accurate about his studies than that he began in Leipzig in 1506, and that after that he assumed the role of a "collaborator" in Aschersleben and Halle. What he had to do with the "conspiracy" against Bishop Ernst of Halle can no longer be ascertained. Perhaps this account refers simply to a loose association of serious and pious citizens united by their criticism of a church that had to a large extent become too involved in worldly and financial affairs. He renewed his studies at Frankfurt on the Oder in 1512, completing the *magister artium* as well as a first-level theological degree, the *baccalaureus theologiae*. After ordination to the priesthood in his home diocese of Halberstadt, he received, through family connections, a benefice at St. Michael's and a teaching position in the Martin School in Braunschweig. During this time he had good connections with well-to-do merchants who were moved, possibly by the tradition of the German mystics, to embrace the true *Gelassenheit* of Christians in the world; the discipleship demanded by Christ of separation from all worldly obligations. He retained his Braunschweig benefice when, after a short time, he took the position of provost and teacher at the Benedictine convent at Frose near Aschersleben.

It was then that Müntzer's theological interests and concern for true Christian piety, active since his youth, impelled him to go to Wittenberg, where the uproar over indulgences had arisen. Apparently he desired in Luther's university to perfect his humanistic education and to intensify his theological studies. Although his own tone is already perceived in his early anticlerical invectives against the Catholic clergy, he can be seen at that time as a disciple of Luther; at any rate, he counted himself as such. But perhaps also at that time he was attracted by the more strongly Augustinian-influenced theology of Luther's colleague, Andreas Bodenstein von Karlstadt, who was calling for a Reformation of a more legalistic character.

Around Easter 1519, Müntzer went to Jüterbog as a temporary replacement for the "Lutheran" preacher, Franz Günther. There he came into conflict with the local Franciscans over his criticism of the ecclesiastical hierarchy and traditional theology. After Günther's return, Müntzer could have returned to Wittenberg; a short while later he became confessor to the Cistercian convent at Beuditz. There he could have studied works of church history and the writings of the so-called German mysticism. He also followed the process of the "Luther affair," and what is more, he could have been present at the Leipzig Debate (1519) between Karlstadt, Luther, and Eck. It is possible that Luther recommended him in 1520 to the Zwickau Town Council as a substitute for the preacher Johannes Egranus at St. Mary's, a parish with clear social tensions. Again, there were difficulties; Müntzer not only sharply attacked the monks and priests, but after the return of Egranus and his own transfer to St. Catherine's he got into conflict with the humanistically minded Egranus over his characteristic theology of suffering and spiritualism. Müntzer did not spare blunt and vivid polemic. Among other charges, he declared that "the monks had such big mouths that you could cut off a pound of flesh, and they would still have mouths enough."[3]

Among the factions in Zwickau, Müntzer supported the weavers, whose trade was in difficulty. It is still undecided whether at that time the so-called "Zwickau Prophets," with their spiritualistic-apocalyptic views, influenced Müntzer or he them.

In the interest of peace within the city, the town council succeeded in expelling Müntzer after his brief year of activity. The following period up to Easter 1523, described by Müntzer himself with the phrase "the wretchedness of my expulsion,"[4] was the time during which his mother died, his father moved to Braunschweig, and he also relinquished his benefice in Braunschweig. He proceeded next to Prague because, as his open letter to the Bohemians and all of Christendom, the so-called "Prague Manifesto,"[5] inferred, he expected there the beginning of the great and final restitution of Christendom. Expelled from Prague, he perhaps stayed in Erfurt and Jena; encountered the Lutheran preacher Lorenz Süsse in Nordhausen; visited Karlstadt, who was then devoted to the mystical tradition, in Wörlitz; and obtained a position as preacher at the Cistercian nunnery at Glaucha near Halle. Yet there was nowhere he could remain because he reproached the Reformation clergy as well as those of the old faith as "testicled, profit-seeking, whore-riding priests,"[6] who only guzzle and carouse, captivating and seducing the people in false faith for their own egotistical, financial gain instead of preaching the true faith. Müntzer was increasingly becoming conscious of his differences with the Wittenberg theology of justification, that appeared to him to be a fundamental perversion of Christendom equal to that of Catholic works-righteousness. According to Müntzer, God does not accept the sinner but rather the one who becomes conformed to Christ through inner and outer suffering. His own sorrowful experiences in "the wretchedness of my expulsion" only confirmed this conception.

In early April 1523, through the mediation of Felicitas von Selmenitz, who perhaps had earlier helped him gain the position at Glauche, Müntzer became the pastor of the Electoral Saxon enclave of Allstedt in the southern Harz. Here he succeeded in winning over not only his colleague, Simon Haferitz, and the congregation, but also the electoral official, Hans Zeiss. Thus in Allstedt, for the first time, he was able to work out his theology in tolerable peace. His accomplishments there included an order of worship in clear German, *The German Evangelical Mass*, the *German Church Service Book*, and a public account of his liturgical activity by which he intended to lead the people to true faith, *Order and Explanation of the German Church Service recently instituted at Allstedt by the servants of God, 1523*.[7] It is no wonder that people streamed to his services from the surrounding areas. When Count Ernst of Mansfeld forbade his subjects under threat of punishment from participating in these services, serious conflicts arose. Müntzer publicly reviled the count and complained to the Electoral Saxon court. He declared he was always ready to defend his teaching, but he rejected a hearing before the Wittenberg Reformers. In this connection he succinctly summarized and clearly demarcated his theology from that of Wittenberg as well as the old faith in two writings: *On Counterfeit Faith* and *Protestation or Proposition by Thomas Müntzer . . . about his teachings*.[8]

When the Allstedters not only refused tributes to the nunnery of Naundorf but pillaged and burned down its Mallerbach chapel, the Electoral Saxon court took action to intervene. But the bailiff and town council did not at first proceed against the responsible parties, defended by Müntzer; when they did begin to act they did so only reluctantly. In the meantime, Luther in Wittenberg was informed of the activities in Allstedt and warned the Saxon court about Müntzer's violent activities. At this time, Duke John, traveling by Allstedt, gave Müntzer the opportunity to preach a sermon in his presence at the castle. In this so-called "Princes' Sermon," *Interpretation of the Second Chapter of Daniel*,[9] Müntzer openly called upon the Saxon princes by virtue of their office to take the lives of his enemies, whom he branded as godless and damned.

This sermon may have been enough for the princes, particularly since Müntzer did not shy away from also declaring before members of his congregation that rulers who did not discharge their office and who acted against the Christian faith "ought to be throttled like dogs."[10] When the Saxon court now began to take more aggressive steps, the town bailiff and council began to dissociate themselves from Müntzer. In this context the covenant his followers had formed for defensive purposes broke up.

Müntzer evaded imminent imprisonment by flight to Mühlhausen in August 1524. In this city a covenant had already developed in 1523 between those striving for religious reform and guild craftsmen disgruntled with the town government. At that time, the town council entertained a compromise, but iconoclasm broke out in June 1524. Müntzer thus arrived as a preacher at the churches of St. Mary and St. Nicholas in the midst of a tense situation that his own activity sharply intensified. When the town council contravened their earlier compromise, a riotous assembly demanded the election of a new council that would at all times be accountable to the community and would preserve "divine righteousness." Müntzer apparently participated in these events and also established an "Eternal Alliance" whose members were recorded on a list. But then when the council overcame the unrest and regained power, Müntzer, with his local colleague Heinrich Pfeiffer, had to flee the city in September 1524.

In the ensuing period Müntzer's wanderings are not very clear until his return to Mühlhausen in February 1525. It is known that he had two tracts printed in Nuremberg: *A Manifest Exposé of False Faith . . . through the Testimony of the Gospel of Luke*[11] and a verbose reckoning with Luther, *A highly provoked Vindication and a Refutation of the unspiritual soft-living Flesh in Wittenberg*.[12] Apparently he also spent a longer time in the upper Rhine area in the Klettgau and Hegau regions, during which time he met with Johannes Oecolampadius in Basel and Balthasar Hubmaier in Waldshut. He also had contact with the rebellious peasants, however their uprising was neither instigated by nor measurably influenced by him. After his return to Mühlhausen he was installed by the congregation, not the town council, as pastor in St. Mary's in the new part of town. A protest by property owners among the petite bourgeoisie and the middle bourgeoisie renewed controversy. This time he was able to push through the "Eternal Alliance" and thereby officially to implement his Reformation. At this point Müntzer, with the members of his "Eternal Alliance," had command over a numerous following devoted to him. When, then, the first reports about the Peasants' War in the southwest and the uprising in the neighboring areas of Würzburg and Fulda reached him, Müntzer believed he recognized in this war the divinely willed final great conflict between the pious and the godless. He sought everywhere to mobilize his followers. Depicting himself as the Old Testament judge Gideon, Müntzer led a band of 300 men to Frankenhausen am Kyffhäuser, where they joined the Thüringian peasants. The advancing armies of the princes demanded in vain the surrender of Müntzer, who was the clerical and spiritual leader of the mass of peasants, and in a threatening letter asked about the affiliation of the adjacent counts and lords with the peasants. On May 15 the peasants were defeated, and Müntzer himself taken prisoner. After the customary inquisitorial hearing assisted by torture, Müntzer was executed on May 27, 1525, in the camp of the princes before the gates of Mühlhausen.

Men can be silenced, but where their writings and words survive the chance exists that they, in a kind of democracy of the dead, may at any time return to speak. What did Müntzer have to say to the people of his time?

Müntzer's Message[13]

It is not very easy to answer this question because Müntzer's extant writings, with the exception of his liturgical works, are thoroughly polemical and do not provide a comprehensive presentation of his theology.

In view of the manifold secular and ecclesiastical grievances at the beginning of the sixteenth century, many people were convinced that the end of the world was directly at hand and that only the intervention of God himself would be able to effect change. This consciousness became even stronger when Luther believed he recognized the prophesied power of the Antichrist in the papacy and thus the final stage for the end of the world. Müntzer also was early on convinced that he was living in the final phase of history. He anticipated the great transformation of the world, an insuperable reformation of all relationships. Christ himself would return in order to separate the pious elect from the godless condemned, and to establish his kingdom and rule, not in some distant beyond but rather here on earth in a chiliastic breaking into history.

Müntzer referred people to these events; he meant the people to participate in them through his preaching and writing. As Daniel interpreted his dream to Nebuchadnezzar, so Müntzer as a new Daniel and prophet drew attention to the signs of the times. As Elijah opposed the priests of Baal, so he intended to be a new Elijah to oppose the priests of the old faith and the "scribes" of the Reformation because both parties have seduced the people, strengthened them in their unbelief, and thereby profited to their own self-seeking advantage. Just as John the Baptist as a preacher of repentance prepared for the proclamation of Jesus Christ, so he intended as a new John to call all Christendom to repentance and conversion. With all that, he believed he was one of those angels who, according to the parable of the weeds among the wheat, is the reaper at the harvest who collects the wheat and destroys the weeds. He rejected the view that the end-time could only be initiated by the action of divine transcendence. Thus he was convinced that in his preaching and proclamation the definitive separation of the pious and godless would occur and that the principal defect of Christendom, the Augustinian *corpus mixtum*, would be ended. What Müntzer had to say to the people, he therefore summarized in a very impressive penitential preaching that was in its principles very simple, clear, and easy to understand.

Müntzer's central point of departure was the order of creation as he read it in the creation account of the first chapter of Genesis. He understood the order of creation to be a given succession in which the earlier creations serve the later ones. Thus the plants are over the earth; the livestock are over the plants; but people are over the whole creation. The creation account thus represents not only a graduated pyramid of existence, but also a pyramid of rulership. Humankind, however, has to serve God. Thus humankind is given the instruction to rule as lord over everything created and to serve God. But it is just this "order" that humans have destroyed through their sin. Instead of relying upon the one transcendent God, humans lost their hearts to the many creatures of this world; basing their trust not upon God but upon possessions, power, honor, and influence. In this relationship all are the children of Adam, "who distorts the order of things and entangles himself with creaturely things, whereas Christ held fast to the Highest and despised creaturely things."[14] This is the source for the thoroughly ascetic, world-denying character of the theology of the Allstedt preacher.

For Müntzer, the turn away from God and toward the world has grave consequences for the person's relationship to the world and the neighbor. Where the person no longer rules over the world, there he or she becomes ruled by it and lives in bondage to it. The result is the distorted relationship to the things of this world. This is apparent in persons' possessive instinct, which ever more arrogates things to him or herself, and even exploits others without mercy. These cravings therefore generate the need and misery of others in whom thereby their own greed is unleashed. For Müntzer this takes concrete form not only in titles of possession, but just as much in immoderate eating and drinking, as well as in sexual voracity. At the same time, this perversion of the created order sets one person over another, and creates mutual fear. Where persons no longer fear God alone as their Lord, they live in fear of one another. This is true not only for the servant's fear before the master, the subject before the prince, but also for the princes themselves, since they cannot properly protect their office for fear of one another. "Since man has fallen from God to serve the creatures, it is only just that he has (to his cost) to fear the creature more than God."[15] For Müntzer, this creaturely fraternity of humankind abrogating lordship materializes in the seeking after glory, honor, and titles that not once gives Christ and God what honors them as the proper Lords. "Alas! Christ, the gentle son of God, is a mere scarecrow or a painted puppet in our eyes compared with the great titles and names of this world."[16] In this way the apostasy of humankind from God also determines sins and deficient, i.e., false, faith, affecting the external relationships of persons to others, to the world, and to God.

This "defect of Adam," however, has been healed in one man, namely Christ. For Christ is the only person who has not lost himself to the creatures, but rather has remained in obedience and in service to his divine Father, even to the extent of suffering external abandonment by God on the cross. It is just in this that Christ is also the model for believers. In this way, in a Trinity conceived as subordinationist, Christ remains under God; the "order" mentioned previously is not only one of creation but is also an order "placed in God and the creatures."[17]

Therefore this is not only an order of governance and creation but also an order of redemption. For just as Christ in his suffering was preserved in this order, so also humankind, which cannot by itself return to the old order of creation and dominion, has to be led by God into suffering. In a process of internal and external suffering, God himself has to free humankind from "clinging" to this world and its creatures.

The order of salvation thereby concerns a process of suffering by which everything must be taken from the person; everything upon which he or she had placed trust must come to nothing. Therefore "the work of God is as bitter as the abyss of hell," and its effect is that God "deprives man of all comfort."[18] Müntzer thus has the entirely consistent conception that the intensity of this suffering corresponds exactly to the extent the person has abandoned him or herself to the world. Everyone will have to go through this purification process which Müntzer understands as purgatory. One must beseech God for this suffering; one must receive this suffering. For whoever does not here experience redeeming suffering and make it his or her own, will have to endure it in hell in an even more grievous form. It is possible that Müntzer also associated this redemption, through universal suffering, with the concept of a final universal reconciliation.

In this process of suffering, however, what the Christian usually designates as faith is destroyed. For Müntzer believes that the habitual Christian faith in God is nothing other than a simulated faith, a "made-up," a fictional faith. Namely, one cannot be consumed by constant concern for food, clothing, and personal security or indulge oneself without restraint in all these things and at the same time depend upon God. "We are boastful and say: I believe, I believe, yet we are nevertheless daily concerned with vain squabbling over and cares for worldly goods."[19] One cannot constantly strive for honor and glory or live in servile fear before the great of this world, and at the same time claim to fear God. "No one can serve two masters." But it is just in this constant effort and activity that people live in false faith. That is why we have to despair not only of ourselves and the world, but even of our faith and our God. "First unbelief has to get the better of counterfeit faith, and one has to stand before God quite helplessly."[20]

Where this happens, one truly follows the suffering Christ, the Son of God. Christ was invariably and entirely obedient to God up to and including suffering. Thus it is only in him that we learn the original order of creation and the later order of redemption. It is not the Christ offered for us in the bread and wine of the Roman Mass, and also not the Christ who vicariously died for us as preached by the Reformers who is able to help us. For both these Christs remain entirely outside us. They are not capable of changing us; they are not able to conquer Adam's defect in us. Both are concerned with only a kind of "honey-sweet" Christ instead of the "bitter" and suffering Christ. One must therefore enter into the passion with Christ himself. One must with Christ entirely surrender one's own will and completely accept the will of God. One must, like Christ on the cross, despair of God's help. In this way one will first really conform to Christ, become one with Christ, and with him become a child of God.

Only when we become like Christ in this manner, and Christ in this manner is in us, can Christ also be for us. Only, then, at this profoundest point of suffering, does God come in order to console us. There God addresses his Son, the Son in us. There we hear God himself speak – and indeed not only in the external Word of the Bible. For Scripture remains a dead letter so long as we do not experience in suffering the living Scripture of the finger of God. That is also why the Scripture and the external Word are unable to call forth faith. For this reason also, all "scriptural scholarship" remains completely useless. For Scripture only shows us that all receive faith only through severe suffering. There it is only just this process of suffering in which God leads us and that testifies to true faith. True faith – very small like a mustard seed – arises first only at the profoundest level of suffering.

Müntzer hardly said anything about how this faith then changes a person's life, how it determines in a new way the relationship to the things of this world and to the neighbor. His interest focussed expressly on the passion, and he had little interest in any way in the concrete new life and the fulfillment of the law of Christ. Müntzer allows the disclosure of the true Christian life only indirectly and in opposition to what he criticized as the consequences of the broken order of creation.

From this it is easily understood why Müntzer neither in Zwickau nor in Prague, nor later in Allstedt and Mühlhausen, began with social-revolutionary demands. Whoever desired in one's own interest to change relationships of property and governance in his or her own favor, only testified once again to dependence on the world and creatures. Only where one in true, self-experienced faith proved by suffering that he or she is able to let everything go (*gelassen*) will that person also be able to change the world. That is why Müntzer begins by preaching repentance and suffering, and then in Allstedt and Mühlhausen implemented corresponding reforms of worship and church orders. For the orders of worship and the celebration of baptism and the Lord's Supper are so structured that they have the task of pointing the hearer to the process of suffering that makes one conform to Christ.

Müntzer's Reformation Programme

Müntzer, however, did not intend to convert only the individual. He expected the great change of the entire world to be effected and led by God. It can be said without exaggeration that Müntzer at least since 1521, if not earlier, awaited the events by which this great "Reformation of the world" would be heralded and consummated.

He went to Prague in 1521 because he expected a special resonance for his anticlerical message in Bohemia on the basis of the Hussite traditions, which, with high probability, he knew.[21] There he intended "to fill the sonorous marching trumpets with the new song of praise of the Holy Spirit."[22] In Bohemia, so he hoped, the new church would begin, the pure church of the pious and the elect, that would be the model for the whole world; here in Bohemia would be "the defense of the Word of God."[23] But his expectation was disappointed.

In Allstedt, Müntzer placed his hope upon the reform-minded princes of Electoral Saxony. Recognizing no difference between the ecclesiastical and civil communities, he demanded the princes, with direct reference to Romans 13, slay the godless. He defined the godless as the Catholic and Reformation theologians, as well as those secular authorities who protected them. Müntzer called upon the princes to carry out this mission even if it endangered their own territories and created personal danger and suffering for them. As Christian princes, they had not only the right but the responsibility to exterminate the godless, just as once the Israelites under Joshua conquered the land of Canaan by the sword. God fought for them, but the swords of the Israelites were the means. So the Christian princes must complete the final destruction of the godless by earthly means. Müntzer emphatically polemicized against the Lutheran thesis that the civil authority has concern only for the peace of the civil community, and is not at all directly responsible for correct worship and the punishment of the godless.

What Müntzer expected of the Saxon princes was a striking violation of public peace. It is understandable that the princes refused such an unreasonable request. For Müntzer their rejection was the reason for founding a "covenant" for the protection of those who came to his services of worship from the Catholic areas around Allstedt. He expressly emphasized this covenant had the function of deterrence. In no case should anyone put personal trust in the covenant; no one should misuse it for social-revolutionary goals. One may not enter an alliance "for the sake of the creatures." Therefore the members of the covenant should continue to fulfill their required public obligations, such as taxes.

From the fall of 1524, Müntzer drew a double conclusion from the princes' rejection of the tasks set forth for them in his sermon. First, he interpreted this refusal by the Saxon princes as their divine judgment and total rejection. Thus he would have nothing more to do with them. Now he could only recognize the princes as tyrants like Nimrod and Herod, established by God in order to lead the pious into suffering. "God has given the world to the lords and princes in his wrath, and will again take it away in bitterness."[24] From here on Müntzer was certain that according to Daniel 7, governance would be given to the people, without however yet knowing who they could be.

Second, Müntzer now also drew a consequence in view of the possibility of individual conversion. Up to this point he had only elaborated on the manner in which the order of creation broken by human sin determined human relationships to the world and fellow humans. But now he came to realize that the present external relationships of possession and governance going back to the broken order of creation impeded the effect of his penitential preaching and the rise of true faith. "What possible chance does the common man ever have to welcome the pure word of God in sincerity when he is beset by such worries about temporal goods?"[25] Müntzer was particularly embittered that both the Reformation and Catholic theologians were prepared to justify with reference to God's commandment an – in his eyes – unchristian order of property.

> Open your eyes! What is the evil brew from which all usury, theft and robbery springs but the assumption of our lords and princes that all creatures are their property? The fish in the water, the birds in the air, the plants on the face of the earth – it all has to belong to them! Isaiah 5. To add insult to injury, they have God's commandment proclaimed to the poor: God has commanded that you should not steal. But it avails them nothing. For while they do violence to everyone, flay and fleece the poor farm worker, tradesman and everything that breathes, Micah 3, yet should any of the latter commit the pettiest crime, he must hang. And Doctor Liar [Luther] responds, Amen. It is the lords themselves who make the poor man their enemy.[26]

According to Müntzer, everything has to lead to the consideration that the kingdom of God must be realized not only in persons in the return to the order of creation, but at the same time also generally in the final transformation of the entire life of the world.

Müntzer and the Peasants' War

Already in the "Princes' Sermon," Müntzer had, with reference to Daniel 7:27, threatened that if the princes did not follow their mission, "the kingdom, power, and might under all of heaven would be given the holy people of the Highest."[27] This basically had been his expectation since the "Prague Manifesto" of 1521. Thus, after this, the "people" are not simply identical with the "common man" but with the "elect."

With this background, it is also understandable why Müntzer supported the South German peasants, and, as the Peasants' War erupted, himself participated in it in Thuringia, even though he did not nearly have the leading role in either the south or the north that has been ascribed to him in Marxist historiography. For the peasants really did fight according to the programmatic declarations in "The Twelve Articles" and the "Memmingen Covenant,"[28] not simply for the improvement of their social conditions; they desired a "Christian Confederation," an order of public peace, in which Christian brotherly love and the common good would be realized as well as the "godly law." In line with these views, they should continue to pay all taxes. When the peasants now turned in particular against the wealthy cloisters and the Catholic nobility, they did so, in Müntzer's eyes, just because the nuns and nobles were the godless and the damned. For this reason, he saw the peasants as the "pious." From his perspective he saw that their battle was the revealed prophesied conflict with the godless that would precede the end-time. And in this final battle, the Christians, as he had with complete consistency warned of "public revolt," not only may, no, must, take up the sword in order to slay the enemy. The apocalyptically interpreted peasants' revolt released the revolutionary power of Müntzer's ideas. Hence, his truly powerful appeal in the last days of the Thüringian Peasants' War:

> Go to it, go to it, while the fire is hot! Don't let your sword grow cold, don't let it hang down limply! Hammer away ding-dong on the anvils of Nimrod, cast down their tower to the ground! As long as they live it is impossible for you to rid yourselves of the fear of men. One cannot say anything to you about God as long as they rule over you. Go to it, go to it, while it is day! God goes before you; follow, follow! The whole business can be read up in Matthew 24, Ezekiel 34, Daniel 7, Ezra 16, Revelation 6, and all these texts are explained by Romans 13.[29]

That Müntzer understood the war as God's war and a holy war in the sense of the Old Testament is proved not least by his departure with 300 men from Mühlhausen for Frankenhausen. Like his self-appellation in his letters, "with the sword of Gideon," this number "300" evoked the miraculous victory of the Old Testament judge, Gideon, effected by God.

It is of interest that Müntzer nowhere expressed anything more specific about the communal life of the saints of the Most High after their earthly victory, and life in the kingdom of Christ after the final destruction of the godless. This was undoubtedly not only because in the weeks leading to the revolt, time was running out. Rather it corresponds throughout to the observation that he also knew he had less to say about the new life of the individual believer. As in the view of the individual, the perspective of the process of suffering through which he or she should come to faith stood in the foreground, so too in the view of the coming kingdom of Christ did the judgment of the godless.

Nevertheless, something may be inferred of the new life from a few suggestions from Müntzer's writings and his statements during imprisonment. He was entirely prepared to make certain concessions to the existing nobility in view of their higher costs of living. But he would no longer recognize rulers' privileges. In this regard the destruction of castles stood as a symbolic act. As Christian brothers – as Müntzer addressed the nobility during the revolt and spoke to Duke George of Saxony, even when a prisoner – the nobility should join the confederation of the peasants. Then they could indeed retain the administration of the land under the control of the community. But otherwise they should be deposed, and in the case of rebellion, be killed. Müntzer thus appears to have had in mind a theocracy controlled by the people. It is doubtful, however, that with the principle *omnia sunt communia*[30] Müntzer actually conceived of the realization of a communism of production and consumption. Indeed, property and its protection belonged, also according to ecclesiastical opinion, really in the world after the fall into sin, whereas in Paradise all was communal. When Müntzer stated that it shall be given to each according to need, the maintenance of property was considered which at the same time should be bound to wholehearted realization of love to the neighbor. In this sense, of course, Luther also intended that everything at our disposition that was concerned with living is to be given for support of the neighbor. Thus, Müntzer attempted to develop concrete formulations for mediating the great utopia of the kingdom of Christ.

That Müntzer interpreted the Peasants' War apocalyptically is clearly seen just before the battle of Frankenhausen. In a sermon, Müntzer summoned the peasants to battle with reference to divine help. That, of all things, just at this point a rainbow-colored solar halo formed, appeared to him to be a heavenly confirmation, for the standard under which the Mühlhausen troops fought was a rainbow, the sign of the "eternal covenant" God had concluded with humankind after the flood.

Nevertheless, the peasants were beaten. The slaughter of the peasants did not, however, cause Müntzer to doubt his theology nor his expectation of the coming kingdom of Christ. Rather, he thought the battle had been lost because the people had not properly understood him, and had sought only their own interests.[31] For this he was ready to die, and expressed his hope that the good and foolish people would learn from this. When, shortly before his execution, he called upon the princes to read the Old Testament books of Kings, he thus consistently referred once again to their responsibility to serve the true worship of God.

Conclusion

In an astonishing way, Müntzer has had a wide-ranging effect even though his writings have hardly been reissued or reprinted. This applies first of all to the "Müntzer legend" of Lutheranism in which he figures as the one with major responsibility for the Peasants' War. A positive development of his concepts, providing his mystical spiritualism as well as his apocalypticism, even though slightly modified and including his death, was given in the apocalyptic interpretations of the time, above all by Hans Hut and the branch of Anabaptism that derived from him. Just with respect to this apocalypticism, this interpretation prospered even during Hut's lifetime in debate with Swiss Anabaptism. Thus later the Hutterian Brethren as pacifist Baptists could separate themselves from the Peasants' War and still maintain Müntzer in honored memory. Müntzer's mystical spiritualism, however, also continued to exert influence in the "Left Wing" of the Reformation, so that the radical Pietist, Gottfried Arnold, in his *Non-Partisan Church History and History of Heretics* (1699–1700), could relate in a deferential manner to Müntzer. But this was only a weak voice in comparison to the strong chorus of confessional condemnation. One can therefore correctly say that it was first the historical and church historical research of the second half of the twentieth century, influenced by different, conflicting conceptions of history which encountered the historical Müntzer and placed him living before our eyes.

Notes

1   Editor's note: The university statutes precluded entrance for degree work before the age of 17. The feast of St. Thomas is December 21.

2   Ernst Bloch, *Thomas Müntzer als Theologe der Revolution* (Frankfurt am Main: Suhrkamp, 1963). The best biographies are those by Günter Vogler, *Thomas Müntzer* (Berlin: Dietz, 1989), Eike Wolgast, *Thomas Müntzer. Ein Verstörer der Ungläubigen* (Göttingen: Muster-Schmidt, 1981), and Hans-Jürgen Goertz, *Thomas Müntzer: Apocalyptic Mystic and Revolutionary* (Edinburgh: T. & T. Clark, 1993).

3   Otto Clemen, "Johannes Sylvius Egranus," *Mitteilungen des Altertumsvereins für Zwickau und Umgegend*, 7 (1902), 18 n. 45.

4   *CTM*, 54; *MSB*, 388.

5   See *CTM*, 352–79.

6   See *CTM*, 367–8; *MSB*, 501, 8 and 30.

7   Müntzer's "Forewords" to the first two liturgical works as well as his *Order and Explanation* are in *CTM*, 166–83. The texts with musical notations are in *MSB*, 25–215.

8   *CTM*, 210–25; 183–209.

9   *CTM*, 230–52.

10 *CTM*, 96; see also 250, 251; *MSB*, 417.

11 *CTM*, 253–323.

12 *CTM*, 324–50.

13 For Müntzer's theology see especially Siegfried Bräuer and Helmar Junghans, eds., *Der Theologe Thomas Müntzer* (Berlin: Evangelische Verlagsanstalt, 1989) and Gottfried Seebass,

"Thomas Müntzer," in *TRE* 23:419, 44–427, 12.

14 *CTM*, 388; *MSB*, 520.

15 *CTM*, 282; *MSB*, 285.

16 *CTM*, 232; *MSB*, 244.

17 *CTM*, 363; *MSB*, 496, 10f.

18 *CTM*, 387; *MSB*, 519.

19 *MSB*, 227 (text cited); *CTM*, 190.

20 *CTM*, 387; *MSB*, 519.

21 See Reinhard Schwarz, *Die apokalyptische Theologie Thomas Müntzers und der Taboriten* (Tübingen: C. B. Mohr, 1977).

22 *CTM*, 362; *MSB*, 495.

23 *CTM*, 360; *MSB*, 494.

24 *CTM*, 151; *MSB*, 463, 19–22.

25 *CTM*, 151; *MSB*, 463.

26 *CTM*, 335; *MSB*, 329.

27 *CTM*, 250; *MSB*, 261, 19f.

28 For these and numerous other documents and accounts of the Peasants' War, see Tom Scott and Bob Scribner, eds. and trans., *The German Peasants' War: A History in Documents* (Atlantic Highlands: Humanities Press International, 1991); see also Gottfried Seebass, *Artikelbrief, Bundesordnung und Verfassungsentwurf. Studien zu drei zentralen Dokumenten des südwestdeutschen Bauernkrieges* (Heidelberg: Winter, 1988).

29 *CTM*, 142; *MSB*, 455.

30 *CTM*, 437: "All things are to be held in common."

31 *CTM*, 160; *MSB*, 473.

Bibliography

Primary Sources

Franz, Günther, ed., assisted by Paul Kirn, *Thomas Müntzer, Schriften und Briefe*, Kritische Gesamtausgabe, Gütersloh: Gerd Mohn, 1968.

Matheson, Peter, trans. and ed., *The Collected Works of Thomas Müntzer*, Edinburgh: T. & T. Clark, 1988. Includes references to other English translations.

Secondary Sources

Bräuer, Siegfried and Helmar Junghans, eds., *Der Theologe Thomas Müntzer: Untersuchungen zu seiner Entwicklung und Lehre*, Berlin: Evangelische Verlagsanstalt, 1989.

Bubenheimer, Ulrich, "Thomas Müntzer," in *OER* 3:99–102.

Goertz, Hans-Jürgen, *Thomas Müntzer: Apocalyptic Mystic and Revolutionary*, Edinburgh: T. & T. Clark, 1993.

Lohse, Bernhard, *Thomas Müntzer in neuer Sicht: Müntzer im Licht der neueren Forschung und die Frage nach dem Ansatz seiner Theologie*, Göttingen: Vandenhoeck & Ruprecht, 1991.

Scott, Tom, *Thomas Müntzer: Theology and Revolution in the German Reformation*, New York: St. Martin's Press, 1989.

Seebass, Gottfried, "Thomas Müntzer" in *TRE* 23:414–36. Exhaustive multilingual bibliography.

——, "Reich Gottes und Apokalyptik bei Thomas Müntzer," *LuJ* 58 (1991), 75–99.

Caspar von Schwenkfeld (1489–1561)

chapter 24

André Séguenny

Caspar von Schwenckfeld was among those laity who quickly embraced Lutheran ideas. This Silesian nobleman, born in 1489 at Ossig, a village in the vicinity of Liegnitz (present-day Legnica), was the author of a theological proposition that very forcefully marked the history of sixteenth-century Protestantism. After attending one of the Latin schools, probably at Liegnitz, he continued his studies for two or three years at the University of Cologne and at the University of Frankfurt on the Oder. His studies probably focussed on classical literature, but he never received a degree. However, the knowledge of literature, canon law, and church history that is evident in his writings testifies to the astonishing breadth of his erudition.

Schwenckfeld entered the service of the prince of Münsterberg-Oels, and then that of Georg de Brieg, where he remained until 1518; he then became counselor to the court of Prince Friedrich II of Liegnitz. He left that service in 1523 owing to hearing problems. He retired to his estate in Ossig, where he devoted himself to promulgating his religious ideas which were, without any doubt, initially instigated by the positions of Martin Luther.

His first steps in the search for a way that could lead people to authentic living faith were characterized, as may be seen in his letter to the bishop of Breslau, Jakob von Salza, not so much by rejection of the Roman Catholic Church as by his hope of promoting a true Christian piety in the heart of that Church. This was an attitude that Luther had once shared with the Christian humanists, in particular with Erasmus, but which he had soon abandoned. Thus, this letter, the first public expression of Schwenckfeld's position, conveyed a humanistic reforming tendency that believed in a possible reform within the church.

It is well known that Erasmus, along with Luther, was one of the most read authors in Silesia. Schwenckfeld certainly knew the humanist's writings very well since he discussed them with Luther during his visit to Wittenberg at the end of 1525,[1] when Luther's passionate response to Erasmus's tract on free will (1524) was already in press.

From Schwenckfeld's account of that conversation, they probably did not discuss the freedom of the will; their meeting was devoted to the sacrament of the Lord's Supper. Thus it is possible that Schwenckfeld did not yet know Luther's categorically negative response concerning free will that later became essential in Schwenckfeldian soteriology. Schwenckfeld's Erasmian attitude is nevertheless apparent in his conception of the sacrament.[2] Moreover his whole perception concerning piety and religious reform appears to reflect the ideas of Erasmus's *Enchiridion*, a book that was widely read in Silesia[3] and which emphasized above all the necessity of the moral renewal of humankind and not that of the reform of the church.

Now the postulate of converting the person, and not only seeking to justify his or her condition as sinner as Luther wanted, became the center of Schwenckfeld's work. In his letter to the bishop of Breslau, he stressed the necessity of letting the Scriptures speak "without any human addition." He considered this the primary obligation of the bishop and his clergy. He saw the source of the peoples' moral decline in the ignorance of the clergy and lack of biblical education. Of course, one may see in this critique the repetition of one of the most important Lutheran demands, but since Schwenckfeld did not present the Scriptures as the source of faith, we are inclined to see once again an Erasmian postulate and not that of *sola scriptura*. Let us also add that in this letter to the bishop, Schwenckfeld opposed being classed as a Lutheran; he presented himself as simply a Christian and nothing else.

All of Schwenckfeld's declarations taken literally have the air of belonging to the programme of the Wittenberg Reformer, however it was still a matter of the transformation of the person and not the pardon of his or her nature as sinner. The letter in question expresses a faith that, far from all dogmatic considerations, desired simply to be worthy of approaching God by the knowledge and imitation of Christ. It was a matter of faith whose source, according to the believer, is the grace of God, but it is evident that it concerns a grace merited and desired by the believer. Put another way, at the source of faith one recognizes already the will and the effort of the person to change and transform his or her nature. This conviction constitutes the foundation of Schwenckfeld's entire thought. It takes first place in his ideas concerning the Sacrament of the Lord's Supper which, in the case of Judas indicates the inefficacy of changing the nature of an evil person.

Not seeing the hoped-for improvement that the Lutheran Reformation would properly have to contribute, Schwenckfeld thought at that time that the reason for this state of affairs is that the people wrongly interpret Lutheran principles such as justification by faith, the bondage of the will, the impossibility of achieving the commandments of God, the value of good works in the work of salvation, and, finally, justification obtained by grace of the sacrifice of Christ.[4] Of course it must generally be admitted that the wrong interpretation of these principles further aggravated the crisis of piety and morality, and it is, according to Schwenckfeld, contrary to the intentions of the Reformer. Schwenckfeld therefore resumed analysis of these arguments, trying in a nevertheless Erasmian spirit to draw out a positive meaning. At first he supported the soundness of the theses to the extent they are formulated, by indicating at the same time the necessity of an interpretation. It is thus true that faith alone justifies, but genuine faith always proves itself by moral change and by its works. It is true that the natural human will spontaneously incline toward evil, but nevertheless it is, in principle, free. Yet this freedom, even if it can be partially regained by persons, should never be considered otherwise than as given by God. It is equally true that human works have no salvatory value in themselves, nevertheless there is no authentic faith without them; thus the accomplishing of works must be seen as the act of God and not as one's own.

If Schwenckfeld accepted the first four theses in their literal wording – though he considered it necessary to accompany them with a commentary – he did not deal this way with the fifth thesis that speaks of justification thanks to the sacrifice of Christ. Schwenckfeld opposed the idea of a passive justification. He affirmed that Christ opened the way of our salvation, but in order to attain salvation we must enter the way that Christ traveled, bearing as he did, our cross. "If we are to be conformed to God, we must first be conformed to Christ, otherwise we clearly come to nothing."[5] To follow the way of Christ means to embrace Christ, to make his life ours, to live in his teaching, but also to endure his anguish and suffering. *Otherwise one will amount to nothing.* According to Schwenckfeld, it is not true that the cross covers our sins; we must see there a proclamation that henceforth it is possible to be saved. The cross is also a call and a challenge which must improve us, but also an assurance that the victory over the flesh is possible; that death may be conquered if only we will to enter the combat.

Schwenckfeld's demand to commit oneself to follow Christ is identical to Erasmus's demand to enter the school of Christ that he had formulated in his *Enchiridion*. Indeed, the idea that Schwenckfeld wanted to transmit to his reader is that of Erasmus: "It is Christ alone who establishes the person."[6] We shall see that all of Schwenckfeld's theological and later pastoral activities were dedicated to show the unconditionality of this thesis. The transformation of the person into the Second Adam, into the spiritual person, will henceforward be the principle subject of Schwenckfeld's reflections. The shift of accent in relation to Lutheranism is significant. Luther's fundamental thesis that the Christian is righteous and sinner at the same time (*simul iustus et peccator*) is completely alien to the intentions of Schwenckfeld. He appears to resume the principle theme of classical Renaissance anthropology, which was to restore dignity to persons and to rehabilitate the power of personal action, in contrast to Luther's desire to justify the person as he or she is. The person without sin is the ultimate object of Schwenckfeld's faith. Therefore we observe that in combating the corruption of the Roman Church, Schwenckfeld retained the anthropological principles which since the Fathers, the Scholastics, and the humanists had animated the religious tradition that Luther himself opposed. Thus Schwenckfeld's attitude at the beginning of his theological career corresponded exactly to that of the humanist Christians.

Schwenckfeld's attitude is apparent in his way of considering the natural person, whom he considered offhand as naturally evil and incapable of proceeding by himself to change his nature. It is true that this judgment thus formulated corresponds exactly to the Lutheran thesis concerning human nature. Schwenckfeld himself also, similarly to Luther, puts the accent on the necessity of grace. However, contrary to Luther, he would no less acknowledge the necessity of the person's first movement, and he required from the person an effort of the will in order for this grace to be given to him or her. Thus everything depends upon God, but nothing can occur without human effort; this is Schwenckfeld's motto.

Schwenckfeld's reflection on the possibility of changing human nature led him to rethink the nature of the Sacrament of the Lord's Supper. The example of Judas constituted for him the proof that the bread that Christ broke and gave to his disciples (Matt. 26:26–8; Luke 22:15–20; Mark 14:22–5) was not the flesh spoken of in John 6:54: "Those who eat my flesh and drink my blood have eternal life." Consequently, Schwenckfeld rejected all the Catholic and Lutheran theories which postulated the real presence of the body of Christ in the bread and wine of the Mass or the service of worship.

Schwenckfeld retained the literal validity of John 6:54 and associated it with verse 58: "This is the bread that came down from heaven, not like that which your ancestors ate, and they died. But the one who eats this bread will live forever." He concluded the real but spiritual existence of the flesh of Christ that is thus accessible, but solely in the act of faith. The physical eating of the bread of the Mass is useless; at most it may aid in revivifying the memory of Christ's sacrifice, which is as much to say as that it has no salvatory signification. There is the great danger therefore that those who practiced communion as proposed by the Catholics and the Lutherans, and who do not have faith and have not changed their lives, may believe they are saved.

Thanks to the interpretation of Valentin Crautwald, an erudite canonist and friend of Schwenckfeld, Schwenckfeld was successful in demonstrating that the words of Christ, "this is my flesh," did not designate the material bread broken by Christ, but intended to define the flesh of Christ as the bread without which life eternal is impossible (John 6:58).

Schwenckfeld presented his conclusions to Luther, who categorically rejected them. Henceforth it was clear that their respective views of faith were incompatible. In addition to theology, their understandings of the social role of the church differed. The social realism of the Reformers, not only Luther but also Bucer and Calvin, compelled them to organize a new church that would be able to impose discipline upon people inclined to neglect social and ethical obligations, and easily influenced by very dangerous social claims. In contrast, Schwenckfeld's proposition was addressed to the individual and neglected the person's social rootage. He spoke of the interiority of faith, ignoring the role that may be played by the social environment. It was a very elitist vision, and thus it is not surprising that it was a social as well as moral elite who adhered to Schwenckfeld's ideas.

This may perhaps explain a part of the reason for the constant animosity of the Protestant clergy toward Schwenckfeld. Indeed, Bucer and Frecht, as well as the Swiss theologians, fiercely battled Schwenckfeld and sought to warn the town councils of southern Germany against him when he journeyed there after leaving his native Silesia. The clergy very quickly reported the danger that Schwenckfeld's ideas represented to their efforts to reconstruct the institutional church on new foundations, having as much power, if not more, than the old church. Finally, Schwenckfeld's doctrine was, in the manner of a Roman Catholic trial, solemnly condemned during a meeting of the clergy at Schmalkald in 1540. Pursued by the Catholic authorities of the Empire, hounded everywhere by the Protestants, Schwenckfeld continued to write and to teach hidden in the homes of friends, nobility or patricians in the cities of South Germany. He died in Augsburg in 1561.

Schwenckfeld left a considerable body of work, as may be seen by the 19 volumes edited in the twentieth century (1907–61) by the American Schwenckfelders. The principle subject of his reflections was always the same: the definition of faith as an interior state that may and must lead the person to a transformation not only of the person's conscience but also body, soul, and flesh. Here is what Schwenckfeld affirmed in 1532:

> If the first Adam, created by the plan of the Creator by his Word was a natural man, upright and perfect, nevertheless he was not created as he shall be only by the grace of God. He has been created in order to manifest the image of God and in order to be like Him, but he has not been the image and parable of God. The breath or the scent of the divine life is breathed into him, but not the life itself. He is destined to eternal glory and divine justification, but he has not yet become this eternal glory nor this righteousness nor this perfection. He is dust and earth; he is the earthly sketch of the Father and a beginning work of God, and not yet a heavenly work. In brief, he is before God a figure and a rough outline (*figurlich, bildlicher mensch*) of the other man, the heavenly and true incarnation of God, the Christ. It is by Him that Adam, created naked, and all other men shall be clothed, molded, beatified, divinized, and introduced to divine glory.[7]

The work of creation has only begun; it shall be individually completed in each separate person, and thanks to Christ, "the first Adam was not created equal to God; he shall approach him only by Christ and his grace."[8]

The problem of the efficacy of the Lord's Supper, the first question posed earlier by Schwenckfeld, he now articulated as that of the continuation of the creation and the role of Christ in accomplishing it. Schwenckfeld did not consider the natural person as a finished being; for the man to become the Man it is necessary that the fleshly man be transformed into the spiritual man, and that signified substantial transformation of his being into that which the Christ possessed. "If we are to be conformed to God, then we must first be conformed to Christ."[9]

But in order better to define this ontological transformation of the person, Schwenckfeld was obliged to brood over the problem of the flesh of Christ, and to compare it to the natural flesh of man.

The idea of the celestial flesh and of the transformation of the natural flesh is of biblical origin.[10] It was also suggested by Luther who, already in 1528, remarked that the body of Christ is glorified: "Christ's body has a far higher, supernatural existence, since he is one person with God."[11]

Nevertheless, Luther did not think that this body would be able to belong to Jesus, the man who lived on earth. This provoked major difficulty in explaining the unity of the two natures of Christ. Luther proposed the theory of the sharing of natures [*comunicatio idiomatum*] but, to tell the truth, "he scarcely asks the question about the real humanity of Christ, nor about the way in which this humanity is included in the work of redemption."[12]

It was otherwise for Schwenckfeld, according to whom there was no substantial difference – in the ontological sense – between the Christ on earth and the glorified Christ, since being man he was God. Schwenckfeld did not want to admit the idea of two Christs, which Luther, in spite of all his precautions, left implied. The Christ before the Passion and the glorious Christ, the humiliated Christ and the Christ of the Trinity, is always the same in his divinity and in his humanity. And his body, presently glorified, is substantially the same as when was living. Is it, however, the body of natural man?

For Schwenckfeld, the difference between the natural man and Jesus was evident. The former, we recall, is the rough shape made by God; it is but a creature. The former possessed a certain resemblance, but it did not possess the perfection of the image. Made of matter, it is condemned to carry the imprint. The image, however, proceeded directly from God, without any mediation, so it was thus engendered and not made, a difference that Schwenckfeld reproached Luther for ignoring. Jesus Christ was not made in a fleshly act, he was engendered in an act by which the Word became a corporal reality. The body of Christ is the bearer of the Spirit of his Father. And to consider him as a natural and earthly body, even like that which is on the way of glorification, as is the case for the body of the righteous person, does not clarify the mystery of the identity of Christ before and after the Resurrection.

Schwenckfeld was conscious that being the body of a man, the body of Jesus was not at all made the same as that of the earthly man. His body represented the place of encountering the divine with the human, because his engenderment was spiritual and his conception was that of faith. In setting forth evidence of this mode of conception of Christ – never contested by the theologians of the different confessions (except by the anti-Trinitarians) – Schwenckfeld drew conclusions from faith that were original and astonishing for their clarity. He affirmed that the difference is that of the conception which involves the difference of the essence and of the quality of the body. The body of Christ engendered by the Father is a divine body, this body is not that of a creature, although his real existence had its support in the flesh of Mary. Thus, "his body (is) not a cursed flesh, but a blessed flesh."[13]

Human nature becomes clear by the mode of conception; in the case of Jesus of Nazareth it is God himself who engendered him. His nature is therefore divine and the flesh that is adjoining is equally so, and yet it is human.[14] It is the true flesh of a man, but it is not that of sin and of the old man. "And although it is identical to that of the latter, it is flesh without sin, the flesh of the new man. . . ."[15]

The body of Christ was from his birth a new flesh, immaculate, flesh of the Spirit, of grace and of truth,[16] although it was given by Mary.

It is a human flesh that protects, says Schwenckfeld, "the truth of the flesh of man,"[17] but it is the fulfillment of it; it is a flesh of the state of perfection. Nevertheless, although the body of Christ may be of divine origin it is not completely free of certain natural difficulties, but not essentials. The earthly existence of Christ required that his body possess some elements which rendered possible his earthly existence. It was a true human body, "fleshly, mortal, suffering,"[18] but marked by the seal of divine paternity. Thus Christ was truly the Son of God according to his two natures, though his flesh did not yet possess final perfection (Lk. 2: [52] *crescebat puer*...; "And Jesus increased in wisdom ... and in divine and human favor") which made him the seed of salvation for humanity, manifesting that the ultimate reason of the incarnation of the Word was the glorification of man in his soul but also in his body.

It is only at the moment of his death, at the end of his earthly itinerary that the glorious body of Christ will be definitively liberated from its physical element and freed from its spatial dimensions. His body will then turn to an infinite clarity.[19]

As if he feared the reproaches that he in fact postulated the dissolution of the human flesh of Christ, Schwenckfeld at once specified that the body became a pure transparency, possessing nevertheless a face and human limbs, but of such a nature that "no painter can paint them, no sculptor can sculpt them." The Christ remains always the same, that is, a man, but at the same time he is an Other, namely the New Man.[20]

Schwenckfeld warned his reader that no example would know how to illustrate in satisfactory manner the mystery of the spiritual body of Christ, but all the same he provides one. He thus evokes the metamorphosis of a simple block of wood into a statue, where the wood acquires "a new form, a new essence, a new genre."[21]

The substance of the wood remains identical, but the sculptor's talented hand has conferred on it a new quality, totally different from its prior state. This example also indicates that matter in itself is morally neutral; it becomes evil or good according to the principle the person imposes on it. Matter docilely submits to the determination of the human will. Thus the spiritual renewal of the person is able to spiritualize the matter; and the matter then becomes the body of the Spirit. Thus matter continues to exist in reality, but in so far as spiritual reality. Christ therefore, perfectly man and perfectly God, is a faithful image of his Father.

Schwenckfeld did not conceal the possibility that God could have given to the Christ-Word a perfectly glorious flesh from the first day of his earthly existence. This possibility is suggested by the Transfiguration (Mt. 17:2). However, God decided otherwise in choosing to unite the Transfiguration to suffering and death. Thus when Schwenckfeld affirmed that the properties of the body of Christ evolved and that that evolution was accomplished by and on the cross, he included that evolution in the logic of the continuing creation.

Jesus, as witnessed by his prayer (John 17:5), was conscious of the process of the complete spiritualization of his body.[22] He knew with certitude that his body still had to submit to a transformation and that his two natures did not yet possess the same degree of perfection. But it concerned only one transformation. His body will always preserve its ontological specificity of the human body, even if it is different from that whose carnal state is the principal. Thus Schwenckfeld wrote that the human nature of Christ "is neither destroyed nor absorbed in God, but the New Adam is still today a true man in a divine and celestial being."[23]

The spiritualization of the body of Christ permits him to be really present in the heart of the Trinity. It is a very important ascertainment, and for two reasons. The first is that the natural man, conscious in the faith of the identity of the nature of his flesh with that of Christ, can feel comforted since that spiritualization is also within his reach. The second is that the creature transformed in the New Man participates nonetheless, by the grace of Christ, in the mystery of the Trinity. That signifies not only the most complete identity between the Creator and his work, but at the same time the acceptance, therefore, the justification of the person.

Only the human nature of Christ, not that of the natural man, carries in it the seed of his spiritualization. For that spiritualization to be realized in the earthly man, it is necessary that he lose his character of a creature made from dust. He must be reborn anew; that must be accomplished by a spiritual act, therefore in and by faith. His body must change into the spiritual body, that of Christ. That is possible thanks to the spiritual body of Christ, who, like a ray of the sun lights up and transforms all things, enlightens the whole body. This is the way that the celestial body of Christ is given to the believer.[24] Before, during his earthly life, "Jesus was not able to sanctify and beatify anyone until his body attained celestial and divine being."[25]

The natural man must receive this light from Christ, but nevertheless there is in the earthly body something that makes it impossible. "Adam," Schwenckfeld wrote, "did not have a flesh of sin, but a flesh that could have sinned, that is, a flesh to which sin could have attached itself."[26] Therefore in turning away from God, he has chosen "the animal and carnal life . . . a hopeless life . . . a life without God against the law of nature and against all that reason can prescribe. . . ."[27]

And Schwenckfeld avers: "In Adam sin had entirely corrupted and destroyed all his flesh. It had made us renegades, very poor, sick, and bestial men. It has brought us curse, shame, infamy, and misery. It has hidden God and all that is divine from us."[28] All men are heirs of Adam, and accepting the same principle of life, they are all sinners.[29]

However, free will has remained. It is the will to choose sin – a choice, from another perspective, without an alternative, ineluctable since one has rejected the Spirit. Schwenckfeld also recognized the existence of the powerful inclination to evil and never denied the deplorable effect of original sin. He observed that same idea in all its dimensions of the human tragedy, but at the same time he did not consider it as an inherited punishment passed on from generation to generation. It is a state of illness, he said, but that illness is freely accepted by each person individually. According to him, it is possible to oppose it either by reason or by the grace of God.[30] Schwenckfeld also affirmed that in the heart of the natural man there was enough of things inscribed and innate for a measure of discerning good from evil and for knowing – at least to a certain point – that he must do good rather than evil, and this knowledge is known as the natural law.[31] And Schwenckfeld stressed with all his power the rule of the old Law. He knew that man cannot fulfill it, but as he wrote in his first interpretation of Lutheran principles, the Law "awakens in us the consciousness of sin, that of our weakness and our sickness."[32] This Law guides us toward the work of Christ and allows his Spirit to be born again.

One would not be mistaken if one concluded that the analysis of the old man, the man of sin, led Schwenckfeld to conclusions radically opposed to those of Luther. He emphasized the role of man for his salvation in proposing, or at least not excluding, a collaboration between God and man; and finally, he affirmed that man must be transformed and not only pardoned as Luther intended. Like Erasmus, Schwenckfeld himself also sought to discover a difficult equilibrium between the grace of God and the free will of man; he did not want to renounce one or the other.

Although the "invitation" to salvation comes from God, it is nevertheless man who calls it forth thanks to the recognition of his condition as sinner and of his desire to change. He must, however, make himself worthy of this invitation beforehand. Schwenckfeld's reasoning always followed from his inner logic: the natural man was an incomplete work of God; but he was not rejected by Him, and the process of creation is not finished. But this continuation of creation demands, in this arena, a consent on the part of the creature. Man can be content with his condition of being incomplete, which Luther considered as definitive, but he can also submit himself to the transforming action of God.

This transformation cannot be defined as the act of creation, since the created being is already there. It concerns the creation since it is the Creator who breathes into it its spirit, the Spirit of God. The condition of the creature as an alienated object changes, and becomes the real expression of the Spirit in which God can be recognized as being Himself. Thus the identity between the Creator, his idea, and the spiritual man is realized. The Word incarnate in Christ now has incarnated itself in man, thus leading him to spiritualization.

Once again, we have here to do with a process and not an act. Schwenckfeld spoke of the necessity of entering the School of Christ, a concept that he surely borrowed from Erasmus's *Enchiridion*. The symbol of this School is the cross. Indeed, there was no other path to God, Schwenckfeld wrote, than that marked by "the cross and suffering, the suffocation of the passion, the contempt of the world, and the same death in the flesh."[33]

The cross is the instrument by which matter is definitively transformed and loses its "materialness." It is like the knife of the sculptor of which Schwenckfeld spoke in relation to the transformation of wood, and which removes all the dross without affecting the substance. The cross is a synonym of suffering.

If the cross represents the decisive moment in the process of the transformation of the carnal body into a spiritual one, and thus becomes indispensable for the glorification of man, it did not change Jesus into God, since he always was God, as Schwenckfeld stressed with reference to Hebrews 5:5 and Luke 1:35.[34] Likewise, it does not transform the natural man into the spiritual man, since that is the work of Christ alone. The action of the cross is limited to a victory over the carnal, to the suppression of the exterior carnality of human nature that hinders the spiritual from asserting itself, just as a seed is impeded by its husk. It is necessary for that work of creation to be able to pass to another stage, that of engenderment. It is also the expression of the love God bears to his creation, love that includes in itself suffering and death.

If the cross interrupts the natural life, it opens at the same time, as Schwenckfeld emphasized, the door to a new existence. The body of the glorified Christ is able now to open to the body of man, to illumine it by his translucent divine humanity. And man starting on the path of Christ, following his steps on the way to the cross, approaches Him more and more, letting himself be embraced by Him.

It is clear for Schwenckfeld that the transformation of man into conformity to Christ (*Christusformig*) results from an individual and direct relationship between the person and Christ. The celestial body of Christ is not accessible except by faith; it is not bound to anything material, even if it might be the bread of the Sacrament. "In heaven, at the side of the Father, and nowhere else, it is necessary that true faith seeks Jesus Christ; our life and blessedness is without external mediation. . . ."[35]

Faith alone and nothing else constitutes the truth of the relationship between God and the person. But we should not be mistaken about this. Schwenckfeldian "faith alone" cannot be understood in the Lutheran sense because it derives from another comprehension of the creation, and from another, this time positive, appreciation of human effort. For Schwenckfeld, "faith alone" signified the refusal of every institutional and sacramental mediation. The only mediator is the glorified Christ, but not as the one who alone may be able to appease the wrath of God and obtain the pardon of humankind's sins, as Luther affirmed, but He is the mediator because He alone can conquer the carnal.

If the rejection of the ecclesiastical institution, Catholic or Protestant, was un-equivocal, that is because Schwenckfeld knew that their pretension to be in exclusive possession of the means of salvation was illusory. On the other hand, if the church, Catholic or Protestant, renounced that pretension, its preaching could be useful for the people and its sacraments could offer an opportunity to remember Christ and his life. But in the period of Schwenckeld's activity, his writings were dominated by a most profound distrust of the church.

Schwenckfeld always sought support for his reasoning in the Bible. Only it was not the Bible that was the source of his questioning. He searched there for the answer, but it was he himself who posed the question. It was his vision of piety and the righteous man which guided him to the Bible and that showed him the way leading to Christ. Thus we also note, next to the difference in the interpretation of the principle of *sola fides*, another acceptance of the Lutheran principle, *sola scriptura*. For Luther, Scripture was the unique source of faith and the promise of pardon. Not so for Schwenckfeld. According to Schwenckfeld, Scripture can and must open the horizon toward that which faith has called, but it is God alone who gives that faith. Scripture comforts the person in his or her quest for faith, but it is not the source. It is the same with the third Lutheran principle, *solus Christus*. According to Luther, Christ is the gift of God offered to humankind, a gift that is accounted for by the love and mercy of God toward his miserable creature. According to Schwenckfeld, the fact of the incarnation of the Word testifies to the continuity of the creation. The incarnation is conceived as a decisive moment of grace by which "a figure or a rough draft," as Schwenckfeld wrote, can be transformed into a true work of God, a work where divine thought becomes a reality.

The theologians of the Lutheran reform were well aware of the difference between their ideas and those of Schwenckfeld. They expressed their total disagreement in solemnly condemning him (along with another Spiritualist, Sebastian Franck) at Schmalkald in 1540.[36]

If Schwenkfeld differed, notwithstanding a certain verbal resemblance, from the mainstream of the Magisterial Reformation, did he differ from Roman Catholicism? Certainly, especially with regard to ecclesiology and the sacraments. Yet it seems possible to discern a certain community with the endeavors of, especially in the enterprise of the Christian humanists, Erasmus in particular, who were concerned to fill the abyss that separated the Creator from his creature, the abyss that Luther considered impassable. They expressed that concern in their consideration of human nature as essentially good in spite of its degeneracy through Adam's sin, by their recognition of free will, and, in conclusion, by their recognition of the necessity of human effort accompanying grace. The radical difference between these two visions of humankind and God set forth fairly early by Luther and Schwenckfeld may be explained with the disillusioned remark by the latter: "As far as I am concerned, I must confess that today, after having recognized the truth, I preferred to join the papists rather than the Lutherans. . . ."[37]

We consider Schwenckfeldianism as a reprise of Erasmian ideas which, although strongly radicalized, postulate the return to the faith of the early church when piety was expressed not by liturgical action but by moral rectitude. Was it possible in the sixteenth century to realize this model of piety? The Reformers who had a bitter experience with the Peasants' Revolt and the Anabaptist utopia at Münster, and who felt accountable for the moral conduct of the people, considered that society could not function without a strong ecclesiastical organization to guarantee social discipline. That attitude of those responsible for the Reformation provoked a lively protest from the social and moral elite, who themselves did not need to be supervised in their Christian and social life. These elites feared that the new Protestant Church would subjugate all public activity to the power of the clergy, thus superseding civil authority. Thus it is not surprising that the patricians and nobles, at least those who were the readers of Erasmus, greeted enthusiastically the Schwenckfeldianism that stressed human liberty in its activity and its proper responsibility in the work of salvation. They were conscious that the process was wanted, decided, and begun by God, but they knew also that its accomplishment depended upon the person alone. This sense suited not only the aspirations of the aristocracy, but equally that of the patricians of the commercial cities, since it gave them a profound sense of their activities. Yet it must not be forgotten that many of the partisans of Schwenckfeld came from the modest beds of the bourgeoisie; they represented a moral elite.

Schwenckfeldianism, persecuted and hounded by Catholic and Protestant authorities, did not die out. Nevertheless, over the course of centuries, it more and more lost its place in society, becoming limited to small circles which often had a familial character. Nevertheless, Schwenckfeld's writings have been widely known throughout all of Europe, and contributed strongly to the spread of his ideas. Even if it is very difficult to estimate their impact, these ideas may be recognized in many of the religious currents which, in the course of the seventeenth century, proclaimed the development of a personal piety that ignored the existence of the institution. The last Schwenckfeldians of Silesia, the fatherland of Caspar von Schwenckfeld, emigrated to the United States in 1734 to evade persecution. Their community, very active and open, was established in Pennsylvania and, in the course of the last century, undertook the considerable, difficult, and costly task of editing Schwenckfeld's works; a task completed in 1961.

Notes

1 *Corpus Schwenckfeldianorum*, 19 vols. (Leipzig and Pennsburg, PA, 1907–61), 2:281. Cited hereafter as *CS*.

2 See Jacques Chomarat, *Grammaire et Rhétorique chez Erasme* (Paris: Les Belles Lettres, 1981), 1:652 and 695–700, where he shows that, according to Erasmus (*Paraphrases*),

> it [the sacrament] does not concern a real sacrifice nor is the sacrament intended as a sensible and efficacious sign bearing grace, but it is a commemoration and a symbol of multiple meaning. ... Flesh and blood are to be understood in a figurative sense; they designate the doctrine, the teaching of Jesus: "I appoint 'my flesh and blood' my teaching; if you consume it eagerly by faith and it enters the womb of your spirit (*in viscera mentis traiceretis*) it shall give life to your soul and you will be united with me. ..." (Jn. 6:54).

3 See Karol Glombiowski, "Über der Verbreitung der Schriften des Erasmus von Rotterdam in Schlesien im 16. Jahrhundert" in Johannes

Irmscher, ed., *Renaissance und Humanismus in Mittel- und Osteuropa* (Berlin: Akademische Verlag, 1962), 209.

4 *CS* 2:26–103.
5 *CS* 2:81, 24–5.
6 Erasmus, *Opera* (Hildesheim: Olms, 1962), 5: 988A.
7 *CS* 4:646, 7–21.
8 *CS* 4:646: 30–5.
9 *CS* 2:81, 24–5.
10 See I Cor. 15:40–4, but also Mt. 17:2; Mk. 9:2; Lk. 9:29.
11 *Confession Concerning Christ's Supper. WA* 26:335, 9–10; *LW* 37:221.
12 Marc Lienhard, *Luther: Witness to Jesus Christ. Stages and Themes of the Reformer's Christology.* trans. Edwin H. Robertson (Minneapolis: Augsburg, 1982), 298.
13 *CS* 6:237, 15–18.
14 *CS* 6:237, 24–238, 15.
15 *CS* 6:238, 1–2.
16 *CS* 8:762, 22.

17 *CS* 6:243, 34.
18 *CS* 8:762, 23–4.
19 *CS* 6:244, 27.
20 *CS* 6:81, 9–10.
21 *CS* 6:239, 18–19.
22 *CS* 8:784, 7.
23 *CS* 8:776, 16–20.
24 *CS* 8:778, 16.
25 *CS* 8:778, 24–8.
26 *CS* 8:275, 23–35.
27 *CS* 9:832, 30–1.
28 *CS* 6:617, 22–5.
29 *CS* 9:837, 20–2.
30 *CS* 12:571, 25–7.
31 *CS* 7:369, 22–5.
32 *CS* 2:72, 3–5.
33 *CS* 2:47, 22–3.
34 *CS* 8:790, 24.
35 *CS* 2:503, 37–504, 1.
36 *CR* 3, cols. 1985–6.
37 *CS* 3:106 (1528).

Bibliography

Primary Source

Corpus Schwenckfeldianorum, 19 vols., Leipzig and Pennsburg, PA: 1907–61.

Secondary Sources

Erb, Peter, *Schwenckfeld in his Reformation Setting*, Valley Forge, PA, 1978.

——, ed., *Schwenckfeld and Early Schwenckfeldianism*, 2 vols., Pennsburg, PA, 1986.
McLaughlin, R. Emmet, *The Freedom of Spirit, Social Privilege, and Religious Dissent*, Baden-Baden, 1996. Includes a bibliography of works edited in the twentieth century.
Schultz, Gerhard, *Caspar Schwenckfeld von Ossig (1489–1561): Spiritual Interpreter of Christianity, Apostle of the Middle Way, Pioneer in Modern Religious Thought*, Norristown, PA: 1946.

Menno Simons (1496–1561)

Sjouke Voolstra

"A life full of danger," the title of the catalogue and exhibition in the Frisian capital of Leeuwarden commemorating the 500th anniversary of the birth of Menno Simons, conveys how the Frisian reformer and many of his contemporaries experienced the times in which they lived.[1] Menno himself wrote:

> We perceive and experience in our own lives the truth of what was foretold by the prophets, Christ and the apostles about the exceedingly dangerous pressure, the suffering and need, the persecution, the danger, the anguish and false teachings in these latter times – so dangerous and so dreadful that God must shorten these days if we are not to be lost.[2]

When this apocalyptic lamentation appeared, it was four years since Menno had exchanged his comfortable life as a well-paid parish priest for the uncertain existence of a persecuted dissenter in exile. From January 1536 to the spring of 1544, he and his family found refuge in the province of Groningen and the county of East Friesland, from where he regularly risked his life to visit Friesland and Holland. After a disputation with Johannes à Lasco in Emden, he found a new field for his missionary activities from the spring of 1544 to the spring of 1547 in the Cologne diocese of the reformist bishop, Hermann von Wied. When the tolerant bishop was replaced by the strict Catholic, Adolf von Schaumberg, in February 1547, Menno Simons sought refuge in the Hanseatic towns of Lübeck and Wismar on the Baltic Sea. These towns were the bases for his travels until November 1554, when he had to leave the town of Wismar after a disputation with Martin Micron. His last refuge was on the estate of the nobleman Bartholomeus von Ahlefeldt, lord of Oldesloe. He also set up a printing shop there for his own works. After 22 years of travelling and hardship, he died in Wüstenfeld on Friday January 13, 1561, at the age of 66. He was buried in his cabbage garden.

His successors had great respect for this life of deprivation. The martyr Valerius Schoolmeester, awaiting his own sentence of death in the prison of Brouwershaven in January 1568, wrote: "I have heard it said that the pious Menno left very little and great poverty after his death. I would prefer to hear that than that he had left one or two hundred guilders, or house, or land to his children. It bears good witness to him, with which he puts many others to shame."[3]

Even Menno's opponents did not find much fault with his life. In fact, general opinion concerning the Anabaptists was that they led exemplary lives, but unfortunately cherished strange ideas on the grounds of their primitive interpretation of the Bible. Thus Albert Hardenberg wrote to his friend Melanchthon:

> Anyone who has had only stupid teachers can scarcely teach with understanding. Those who fled the monasteries without learning and without correct judgment, or those who are merely self-taught have done much damage to the church. Such a one is a certain Menno Simons, whom I had known as a priest in the country. After he had read seditious books without discrimination and had taken the Holy Scriptures into his hands without judgment and formal education, he caused such harm among the Frisians, Belgians, Dutch, Menapiers, Saxons and Cymarians, even throughout Germany, Gaul and Great Britain and all the surrounding countries that posterity has not sufficient tears to weep on this account.[4]

The Humanist Hardenberg, himself suspected of reformist ideas, had been in hiding in his mother monastery in Aduard since 1540, after his studies in Louvain. He preached and taught in the surrounding area, the west district of the province of Groningen. Menno Simons had taken refuge in that same area after leaving his Friesland parish of Witmarsum on January 12, 1536, with his wife Gertrude, whom he had married after relinquishing his priesthood. Here, in comparative safety, Menno devoted himself to studying the Bible and preparing his first writings for printing. This area, however, also served as the first operational basis for his journeys to Holland, Friesland, and East Friesland, where he preached and baptized; a right conferred on him when he was ordained elder or bishop by Obbe Philips in the city of Groningen in the winter of 1536–7.

The paths of Hardenberg and Menno crossed again later. Hardenberg joined the staff of Archbishop von Wied after leaving the monastery, and Menno Simons too chose domicile in von Wied's diocese from the spring of 1544 to 1547, accompanied by his fellow elder, Dirk Philips. In this period, Hardenberg and Johannes à Lasco drafted the written refutation of Menno Simons's teachings on the incarnation of Christ. They also frustrated Menno Simons's missionary activities, by preventing him from a disputation with the ministers in Bonn.[5]

Hardenberg's response to Menno Simons reveals knowledge of his ideas and activities. His reproach of Menno for a lack of formal education reveals the character of this humanist-educated theologian. Furthermore, the radicalism of Menno's plans for reform, with the inherent danger of a split in society and loss of government support, did not agree with his own reformational humanist objective of gradually changing the church from the inside.

Hardenberg's criticism raises the following three questions: (1) What knowledge did the "self-taught" Menno have at his disposal? (2) What were the intentions of his reform programme? (3) What problems did he encounter in its implementation?

How did the self-taught Menno Simons acquire his knowledge? Menno was ordained as a priest in the spring of 1524 and accepted a vicarship in Pingjum, the

Frisian village of his father. According to Menno himself, it was here that he commenced his independent study of the Bible two years later, prompted by his growing doubts concerning the miracle of the Mass.[6] These doubts must have been nourished by the spiritual interpretation of the Eucharist, which was strongly gaining in popularity in reformational humanist circles in the Low Countries in those years. Following Wessel Gansfort, Cornelis Hoen had already made a critical comparison between official ideas on the physical presence of Christ in the bread and wine, the consecrated elements of the Lord's Supper, and the more spiritual interpretation in John 3:36 and 6:54. Hinne Rode had been dismissed from his position as rector of the Hieronymus school in Utrecht in 1522, as a result of his rejection of the doctrine of transubstantiation. On Hoen's instructions, he had tried in vain to win Luther over to this anti-sacramentalist interpretation, but he had been more successful with the Swiss Reformers Oecolampadius and Zwingli. Through their writings, the symbolic interpretation of the Lord's Supper became widespread, particularly in East Friesland, where Hoen was to become a minister in Norden in 1527. Menno himself provides no definite answer on how new ideas of this kind reached him. It is obvious that they were general knowledge. In 1525, the whole of Holland and Friesland knew of Rode's ideas, which were the subject of much discussion in many a sitting room, presbytery, and inn.

Menno probably worked in the church before his ordination as a priest, pending a vacancy in his native region. It was not unusual for someone to assist a parish priest during worship and with schoolteaching, in preparation for the priesthood. Menno did not become a priest until he was 28 years of age, while the official age for the priesthood was 23, and often even younger in practice. Training for the priesthood was not organized before the Council of Trent and so it is not clear where Menno received his training and what the quality of that training was. The quality of the Roman Catholic clergy has wrongly been underestimated, due to reformational anticlerical polemics. Around 1500, almost half of the clergy in prosperous Friesland had attended a university, although Menno did not belong to this half.[7] It would appear most likely that he received the knowledge necessary for pastoral duties from an educated priest, who was usually prepared to give such teaching for payment. It is less probable that he attended a monastery school, since these generally only trained members of their own orders. Despite this non-academic education, however, Menno betrays a respectable knowledge of a humanist-flavored Latin in his writings, which he likes to display in Latin marginalia and prologues in his works.

Erasmus was not unknown to Menno, and he shows a certain knowledge of the pedagogical and exegetical works of "that extremely wise and very well-educated Erasmus" in his own works from the start.[8] Menno's theology therefore shows implicit humanist traits, with its emphasis on will above intellect, the moral interpretation of the Bible, and the dichotomy of flesh and spirit. We find few traces of other humanistic features, however, such as attention to style as a means to convince and the presentation of heathen models of morality. After all, these last characteristics are at loggerheads with Menno's rigid wielding of the principle of *sola scriptura* and with his aim to implement bible texts in the most literal and direct manner possible, and so with common sense, instead of "with human wisdom, dialectics or rhetoric."[9]

According to Hardenberg, Menno read the Bible without judgment and formal education. It is uncertain which editions of the Bible Menno used, but he probably commenced his biblical studies in 1524 with a Low German translation based on Erasmus's critical publication of the New Testament. It is also possible that he later used other High German translations printed in Zurich and Strasbourg, as well as that of Castellio. It is difficult to conclude from his manner of quoting from the Bible, which translations he had at his disposal. There is much to be said for the theory that he frequently made his own translations from the Vulgate, possibly with the aid of the Cologne translation of the Vulgate published by Jacobus Liesveldt in Antwerp in 1526. The Erasmus translation definitely continued to serve Menno as an authoritative source, however.[10]

Hardenberg rightly remarks that Menno Simons did not only address himself to Holy Scripture without judgment and formal education, but also that he had read "seditious books without discrimination." This begs the question which literature of a reformatory persuasion – seditious or not – helped to define Menno's thinking. Nowhere does he mention book titles, although he does name authors. In his early writings, he made "the living and sanctifying word of the holy gospel of Jesus Christ" the exclusive fundament of his preaching. He believes that the divine authority of the Scriptures puts the opinions of influential authors like Augustine, Erasmus, Luther, Hoffman, Bucer, and Bullinger into perspective.[11] We can deduce from his autobiographical notes that during his time as vicar of Pingjum (March 1524 to early 1533), Menno studied the ideas on baptism held by the church fathers and by Luther, Bucer, and Bullinger,[12] besides consulting the Reformers in Nördlingen.[13] Every priest acquired some knowledge of patristic literature in the course of his training, while current reformational writings from Germany were to be had from travelling book salesmen in Friesland. The book chests of Menno's predecessor in Witmarsum were forced by the procurator general of the court of Friesland in 1527 and were found to contain works by Luther and others.

Luther was unquestionably the most important source of inspiration for reformational thoughts in the Low Countries in the 1530s. The Dutch reformational humanists were influenced by him and the majority of the population of Holland, Zeeland, and Flanders knew of Luther's teachings in 1525. Only his doctrine on the Lord's Supper was not favorably received in the northern part of the Low Countries, where the spiritual interpretation of the Lord's Supper had already become too generally accepted. What the Anabaptists (Menno included) particularly disliked in Luther was that his emphasis on Christian freedom could be used to justify lax morals.

Menno says that Luther helped him to overcome his fears that the believer would forfeit salvation if he did not follow the old customs of the church, even though these were not based on the Bible.[14] Dissociation from "human injunctions" was generally held to be the core of Luther's theology.[15] At the very time of Menno's awakening reformational consciousness, Luther was an authority for him. Menno voices great respect for "the learned man through whom God worked so powerfully in the beginning."[16] He feels himself to be "a small mosquito in comparison to this elephant."[17]

It is not clear which of Luther's writings Menno read at first hand.[18] The wealth of Luther quotations in Franck's *Chronica* may have served as his most important source.[19] Menno is said to have seen only one short work, *Avoiding the Doctrines of Men* (1522),[20] although this is also referred to by Franck.[21] Menno took Luther's distinction between the Word of God and the words of human beings as the point of departure for his biblicism, even if he did believe that Luther's theology did not transcend the authority of the Scriptures.[22]

In his early writings after his "exodus from Popedom" in January 1536, Menno refers to his continuing research into the biblical legitimacy of infant baptism, in which connection he mentions Origen, Cyprian, Cyril, and Tertullian as examples of "old writers," in addition to Augustine and Eusebius. These sources, as well as his knowledge of the work of Zwingli, specifically the latter's "Sixty-seven Articles," probably also derived from Sebastian Franck's *Chronica*.[23] Where Bullinger, Zwingli's successor, was concerned, Menno read his writing *Von der onverschampten frävel der Widertöufern*, which appeared in 1531.[24] The influence of the Strasbourg ministers was quite significant in the northern Netherlands and one of them, Martin Bucer, was an important interlocutor for Menno.[25]

When Hardenberg refers to "seditious books" which Menno read "without discrimination," he certainly did not have the works of the above-mentioned learned theologians in mind. But who would qualify for this category? In Hardenberg eyes, there is no doubt that they would be Melchior Hoffman, Sebastian Franck, and Cellarius.

We may indeed assume that Menno read works by Melchior Hoffman, the father of Dutch Anabaptism, but we can only speculate on which works these were. Menno certainly did not read them "without discrimination," however, as Hardenberg assumes. If there was one question on which Menno was critical it was precisely the apocalyptic radicalism of prophetic violent Münsterite Anabaptism, a product of Hoffman's ideas, however undesirable this was to the latter. In correction of the false prophets of Münster, Menno poses his pure explanation of the teachings of Jesus Christ which, according to Menno, was directly derived from the New Testament without theological distortions. In this way, he was able to reject the Old Testament-inspired conceptions of an earthly messianic realm, equated with the Anabaptist reformation in Münster. It is remarkable how consistently Menno pursued this implementation of the "simple command of Christ."

It is difficult to trace direct references to or borrowings from the writings of Melchior Hoffman and Bernard Rothmann in Menno's works. What appealed to Menno in their struggle for radical piety and newness of life is only hinted at. The call to sincerity and piety which he heard from the pre-Münsterite messengers, like Hoffman and his apostles, made a deep impression on Menno, and finally won him over to their cause after a prolonged spiritual struggle. He continues to sympathize with these "true penitents," despite the fact that some of them, according to Menno, acted a little wrongly and strayed when they did not trust exclusively the effect of the preaching of God's word, but also trusted violence to accomplish their commission to purify and reform the world.[26] Despite a difference in insight as to the fulfillment of the prophecy, Menno always remained inwardly affected by the manifestations of true penitence shown by the first Anabaptists, with whom he also came into contact in his own parish of Witmarsum after 1530.

Menno used the works of Franck for the historical and theological foundations of his own program; not only Franck's *Chronica*, but also the *Paradoxa* (Ulm 1534), from which he liked to cite adages from classical authors. In general, Franck will have sustained Menno in his criticism of Luther's Word Theology, which they both regarded as the most important reason why moral improvement was failing to develop. Menno was, however, unable to follow Franck in his spiritualism and corresponding rejection of the visibility of the congregation restituted in accordance with the example of the New Testament.

What is finally remarkable is Menno's knowledge of Cellarius (Martin Borrhaus), who was controversial in reformational circles and to whose work, *De immensis operibus Dei* (Strasbourg 1527), Menno refers.[27] Cellarius enjoyed the friendship of the Strasbourg reformer Capito for a long time, until he fell into disfavor with Zwingli, Oecolampadius, and Bucer on suspicion of Anabaptist sympathies. His critical attitude toward infant baptism would have particularly appealed to Menno. Cellarius had considerable influence in the county of Gulik and the bishopric of Cologne, the region where Menno also worked. There is no doubt that Hardenberg would not have found Cellarius to be orthodox in reformational doctrine either.

Menno's work as a reform-minded priest and later as scribe and elder of the peaceful Anabaptists is characterized by his tireless struggle to offer a program directly derived from the Scriptures to all earnest believers – those who were most deeply convinced of the necessity of profound reformation of faith and morals – in order thus to assure their salvation on the Day of Judgment, which he knew to be imminent. In his opinion, the only thing that showed whether true believers profoundly knew the word of Christ was whether they had the spirit of Christ, as in the days of the apostles.[28]

He envisaged the restoration of the original Christian Church, consisting of believers who possessed the disposition of Christ. These were those who, reborn through hearing His Word alone, had become new creatures and thus inspired to lead lives of submission, true charity and moral purity. He felt compelled to preach this missionary message, since time was short! According to him, there is "verily no teaching but God's word alone which can lead to eternal life,"[29] although we must remember in this context that just as every heretic has his own justification, likewise every reformer trims the Bible to his own interpretation.

Let us now take a look at the constituent elements of Menno's ideas on the true faith. He softened the rough edges of Hoffman's apocalypticism and prophecy. In Menno we find no concrete location and exact date for the Kingdom of God; the Age of Grace has already dawned in Christ. He consequently explains Mark 1:15, "The time is fulfilled, and the kingdom of God has come near; repent, and believe the good news," as a prolegomenon to his *Fundament*. No other kingdom of peace will precede the second coming of Christ, and he therefore adamantly rejects the Münsterite ideas on this theme, with their visible kingship, polygamy, and use of violence. He also dismisses the spiritualist option of reform which, briefly put, says that if your inner being alone is pure, then outward things are of no matter – ideas he encountered in his formidable rival and fellow elder David Joris.

Thus Menno sets the tone of his Christocentric, biblicist programme of reformation, distinguishing his teachings from Roman Catholicism, revolutionary Anabaptism, and spiritualism. Following Erasmus, he no longer interprets true penitence as the acceptance of the sacrament of penance, but as making visible the fruits of penitence

– the moral betterment of life. In this way, Menno makes the doctrine of sanctification the very heart of his theology, in line with the entire Anabaptist movement.

"No one may boast of grace, forgiveness of sins and the virtues of Christ, before he has borne the true fruits of penance" is the *cantus firmus* of his thinking.[30] This appeal for true penitence has a strongly apocalyptical significance for true revivalists, of whom Menno is one, and is therefore a better reflection of the essence of his theology than "betterment of life," which can also be interpreted in a strictly moral sense. The Law and the gospel permanently presuppose and define each other and the fear of God's demanding justice continues to be present in all phases of belief. Total freedom from the Law is out of the question. The fear of God is the ultimate criterion for damnation or salvation. Romans 8:13 frequently appears in Menno's work, "For if you live according to the flesh, you will die; but if by the Spirit you put to death the deeds of the body, you will live." A resultant tendency to melancholy, legalism, and perfectionism was characteristic of the Melchiorite Anabaptists from the very beginning.

According to Menno, this demonstration of true penitence out of fear of the imminent Day of Judgment, expressed in the struggle for identification with the disposition, defencelessness, and sinlessness of Christ, is preconditional to the full receipt of grace. Menno's and Luther's paths diverge at this point. Even if Menno and Luther share the conviction that faith must focus on God's promise of the forgiveness of sins, irrespective of one's own righteousness or unrighteousness, this faith concerning God is not merely trust in the forgiveness of sins. True faith bears fruits; it works through love; it voluntarily does all righteousness; it causes the eradication of fallen human nature; it crucifies lust and desire; it glories in the cross of Christ; it renews; it causes to be reborn; it makes the believer alive, willing, obedient and peaceful in Jesus Christ.

Menno defines faith equally as a gift and a power conferred by God. It penetrates the opened heart or the conscience and grants the certainty of salvation. As a consequence, the penitent believer acknowledges that both the Law and the gospel are just and true.[31] Faith is the simultaneous acceptance of the promise of the forgiveness of sins and acceptance of the injunction and opportunity to live by God's commandment. Menno therefore bases *sola fide* on Habakkuk 2:4 ("Look at the proud! Their spirit is not right in them, but the righteous live by their faith"), and not on Romans 1:17 ("For in it the righteousness of God is revealed through faith for faith; as it is written, 'The one who is righteous will live by faith'"), as Luther does.[32] Faith and obedience to the Law remain inextricably intertwined with each other. Christ cannot be the Savior of perpetually impenitent sinners. Furthermore, faith is primarily held to be voluntary subordination to the gospel as the new Law of Christ.[33] A logical consequence is that a penitent faith of this kind cannot be supposed of children. Baptism and the Lord's Supper, too, only have significance if administered to people in whom faith has brought about a visible change in thought and deed.

Starting from this concept of faith, founded on a traditional Catholic doctrine of grace, Menno designed his blueprint for the church of Christ, in sharp contrast to the church of the Antichrist, which he holds to mean the Roman Catholic Church as well as subsequent rival Protestant groups. Menno's church of the narrow path has the following characteristics: a biblical doctrine unfalsified by church and theology, the administration of baptism and the Lord's Supper to true penitents and therefore not *ex opere operato* to minors and people living in public sin, obedience to faith instead of cheap grace, sincere brotherly love without disdain for one's neighbour, bearing frank witness to God and Christ instead of not daring to admit openly to the Reformed faith, and willingness to suffer for the faith instead of persecuting true believers.[34]

This concept of faith presumes a doctrine of grace in which all emphasis is placed on its effectiveness. The only difference with the Catholic interpretation is that this grace is not mediated through sacraments but through the hearing of the Word of God. This is the reformist interpretation of Menno Simons. The consequent doctrine of justification has a twofold nature. The first justification through the death of Christ on the cross is the universal forgiveness of original sin and sins committed before conversion. The second justification only comes about, however, when the believer personally accepts this offer of universal grace and persists in the manifestation of the received identification with Christ.[35] Refraining from public sin is therefore a possibility that is part of the new life. Menno's understanding of the concept of sin is mainly concerned with its deliberate and public nature, although he does not deny that the believer continues to be tormented by his sinful nature after repentance and baptism. Thus he dissociates himself from the radical spiritualism of his rival David Joris, which assumes that it is possible to banish the inner impulse to sin, as a result of which the Law loses its function completely.

The call for true penitence in the evangelical sense leads to a division between the penitent and the impenitent, between the true church and the false church, between a society which demonstrates the disposition of Christ and a society of Christians in name only. With the Last Judgment in sight, the church – coincident with society in Menno's day – could no longer remain a *corpus permixtum*, in which the righteous and the unrighteous could not be visibly distinguished and where ultimate salvation depended solely on God's hidden ordinance. Therefore, the restoration of free will to the truly penitent believer and God's predestination are mutually exclusive. Believers are urged to anticipate the great purge that is at hand, by purifying themselves of sin and godlessness. In this respect, there is no difference whatsoever between Menno and the missionary urge to purify which characterizes early Anabaptism. He only repudiates violent means to precipitate this purification.

Menno is not concerned with a superior morality alone, but also with the correct interpretation of the biblical message; not only with life, but also with doctrine. For these two presuppose each other; doctrine and life, both of a new quality and arising from an earnest understanding of the unfalsified, pure Word of God. And where is that Word revealed in a purer form than in Jesus Christ, wonders Menno? The Word of God became flesh in Jesus Christ (Jn. 1:14) and this is where the heart of Menno's theology beats, in his understanding of the person and work of Christ, with a strong emphasis on the doctrine of incarnation. Only this Word become flesh, only Christ has authority. No other foundation but Christ can therefore be laid for a penitent faith and a church cleansed of the stains of Roman Catholicism. As a consequence, the passage "For no one can lay any foundation other than the one that has been laid; that foundation is Jesus Christ" (1 Cor. 3:11) becomes his device and appears on the title page of almost all his printed works.

The incarnation doctrine and discipline became the most controversial tenets of the teaching of Menno. After the fall of Münster, the spiritual inheritance of Anabaptism disseminated in the Netherlands included Hoffman's incarnation doctrine, his ideas on charismatic leadership which led to the institution of elders endowed with arbitrary authority over teachings and morals, and his respect for Christian government charged with furthering the Anabaptist reformation. Menno continued to be influenced by these ideas, and when he does not explicitly mention Melchior Hoffman as the *auctor intellectualis* of these convictions, then this is done for apologetic reasons, since he does not wish to be identified with Melchiorism in its Münsterite form. After all, Bernard Rothmann, the court theologian of King Jan van Leiden, also voiced the same ideas.

Before he broke with the Roman Catholic Church in 1536, Menno had already come into contact with Hoffman's teaching that, in its incarnation in Jesus Christ, the Word had not taken on flesh from Mary, a human nature which carried the traces of the Fall. Menno was not unorthodox in this respect. The doctrine of the Immaculate Conception of Mary was not yet church dogma in his times, in fact the struggle between the maculatists and the immaculatists would not be decided in favor of the adherents of the sinless conception of Mary until 1854.[36] Through continuing bible study Menno overcame his original resistance to this doctrine inherited from Hoffman. Menno deepened and defended the Melchiorite incarnation doctrine in disputations with reformed theologians like Gellius Faber, Johannes à Lasco, and Martin Micron, and with his fellow elder Adam Pastor. The written records of this defense constitute a substantial quantity of the works which form his legacy.

Menno's constant occupation with this doctrine is a product of his need to associate the heart of reconciliation, which is God's ineffable love, with the subjective and spiritual assumption of this, resulting in rebirth and the sanctified life which follows it. God did not reconcile the world through the flesh of Adam, but through the eternal Word, his Son, who became the equal of the first Adam in all things, with the exception of unrighteousness, disobedience, and sin.[37] God gave himself. He "gave the heart from his body for us in death."[38] God's overwhelming love is diminished by a more adoptionist incarnation doctrine, which explicitly emphasizes the complete identification of divine nature with sinful human nature as a precondition for reconciliation. In short, if Christ does not embody the holiness of God completely and indivisibly, how can those who believe in him become completely holy? How else can a church without spot and wrinkle arise from the preaching of God's Word? Menno therefore consistently ascribes the absence of sanctified life among other groups – and their ministers in the first place – to their erroneous understanding of the incarnation of the Word of God.

In addition to Genesis 3:15 and Hebrews 2:15–17, Menno cites John 1:14 as the most important place of proof for his incarnation doctrine. He based his contention on the Vulgate, *Verbum caro factum est*, the Word became flesh, and he saw the complete godliness, holiness and sinlessness of Christ guaranteed in this text. He is not concerned with theological speculations on the question of the relationship between the divine nature and the human nature of Christ. That remains incomprehensible. Although forced into such speculation by opponents, he was ultimately concerned solely with the ethical purport of reconciliation, since grace without sanctification is no grace at all. This is what makes or breaks his conviction that only the believer who is reborn out of this Word alone can also demonstrate the disposition of Christ.

This theology of sanctification makes great demands of the discipline that must be practiced in order to maintain the high ethical standards of the congregation of true penitents. The question of the areas of private and public life to which discipline had to be applied, the biblical guidelines according to which this should be done, and who had the required authority, led to significant divisions in Dutch Anabaptism during and after Menno's lifetime. For Menno, the first principle of discipline was that it was only permitted to correct public sins. By taking this stance, he dissociated himself from the ideas of David Joris that secret sins, particularly of a sexual nature, had to be confessed and punished. The church is entitled to judge in outward matters; the inner self is judged by God alone.

According to Matthew 16 and 18, the church has the power to attribute and forgive sins. The true church is recognizable by its good discipline; church being understood as a visible community with its own church law analogous to the Roman Catholic tradition, with the exception that this law must now rest on exclusively evangelical pillars. The Magisterial Reformation, in contrast, opted for an invisible church and a government that exercised discipline with or without the assistance of the church. Should this power to cut sinners off from the congregation be exercised after a number of previous admonishments, in accordance with Matthew 18:15–17, or may the leaders also proceed directly to placing a sinner outside of the congregation? Must the transgressor be shunned to such a degree that association with the spouse should also be broken off as a result? Does the marriage bond not prevail over the demand to shun the sinful spouse? The New Testament provides no unequivocal answer to these questions, and neither does Menno.

Menno's views on this subject are changeable therefore, and led to his being called a "weathercock." An assessment of his position should take into consideration that correct disciplinary practice can only gradually start to take shape in a movement in the process of consolidation. In addition, we see a struggle for jurisdiction developing between the elders of the first and second generations. In 1555–6, Menno Simons had to give way to the leaders of the rigorist Flemish Anabaptists, whose self-appointed leader was Leenaart Bouwens and whose radicalism was derived in part from the fact that they had recently escaped from atrocious persecution. Furthermore, they were refugees in the northern Netherlands and their social position was uncertain as a result, which led to animosity with the already consolidated congregations. Menno had to pass under the yoke of the new leaders and he was forced into the camp of the hard-line excommunicators, although he had always been in favor of the moderate practice of excommunication and shunning since he became a leader. From this time on, he defended in writings not only the exclusion of deliberate sinners without previous admonishments, but also the complete shunning of spouses. This was required in conformity with the maxim that the spiritual should not yield to the fleshly, but the fleshly to the spiritual. A Christian is joined to Christ in matrimony in the spiritual sense, and the heavenly marriage is therefore superior to the earthly one.

The implementation of Menno's program of reform for church and society did not proceed without difficulties. The emphasis on the sanctification of life, founded in Christology and manifested in severe discipline, forced the community of saints to dissociate itself from the society surrounding it, which could scarcely be governed in accordance with this strict moral code. This process took place in the 1560s, when it became clear that Menno and his followers could expect no support from reformist governments, despite their constant appeals to such authorities. For the Mennonites (and for the Reformed as well), discipline was an indispensable means of loosening their ties with a society marked by Roman Catholic religious practice and of creating a distinct profile for themselves as a purified church built on evangelical foundations. The lack of government support for a religious-ethical revival throughout society, however, meant that the scope of the rigorist practice of discipline remained restricted of necessity, and the urge to purify felt by Menno's followers subsequently focussed on the church itself. The Mennonites therefore compromised first on the points of incarnation doctrine and discipline during the progressive assimilation of the Anabaptist movement into the tolerant Netherlands of the seventeenth century. Where they had won their independent position from the Roman Catholic Church and the other reformational groups in the sixteenth century, it now became important, in the light of a dwindling eschatological consciousness, to find a place in the religiously multiform society of the Republic of the Netherlands.

At the start of Menno's career, the spiritual climate in the regions where he worked was such that he could cherish a justified hope of being able to secure the help of a government for his reform plans. In East Friesland in particular, which opposed the Hapsburg expansion, it appeared as if it would be possible to reap a harvest from the new ideas sown by reformational humanist ministers and Anabaptist missionaries. The authorities were called on to suppress Roman Catholic idolatry, such as the elevation of the host, auricular confession, and the veneration of saints by means of statues. In this way, a religious practice developed in the 1530s in which a clear distinction was made between the way in which God worked inwardly and outwardly. External matters, such as preaching and the sacraments, were considered useful only to the extent that they were signs of internal inspiration by God. This spiritualism was an effective breeding ground for Anabaptism, which could also count on sympathy among the lower nobility at first. But the violent religious politics of the House of Hapsburg ultimately caused all hope to evaporate of a radical renewal of church and society on the basis of divine law.

This raises the question of Menno's ideas on the role of government and the use of violence, in view of the political and social reality of his times. In his opinion, the spiritual and worldly regiments, church and government, should not be mixed. Menno agreed with Luther on that point. For Menno, however, this meant first and foremost that the authorities should not use the worldly sword to impede attempts at reform. True Christian government had to realize that it should not fight the truly pious (by which Menno meant his own coreligionists primarily) with fire and sword. He makes continual appeals to the authorities to read his writings without bias, to compare his teachings and life with theirs and not to equate the whole Anabaptist movement with the Münsterite Anabaptists. He hopes that, edified by his apologia, they will show themselves to be a "Christian, wise, true and god-fearing government."[39] This implies that they will halt persecution and give Menno and his followers freedom to enter disputations with all scholars, in order to ensure the continuation of the preaching of the pure gospel. Government without responsibility for religion is an alien idea to anyone living in the sixteenth century, but the question was, which religion was the true religion that was to be fostered by the government? The government would, after all, be held accountable at the coming Day of Judgment, whether it encouraged the true, evangelical religion or not.

Menno's ideas on Christian government are reminiscent of Erasmus's image of the pious monarch. In Menno's view, leaders should boast more of their piety than their noble birth.[40] Offensive wars are condemned, as is the excessive use of force by the authorities, and pious kings from the Old Testament are held up as examples to the authorities. Revolt is out of the question in Menno's view. In accordance with the traditional interpretation of Romans 13, the government should be obeyed in worldly matters, and Menno also places responsibility for the moral and religious order within its jurisdiction. The government should educate souls instead of killing them – educating them in the true evangelical teachings, of course. This is why Menno calls on all the monarchs of his day to remove all false teachers, just as their Old Testament predecessors had wiped out the false prophets. He even incites governmental disobedience, with his call not to carry out imperial edicts.[41] Finally, rulers were to moderate their immoderate conduct and themselves become models of evangelical, God-fearing and Christian life.

Menno's ideas on violence are strongly influenced by his aversion to Münsterite Anabaptism. He shares Hoffman's belief that the use of violence to further evangelical doctrine is the exclusive right of legitimate government and not of subjects. In contrast to the Münsterites, who used violence to purge religion of unbiblical practices, Menno only wants to fight with spiritual weapons, which is to say through missionary preaching.[42] General defencelessness is therefore not preached by Menno. His rejection of violence should primarily be interpreted against the background of the violent persecution to which the reformists were subjected by governments. He orders the persecuted believers to renounce violent resistance and calls on the government to carry out no executions in questions of religion.

Menno's rejection of the death penalty is also given a more general purport. The question raised in discussions with Johannes à Lasco and Martin Micron was that if a pious government is permitted to use violence in worldly matters, is it possible for true Christians to enter public service?[43] This is permissible, according to Menno, to the extent that no death penalties are pronounced. Can such a true, Christian government be found? Menno doubts this in the extreme, because the average government does not know the kingdom of Christ.[44] Otherwise they would not persecute the true followers of Christ. If the authorities knew the teachings of Christ, the walls, soldiers, and weapons would no longer be needed.[45] Menno's considerations clearly echo Luther's view on the true Christian in his *Temporal Authority: To What Extent It Should Be Obeyed* (1523), but without any reference to Luther's conviction that also the true non-resistant Christian, out of responsibility for the neighbor, cannot avoid participation in violence.[46]

Menno subjected not only the government, but also the clergy and the ordinary people, to the criticism of Christ's teachings. His aim is a religious-ethical revival in all sections of the population. Menno rejects the worldliness of the clergy when, drawing on his own experience, he writes in his autobiographical notes of seeing his career as a village priest as having been marked by the longing for a quiet, easy, sensual life in the way of the flesh.[47] The clergy is called to embrace evangelical doctrine and to lead the irreproachable life which is its consequence. They must no longer allow themselves to walk on the leash of the authorities who persecute true believers.

With respect to ordinary people, Menno adopts the position of a preacher of penance and morality. Hundreds of thousands of people have been born Christians in name, but their immorality will ensure that they never inherit salvation, he says threateningly.[48] They are out of control because they have no knowledge of evangelical doctrine and lack the right spiritual leaders, and their violence, sensuality, and immoderation are sharply denounced. Menno rejects the thoughtless swearing of oaths and usury, and reproves employers for abuse of power relating to the dismissal, illness, and sexual intimidation of their employees. Menno called on all walks of life to shape a new society directly subject to divine righteousness, knowledge of which has become possible in Christ and the apostolic teachings. He envisions a purified *corpus christianorum* as a virginal bride who longs passionately for the arrival of her Bridegroom. Here is the *communio sanctorum* of truly penitent Christians: sanctification in all aspects of life, in accordance with the disposition of Christ and his guidelines.

To this day, there is still a difference of opinion on how and to what extent the love of God can be active in all aspects of life. Hardenberg will probably have concluded that the simple manner in which the self-taught Menno Simons wished to apply the biblical witness of Christ's love, forgiving nature and nonviolence to recalcitrant reality must, of necessity, lead to irresponsible behavior which can only result in unrest, chaos, and division. Menno Simons explored the frontiers of this exalted ideal and personally experienced the resistance to it. It is why he became a radical reformer in exile.

Notes

1 The catalogue was compiled by B. Rademaker-Helfferich (with a contribution from S. Zijlstra): *Een leven vol gevaar. Menno Simons (1496–1561), leidsman der dopers* (Amsterdam: Algemene Doopsgezinde Sociëteit, 1996).

2 *Dat Fundament des Christelycken Leers doer Menno Simons op dat aldercorste geschreven* (1539–40), ed. H. W. Meihuizen (The Hague: Martinus Nijhoff, 1967), 5 ('voerreden'). (Cited hereafter as *Fundament*).

3 [Valerius Schoolmeester,] *Proba Fidei. Oft de Proeve des Gheloofs* (s.l., 1569), 30. For the life and teachings of this Anabaptist field preacher see S. Voolstra, "Valerius Schoolmeester (overleden omstreeks 1569). Leven en leer van een menniste hageprediker in Zeeland in de Reformatietijd" in A. Wiggers et al., eds., *Rondom de kerk in Zeeland* (Derde verzameling

bijdragen van de Vereniging voor Nederlandse Kerkgeschiedenis) (Delft: Eburon, 1991), 106–33.

4 Cited in W. Jansen, "Reformhumanistische kritiek op dopers radicalisme in de zestiende eeuw," *Tijdschrift voor Nederlandse Kerkgeschiedenis* 1/2 (1998), 6.

5 Jansen, "Reformhumanistische kritiek," 9, n. 13.

6 See Menno Simons's autobiographical notes on his "exodus from Popedom" in *Opera Omnia Theologica, of alle de godtgeleerde werken van Menno Simons* (Amsterdam: Joannes van Veen, 1681) (cited hereafter as *Opera Omnia*), 256–9; *The Complete Writings of Menno Simons, c.1496–1561*, trans. Leonard Verduin, ed. John Christian Wenger (Scottdale, PA: Herald Press, 1956) (cited hereafter as *Complete Writings*), 668–74.

7   The level of education of the Frisian clergy is discussed in S. Zijlstra, *Het geleerde Friesland – een mythe? Universiteit en maatschappij in Friesland en Stad en Lande ca. 1380–1650* (Ljouwert: Fryske Akademy, 1996).

8   *Verclaringe des christelijcken doopsels* (Antwerp: M. Crom, 1539), D8vo; *Opera Omnia*, f. 408b; *Complete Writings*, 248. For a consideration of the influence of Erasmus on Menno, see C. Augustijn, "Erasmus and Menno," *Mennonite Quarterly Review* 60 (1986), 497–508; idem, "Der Epilog von Menno Simons 'Mediation'" in J. G. Rott and S. L. Verheus, eds. *Anabaptistes et dissidents au XVIe siècle. Actes du Colloque international d'histoire anabaptiste du XVIe siècle tenu à l'occasion de la XIe Conférence Mennonite mondiale à Strasbourg, juillet 1984* (Baden-Baden and Bouxwiller, 1987) (Bibliotheca Dissidentium scripta et studia 3), 175–88.

9   "Voorreden" to *Meditatie . . . op den XXV. Psalm* [1539]. *Opera Omnia*, f. 163; *Complete Writings*, 65.

10   Menno Simons and Adam Pastor used "den Testamenten vnde vordütschinge Erasmi" as the authoritative Bible during their disputation on the Trinity in Lübeck in 1552. See S. Cramer, ed., *Bibliotheca Reformatoria Neerlandica V: Nederlandse Anabaptistica (geschriften van Henrick Rol, Melchior Hoffman, Adam Pastor, De Broederlicke vereeninge)* ('s-Gravenhage: Martinus Nijhoff, 1909), 356–7, 451, 545.

11   *Fundament*, 117.

12   *Opera Omnia*, f. 256b; *Complete Writings*, 669.

13   *Fundament*, 70. This refers to the work of the Lutheran minister Diepold Gerlacher (alias Billicanus), "Renovatio Ecclesiae Nordligensis . . . per Diaconos ibidem 1525" and possibly the "Nördlinger Messe 1522" by Kaspar Krantz, the former Carmelite prior in Nördlingen. The text of these writings can be found in E. Sehling, ed., *Die Evangelische Kirchenordnungen des 16. Jahrhunderts* (Bd. XII: Kirchenordnungen der Freien Reichsstadt Nördlingen) (Tübingen: J. C. B. Mohr, 1963), 271ff.

14   *Opera Omnia*, f. 256a; *Complete Writings*, 668: "I was in so far helped by Luther, however, that human injunctions cannot bind unto eternal death."

15   Compare the content of the fifth thesis of the reformational disputation in the vernacular in Oldersum (East Friesland) in June 1526, under the protection of Ulrich van Dornum, in whose district Menno Simons too would later seek a safe refuge. This thesis dealt with the question of whether old customs which were in force in the church for centuries should continue to be observed. See Menno Smid, *Ostfriesland im Schutze des Reiches* (Bd. VI: Ostfriesische Kirchengeschichte) (Pewsum: Deichacht Krummhörn, 1974), 123ff.

16   *Fundament*, 49.

17   *Opera Omnia*, f. 404b; *Complete Writings*, 242.

18   See Christoph Bornhäuser, *Leben und Lehre Menno Simons. Ein Kampf um das Fundament des Glaubens (etwa 1496–1561)* (Beiträge zur Geschichte und Kirche der Reformierten Kirche, XXXV) (Neukirchen: Neukirchener Verlag, 1973), 174–5 (Exkurs I: "Welche Schriften Luthers kannte Menno Simons?").

19   Sebastian Franck, *Chronica Zeitbuch unnd Geschichtsbibell* (Straszburg, 1531). Menno probably did not quote from this confiscated first edition, but from the second edition of 1536, III, ff. 168r–171r.

20   According to Bornhäuser, *Menno Simons*, 54–5.

21   Franck, *Chronica*, III, f. 168vo.

22   *Fundament*, 171.

23   *Fundament*, 71. According to Gerardus Nicolai, the editor of Bullinger's *Tegens de Wederdoopers* (1617) I, c.6, f. 12a.

24   K. Vos, *Menno Simons (1496–1561). Zijn leven en werken en zijne reformatorische Denkbeelden* (Leiden: E. J. Brill, 1914), 71.

25   See his reference to the "Argentinenses," for example, in *Fundament*, 50 and 68, where Menno considers the content of Martin Bucer's *Quid de Baptismate infantium . . . sentiendum* (Straszburg, 1533).

26   *Fundament*, 202–3.

27   *Fundament*, 71.

28   *Fundament*, 204.

29   *Fundament*, 212.

30   *Fundament*, 19.

31   *Opera Omnia*, ff. 75b–76a; *Complete Writings*, 328–9.

32   *Fundament*, 28.

33   *Fundament*, 28.

34   *Opera Omnia*, ff. 300b–301a; *Complete Writings*, 739ff.

35   See Hans-Georg Tanneberger, *Die Vorstellung der Täufer von der Rechtfertigung des Menschen* (Stuttgart: Calwer Verlag, 1999), 218–32.

36   See S. Voolstra: *Het Woord is vlees geworden. De melchioritisch-menniste incarnatieleer* (Kampen: J. H. Kok, 1982), 128ff.

37 *Opera Omnia*, f. 526a; *Complete Writings*, 428–9.
38 *Opera Omnia*, f. 315a; *Complete Writings*, 766–7.
39 *Fundament*, 5; 31ff.; 161ff.
40 *Fundament*, 183.
41 *Fundament*, 180.
42 *Opera Omnia*, f. 445a: *Complete Writings*, 304.
43 See Martin Micron's report of the discussion of this question: *Marten Mikron, Een waerachtigh verhaal der t'zamensprekinghen tusschen Menno Simons ende Martinus Mikron*

van der menschwerdinghe Iesu Christi (1556), ed. W. F. Dankbaar (Documenta Anabaptistica Neerlandica III) (Leiden: E. J. Brill, 1981), 29ff.
44 *Opera Omnia*, f. 445ab; *Complete Writings*, 304–5.
45 *Opera Omnia*, f. 455ab; *Complete Writings* 320.
46 *WA* 11: 229–81; 248, 36ff.
47 *Fundament*, 185–7; *Opera Omnia*, ff. 256a–257a; *Complete Writings*, 668–71.
48 *Fundament*, 193.

Bibliography

Primary Sources

Opera Menno Symons, ofte Groot Sommarie. s.l., 1646.
Opera Omnia Theologica, of alle de godtgeleerde werke van Menno Simons, Amsterdam: Joannes van Veen, 1681.
The Complete Writings of Menno Simons, c.1496–1561, trans. Leonard Verduin, ed. John Christian Wenger, Scottdale, PA: Herald Press, 1956.
Dat Fundament des Christelycken Leers doer Menno Simons op dat aldercorste geschreven (1539–40), ed. H. W. Meihuizen, The Hague: Martinus Nijhoff, 1967. First edition of the "Fundamentboek;" not in *Opera Omnia* or *Complete Writings*.

Secondary Sources

Bornhäuser, Christoph, *Leben und Lehre Menno Simons. Ein Kampf um das Fundament des Glaubens (etwa 1496–1561)*, Beiträge zur Geschichte und Kirche der Reformierten Kirche, XXXV, Neukirchen: Neukirchener Verlag, 1973.
Brunk, Gerald R., ed., *Menno Simons: A Reappraisal. Essays in Honor of Irvin B. Horst on the 450th Anniversary of the Fundamentboek*, Harrisonburg, VA: Eastern Mennonite College, 1992.
Krahn, Cornelius, *Menno Simons (1496–1561). Ein Beitrag zur Geschichte und Theologie der Taufgesinnten*, Karlsruhe: Heinrich Schneider, 1936; 2nd ed. Newton, KS: Faith & Life Press, 1982.
Meihuizen, H. W., *Menno Simons. Ijveraar voor het herstel van de nieuwtestamentische Gemeente*, Haarlem: H. D. Tjeenk Willink & Zoon NV, 1961.
Voolstra, Sjouke, *Menno Simons: His Image and Message*, North Newton, KS: Bethel College, 1997.
Vos, K., Menno Simons (1496–1561). *Zijn leven en werken en zijne reformatorische Denkbeelden*, Leiden: E. J. Brill, 1914.

Trajectories of
Reformation Theologies

Carter Lindberg

There is no conclusion to our volume. The theologians of the Reformation may have died, but they have not faded away. And even if some of the Reformers "in the wings" are no longer household words in contemporary theological reflection, their concerns continue to leaven the theological lump one way or another. The Reformation theologians – blessed *and* cursed – by their denominational heirs have always served at least as compass points for their churches' theologians. The history of their readings and mis-readings has been a minor scholarly industry in itself.[1] Our concern here is not to review the many histories of interpretations, but to suggest the impact of the trajectories of Reformation theologies upon modern theology.

The impact of Reformation theological trajectories – for good or ill – can of course be examined in later individual theologians. Random examples include Luther's theological motifs of the law–gospel dialectic and justification in Tillich's method of correlation, and his understanding of justification by grace alone through faith alone as acceptance of one's acceptance in spite of being unacceptable. Feuerbach developed his theory of religion as projection in relation to Luther's affirmation that faith creates God. Hegel viewed the Reformation as the source of true subjectivity and the dawn of a new age. Flacius's contribution to a theological understanding of adiaphora and theologically grounded political resistance found resonance in Bonhoeffer's stance against National Socialism. Barth's revelational positivism reflects the Magisterial Reformers' emphasis upon the Word of God, *extra nos*, standing over against the world and culture.[2] The significance of Reformation studies in general and the Luther Renaissance in particular for evangelical responses to the perceived bankruptcy of liberal theology after the First World War has often been discussed.[3] Müntzer's emphasis that Spirit-inspired faith in the heart "is identical with that in the hearts of the elect throughout the earth," including the Turks,[4] foreshadows the experiential-expressive model of liberal Protestantism in which different religions are diverse expressions of a common core experience.[5]

Karlstadt's theology of regeneration, with its focus on obedience to the Law of God, runs through consequent renewal movements from Pietism to contemporary charismatics.[6] "With his theology of rebirth and sanctification, Bodenstein was a forerunner of Pietism."[7] The theological trajectories of Karlstadt and Müntzer lead through Valentin Weigel, Johann Arndt, Johann Valentin Andreae, and others into Pietism, and influenced the Pietist claim that the "first Reformation" initiated in the sixteenth century was incomplete, for it was only a reform of doctrine. The "second Reformation," as Pietism understood itself, was the reform of life. Thus the radical Pietist Gottfried Arnold emphasized that the reform of doctrine initiated by Luther must be completed by the reform of the Christian life, by a *theologia experimentalis.* And Christian Hoberg, another radical Pietist, affirmed that without rebirth, justification is a fiction.[8] Later, John Wesley could praise Luther for his recovery of justification while lamenting that Luther was ignorant of, or at least confused about, the doctrine of sanctification.[9] These positive and negative trajectories continue to echo in contemporary ecumenical dialogues.[10]

Other trajectories influencing modern theology include the "peace church" perspectives on separating church and state, as well as conscientious objection to war stemming from Menno Simons and other Anabaptist groups, as well as the revived interest in spirituality with roots in Roman Catholic theologians such as Teresa and Ignatius. Those interested in the contributions of women to theology are discovering an expanding field of research in Reformation studies.[11]

The trajectories of Reformation theologies not only impacted later individuals and movements, but also were of seminal significance in the development of specifically modern concerns.[12] Most obvious among the theological concerns is the development of hermeneutics. The *sola scriptura* watchword impelled intense biblical study. And the concern for vernacular bibles so famously voiced by Erasmus[13] impelled translations and hence also raised numerous hermeneutical issues. One of the most notorious cases was Luther's addition of the word "alone" to his translation of Romans 3:28 so that the verse read: "We hold that a man is justified without the works of the law, by faith *alone.*"[14] Yet it is clear from our chapters that Protestants by no means had a corner on biblical studies and hermeneutical issues. All parties became engaged in biblical studies and the writing of commentaries. "One of the surprising conclusions of the study of sixteenth-century exegesis is how difficult it is to identify confessional biases in biblical commentaries."[15]

Along with the rise of hermeneutics and intimately related to it was the rise of critical historical studies. Historical study was stimulated both by the debates over the relationship of Scripture and tradition, and by the issue of papal authority in relation to the early ecumenical councils. Theologians strove to prove that the history of the church supported their reading of the Bible. Thus Flacius not only stimulated biblical hermeneutics with his *Clavis scripturae sacrae,* he also was involved with a group of scholars in writing a history of the church from its beginning to the fifteenth century, titled *Historia Ecclesia Christi,* also known as the "Magdeburg Centuries." The goal was to demonstrate both the deviance of the Roman Church from the early church and the Reformation recovery of primitive Christianity. In the process, the tripartite periodization of history as ancient, medieval, and modern was introduced into the schema of universal history. To counter this Lutheran church history, the Catholic scholar Caesar Baronius produced a church history that defended the institution through a year-by-year analysis, hence the title *Annales Ecclesiastici.* The radical wing of the Reformation found its historical defense in tracing the true church through the succession of martyrs, and later in Gottfried Arnold's so-called "impartial" history of the church and heretics: *Unparteyische Kirchen und Ketzer Historien vom Anfang des Neuen Testaments biss auf das Jahr Christi 1688*. In contrast to the Lutheran hermeneutic of justification by grace alone and the Catholic hermeneutic of ecclesiastical authority, Arnold's key to the history of "true" Christianity is the conversion experiences and exemplary lives of persons, even those deemed heretical by theological and ecclesial standards. Religious experience was displacing doctrine. This concern with individuals and their conversion experiences foreshadows modern interests in biographical and psychological studies of historical figures.[16] Arnold's turn to those historically marginalized by the institutional church as models of faithful discipleship may also foreshadow the modern liberation theologies which speak of history from the "underside." That we today may not confidently share Arnold's claim to impartiality reflects the further development of the critical historiography rooted in the Reformation period.

A striking aspect of all the Reformation theologians examined in this volume is that each and every one of them focussed on ministry. Theology for them was not an abstract academic enterprise, but rather was always related to ministry through Word, Sacrament, and service. Theology for them was indeed always "practical" in the sense that it was addressed, in Loyola's terms, to "ways" of ministry. The Reformation theologians were not embarked upon a quest for relevance or engaged in developing plausibility structures. Rather, convinced that the gospel is not only implausible but scandalous, they proceeded to proclaim God's salvation of lost humankind. The Reformation theologians insofar as they were professional theologians would probably be puzzled or upset by the modern seminary or school of theology with its fragmentation of theology into many specialized departments and compartmentalized faculties. The refrain throughout the above chapters is the recovery of biblical preaching and pastoral theology. The Reformation theologians were not interested in academic "objectivity" in the sense of critical distance from the subject of their study. The Bible to them was not ancient literature but the present Word of God. Hence Erasmus rendered the opening of the Gospel of John with the term *sermo* instead of the customary *verbum* or *logos*: "In the beginning was the *sermon*." Yet what was astonishing and disturbing to contemporaries was not primarily the translations but the content of the Scriptures. The Reformers strove to make accessible the cross as "scandal to the Jews and foolishness to the Greeks" (1 Cor. 1:23). The translators were preachers, and the preachers were translators.[17] Theology was not an autonomous academic enterprise, but a study of *sacra pagina*, the Bible, in service to the Christian community.

Here, too, our contributors remind us that the Reformation did not begin in divisiveness, but rather that the early years were marked by a corporate effort to bring the gospel to bear upon church and society. We are reminded of the humanist circles such as that of Meaux led by Lefèvre and reforming circles in Wittenberg, Zurich, Strasbourg, and elsewhere. Months before the posting of the *Ninety-five Theses*, Luther could write of the development of "*our* theology."[18] And even at the first signs of divergence among the Wittenberg theologians in 1521–2, Luther publicly eschewed party names: "I ask that men make no reference to my name; let them call themselves Christians, not Lutherans."[19] Likewise, reformers such as Argula von Grumbach and Katharina Schütz Zell refused any party designation. The humanists, too, thought all reformers were engaged in the common cause of recovering the Christian tradition.[20] In those heady days, theology came out of the academic closet and into the public domain of a communal endeavor to reform the church through the restoration of primitive Christianity. The cry *"ad fontes"* was not an appeal for intellectual achievement for its own sake but for the recovery of a critical norm and inspiration for the present. To state the obvious: "It is important to remember that the Reformation began as an intra-Catholic debate."[21]

Yet, within a few years after the *Ninety-five Theses*, the common cause began to fragment. Karlstadt literally removed himself from the Wittenberg scene; Müntzer shifted from deference to Luther to excoriation of him. And by 1524, Erasmus went for Luther's jugular vein with his *On the Freedom of the Will*.[22] The center no longer held. Some commentators have suggested that the growing dissension stemmed from alternative strategies and tactics for implementing reforms. Should reform be radical or gradual? Should reform be coerced or free? Is the church inclusive or exclusive? Reformers such as Karlstadt advocated rapid and total displacement of the old by the new. Karlstadt challenged "every congregation, be it small or large," to "see for itself and do what is right and good without waiting for anyone."[23] Here we see the beginnings of a congregational ecclesiology. Here too is the beginning of that later puritanism expressed by Robert Browne's tract: *A Treatise of Reformation without Tarrying for Any* (1582).[24] Similar conflicts arose in Zurich between Zwingli and his initial followers.

There is something to be said for the argument that the early Reformation exemplified the perennial liberal-radical debate over gradual change and sweeping reform.[25] On the other hand, the argument can be made that the differing trajectories between the Magisterial and Radical Reformers (and humanists) were fundamentally rooted in differing theologies rather than strategies.[26] Was the restoration of primitive Christianity to be understood in terms of doctrine or patterns of behavior? The latter are subject to external control; the former are not, or at least less so. Furthermore, the strategy for reform is not innocent of theology. These are old issues, of course, going back to the earliest Christian communities and their struggles over ritual purity, the use of foods sacrificed to idols, the scope of Christian liberty in relation to the neighbor and the weak in the faith, the role of the law in light of the gospel, the relationship of the church to civil society. These and other issues once again came forcefully to the fore in the Reformation as the biblical language and message was recovered and applied to the times. The question here is not whether the Reformation theologians succeeded in this task,[27] but rather their faithfulness to the tradition and what theological resources they provide for present theological reflection and proclamation.

Notes

1 For a start, see the volume by A. G. Dickens and John Tonkin with Kenneth Powell, *The Reformation in Historical Thought* (Cambridge: Harvard University Press, 1985), as well as the titles listed in n. 2.

2 The numerous studies on Luther's influence upon later theologians are listed annually in the extensive "Lutherbibliographie" of the annual *Lutherjahrbuch.* See also, for example: Ulrich Asendorf, *Luther und Hegel: Untersuchungen zur Grundlegung einer neuen systematischen Theologie* (Wiesbaden: Steiner Verlag, 1982); Oswald Bayer, *Theologie* (Handbuch Systematischer Theologie, 1) (Gütersloh: Gütersloher Verlagshaus, 1994); Heinrich Bornkamm, *Luther im Spiegel der deutschen Geistesgeschichte* (Göttingen: Vandenhoeck & Ruprecht, 2nd ed., 1970); Robert Kolb, *Martin Luther as Prophet, Teacher, and Hero: Images of the Reformer, 1520–1620* (Grand Rapids: Baker Books, 1999); Walther von Loewenich, *Luther und der Neuprotestantismus* (Witten: Luther-Verlag, 1963); Jaroslav Pelikan, ed., *Interpreters of Luther: Essays in Honor of Wilhelm Pauck* (Philadelphia: Fortress Press, 1968).

3 The most recent contribution to the discussion is James M. Stayer, *Martin Luther, German Saviour: German Evangelical Theological Factions and the Interpretation of Luther, 1917–1933* (Montreal and Kingston, Ont.: McGill-Queen's University Press, 2000).

4 *CTM* 111.

5 A perspective expressed by Lessing's fable of the ring, but also foreshadowing perhaps Schleiermacher's view of religion in terms of the feeling of unconditional dependence. See George Lindbeck, *The Nature of Doctrine: Religion and Theology in a Postliberal Age* (Philadelphia: Westminster Press, 1984), 31–55. See also my review essay, "Müntzeriana," *LQ* 4 (Summer 1990), 195–214, 202–3.

6 See my *The Third Reformation? Charismatic Movements and the Lutheran Tradition* (Macon: Mercer University Press, 1983).

7 Ulrich Bubenheimer, "Andreas Rudolff Bodenstein von Karlstadt" in *Andreas Bodenstein von Karlstadt. 500–Jahre-Feier* (Karlstadt: Arbeitsgruppe Bodenstein, 1980), 40. Bubenheimer points not only to substantive theological agreement, but to the seventeenth-century reprint of Karlstadt's central work on *Gelassenheit,* and his rehabilitation by the radical Pietist, Gottfried Arnold.

8 The historical richness and complexity of transdenominational and transnational Pietism cannot be pursued here. For a brief introduction see Johannes Wallmann, *Der Pietismus* (Göttingen: Vandenhoeck & Ruprecht, 1990); for more extensive exposition see the four-volume study under the general editorship of Martin Brecht, *Geschichte des Pietismus* (Göttingen: Vandenhoeck & Ruprecht, 1993ff.). For Hoberg see Martin Schmidt, *Pietismus* (Stuttgart: Kohlhammer, 1972), 14.

9 John Wesley, *The Works of John Wesley* (London: Wesleyan Conference Office, 1872), 7:204.

10 See for example, David Fergusson, "Reclaiming the Doctrine of Sanctification," *Interpretation* 53/4 (October 1999), 380–90, and my "Do Lutherans Shout Justification But Whisper Sanctification," *LQ* 13/1 (Spring 1999), 1–20.

11 For an introduction to this subject see Merry E. Wiesner-Hanks, "Women," *OER* 4:290–8 and Merry E. Wiesner, *Women and Gender in Early Modern Europe* (Cambridge: Cambridge University Press, 1993). Of the many sources becoming available see for example, Erika Rummel, ed., *Erasmus on Women* (Toronto: University of Toronto Press, 1996); Merry Wiesner-Hanks and Joan Skocir, ed. and trans., *Convents Confront the Reformation: Catholic and Protestant Nuns in Germany* (Milwaukee: Marquette University Press, 1996); Theresa M. Kenney, ed. and trans., *"Women Are Not Human": An Anonymous Treatise and Responses* (New York: Crossroad, 1998). A random sampling of theological journals also suggests the breadth of research. For example: Matthieu Arnold, "La Réforme Fut-Elle Féministe? Simples Remarques sur Luther et les Femmes," *Foi et Vie* 98 (July 1999), 35–50; Marion Obitz, "Katharina Zell – Kirchenmutter, Publizistin, Apostelin, Prophetin," *Evangelische Theologie* 60/5 (2000), 371–88; Gisela Möncke, "Margareta von Treskow, eine unbekannte Flugschriftenverfasserin der Reformationszeit," *ZKG* 108/2 (1997), 176–86.

12 The association of the Reformation with the initiation of the modern age is a long tradition. See, for example, Gerhard Ebeling, "Luther

and the Beginning of the Modern Age" in H. A. Oberman, ed., *Luther and the Dawn of the Modern Era* (Leiden: E. J. Brill, 1974), 11–39; Richard van Dülmen, "The Reformation and the Modern Age" in C. Scott Dixon, ed., *The German Reformation: The Essential Readings* (Oxford: Blackwell, 1999), 193–219; and Heinz Schilling, "Luther, Loyola, Calvin und die europäische Neuzeit," *ARG* 85 (1994), 5–31.

13 I desire that everyone including women read the Gospels and the Pauline letters. These ought to be translated into all languages.... Thus I would like the farmer to sing Scripture as he plows, the weaver to hum it as he weaves, the traveler to pass the boredom of his journey with such stories. Let the conversation of all Christians therefore relate to Scripture.

Gustav Benrath, ed., *Wegbereiter der Reformation* (Bremen: Carl Schünemann Verlag, 1967), 529; English translation in my *The European Reformations Sourcebook* (Oxford: Blackwell, 2000), 48.

14 *LW* 35:182, 187–9, 195.

15 David C. Steinmetz, "The Intellectual Appeal of the Reformation," *Theology Today* 57/4 (January 2001), 459–72, 461 n.3. Steinmetz cites Kenneth Hagen, *Hebrews Commenting from Erasmus to Bèze, 1516–1598* (Tübingen: Mohr, 1981), 98: "Denominational lines of interpretation are virtually non-existent."

16 See Jaroslav Pelikan, *Historical Theology: Continuity and Change in Christian Doctrine* (London: Hutchinson, 1971), chapter two: "The Evolution of the Historical;" Robert L. Wilken, *The Myth of Christian Beginnings: History's Impact on Belief* (Garden City: Anchor Books, 1972), 104–29; and Cyriac K. Pullapilly, *Caesar Baronius: Counter-Reformation Historian* (Notre Dame: University of Notre Dame Press, 1975).

17 See Albrecht Beutel, "Luthers Bibelübersetzung und die Folgen," *Evangelische Theologie* 59/1 (1999), 13–24; and Walter Mostert, "Scriptura sacra sui ipsius interpres: Bemerkungen zum Verständnis der Heiligen Schrift durch Luther," *LuJ* 46 (1979), 60–96.

18 My emphasis. Letter to John Lang, May 18, 1517. *LW* 48:41–2.

19 *LW* 45:70.

20 See Leif Grane, *Martinus Noster: Luther in the German Reform Movement 1518–1521* (Mainz: Zabern, 1994) and Helmar Junghans, *Der junge Luther und die Humanisten* (Weimar: Böhlaus, 1984).

21 Steinmetz, "The Intellectual Appeal of the Reformation," 459.

22 "My dear Erasmus.... You and you alone have seen the question on which everything hinges, and have aimed at the vital spot; ..." *LW* 33:294.

23 *Whether We Should Go Slowly and Avoid Offending the Weak in Matters Pertaining to God's Will*, 1524. E. J. Furcha, ed. and trans., *The Essential Carlstadt* (Waterloo: Herald Press, 1995), 253.

24 The second volume of Hermann Barge's biography of Karlstadt is subtitled "The Champion of Lay Christian Puritanism." *Andreas Bodenstein von Karlstadt*, 2 vols. (Leipzig, 1905; repr. Nieuwkoop: De Graaf, 1968). Robert Browne (c.1550–1633) was a Puritan separatist.

25 See Ronald J. Sider, ed., *Karlstadt's Battle with Luther: Documents in a Liberal-Radical Debate* (Philadelphia: Fortress Press, 1978) and James S. Preus, *Carlstadt's "Ordinaciones" and Luther's Liberty: A Study of the Wittenberg Movement 1521–22* (Cambridge, MA: Harvard University Press, 1974).

26 See my "Conflicting Models of Ministry – Luther, Karlstadt, and Muentzer," *Concordia Theological Quarterly* 41/4 (October 1977), 35–50.

27 The *question mal proposée* answered in the negative by Gerald Strauss, *Luther's House of Learning: Indoctrination of the Young in the German Reformation* (Baltimore: Johns Hopkins University Press, 1978). See the responses by James Kittelson, "Successes and Failures in the German Reformation: The Report from Strasbourg," *ARG* 73 (1982), 153–74; and "Visitations and Popular Religious Culture: Further Reports from Strasbourg" in Kyle C. Sessions and Phillip N. Bebb, eds., *Pietas et Societas: New Trends in Reformation Social History. Essays in Memory of Harold J. Grimm* (Kirksville: Sixteenth Century Journal Publishers, 1985), 89–101.

Glossary

For information on other Reformers and major figures in church history, see *OER*, *TRE*, *The Oxford Dictionary of the Christian Church*, *The Westminster Dictionary of Church History*, and so on. An especially useful book is Mark Greengrass, *The Longman Companion to The European Reformation c.1500–1618* (London: Longman, 1998), that includes chronologies and mini-biographies. Heiko A. Oberman, *The Harvest of Medieval Theology: Gabriel Biel and Late Medieval Nominalism* (Cambridge, MA: Harvard University Press, 1963) includes a glossary of late medieval theological terms, and Alister E. McGrath, *Iustitia Dei: A History of the Christian Doctrine of Justification* (2 vols., Cambridge: Cambridge University Press, 1986) includes in Volume 1 a glossary of terms relating to justification. Also useful is Richard A. Muller, *Dictionary of Latin and Greek Theological Terms* (Grand Rapids: Baker Books, 1985).

ad fontes "To the sources." Humanist motto for the endeavor to find the earliest reliable sources of classical antiquity, including the Bible and church fathers.

adiaphora "Things indifferent." Ceremonies, liturgical actions and vestments, and traditions Reformers were willing to tolerate because they were neither explicitly rejected nor stipulated by Scripture. Major controversies arose among German Lutherans (1548–52) and English Anglicans (1550–73) over what constituted adiaphora and whether adiaphora may be conceded under political pressure.

affair of the placards On October 17/18, 1534, placards or posters denouncing the Mass as an abomination were posted in Paris and various other cities in France. The audacious affixing of a placard to Francis I's chamber door at Amboise incited the king's persecution of Protestants.

Anabaptism "Rebaptism." Pejorative designation of those Reformation communities that advocated a profession of faith as a condition for baptism. Since the first generation of these communities had been baptized as infants, the practice was condemned as "rebaptism."

Anfechtungen Luther's term for the profound anxiety and fear in the experience of divine wrath. Sometimes translated as "temptations," the term is better understood in light of its verbal root as divine or demonic "assaults" upon conscience and faith; despair; spiritual conflict.

Antinomianism   The view that since justification is by grace alone apart from works of the law, Christians are freed from observance of the law.

apocalyptic   The "revelation" or "unveiling" of things normally hidden concerning the future end of the world. Apocalyptic literature and expectations often reflect dreams and visions filled with symbols concerning impending disasters and social upheavals associated with the end of the world and the Last Judgment.

Augsburg Interim   The 1548 intermediate religious settlement following Charles V's defeat of the Protestant Schmalkald League. The Interim was designed as a provisional basis of agreement until the conclusion of the Council of Trent (1545–63).

Book of Concord   The 1580 Collection of Lutheran confessional writings.

Cabbala   A variety of Jewish mysticism that used esoteric methods of biblical inter-pretation, including numerology, in order to reveal hidden meanings and doctrines in the Hebrew texts. Christian scholars such as Reuchlin used these methods to "discover" Christian doctrines in the Hebrew Bible or Old Testament.

celestial flesh Christology   A monophysite Christology associated with such "Radical Reformers" as Schwenckfeld, Hoffman, and Simons. The concern was to preclude any thought that Christ participated in the sinful substance of the creature. Hence Jesus was born *out of* not *from* Mary.

character indelibus   The indelible character imprinted upon the soul in the Roman Catholic theology of the sacraments of baptism, confirmation, and ordination that cannot be lost even by the gravest of sins.

chiliasm   Greek for "a thousand;" posits Christ will return to earth for a thousand-year reign before the final consummation of history.

Church Fathers   Theologians of the "Patristic Age" (end of the first to close of the eighth century); the focus of the humanists' "return to the sources." St. Augustine (350–430) was of particular importance to theologians of the late medieval and Reformation periods.

Company of Pastors   The collective clerical leadership of the Genevan church set forth in Calvin's *Ecclesiastical Ordinances* in 1541 and 1561 that included responsib-ility for mutual education, edification, and approval of candidates for the ministry as well as relations with the civil government.

communicatio idiomatum   Latin form of a Greek phrase meaning "exchange of the properties." Applied to Christology by Cyril of Alexandria (d. 444) to affirm that while the human and divine natures of Christ are separate, the attributes of one may be predicated of the other due to their union in Christ's one person. The Council of Chalcedon (451) confessed the one person Christ's true divinity and true humanity in two natures united "unconfusedly, unchangeably, indivisibly, inseparably." The phrase played a significant role in Luther's Christology and theology of the Lord's Supper, especially in his conflict with Zwingli.

conciliarism   The medieval development that final church authority is located in a general council rather than the pope. Leading theorists of conciliarism included the French theologians Jean Gerson (d. 1429) and Pierre d'Ailly (d. 1420). Papal opposition to conciliarism was formulated in Pius II's 1460 bull *Execrabilis* that condemned appealing from the pope to a general council.

Confession   A statement of faith by a Protestant church. For example, the *Augsburg Confession* (1530) expresses the doctrinal position of Lutheranism, and the *First Helvetic Confession* (1536) that of the early Reformed church. A Confessional Church is a church that defines itself with reference to such a document.

Consensus Tigurinus   The "Zurich Agreement" on the doctrine of the sacraments reached by Bullinger and Calvin in 1549 that united the Reformed churches of Zurich and Geneva.

consubstantiation   A medieval scholastic theology of the Eucharist that holds Christ's presence by virtue of the omnipotence of God. Although all the Protestant Reformers rejected the doctrine of transubstantiation, Luther emphasized a strong doctrine of the real presence of Christ in the Lord's Supper in bitter eucharistic debates with Reformed theologians. Hence, while Luther himself never used the term, it was applied to him and his followers by the Reformed.

coram deo   In the presence of God or before God, in contrast with *coram hominibus*, in the presence of humans.

Corpus Christi   Special commemoration of the "body of Christ" in the Eucharist arose in the thirteenth century largely due to the influence of the nun Juliana. Corpus Christi Processions on the Feast of Corpus Christi, the Thursday after Trinity Sunday, were civil as well as religious events. In the Reformation period these processions affirmed popular belief in transubstantiation in opposition to Protestant eucharistic theology.

Council of Trent   The Roman Catholic Council (1545–63) concerned with internal theological and moral reform and external reaction to Protestant criticism.

Devotio moderna   The fourteenth-century movement of spiritual renewal originating in the Low Countries in the circle around Geert de Groote, that received classic expression in Thomas à Kempis's (d. 1471) *Imitation of Christ*. In the form of the Brethren of the Common Life it exercised influence upon various humanists and Reformers, including Erasmus and Luther.

Discalced Carmelites   The Order of Carmelite Sisters ("Our Lady of Mount Carmel"), founded in the Low Countries in 1452, spread through France, Italy, and Spain. In Spain reform of the order was led by St. Teresa. Discalced (from Latin "unshod') signifies the reformed order whose members went barefoot or used sandals.

Docetism   A christological heresy which emphasized that Jesus Christ was a purely divine being who only had the "appearance" of being human.

Donatism   An early church schismatic movement in North Africa that insisted upon the moral purity of the church and claimed that the validity of the sacraments depended upon the purity of the priest. St. Augustine, among others, condemned the Donatist view that the message depends upon the messenger.

Ecclesiastical Ordinances   The basic document of Genevan church order accepted by the city council upon Calvin's return to Geneva in 1541. The *Ordinances* set forth Calvin's program of discipline and church polity based on the fourfold office of pastor, teacher, elder, and deacon.

Enthusiasts   From the Greek term meaning "God within-ism," and indicating divine possession. A pejorative label for those claiming direct inspiration by the Holy Spirit. Luther referred to Enthusiasts as *Schwärmer*, sometimes translated as "fanatics."

Eucharist Literally, "thanksgiving." The term refers to the Sacrament of the Lord's Supper also known as "the Mass" and "Holy Communion."

Eschatology The area of theology that deals with the "last things": resurrection, hell, eternal life, the Last Judgment.

evangelicals Self-designation of reforming movements that claims their teaching is rooted in the gospel. Interchangeable with the term "Protestant" that came into use after the "protest" of the Evangelicals at the 1529 Diet of Speyer.

exegesis Explanation and interpretation of texts; methods used to interpret Scripture are referred to as "hermeneutics."

extra Calvinisticum "The Calvinist extra." A Lutheran polemical term for the Reformed doctrine that the Son of God exists "also beyond the flesh" (*etiam extra carnem*); i.e., although Christ's humanity is entirely dependent upon the divinity, the divinity is not dependent upon the humanity. In the Incarnation, the Word of God while united with the human nature of Jesus is to be conceived as outside of (*extra*) the human nature.

facere quod in se est "To do that which is within one." The *via moderna*, the theological school associated with Occam and Biel, posited that a person on the basis of the natural powers within him could fulfill the commandments and therefore love God above all else and thus earn the infusion of divine grace.

fides ex auditu "Faith by means of hearing," the Vulgate translation of Romans 10:17, became a Protestant phrase for the salvific importance of preaching and hearing the Word.

forensic justification An expression of justification by grace alone in the legal imagery of a declarative verdict. God, the Judge, declares the sinner righteous.

Formula of Concord The last of the Lutheran Confessional writings (1577) that resolved a number of intra-Lutheran theological disputes.

Gelassenheit A term from the German mystical tradition for self-renunciation and complete surrender to the will of God. There is no precise English equivalent.

gemina praedestinatio Double predestination.

Gnesio-Lutherans The Lutheran party claiming to represent the "genuine Lutheran" position led by Matthias Flacius and others claiming true continuity with Luther's theology. Opposed to the "Philippists," the Lutheran party associated with Philip Melanchthon (q.v.).

Gnosticism From the Greek *gnosis* (knowledge). A complex and varied dualistic religious movement prominent in the second century that posited a saving knowledge that enabled escape from the material world, regarded as evil, and access to the spiritual world, regarded as good.

hermeneutics *see* **exegesis**.

hermetic writings Mystic writings from the first through third centuries attributed to Hermes Trismegistus, a designation for the Egyptian divinity of all knowledge, which speak of the soul's ascent to God through knowledge.

humanism The Renaissance movement of education and reform of church and society based on the recovery of classical Greco-Roman, biblical, and early church literature. Humanist advances in rhetoric, philology, and textual criticism contributed to the development of Reformation theologies.

iconoclasm The destruction of religious images ("icons") and statues.

indulgence The medieval doctrine that the church may partially or completely (plenary indulgence) remit the temporal penalty or "debt" due to sin after the guilt is forgiven. The resource for indulgences was the treasury of merit acquired by Christ and the saints. By the late Middle Ages indulgences were extended to sinners suffering in purgatory.

infralapsarian/supralapsarian Terms associated with Reformed theologies of predestination in which the divine election and reprobation of individuals was decreed after (infralapsarian) or before (supralapsarian) the fall of Adam.

Magisterial Reformation Reference to the Lutheran and Reformed communities in distinction from the "Radical Reformation" of the Anabaptist communities. The term refers both to origin of the Reformation in the universities (*magister* = teacher) and a positive view of culture and politics that expected the support of magistrates for reforms.

Marcionitism From Marcion (d. c.160), condemned as a heretic and whose affinities with gnosticism appear in his dualistic antithesis of the Old Testament "God of law" with the New Testament "God of love." Marcion rejected the Old Testament and strove to purge Christianity of all Jewish influence.

Monophysitism The Christological heresy condemned by the Council of Chalcedon (451) that Christ's humanity is absorbed by his divinity, so that there is only one nature in Jesus Christ.

Münster/Münsterites The city of Münster in Westphalia was the site of a major uprising by radical Reformers in 1534–5.

mysticism The personal union of love and will with God through religious experience, with various expressions in medieval theology (e.g., Meister Eckhart, Bonaventure, Tauler).

nominalism *see via moderna*

Peasants' War The major armed revolt of 1524–6 that involved a complex network of social and religious motivations.

Pelagianism The fifth-century heresy named after the British monk Pelagius (c.360–420) that persons may take the first steps toward salvation without the assistance of divine grace. Associated with the possibility of moral reform through human free will. A frequent charge leveled against opponents in controversies over justification.

Philippists The followers of Philip Melanchthon in the intra-Lutheran theological conflicts following the death of Luther. *See also Gnesio-Lutherans.*

Philosophia Christi "The philosophy of Christ." Erasmus's phrase for reform through moral improvement, education, and the imitation of Christ.

Prophecyings Regular, required biblical studies in Zurich established by Zwingli, designed to retrain and educate the city clergy. The name "Prophecy" for this Bible school was taken from 1 Cor. 14:26–33.

Protestant Orthodoxy The designation for late sixteenth and seventeenth-century Protestant theological systems that utilized scholastic methodology.

Realism *see via antiqua*

Reformed The designation for the Calvinist churches and their followers (French: *églises réformées*; German: *reformierte Kirchen*).

reprobation In the doctrine of double predestination, reprobation designates God's inscrutable incitement to sin of those foreordained to condemnation.

Roman Inquisition   Also known as "The Holy Office," established by Pope Paul III in 1542 as the final court of appeal in heresy trials.

Sacramentarians   Luther's term for theologians (such as Zwingli) who maintained that the bread and wine in the Eurcharist were the body and blood of Christ in only a "sacramental" or "metaphorical" sense. The designation came to be applied to all who denied the doctrine of the Real Presence of Christ in the Eucharist.

St. Bartholomew's Day massacre   The massacre of thousands of French Protestants, instigated apparently by the Queen Mother, in and around Paris on August 24, 1572.

Schwärmer   *see* **Enthusiasts**

Sentences   Peter Lombard's (d. 1160) *Four Books of Sentences* was the standard textbook of theology in the sixteenth century.

simul iustus et peccator   Luther's theological anthropology affirms that the Christian is "righteous and sinner at the same time."

Sorbonne   The theological college of the University of Paris (founded c.1257 by Robert de Sorbon). Its faculty strongly opposed reforming movements in France.

soteriology   From the Greek *soter* (savior). Doctrine of salvation.

synecdoche   Figure of speech that puts the part for the whole (e.g., "50 sail" for "50 ships"). Used in eucharistic controversies.

theodicy   The justification or explanation of God's goodness in the face of the presence of evil in the world.

transubstantiation   The doctrine affirmed at the Fourth Lateran Council (1215) that the elements of bread and wine become the substance of the body and blood of Christ at their consecration in the Mass.

Tridentine   Refers to the Council of Trent (1545–63) and the Roman Catholic Church following the Council.

ubiquity   Omnipresence. The term is associated with Lutheran emphasis upon the Real Presence of Christ in the Eucharist in light of the conviction that Christ, in his human as well as divine nature, is everywhere present.

Vestiarian Controversy   Dispute over clerical dress (vestments) in the Church of England in the 1550s and following years. Puritans rejected traditional vestments as "popish." *See also* **adiaphora**.

via antiqua, via moderna   "The old way" refers to the medieval scholastic theology associated with Thomas Aquinas; "the modem way" refers to the scholastic theology stemming from William of Ockham and Gabriel Biel. Luther was trained in the *via moderna*, whereas Zwingli resonated more with the *via antiqua*.

Vulgate   The Latin translation of the Bible stemming mainly from Jerome (c.342–420) and designated the only authentic Latin version by the Council of Trent in 1546.

Index